Beyond the Transition Phase of WTO

The Editors

Dipankar Sengupta is Fellow (Economics) at the Centre de Sciences Humaines, New Delhi. Prior to this, he taught economics at the School of International Studies, Jawaharlal Nehru University, New Delhi. He was educated at the University of Calcutta and at the Centre for International Trade and Development, Jawaharlal Nehru University and his areas of interest include International Political Economy, Industrial Organisation Theory and Indian Economic Development and has published extensively on these subjects.

Debashis Chakraborty is Research Associate at the Rajiv Gandhi Institute for Contemporary Studies, New Delhi. He was educated at the University of Calcutta and at the Centre for International Trade and Development, Jawaharlal Nehru University and his areas of interest include International Trade, the interface between Law and Economics and Indian Economic Development. He has presented and published papers at various academic and policy forums in India and abroad.

Pritam Banerjee was formerly a Trade Policy analyst with the Confederation of Indian Industry. He has also been with the World Bank as a consultant in Washington DC. He was educated at Illinois Wesleyan University, London School of Economics and the Centre for International Trade and Development, Jawaharlal Nehru University, New Delhi. His primary interests include GATS, International Services Supply Chains and Trade Facilitation in Services.

Beyond the Transition Phase of WTO

An Indian Perspective on Emerging Issues

EDITORS

DIPANKAR SENGUPTA
DEBASHIS CHAKRABORTY
PRITAM BANERJEE

Published by Academic Foundation
in association with
Centre de Sciences Humaines,
New Delhi

Academic Foundation
NEW DELHI

Centre de Sciences Humaines (Centre for Social Sciences and Humanities): Created in 1989, the CSH is part of the network of research centres of the French Ministry of Foreign Affairs. The Centre's research work is primarily oriented towards the study of issues concerning the contemporary dynamics of development in India and South Asia. The activities of the Centre are focused on four main themes, namely: Economic transition and sustainable development, political dynamics, institutional set-up and social transformations, regional dynamics in South Asia and international relations and urban dynamics.

Centre de Sciences Humaines, 2 Aurangzeb Road, New Delhi 110 011, India
Tel: (91) 11 30410070
Fax: (91) 11 30410079
Email: public@csh-delhi.com
Website: http://www.csh-delhi.com

First published in 2006 by
Academic Foundation
4772-73 / 23 Bharat Ram Road, (23 Ansari Road), Darya Ganj, New Delhi - 110 002 (India).
Phones : 23245001 / 02 / 03 / 04. Fax : +91-11-23245005. E-mail : academic@vsnl.com
www : academicfoundation.com

Published in association with :
Centre de Sciences Humaines,
New Delhi

Beyond the Transition Phase of WTO: An Indian Perspective on Emerging Issues
Edited by Dipankar Sengupta, Debashis Chakraborty and Pritam Banerjee

ISBN 81-7188-510-1

Designed and typeset by Italics India, New Delhi.
Printed and bound in India.

Contents

Section III

Barriers to Trade: A Topical Analysis

Section IV

Services and E-commerce: The Emerging Sectors

Acknowledgements

This volume was conceived almost two years ago and is the result of our dissatisfaction over the then current literature on the WTO and its failure to educate the interested public about what the relevant issues were and where India's interests lay. (We have no doubt that some other scholars after reading this volume will think similarly and set off on a similar venture!) We felt that for most people, debates on the WTO were conducted using too much jargon or techno-speak when the very same ideas could be communicated using simple language without the loss of academic rigour. We also felt that the implications of the WTO regime on the emerging new economy, as well as issues like biotechnology and genetically modified crops, were unjustly neglected. We, therefore, decided to compile a volume that would be addressed to lay persons and specialists alike, where the issues — both current as well as emergent — would be introduced and the appropriate positions that India should take be discussed.

While this volume was supposed to have taken, at most, a few months from conception to publication, the difficulties that go with such an effort soon made themselves visible. It became clear that given the breadth of issues that would have to be covered, a large number of specialists would have to be involved. Secondly, the arrogant economists that we were, it came home to us that great many of these issues could only be dealt with by specialists in Trade and Environmental Law. As we started to feel overwhelmed by the sheer magnitude and the complex nature of our venture, the eagerness of the contributors to this volume and the effort that they put into their individual chapters made our burden much lighter. The contributors were their own stern taskmasters who were unsatisfied with what they had written even when we the editors thought that their contributions passed muster.

As we changed the thrust of the volume midway to focus on emerging issues, the contributors too displayed exemplary flexibility. In any case, most chapters were projective in nature. But as we thought it appropriate to include new areas, new contributors — given the onerous responsibility of covering new areas — handed in their chapters in record time.

Thus, when we look to the volume in its current shape and form, we are humbled by the faith reposed in us by the contributors — all scholars of repute — who come from a range of prestigious institutions in India and abroad.

We thank Centre de Sciences Humaines (CSH), New Delhi and its Directrice, Dr. Veronique Dupont, for supporting this publication. We cannot fail to thank those who have indelibly influenced our approach to this subject — Professors Ashok Guha, Manmohan Agarwal, Alokesh Barua, Bibek Debroy, Arjun Sengupta and Dr. Jayanta Roy. We must also thank Attreyee Roy Choudhary publications-in-charge CSH but for whose constant prodding the volume would have probably come out an year later! Rituraj and Sanu Kapila of Academic Foundation were of course most understanding about the delays; apparently they had seen all this before! We also thank our colleagues at CSH, Rajiv Gandhi Institution of Contemporary Studies and the Confederation of Indian Industry — who have never doubted that the volume once published would justify all delays that accompanied the making of it. Lastly, we must acknowledge the institution where we, the editors were first introduced to the great debates in international economics, the Centre for International Trade and Development Division in the School of International Studies, Jawaharlal Nehru University, New Delhi.

We hope that in compiling this volume we fulfil the role that Dr. Frederic Grare, the former Director of CSH (and now at the Carnegie Endowment for International Peace) envisaged for this institution: to be at the forefront of debates on issues that are of current and future interest to South Asia and to inform the interested public, researchers and policymakers of what lies ahead as well as the options available to them.

— Editors

Contributors

Alice Pham is Researcher at Consumer Unity and Trust Society (CUTS) International, Jaipur.

Amir Ullah Khan is Fellow at the India Development Foundation, Gurgaon.

Anirudh Shingal is Consultant with the World Bank, Washington D.C.

Debashis Chakraborty is Research Associate at the RGICS, New Delhi.

Dipankar Sengupta is Economics Fellow, Centre de Science Humanines, New Delhi.

Els Reynaers is Legal Adviser in M.V. Kini & Co, New Delhi.

Julien Chaisse is affiliated to the Institut d'Etudes Politiques d'Aix-en-Provence, University of Aix-Marseille III as a teacher and a researcher.

K.D. Raju is Assistant Director, Amity Institute of Global Legal Education and Research, New Delhi.

Mayank Sinha was formerly Research Associate, Global Agreements, Legislation and Trade (GALT), The Energy Research Institute (TERI), New Delhi.

Nilanjan Banik is Assistant Professor, Madras School of Economics, Chennai.

Nitya Nanda is Policy Analyist at CUTS International, Jaipur.

Nivedita Dutta is enrolled in the Ph.D. Economics programme in the Indian Institute of Technology, Mumbai.

Pavel Chakravarty is Research Associate, GALT, TERI, New Delhi.

Pradeep S. Mehta is the Secretary-General of CUTS International, Jaipur.

Pritam Banerjee was formerly Trade Analyst with the Confederation of Indian Industry.

Sachin Chaturvedi is Fellow, Research and Information System for the Non-Aligned and Other Developing Countries (RIS) and Managing Editor, Asian Biotechnology and Development Review, New Delhi.

Sandwip Kumar Das is Professor at the International Trade and Development Division, JNU, New Delhi.

Saon Ray is Assistant Professor at TERI School, New Delhi.

Saurabh Bandyopadhyay is Economist at the National Council of Applied Economic Research (NCAER), New Delhi.

Subhodip Ghosh is an Economist at Bengal Chamber of Commerce and Industry, Kolkata.

Suparna Karmakar is Consultant at the Indian Council for Research in International Economic Relations, New Delhi.

Swapan K. Bhattacharya is Associate Professor, Indian Institute of Public Administration, New Delhi.

S.R. Rao is Director, Department of Biotechnology, Ministry of Science & Technology, New Delhi.

Toposhmito Sengupta is Research Associate at NCAER, New Delhi.

Upasana Gaur was formerly Research Associate, GALT, TERI, New Delhi.

Yashika Singh is Leader, Economic Analysis Group, Dun and Bradstreet Information Services India Pvt. Ltd., Mumbai.

Glossary of Acronyms and Terms

Acronyms

AB	Appellate Body
AIA	Advanced Informed Agreement
AICTE	All India Council for Technical Education
AIDS	Acquired Immune Deficiency Syndrome
AITUC	All India Trade Union Committee
AMS	Aggregate Measurement of Support
AoA	WTO Agreement on Agriculture
APEC	Asia Pacific Economic Council
APEDA	Agricultural and Processed Food Products Export Development Authority
AQIS	Australian Quarantine and Inspection Service
ASEAN	Association of South-East Asian Nations
ASEM	Asia Europe Meeting
ATC	Agreement on Textiles and Clothing
ATV	Anti-retroviral
B2B	Business to Business
BIS	Bureau of Indian Standards
BoP	Balance of Payments
BPO	Business Process Outsourcing
CAG	Comptroller and Auditor General
CAGR	Compounded Annual Rate of Growth
CAP	Common Agricultural Policy
CAT	Common Admission Test

CBD	Convention on Biological Diversity
CBEC	Central Board of Excise and Customs
CIF	Cost Insurance Freight
CII	Confederation of Indian Industry
CIS	Commonwealth of Independent States
CIT	US Court of International Trade
CITES	Convention on International Trade in Endangered Species
CITU	Centre of Indian Trade Unions
CL	Compulsory Licenses
CLRI	Centre of Leather Research Institute
CMIE	Centre for the Monitoring of the Indian Economy
COP	Conference of the Parties
CPC	Central Product Classification
CTE	Committee on Trade and Environment
CTESS	Committee on Trade and Environment Special Session
CTG	Council for Trade in Goods
CWI	Consignment Wise Inspection
DBT	Department of Biotechnology
DDA	Doha Development Agenda
DDT	Dichloro-Dyphenyl-Trichloroethane
DEC	Distance Education Council
DGCI&S	Directorate General of Commercial Intelligence and Statistics of India
DGFT	Directorate General of Foreign Trade
DGHS	Directorate General of Health Services
DGS&D	Directorate General of Supplies and Disposal
DMD	Doha Ministerial Declaration
DPCO	Drug Price Control Order

DSB	Dispute Settlement Body
DSM	Dispute Settlement Mechanism
DSU	Dispute Settlement Understanding
EC	European Communities
EDI	Electronic Data Interface
EIC	Export Inspection Council
EMR	Exclusive Marketing Right
ERP	Effective Rate of Protection
ESA	US Endangered Species Act, 1973
ESCAP	Economic and Social Commission for Asia and the Pacific
ETE	Export Tax Equivalent
EU	European Union
F&FP	Fish and Fishery Products
FAO	Food and Agricultural Organisation
FDI	Foreign Direct Investment
FoB	Free-on-Board
FSC	Foreign Sales Corporation Tax Exemption
FSMSC	Food Safety Management Systems based Certification
G3	The big 3 economies i.e. USA, Japan and the European Union
GATS	General Agreement for Trade in Services.
GATS+	Market Access Commitments beyond General Agreements for Trade in Services.
GATT 47:	General Agreement on Tariffs and Trade 1947
GATT 94:	General Agreement on Tariffs and Trade 1994
GATT	General Agreement on Tariffs and Trade
GDP	Gross Domestic Product

GEAC	Genetic Engineering Approval Committee
GFRs	General Financial Rules
GM	Genetically Modified
GPA	Government Procurement Agreement
GSP	Generalised System of Preferences
H1B	Temporary Highly Skilled Worker (at least college graduate) in the USA.
HACCP	Hazard Analysis Critical Control Point
HIV	Human Immunodeficiency Virus
HMS	Hind Mazdoor Sabha
IBSC	Institutional Biosafety Committees
ICFTU	International Confederation of Free Trade Unions
ICT	Information and Communication Technology
IGNOU	Indira Gandhi National Open University
IIMs	Indian Institute of Management
IITs	Indian Institute of Technology
ILO	International Labour Organisation
IPPC	International Plant Protection Convention; International body for plant safety
IPQC	In Process Quality Control
IPRs	Intellectual Property Rights
IRRI	International Rice Research Institute
IS	Payments based on Input use
ISO	International Standards Organisation
IT	Information Technology
ITA I & II	Information Technology Agreement
ITES	Information Technology Enabled Services
ITI	Industrial Technical Institutes
ITS	Information Technology Services

JEE	Joint Entrance Examination
KBA	Knowledge Based Assets
KPO	Knowledge Process Outsourcing
LDCs	Least-Developed Countries
LMOs	Living Modified Organisms
LTA	Long Term Arrangement
MAFF	Ministry of Agriculture, Forestry and Fishery
MEA	Multilateral Environmental Agreement
MFA	Multi-Fibre Arrangement
MFN	Most Favored Nation
MFPI	Ministry of Food Processing Industries
MNCs	Multinational Corporations
MNP	Movement of Natural Person (cross border movement of skilled labor)
MoEF	Ministry of Environment and Forestry
MOP	Meeting of the Parties
MPS	Market Price Support
MRA	Mutual Recognition Agreement (for Technical standards and qualifications)
NAFTA	North American Free Trade Agreement
NCB	National Competitive Bidding
NET	National Eligibility Test
NGO	Non-Governmental Organisations
NIEO	New International Economic Order
NITRA	Northern India Textile Research Association
NPC	Nominal Protection Coefficient
NT	National Treatment
NTBs	Non-Tariff Barriers
OECD	Organisation for Economic Co-operation and Development
OGL	Open General Licence

OIE	Office International des Epizooties (World Organisation for Animal Health)
OP	Payments Based on Output
PBIC	Plant Breeding International Cambridge Ltd.
PCP	Penta-Chloro-Phenol
PFY	Polypropylene Filament Yarn
PIHEAD	Promotion of Indian Higher Education Abroad
PPM	Parts Per Million
PSE	Producer Support Estimate
PSF	Polyester Staple Fibre
PSI	Pre-Shipment Inspection Agreements
PTA	Preferential Trade Agreements
PVP	Plant Variety Protection
PWD	Public Works Department
QR	Quantitative Restrictions
RCA	Revealed Comparative Advantage
RCGM	Review Committee on Genetic Manipulations
REC	Relative Export Competitiveness
RIS	Research and Information System for Developing Countries
RTA	Regional Trade Agreement
SDT	Special and Differential Treatment
SEZs	Special Economic Zones
SME	Small and Medium Enterprises
SOEs	State-owned Enterprises
SPS	Sanitary and Phyto-Sanitary Measures
SSI	Small Scale Industry
STO	Specific Trade Obligation
TBT	Technical Barriers to Trade

TCMTB	Thio-Cyano-Methyl-Thio-Benzothiazole
TEDs	Turtle Excluder Devices
TF	Trade Facilitation
TPR	Trade Policy Review
TPRM	Trade Policy Review Mechanism
TRIPS	Trade-Related Aspects of Intellectual Property Rights
TSE	Total Support Estimate
TUFS	Technology Upgradation Fund Scheme
TUPE	Transfer of Undertakings and Protection of Employees (legal norm designed to protect workers in outsourced deals in Europe).
UGC	University Grants Commission
UN	United Nations
UNCITRAL	United Nations Commission on International Trade Law
UNCTAD	United Nations Conference for Trade and Development
UNEP	United Nations Environment Programme
UNESCO	United Nations Educational, Scientific and Cultural Organisation
UPOV	Union for the Protection of New Varieties of Plants
US/USA	United States of America
USAID	United States Agency for International Development
USDA	United States Department of Agriculture
VER	Voluntary Export Restraints
WCO	World Customs Organisation
WTO	World Trade Organisation

Terms

Amber Box	The subsidies falling under this category refer to the ones in place for supporting the prices or the production of agricultural products, and these subsidies need to be reduced or eliminated in accordance with AoA.
amicus curiae	Person or organisation that files a legal brief with the court expressing its views on a case involving other parties because it has a strong interest in the subject matter of the action
acquis	Strictly speaking means "acquired" and refers in a supranational or international context to a body of laws, rights and obligations that must be accepted as a complete binding set by the Parties desirous of being part of such regional or international forum
Blue Box	The subsidies falling under this category refer to the direct payments to agricultural producers. These payments must be part of programs aimed at limiting agricultural production and must conform to certain specified production-related criteria, and need not be reduced or eliminated
CAIRNS	Group Argentina, Australia, Bolivia, Brazil, Canada, Chile, Colombia, Costa Rica, Guatemala, Indonesia, Malaysia, New Zealand, Paraguay, Philippines, South Africa, Thailand, Uruguay.
Codex	*Codex Alimentarius* Commission: International standard-setting agency for food safety
chapeau	Head note or first paragraph of Article XX GATT 1994

demandeurs	WTO jargon for WTO Members who support and 'demand' a particular negotiating approach, strategy, or outcome
de minimis	Lacking significance or importance so as to be beneath judicial notice
ex ante	Based on prior assumptions or expectations
ex post	After the fact
GATT à la carte	System where GATT parties could choose whether they wanted to adhere to the various Agreements and to pursue disputes through the general GATT or special GATT Dispute settlement mechanisms
Green Box	The subsidies falling under this category refer to government-funded ones not involving direct price support, and according to AoA, these subsidies need not be reduced or eliminated.
ipso facto	By virtue of that fact.
lex generalis/ lex specialis (rule)	Legal interpretation rule according to which the more specific provision of a statute or treaty prevails over the more generally phrased provision (*lex specialis generalia specialibus non derogant)*
lex posterior (rule)	Legal interpretation rule according to which the law adopted "later in time" shall prevail over a previously adopted law
obligation de résultat	French for "result-oriented obligation" which stems from contract law in civil law countries indicating a liability to achieve an agreed result (for which only limited exceptions can be invoked in the event of a failure to achieve the said result)
ratione materiae	Relevant reasons

stare decisis	The legal principle according to which the precedent decisions by the courts bind the courts in future decisions involving other parties as well.
E-Visa	Economic Visa, i.e. visa for specific contractual service allowing skilled workers to work abroad for specific periods.
W 120	GATS Services Sectoral Classification List

Introduction and Editors' Note

India at the WTO: The Story so Far...

Background

It may be argued that India's positions taken at the WTO during its transition phase (used here to mean the period of ten years ending on 31st December 2004 allowed to developing countries to bring their legislation in line with WTO provisions e.g. the Agreement on Agriculture) or its predecessor body the GATT were in reality reflections of domestic policies followed in the earlier period and the role and importance they assigned to international trade. This is an unexceptional stand to take and would be expected to be rationally true for any economy. What is probably different for India is that in the nineties there was a lag between the change in economic policy and its implications for international trade and the corresponding change in negotiating stance at the GATT or WTO. In many cases the lag was a product of uncertainty and domestic opposition to the process of liberalisation itself, which manifested in confusion regarding India's stance and negotiating style as she attempted to influence the shape of global economic governance. This confusion originated from the lack of intimacy with the system, and the initial participation of India took place in the midst of structural adjustment with a mindset that had not fully accepted the framework under which a market economy functions.

At the time of independence India's share in world trade was 2 per cent, which declined to around 0.4 per cent over the next two decades, thanks to the import substitution policy followed. India made no significant tariff concessions either at the Kennedy or Tokyo Rounds of Trade Negotiations, since it would have defeated the very purpose of the import-substituting industrialisation process. A major proportion of India's lost market was captured by the East and South-East Asian countries.

There was a half-hearted effort made in the seventies to boost exports, resulting in the increased export of garments, gems and jewellery and several engineering goods. In the late-eighties, a more serious effort followed, which, however, in the face of liberalisation of import licenses ended up by worsening balance of payments. The chief reason behind the inability of exports to grow was that it was still considered as an instrument of financing the imports necessitated by a growing economy, and not an independent policy variable capable of enhancing economic growth by itself.

But there was a qualitative difference induced by a quantitative factor of the liberalisation exercise. Imports grew so rapidly due to rising GDP growth that exports too needed to grow rapidly as well. Thus India could not remain content with the sedentary pace of export growth as was witnessed in the 1970s. However in order to achieve this, tariff concessions made by India's trading partners were of vital importance and as such they would hardly be forthcoming if India did not give concessions in return.

However, certain other developments started playing a major role. Developed countries at one time not all that concerned about competition from developing countries started to change their attitudes once goods from East Asia started to out-compete local products. As de-industrialisation started to take place and jobs started to get lost, protectionism in Asian economies started to draw ever-increasing attention. From simply negotiations on Tariff Reductions, the Uruguay Round of Trade Negotiations which started in 1986 aimed at setting up a New Global Economic Order where Trade in Goods *and* Services would be carried out in an international regime where there existed clear, enforceable international trading rules. Not only were drastic tariff reductions called for, quotas were sought to be replaced by their respective tariff equivalents. Certainly in 1986, the international regime that was envisaged was not compatible with the economic regime that existed in India at that point of time. It is another story, that when this regime finally came into place, India's economic regime had changed. For one, a stronger Intellectual Property Rights regime was incompatible with India's domestic patents regime that recognised only process patents for items like medicine. While Indian pharmaceuticals flowered and prospered under this regime as they were able to reverse-engineer almost any drug produced/developed abroad (thus free-riding on the inventions of others) while at the same time ensuring (through India's drug price control orders) that drug prices in India were among the lowest in the world, the same regime also ensured that Indian companies did not invest in molecule development. Similarly to allow free movement of capital was also not compatible with a regime that depended on licences and quotas to direct investment. In short India's licence –quota regime was incompatible with what was being proposed.

India After 1991

That India disbanded the Nehru-Mahalanobis Model in 1991 was not due to its incompatibility with the coming global order but because it was deemed to have failed in her pursuit of economic growth and economic development (however defined). But by doing so, it became willy-nilly *compatible* with a WTO governed international trading order even if arguably some provisions militated against Indian interests. What made this order *essential* to Indian interests was the fact that after 1991, the stated objective of the policy-makers to go for an export-led growth strategy rather than one where aggregate demand was led by state expenditure (see Figure 1).

Figure 1[1]

Export and Government Expenditure as Proportion of Aggregate Demand

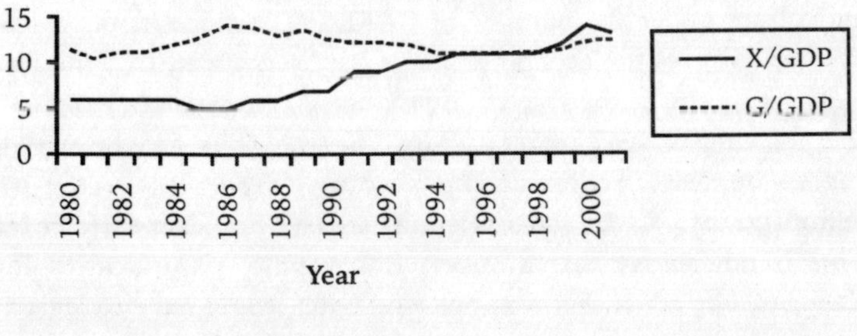

1. Calculated from WDI 2004 CD-ROM, World Bank. Here Government Expenditure is total government expenditure less interest payments as it is this figure that influences aggregate demand.

Thus the goal of open markets world-wide became imperative indeed crucial for economic growth. To this end, allowing reciprocal access became inevitable and in so far as this facilitated cheap capital goods or inputs, even welcome. That certain sectors promoted by the state would face import competition was no longer important; the sword-arm of economic growth would be the export sector and these would be in areas where India had a comparative advantage.

But at the time when the P.V. Narasimha Rao-Manmohan Singh duo introduced the programme of economic reforms, this was stated in defensive terms; that India had no choice but to globalise. Thus on issues like foreign direct investment there was a good amount of diffidence with India arguing for investment only in selected areas, 'in silicon chips not potato chips.' So while trade in goods was acceptable, acceptance of foreign direct investment was not. Additionally, a stronger regime on property rights (especially, on pharmaceuticals) was not seen to be in India's interests as that would mean Indian patients paying a higher price for medicine while the Indian drug manufacturer would no longer be able to reverse-engineer the latest drugs with impunity. While FDI could conceivably produce some gainers in India (undoubtedly, the consumers), a strong Intellectual Property Rights regime would cause all to lose (save the Indian innovator then a nascent class). India's firm opposition to an agreement on both these issues, given the furious opposition domestically to concessions on TRIPS and TRIMS, saw to it that India was left isolated and the Dunkel Draft which became the basis of the WTO agreement contained a strong regime on both these issues. A similar event was noticed on the question of including agriculture under the purview of GATT/WTO, since it was considerd the backbone of the economy. It was hardly doubted that the farmers would lose out in the face of international competition, coupled with the granting of seed rights to MNC firms.[2] Thus for the first time, India's domestic economic regime came to be constructed by her commitments to an international treaty, not domestic interest. This is not to say that a strong IPR regime is inimical to India's interests, but when that was not why India would have to legislate to ensure it.

---

2. Sharma, Devinder, *GATT-WTO: Seeds of Despair*, Konark Publishers Pvt. Ltd., 1995.

However, two years after the introduction of economic reforms, the economy started to grow, mainly being powered by exports lending credibility to the government and discrediting all those who had prophesied doom for the economy following reforms. Unlike the growth in the eighties that had given rise to a BoP crisis, this export-led policy ensured an improvement in the BoP instead. It is on this economic 'high' that the government (isolated in its bid to have its way on both investment and intellectual property rights) signed on to the Merrakech Agreement. What was worse was the fact that for the ten years the Multifibre Agreement enabled the developed countries to place quotas on exports of textiles and garments from countries like India in favour of countries like Bangladesh. What made the agreement palatable was that the first ten years after the formation of the WTO was announced to be its transition phase, during which the member countries were allowed to bring their legislation in line with WTO norms.

In all, India did not adopt a pro-active approach at the multilateral level in the Uruguay Round of Negotiation although she participated in the process since 1986 (Table 1). Although the country became a signatory member of WTO in 1994, in spite of the internal debate over inclusion of agriculture and TRIPS, it was still unsure about the negotiation strategy to be pursued. The initial response of India boiled down mainly to demand for increased market-access and extended coverage of special and differential treatment to developing countries.

The major reason for the relative inaction of India in multilateral forum during the later phase of Uruguay round was the higher export growth rate the country witnessed during the early-nineties. After the liberalisation in 1991, India experienced a double-digit growth in exports, something spectacular in India, going by past experience.[3] In other words, there was no immediate compulsion for adopting a pro-active negotiating strategy for obtaining higher penetration into principal export markets. It may be stated out here, that unlike growth in the 1980s which was debt-led and thus unsustainable, this growth in the frist half of the nineties was

3. The export growth rate during 1993-94 and 1994-95 was 20.0 and 18.4 per cent respectively, as compared to the rates of 5.3 and 4.6 during 1996-97 and 1997-98 in that order.

Table 1

India at the WTO Meetings[4]

No. of Ministerial	Place of Occurrence	Year	Outcome	India's Role
1	Singapore	1996	Information Technology Agreement was signed. In addition, four new issues were discussed, Trade and Investment, Competition Policy, Transparency in Government Procurement, and Trade Facilitation.	Mere presence.
2	Geneva	1998	Global E-commerce Agreement was signed. Also, the implementation issues were discussed.	Mere presence.
3	Seattle	1999	The negotiations failed as several developed countries wanted to incorporate environmental and labour-standard related issues under the wings of WTO. The move was strongly opposed by developing countries.	Was vocal against introduction of environmental and labour-standard related issues under WTO.
4	Doha	2001	A new round was launched and the concerns for developing countries like India (e.g. TRIPS and Public Health) were attended. The market access and implementation issues were also given due notice.	Mostly singled out in its protest. However, made its presence and position felt for the first time.
5	Cancun	2003	The members could not arrive at a common viewpoint even on the last date of the conference. The ministerial decided to take stock of progress in negotiations and other work under the Doha Development Agenda. The developing country solidarity at the ministerial was formed for the first time.	Actively protested against EU-US draft on agriculture jointly with other developing countries.
6	Geneva	2004	Five member countries came forward to create an atmosphere for initiating multilateral negotiations once again.	Played a constructive role in the process while protecting developing countries' interests.

Source: Compiled from WTO Ministerial Declarations and other documents.

accompanied by a falling Central government debt-GDP ratio. As compared to the 1980s when this ratio rose from 39 per cent in 1980 to (Figure 2) to 51 per cent in 1990, the ratio actually fell to

4. Chakraborty, Debashis and Dipankar Sengupta, *Learning Through Trading: India's Decade Long Experience at the WTO*, forthcoming South Asian Survey.

47 per cent in 1996 when the economy boomed. This ratio started to rise only after the economy started faltering.

Figure 2

Trends in the Debt-GDP Ratio

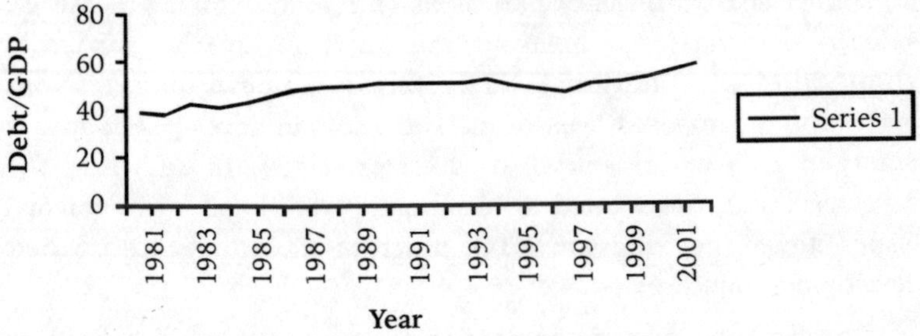

Unfortunately India allowed herself to be guided by this mindset even during early days of WTO. The first two ministerial meetings were held at Singapore (1996) and Geneva (1998) respectively, where various provisions of the agreement were discussed and the state of their implementation was reviewed. In addition, two new agreements, namely Information Technology agreement and Global E-Commerce agreement were signed in these meetings. This was at a time when India's IT exports started to take off! Fortunately the agreements inked on these issues have actually helped e-commerce and not gone contrary to India's interests. The Singapore ministerial was particularly important as it agreed to discuss in future on four issues, (1) Government Procurement, (2) Trade and Investment, (3) Trade and Competition Policy, and (4) Trade Facilitation – collectively known as Singapore issues. In addition, the negotiation over implementation of other Uruguay round provisions was also in progress, the extent and coverage of which was debated among members.

The road between Singapore and Seattle was not a rosy one for India owing to a number of reasons. First of all, the export growth rate decelerated in the second part of the nineties. The disadvantages faced by the export sector were intensified after the East Asian crisis, when the exchange rates of a number of countries in that region were devalued. On the other hand, the service sector fast emerged as a major foreign currency-earner, and the urgency to ensure free trade in this arena (or, at least in Mode 4, i.e., movement of professionals) was intensely felt. It was noticed while tariff barriers decreased to some extent in the post-WTO period; several WTO-compatible non-tariff barriers through usage of higher standards (e.g., SPS-TBT measures) and contingency provisions (e.g., anti-dumping measures, safeguard provisions) have sprung up, limiting the impact of elimination of traditional NTBs (e.g. – import quota). Non-realisation of proposed level of market access in developed countries emerged as a major source of dissatisfaction. In addition, the developed countries wanted to incorporate labour and environmental issues under the wings of WTO, much to the annoyance of their developing counterparts.

However, the most important factor responsible for enhancing India's participation in WTO negotiations was the outcome of the dispute settlement cases involving her. In general, the period between 1995 and 1998 witnessed a substantial rise in the number of cases in WTO's dispute settlement mechanism. India was among one of the victims of this provision as a number of developed countries moved to the dispute settlement body complaining about the WTO-compatibility of Indian policies. The complaints revolved mainly around IPR, import provisions on BoP grounds, custom duties and trade and investment in motor vehicles sector. A total of thirteen cases were filed against India during this period. While India lost in most of the cases, the others were 'amicably' settled, implying opening up of the domestic market. However, the cases like the 'shrimp-turtle' dispute (DS 58) proved that traditional export items of India are very much vulnerable to external barriers.[5] On the other hand, India won three cases on import provisions of textile products during this period. But the non-realisation of market access proposed during Uruguay round and increase in NTBs, coupled with forced liberalisation (i.e. substantial opening up of domestic market after numerous defeats/setbacks at the DSB) caused India to seriously weigh a pro-active negotiating strategy in association with other

5. In addition, the battle over 'Texmati' to protect 'Basmati' as a geographical indication with RiceTech is worth mentioning.

developing countries. However, it should be pointed out that a few of the other developing countries were thinking along this line. As Sally (2000) points out, "*.. there are issues on which all developing and transition countries have common interests, such as resistance to trade sanctions to enforce labour and environmental standards, credit for unilateral liberalisation, and technical support for dispute settlement. Here a united front would enhance bargaining power.*[6]"

In the Seattle Ministerial (1999), India was vocal at the multilateral forum for the first time, protesting against a developed country initiative to incorporate labour and environmental standards under the aegis of the WTO. Due to the protests of the developing countries, the developed countries were not successful in incorporating this element in the agenda. The Ministerial meeting ultimately ended in failure as the members could not arrive at a mutually agreeable solution. The then Commerce Minister Mr. Maran viewed the Seattle outcome as a success for India as for the first time, developing and poorer countries were united in mutual interest.[7] The Ministry of Commerce officially held the view that another ministerial meeting should be convened only after arriving at a broad consensus among members on major issues, and the agenda for it must include removal of the contentious non-trade related issues and the concerns of developing countries over product patents. In connection with the latter point, India also became vocal in favour of introducing a system for granting of Exclusive Marketing Rights (EMRs) to the applicant countries fulfilling certain conditions.[8]

During the Seattle-Doha period, India, for the first time, started communicating its dissatisfaction over several issues and sharing its position with other countries at various appropriate forums[9] of WTO

6. Sally, R. (2000) "Developing Country Trade Policy Reform and the WTO", *Cato Journal 19(3)*: 403-423.
7. *WTO Newsletter*, Ministry of Commerce, Nov.-Dec., 1999, (Excerpts from the Commerce & Industry Minister Murasoli Maran's reply to the short-duration discussion on the Seattle meet in the Rajya Sabha on 9/12/99).
8. *WTO Newsletter*, Ministry of Commerce, various issues.
9. For instance, Mr. Murasoli Maran, the then Union Minister of Commerce & Industry presented India's positions and concerns at the informal meeting of WTO Trade Ministers held in Mexico City during 31st August and 1st September 2001. In addition, India submitted various proposals towards the ministerial meeting, e.g., a proposal on agriculture on 15th January 2001 – stressing flexibility for developing countries in the manner of providing subsidies to the key farm inputs, for ensuring food security and other important measures.

and other international bodies. Broadly speaking, a clearly distinguishable and proactive stand emerged before the Doha ministerial, and India became particularly concerned with (i) non-realisation of anticipated benefits (e.g. - Agreement on Textiles and Clothing and Agreement on Agriculture), (ii) inequities and imbalances in WTO (TRIPs, Subsidies, Anti-dumping etc.) and (iii) non-binding nature of special and differential provisions (market access, DSB etc.).[10] In short, India strongly objected to the inclusion of any new issue in the negotiating agenda before realisation of Uruguay round promises, the non-implementation of which was costly to developing countries.[11]

TRIPS and DSB (this time, India was a complainant) provisions also played a crucial role during this period. An Indian firm, Cipla, was exporting a generic version of HIV/AIDS drugs to South Africa at an affordable price in early-2001. However, under massive pressure from a number of countries, South Africa finally stopped importing the drug. This was a major source of discontent to the African countries and India.[12] Months before the Doha ministerial, India in association with 46 other developing countries submitted a joint proposal on "TRIPs and Public Health". The proposal demanded the WTO should ensure that the TRIPs Agreement does not infringe upon the sovereign right of the members to formulate their own public health policies and adopt measures for providing affordable access to medicines. On the other hand, at the DSB India successfully challenged a number of cases related to textile products, and the sequence of events compelled it to stress more on a pro-active strategy.

However, during the Doha meeting, India was isolated on various issues, and surprisingly Pakistan emerged as a major ally in most of

10. *WTO Newsletter*, Ministry of Commerce, June/July, 2001.

11. For instance, the scenario in case of tariff reform and agriculture had been highlighted in details in the World Trade Organisation Special Study No. 6, entitled "Market Access: Unfinished Business - Post-Uruguay Round Inventory and Issues" (2001). Many economists have focused on the non-tariff barriers on Indian economy in particular. Bhattacharya (1999), 'Non-Tariff Measures on Indian Exports: An Assesment' Occasional Paper No. 6, Indian Institute of Foreign Trade, provides a detailed analysis.

12. Dasgupta, Subhendu "Their Rules Our Rights: Intellectual Property Rules and Right to Health", in Byasdeb Dasgupta *et al.*, (Eds) *WTO and TRIPS: Indian Perspective*, University of Kalyani, 2003.

the tussles.[13] EU, US and other developed countries were in favour of initiating a new round, and as things turned out, several developing countries were either not averse to this concept, or, at best, indifferent to it. In addition, a formidable section of developing countries also favoured discussion on the Singapore issues.[14] In spite of the isolation, India held its stand that any new round or topic of discussion should only be put in the agenda after realisation of the Uruguay Round commitments. The polar difference between the two sides made India's voice particularly audible for the first time at a ministerial meeting. At the end, after a series of negotiations, India consented on a joint ministerial declaration, widely known as, 'Doha Development Agenda'. Although India's concerns were morally acknowledged, the effectiveness of future market access still depended on the reforms carried out in developed countries.[15] In other words, the absence of sufficient bargaining power, due to lack of any strategic alliance with other developing countries, constrained India's success. However, the then Minister of Commerce, Mr. Maran commented that *"In sum, the Doha mandate will not in any way harm us; on the contrary, we have substantial gains.*[16]*"* Officially, India identified the following areas as gains in the Doha ministerial:[17]

- Implementation issues were given due importance.

---

13. See Singh, Yashika (2001), "India at the Fourth Ministerial Meeting in Doha: Déjà vu – again?" *RGICS Working Paper No. 32*. So in a sense, the credit goes to Ministry of Commerce, which managed to achieve a feat which must have been envied by Ministry of External Affairs!
14. It needs to be noted that India has not been completely inactive on Singapore issues. During 2003 India submittd a number of joint proposals to WTO in association with several developing coutries (Document No. WT/GC/W/522 dated 12 December, WT/GC/W/514 dated 28 August, WT/GC/W/513 dated 23 August). The proposal asked a number of clarifications on the extent and coverage of Singapore Issues.
15. T.C.A. Anant (2001) summarised the problem to be, "The consequence of the government's approach to the WTO and to trade negotiations is to create a self-fulfilling prophecy. Our flawed rejectionist approach to negotiations, with the absurd threats to leave, imply that we are unable to address our own immediate trading concerns," and also termed the stance of the country on implementation issues as 'unreal'.
16. *WTO Newsletter*, Ministry of Commerce, Oct.-Nov. 2001 – Statement by Mr. Murasoli Maran, Minister for Commerce and Industry – in the Rajya Sabha on 21/11/2001 and in Lok Sabha on 21/11/2001 – Regarding the Fourth Ministerial Conference of the WTO.
17. *WTO Newsletter*, Ministry of Commerce, Oct-Nov 2001.

- ILO had been acknowledged as the appropriate forum for discussing labour-related concerns.
- Market access issues in agriculture were discussed, and Special and Differential Treatment for developing countries was focused.
- In services, the importance for ensuring free movement of natural persons has been acknowledged.
- A separate declaration on TRIPS and Public Health was included in the Doha Development Agenda, in which India played a key role.
- Negotiations in the area of market access on non-agricultural products were discussed, while the special needs and interests of developing countries were acknowledged.[18]
- The Council for TRIPS was assigned to address the issues of biological diversity, protection of traditional knowledge and folklore.

Buoyed by the success achieved at Doha, India tried to utilise the two-year period before Cancun in a much productive manner and coalition-formation experience with other developing countries were fruitful not only for general agreements that affected merchandise and services trade, but also in case of institutional arrangements like dispute settlement.[19] The movement towards a pro-active strategy at the WTO was accompanied towards implementing an increasingly WTO compatible regime at home (Table 2) and frustration mounted

18. India has a reason to pursue this, as it stands to gain heavily from the market access generated. Chadha *et al.* (2003) note that if only Uruguay Round commitments are fully implemented, then India's welfare gain reaches 0.68 per cent (US $ 2.8 billion over its 2005 GDP). However if the Doha round agenda is implemented as well, then the gain would amount to 1.67 per cent (US $ 7.0 billion). Rajesh Chadha, Drusilla Brown, Alan Deardorff and Robert M. Stern, "Computational Analysis of the Impact on India of the Uruguay Round and the Doha Development Agenda Negotiations", in Aaditya Mattoo and Robert M. Stern (Eds) *India and the WTO*, World Bank and Oxford University Press, 2003, pp. 13-46.
19. India has submitted two proposals to WTO along with several other developing nations. The first proposal submitted on 23rd September 2002 and the partner countries were Cuba, Honduras, Malaysia, Pakistan, Sri Lanka, Tanzania and Zimbabwe. The second proposal dated 9th October 2002 was submitted in association with Cuba, Honduras, Indonesia, Malaysia, Pakistan, Sri Lanka, Tanzania and Zimbabwe. The two proposals suggested a number of modifications in the DSU agreements, and imposition of a mechanism to ensure strict compliance to these by developed countries has also been sought.

at not obtaining the desired level of market access in principal export destinations. In Cancun, India principally negotiated over liberalisation of agricultural trade and trade in services; in particular Mode 4 of the later.[20] In line with the concern raised at Doha, India was, extremely, particular about ensuring transparency in the negotiations to take place in Cancun ministerial. While in case of Mode 4, India's concern circled around transparency in granting of visa procedures in developed countries and various other procedural bottlenecks; the debate over agricultural trade circled around the distortions caused by the subsidisation schemes of EU and US, where the realised PSE or AMS levels are quite high. Since the Doha round, EU has promised to reform its domestic policies on several occasions, but has delivered little. To make things worse, a few days ahead of Cancun, EU and US jointly came up with a proposal; completely bypassing the issue of agricultural reform in Cancun Ministerial, focusing on non-agricultural tariff related issues instead. Several developing countries, led by India, Brazil and China, came out with an alternate proposal, and successfully blocked the EU-US plan. The emergence of G-20 as a bargaining group, and the solidarity between them marked the beginning of a new era in WTO negotiations.

The Developing Country members (G-20 and others) made it clear that the 'Derbez Draft' released at the ministerial, could not be taken as a basis of negotiation in future. For more than seven months, there was a deadlock in negotiations, and only in July 2004 five member countries, including India, came forward for a discussion. The discussion, although not entirely fruitful, at least

20. "The limitations existing in these commitments include restrictions on the entry and stay of service providers, limits on duration of stay, quantitative limits on visas, economic needs test (ENT), lack of recognition of qualifications and payment of social security taxes. India has submitted a proposal on "Liberalisation of Movement of Professionals under General Agreement on Trade in Service (GATS)" during the ongoing Services negotiations at the WTO...... The strategies suggested include delinking of commitments from Mode 3 by inclusion of a category of independent professionals in the horizontal commitments, establishment of multilateral norms to reduce the scope for discriminatory practices in use of ENT: exemption from Social security contributions; transparent and objective administration of visa regimes and separation of temporary service providers from permanent labour flows by introducing separate visa procedures; establishment of multilateral norms to facilitate Mutual Recognition Agreements (MRAs) among member countries, and exemption from social security contributions for developing country professionals. The proposal also seeks specific sectoral commitments on Mode 4 from developed countries." WTO Newsletter, Ministry of Commerce, September 2002.

Table 2

A Comparative Analysis of the Two Trade Policy Reviews on India[21]

Policies Praised	Policies Where Further Reform Advocated
Trade Policy Review (1998)	
• Rapid reform in tariff rates over 1993-94 to 1997-98. • Overall economic reform measures. • Amendment in Copyright law in line with TRIPS.	• Complex structure of tariff regime and tariff escalation. • Import restriction on consumer goods. • Restrictive import licenses and other procedural hassles on imports. • Presence of indirect subsidies, export subsidies and other incentives. • Unfinished compliance with TRIPS. • Reform in case of agricultural products. • Transparency in decision making. • Reform in services.
Trade Policy Review (2002)	
Policies Praised	*Policies Where Further Reform Advocated*
• Simplification of tariff structure. • Complete elimination of quantitative restrictions. • Reduction in export restrictions. • Review of FDI policy. • Move towards full conformity with TRIPS • Significant reform in certain key service sectors e.g.-telecommunication, financial services and to some extent in infrastructural services.	• Increase in use of contingency measures on imports. • Wide range of price and distribution controls in agriculture. • Existence of certain commodity specific entry restrictions.

Source: Compiled on the basis of the Country Review on India (WTO – 1998, 2002).

21. Chaisse, Julien and Debashis Chakraborty, "Disputes Resolution in the WTO: In the Light of Chinese and Indian Involvements" in Bibek Debroy and Mohd. Saqib (Ed.) *Future Negotiation Issues at WTO: An India-China Perspective*, pp. 377-432, New Delhi: Globus Books, 2004.

paved the path for future negotiations along the declaration, known as 'July text'. In addition, the intensity of proactive approach was further noticed in the sharp increase in the number of joint submissions at WTO, ranging from agriculture to services. Interestingly, the Indian submissions to WTO, both joint and individual, stressed both export promotion (enhancement of market access) and domestic protection (e.g. provision of special products, special safeguard mechanism in agriculture) much vigorously. On the other hand, domestic reforms have been regularly undertaken in order to enhance compliance with WTO. The adoption of the 2005 Patents Ordinance and its subsequent tabling in Parliament, in spite of the domestic opposition, is the best example of it.

Table 3

An Analysis of India's Submissions at WTO[22]

(Number of Submissions)

Subject Area	*1997*	*1998*	*1999*	*2000*	*2001*	*2002*	*2003*	*2004*	*Total*
Agriculture	7 (-)	7 (-)	0 (-)	5 (3)	6 (1)	1 (-)	6 (4)	2 (2)	34 (10)
Competition Policy	1 (-)	3 (-)	0 (-)	1 (-)	0 (-)	2 (-)	0	0	7 (-)
Dispute Settlement	0	0	0	0	0	4 (3)	1 (1)	0	5 (4)
Environment	2 (-)	2 (-)	0	3 (-)	0	0	1 (-)	0	8 (-)
General Council	0	4 (-)	29 (9)	1 (-)	7 (5)	1 (1)	8 (7)	1 (1)	51 (23)
Investment	1 (-)	1 (-)	4 (-)	1 (-)	1 (-)	4 (1)	0	0	12 (1)
Non-Agricultural Market Access	0	0	0	0	0	1 (-)	4 (1)	0	5 (1)
WTO Rules	0	0	0	0	0	2 (-)	5 (-)	0	7 (-)
Services	3 (-)	1 (-)	0	2 (1)	1 (1)	1 (-)	5 (3)	5 (4)	18 (9)
TRIPS	0	0	2 (-)	7 (2)	4 (4)	4 (3)	1 (1)	1 (1)	19 (11)

(The numbers in the parenthesis indicates the number of joint submissions)

22. Chakraborty, Debashis, "India's Participation in WTO Negotiations: The Changes in Attitude and Emphasis", Paper for Presentation at the Conference on *WTO, FTA and RTA*, Organised by Center for WTO Studies, College of International Affairs National Chengchi University, Taiwan, April 22, 2005. Submissions under service trade include informal submissions to WTO as well.

However, if we are to measure the trajectory of India's learning curve by a sector-by-sector basis, two areas stand out immediately. The first is anti-dumping, where India has transformed itself from the major affected country to an aggressor becoming quick to intiate investigations. While in the mid-nineties, it was one of the major affected countries, during the last two years it has topped the list by being the initiator of the maximum number of anti-dumping investigations[23] (Table 4). The last two cases faced by India at the WTO have been on account of these investigations. In fact, the last case has been lodged by Bangladesh (the first time, a developing country has filed a complaint against India at the WTO). The second area where India has evolved is with regards to its outlook towards regional trading arrangements. Not too long back, India was unhappy with the growth of regional trade agreements, which was constraining its market access.[24] However, from 2003 onwards, i.e., from Cancun days, it has initated negotiations on preferential access with a number of developing countries, which would clearly help it in guaranteeing an assured export market on one hand, and an ally in future negotiations on the other.[25]

Also indicative of India's evolution is the proactive nature of its services negotiations. The shrill rhetoric of the pre-1994 period of the simplistic equation of free flow of capital with labour has been replaced by a more nuanced approach that fully recognises the concerns of countries receiving immigrants. This has been no doubt due to her performace in IT and IT enabled services where cross-border service will be increasingly important in the years ahead. But also the nature of movement of natural persons that India's IT exports require enable India to qualify demands for concessions on Mode 4 laying stress on educated labour (a move that does not rise visions of immigrant hordes taking over host countries).

---

23. *WTO Annual Report* (2004), p. 47. While during the calendar year 1997 India imposed 13 anti-dumping cases against other countries, during July 1, 2001 to June 30, 2002 and July , 2002 to June 30, 2003 it lodged 76 and 67 cases respectively.

24. *India and the WTO*, Newsletter of the Ministry of Commerce, Government of India, Vol. 1, No. 8, August 1999, p. 3.

25. Chakraborty, Debashis. and Arnab Kumar Hazra, "Preferential Trade Agreements and India: The State of Affairs," *RGICS Working Paper No. 48*, March 2005.

Table 4

A Comparison of Anti-Dumping Cases between EU, India and the US[26]

Period	*India*		*EU*[27]		*US*	
	A	*B*	*A*	*B*	*A*	*B*
1 January 1995 – 31 December 1995	5	3	33	21	13	6
1 January 1996 – 31 December 1996	20	10	23	35	21	21
1 January 1997 – 31 December 1997	13	7	41	59	16	15
1 January 1998 – 31 December 1998	33	12	21	42	22	15
1 January 1999 –30 June 1999	40	6	32	20	28	7
1 July 1999 – 30 June 2000	27	11	49	32	29	10
1 July 2000 – 30 June 2001	37	–	29	–	77	–
1 July 2001- 30 June 2002	76	12	23	39	58	11
1 July 2002 – 30 June 2003	67	12	15	32	29	12

It is pertinent to point out what the WTO does for India - by supplementing India's internal market with the global market offers India the opportunity to utilise its most abundant factor labour, both skilled as well as not so skilled:

- it offers the opportunity to supplement its meager capital with investment from the rest of the world to enhance growth,
- it allows Indian entrepreneurs to plan for global markets given the fact that their export destinations have to be governed by laws that are WTO compatible and thus are rule based and not run by administrative fiat.

How India *utilises* this opportunity is a separate matter For example, India's export performance depends on a great deal on what the state delivers on the infrastructure front India's infrastructure is woefully inadequate to cater to industry as well as agriculture, and erodes competitiveness in both sectors. This can either be remedied by investment by the state and/or by instituting reforms to let the market participate in the solution of this problem.

---

26. Chakraborty (2005), op. cit.

27. The data includes the anti-dumping measures imposed on individual EU member states as well.

This is true to varying degrees whether it be irrigation, port facilities, railways or power. It is India's shortcomings in this area as well as irrational policies that limit firm size (to deny scale economies) in precisely those areas where India possesses comparative advantage that has led to the Indian exporter to be at a disadvantage *vis a vis* his Chinese counterpart, not necessarily (as some argue[28]) because the Chinese worker is more productive. It must be pointed out however that an agreement of Trade Facilitation will in all probability improve India's capacity to engage in international trade significantly.

Equally important, it must be remembered that India cannot be seen as any other LDC. India's (and certainly China's) level of development has endowed both economies with Industrial structures and institutions with the help of which they can mount export initiatives in an array of different sectors. In the same vein, both countries (certainly India) can use provisions on TRIPS to provide for cheap medicine against pandemics like AIDS. In this situation India's performance in the global economy under the aegis of the WTO will be better than a uni-commodity LDC and therefore its negotiating positions are different. For example, where many LDCs with an employment problem would be interested in securing concessions on the movement of natural persons, India would be satisfied with concessions in the area of cross-border services and consumption abroad, given the phenomenal growth in Business Process Outsourcing aided by revolutionary developments in telecommunications, Information Technology that have utilised India's large pool of English-speaking professionals.

With regard to the stated objective of WTO, to achieve policy coherence with the bank or the fund, this must be some time off. Given the dual nature of the economy in India where given severe institutional shortcoming markets do not clear (leading to situations that there exist massive food surpluses along with underutilised labour) Keynesian policies even when they breach the demands for, fiscal discipline cannot be wished away. Indeed, if deficits are due to productive expenditure (irrigation projects, placing orders with

---

28. Sikdar, S, *Contemporary Issue in Globalisation, An Introduction to Theory and Policy in India*, Oxford University Press, 2002.

Bharat Heavy Electricals Limited to build power plants), they may be totally non-inflationary.[29] It may be noted, however, that had government procurement been taken for discussion at the WTO, Keynesian policies aimed at boosting domestic demand even via productive expenditures may not have been compatible under WTO law.

To summarise, the problem areas on freeing international trade are yet to be resolved, and it is unlikely that the scenario would drastically change from January 2005 onwards. While tariff barriers have declined over the last ten years, newer standard-related and procedural non-tariff barriers have been devised to protect the market. Even the effectiveness of tariff reduction in strategic areas has been subjected to questions. In agriculture, the debate over subsidisation issue is far from over, and the tussle between developed and developing countries is likely to intensify in coming days. In industry, the increasing use of contingency and safeguard measures has turned out to be another major source of dispute. Within industry, two sectors need special attention, where post-transitory phase scenario has a significant implication on developing countries– Pharmaceutical and Textile sector. While the public health related concern in case of TRIPS is quite high in developing countries like India, especially in a product patent regime, the MFA phase-out might turn out to be a boon (if India responds swiftly enough). In case of services, the conflict of interests between developed and developing countries in liberalisation of various modes is playing the key role with no global agreement in sight. Finally, the effectiveness of WTO rules like special and differential treatment and dispute settlement procedures in protecting the interest of developing country members has often been questioned, and an in-depth study of the same is the need of the hour and it is precisely this that volume attempts to accomplish.

About This Volume

While the preceding sections have provided a narrative of what has transpired in some key sectors of the Indian economy in so far

29. Rakshit, M. "The Uses and Abuses of Fiscal Policy" in R.E.B. Lucas & Papanek, G. edited *The Indian Economy: Recent Developments and Future Prospects*, Oxford University Press, New Delhi, 1988.

as they are related to the external sector, the main objective of the volume is geared to throw light on the available options and concerns of India in areas that are of interest to her in the *post-transition* period. Thus this volume aims to be almost entirely projective in outlook.

Therefore the analyses contained in this book are not merely concerned at short-term outlooks and tactics, but is geared at long term strategies and interests. To this end the volume mainly focuses on the key areas (e.g. trade in services) where global agreements have not yet been negotiated and areas where it is unlikely that a globally binding agreement will be arrived in the near future. But the volume also looks at areas which are likely to be affected by changes induced by recent developments in the WTO regime like textiles and garments. Similarly issues on agriculture where the international trade regime is far from stabilisation have to be examined for impact and appropriate strategy. By this criterion, a key sector like automobiles has been excluded as the international trade regime under which this sector will operate has since stabilised. On the other hand, a discussion on seed protection and genetically modified crops and indeed biotechnology itself is paramount as biological innovations occupy a central place in India's agricultural strategy and the tensions between breeders' rights and plant variety protection have not yet been resolved. Likewise, services and e-commerce has been dealt with as the international regime is still in its formative stage and given India's present and potential prospects it is vitally important that the trajectory of this regime along with India's negotiating positions and strategies be analysed. In the same vein, we discuss trade facilitation which is on the WTO agenda, as well as government procurement and competition which are not, as the Indian government adopts an increasingly proactive approach even though no formal agreement obliges her to do so. However the trajectory of such reforms must be made with reference to some form of an international regulatory framework that is likely to be in place sometime in the future.

The volume is divided into six sections with each of them dealing on a different aspect of India's participation in WTO. The Sections are briefly discussed below:

Section I deals with relevant WTO issues in agriculture such as SPS-TBT measures and agricultural subsidies, which are very much part of India's current concerns. However, future concerns like seed protention and farmer's right and the problem of genetically modified crops, are also equally important. The three chapters in this section attempts to frame appropriate responses to these questions from an Indian standpoint.

Section II covers the issues related to industry. The major segment of the economy is the textile and garments sector and MFA phase-out is expected to benefit it enormously. However, how far the industry is likely to gain, given the state of affairs that prevails in this industry, is a major question, and the possible consequences are analysed. However, the WTO does not merely affect our ability to export: TRIPS, for example, in the Indian context, puts constraints on domestic industry which is duly analysed. Finally the increasing use of contingency measures threatens to limit India's export potential substantially, and analyses of those provisions are included in this section as well.

Both Sections have notes detailing India's trade performance in agricultural and non-agricultural goods.

Section III deals with barriers to trade and commences with a survey. Since Seattle, the developing countries have opposed developed countries attempts to include environmental or labour standard related issues under the aegis of the WTO. While labour standards are not part of WTO so far (contrary to popular belief, most of the labour standard related barriers are imposed by civil society bodies, and therefore not NTBs by definition), environment-related provisions come indirectly through trade in hazardous products. Owing to the growing importance of standards in the global trading system, separate chapter on environmental standards used as NTBs is included in Section III which is devoted to the analysis of trade barriers. In addition, much has been said about the potential conflicts between the Multi-lateral Environment Agreements and the WTO system and their potential implications. A detailed analysis of it comes under this section. Finally, a chapter that deals with the issue of social clauses and the related options is also included here.

Section IV deals with services and e-commerce i.e. the emerging sectors. This is not to downplay the importance of agriculture or manufacturing sector in the Indian economy but to take cognizance of the growing importance of services in India and its contribution to exports. Analyses that try to map out appropriate future negotiation strategy in services are included in this section. Also incuded are studies that deal with sectors of immense importance, where India has the potential of becoming a major player in the global market i.e. telecom and education. In addition there is also a chapter that examines India's options in the world of e-commece and the performance of Indian firms in adapting themselves to rapidly evolving global conditions.

Section V concentrates on future concerns. The growing incidence of Regional Trading Arrangements is a point of concern for India, and it needs to be examined what this holds for the country and how she has responded to this trend. In addition, the working of the 'safety valve' of WTO, the Dispute Settlement Mechanism (DSM) has been questioned at times. Thus this volume also includes an analysis of the working of the DSM and reform of the same in the light of pertinent concerns raised by India and other countries are mentioned. This is followed by a discussion on what standard-related barriers hold in the future for Indian exports i.e. an analysis of precautionary principles, which also finds its entry into WTO through disputes at times and which is included here. Finally an analysis on the concerns originating from Biotechnology related issues , an area which operates under several regimes including the WTO and the Cartagena protocol is discussed here.

Finally Section VI deals with the Singapore issues. Our decision to put it at the end does not mean that they are not important from an Indian perspective. However, in the light of India's disinterest in discussing most of these issues imply that movement towards a unified global regime governing these subjects will not fructify now. In the current analysis, we include three Singapore issues - Trade Facilitation (which is on the agenda) as well Government Procurement (given its importance in any mixed economy) and Competition Policy, which while not on the agenda are areas that are immensely important for India and where India has been proactive on its own.

Section I

Agriculture and Exports: What Lies Ahead

Although the proportional share of agriculture in India's trade basket is declining, it still is an important component of exports. The potential threats to this sector originate from three principal sources-higher standards and subsidies in developed countries and the debates over farmers' right on the seed to be used for sowing.

The standards-related problems in agriculture, mostly on SPS-TBT, originate from the variation and lack of conformity across the member countries' domestic regulations. Pritam Banerjee details the problems faced by Indian exporters on this front, elaborating on the government's trade diplomacy followed so far to counter trade losses. Banerjee emphasises the role that Indian standard-guaranteeing institutions have to play in this regard to evade SPS regulations. Where multilateral fora are concerned, India should coordinate with countries like China and CAIRNS group to ensure proper working of potentially trade-distorting provisions of the SPS agreement. Furthermore, Banerjee suggests adoption of aggressive moves to get bilateral recognitions of India's laboratory with major trading partners on various applied standards; protecting Indian consumers from unhealthy imports at the same time.

The other major problem concerning agriculture is the continuation of domestic subsidy policies in a number of developed countries. Citing their WTO-incompatibility on a case-by-case basis and focusing on the negotiation trends over the last decade, Debashis Chakraborty and Yashika Singh argue that this scenario is not likely to change significantly in the post-transitory phase. Welcoming the formation of G-20 and later that of G-33, the authors have concluded that in order to get increased market access from the developed countries in agriculture, the developing countries must continue on the track of collective proactive bargaining policy already adopted (i.e., negotiate jointly).

The debate on the granting of intellectual property right on seeds and its implications on developing country farmers have been a major area of concern, and also the driving motive for opposing inclusion of TRIPS under WTO. Amir Ullah Khan presents an Indian perspective on this issue by analysing the Indian and the global seed industry. So far the domestic research has been dominated by public sector, which has focused on generation, testing and diffusion of relevant technologies. However, the scenario is slowly changing and the stronger intellectual property right would provide incentives to innovators to spend money in research. More dynamism is expected in research trends in seed industry, as private sector has a sizeable presence in many crops. Although the idea of seed protection does not receive an unmixed welcome in India, as NGOs and environmentalist groups are extremely vocal about the impact of these developments on bio-diversity, on the whole it is likely to benefit the agriculture sector. In addition, the debate over the genetically modified organisms (GMOs) is another area of discord among WTO members. While Argentina, China and the US are major producers of the GM crops and therefore wants free trade in these items (corn, soya etc.), EU and African countries are not quite willing for it and insists for labeling these products. In the Indian context, the debate over Bt Cotton is yet to be over. Khan provides a detailed overview of the developments on that front in India, and argued guaranteeing property right would benefit the industry through enhanced incentive for research and development.

1

SPS-TBT Measures: Harmonisation and Diversification?

PRITAM BANERJEE

Introduction

As the WTO led multilateral regime on trade reduces tariff protection and opens up markets, especially in hitherto heavily protected sectors like processed agriculture and marine products, countries will try and protect such markets through other, non-tariff means. This precisely what makes Technical Barriers to Trade (TBT), and in that context Sanitary and Phyto-Sanitary measures (SPS), so important for any future discussion on trade policy and trade diplomacy. There is absolutely no doubt that Non-Tariff Barriers (NTB), especially TBTs, will become the cornerstone of protectionist measures, and the main area of trade disputes of the future. Given India's strong interest in the exports of processed food (both agricultural and marine), such TBTs, especially the SPS related measures, become very important for Indian policy-makers. This article makes an attempt to lay out the issues related to TBT, in particular the SPS agreement, from an Indian point of view, keeping in mind Indian interests.

It was quite clear by the end of the Doha Development Round (DDA) that domestic regulation affecting imports through technical requirements, testing, certification, and labeling represent one of the most important new areas for focus in continuing trade liberalisation efforts. Mandatory regulations imposed by governments at the border can produce serious distortions in commercial markets. Domestic regulatory systems may restrain trade and limit market entry through environmental, health, or safety mandates not based on international norms, for example. These types of market-access requirements may or may not be discriminatory within the context of WTO disciplines, including commitments undertaken by WTO members in the Agreement on Technical Barriers to Trade or Agreement on the Application of Sanitary and Phyto-sanitary Standards. In sum, whether sanctioned or not under multilateral trade rules, technical regulations imposed on trade in goods and agricultural products are affecting trade patterns, the ability of producers to enter new export markets, and also consumer costs. Important questions remain, however, the answers to which will directly affect trade policy choices and the success or failure of liberalisation efforts in which developing countries like India have a direct stake.

Industry calls to focus on costs of regulatory barriers to trade have accelerated over the past decade. There have been few attempts, however, to determine the economic impact of differing standards and conformity assessment requirements based on rigorous empirical analysis and research.

On the face of it, there is nothing wrong with the TBT and SPS agreements in the context of the WTO *per se*. In essence, the TBT agreement commits the WTO members to use international standards whenever possible and not to introduce national standards that favour domestic production. The agreement on Sanitary and Phyto-Sanitary products establishes the principles that WTO members need to produce scientific evidence when they appeal to the protection of health in order to justify a trade restrictive measure. These two agreements thus provide specific arguments that can justify discriminatory measures. Technical barriers covered by the TBT can thus be challenged in terms of their conformity with respectively the TBT and SPS agreements. These actions will then typically question the validity of the justification behind the trade restrictive measures. One also cannot ignore the fact that the issue of human and animal health and plant protection is getting very high in several developed countries' agenda fuelled by recent cases of food poisoning, spread of pests among animals and environmental contamination. International trade is perceived as a magnifier of such problems. While appreciating that in several cases these concerns are genuine, developing countries fear that developed countries may use SPS measures for protectionist purposes.

Thus the major difficulty in dealing with SPS measures is to distinguish those measures which are justified by a legitimate goal and have a scientific justification from those which are applied to shield domestic producers, developing country concern is well founded. This need for specialist scientific or technical knowledge makes restrictions imposed for health and safety much more difficult to challenge than some other barriers to trade. While the requirements for SPS measures to be based on scientific evidence helps secure trade policy objectives, it is perceived by environment and consumer protection groups as a dangerous limitation on the right of governments to take precautionary measures to protect their citizens and the environment against risks which can have irreversible effects. Differences between "sound science" and the "precautionary approach" to health and safety are causing acute tensions among countries. Among the other difficulties identified by the developing countries on application of SPS to trade are the high cost of adaptation, the irrelevance of foreign standards to local conditions, the lack of timely and adequate information and consequent transaction costs, the difficulties in understanding the requirements as well as testing and monitoring them, the perceived lack of scientific data for specific threshold or limiting values and the uncertainty that arises from rapidly changing stringent requirement in overseas market.

The situation is further complicated by the emergence of biotechnology and international trade in biotechnology products. Because of the scientific uncertainty related to the impact of biotechnology products on health and on the environment and because of strong consumer resistance in some countries to production and consumption of these products, restrictive trade measures affecting bio-engineered products are increasingly being implemented by a number of governments. Developing countries are facing several challenges in this field. As exporters, they may have to prove that their products do not contain any bio-engineered inputs. This may imply a system of certification and segregation that can be rather costly and burdensome. As importers, those developing countries that have imposed trade restrictive measures affecting bio-engineered imports are in a rather difficult position to justify the scientific basis of their trade measures.

The Doha Ministerial Decision on Implementation-Related Issues and Concerns provides some flexibility to developing countries in relation to the time frame for compliance with the SPS measures, to the interval between the publication of a SPS measure and its entry into force, to the issue of equivalence, to developing country participation in the international standard-setting activities, and to technical assistance.

For developing countries the most promising option to maintain and expand their agricultural and food exports is to become able to respond to the exigencies which are emerging in their target markets by providing high quality and safe products. This implies building up knowledge, skills and capabilities. Strengthening domestic capacities in the SPS domain would also help developing countries to identify products that they may wish to keep out of their markets because of the actual or potential negative impact on local people's health and safety, animal health or the environment. However, for this goal to materialise, developing countries need the support of their developed partners, of the international trade organisations and of technical organisations. They also need a multilateral legal framework, which facilitates the achievement of such a result.

The Article 9 of the SPS Agreement in this context talks about technical assistance and capacity building in the first instance. On the other hand, a relaxation (Article 10 and 14) for the least developed countries is also provided. Notwithstanding these concessions, developing countries' fears on SPS becoming increasingly important in the future and developing into significant barriers to trade have come true. Although the SPS agreement has established certain standards for the application of measures, disagreements between countries about these measures often involve complex issues not specifically addressed by the texts of the agreements. First, the agreement requires measures to be based on scientific principles, but scientific research on certain topics may not exist or existing research may be inconclusive.

Given this brief background, this chapter shall investigate the issue of SPS-TBT on the following lines:

- Section 1 defines the concepts of Non-Tariff Barriers (NTBs), Technical Barriers (TBTs) and SPS.

- Section 2 takes a brief look at Indian trade diplomacy on SPS-TBT issues.
- Section 3 takes a broad overview of SPS-TBT and its relevance to India and its agricultural sector.
- Section 4 takes a specific look at some important SPS-TBT related problems that Indian agricultural sector faced and the strategy adopted by the Indian Government to face up to them.
- Section 5 analyses some of the domestic policy steps taken to meet the SPS-TBT challenges facing Indian agriculture.

The chapter ends with a conclusion and some policy recommendations.

Defining the Concepts: NTB, TBT and SPS

SPS and TBT come broadly under the term NTB. It is important at this stage to define the scope of NTB in general, and SPS and TBT in particular.

Hillman[1] defines NTBs as "Any governmental device or practice other than a tariff which directly impedes the entry of imports into a country and which discriminates against imports, but does not apply with equal force on domestic production or distribution." This definition includes standards of identity, measure, and quality, SPS measures, and packaging measures.

However, distinguishing an NTB from a legitimate regulation for protecting consumers can be difficult. That is why other authors emphasise that the term "barrier" should not be applied to measures that may have an incidental effect of restricting trade but whose principal objective is to correct market inefficiencies. On the basis of a definition of NTBs given by Baldwin,[2] who restricted the concept to measures that decrease world global revenue, trade-restricting regulations that have overall positive welfare effects should not be considered NTBs. A third definition of NTBs relies on the idea that

1. Hillman, J.S. 1991. *Technical Barriers to Agricultural Trade*. Boulder, CO: Westview Press.
2. Baldwin, R 1970. *Non-Tariff Distortions in International Trade*. Washington D.C.: Brookings Institution.

a regulatory measure should be compared to the measure that would have been implemented if it had been designed for domestic purposes only. Fisher and Serra,[3] for example, characterise a standard (in an open economy) as non-protectionist if it corresponds to the standard that the social planer would use if all firms were domestic. This makes it possible to account for the welfare-enhancing effect of a standard in the presence of negative externalities.

What is TBT?

A category of non-tariff barriers to trade, TBTs are the widely divergent measures that countries use to regulate markets, protect their consumers, or preserve their natural resources (among other objectives), but they also can be used (or perceived by foreign countries) to discriminate against imports in order to protect domestic industries. TBTs with the greatest impact on agriculture are the various sanitary and phyto-sanitary (SPS) measures designed to protect humans, animals, and plants, from diseases, pests, and other contaminants. Examples of TBTs, other than SPS measures, are rules for product weight, size, or packaging; ingredient or identity standards; mandatory labeling; shelf-life restrictions; and import testing and certification procedures. While in general terms SPS can be considered to be a sub-category within the larger group of TBT, in the WTO context, especially with regards to disputes, a distinction is made between SPS and TBT, as two separate agreements exist in within the WTO for SPS and TBT.

The SPS Agreement is a new agreement concluded during the Uruguay Round, a plurilateral Agreement on Technical Barriers to Trade (TBT), applying only to those countries that chose to accept it, had already been negotiated during the Tokyo Round (1974-1979). The TBT agreement, while not primarily negotiated, having SPS concerns in mind, covered, nevertheless, requirements for food safety, animal and plant health measures, inspection and labelling. This Agreement was modified during the Uruguay Round and constitutes an integral part of the Final Act of the Uruguay Round, thus applying to all WTO Members. It covers all technical

3. Fisher, R., and P. Serra. 2000. "Standards and Protection." *Journal of International Economics* 52: 377-400.

regulations and voluntary standards and the procedures to ensure that these are met, except when these are sanitary or phyto-sanitary measures as defined by the SPS Agreement. The TBT Agreement also covers measures aimed at protecting human health or safety, animal or plant life or health.

To identify whether a specific measure is subject to the provisions of the SPS or the TBT Agreement, it is necessary to look at the purposes for which it has been adopted. As a general rule, if a measure is adopted to protect *human life* from the risks arising from additives, toxins, plant and animal-carried diseases; *animal life* from the risks arising from additives, toxins, pests diseases, disease-causing organisms; *plant life* from the risks arising from pests, diseases, disease-causing organisms; and a *country* from the risks arising from damages caused by the entry, establishment or spread of pests, this measure is a SPS measure. Measures adopted for other purposes, to protect human, animal and plant life, are subject to the TBT Agreement. For instance a pharmaceutical restriction would be a measure covered by the TBT Agreement. Labeling requirements related to food safety are usually SPS measures, while labels related to the nutrition characteristics or the quality of a product falls under the TBT discipline.

Indian Trade Diplomacy: TBT and SPS in the Multilateral Trading Order

The principal aim of the GATT, which had its first round of negotiations in 1947 at Geneva, was substantial reduction in ALL barriers to trade, both tariff and non-tariff. Unfortunately such non-tariff barriers to trade received little attention in the five subsequent rounds of the GATT that focused mainly around the issue of tariffs reduction. India must shoulder some responsibility for this lapse. As a leading developing country member of both the GATT and UNCTAD; it did little to bring such issues to the fore. It was the Tokyo Round (1974-79) that set the stage for addressing NTB's as a major impediment to world trade. It was the Uruguay Round (1986) that saw the emergence of NTB's in the agenda of economic diplomacy for many developing countries who finally realised the potential of such NTB's to distort trade. India was in the forefront of the economic diplomacy to address the issue of NTB's during the

Uruguay Round. It has been alleged that India paid the price for the lack of preparation earlier at the Uruguay Round and could have engaged in issues such as NTB's more effectively had it not been for its insular attitude at earlier rounds i.e. Tokyo and Kennedy Rounds.[4] The following few paragraphs discuss the broad history of negotiations on products standards in NTB's with respect to agricultural trade in WTO, and India's role and stance in such economic diplomacy. The specific context is the negotiations on SPS, as they remain the crux of NTB's in agriculture.

When the Uruguay Round started, there was a consensus that the time had come for reform of international agricultural trade. The Punta del Este Declaration, which launched the Round in September 1986, called for increased disciplines in three areas in the agricultural sector: market access; direct and indirect subsidies; and sanitary and phyto-sanitary measures. On the latter, the negotiators sought to develop a multilateral system that would allow simplification and harmonisation of SPS measures, as well as elimination of all restrictions that lack any valid scientific basis.

At the beginning of the Round the negotiating positions were the following. The United States and the European Communities (EC) were proposing broad harmonisation efforts, based upon the expertise of international organisations. The EC was calling for all standards to be based on scientific evidence. The Cairns Group of seventeen countries[5] endorsed the broad recommendations toward harmonisation proposed by the EC and the United States. The Cairns Group included several developing countries with strong interest in agricultural exports and thus they naturally suggested that the burden of justification of SPS measures should be placed upon the importing country. Japan supported harmonisation efforts based upon the work of international organisations; the improvement of notification and consultation procedures and of the dispute settlement mechanism; and special allowances for developing countries. However, Japan also supported the idea that international

4. Srinivasan, T.N., *Developing Countries and the Multilateral Trading System: From the GATT to the Uruguay Round and the Future*, Westview Press, 1998.

5. Argentina, Australia, Bolivia, Brazil, Canada, Chile, Colombia, Costa Rica, Guatemala, Indonesia, Malaysia, New Zealand, Paraguay, Philippines, South Africa, Thailand and Uruguay.

standardisation bodies should develop guidelines rather than standards, thus providing countries with more flexibility in drafting SPS regulations. Developing countries, led mainly by India, strongly advocated the removal of sanitary and phyto-sanitary measures that acted as non-tariff barriers to trade. They supported the international harmonisation of SPS measures to prevent developed countries from imposing arbitrarily strict standards. In some ways India's demands mirrored that of the Cairns group in the specific context of TBT and SPS in agriculture, as the objective in general was to introduce transparency and reduce barriers to exports to large developed country markets. The similarity reflected the fact that several export-oriented developing countries are members of the Cairns Group.[6]

The Working Group on Sanitary and Phyto-sanitary Regulations, which was formed in 1988, produced a draft text in November 1990. First of all, the discipline related to SPS measures was included in a separate draft agreement. Secondly, a consensus was reached by the parties on the following points: SPS measures should not represent disguised trade barriers; should be harmonised on the basis of international standards, guidelines and recommendations and of generally-accepted scientific principles; special consideration should be taken of developing countries and their difficulties in meeting standards; transparency should be ensured in setting regulations and in solving disputes; and an international committee should be established to provide for consultations regarding standards. However, several areas remained unsettled: there was no agreement on whether and under what circumstances, countries could implement domestic measures stricter than international standards, or on whether economic considerations or consumer concerns, other than health-related concerns, should be taken into account in the risk assessment. The issues of inspection and approval still remained an area of dispute. It is worth noting that progress on SPS-related issues continued to outpace many other sectors within agriculture. Due in large part to the agriculture deadlock, the Round, which was supposed to be concluded by December 1990, was adjourned. In December 1991 the Director General of the General Agreement on Tariffs and Trade (GATT) issued the so-called "Dunkel Draft" with

6. Stewart, T.P. Editor (1993) *The GATT Uruguay Round: A Negotiating History*, Kluwer Law and Taxation Publishers, Deventer – Boston.

the intention to move the talks toward completion. The draft incorporated proposals on sanitary and phyto-sanitary issues. The Dunkel text closely followed the draft text produced by the Working Group in November 1990, while providing for more stringent national regulations and excluding economic considerations. The final text of the Agreement on the Application of Sanitary and Phyto-sanitary Measures that were approved at the end of the Uruguay Round was largely based on the Dunkel text. It fulfils the general objectives of the Punta del Este Declaration in this area.

The thrust of India's economic diplomacy *vis-à-vis* SPS received a boost post the 2nd WTO Ministerial Conference in May 1998. Indian negotiators in the WTO realised that while on one hand Indian food processing industry had export aspirations, such aspiration might be curtailed by SPS and TBT measures that were yet to address the needs of emerging economies such as India. India fired its first salvo in its submission to the Committee on Sanitary and Phyto-sanitary Measures dated 23 July 1998.[7] The Indian submission questioned the transparency of the SPS agreement and proposed that new SPS measures adopted by members need to provide adequate time for other interested Members to raise concerns. The submission further states that notification of new SPS measures does not provide sufficient information to enable Members to become acquainted with them. Often only a very brief description of the proposed measure is given and that is wholly inadequate. This necessitates that the details of the measure have to be then obtained from the Enquiry Points and by the time that these details are actually obtained, the last date for comments is invariably past. Similarly, the main legislation on the measures being amended or adopted is also usually not available and its procurement too takes a long time, which further delays the process.

India quickly followed up this submission with another dated 24 September 1998[8] on another issue very close to the heart of many developing countries, that of harmonisation of standards. India maintained that even though the SPS Agreement lays considerable emphasis on countries using international standards in their SPS regulations, curiously enough, the SPS Agreement does not define in

7. WTO Document G/SPS/GEN/86.
8. WTO Document G/SPS/GEN/94.

precise terms when a standard should be considered as an international standard. The Indian submission proposed that, given the diverse conditions prevailing in the developed and the developing countries, it may be more appropriate to harmonise standards of a particular region where similar conditions prevail and where the population also has more or less similar immunity levels. The regions that do not have duly harmonised regional-standards should be encouraged to do so. The Indian submission also addressed the issue of Institutional Politics of standards formation in this submission. It stated that "Presently, there are two major international organisations in the area of standards for foods, namely, the International Organisation for Standardisation and the Codex Alimentarius Commission. These organisations are following different standards formulation procedures. The procedures followed by the ISO involve voting by letter ballot in which all members have an equal vote. In the Codex, the decision on acceptance of standards is on the basis of the decision taken at its meetings in which the extent of participation of developing countries is uncertain as discussed above. Therefore, it needs to be ensured that standards formulation procedures are harmonised at the international level". This particular submission received wide support from several developing countries and the Cairns group.

India made a bid to pre-empt negotiations on TBT and SPS at the Third WTO Ministerial Conference at Seattle. India submitted a proposal regarding SPS measures to the General Council dated June 1999,[9] the main focus of which was the "reform of arbitrary and restrictive sanitary and phyto-sanitary measures that continue to represent a major obstacle to international trade of agricultural products". India held that SPS measures create obstacles to free and fair trade in two ways. First such measures are often developed in a non-transparent manner and developing countries invariably do not get adequate opportunity to respond to the proposed measures. Secondly, there never is a reasonable interval between publication of new SPS/TBT measures and its entry into force. Despite the fact that Paragraph 2 of Annex B of the Agreement stipulates that Members shall allow a reasonable interval between publication of a sanitary or phyto-sanitary regulation and its entry into force in order to allow

9. WTO Document WT/GC/W/202.

producers, particularly in developing countries, to adapt their products and methods of production to the new requirements, this has rarely been done. The provisions of this paragraph should therefore be made mandatory and what constitutes a "reasonable interval" should be specified. The issue of MRAs featured strongly in this submission; it held that though the SPS Agreement encourages Members to enter into MRAs, so far developed countries have shown little inclination to include developing countries into such agreements. It was proposed by India that (i) MRAs are developed in a transparent way; (ii) they should be open to parties that may wish to join them at a later stage; and (iii) they should contain rules of origin which allow all products which pass the conformity assessment procedures to benefit from the MRA. India made bold recommendations during the negotiations leading up to the Doha Development Round (DDA).[10] It was proposed by India that if an SPS measure created a problem for more than one developing country, then it should be withdrawn. Further, it was also suggested by India that if an SPS measure created problems for several developing countries but could not be withdrawn, the country adopting the measure should reconsider the same and provide the necessary technical assistance to enable developing countries to adapt to such measures. Post-Doha, the Indian economic diplomacy has mostly focused on issues of the variation of measures and 'trade harassment' of many developing countries by major economic powers and the lack of progress in implementation in areas like MRAs.

Indian negotiators have repeatedly used FAO reports to buttress their arguments. FAO's investigation has revealed that more developing countries are experiencing trade obstacles due to SPS measures. A major problem is that there is a lack of mutual recognition of inspections and standards. Several major importing countries are asking for 'sameness' in the process, rather than 'equivalence'. Moreover, so far, only a handful of equivalence agreements have been agreed upon, all amongst developed countries. The variation and stringency of measures for imported food products can be gleaned from the example of imported poultry meat. The different standards raise the issue of how arbitrary standard setting can be. Of the 135 countries that are WTO members, 15 are

10. WTO Document G/SPS/GEN/197.

currently allowed to export fresh, chilled or frozen poultry meat to the EC, five may export to the US, one to Canada and none are allowed to export to Australia. FAO rightly comments that indeed, 'Trade harassment' is 'considered a common problem'[11]. India has always found widespread support for its stand on SPS-TBT among developed countries, and often among the Cairns Group members. India has not allowed itself to be limited to such groupings and has followed a pragmatic negotiating strategy that has seen it ally with US and Canada on some occasions. The next section deals with India's main disputes *vis-à-vis* SPS and the submission of concerns over SPS-TBT that India was party to, and this shall reveal a fuller picture of India's wide spectrum of economic diplomacy in this area.

India's Agricultural Trade: Issues and Problems with SPS-TBT

Although agriculture sector share in the national income has shown a decline from 55 per cent in the early-1950s to about 30 per cent in the 1990s and about 24 per cent in the recent years, nearly two-third of the population of the country derive their livelihood support directly from the agriculture and allied activities. This is an indication that agricultural production dynamics has a strong bearing in our discussion on agricultural exports.

The Indian agricultural sector since the economic reforms programme in 1991 has been witness to a number of changes. The most dominant amongst these has been conscious attempts to address the WTO obligations in a whole spectrum, starting with the domestic farm and farmer level to the consumers. In the light of rapidly changing food habits as well as the food basket, the agro-food and processing sectors need to be keyed into addressing such emerging challenges.

Agricultural exports, against this backdrop, constituted nearly 17 per cent of the total exports from India during 1990-91. The share of agricultural exports during 1996/97 was around 20 per cent. After 1996-97 there is consistent declining trend.[12]

11. FAO 1999, Symposium on Agriculture, Trade and Food Security: Issues and Options in the Forthcoming WTO Negotiations from the Perspective of Developing Countries, Paper No 3.

12. *Economic Survey 2001-2002*, Ministry of Finance, Government of India.

But while exports of agro-foods as a whole have declined, the composition within the basket of agricultural exports has shown another definitive trend that is worth exploring. In the decade of the 90's, agriculture production that involved value addition to primary agricultural produce showed positive growth rates in exports, while exports of primary agricultural produce declined rapidly. In 1998, primary agriculture produce (Cereals, Tea, Coffee and Tobacco) comprised 8 per cent of India's total export (in terms of earnings) while processed agricultural exports (processed meat, marine, vegetables and fruit products) were around 7.6 per cent of India's total exports. In 2003, share of primary agricultural produce in India's export basket had declined to around 4.4 per cent while that of processed agricultural exports had increased to 7.9 per cent. In 2002, processed agricultural goods comprised around 68 per cent of the total agricultural goods exported from India in terms of earnings, compared to only 40 per cent in 1998.[13]

This trend has important implications for Indian agricultural sector. As Food processing is expected to emerge as one of the largest sectors in India in terms of turnover, employment as well as export earnings,[14] issues of global market access for Indian processed foods assume a very important dimension in India's future economic diplomacy and trade strategy. As discussed before, it can be reasonably expected that tariff barriers to processed agricultural produce will come down substantially, given the trend in WTO agricultural negotiations. Thus, agricultural subsidies and TBT-SPS will emerge as the two main areas of contention as they will be used as tools to protect domestic agriculture and deny market access.

Such concerns regarding TBT in general and SPS in particular as constraints on the global trade in agriculture are borne out by the rising incidence of TBT and SPS notifications in the WTO and related concerns raised by members. Agriculture and food products account for about nine per cent of world merchandise trade,[15] but were specifically targeted in 28 per cent of all notified TBT measures during 2001. Moreover, 32 per cent of all specific trade concerns raised in the TBT Committee have concerned agro food products, as

13. Director General of Foreign Trade (DGFT), Ministry of Commerce, India.
14. FAIDA Report: CII and McKinsey, 2001.
15. ITC-WTO Trade Figures, 2001.

well as 62 per cent of all TBT-related disputes.[16] Hence, technical measures and their possible trade impacts seem to be more controversial for agro-food products than for other merchandise. However, most TBT-related disputes also involve and are often mainly about alleged violations of other parts of international trade law, so that the absolute number of disputes should be interpreted with care. About 28 per cent of the TBT notifications in 2001 specifically concerned agro-food products. Of these, a quarter referred to broad categories of agriculture and food products, a further fifth to beverages and tobacco, and almost 15 per cent each to field crops and livestock products. Almost half of all TBT notifications concerning agro-food products in 2001 stated as their objective either consumer information and labeling or prevention of deceptive practices and consumer protection. More than 240 requests for consultations that had been formally raised during 1995-2001, 27 concerned alleged violations of the TBT Agreement. During 1995-98, there were four to seven new consultation requests per year, while subsequently the number of new cases fell to one to three. Seventeen cases, i.e. more than three-fifths of all TBT-related cases, concerned agro-food products. However, in all these cases violations of other parts of international trade law were also alleged. Consultation requests of 10 of the agro-food cases also alleged violations of the Agreement on Sanitary and Phyto-sanitary Measures (SPS Agreement) and concerned indeed often mainly to SPS issues. The alleged violation of the TBT Agreement was in these cases generally related to some part of the regulation or standard that was not of a sanitary or phyto-sanitary nature, such as a labeling requirement.

At this point it becomes important to flag what exactly are India's concern *vis-à-vis* the TBT in agriculture, particularly within the context of SPS. Trade impact of SPS-TBT can be placed under three main categories:

1. Prohibit trade by imposing an import ban or by prohibitively increasing production and marketing costs.
2. Trade diversion can take place due to discrimination on the SPS/TBT measures applied among between different partners.

16. WTO Tables, 2003.

3. Reduce overall trade flows by increasing the costs of doing trade i.e. transactions costs of accessing international markets.

India is a signatory to the SPS Agreements and recognises the basic principle of protecting consumers from health hazards and the sovereignty of individual countries to set standards of health and safety they deem to be fit. India's concerns with SPS agreement (and such concerns are widely shared by other developing economies) are with the flawed working of the mechanism of the SPS and TBT agreements within the WTO and lack of implementation and violation of some of the basic tenets of these agreements by developed countries. Such concerns can be categorized under the following heads:

Harmonisation Issues

Different sets of standards in different countries increases the cost of compliance, a vital issue for the competitiveness of developing country exporters. Different sets of measures will result in multiple tests and requirements, forcing the exporter to seek separate sets of certification to access different markets, increasing costs. India and several other developing countries have been pushing for harmonisation of standards acceptable globally on a product-by-product basis. An emergency safeguard clause that will allow countries to adopt a higher level protection than such a global norm will be allowed for specific periods to tide over unusual circumstances or severe health and safety challenges such as the Bird flu case in South-East Asia. India, along with other developing countries believe that a stringent global norm coupled with an emergency mechanism provided enough protection and can be used as the basis for harmonisation of standards.

Institutional Politics of Standards Formation in International Bodies

Article 3 of the SPS Agreement encourages countries to use international standards as a basis for their regulations. In Annex 'A' it recognises for food-safety, the standards, guidelines and recommendations established by the Codex Alimentarius Commission, for animal health those developed by the International

Office of Epizootics (OIE), and for plant protection those developed under the auspices of the Secretariat of the International Plant Protection Convention (IPPC). For matters not covered by these organisations, standards developed by "other relevant international organisations open for membership to all Members", as identified by the SPS Committee, are recognised.[17] For TBT related issues that are not covered by these institutions, the ISO (International Standards Organisation) is accepted by the TBT as the relevant organisation.

Developing countries, often led by India,[18] have repeatedly expressed their concern about the way in which international standards are developed and approved in such bodies. Developed countries often hold the edge in terms of scientific data and knowledge. Developing countries do not have the institutional capacities to match the developed world in terms of research and technical capacities and as a result their participation is very limited from the point of view of both numbers and effectiveness. As a consequence of the inadequacy of the process, international standards are often inappropriate for use as a basis for domestic regulations in developing countries and these countries face problems when they have to meet regulations in the importing markets developed on the basis of international standards.

Under the present rules, the Codex Alimentarius Commission and the OIE adopt standards, guidelines and recommendations by a simple majority of votes cast, when adoption by consensus proves to be impossible to achieve. Because of the simple majority rule, some Codex standards were adopted or rejected by a relatively small majority with a large number of member countries not voting in favour. It is obvious that such an institutional framework will act as an impediment to any moves towards harmonisation. A good example is the revised standard for natural mineral waters was approved by 33 votes in favour, 31 against and 10 abstentions.[19]

---

17. *WTO Handbook on Trade, 2003*.
18. Wilson, John (2002). *WTO Rules and Developing Countries*, World Bank.
19. Stewart, T.P. and D.S. Johanson (1998) "The SPS Agreement of the World Trade Organisation and International Organisations: The Role of the Codex Alimentarius Commission, the International Plant Protection Convention, and the International Office of Epizootics", *Syracuse Journal of International Law and Commerce*, Fall 1998.

Protectionist Trade Politics and the Use of Standards

India in association with several developing countries has pointed out that SPS and other such Technical Standards are often used deliberately as protectionist measures. A very common occurrence *vis-à-vis* agricultural produce is delaying tactics used by customs to clear such produce citing health and safety reasons under the aegis of the SPS. Given the perishable nature and high cost of preserving and storing such produce, such delays often result in the loss of the whole consignment. Such losses are potentially disastrous for developing country exporters. Another protectionist tactic is to keep changing the 'goalposts' i.e. periodically change standards for a product to force exporters to seek new certification and technical inputs that meet the requirements of the new standards. With such frequent changes in standards and specifications, the cost of 'keeping up' with such measures are often beyond the capacity of smaller exporters in many developing countries. The reason that many developed countries avoid the entire issue of harmonisation is because harmonisation will eradicate such practices. It is precisely the same reasoning that informs the developed world reluctance to enter into Mutual Recognition Agreements (MRAs) with developing country trade partners. MRAs can take several forms. They can be limited to testing methods, they can cover conformity assessment certificates, or they can be full-fledged and include the standards themselves. MRAs of the first type entail only limited savings in international trade, but play an important role in building up confidence between laboratories in different countries and usually represent a necessary step towards the conclusion of broader MRAs. MRAs on conformity assessment improve market access by avoiding duplicative testing and the related costs, by reducing possible discrimination against foreign products and by eliminating delays. MRAs of the third type require that parties consider their domestic requirements as equivalent, with the consequence that a good that can be legally sold in one country may be legally sold in the other(s). Article 4.2 of the SPS Agreement makes reference to this last type of MRA.

The impact of protectionism that arises out of SPS and TBT measures can have major impact in India, especially given the increasing importance of the food sector and its exports in the Indian economy. The following section deals with the impact of SPS on

Indian exports and the moves made by the Indian Government to deal with such protectionism.

India's Agricultural Exports and SPS-TBT: Problems and Solutions

It is important at this point to have a brief exposure to the type of TBT-SPS problems faced by Indian exporters in the food and food processing industry, followed by how India has faced up to such problems.

Major Problems Faced by Indian Exporters on SPS-TBT Front: A Few Major Case Histories[20]

1. **Aflatoxins in Peanuts**: In 1999 EU imposed new tolerance limits for aflatoxin contamination in peanuts, as well as a new testing procedure based three tests, material drawn randomly from a 30 kg sample. If *any* of the three tests is found to be over the limit, the entire lot is rejected. This revised standard is stricter than the one imposed by Codex. FAO Experts have concluded that if such a measure is imposed, the risk probability of eating a contaminated nut for every EU citizen will be one nut in every 27 years, far below the possibility of any conceivable health risk. Needless to say, such stringent standards are unnecessary.
2. **Mango Pulp**: EU requires that record be kept for *each* delivery of raw mangoes by farmers, making it traceable to the particular farm it came from. For pulp processing units this is a very cumbersome and expensive process. In a country like India, where most of such pulp processing units are in the small scale sector, the impacts of such requirements are disastrous. It has been pointed out by experts in the World Bank that it would be far more efficient and effective to ensure that pulp processing plants observe strict quality control of inputs during production to prevent contamination rather than bother to maintain records of where such inputs originated.

20. Wilson, John (2002). *WTO Rules and Developing Country Concerns*, World Bank.

3. **Milk Products**: EU and Japanese standards for milk and milk products demand quality control measures at the source rather than at the point of packaging (milk) or processing (milk products). This involves laying down norms for animal care, types of feed and standards on cleanliness of animal pens. In India, with its vast cattle population, such norms are impossible to implement on a large scale. Moreover, it will drive out several small-scale producers who provide the inputs to larger processors of milk e.g. Amul and operation Flood. Once again, World Bank experts on the topic hold that it is far easier and more efficient to control quality of inputs at the stage of packaging and processing, rather than trying to control it at the stage of primary production that might be spread out over a large number of such primary producers. There is an EU norm that demands that milk from only such cows or buffaloes that yield over 2 liters per day be used. Such requirements are difficult to meet in cattle from most parts of India. The OIE holds that this particular measure is too stringent and has no scientific basis.

4. **Egg Products**: Japan has rejected several consignments of egg products from India citing high levels of contamination. When these consignments were re-tested in Indian labs in Bangalore, the Japanese claims were found to be without basis. The consignment was further tested in Belgium in ISO certified labs, and they upheld the Indian findings that the consignment was contamination-free. Despite this, Japan has refused to accept results from Indian labs on *any* egg and egg-based product, causing the EIC great concern.

5. **Packaging, Marking and Language Barriers**: Indian food and processed food exporters have faced specific TBT issues in areas of packaging, marking and language barriers. In some EU countries (France, Denmark and Spain), texturised yarn must be supplied in equal length-packages, thus creating additional costs for exporters. The EU parties have never explained the logic behind such a norm. German norms for engineering products are very problematic as they are never provided in English, and Indian exporters have to incur extra costs to get them translated.

Meeting the Challenge on SPS-TBT: India's Response to Trade Protectionism

Having looked at some of the principal problems faced by Indian exporters *vis-à-vis* SPS-TBT, it is interesting to see how the Government reacted to it through submissions on trade-concerns to the SPS committee.

The only specific trade concern raised directly by India at the SPS committee was regarding the *Aflatoxins* controversy. India took this issue with the EU directives on maximum levels for certain contaminants (aflatoxins) in foodstuffs in a submission dated March 1998.[21] India built a wide coalition of interested parties and was supported by developed countries that have problems with market access on agricultural products to EU like US and Canada, members of the Cairns group like Mexico and other developing nations like Turkey, South Africa, Pakistan and Uruguay. This wide-ranging coalition had its own advantages as it led to the *aflatoxins* issue being perceived as a genuine trade concern, not the usual partisan North-South divide on SPS-TBT issues. The submission has since forced the EU to revise the maximum levels of aflatoxins acceptable for some products and sampling procedures have also been revised.

Over the years India's approach to dealing with its concerns have become even more pragmatic, and India has leveraged wide-ranging concerns of several countries to promote product-specific problems of Indian exporters. This strategy has added legitimacy, and provides support to India's concerns in the SPS committee. Two excellent examples of such strategy are the submissions made by ASEAN on Australian import restrictions on fresh-tropical fruits (dated March 2000)[22] and the submission made by US on Swiss import requirements (more stringent than Codex norms) for meat and egg products (dated September 1998).[23] Both these submissions were strongly supported by India, and in effect, brought to light India's concerns *vis-à-vis* Mangoes (with the EU) and egg products (Japan). Australia was forced to respond, and reported that "Indian authorities

21. WTO Documents G/SPS/N/EEC/51, G/SPS/GEN/50, G/SPS/GEN/52, G/SPS/GEN/54.
22. WTO Document G/SPS/GEN/189
23. WTO Document G/SPS/GEN/321.

had provided helpful information regarding the efficacy of treatment for pests in mangoes". This has led to negotiations that will eliminate barriers for Indian mangoes in Australian markets and will hopefully serve as a precedent for other important markets for Indian exporters. The Swiss are yet to respond to the submission, but the issue has been raised, and it is expected that all countries that have SPS related-barriers in meat and egg products, will have to engage in negotiation and will not be able to ignore India's concerns. Another aspect of India's pragmatism is that it has aggressively negotiated MRAs, especially with the EU, a market with which it has had the maximum SPS-TBT related problems. In the next section, India's efforts to prepare itself to face challenges from SPS and TBT related-measures are discussed in some detail, including the MRAs it has negotiated with the EU. The Ministry of Commerce and the EIC (Exports Inspection Council) have drawn up ambitious plans for furthering Indian interests through more MRAs in the future.

Domestic Policy Steps to Meet the SPS-TBT Challenge: Role of Institutions

In light of the following sections, it becomes important to have some idea on the measures adopted by in India to meet SPS requirements and establish systems that allow Indian exporters to negotiate SPS and TBT related-impediments to market access. This is especially because..

> *"..the acceptance or rejection of any export consignment would primarily depend on the domestic inspection and certification procedure adopted for the agriculture and food products export from India, on the other hand, the import procedures in the destination market will be crucial in as much as the SPS measures are concerned[24]".*

The processed food exports from India are handled by two apex-level agencies, namely, Agricultural and Processed Food Export Development Authority (APEDA) and Marine Products Export Development Authority (MPEDA). The Ministry of Food Processing Industries (MFPI) is the nodal government-entity and is proactively involved in the food processing industries within the macro issues of policies and plans for the sector. MFPI is charged with the implementation of various food safety and quality concerns codified

24. Mehta, R., M. Saquib and J. George (2002). "Addressing SPS Agreement: A Case Study of Select Processed Food Products in India," *RIS Discussion Paper 39.*

in various legislations. MFPI is closely associated with the Codex Contact Point in India, namely, the Directorate General of Health Services (DGHS) in the Ministry of Health and Family Welfare.

The business of this nodal ministry (MFPI) is organised under broad categories and it involved APEDA, MPEDA and the EIC (Exports Inspection Council) to evolve systems that will certify quality of Indian exports in each and every one of these product categories over a period of time. The product categories are:

1) Fruit and Vegetable-Processing Industry (including freezing and dehydration).
2) Food-Grain Milling.
3) Processing and Refrigeration of Agricultural Products, Dairy Products, Poultry and Eggs; Meat Products.
4) Processing of Fish (including canning and freezing).
5) Bread, Oilseeds, Meals (edible), Breakfast Foods, Biscuits, Confectionery, Malt Extract, Protein Isolate, High Protein Foods, Weaning Foods and Extruded Food Products.
6) Beer including non-alcoholic beer.
7) Alcoholic drinks from non-molasses.
8) Aerated Waters and Soft Drinks.

The MFPI has also provided for technical assistance and advice to the Fish Industry (i.e. the Development Councils for Fish Processing Industries) and a special unit to promote processed-food exports from India's North-Eastern states (i.e the North Eastern Regional Agricultural Marketing Corporation).

Export Inspection Council (EIC) and its related agencies provide certification and inspection services to the Indian export as well as other industries, both in regulatory areas as well as on voluntary basis. During the year 2000-01, the following three types of export-inspection and certification systems continued to be operational for agriculture and food products:[25]

- Consignment-wise Inspection (CWI)
- In Process-Quality Control (IPQC)

25. Most of the information provided in this section has been gleaned from EIC Annual Report 2002.

- Food Safety Management Systems-based Certification (FSMSC)

Consignment-wise Inspection (CWI)

Under the Consignment-Wise Inspection (CWI), each export consignment is inspected and tested by the recognised inspection agencies. Samples are drawn on the basis of statistical sampling plans, inspected and tested for verifying the conformity of products to the prescribed standards. Tests are carried out in the field and/or in the recognised inspection-agencies' laboratories.

In Process Quality Control (IPQC)

The In-Process Quality Control (IPQC) system lays emphasis on the responsibility of manufacturers/processors in ensuring consistency in quality during all stages of production by adopting quality control drills and exercising control on raw materials and bought-out components, manufacturing process, packing and final testing. Manufacturing and processing units, adjudged as having adequate levels of quality control in all these areas, are approved by EIC based on the assessments. Units approved under this system are eligible to get certificate of export worthiness without further verification of the quality of the out-going consignments by EIC and random spot-check of the consignments is carried from time to time. Under the simplified inspection procedure, such units have been given the option, either to issue certificate of inspection of export worthiness on their own or to obtain certificate of inspection from EIC.

Food Safety Management Systems based Certification (FSMSC)

In view of growing concern in the world over regarding health and safety parameters of food items being imported, international standards on Food Safety Management Systems like HACCP/GMP/GHP have been developed. Based on such standards, which are being prescribed by several of India's trading partners of European Union, EIC has introduced certification of product-quality integrated with the systems-approach.

EIC Special Measures to Deal with Fish and Marine Product Exports

Under the Export of Fresh, Frozen and Processed Fish and Fishery Products Act., compulsory pre-shipment certification of Fish and Fishery Products (F&FP) is being carried out by EIC. As on 31 March 2001, there were 108 units approved to process F&FP for export to European Union and rest were approved for processing F&FP for export to countries other than EU. These include eight freezer vessels approved for EU.

EIC's Current Mutual Recognitions Agreements

1) *Basmati* Rice by European Comission (for Certificates of Authenticity). This is in conjunction with APEDA.
2) Black Pepper by United States Food & Drug Administration (USFDA) (as per which, any consignment of black pepper from India, not accompained by EIA's certificate, is detained on arrival in USA).
3) Fish & Fishery Products by European Commission (as per which, the processing units are specifically approved for export to European Union and the names of approved units-sent to the European Commission for formal notification, after which they can export to EU countries).
4) Fish and Fishery Products by Australian Quarantine & Inspection Service (AQIS) Australia's official import control agency (as per which, seafood consignments from India accompanied by EIC's certificates will undergo only random verification sampling, not exceeding 5 per cent of the consignments, and health certificates issued by EIC will be accepted).

Conclusion

The above sections provide a clear indication that India cannot ignore or procrastinate on issues related to SPS and TBT as they are of vital interests to our exporters of agricultural products. Since agriculture employs such a large proportion of the population and given the large employment-generating ability of the food processing sector in India, exports of processed food products are very important to India's future growth plans. SPS and TBT are also tools by which the Government of India can maintain quality of food-related imports into India and safeguard Indian consumers. The recent outbreak of Bird flu in the ASEAN countries and the rapidity by which this contagion spread across countries is a clear indication that in a globalised world, there is a necessity for such safeguards.

India's strategy *vis-à-vis* SPS-TBT will have to take three important dimensions i.e. domestic, bilateral and multilateral.

Domestic Policy

Post-WTO experience, abundantly, indicates that Indian food industry will have to adopt HACCP as a strategic food quality management system. HACCP is a logical system that emphasises hygiene and prevention of contamination in the production process. While big companies are incurring high costs to implement HACCP, small firms can effectively employ the essence of HACCP as well. For this purpose, government may give subsidy for the initial fixed costs associated with its implementation, and the recurring costs can be (and should be) borne by the respective enterprises.

Indian food industry does not have a trained manpower to handle post-harvest quality management practices and food-processing activities. There is an urgent need to train labourers engaged in post-harvest practices and shop-floor workers engaged in food-processing activities.

Setting-up of farm schools on the lines of Industrial Technical Institutes (ITI's) should be given priority, where essentials of hygiene, food-handling practices and processing are taught in certificate courses. Such training be made mandatory to hire workers on farm or in processed-food sector.

India requires many more state-of-the-art testing and analysis-laboratories that are specialised to meet the needs of the food-processing industry. It is quite possible to build eight such regional labs across the country with the help of bodies like the APEDA and MPEDA. The next step of course will be to get these labs certified by ISO as meeting every international standard and practice.

Multilateral Policy

The Article 3.3 of SPS as discussed earlier, is quite discriminatory. It allows countries to impose standards stricter than the ones suggested by the international standards—setting bodies. In the coming rounds of re-negotiation, India must oppose this article that undermines the importance of the principle of harmonisation of food standards. In order to do this, it must work on building an alliance comprising of the Cairns Group and other developing countries including China. This alliance should be specific to the SPS and TBT committees to prevent dilution over other issues.

India should suggest the formation of 'Convergence Committees' on specific product groups within the processed-food sector. These product groups should be based on export-interests of developing countries. A multilateral 'convergent' standard, acceptable by all parties, should be developed for each of these product groups. This product-by-product approach will go further towards convergence than trying to force the issue as a whole.

Bilateral Policy

India should make aggressive moves to get bilateral recognitions of its labs with major trading partners. Such recognition will give teeth to India's quality control and testing measures.

India should identify important product lines and aggressively pursue MRAs with major trading partners on standards of such products. Such MRAs go a long way in reducing transaction costs for Indian exporters and it is easier to negotiate than any multilateral initiative.

India should take up the issue of bilateral PSI (Pre-shipment Inspection) of product quality that allows Indian exports to be subject to only sample checks rather than consignment checks. The savings made by Indian exporters due to such agreements will be enormous.

One hope is that India will successfully negotiate challenges thrown up by the SPS-TBT and emerge as one of the most successful exporters of food and food related products, at the same time, protecting Indian consumers from unhealthy imports.

2

Agricultural Subsidy: The Major Hurdle to Free Trade

DEBASHIS CHAKRABORTY
YASHIKA SINGH

Introduction

Protectionist measures in agriculture, on seemingly rational grounds of national interest, are not uncommon.[1] Support measures in agriculture took off in post-war Europe (and later in US) in order to protect the interests of local farming community. However, these measures, on the one hand, have caused distortion in the domestic market, and (at the international level) affected the comparative advantage of developing countries, on the other.[2] The opposition of several key players[3] did not allow the question of agricultural reform at the multilateral level to be addressed before Uruguay Round of negotiations, with the intention of removing severe distortions present through support measures and restrictive import policies. Although 123 members participated in the Uruguay Round of

1. For a detailed analysis of economics behind the support measures, see *The Political Economy of Agricultural Protection*, Anderson and Hayami (1986).
2. "Government intervention... in the interests of food security, maintaining farm incomes, and preserving the farming population had become progressively costly and distortionary .. In 1990, for the Organisation for Economic Cooperation and Development (OECD) countries alone, total transfers associated with support policies had peaked at US $ 300 billion. About 40 per cent of this came from government budgets; the reminder was paid by consumers through higher domestic prices resulting from trade barriers, amounting to as high as 2 per cent of the GDP (Kelly and McGruik 1992).", Gulati and Narayanan (2003), p. 6.
3. Interestingly, there exists a striking similarity in the approach of developed and developing countries towards agricultural support-measure reform, where irrespective of their development status, they are willing to favour protection with the fear of losing out in the face of international competition. An important qualitative difference must be borne in mind, while developed countries generally support agriculture through high output prices; developing countries do the same through lower input prices.

negotiations (a steep increase as compared to the earlier rounds), the course of implementing reform has never been a rosy one. The Uruguay Round itself witnessed an increase in the support measures, a major source of which was the government budget of respective members,[4] a trend that is still operative.[5]

The recent negotiations to tackle this issue may be sub-divided in three phases. The first phase was initiated in March 2000 and continued upto March 2001, when more than hundred countries submitted proposals outlining the commitments that they were seeking and willing to make. This was a starting position for the negotiations to take place. The second phase was launched with a stocktaking meeting in March 2001, while the third phase began in March 2002 with the Doha Declaration as a reference. The modalities included - setting out scope of the negotiations, the methodology to be followed during actual process, and the end-results expected; and were scheduled to be finalised over a 12-month period, ending in March 2003.[6] Based on these modalities, members were supposed to submit comprehensive draft schedules, by June 2003. It is important to ensure observance of various commitments by member countries before the implementation phase of WTO came to an end in December 2004.[7] However, the possibility of compliance with this deadline looks extremely bleak in the light of the outcome of Cancun Ministerial meeting in 2003, supposed to look into issues pertaining

4. See Kelly and McGruik (1992). In addition, Borrell and Pearce (1999) have shown that Uruguay Round negotiations hardly contributed to liberalising the international trade in sugar.

5. As put by WTO Annual Report (2003), "The disciplines on trade distorting subsidies contained in the WTO Agreement on Agriculture (AoA) have also capped support to this sector; nonetheless, support for agriculture remains high, particularly in many of the major industrialised countries, and continues to have a considerable impact on agricultural markets." p. 20.

6. While the problems of market access or subsidy issues were addressed during the negotiations, various non-trade concerns including food security, environment, structural adjustment, rural development, poverty alleviation, etc. were also discussed. Naik and Singh (2003), p. 7.

7. The WTO Committee on Agriculture earlier faced a March 2003 deadline for agreeing on modalities for the negotiations to conclude by 2005. "At the November 2001 Doha Ministerial Conference, the agriculture negotiations became part of the single undertaking in which virtually all the linked negotiations are to end by 1 January 2005." The current negotiations, http://www.wto.org/english/tratop_e/agric_e/negoti_e.htm. However, given the current scenario, this seems highly unlikely.

to global free trade as well as the working of the Doha Ministerial Agenda and casts a doubt over the success of future rounds.[8]

The current analysis focuses on the present scenario and tries to formulate a suitable negotiation strategy to be followed by the developing countries like India.[9] The chapter is organised along the following lines. First, the WTO agreement on agriculture (henceforth AoA) is described briefly and various provisions are outlined. Second, the measurement issues and a cross-country perspective are provided. Third, the Indian scenario is described with the potential threats. Fourth, the recent multilateral negotiation process is reviewed. Finally, the relevant policy issues with a focus on India's negotiating strategy are discussed.

The Agreement of Agriculture

The WTO (1994) AoA requires the member countries to observe four basic conditions. First, MFN treatment needs to be offered to other members, resulting in improved market access. Second, level of subsidisation, both export and domestic support measures have to be curtailed; the extent of which depends on the development level of the particular country. Third, all quantitative restrictions and other NTBs need to be phased out and converted into tariff barriers, while reducing the overall tariff protection extended to the agricultural sector. Finally, the sanitary and phyto-sanitary (SPS) conditions should not be erected in a trade-restricting manner. The deadlines specified in the agreement for fulfilling various reduction commitments are shown in Table 2.1.

Although the liberalisation in agricultural trade has been substantial in the post-WTO period, several concerned areas are yet to be taken care of. The tariff reduction has covered sectors

8. Naik and Singh (2003) notes, "The supports provided in the developed countries have depressed prices, reduced returns, increased risk and reduced incentive to invest and adopt new technology in the developing countries. Continuation of this situation would result in low productivity, further reduction in returns and possibly, exit of farmers from the only occupation they are dependent on for their livelihoods.", p. 60. The suicide attempt of Korean farmers in streets of Cancun brought this burning issue to limelight once more.

9. WTO Deputy Director-General Andrew Stoler rightly said that the "outcome of the agricultural negotiations will depend heavily on EU internal reforms, including decisions made about EU enlargement and food safety." www.useu.be, June 19, 2002.

Table 2.1

Reduction Commitments to be Fulfilied by WTO Members

(Percentage)

Nature of Reduction Commitment	*Developed Countries 6 Years (1995-2000)*	*Developing Countries 10 Years (1995-2004)*
Average reduction in tariff rate	36	24
Minimum tariff cut per product	15	10
Total AMS cut for domestic sector (base period 1986-88)	20	13
Value of export subsidy	36	24
Quantities of subsidised export	21	14

Source: WTO Text (1994).

adequately, but veiled protectionism is still operational in the form of 'tariff escalation' and 'tariff peaks'[10]. Similarly, SPS measures are much more harmonised currently, than they were eight years back at the time of inception of WTO. However, the stringent norms used by several members still pose a major threat to developing country exports.[11] In spite of the problems in these fields, the actual hurdle in freeing agricultural trade is the question of subsidisation. Several WTO member countries enjoy a synthetic price advantage, buoyed by huge agricultural subsidies, while the main losers are the poor developing countries, mostly dependent on primary produce as a major source of export earning. Besides, in the presence of this hefty

10. "As required by the Uruguay Round Agreement on Agriculture, all agricultural tariffs are bound, but in many cases, these bindings are at very high rates and offer limited market access opportunities... Tariffs tend to increase with the level of processing. There are signs of escalation in most countries' tariff structures." WTO Special Study (2001), p. 3. WTO Annual Report (2003) notes, "Even in industrialised countries, where average tariff protection is low, tariff 'peaks' exist in certain sectors, notably agricultural products, textiles, clothing and footwear. These peaks constitute *prima facie* evidence that the domestic dead-weight and net welfare losses caused by tariff protection as well as the costs to consumers could be high. The losses and costs to consumers are also likely to be high in developing countries, where overall tariff protection tends to be relatively high." p. 11. In addition, for details see Mehta and Mohanty (1999) and Singh (2000).

11. The protective SPS measures of the EU and US, as obtained from, "National Trade Estimates", by United States Trade Representative and "Report on United States' barriers to Trade and Investment" by European Commission, are representative of the current scenario. For detailed analysis see ESCAP (1999), Otsuki *et al.*, (2000) and Maskus and Wilson (2001). The potential threat to India has been outlined in Bhattacharya (1999), Chaturvedi and Nagpal (2002), Mehta *et al.*, (2002), and Mohanty and Manoharan (2002).

subsidisation (domestic as well as export) programme in developed countries, the actual level of increased market-access generated through lowering of tariff and other quantitative restrictions gets nullified to a large extent.[12]

Subsidy Levels: The Major Problem

Before presenting the global scenario on subsidisation policy, a brief account of various measures to calculate the same would not be inappropriate here. The extent of domestic subsidy given to the agricultural sector is generally calculated through aggregate measurement of support (AMS). The members, according to their commitment, have to keep their support measures within the bound rate specified in the members' schedule. The AMS could further be sub-divided in two categories, product specific AMS and non-product specific AMS. The product specific AMS is calculated for each basic agricultural product receiving market price support, non-exempt direct payments, or any other subsidy that is not exempted from the reduction commitment in the AoA. On the other hand, the non-product specific AMS has to be calculated using non-exempt direct payments that are not based on price differential and is generally estimated using budgetary expenditures.[13] A new measure named Producer Support Estimate (PSE), devised by OECD, is most commonly used to measure the level of subsidisation. PSE is an indicator of the annual monetary value of gross transfers from consumers and taxpayers to support agricultural producers at farm-gate level, arising from policy measures, regardless of their natures, objectives or impacts on farm production or income.[14] The percentage PSEs cited in this analysis is the ratio of the PSE to the value of total

---

12. The concentration of subsidisation in the developed world has been noted by Jank *et al.*, (2003), "Indeed, more than 95 per cent of domestic support measures and export subsidies are concentrated in the US, EU and "like-minded" protectionist countries." p. 33. The "like-minded" countries consist of Japan, Korea, Czech Republic, Hungary, Iceland, Norway, Poland and Switzerland.

13. However, all domestic support measures are not included in calculation of AMS. Most of the AMS components fall in the amber box measures and therefore constitutes only around 40 per cent of total support to agriculture. Gulati and Narayanan (2003).

14. The measure has replaced the earlier 'PSE', index i.e., Producer Subsidy Equivalent, also devised by OECD. PSE is much more robust measure of farm support as compared to AMS technique. For details, see Gulati and Narayanan (2003), pp. 13-15.

gross farm receipts as measured by the value of total production at farm-gate prices, inclusive of budgetary support. In Figure 2.1, the current scenario in four countries is provided, whose subsidisation policies have caused a tremendous dissatisfaction among their developing counterparts.[15] Although PSE index is highest in Japan, the level of subsidisation in EU creates much wider distortion due to its larger domestic market size and presence in global export market.[16]

Figure 2.1

Trends in Producer Support Estimates (1986-2001)

(Per cent)

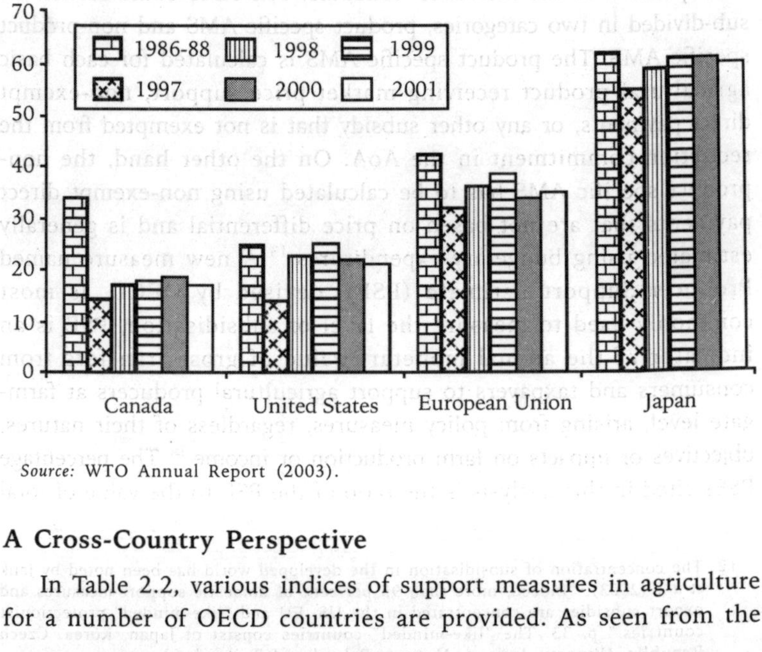

Source: WTO Annual Report (2003).

A Cross-Country Perspective

In Table 2.2, various indices of support measures in agriculture for a number of OECD countries are provided. As seen from the

15. However, Canada has now become an active member of CAIRNS group, the coalition of major agricultural exporters, and more serious on liberalisation of agricultural trade than it was before. But certain areas like dairy sectors are still heavily subsidised.
16. The fact that the joint share of EU and US in world exports accounts for more than 20 per cent as seen from *International Trade Statistics* (2002) further aggravates the seriousness of the problem.

Table, higher support measures are provided in the countries located in Europe and North America, although Japan and Korea are not far behind.

Table 2.2

Selected Indicators of Support to Agriculture in OECD Countries, 2001[17]

Country	*Agriculture's share of GDP (per cent)*	*TSE (per cent share of GDP)*	*Percentage PSE (per cent)*	*MPS + OP[a] (per cent)*	*IS[a] (per cent)*	*Producer NPC*	*Consumer NPC*
Australia	3.3	0.3	4	3	66	1.00	1.00
Canada	2.2	0.7	17	53	9	1.11	1.15
Czech Republic	3.6	1.2	17	41	19	1.06	1.06
EU	2.1	1.4	35	62	6	1.33	1.41
Hungary	3.7	1.4	12	30	56	1.01	1.00
Iceland	9.6	1.6	59	74	10	2.11	1.68
Japan	1.1	1.4	59	93	5	2.36	2.12
Korea, Rep. of	4.9	4.7	64	93	3	2.64	2.47
Mexico	5.5	1.3	19	57	12	1.17	1.21
Norway	1.5	1.4	67	56	22	2.27	1.94
Poland	4.1	1.0	10	70	27	1.07	1.07
Switzerland	1.2	1.9	69	59	5	2.39	2.33
Turkey	14.1	4.3	15	81	9	1.15	1.16
US	1.4	0.9	21	55	15	1.15	1.13
OECD Average	—	1.3	31	69	8	1.31	1.37

Source: WTO Annual Report (2003).

United States: While a number of instances indicating extensive support to domestic agricultural sector could be cited, only the case of sugar industry is discussed here as a classic example. The support provided to domestic producers at the cost of the consumers has created severe distortions, as reflected from the huge differential between domestic and world price in Table 2.3. As clearly seen from the Table, the huge subsidy cushion has protected the producers to

17. Note: a - Per centage share of PSE; TSE = Total Support Estimate; PSE = Producer Support Estimate; MPS = Market Price Support; OP = Payments based on Output; IS = Payments based on Input Use; NPC = Nominal Protection Coefficient.

such an extent that the decline in international price has not been reflected in the domestic price on more than one occasions. Groombridge (2001) in his analysis described the US policies to be highly trade distorting.[18] Borrell and Pearce (1999) have also noted the huge distortion caused by subsidies in the US in their analysis and worried about the resulting consequences.[19]

Table 2.3

US and World Prices for Raw and Refined Sugar, 1985–98

(Cents per Pound)

Year	*US Raw Cane Sugar*	*US Wholesale Refined Beet Sugar*	*US Retail Refined Sugar*	*World Raw Sugar*	*World Refined Sugar*
1985	20.34	23.18	35.34	4.04	6.79
1986	20.95	23.38	35.08	6.05	8.47
1987	21.83	23.60	35.28	6.71	8.75
1988	22.12	25.44	36.60	10.17	12.01
1989	22.81	29.06	40.03	12.79	17.16
1990	23.26	29.97	42.78	12.55	17.32
1991	21.57	25.65	42.80	9.04	13.41
1992	21.31	25.44	41.53	9.09	12.39
1993	21.62	25.15	40.54	10.03	12.79
1994	22.04	25.15	39.99	12.13	15.66
1995	22.96	25.83	39.83	13.44	17.99
1996	22.40	29.20	41.79	12.24	16.64
1997	21.96	27.09	43.26	12.06	14.33
1998	22.06	26.12	42.98	9.68	11.59

Source: Groombridge (2001).

18. "Nowhere is there a larger gap between the U.S. government's free-trade rhetoric and its protectionist practices than in the sugar programme. Through preferential loan agreements and tariff-rate quotas, the U.S. government thwarts price competition to maintain an artificially high domestic price for sugar—a price that can be twice the world market price or higher... The U.S. sugar programme is a classic case of concentrated benefits and dispersed costs: a very small number of sugar cane growers receive enormous benefits, while the costs of providing those benefits are spread across the U.S. economy, specifically to consumers and confectioners." p. 1.

19. "(sugar) producers in the United States, Mexico, Indonesia and Eastern Europe are also heavily dependent on subsidies.", p. 6.

Apart from domestic support policies, US provides export subsidies to the domestic producers as well. In 1997, WTO in response to an EU appeal (DS108) has ruled that the US unfairly subsidises the exports of its multinational companies by giving them a special tax break - the so-called *foreign sales corporation tax exemption* (FSC). The FSC tax break is worth about $3bn a year to US companies (includes all types of exports).[20]

European Union: The subsidisation policy of EU, the biggest single market, and a major exporter of agricultural products, is of extreme importance in this regard. In the following Table, an account of the time trend of support-measures in EU and US is provided. It is seen from the Table that although PSE to three principal crops has been curtailed to some extent, concern areas still remain.

Table 2.4

Producer Support Estimate in EU and US for Selected Commodities

(USD mn)

Commodities	*1986-88*	*2000-2002*	*1999*	*2000*	*2001*	*2002p*
Wheat						
European Union	8,673	8,982	11,424	9,170	8,278	9,498
United States	4,801	3,993	5,725	5,388	3,980	2,611
Sugar						
European Union	3,179	2,172	3,500	2,409	1,798	2,308
United States	1,153	1,223	1,529	1,204	1,287	1,175
Rice						
European Union	440	247	157	125	313	303
United States	868	924	782	886	995	891

Source: OECD, PSE/CSE database 2003.
Quoted from Naik and Singh (2003).

20. The panel found that the United States had acted inconsistently with its obligations under Article 3.1(a) of the Subsidies Agreement as well as with its obligations under Article 3.3 of the Agreement on Agriculture. Although the appellate body reversed certain provisions of the panel ruling, it concluded that the United States acted inconsistently with its obligations under Articles 10.1 and 8 of AOA by "applying export subsidies, through the FSC measure, in a manner which results in, or threatens to lead to, circumvention of its export subsidy commitments with respect to agricultural products.", WTO Case Updates, WT/DS/OV/16, 17 October 2003. US although reacted angrily to the ruling by claiming the policy to be WTO-compatible, promised to abide by the findings.

The basic purpose of the EU Common Agricultural Policy (CAP) is to protect the domestic farmers, thereby leading to serious distortions over the years. WTO Trade Policy Review Report (2000) has shown that the PSE has actually increased to 49 per cent in 1999 from 45 per cent in 1998 and 38 per cent in 1997.[21] To cite a classic example, EU, at one point of time, was a net importer of sugar, but turned into net exporter through a policy mix of import restriction and domestic subsidisation. However, many developing countries could still produce sugar at a much lower price. Similarly, for dairy products, extensive subsidisation scheme played a key role in creating self-sufficiency domestically as well as an export surplus in global market. To maintain this situation, EU keeps a close watch over the prices, so that no product could reach EU at a price lower than the prevailing one.[22] This huge volume of subsidy often creates problems relating to overproduction and boils down to substantial welfare loss for the consumers.[23] In the early nineties, overproduction reached a peak and EU was seriously considering destruction of 20 million metric tonnes of beef, butter and grain, as the storage cost escalated with no possibility of shortfall in supply in recent years.[24] However, EU was not ready to consider marketing this surplus domestically as that would lower prices, a proposition completely unacceptable to producers.

Japan: The support policies followed by Japan, another country with a highly restrictive agricultural regime, buoyed by huge subsidy, have created severe distortions in foodgrains sector. Various WTO

---

21. Consequently, the CSE has declined to –33 per cent in 1998 from –25 per cent in 1997, and further down to –36 per cent in 1999. WTO Trade Policy Report, European Union (2000), Table IV.6, p. 98. In particular, the subsidy level to livestock and meat products is another area of concern.
22. The import levies were reviewed every two weeks. Sharma (1995).
23. Farm subsidies account for just under half of the EU's annual budget. European Union spends the equivalent of $53.5 billion a year on the CAP. In contrast, the U.S. government limits such spending to $19.1 billion a year under WTO agreements.
24. Critics have pointed out more than once that CAP promotes overproduction of grains, beet sugar and other products, which are then exported to Third World markets. Gulati and Narayanan (2003) have pointed out a one-to-one correspondence between commodities with high PSE and high export subsidy (pp. 31). The WTO Special Study (2001) notes, ".. the potential impact of export subsidies on agricultural markets is still significant. Also, between 1995 and 1998, the average use of export subsidy commitments has increased for 10 of the 25 countries with reduction commitments, while it declined only for 5 of them." p. 4.

Trade Policy Reviews on Japan has pointed out that PSE during a significant period of nineties to major crops and livestock products remained very high, while the price was borne by the consumers. The Trade Policy Review Report (2000) notes, *"The support received by farmers in Japan and the costs to consumers of agricultural products remain above the OECD average and have increased since 1997."*[25]

The Indian Scenario

In light of the above observations, the subsidy scenario in India deserves attention, which in the global platform has earned reputation as a country favouring protection of its primary sector heavily. The notion was generated by India's long-standing history of restrictions in this front and has further been fuelled by the move to block import of certain primary products through quantitative restrictions on BoP ground even in the post-WTO period. A number of countries appealed to WTO Dispute Settlement Body on this account and India's policy was ruled as WTO-incompatible.[26] Since then India has brought its import policy in line with the WTO directive. However, opening up of agricultural sector or lowering subsidy level in this country is still taken with a pinch of salt.

India did not raise concern over the issue of subsidisation until recently. This was not because India had vested interests in not raising the issue due to its own agricultural support programmes. On the contrary, as Table 2.5 illustrates, historically, overall support to agriculture in India has been negative since the beginning of Uruguay Round of negotiations. It is more likely that India felt the need to raise concern on the issue of agricultural support in developed countries when it realised the distortions caused by such policies in the international market, which not only get transmitted to the domestic market through disappearing barriers, but also, severely harm India's ability to export agricultural products.[27]

---

25. WTO Trade Policy Report, Japan (2000), p. 86. The report acknowledged an increase of 14 per cent and 15 per cent in PSE and CSE respectively during 1997 and 1999, indicating an increase in support to agriculture. However, the value of AMS decreased by 4.8 per cent over 1996-97.
26. For details, see WTO disputes DS90 (involving US), DS91 (involving Australia), DS92 (involving Canada), DS93 (involving New Zealand), DS94 (involving Switzerland) and DS96 (involving EU). India lost the case against US, while others were amicably settled.
27. For detailed analysis of India's prospects in case of removal of all support measures in case of some important commodities, see Naik and Singh (2003).

Table 2.5

AMS for Selected Commodities with Fixed Reference Prices[28]

Year	*Product Specific AMS*	*Non-Product Specific AMS*	*AMS*
	(as per cent of the value of production of commodities covered)		
1987	-33.23	4.22	-29.02
1988	-24.73	5.19	-19.54
1989	-29.79	5.02	-24.77
1990	-32.83	6.19	-26.64
1991	-27.60	5.87	-21.73
1992	-57.50	7.52	-49.99
1993	-46.60	6.82	-39.77
1994	-51.06	5.67	-45.39
1995	-38.58	6.81	-31.77
1996	-39.32	7.89	-31.43
1997	-40.68	7.49	-33.19
1998	-33.18	6.86	-26.32
1999	-39.75	6.00	-33.76
2000	-32.78	7.16	-25.62

Source: Gulati and Narayanan (2003).

Apart from AMS figures, the overall level of PSEs provided to Indian agriculture shown in Figure 2.2, clearly testifies negative support throughout the Uruguay Round' negotiation period, which reached a trough in 1996-97. Gulati and Narayanan (2003) note that the variation in PSE is not caused by government action, but other factors like devaluation (1991), movement in world prices etc.[29] Therefore, the net taxation of Indian agriculture becomes obvious. In this scenario, India stands to gain only if domestic subsidy level in the developed countries is lowered, i.e., when the unfair price advantage is withdrawn. Agricultural products accounts for around 14 per cent of India's export basket in value terms and most of them

28. "Selected commodities include rice, wheat, maize, sorghum, bajra, barley, arhar, gram, soyabean, rapeseed and mustard, groundnut, sunflower, cotton, jute and sugar, which comprise roughly 46 per cent of the value of output of the Indian agricultural sector." Gulati and Narayanan, p. 18.

29. For instance, world price slumped in 1987, causing an increase in PSE in India where agriculture is discriminated (implicitly taxed) in terms of low price. On the other hand, high world cereal price during 1995-97 caused a sharp reduction in PSE.

are fairly price competitive. However, Naik and Singh (2003) have pointed out that the competitiveness would be seriously hampered if the current level of subsidisation in EU and US continues.

Figure 2.2

PSE Level in India

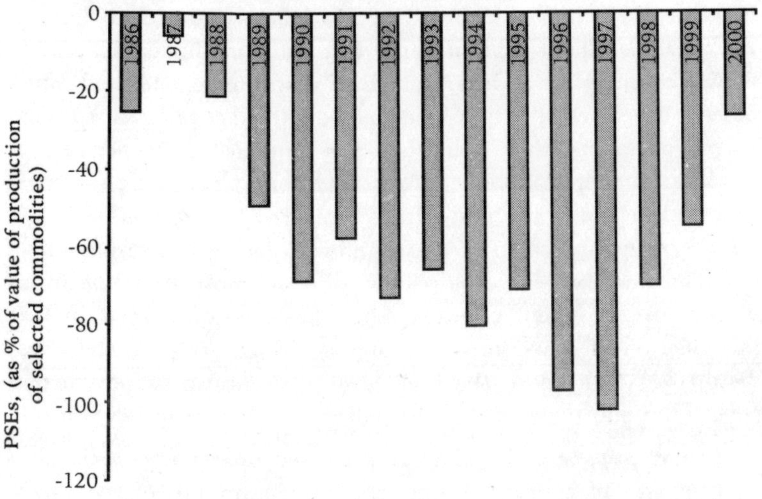

Source: Gulati and Narayanan (2003).

Threat to India and Other Developing Countries

The subsidy level in case of the developed countries is quite high for rice, wheat and sugar, the usual developing country export items. Now the developed country exporters are capable of serving the international market at a synthetic low price as the gap is bridged by the subsidy. Even in cases they could compete, the developing country exporters suffer a heavy loss because of the downward pull in the price. However, apart from the export market loss, there is a possibility that the subsidised exports of several OECD countries might displace the developing country producers at their home markets. U.S. Department of Agriculture in 2001 estimated the full elimination of distorting policies in global agricultural trade to result in an annual world welfare gain of US$56 billion.

Domestic Support: The level of support to farmers in OECD countries decreased from an estimated US$356 billion, or 1.4 per cent of GDP for the OECD as a whole in 1999 to US$ 235 billion (EUR 249 million) in 2002, which is still insufficient to ensure free trade in agriculture. In addition, the prices received by OECD farmers in 2002 were on average 31 per cent above world prices as compared to 30 per cent in the earlier year. The Total Support Estimate (TSE) was as high as US$ 318 billion (Euro 338 billion) in 2002 *(OECD, 2003)*. The presence of production-linked support in OECD countries is another source of discontent. Naik and Singh notes, "The share of output-based support (market price support and output payments) and input subsidies remained at 76 per cent of producer support in 2002 ... These measures are among the most production and trade distorting, and are the least effective in transferring income to farmers or in targeting the provision of environmental benefits. The reduction in the most distorting forms of support in some countries has been accompanied by the introduction of other forms of support, which are potentially less distorting[30]." In short, the high level of domestic support makes penetration into those markets by Indian exporters extremely difficult.

Export Support: The distortion caused by export subsidies is another area of concern. While, the overall amount of the export subsidies is showing a decreasing trend over the years, the problem is far from being solved. The level of subsidisation in EU and US causes a heavy loss for the developing countries and India is no exception to this. The potential loss to Indian exporters is very high owing to the fact that the export share of primary products in India's export basket has improved from around 8 per cent in 1987-88 to around 14 per cent in 2002-03. The hefty subsidisation programmes would lower the export earning opportunities of Indian exporters, originating from the improved market access in post-WTO period. Naik and Singh (2003) conducted a detailed price analysis for major commodities and reported heavy loss of Indian exports due to the distortions in the world market for them, and worse, sometimes in

---

30. TSEs for many countries are greater than 1 per cent of their GDP, and in particular, EU countries, Japan, Iceland, Korea, Norway and Switzerland have much higher PSEs even within the OECD countries. Naik and Singh (2003), p. 40.

their domestic markets.[31] They also feared that the recent (2001-02) downfall in US export of wheat might not benefit the developing countries, as "Farm Bill", the instrument to assist the farmers in US would help the producers to compete in the international market. The scenario is best understood from Figure 2.3, which shows that the individual export subsidy level of EU or US far exceeds the same for the rest of the world.

Figure 2.3

Export Subsidy in Major Players

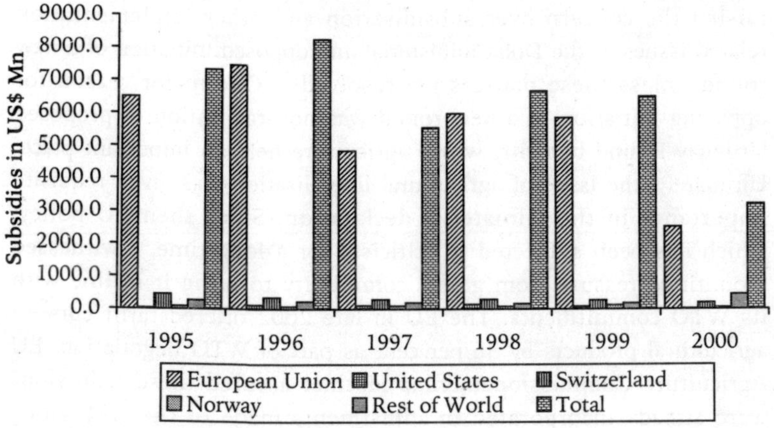

Source: Economic Research Service (ERS) calculations from WTO export subsidy notifications http://www.ers.usda.gov/db/wto/ (Quoted from Naik and Singh, 2003).

Recent Trends in Negotiation

The introduction of agriculture under the purview of GATT witnessed a huge protest from the developing countries, who viewed the event as a calculated move by their developed counterparts. The majority view was that the developed countries are interested in liberalising agriculture only after consolidating their position with

31. "In fact in some cases, such as cotton in India, the efficient producers are unable to compete in their own domestic market. Cotton imports in India have increased substantially due to the availability of cheap US cotton, as a consequence of the subsidies provided by the US to their farmers.", p. 60.

subsidisation schemes for a long time. The developing country suspicion did not vanish even when in 1987 US called for complete phase-out of all trade distorting subsidies by next 10 years (the present experience testifies that they were right in doing so!!). India witnessed an internal debate over the eight-year negotiation period on the issue of joining WTO, the main point of concern being TRIPS and agriculture. From 1995 onwards, WTO came into existence. However it has been shown in Chakraborty and Singh (2004) that although the concern over agricultural trade liberalisation was there all the time, explicit focus was lost during Geneva and Seattle ministerial, and surfaced in Doha only.[32] India was quite active in raising the concern over subsidisation and other implementation related issues at the Doha ministerial and opposed initiation of a new round unless these matters are resolved.[33] One major reason for opposing initiation of a new round was non-realisation of proposed Uruguay Round benefits, where agriculture held an important place. Ultimately, the issue of agricultural liberalisation was given requisite importance in the ministerial declaration. Since then EU policy, which has been subjected to criticism for a long time,[34] witnessed mounting pressure from global community to bring it in line with its WTO commitments. The EU in late 2002 offered tariff cuts on agricultural products by 36 per cent as part of WTO negotiation. EU Agriculture Commissioner Franz Fischler assured these reductions were already incorporated in adjustments made to the CAP along

32. This could partly be explained by the fluid state of the negotiation process during the first two phases and in earlier times.

33. While inaugurating the International Conference on "Concerns of Developing Nations in the WTO Regime" organised by The Institute of Chartered Accountants of India in collaboration with United Nations Conference on Trade and Commerce, and Ministry of Commerce, in New Delhi on August 20, 2001, the Prime Minister, Shri Atal Bihari Vajpayee said, "Six years of the existence of the WTO have not reduced the relevance of this principle in the least. On the contrary, the still unmet promises and unfulfilled obligations of the developed nations made in the Uruguay Round have cast the legitimate concerns of the developing nations into a sharper focus in the run-up to the Doha Ministerial Conference. This is, indeed, the rationale for India's insistence that the incomplete agenda of the Uruguay Round should be first completed, before starting any new round of trade negotiations. India's position is shared by many developing nations, and also by many people in the developed nations." India and the WTO, August 2001, pp. 11. However, Singh (2001) has shown that India was mostly alone in this pursuit.

34. EU practically stalled agricultural subsidy reform, as it bought time at each occasion to bring its domestic regulations in line with the WTO obligations. This in turn made any further progress in agricultural negotiation impossible.

with offering duty-free, quota-free access for primary exports from developing countries.[35] However, the concerned quarters felt that the proposal falls far short of what was needed to help developing nations. The prime objection against the move was the fact that although reduction in export subsidies for wheat, oilseeds, olive oil and tobacco was discussed, dairy products and sugar industries were excluded from any commitments. The US also rejected the claim that the EU proposals are likely to create a new beginning.[36]

In June 2003, EU came out with a new scheme when the farm commissioner Franz Fischler announced that the ongoing farm support policy would be dramatically revised, proposing subsidy levels to be based on farm existence rather than production, where the bulk of direct payments would no longer be linked to production.[37] The scheme boosted global hope to arrive at a concensus during the negotiations in the due Cancun Ministerial, as trade talks had been almost stalled because of EU's apathy towards reducing production- and trade-distorting subsidies, although the proposal did not necessarily reduce subsidy spending as a whole.[38] Some EU members stressed their sincerity in decoupling payments from production so as to devote more funds for environmental and rural

---

35. However, the move is not an open-ended one. "The cuts in subsidies and tariff are conditional on similar cuts from other developed countries, particularly the US. The US, Canada, Japan, Australia and the 15 EU members would also cut export subsidies by 45 per cent and domestic subsidies as part of the deal.", http://news.bbc.co.uk, 16 December, 2002.

36. In March 2003 EU was widely criticised by US on account of inaction in offering a suitable proposal for elimination of agricultural export subsidies. US considered the EU attitude to be disappointing owing to the absence of any commitment in reduction of export subsidies — no timelines, no reductions, nothing that helps to clarify the issue.

37. In short, most of the old premiums paid under the CAP were proposed to be merged into a 'single farm payment' independent of production and linked to compliance with environmental, food safety and animal welfare standards. The single farm payment was supposed to enter into force in 2005, although member states were allowed to apply for a transitional period until 2007. Funds saved through cutting support to big producers will be shifted to the rural development pillar of the CAP. However Naik and Singh (2003) pointed out that "...the changes will allow most subsidies to be shifted to the 'green box' under the Agreement of Agriculture, hence considered to be non-trade distorting or minimally trade-distorting.", p. 59.

38. Pascal Lamy commented that the negotiation would be successfully completed only if United States and other trading partners were willing to put their own farm programmes on the negotiating table, "referring to the legislation signed last year that boosted U.S. crop and dairy subsidy payments by $57.1 billion US from the previous farm bill." www.producer.com, July 8, 2003.

purposes. Major global players cautiously praised this decoupling proposal, while countries like Australia openly expressed dissatisfaction over this announcement.[39]

The effectiveness of the new scheme in reforming CAP shortly faced serious questions. The major obstacle came in early July from the French Government, when it refused to consider reductions in subsidies to its farmers. The French President Jacques Chirac announced that the current subsidy reform proposal of EU to be unacceptable, although he assured that France would actively participate in the reform process.[40] A compromised policy was put forward, which, however, failed to satisfy most of the key players. Initiation of a new discussion within EU clearly put a question mark on the success of the new plan, and brought a massive disappointment to the exporters from the LDCs. US trade representative Robert Zoellick pointed out in a press conference that the success of Cancun ministerial is dependent on EU's ability to reform CAP successfully.[41]

However, the climax reached its peak a few days ahead of Cancun, when EU and US (the major critic of EU even a couple of days back) jointly came up with a proposal to 'liberalise' agricultural trade.[42] The proposal by these two countries, although seemingly discussed the possibility of freeing agricultural trade from subsidies, actually made no definite promise to lower the same in their own territory.

---

39. In Canberra, Australian Minister for Agriculture, Fisheries and Forestry, Mr. Warren Truss said, "After weeks of debate and with a mountain of evidence that the CAP needs to change, EU ministers have adopted what can best be called a marginal and mediocre change. Unfortunately, self-interest has again ruled the day and the addiction to subsidies prevails.", http://www.affa.gov.au/ministers/truss/releases/03/03179wt.html, 27 June 2003.

40. http://deltafarmpress.com/ar/farming_eu_subsidy_reform_2/, June 27, 2003. As of now Sweden, U.K., Denmark, Netherlands and Germany are in favour of the reforms while France, Spain and Ireland maintain a stance that is the polar opposite to the former group.

41 *"You probably know our proposal was called a Swiss 25, which means no tariff in agriculture would be higher than 25 per cent and it would take our average tariff down from 12 to 5 per cent.. So for developing countries that would like us to cut subsidies there are really two elements for us: one is we've got to bring European and Japanese levels down. The European cap on what's called the amber box domestic subsidies that distort production is, depending on exchange rates, about $65 billion, and ours is $19.1 billion so we've got to bring that down and harmonise it."*

42. The attitude of US is hardly surprising as pointed out by Groombridge (2001) and others from time to time. The detailed proposal could be seen from the August 2003 issue of the India and the WTO newsletter.

In contrast, they actually planned to bypass the issue of agricultural reform in Cancun Ministerial, and decided to focus on non-agricultural tariff related issues. To combat this move several developing countries, led by Brazil, India and China, promptly came out with an alternate plan.[43] The proposal was directed at Cancun WTO negotiations, demanding immediate action to end export dumping and production subsidies and improvement of market access. A comparative analysis of the two plans over the major issues is shown in the following Table.

Table 2.6

A Comparison Between EU-US and Developing Country Plans

Area	*Developing Country Proposal*	*EU-US Proposal*
Export Competition	Elimination of all export subsidies, with a quicker time-frame for products of interest to developing countries.	Elimination of export subsidies only in certain sectors and simply reduce them in other sectors.
Domestic Support	Substantial reduction of all subsidies, including those currently classified as minimally distorting, such as the "blue box" (to be eliminated) and the "green box" (some items to be capped).	Continuation of the blue box and no capping or any other new discipline on the green box.
Market Access	Strong differentiation between developed and developing countries, in line with the need to rebalance the agreement, which currently works in favour of developed country farmers.	Increased market access across the board.

Source: Constructed from *www.oxfamamerica.org/art5865.html*

At Cancun, the dissatisfaction reached its peak, as a result of which no clear consensus could be arrived at even before the last day of the ministerial conference. During the ministerial meeting, EU and US came out with a draft declaration, again with little promise

43. The other members of the group are Argentina, Bolivia, Chile, Colombia, Costa Rica, Guatemala, Mexico, Paraguay, Peru, Thailand and South Africa. The detailed proposal has been outlined in the August 2003 issue of WTO Newsletter of Ministry of Commerce, Government of India.

in this front, only to be rejected by the developing countries. India expressed its disappointment over the fact that these two developed countries kept on harping their eagerness to discuss market access issues, but not the area of subsidisation. Without addressing the question of subsidisation, the distortions already present could not be removed, and negotiating on market access is meaningless. Little development has been achieved since then in this front.

The negotiating situation is very complex owing to the conflicting views of the Members with regard to the extent of reform under the three principal categories. These divergences in views have of course been a feature of agricultural negotiations from the beginning, but what is worrying is the lack of common ground being achieved in recent negotiations. Naik and Singh (2003) have focused on the various stands of the countries/blocs, which has been presented in Table 2.7. These, of course, represent initial stands of the countries or groups, i.e. prior to the Doha-Cancun set of negotiations. Country positions largely conform to these basic starting positions, with negotiations hoping to bring changes within the parameters of these positions. Since then, little development has been witnessed, although the members have agreed to negotiate on the basis of the new 'July 2004' text as described later.

The Potential for Future Reform

No agricultural subsidy reform measure is likely to be successful without serious commitment from the EU and the US. The only positive development in this front might occur if the 2003 EU proposal for de-coupling of CAP subsidies by formulating a single farm payment independent from production is implemented. However, as already mentioned, EU is divided over this issue, While the original proposal promised full de-coupling of agricultural subsidies, the compromised policy allows EU member states to maintain a link between subsidies and production under defined conditions. The international community is already dissatisfied over this change, and Cairns' Group had already expressed unwillingness to accept anything but full de-coupling. However, the changed policy is in any case not going to result in a much lower support to farming sector in the coming days. While there is a glimpse of hope in case of EU reform, the future for reform in US front is absolutely bleak.

Table 2.7

A Summary of Country Positions at the AoA Negotiations

Countries/Groups	*WTO AoA "3 Pillars"*		
	Market Access	*Domestic Support*	*Export Subsidies*
1. The African Countries	Tariff reductions based on Final Bound Rates; Review Article 5 of AoA.	Progressively reduce domestic support measures; basic criteria for Green Box Support should be strengthened; domestic support should allow developing countries to meet NTCs like poverty alleviation, food security etc.	Export subsidies should be substantially and progressively reduced, with a view to their eventual elimination. Urgent action should be taken to the development of agreed disciplines to govern the provision of export credits, export credit guarantees and insurance programmes.
2. ASEAN	Tariff reductions and elimination of tariff peaks and escalation.	Domestic measures under development programmes of developing countries must be exempt from reduction commitments; elimination of AMS from developed countries; review Green Box Measures.	Eliminate all forms of export subsidies and commit to their unconditional prohibition; Disciplines in export credits, guarantees and insurance programmes should be developed.
3. CAIRNS' Group	Deep cuts or elimination of agricultural tariffs on bound rates.	Elimination of domestic support measures starting with an initial 50 per cent down payment; review Green Box criteria.	Elimination and prohibition of all forms of export subsidies starting with a reduction (e.g. not less than 50 per cent) in both outlays and volumes in the first year of the implementation period.

Contd...

...Table 2.7 Contd...

Countries/Groups	WTO AoA "3 Pillars"		
	Market Access	*Domestic Support*	*Export Subsidies*
4. European Communities	Tariff Reductions based on the UR formula; Introduced NTCs like precautionary principle, GIs into AoA;Maintain SSG.	Maintain Green and Blue Box Measures; Specific disciplines for Amber Box; reduce *de minimis* levels	Reductions can be negotiated provided that all forms of support to exports are treated on a common footing (i.e. export subsidies, export credits, food aid, state trading enterprises); Specific WTO rules and disciplines should be developed to cover export credits.
5. India	Initial reduction of 50 per cent on bound tariffs by developed countries;Strong accent on food security as a NTC; Create safeguard mechanism similar to SSG for developing countries.	Flexibility to developing countries in the manner of providing subsidies to key farm inputs; total domestic support should be brought below *de minimis* levels within three years by developed and five years by developing countries; all measures taken for NTCs like poverty elevation; food security etc. should be exempt from reduction commitments.	Elimination of export subsidies in the first 2 years of implementation with a down-payment of 50 per cent on the level used in 2000; No rolling over of unused export subsidies.
6. Japan	Built around the concept of multifunctionality, tariff reductions should give flexibility to individual products; Maintain SSG.	Maintain current rules and disciplines on domestic support; determine AMS commitments in a realistic manner; maintain Blue Box.	Further reduction in the amount of export subsidies and the volume of subsidised exports by binding the level of the unit value of export subsidies that will be progressively reduced during the implementation period.

Contd...

...Contd...

Countries/Groups	*WTO AoA "3 Pillars"*		
	Market Access	*Domestic Support*	*Export Subsidies*
7. Transition Economies	Flexibility provisions, such that low tariffs are exempt from further reductions.	Include specific provisions in AoA which exempt investment subsidies and input subsidies from reduction commitments.	
8. The Developing Country Group/ Like Minded Group	Reduction in tariff escalation and tariff peaks.	All domestic support to be collapsed into a single "General Subsidies" box; with a set of criteria; A common level of support should be allowed, e.g. 10 per cent of this one box.	Dumping must be prohibited and export subsidies of all forms by developed countries must be eliminated immediately.
9. USA	Substantial reduction and/or elimination of tariff disparities within different countries; Eliminate SSG under Article 5.	Simplification of the domestic support disciplines into two categories; exempt support and non-exempt support.	Reduce to zero the levels of scheduled budgetary outlays and quantity commitments through progressive implementation of annual reduction commitments over a fixed period; conduct ne gotiations for export credit programmes in the Organisation for Economic Cooperation, and apply disciplines to all users.
10. Small Island Developing States	SSG to developing countries.	Higher *de minimis* level for SIDS.	

Source: Quoted from Naik and Singh (2003).

The US Farm Bill 2002 is estimated to cost more than US $100 billion during the next six years and $180 billion over a 10-year period, providing huge subsidy payments to large cotton and grain farmers, thereby significantly affecting developing country exports.

India stated that the elements of the so-called "Derbez Draft",[44] which emerged as the basis for future negotiations at Cancun, is mostly conducive to developed country positions. The draft has been completely unsympathetic towards developing country interests. The worst example of the inefficiency contained in the draft was related to the cotton subsidy in EU/US and the impact on African countries. In stead of asking EU/US to lower their subsidy in the cotton sector in the first place, which would have been a much easier solution, the draft promised consultancy support to these affected countries for diversification of agriculture. Clearly the proposal directly hurt the natural advantages of the countries concerned. As a consequence, after the failure at Cancun, the agricultural negotiation reached a deadlock since no country was willing to compromise their position. In the following period, apart from the G-20 grouping formed at Cancun, India became part of another network called G-33, whose main objective was to ensure provision of special products and special safeguard mechanisms for developing countries. The idea behind the demand for designating 'speciai products' is that developing countries should have more flexibility for certain products based on the criteria of food security, livelihood security and rural development. On the other hand, 'special safeguard mechanism' was supposed to be a contingency tool for developing countries to restrict market access if faced with unusual scenario.[45] Ultimately, five countries, Australia,

44. The most obvious basis for further agricultural negotiations is (arguably) the Annex to the Revised Ministerial Draft issued by the Mexican Foreign Secretary and the Cancun Conference Chair Luis Ernesto Derbez on 13 September 2003, popularly known as the "Derbez Draft" (JOB (03)/156/Rev. 2). The Derbez Draft had not found support from any quarter. Most countries feel that the Derbez Draft is far too close to the EU-US Text, and would prefer the G-20 Draft to be the basis of negotiation. On the other hand, EU and US have resented the Draft's provisions on domestic support. India had earlier found the Draft to restrict its flexibility in negotiations, and had shown a preference for developing a wholly new approach based upon features of all negotiation submissions.

45. On May 7, 2004, India submitted a proposal to the WTO in association with the G-20 countries where it commented on the 'blended formula' approach adopted (Documnt No. TN/AG/GEN/9). On June 1 2004, India with the G-33 countries submitted another draft to WTO, which demanded increased market access to the developing countries at the earliest (Document No. JOB(04)/65).

Brazil, EU, India and the US came forward in July 2004 to discuss the future course of discussion at Geneva. The discussion lasted two weeks, during which both Brazil and India expressed their dissatisfaction over various issues. On July 31 2004, the countries came up with a draft declaration, which would be the basis of discussion in the future. The July 2004 draft is much sympathetic towards developing countries than the Derbez draft.

On one hand, it acknowledges the need for subsidy reform in cotton, and agrees to allow developing countries to have 'special products' and 'special safeguard mechanism', on the other. However, the draft text has a number of unresolved areas, e.g. – 'appropriate number' of sensitive products, 'appropriate number' of special products', methodology to be adopted for tariff reduction, determination of 'historical period' for reduction in blue box measures and many others. Therefore it is unlikely that future negotiations would be a smooth sailing for developing countries, and there is a high probability that the Cancun experience might be repeated at the upcoming Hong Kong (December 2005) ministerial.

However, the July 2004 text is only a means, and not the end. The developing countries still need to negotiate hard to ensure substantial lowering of subsidies in their developed counterparts. Several studies have focused on the possible direction of the global negotiations with explicit stress on subsidisation reform policies. Wickman (2003) has recommended a radical change in the current system by re-nationalisation of agricultural subsidy programmes combined with elimination of export subsidies and fast reduction of import duties over a period of five years.[46] The policies recommended by him includes immediate dismantling of all price-rigging schedules, abolition of all export subsidies, reduction in import duties and phasing them out step by step; reduction and abolition of farm subsidies over a 5-year-period (20 per cent annually) and re-nationalisation of subsidy programmes for agriculture. Naik and Singh (2003) have favoured phasing out of

46. According to Wickman re-nationalisation of agricultural subsidy policy will reduce the effects of the agricultural lobby, which represents only a small portion of the European economy and population. Agriculture contributes only 3 to 4 per cent to the EU's combined GDP but takes half the EU budget. Source http://www.timbro.se/bokhandel/pdf/000011.pdf.

amber and blue box subsidies over a proposed 'balancing period' of 5 years (2005-2010) and a restriction (the study proposed the limit to be 5 per cent of agricultural production) on green box subsidies. Elimination of all export subsidies, tariff peaks and tariff rate quotas, bar on developed country exports aided by blue box measures has also been advocated by the study. However, the current status of negotiations makes implementation of any of these provisions in near future extremely unlikely.

Conclusion: India's Negotiation Strategy – Past, Present and the Future

Any negotiating strategy on the part of India has necessarily to contain elements pertaining to market access, i.e. discussions and offering of commitments on tariff reductions in agriculture. While a complete discussion on the issue of market access is outside the scope of this paper, it must be pointed out that tariffs are going to be an equally contested area under agricultural negotiations. In fact, the highly subsidising developed countries might ask for ambitious commitments on tariff cuts in return for any commitments that they make on the issue of support and subsidies. In such a scenario, it becomes doubly important for India to keep pushing for reforms in agricultural policies of the subsidising countries. In the light of the above observations, let us focus on the last section, India's past and present performance and a proposed future negotiating agenda.

Past: The discussion of the past strategy is rather an easy exercise, since India did not possess one in the earlier days. What it had, could at best be described as a stance, which opposed the continuation of subsidy policies in EU/US and other countries and sought for ready withdrawal of them.[47] However, the option of adopting a dominant strategy was never explored. Alternatively, it could be argued that the

47. The major reform proposals by India for calculating AMS in late nineties included - (i) setting product-specific AMS as compared to total AMS, (ii) further sharp reduction in *de minimis* limits, (iii) allowing developing countries to recalculate AMS/revise schedules, (iv) raising *de minimis* levels, (v) obtaining even higher de minimis level for basic foodstuffs, (vi) exemption of strictly food security measures and (vii) correction/clarification of methodological problems. Concern over subsidy level in developing countries and the corresponding loss of developing countries was also noted. In addition, universal accessibility to the special safeguard clause (SSG) was favoured since the same was denied to most developing countries by linking it with tariffication process. India and the WTO, May 1999.

consequences of freeing agricultural trade were not taken into account previously, as India was not globally a major player. On the other hand, negotiation for reducing subsidies in foreign markets would have involved opening up of domestic market to others in a reciprocal basis, for which India was not prepared. Therefore no explicit stress was laid in this regard. However after losing the case on import restriction against US in the late-nineties, India had to face free import of primary products, buoyed with farm subsidy. On the other hand, export promotion became a major objective, where it witnessed a potential loss of competitiveness in a number of key products to countries with synthetic price advantage inculcated through subsidisation programmes. This too simultaneously contributed in the evolution of a dominant negotiation strategy.

Present: The present stance of India as reflected in the joint proposal to WTO with other developing countries as well as the July 2004 meeting has been discussed earlier. The country is rightly moving forward with cautious steps and not committing for further liberalisation at multilateral forum before getting the developed countries' responses.[48] Unlike the general demand for withdrawal of support measures in the past, the country has presented its case to the world by submitting a time bound sector-specific plan for removal of subsidisation-programme. Moreover, the proposal has been placed at various international forums in pre- and post-Cancun days to build a solid case. In addition, the country has learned the value of unity (from the bitter experience of Doha), as witnessed from Cancun ministerial. The constituents of the recently formed developing countries' group are bound by the close bond of mutual interest, and therefore, are not likely to yield to the pressure of the developed countries. However, it must be noted that nothing has been achieved so far, and there is no time to be self-satisfied. The group has been able to stall the EU/US plan for the time being, but have definitely not settled it for good. On the contrary, the failure at

48. Statement by India in General Council Meeting on the revised Draft Cancun Ministerial text (26.08.2003), *India and the WTO*, August 2003.

"Mr. Chairman, if some of the major developed countries are not in a position to have a high level of ambition in the reduction of subsidies, how can they expect the developing countries to ambitiously reduce their tariffs which is the only instrument available to them for protecting their farmers. For India, with over 650 million people dependent on agriculture for their livelihood, it becomes all the more important that the agricultural negotiations do not become a tool to impoverish them further."

Cancun gave EU/US the perfect excuse to continue their subsidisation programme for ten more months. Furthermore, although July 2004 text is a major step towards initiating the discussions again, there exist so many potential disputes in the text.[49] Hence the issue of future reform agenda needs serious attention.

Future: The final question revolves around the future of India's negotiating strategy. The analysis shows that it seems unlikely for EU/US to withdraw the current level of support. On the other hand, there is every reason to believe that they are going to exploit all the loopholes in the agreement to maintain the ongoing support level. The only way to extract benefits from them is to move through collective action. The most important achievement of India in the Cancun conference and in the subsequent period is pushing forward its agenda through formation of a formidable group of developing countries, something not witnessed earlier. Although at Doha India raised a very genuine concern, it could not extract any tangible benefit there, as it was completely alienated, even by the developing countries as viewed from Singh (2001). However, the same was not repeated in Cancun, thanks to the developing country solidarity. In future, the success of subsidisation reform will depend on the solidarity of this group. We broadly agree with the reform proposals submitted by India and other developing countries at Cancun and in the subsequent period. However, keeping the ongoing scenario in mind, we propose the following four areas to be incorporated in India's future negotiation:

1. ***Stepping Up Negotiation Strength Through Alliance***: As seen from Table 2.7, developing countries/blocs regarding the three modes of liberalisation held conflicting views even two years back, many of which have not evapourated in spite of the growing developing country soliderity. However, they could still cooperate among themselves owing to the common interest of curtailing subsidisation programmes in developed countries. The strength of bloc formation has been witnessed in Cancun, and this lesson should be part of all future negotiations. It is quite clear by now that EU and US are the major opponents in

49. Chakraborty, Debashis, "Recent Negotiation Trends on Agriculture under WTO", New Delhi: *RGICS Working Paper No. 47*, 2004.

this regard. In order to mitigate the minor differences in outlook towards reform among developing countries, India should follow a give-and-take basis. It has been shown by Gulati *et al.*, (1996) and Chakraborty and Singh (2004) that Indian agricultural products are not price uncompetitive, and therefore granting preferential treatment in domestic market is not likely to lead to a disaster. India should try to win the support of other developing countries through this channel. In addition, alliance with other interested parties like Cairns group, consisting of 14 agro-exporting nations, is another important option and not worth negligence.[50] The group is pushing hard for reforms in the agricultural subsidisation programmes in general, and CAP in particular for a long time. In addition, they are quite sympathetic to the special and differential treatment measures required to enable developing and least developed countries to address their legitimate and varied needs, including agricultural and rural development, food security, and subsistence and small scale farming for the development of domestic food production. The bargaining power of this group is much stronger in comparison with any developing country. India is not likely to suffer by granting them preferential treatment in response to their support against EU/US. Search should also be on for other potential allies. The formation of G-33 in the post-G-20 period shows India is vibrant on that front.

2. ***Push for De-Coupling of Subsidy***: Direct negotiations to restrict EU flow of subsidy, which causes maximum distortions due to its larger market share in primary exports, have not delivered desired results. Any future negotiation must focus on de-coupling of CAP subsidies by formulating a single farm payment independent from production in the short run. The intra-EU tension on this issue is already obvious. Second, the negotiation strategy so far has concentrated on curtailing the subsidisation level across the board. Instead it should focus on restraining the EU subsidy scheme only to non-traded

50. A number of countries like Argentina or Colombia, who are with India within the developing country group, are members of CAIRNS group. Therefore, India might use their connection to exploit the CAIRNS group lobbying power.

agricultural production. This, once achieved (although a difficult goal), would put tremendous pressure on EU budgetary support and is bound to affect subsidy level as a whole, in future. Again, the negotiation should be carried on in association with interested groups like Cairns group along with other developing countries; since the group is ready to support any developing country in the agricultural trade reform related agenda. A similar agenda needs to be pressed in negotiations with US as well.

3. *Qualitative Aspects*: The blue and amber box measures should be completely eliminated within a specified time frame, in place of negotiating to put a futile cap on them – a negotiation that has practically delivered nothing. This is not likely to cause a major problem for the developing countries, as their support level is in any case much lower as compared to their developed counterparts. In addition, the negotiations must ensure a restriction on the maximum possible amount in green box measures as well. In the face of global protest, the proposed reform measures of EU/US often involve minor reshuffling of support measures in blue/amber box merely to green box, in an attempt to gain legitimacy. The proposed de-coupling of CAP subsidies would have involved one such move. The green box measures contribute to rural infrastructure and implicitly lower fixed cost of agriculture in rich countries, and adversely affect competitiveness of the developing countries. Naik and Singh (2003) notes that the developed countries account for 88 per cent of total green box subsidies, and the magnitude of trade distortion in their favour is quite obvious. To counter this, the green box subsidy measures should be limited to less than 5-7 per cent of the total value of the agricultural production.

4. *Special and Differential Treatment for Developing Countries*: The continuation of the subsidisation schemes in developed countries is open proof of the fact that developing countries are yet to reach a level-playing ground. Therefore, in future negotiations, India must make an attempt to ensure allowance of special and differential treatment in green box measures for developing countries. Additional safeguard measures must also

be ensured to combat unforeseen circumstances of national emergency and non-trade concerns. India has already voiced this concern to WTO with regard to the 'special products' and 'special safeguard mechanisms'.

In the post-July 2004 situation, there are some signs that the US and EU may make minor concessions to their intransigent positions. US has taken a step back from the original EU-US joint position and has made a move towards to its original position of calling for elimination of all export subsidies by a certain date. The EU has also engaged in talks with G-20 and G-33. How much of the political rhetoric would transfer into actual commitments is debatable. Yet, the positive aspect is the continued belief in the WTO as a forum to resolve these issues, and that almost all major Members are calling for "flexibility" in negotiating strategies. In the long run, India must continue to gather and consolidate support with other developing countries to push for reforms in agricultural policies of agri-subsiding countries, as they are a pre-condition to any commitments on market access.

References

Anderson, K. and Y. Hayami (1986). *The Political Economy of Agricultural Protection*, Boston, London and Sydney: Allen and Unwin.

BBC News, "EU offers WTO farm subsidy cuts," http://news.bbc.co.uk/1/hi/business/2581963.stm, 16 December.

Bhattacharyya, B. (1999). "Non-Tariff Measures on Indian Exports: An Assessment," *Occasional Paper No. 16*, Indian Institute of Foreign Trade.

Brink Lindsey *et al.*, (1999). "Seattle and Beyond: A WTO Agenda for the New Millennium," *Cato Institute Trade Policy Analysis No. 8.*

Centre for Monitoring Indian Economy Pvt. Ltd. (CMIE) (2002). Economic Intelligence Service, *Agriculture*, December.

Chakraborty, Debashis (2004). "Recent Negotiation Trends in Agriculture under WTO: Mutual Consensus During Transitory Phase?," *RGICS Working Paper No. 47.*

Chakraborty, Debashis and Singh, Yashika, "Agricultural Subsidisation: Options and Challenges for India," Paper presented at the Conference, *Looking Beyond Cancun: The Trend in Trade Talks*, jointly organised by RGICS and Liberty Institute, March 24, 2004, New Delhi.

Chaturvedi, Sachin and Nagpal, Gunjan (2002). "WTO and Product-related Environmental Standards: Emerging Issues and Policy Options before India," *RIS Discussion Papers 36.*

Delta Farm Press, (2003). "EU subsidy reform on hold... again," http://deltafarmpress.com/ar/farming_eu_subsidy_reform_2/, Jun 27.

ESCAP study by United Nations (1999). "Non-Tariff Measures with potentially Restrictive Market Access Implications Emerging in a Post-Uruguay Round Context," *Studies in Trade and Investment 40*, United Nations.

GATT Agreements: *Final Text of Uruguay Round 1994.*

Government of India, *India and the WTO*, the monthly Newsletter of Ministry of Commerce (various issues).

————. *Economic Survey*, Various Issues.

Groombridge, Mark A. (2001). "America's Bittersweet Sugar Policy," *Trade Briefing Paper, No 13*, Cato Institute.

Gulati, Ashok and Narayanan, Sudha (2003). *Subsidy Syndrome in Indian Agriculture*, Oxford University Press.

Gulati, Ashok, Sharma, Anil, Sharma, Kailash, Das, Shipra, and Chhabra, Vandana (1996). *Export Competitiveness of Selected Agricultural Commodities*, NCAER, Global Business Press.

Jank, Marcos Sawaya, Fuchsloch, Ian and Kutas, Géraldine (2003). *Agricultural Liberalisation in Multilateral and Regional Trade Negotiations*, Inter-American Development Bank, Washington, DC.

Maskus, K.E., and Wilson, J.S., (Ed.) (2001). *Quantifying the Impact of Technical Barriers to Trade: Can it be Done?*, Ann Arbor: University of Michigan Press.

Mehta, R. and Mohanty, S.K. (1999). *WTO and Industrial Tariffs: An Empirical Analysis for India*, Research and Information System for the Non-Aligned and Other Developing Countries.

Mehta, Rajesh, Saqib, M. and George, J. (2002). "Addressing Sanitary and Phyto-sanitary Agreement: A Case Study of Select Processed Food Products in India," *RIS Discussion Paper 39.*

Mohanty, S.K. and Manoharan, T.R. (2002). "Analysis of Environment related Non-tariff Measures in the European Union: Implications for South Asian Exports," by, *RIS Discussion Paper 38.*

Naik, Gopal, and Singh, Yashika (2003). "Doha Round Negotiations: Agriculture," *Working Paper No. 217*, Indian Institute of Management Bangalore, November.

OECD (2003). *Agricultural Policies in OECD Countries Monitoring and Evaluation: 2003 Highlights.*

Otsuki, Tsunehiro, Wilson, John S, Sewadeh, Mirvat (2000). "Saving Two in a Billion: A Case Study to Quantify the trade effect of European Food Safety Standards on African Exports," *World Bank Policy Research Working Paper No 2563.*

Press conference of U.S. Trade Representative Robert Zoellick during an OECD meeting, April 30, Paris.

Sharma, Devinder (1995). *GATT-WTO: Seeds of Despair*, Konark Publishers Pvt. Ltd.

Singh, Yashika (2000). "EU Trade – Tariff and Non-tariff Hurdles," *RGICS Working Paper No. 13.*

———. (2001). "India at the Fourth Ministerial Meeting in Doha: Déjà vu – Again?" *RGICS Working Paper No. 32.*

The United States Mission to the European Union (2002). "U.S. cites support in WTO for eliminating Agriculture Export Subsidies," www.useu.be, Brusselles, Belgium, June 19.

The Western Producer (2003). "EU revamps farm subsidies," http://www.producer.com/articles/20030703/market_quotas/20030703mkt05.html, July 8.

Third World Network, "India: Flood of food imports could destroy Indian agriculture," by Binu S. Thomas, August 30, http://www.twnside.org.sg/title/flood-cn.htm.

Wickman, Kurt, "Whither the European Agricultural Policy? - A Viable Reform of the CAP in the Context of An Enlarged EU and the Doha Development Round," Timbro, 2003, http://www.timbro.se/bokhandel/pdf/000011.pdf.

World Trade Organisation "WTO Annual Report" (various issues).

———. (1999). "WTO: Trading into the future."

———. (2001). Special Studies No. 6, "Market Access: Unfinished Business - Post-Uruguay Round Inventory and Issues."

———. (2000). Trade Policy Review, European Union.

———. (1997). Trade Policy Review: European Union.

3

Seed Protection and Genetically Modified Crops: Sentiment and Emotion

AMIR ULLAH KHAN

An intense debate is going on around the world to ascertain the extent to which Intellectual Property Rights should be protected. And nowhere has this subject been more controversial than in the seed industry that now grapples with the issue of plant breeding[1] and genetically modified varieties. Enforcement of the new regime of protecting intellectual property has met with vociferous opposition from various quarters. The opposition is on grounds of disproportionate accrual of profits to multinational corporations; destruction of the domestic gene pool; and inadequate productivity gains to farmers. The debate around genetically modified organisms evokes so much sentiment that any objective discussion becomes difficult. The amendments to the *Patent Act* were passed by the Parliament and have become law. The government has also proposed amendments to the *Seeds Act* and tabled it in Parliament. The fear expressed in some quarters is that both these may adversely affect the interests of farmers. Farmers may not be able to reuse farm-saved seeds for the next cropping season as the new laws will supersede the provisions in the *Plant Varieties Protection & Farmers' Rights Act*, 2001.

The intention of the proposed amendments to the *Seeds Act* is to strengthen the corporate seed sector. These amendments are being opposed by some NGOs and farmers' groups. Similarly, there is a

1. Plant breeding started with a rediscovery of Mendel's laws of inheritance in the early days of the twentieth century. The techniques used were Pureline selection, Hybridisation and Polypoid breeding. The cornerstone of all plant breeding is the conscious introduction of genetic diversity into populations by intercrossing or mating selected germ plasm with outstanding characters that complement one another. And the selection of superior plants with genes for desired traits until higher levels of improved adaptation, genetic uniformity and agronomic stability are reached. Biotechnology is the use of biological organisms for the attainment of commercial ends.

demand that the seed sector remain unaffected in the new patent regime. Faced with pressures, the government made some changes in the definition of "inventive step" in section 2 (1a). It says: "New invention means any invention or technology which has not been anticipated by publication in any document or used in the country or elsewhere in the world before the date of filing of patent application with complete specification, i.e. the subject matter has not fallen in the public domain or that it does not form part of the state of the art."

The food sector will have to face new challenges in the new patent regime. Different processes and products will become patentable. Article 31 (b) of the TRIPS agreement defines the terms for commercial use to check monopolies and encourage competition. The TRIPS agreement has not defined micro-organisms and microbiological processes. However, when the issue of patenting micro-organisms comes up there will be differing views. The moot question is whether micro-organisms, existing freely, are patentable or their mere isolation in pure form are patentable or the human invention involved in establishing a level of novelty in the discovered micro-organism.

The primary argument is the ethical. H.G. Wells and Mary Frankenstein both laid the foundations with their classical characters. Both Dr. Moreau and Frankenstein's creator dabble with life and modify genetic resource, resulting in horror and mayhem. On the other hand is the 'natural' resource argument. Public goods, it is felt are no longer freely accessible, but have become 'economic' resources, to be privatised. And in this process, the commons jointly held and nurtured by communities, are getting captured and held by private corporations to the exclusion of local communities.

New technology has always met with skepticism and suspicion, but where it concerns living organisms, the problem has been far too acute. Biotechnology has thrown up new opportunities and challenges for agriculture. Recombinant DNA technology involves a process where a single gene responsible for a particular trait is isolated. In Genetic Engineering, gene splicing is used to create mutant strains of microorganisms for industrial or medical use. Mixing two or more strains of a particular crop so that the best qualities of each can be distilled creates hybrid seeds. In case of tissue culture, plants are grown in controlled situations so that they grow to precise specifications. The bamboo plant can now flower in a few weeks time compared to the forest tree that takes at least 80 years.[2]

In agriculture, technological change can either emphasise labour-saving or land-saving technologies broadly associated with biological innovations.[3] The distinction should however not be overdrawn. In particular, varieties can be developed so that the crop is more efficiently harvested by mechanical means. Hayami and Ruttan (1985) argue that resource endowments are the principal determinants of particular patterns of technological change. In particular, in labour-abundant and land-scarce countries such as India, biological innovations occupy the central place in technology development. de Janvry, Sadoulet and Fafchamps (1989) question the direct link between resource endowments and technological bias. They point out that large farmers face different factor costs than small farmers for labour and capital. As a result, technological development can be labour saving even in countries that are labour-abundant. The generation and diffusion of new yield improving technologies is critical to sustaining agricultural growth. As varietal development is embedded in seeds, they are the principal vehicles for delivering new technologies. Indeed, new seeds were the basis for the green revolution.[4] Yet the seed industry has been a neglected subject of research. In the recent past, some literature has grown on the seed industry and issues related to genetically modified seeds and hybrids.[5]

The Indian Seed Industry

The Indian seed industry as with the Indian agriculture sector as a whole is extremely heterogeneous. The major distinction that can

2. Two other new concepts finding their way into modern terminology are Biosurfactants and Bioleaching. Bacteria that work like surfactants – cleaning agents in household detergents – work on oil deposits trapped in rock and help the oil flow are called biosurfactants. In Bioleaching, micro-organisms are used to leach ore and therefore help in extracting important minerals from below the earth's surface.
3. This argument seems relevant for situations where there are large disparities in size of farms such as between ranches and holdings of small farmers. As a result, agricultural growth in India and similarly endowed countries stems primarily from rising productivity of land.
4. The dependence on high quality seeds and other inputs continues and even today farmers all over the country are willing to pay more for varieties that promise higher productivity, better weed resistance and lower dependence on pesticides and fertiliser.
5. This includes Basant (1995), Morris, Singh and Pal (1998), Tripp and Pal (2000a, 2000b), Turner (1994), Pray, Ramaswami and Kelley (2001) and Shiva and Crompton (1998). Pray and Ramaswami (1991) is an early work surveying the state of seed industry in developing countries.

be made is between hybrids and open-pollinated varieties. Seeds of open pollinated varieties can be reproduced for many generations with little deterioration in quality. As a result, beyond the initial purchase, farmers can multiply their own seed. This is not a viable strategy with hybrids because they suffer noticeable declines in yields in subsequent generations. As a result, hybrid seeds tend to be repeatedly purchased. Rice and wheat are principally open-pollinated varieties. It is much harder to develop hybrids for naturally self-pollinated crops (e.g., rice, wheat) than for cross-pollinated crops (e.g. maize).[6] Hybrids dominate in coarse cereals consisting of sorghum, pearl millet and maize. Hybrids are also important in cotton and oilseeds.

The Indian seed industry comprises a large public sector and a growing private sector. The public sector consists of the National Seed Corporation, the State Farm Corporation of India and thirteen State Seed Corporations. These corporations multiply and market varieties bred by public sector institutions. Estimates of the number of private seed firms range between 200 and 500. Private seed firms vary widely with respect to size, research capacity and product segments. Plant breeding research however is conducted only in larger firms.

In the private sector there is strong functional integration unlike in the public sector, where research is separated from seed production and marketing. Also the private sector focuses largely on hybrid seed. It is therefore unimportant in the product segments of wheat and rice except as a seller of public varieties and hybrids.[7] On the other hand, the private sector is a major player in the hybrid seed markets of vegetables, sorghum, oilseeds, maize, cotton and pearl millet. In terms of ownership, private firms are closely held and not listed in the stock exchanges although some of the large firms have sold equity to foreign seed companies. Foreign firms maintain a presence through equity stakes in Indian firms, technical alliances or through wholly owned subsidiaries.

Seed firms outsource the production of seeds to contract growers. These growers are supplied with the foundation seed used to produce

6. Rice hybrids have been developed but have not met market success yet.

7. However, especially for the large firms, the sale of public varieties and hybrids is not their mainline activity.

commercial seed. The seed industry is one of the earliest examples of contract farming in India. For the cereal crops of rice and wheat, the principal sources of seeds are the farmers themselves. Seed saved from the preceding crop supplies nearly 90 per cent of requirements in these crops.[8] The value of the seed market is conservatively estimated at a billion dollars. The seed industry was probably half this size in the early part of the 1990s (Shiva and Crompton, 1998). It has grown rapidly in the last decade. Estimates of the share of the private sector range from 60 per cent to 70 per cent (Shiva and Crompton, 1998). Because the private sector sells high value hybrids, their share in value terms is greater than in volume terms.

The Global Seed Industry

Globally, seed business is a part of a larger agricultural business consisting of agro-chemicals. In the last decade or so, there was a wave of consolidation involving pharmaceutical and agricultural businesses. However, in recent years, this trend has weakened and even reversed as these "life sciences" firms have spun off their agricultural business primarily because investors perceived the earnings from agriculture to be more volatile primarily on account of the controversies over Genetically Modified food. Some major players in the seed sector today are Monsanto, which has acquired DeKalb Plant Genetics, the international seed business of Cargill and Plant Breeding International and many other smaller firms, Aventis Crop Science was taken over by Bayer, Syngenta is the agriculture arm of the merger between Novartis and AstraZeneca, Dow Agro Sciences which acquired Cargill Hybrids and DuPont which acquired PioneerHiBred.[9] The top five – AstaZeneca, DuPont, Monsanto, Novartis, Aventis control the global GM seed market almost entirely.

8. These figures vary by crop and by state. See Sidhu (1999) for sources of seed for principal crops in Punjab.

9. According to a report released by the Rural Advancement Foundation International (RAFI), a shrinking number of colossal companies — nicknamed the "Gene Giants" — dominate global sales of seeds and agrochemicals, The top five Gene Giants (AstaZeneca, DuPont, Monsanto, Novartis, Aventis) account for nearly two-thirds of the global pesticide market (60 per cent), almost one-quarter (23 per cent) of the commercial seed market, and virtually 100 per cent of the transgenic (genetically engineered) seed market. Five years ago, none of top five Gene Giants appeared on the list of leading seed corporations. In fact, three of the top five companies didn't even exist. Zeneca and Astra merged to form AstraZeneca; Rhone Poulenc and Hoechst became Aventis; Ciba Geigy and Sandoz became Novartis; and DuPont swallowed Pioneer Hi-Bred in 2005.

The consolidation in the global seed industry is attributed to rising cost of research, the patenting of life forms and the need to control access to elite germplasm. The impact of these changes in India has so far been limited to changes in ownership rather than to a dramatic reduction in seed companies. In the United States, corporate control is most prominent in the livestock sector where producers are contractually tied to agri-businesses in the supply of inputs as well as in marketing. It is not clear whether smallholder agriculture offers greater or lesser opportunities for corporate control. As issues of market structure have traditionally been analysed by looking at the market shares of the leading seed firms, there has not been much research on the market structure at the micro level. How do firms compete at the retail level? What choices do farmers exercise?[10] In the absence of farmer education, quality regulation fails to protect farmers and neither does it reduce barriers to entry that are created by branding.[11]

Global Policy and Regulation

Since genetic engineering and DNA treatment have become specialised disciplines, the scope for invention in micro-organisms and tissue culture has grown and now this is an established technology that requires enormous amounts of ingenuity and hard work and patience and deserves the same incentives that any invention in any other field does. In 1980, the Budapest Treaty on the international deposition of micro-organisms came into force. All biological material is to be deposited in recognised depositories. All signatories of the Paris Convention are eligible to membership in this treaty.

---

10. Public hybrids sold under private brand names are sometimes sold at premiums reflecting the farmers' perceptions of quality. Tripp and Pal (2000) studied the information flow between seed firms and farmers in the pearl millet market of Eastern Rajasthan. They found that even in areas where the use of private hybrids is extensive, while farmers can recall the brand or the company that produced their seed they couldn't often distinguish between a company's hybrids. This is possibly because companies invest resources in advertising company brands rather than in communicating information about the varieties. As established seed companies have reputations to protect, branding is a convenient short cut for communicating product quality. Branding is also an entry barrier to small and new firms that cannot afford advertising or do not have past reputations to build on. Ideally, seed certification should provide the route for small firms to convey signals about their product quality. However, Tripp and Pal find that farmers do not use such information. The farmers in the survey could not explain the difference between certified and truthfully labeled seed.
11. See Tripp and Louwaars (1998) for analysis of seed regulation that is appropriate to the state of development of the national seed system.

The biodiversity convention and the Rio Summit in 1992 regulate the illegal flight of genetic material sources. This convention was signed by 65 countries and came into force from December 1993. India ratified the same in February 1994. The convention accords sovereign rights to nations over their genetic material and biological resources. Access to this has to be mutually agreed upon and subject to prior consent of the contracting parties. The present legislation in India[12] stipulates that any export of genetic material can only be done after authorised bodies like the National Bureau of Plant Genetic Resources[13] approve the transfer of such material. These agencies process the requests from any foreign agency within three months. Violation of the legislation[14] implies confiscation of the material and a fine not less than Rs.1000 or five times the value of the material being taken out.[15] In the US, plant varieties were protected from as early as 1930 when plant patents were sealed for asexually reproducing plant varieties. Now the patent system has been extended to cover sexually reproducing varieties through the *Plant Variety Protection Act* of 1970. In U.K. the protection of patents on plant varieties is covered under the *Plant Varieties and Seeds Act* 1964.

Article 27(3) (b) of TRIPS says *Members shall provide for the protection of plant varieties either by patents or by an effective sui generis system or by any combination thereof.* Article 27 on patentable subject

---

12. The Ministry of Environment and Forests, Government of India has imposed a ban on export of genetic material. This was necessitated by the arrest of two Germans who were illegally carrying away butterflies. This resulted in a general feeling that there is an urgent need to strictly implement the legislation curbing illegal flight of genetic material from the country. What is needed is a more comprehensive legislation that takes cognizance of the issue of disease ridden genetic material or live organisms being brought into the country. There is another general feeling that India has been consistently losing its rich genetic resources over the last 25 years.

13. Other bodies are Indian Agricultural Research Institute, Wildlife Preservation, Indian Veterinary Research Institute, National Bureau of Animal Genetic Resources and National Bureau of Fish Genetic Resources.

14. In Australia as soon as one arrives at any international airports neon signs urge the passenger to declare any genetic material or live organisms. Failure to do so would mean jail or a fine up to 50000 dollars. In India no airport insists on any such declaration.

15. At present India has no mechanism to stop anybody from smuggling germplasm out of the country. Therefore a situation where we find some Germans carrying butterflies in their suitcase. Also of interest is the controversy over a Japanese institute carrying research using micro-organisms brought from Japan in Pondicherry and Meerut. The Japanese call it EM Technology and claim these friendly organisms can enrich soil, kill pests, clear wastes etc. How did these micro-organisms enter the country in the first place?

matter states "Subject to the provisions of paragraphs 2 and 3, patents shall be available for any inventions, whether products or processes, in all fields of technology, provided that they are new, involve an inventive step and are capable of industrial application" (Article 27.1). Thus, three conditions must be satisfied before a patent can be granted. The invention must be new, there must be an inventive step so that the invention is non-obvious and the invention must be useful in the sense of commercial or industrial application. If these three criteria are met, product and process patents must be available in all fields of technology.

"Members may exclude from patentability inventions, the prevention within the territory of the commercial exploitation of which is necessary to protect ordre public or morality, including to protect human, animal or plant life or health or to avoid serious prejudice to the environment, provided that such exclusion is not made merely because the exploitation is prohibited by their law" (Article 27.2). *"Members may also exclude from patentability: (a) diagnostic, therapeutic and surgical methods for the treatment of humans or animals; (b) plants and animals other than micro-organisms, and essentially biological processes for the production of plants or animals other than non-biological and microbiological processes. However, Members shall provide for protection of plant varieties either by patents or by an effective sui generis system or by any combination thereof. The provisions of this subparagraph shall be reviewed four years after the date of entry into force of the WTO Agreement"* (Article 27.3).

A *sui generis* system means a system that is specifically designed to protect plant varieties. The obvious model for this is the protection of a plant breeder's right (PBR). If such protection is to be granted, the plant variety in question must possess the criteria of novelty, distinctness, uniformity and stability. The most obvious guidelines for PBR are those framed in the International Conventions for the Protection of New Varieties of Plants, also known as the UPOV[16] (*Union Pour le Protection des Obtentions Vegetals*) Conventions of

16. Plant breeders' rights as recognised by the UPOV are the rights given to the breeders of new varieties of plants to prevent others from commercially exploiting the same varieties. France led the movement for the protection of new varieties of plants – UPOV in 1957. This was recast as a new UPOV in 1961, revised in 1972, 1978 and 1991. The 1991 UPOV convention could not come into force because of the difficulties involved. The duration of protection according to the 1978 act was 15 years from the date of grant. The 1991 convention hikes it up to twenty years. The government's right to compulsory licensing has been discouraged by UPOV 1991.

1978 and 1991, although the Uruguay Round agreement makes no reference to the UPOV Conventions.[17] Although there is no explicit provision, under UPOV 1978, the farmer can exercise the freedom to save or retain seeds, derived from protected plant varieties, for own use in future sowing periods. There is no explicit objection to limited and non-commercial exchanges of seeds. But commercial sales or multiplication of propagating material are prohibited.

India is endowed with 6.5 per cent of the world's stock of plant and animal species. There are an estimated 45,000 species of wild plants and 77,000 species of wild animals in India. Documenting this germplasm is not going to be easy. But if this can be done, legislation can be introduced to protect the Indian germplasm. And with its strength in biotechnology, India ought to be able to exploit the better patent protection in other countries.

The two major international agreements, the Agreement on 'Trade-Related Intellectual Property Rights' (TRIPS) of the WTO and the United Nations 'Convention on Biological Diversity' (CBD), are now shaping domestic regimes of member states with respect to biological resources and indigenous knowledge. The Food and Agricultural Organisation defines Biodiversity thus- *'Biological diversity denotes the variety of life forms, the other ecological roles they perform and the genetic diversity they obtain. Genetic diversity occurs at the gene level (the molecular level), the individual level, the population level, the species level and the ecosystem level.'* TRIPS engenders privatisation of biological resources by allowing patents to be granted on biological materials and associated indigenous knowledge, and the CBD acknowledges that local communities have rights over bio-resources and indigenous knowledge.

Policy and Regulation in India

The government regulates the seed industry and the seed trade in various respects. The *Seed Act* of 1966, the *Seeds Control Order* of 1983, and the *Seeds Policy* of 1988 are the major components of policy specific to the industry. The seed industry has also been subject to policies relating to industrial licensing and direct foreign investment

17. The original UPOV Convention goes back to 1961, but it was revised in 1972, 1978 and 1991.

that are applicable to all industry. There have been two recent developments. In September 2001, the *Plant Variety Protection and Farmer's Rights Act* came into being. In June 2002, the government announced a new seeds policy that significantly alters the framework of regulation.

There are numerous laws that govern agriculture and its allied activities, foremost in this is the *Plant Variety Protection and Farmers' Right Act* of 2001 (PVP) that deals with intellectual property in this sphere of economic activity. The need for such a law arose due to India signing the Trade Related Intellectual Property Rights (TRIPS) agreement. Its rules devised in 2003, provides the framework for farmers to register new plant varieties and extant varieties including those available in India which are notified under the *Seeds Act*, 1966, varieties about which knowledge is 'common', implying that such knowledge resides in the public domain.

Member States need to provide protection to plant varieties either through patents or a *sui generis* system or a combination of the two. *Sui generis* here refers to a system that protects the rights of the plant breeders. This alternative is the most appropriate choice of 'protection' for countries such as India where knowledge of plant varieties or microorganisms and the products thereof, are not the monopoly of individuals, but shared by the entire community. Knowledge is community-oriented in the sense that discoveries and innovations are considered the result of their cumulative efforts. But this still does not make it 'public' in the 'common heritage of mankind' sense so that anybody might have access to the geographical area or the biotic resources typical to it.

The varieties developed by breeders need to be registered and they have the right to "produce, sell, market, distribute, import or export". Further, there are stringent measures incorporated in the Act to punish infringements of intellectual property. The use of a registered name and denomination are some of the violations that can be penalised by either specifying a monetary penalty or by jail terms or a combination. In fact the provisions are so stringent that the onus of proving innocence in case of infringement is on the violator. The same is true for falsely using a denomination.

At the same time, the Act recognises that over the years farmers have bred several varieties of seeds and explicitly states that they are "entitled to save, use, sow, re-sow, exchange, share or sell farm produce including seed". However, farmers too would be required to register their seed varieties which they can do with the help of non-government organisations; the only restriction being that farmers cannot brand the seeds with the breeder's registered name.

An alternate method of protecting property rights is through the *Geographical Indications of Goods (Registration and Protection) Act*, 1999, that was adopted by the Ministry of Law and Justice and Company Affairs, India, as the domestic aspect of the general GI law that was formulated under the purview of the TRIPS. It refers to a country (or a place situated therein) as being the country or place of origin of a product – agricultural, natural or manufactured – typically referring to a quality, reputation and distinctiveness which is essentially attributable to the fact of its origin in that defined geographical locality, region or country.

The *Biological Diversity Act, 2003*, too seeks to provide for conservation of biological diversity, sustainable use of its components and fair and equitable sharing of the benefits arising out of the use of biological resources, knowledge and related matters. It is aimed to protect the conservers of biological resources, their byproducts, creators and holders of knowledge and information relating to the use of biological resources, innovations and practices associated with such use and application. The PVP can be read as a subset of this legislation as it tackles only one component of a much wider debate.

Underlying these three new laws is an older legislation that concerns itself with phyto-sanitary measures in the country. The *Seeds Act* of 1966 and the consequent Seed Rules of 1968 administer the sale and classification of seeds. The Act defines the quality of seed to be sold and helps to notify different kinds of seeds for different States or geographical areas. The requirement of marking or labeling the same is encompassed under this Act, and is necessary for transacting seeds in India. For selling, exporting or importing seeds, a license is required under the Seeds (Control) Order, 1983.

The *Seed Act* of 1966 and the *Seeds Control Order* of 1983 provide statutory backing to the system of variety release, seed certification and seed testing. Varieties are released after evaluation at multi-location trials for a minimum of three years. Varieties approved are "notified" which is a prerequisite for certification. While all public sector varieties go through this process, it is not mandatory for private varieties.

Certification is a process that certifies that seed is of a specified variety and is of acceptable genetic purity. Usually, seeds are also tested for physical characteristics such as germination capacity, analytical purity and pathogen levels. Certification requires that the certifying agency has access to the parent lines of the variety. While all public sector varieties are certified, the process is voluntary for private varieties. Often private seed firms do not submit their varieties for certification either because they do not wish to go through the time consuming process of notification or because they have their own quality control processes. However, uncertified seeds are required to be truthfully labeled listing quality attributes on the label.

The seed control order brings seeds within the scope of the *Essential Commodities Act* that regulates the marketing of essential items. All seed sales outlets have to be licensed and must observe certain marketing practices such as public display of stocks and prices. Major changes in this system of regulation find place in the *National Seeds Policy* of 2002. Variety registration will now be mandatory for all varieties, new and extant. The evaluation will be done over three seasons of field trials. However, certification will continue to be voluntary. The emphasis on registration in the new seeds policy ties in with the demands of the *Plant Variety Protection and Farmer's Rights Act* passed in 2001. This Act provides for plant breeder's rights, which requires extant and new plant varieties to be registered on the basis of characteristics relating to novelty, distinctiveness, uniformity and stability.

Besides regulating quality, the government has also controlled imports and exports of seed. The *Seed Policy* of 1988 allowed limited imports of commercial seed. Curbs were removed from imports of seeds of vegetables, flowers and ornamental plants. Seeds of coarse cereals, pulses and oilseeds could be imported for upto two years provided this finally led to technology transfer in the form of parental lines/breeder seed. The policy of 2002 allows imports and exports of seeds of all crops. However, all imported seed is also required to go through the process of registration.

Prior to 1991, the seed industry was also subject to the policies on industrial licensing and foreign direct investment that applied generally. The seed sector was reserved for the small-scale sector and the entry of foreign firms was tightly regulated.[18]

The Growth of the Private Sector

In the past, the public sector was the principal vehicle for the development and diffusion of new seeds. Indeed, the seed industry in India had its beginnings in the early-1960s with the establishment of the public sector National Seeds Corporation. The NSC provided foundation seed, training and technical assistance to state governments and private companies. The Terai Seed Development Corporation established in 1969 became the model for state seed corporations established in the 1970s and 1980s.[19]

The primary purpose of these and related public sector organisations such as the state seed certification agencies was to produce, certify and distribute high quality seeds that were the product of public research. But they also stimulated private sector activity through distribution of foundation seed and through the creation of expertise in seed technology, processing and distribution (Candler, 1995).[20] As the import of commercial seeds was prohibited and foreign direct investment not permitted, private sector activity depended on home grown firms. Consequently, it grew in bursts and spurts focusing first on vegetables and later on sorghum and pearl millet.

The obstacles to private industry were not just their lack of capabilities in research or access to capital and technology. There was also lack of confidence, on the part of the government, in leaving these activities to the market. Probably, the most important is the fact that with certain kinds of varietal development, the innovator cannot

18. In 1987, the seed industry was de-reserved allowing the entry of large firms and foreign firms with equity stake in joint ventures of not more than 40 per cent. In 1991, reforms allowed the entry of firms with majority foreign equity.

19. The Rockfeller Foundation and the World Bank were closely associated with India's seed programme in those initial years through grants, credits and technical assistance.

20. B.R. Barwale, the founder of MAHYCO, India's largest private seed firm, began his career producing and marketing vegetable seeds developed by ICAR and later graduated to producing hybrid maize with seed supplied by the Rockfeller Foundation that was developed in a joint research programme between ICAR and the Rockfeller Foundation (Padmanabhan, 1998).

appropriate a significant enough share of the gains leaving little incentive for private effort. This is certainly true for seeds of open-pollinated varieties (which include rice and wheat) that can be reproduced by farmers for their own use or sale to other farmers.

In recent years, the private seed industry has grown sizably in many crops. Regulatory reforms have eased the restrictions on the entry of large and foreign owned private firms into this industry. It is also expected that the strengthening of intellectual property rights and the new technologies of genetic selection offered by biotechnology would make this sector even more attractive for private investment. These developments have affected the structure of the seed industry worldwide. In the United States, private spending for food and agricultural research tripled in real terms in two decades. As a result, the private sector invests considerably more in food and agricultural R&D than the government. Furthermore, private research has expanded its range of activities. While earlier most private research in the U.S. was for farm machinery, new food products and processing methods, the private sector has since developed research capabilities in plant breeding that was once a traditional area of public sector research (Fuglie *et al*, 1996).

In India too, private sector spending on seed R&D is rapidly growing. According to one estimate, R&D effort (measured by rupee investments, technical personnel, size of experiment stations) in the private sector tripled within a short span of about 8 years. This period was associated with changes in government policy towards the seed industry as well as the industry wide economic reforms. The same study concludes that about 50 per cent of the observed increase in R&D was attributable to the liberalisation in government policies that allowed entry into the seed industry by large domestic firms as well as foreign firms (Pray, Ramaswami and Kelley, 2001).

The growing importance of the private seed industry has prompted new policy concerns. Broadly speaking, there are three inter-related issues. First, is the issue of efficiency. Since the entry of private players is possibly only because of greater appropriability (of the gains from higher productivity), does the exercise of resulting monopoly power reduce social gains and in particular, the benefits to farmers and consumers? The earlier literature that estimated the gains to agricultural research typically assumed competitive markets and therefore does not address the new situation.[21] This question is important because some of the regulatory reform, like the *New Seed Policy* of 1988, was explicitly motivated by the objective of facilitating rapid technology transfer from the private sector (and in particular, the multinational seed firms) to farmers. The *Seed Policy* of 2002 is even more direct in its goal of fostering the growth of a private seed industry. The last decade has seen the entry of major international seed firms into the Indian market. However, it has also been accompanied by consolidation of the industry through mergers and acquisitions. The entry of large firms, backed presumably by formidable marketing and technological prowess, has also raised fears about the viability of smaller seed firms.

All this has raised a number of questions. Would the products of private technology suppliers be so high priced that small farmers would not be able to afford it?[22] Do these developments call for a redefinition of the priorities of the public sector whether in terms of research, seed production, certification and environment regulation? On the one hand, there is now considerable expertise outside the public sector that is capable of applied plant breeding, seed production, seed certification and testing. On the other hand, the public sector constitutes a countervailing power in the marketplace. Furthermore, it is still the major supplier of seeds of open-pollinated varieties.

The Gains From Research

In India, private technology suppliers had a form of intellectual property rights protection in the form of hybrids. How has this helped private firm appropriate gains from improved seed? Evidence from the United States suggests that for crops grown with hybrid seed like sorghum and maize, seed companies capture between 35 to 48 per cent of the gains (Fuglie, *et al.*, 1996). For India, Pray *et al.*, (1991) calculated that seed companies captured 18.5 per cent of the yield increases of hybrid sorghum and 6 per cent of the gains from pearl millet hybrids. These estimates were based on yield data from

21. This research showed that payoffs to agricultural research generally are high and that therefore more resources should be invested in research and development and in alleviating the factors that constrain adoption of new technologies at the farm-level.

22. Such issues are not exclusive to private research; they were debated vigorously in the context of the Green Revolution technologies as well although the concerns there were not with the price of seed but with the cost of complementary inputs.

1986 and 1987. This fact is also relevant for stimulating private investments in plant breeding. In India, private R&D expenditures by seed companies as a proportion of their sales are estimated to have risen from 3.6 per cent to 6.9 per cent between 1987 and 1996 (Pray, Ramaswami and Kelley, 2001). About half the increase in the R&D ratio was due to the development of hybrids of rice and rapeseed that became commercially viable during this period.

The only partial appropriation of gains by private seed firms suggests that new hybrids reduced the efficiency price of seed. This is consistent with the evidence of Ramaswami, Pray and Kelley (2002) who showed that private hybrids in coarse cereals have become important enough to contribute to increases in average district yields in Andhra Pradesh, Karnataka and Maharashtra. The social gains of these private hybrids must be reckoned to be particularly high because (a) of their success in the pre-dominantly poorly endowed regions of the semi-arid tropics and because of (b) the greater importance of coarse cereals in the cereal budgets of poor households relative to the richer households.

With the enactment of the *Plant Variety Protection and Farmer's Rights Act*, protection has been extended to the rights of breeders of open-pollinated varieties. Following the experience of hybrids, could we then expect that this would enable breeders of open-pollinated varieties to appropriate some of the gains of the improved seed? And would it provide substantial incentives for investment in breeding for open-pollinated varieties?

In the United States, which has had the longest experience with plant breeders' rights, seed companies appropriate about 12 to 24 per cent of yield gains from improved non-hybrid varieties (Fuglie, *et al*, 1996). The extent of appropriability is significantly lower here compared to hybrid seed. Further, plant breeders' rights did not stimulate investments uniformly in all crops. While investments in soybean breeding increased substantially, impacts on small grains (wheat, rice, barley, oats, rye and triticale) were insignificant (Fuglie, *et al*, 1996). This reflects the seed industry's perceptions about future grain sales, technological opportunities and research costs which are not uniform across crops. Hence, even in the U.S., public breeding continues to be an important source of finished varieties for some major field crops. In an evaluation of plant breeding rights in the U.S.,

Butler and Marion (1985) concluded that the "... (plant breeders rights) has resulted in modest private and public benefits at modest private and public costs".

Could it be otherwise in India? If anything, the Indian regulation affords a lesser degree of protection to breeders' rights than the American legislation. The farmer's right to save, use, exchange and sell seed limits the breeders' rights.[23] Of these it is the right to exchange and sell seed that limits appropriability. If farmers had only the right to save and use seed, without the right to sell, the seed becomes like a durable good that could be priced appropriately. Such pricing cannot be sustained when competition (to the seed company) arises from farmers themselves.[24]

Enforcement of intellectual property rights is an issue that is sometimes ignored in evaluating policies. Yet, from the point of view of a seed firm, its ability to enforce its rights of intellectual property is paramount. Theft of parental lines, theft of foundation seeds (by contract growers) and the sale of counterfeit seed are some of the threats to the intellectual property of a seed company (Shiva and Crompton, 1998). If there was stronger enforcement of existing laws for trade secrets (to protect parental lines), contracts (to protect foundation seeds) and trademarks (for action against counterfeit seeds), they could have a significant impact on hybrids as well. Inability to protect parental lines means that Indian varieties are usually double-cross hybrids that have 10-15 per cent lower yields than single-cross hybrids.

Conclusions

India has invested considerable resources in public sector agricultural research. Within this framework, the focus has been in generating, testing and diffusing relevant technologies. The public sector driven picture of agricultural research has, however, been changing. Because of new technologies and stronger intellectual

---

23. Farmers are not, however, entitled to sell branded seed of a protected variety under the brand name.

24. The Plant Variety Protection and Farmers Rights Act has been criticised especially by NGOs because they believe that it provides the legal framework for trans-national firms to monopolise the Indian seed industry. A fairly typical assertion is the following. "A much greater threat to farmer comes (from)...the likely loss of Indian markets in future...This is evident from the Plant Variety Protection and Farmer's Rights (PVPFR) Bill ... facilitating industries to obtain seed monopolies." (Utkarsh and Satheesh, 2002).

property rights, innovators can now appropriate a significant enough share of the gains from research. This has transformed the seed industry as the private sector has grown to be a sizeable presence in many crops. As the payoff to research and higher agricultural productivity is high in poor countries, the investment of private capital in agricultural research contributes to economic development.

The appropriability of research gains is made possible by monopoly power in the hands of seed suppliers. The growth of private seed industry has occurred in the context of global capital flows, the agreements on intellectual property rights and patents at the WTO and continuing applications of biotechnology to crops and livestock. NGOs and in particular, environmentalists have strong misgivings about the impact of these developments on bio-diversity and low input agriculture is cited by them as the only sustainable form of agricultural development. For economists, it is often not clear what is objected to: market forces, trans-national companies, monopolies, patents or biotechnology itself.

GM and Indian Agriculture – A Timeline

March 1991	The first Indian transgenic fish was generated in Madurai Kamaraj University (MKU) in 1991 using borrowed constructs. India has developed experimental transgenics of rohu fish, zebra fish, cat fish and singhi fish. Genes, promoters and vectors of indigenous origin are now available for only two species namely rohu and singhi for engineering growth. Transgenic rohu recently produced from indigenous construct at Madurai Kamaraj University has proved to be eight times larger than the control siblings. This transgenic rohu attains 46 to 49 gram body weight within 36 weeks of its birth. In India, research in transgenic fish was initiated in (MKU), Centre for Cellular and Molecular Biology (CCMB), Hyderabad and National Matha College, Kollam with borrowed constructs from foreign scientists.
March 31, 2002	The Genetic Engineering Approval Committee (GEAC) conditionally approves the commercial cultivation of Bt Cotton varieties belonging to Mahyco-Monsanto for a period of three years.
May, 2002	The Department of Biotechnology (DBT) gives the go-ahead signal to the Tamil Nadu-based private seed producing firm, Rasi Seeds Company Ltd (RSCL), for conducting 'multi-location contained replicated research trials in open fields using transgenic Bt Cotton containing the Cry 1A(c) gene' during *kharif* season 2002.

Contd...

...Contd...

June 13, 2003	The Genetic engineering approval committee (GEAC) struck down the plea made by Rasi Seeds for commercial cultivation of its genetically modified (GM) RCH 2 Bt cotton seeds in the South, saying the product needs further field trials and evaluations.
January 13, 2004	The Union Agriculture Ministry asked the Gujarat government to take action against the manufacturers and vendors of spurious Bt cotton seeds.
January 18, 2004	The Agriculture Ministry said that the area under Bt Çotton was negligible. *"In 2002-03, the first year of its approval for commercial cultivation, Bt cotton covered an area of only 38,038 hectare representing 0.51 per cent of the area under cotton in the period. In 2003-04 with good monsoon rains the area under Bt cotton increased to 92,000 hectare. This area coverage under Bt cotton is almost neligible as compared to over 9 million hectare under cotton crop in the country. This points to the low acceptability of Bt cotton by farmers"*, reports an internal report of the agriculture ministry. The agriculture ministry's findings ran down the hype created by US based International Service for the Aquisition of Agri-biotech Association (ISAAA). The ISAAA study has claimed that the Bt cotton area in India has increased to 100,000 hectare in 2003-04, while the government estimate put it at 92,000 hectare.
February 10, 2004	Study released by entomologists at IARI cast doubts on the long-term benefits of Bt Cotton. It found that the protection afforded by Bt gene is at best for six years.
April, 2004	GEAC approves yet another Bt transgenic cotton, RCH 2 for commercial cultivation in the central and southern parts of the country.

References

Basant, R., "Seed Industry in India: Issues Arising from GATT," *Vikalpa*, 20, 3, 21-41.

Butler, L.J. and B.W. Marion (1985). "The Impacts of Patent Protection on the U.S. Seed Industry and Public Plant Breeding," *Monograph 16*, Madison: Research Division, College of Agricultural and Life Sciences, University of Wisconsin.

Candler, W. (1995). "Impact Evaluation Report, Bangladesh: Cereal Seeds Project, India: National Seeds Projects I and II, Pakistan: Seeds Project," *Report No. 14761*, World Bank.

de Janvry A., E. Sadoulet and M. Fafchamps (1989). "Agrarian Structure, Technological Innovations, and the State," in P. Bardhan, (ed.) *The Economic Theory of Agrarian Institutions*, Oxford University Press.

Falck-Zepeda, J.B., G. Traxler and R.N. Nelson (2000). "Surplus Distribution from the Introduction of a Biotechnology Innovation," *American Journal of Agricultural Economics*, 82, 2, 360-369.

Fuglie, K., N. Ballenger, K. Day, C. Klotz, M. Ollinger, J. Reilly, U. Vasavada and J. Yee (1996). "Agricultural Research and Development," Economic Research Service, U.S. Department of Agriculture, *Agricultural Economic Report No. 735*, May.

Hayami Y. and V. Ruttan (1985). *Agricultural Development: An International Perspective*, Johns Hopkins University Press: Baltimore.

Morris, M. L., R.P. Singh and S. Pal (1998). "India's Maize Seed Industry in Transition: Changing Roles for the Public and Private Sectors," *Food Policy*, 23, 1, 55-71.

Moschini, G. and H. Lapan (1997). "Intellectual Property Rights and the Welfare Effects of Agricultural R&D," *American Journal of Agricultural Economics*, 79, 4, 1229-1242.

Padmanabhan, R. (1998). "Honour for a Seedsman," *Frontline*, Volume 15, No. 23, November, 07-20.

Pray, C. and B. Ramaswami (1991). *A Framework for Seed Policy Analysis in Developing Countries*, International Food Policy Research.

Pray, C., B. Ramaswami and T. Kelley (2001), "The Impact of Economic Reforms on R&D by the Indian Seed Industry," *Food Policy*, 26, 587-598.

Pray, C., S. Ribeiro, R.A. Mueller, and P. Parthasarathy Rao (1991). "Private Research and Public Benefit: The Private Seed Industry for Sorghum and Pearl Millet in India," *Research Policy*, 20, 314-324.

Economic Times (2003). "States Asked to Report Bt Cotton Performance," 17 April.

Financial Express (2003). "Panel Rejects Rasi Seeds' Bt Cotton Bid," June 14, 2003.

Government of Andhra Pradesh (2003). *Performance Report of Bt Cotton in Andhra Pradesh During kharif, 2002*,Department of Agriculture, Hyderabad.

Liu, Yong-Biao, Bruce E. Tabashnik *et al.*, (1999) "Development Time and Resistance to Bt Crops," *Nature*, 400: 519.

Qaim, M. and D. Zilberman (2003). "Yield Effects of Genetically Modified Crops in Developing Countries," *Science*, 299, 900-902.

Rowell, Andy (2003). "Debate, What Debate?" *The Ecologist*, July/August, pp. 36-37.

Sahai, Suman (2003). "Genetically Modified Crops in India: Some Issues," *Gene Campaign*, New Delhi.

4

Agricultural Sector: Trends in Export and Import

PAVEL CHAKRAVARTY

This chapter is compilation of tables that detail India's Trade in Agricultural commodities after economic liberalisation. They are added as references with which the chapters in this section may be read.

Table 4.1

India's Agricultural Trade in Post Reforms and WTO Period

Year	*Agricultural Export (US $ million)*	*Agricultural Import (US $ million)*	*Export surplus (US $ million)*
1990-91	2063.74	788.60	1275.14
1991-92	2586.72	546.97	2039.75
1992-93	2475.27	802.48	1672.79
1993-94	3385.66	757.97	2627.69
1994-95	4314.38	1757.79	2556.59
1995-96	6261.69	1613.28	4648.41
1996-97	6579.13	1782.27	4796.86
1997-98	6551.03	2317.87	4233.16
1998-99	6107.06	3312.29	2794.77
1999-00	5756.48	3256.21	2500.27
2000-01	6195.90	2224.13	3971.77
2001-02	6137.42	2826.13	3311.29
2002-03	6913.40	3327.83	3585.57

Source: Economic Survey (various years).

Exports

The table below sets out the top export items.

Table 4.2

List of Major Export Items at 2-digit Level in the Post Reform Period

Code	*Name*	*Average Percentage Share (post reform)*
3	Fish and crustaceans, molluscs and other aquatic invertebrates.	20.65
9	Coffee, tea, mate and spices.	17.52
10	Cereals.	11.34
23	residues and waste from the food industries; prepared animal fodder.	10.10
8	Edible fruit and nuts; peel or citrus fruit or melons.	10.83
12	Oil seeds and oleaginous fruits; miscellaneous grains, seeds and fruit; industrial or medicinal plants; straw and fodder.	4.58
24	Tobacco and manufactured tobacco substitutes.	4.57
7	Edible vegetables and certain roots and tubers.	3.87
2	Meat and edible meat offal.	3.70
13	Lac; gums, resins and other vegetable saps and extracts.	3.41

Table 4.3

List of Major Export Items at 2-digit Level in the Pre-WTO Period

HS Code	*Name*	*Average Percentage Share (pre-WTO)*
3	Fish and crustaceans, molluscs and other aquatic invertebrates.	19.47
23	residues and waste from the food industries; prepared animal fodder.	16.90
9	Coffee, tea, mate and spices.	16.79
8	Edible fruit and nuts; peel or citrus fruit or melons.	12.01
10	Cereals.	8.37
12	Oil seeds and oleaginous fruits; miscellaneous grains, seeds and fruit; industrial or medicinal plants; straw and fodder.	3.70
24	Tobacco and manufactured tobacco substitutes.	3.57
2	Meat and edible meat offal.	3.17
7	Edible vegetables and certain roots and tubers.	2.98
15	Animal or vegetable fats and oils and their cleavage products; prepared edible fats; animal or vegetable waxes.	2.95

Table 4.4

List of Major Export Items at 2-digit Level in the Post-WTO Period

HS Code	*Name*	*Average Percentage Share (post-WTO)*
10	Cereals.	19.72
3	Fish and crustaceans, molluscs and other aquatic invertebrates.	17.04
9	Coffee, tea, mate and spices.	15.77
23	residues and waste from the food industries; prepared animal fodder.	12.18
8	Edible fruit and nuts; peel or citrus fruit or melons.	7.17
12	Oil seeds and oleaginous fruits; miscellaneous grains, seeds and fruit; industrial or medicinal plants; straw and fodder.	4.08
13	Lac; gums, resins and other vegetable saps and extracts.	3.50
15	Animal or vegetable fats and oils and their cleavage products; prepared edible fats; animal or vegetable waxes.	3.18
24	Tobacco and manufactured tobacco substitutes.	3.19
2	Meat and edible meat offal.	3.05

Table 4.5

Items Identified at the 6-digit Level on the Average Percentage Share Basis

Code	*Name*	*Average Percentage Share*	*Rank*
100630	Semi-milied or wholly milled rice, whether or not polished or glazed.	21.54	1
30613	Shrimps and prawns frozen	19.85	2
80132	Shelled cashew nuts	8.76	3
230400	Oil-cake and other solid residues, whether or not ground or in the form of pellets, resulting from the extraction of soya-bean oil.	8.55	4
100190	Other(wheat seed, mueslin, wheat for human consumption)	7.28	5
170199	Other (cane sugar-candy, refined sugar cubes)	6.88	6
30379	Other frozen fish, excluding livers and roes	5.81	7
2023000	Boneless of bovine animals, frozen	5.41	8
90240	Other black tea (fermented) and other partly fermented tea	4.83	9
90111	Coffee neither roasted nor decaffeinated	3.37	10
		100	

Table 4.6

India's Export Destinations of the Items (items identified on the basis of average percentage share)

Importing Country	*Code*	*Name*	*Average Percentage Share*
China	30379	Other frozen fish, excluding livers and roes	13.36
Taiwan (Taipei)	30379	Other frozen fish, excluding livers and roes	5.93
Japan	30379	Other frozen fish, excluding livers and roes	5.46
Total			**100**
USA	30613	Shrimps and prawns frozen	17.00
Japan	30613	Shrimps and prawns frozen	16.45
UK	30613	Shrimps and prawns frozen	2.98
Total			**100**
USA	80132	Shelled cashew nuts	25.67
Netherlands	80132	Shelled cashew nuts	6.825
Total			**100**
Italy	90111	Coffee neither roasted nor decaffeinated	11.36
Germany	90111	Coffee neither roasted nor decaffeinated	8.46
Belgium	90111	Coffee neither roasted nor decaffeinated	4.56
Spain	90111	Coffee neither roasted nor decaffeinated	2.75
Total			**100**
UK	90240	Other black tea (fermented) and other partly fermented tea	8.33
Russia	90240	Other black tea (fermented) and other partly fermented tea	7.65
Iraq	90240	Other black tea (fermented) and other partly fermented tea	6.66
Total			**100**
Bangladesh	100190	Other (Wheat seed, mueslin, wheat (not seed) for human consumption)	14.73
Philippines	100190	Other (Wheat seed, mueslin, wheat (not seed) for human consumption)	9.82
Indonesia	100190	Other (Wheat seed, mueslin, wheat (not seed) for human consumption)	5.13
Total			100

Contd...

...Contd...

Importing Country	Code	Name	Average Percentage Share
Saudi Arabia	100630	Semi-milled or wholly milled rice, whether or not polished or glazed.	14.65
South Africa	100630	Semi-milled or wholly milled rice, whether or not polished or glazed.	4.90
Bangladesh	100630	Semi-milled or wholly milled rice, whether or not polished or glazed.	3.30
Philippines	100630	Semi-milled or wholly milled rice, whether or not polished or glazed.	3.23
Total			**100**
Sri Lanka	170199	Other (cane sugar refined/candy,sugar cubes)	10.60
Malaysia	170199	Other (cane sugar refined/candy,sugar cubes)	8.34
Indonesia	170199	Other (cane sugar refined/candy,sugar cubes)	8.19
Bangladesh	170199	Other (cane sugar refined/candy,sugar cubes)	6.35
Total			**100**
Indonesia	230400	Oil-cake and other solid residues, whether or not ground or in the form of pellets, resulting from the extraction of soya-bean oil.	7.07
Viet Nam	230400	Oil-cake and other solid residues, whether or not ground or in the form of pellets, resulting from the extraction of soya-bean oil.	6.79
Korea Republic (South)	230400	Oil-cake and other solid residues, whether or not ground or in the form of pellets, resulting from the extraction of soya-bean oil.	6.78
Bangladesh	230400	Oil-cake and other solid residues, whether or not ground or in the form of pellets, resulting from the extraction of soya-bean oil.	5.03
Singapore	230400	Oil-cake and other solid residues, whether or not ground or in the form of pellets, resulting from the extraction of soya-bean oil.	5.01
Total			**100**
Malaysia	2023000	Boneless of bovine animals, frozen	14.65
Philippines	2023000	Boneless of bovine animals, frozen	8.68
Total			**100**

In this part, we attempt to see whether the export destinations are favorable trading points for India or not. To meet this objective, we calculate the Trade Intensity Indices for those countries, which could be defined as:

T_{ii} = ((India's export of the specified commodity to that country/ India's total agricultural export)/(World export of that commodity to that country/Total world's agricultural export)).

If $T_{ii} > 1$ => it is a favorable trading position for India

$T_{ii} < 1$ => it is not.

Table 4.7

Trade Intensity Index for Different Export Destinations of India Based on the Items (Selected on the Basis of Average Percentage Share)

Code	*Country*	*1997*	*1998*	*1999*	*2000*
030379	China	20.20	13.15	18.15	17.31
	Taiwan	1.36	1.95	2.13	6.29
030613	USA	10.14	10.78	12.16	13.98
	Japan	45.76	40.01	36.40	30.07
080132	USA	—	—	—	—
	Netherlands	—	—	—	—
090111	Italy	12.24	12.75	10.94	10.22
	Germany	14.52	12.16	12.93	10.95
090240	UK	14.13	11.79	12.44	11.09
	Russia	19.43	13.43	15.06	10.83
100190	Bangladesh	—	—	—	16.85
	Philippines	—	—	—	5.61
100630	Saudi Arabia	22.47	16.12	26.81	28.20
	South Africa	—	—	—	—
170199	Sri Lanka	4.51	—	—	7.02
	Malaysia	—	—	—	—
230400	Indonesia	8.50	8.51	9.13	10.09
	Vietnam	2.48	3.00	5.37	5.91
02023000	Malaysia	2.08	14.09	12.60	15.07
	Philippines	0.93	6.46	6.30	8.67

The above table has been calculated given available data. Except for the product '02023000' in the year 1997 all the Tii values are well above 1. So, it can well be concluded that as India's agricultural exports are increasing to the very export destinations that are favorable for India.

Imports

The table below sets out the top import items.

Table 4.8

Identification of Sensitive Import Items at the 6-digit Level on the Average Percentage Share Basis

Code	*Name*	*Average Percentage Share*	*Rank*
15111000	Crude Palm Oil and its Fractions	32.71	1
15071000	Soya Bean Crude Oil whether or not Degummed	17.35	2
15119000	Refined Palm Oil and its Fractions	9.23	3
7131000	Peas (*Pisum Sativum*) Dried and Shelled	8.33	4
80131	Cashew Nuts Fresh/Dried in Shell	7.08	5
7132000	Chickpeas (Garbanzos) Dried and Shelled	5.56	6
15079000	Other Soya Bean Oil and Its Fractions	4.28	7
151620	Vegetable fats and oils and their fractions	1.98	8
8021100	Almonds Fresh or Dried in Shell	1.84	9
80410	Dates	1.70	10
		100	

Table 4.9

India's Sources of Import of the Products (Identified on the Basis of Average Percentage Share)

Exporting Country	*Importing Country*	*Code*	*Name*	*Average Percentage Share*
Tanzania	India	80131	Cashew Nuts Fresh/Dried in Shell	14.16
Cote d'Ivoire (Ivory Coast)	India	80131	Cashew Nuts Fresh/Dried in Shell	10.31
Guinea-Bissau	India	80131	Cashew Nuts Fresh/Dried in Shell	7.29
Indonesia	India	80131	Cashew Nuts Fresh/Dried in Shell	5.03
Total				100

Contd...

...Table 4.9 Contd...

Exporting Country	*Importing Country*	*Code*	*Name*	*Average Percentage Share*
Iran	India	80410	Dates	27.09
Pakistan	India	80410	Dates	17.61
Total				**100**
Nepal	India	151620	Vegetable fats and oils and their fractions	42.43
USA	India	151620	Vegetable fats and oils and their fractions	4.44
Total				**100**
Canada	India	7131000	Peas (*Pisum Sativum*) Dried and Shld.	21.73
France	India	7131000	Peas (*Pisum Sativum*) Dried and Shld.	10.77
Australia	India	7131000	Peas (*Pisum Sativum*) Dried and Shld.	7.03
Myanmar (Burma)	India	7131000	Peas (Pisum Sativum) Dried and Shld.	5.21
Total				**100**
Canada	India	7132000	Chickpeas (Garbanzos) Dried and Shld.	12.92
Iran	India	7132000	Chickpeas (Garbanzos) Dried and Shld.	11.28
Australia	India	7132000	Chickpeas (Garbanzos) Dried and Shld.	7.95
Myanmar (Burma)	India	7132000	Chickpeas (Garbanzos) Dried and Shld.	5.41
Total				**100**
USA	India	8021100	Almonds Fresh or Dried in Shell	45.06
Australia	India	8021100	Almonds Fresh or Dried in Shell	1.88
Afghanistan	India	8021100	Almonds Fresh or Dried in Shell	1.35
Total				**100**
Argentina	India	15071000	Soya Bean Crude Oil whether or not Degummed	34.79
Brazil	India	15071000	Soya Bean Crude Oil whether or not Degummed	12.71
USA	India	15071000	Soya Bean Crude Oil whether or not Degummed	1.42
Total				**100**
Argentina	India	15079000	Other Soya Bean Oil and Its Fractions	28.85
Brazil	India	15079000	Other Soya Bean Oil and Its Fractions	11.89
USA	India	15079000	Other Soya Bean Oil and Its Fractions	8.61
Total				**100**
Indonesia	India	15111000	Crude Palm Oil and Its Fractns.	25.29
Malaysia	India	15111000	Crude Palm Oil and Its Fractns.	23.34
Total				**100**
Indonesia	India	15119000	Refined Palm Oil and Its Fractions	26.09
Malaysia	India	15119000	Refined Palm Oil and Its Fractions	23.43
Total				100

Conclusion

The unusual performance of Indian agriculture in the world market where the initial surge in growth could not be sustained indicates the size of the task that must be accomplished in this sector. This and the surge in imports in the post-WTO phase indicate that Indian agriculture (or at least parts of it) are high cost; i.e. the fall in international prices worldwide inconveniencing Indian producers indicate that there are more efficient economies in the field of agriculture. The areas where India seems to have some advantage are the labour-intensive sectors; the growth in cereal exports are a matter of off-loading stocks the costs of storing which have become too much to bear and yet continue to pile up given the high support prices.

Section II

Indian Industry: The Impact of WTO Within and Without

In the current section, we deal with issues pertaining to Indian industry. The first two papers explicitly consider the impact on the industry, namely textile and pharmaceuticals. However, the recent upturn in the use of contingency measures (e.g. – anti-dumping duites) could seriously hurt Indian export interest, and the chapters that follow looks into that aspect.

Saurabh Bandhyopadhyay and Toposhmito Sengupta attempt to identify sectors in the textile industry where India has a comparative advantage or disadvantage following further to examine India's position *vis-à-vis* its competitors in the backdrop of MFA phase-out. They attempt to identify factors responsible for the relatively poor performance of the textile sector and set future policy implications. Bandhyopadhyay and Sengupta blame state policy regarding inflexible labour laws, reservation of garments for the small scale sector, policy biases against synthetics, transaction costs of business and lack of brand equity being factors that may prevent India from taking full advantage of the MFA phase-out. They point out that while many of these misguided policies have begun to be tackled, the old mindset about controlling the industry remains.

Subhodip Ghosh argues that the Indian pharmaceutical industry has come of age and it can not only co-exist with TRIPS but also make the use of it to its advantage. IPRs are essential to economic innovation and foster an environment where investment in new technologies and products are taken up. Ghosh argues for moving from tired intellectual formulations about TRIPS and opines that the real agenda should be an action plan to deal with medicines that are needed but may not be provided for the market. In this respect the paper points out that there are divisions and debates in the West as well and the final contours of TRIPs and the elbow space that generic drug makers will have is not yet known. In addition, the paper briefly discuses the features of the recently adopted Patents Ordinance (2005), commenting on its future implications.

The anti-dumping agreement has become uniquely important for India, as it has successfully transformed itself from the affected to the violator in recent years, emerging as the most frequent user of this provision. The concern over this increased usage has been highlighted in various WTO studies, and the recent lodging of cases by EU and Bangladesh against India testify that. Nilanjan Banik focuses on the anti-dumping agreement in general, and India's negotiating policy for future in particular. Through an empirical analysis, Banik establishes that anti-dumping provisions have indeed a negative impact on Indian exports, and globally developed countries are the major users of this provision. Based on the experiences, Banik has argued in favour of a special and different treatment for developing countries and called for systemic reform of the anti-dumping agreement.

5

Cotton Textile Industry in India: Implications for MFA Phase Out

SAURABH BANDYOPADHYAY
TOPOSHMITO SENGUPTA

Introduction

The textile industry has always been considered critical from the perspective of generating employment (next only to agriculture) and foreign exchange earnings. In terms of value addition, the industry stands next only to chemicals, accounting for 12.5 per cent of the manufacturing value addition (CMIE, 1998). Indian households spent 16 per cent of their income on textiles, as compared to 6 per cent-7 per cent of income by citizens of Japan, the USA, Sri Lanka and the Philippines (Venkatesan *et al.*, 1999). It is the second largest in terms of direct employment (about 35 m people). Besides, it has a very important role to play where the country's 'macroeconomy' is concerned. To put things in perspective, the sector contributes to almost 14 per cent of the industrial production and about 35 per cent of the gross export earnings. The sector's contribution to the GDP stands at over 6 per cent. Due to all of the above, the growth of the industry has a bearing on the development of the economy, especially exports.

It has to be kept in mind that the Indian textiles is an integrated sector, as the industry not only grows its own raw materials (cotton, jute, silk and wool) but also processes the same into high value products like fabrics and garments. India exports a large portion of its textile produce. Despite quota restrictions, Indian textile exports have grown at a CAGR of over 17 per cent in the period FY93 to FY01. Our main competitors in the textile sector include countries like China, Bangladesh, Indonesia, Sri Lanka and Pakistan. Like India, these countries too are cost-effective textile producers due to the advantage of lower labour costs, which account for a significant portion of the cost of converting fabrics into garments. The major markets for India have been the US and the EU (despite having quota restrictions). UAE, Japan and Switzerland are amongst the top non-quota export destinations. In this context, one may recall that first time Quotas were imposed by USA and EC in the late-1960's. While the USA imposed quotas under the Long Term Arrangement (LTA) from 1962 on items like Print cloth; Twills, Sateen and Duck Fabrics, the EC member states like Germany, France, and Italy imposed restrictions on cotton fabrics and made-up articles in terms of the Second LTA signed in 1967. Subsequent years saw a comprehensive set of restrictions under the aegis of the Multi-Fibre Arrangement (MFA) negotiated in 1974. Given this background, the complete elimination of quotas in the year 2005, will undoubtedly herald a new era in the global trading system in textiles and clothing.

In view of its national importance, this chapter intends to look at the changes in Effective Rate of Protection (ERP) on the Indian textile industry and forecast its output response in the absence of quota restriction from 2005. In the process of identifying the sunrise and sunset segments within the textile sector, the objective is to test the hypothesis that a fall in ERP for the sunset segment is going to be harmful, and there is a need for protecting the same. On similar grounds, it is necessary bringing down ERP for the industries performing well, i.e., for the sunrise segments.

However, there is a caveat to this hypothesis. Going by the commitments of globalisation and liberalisation (as enshrined in the WTO Agreement), it may be difficult for a member-nation to carry on with protection. The short-run solution lies in way of providing subsidies. This is possible, as the present agreement requires a fall in subsidy at aggregate level (two-digit level) and not at a higher disaggregated levels (say at a six-digit or eightdigit level), like the case for agricultural inputs. For instance, it is perfectly possible for the government to give a higher amount of subsidy in the production of red colour pure cotton shirts (representing a six-digit level of classification) and yet show a fall in subsidy in the production of cotton (representing a two-digit level of classification). This happens when the government gives a higher amount of subsidy for producing red colour cotton shirts at the cost of cutting subsidy by a greater amount for producing other items, say, blue colour cotton shirts, at the same disaggregated level. To put it simply, the government can cross-subsidise production at a disaggregated level provided it can show a fall in subsidy at a higher aggregated level.

Unfortunately, in the long run such a solution is not viable. Besides being a cause of distortion, excessive protection can cripple domestic industry. What is needed is to make the *sunset* segment of the textile industry efficient. This study examines ways of achieving this objective.

The study uses the Relative Export Competitiveness Index (REC) and the Revealed Comparative Advantage Index (RCA) for identifying *sunset* and *sunrise* segments in the textile industry. ERP is calculated following Corden's Method, concentrating only on tradable inputs. The paper is divided into five sections. The next section deals India's position in the textile sector in congruence with Multi-Fibre Arrangement (MFA). Section 2 looks at those sectors in which India has a competitive advantage or disadvantage. In Section 3, the exercise is carried out regarding calculation of Effective Rate of Protection. Section 4 examines India's position *vis-à-vis* its competitors and deals with conclusion and policy prescription.

MFA and India's Position

Since 1995, MFA has been taken over by the Agreement on Textiles and Clothing (ATC). Basically, MFA is a framework for bilateral agreement that proposes quota-limiting imports into countries whose domestic industries face serious damage from rapidly increasing imports. From its inception, MFA dealt with textile exports originating mainly from developing countries. On the other hand, ATC provides a blueprint for removal of restrictions on textile exports originating mainly from developing nations. The integration process is to be carried out in four stages. The integration process is represented schematically below in Table 5.1.

As revealed by Table 5.1, the first phase calls for integrating product categories accounting (at least) 16 per cent of the importing countries total volume of textile and clothing imports (with 1990 as a base year), into WTO. Article 2.6 of the ATC Agreement states that- *'the products to be integrated shall encompass products from each of the following four groups: tops and yarns, fabrics, made up textile products and clothing.'* On 1 January 1995, 16 per cent of textiles and clothing exports was thus liberalised. This however does not imply that 16 per cent of textiles and clothing export from any country that face MFA restraints will be liberalised. For, liberalisation may include products that any specific nation does not export. For example, in case of India, 90 per cent of its exports was liberalised only after the end of 2004. At the beginning of the second phase, an additional 17 per cent was to come into the existing framework and by the end of 95th month (with start of the third phase) a further 18 per cent was to be added. Now with the end of ten-year period, all product categories will be free from all restrictions.

Table 5.1

Integration with the Principles of GATT

Steps	*Percentage of Products to be brought under GATT (including removal of any quota)*	*How Fast Remaining Quotas Should Open Up, (if 1994 rate was 6 per cent)*
Step 1 1 Jan. 1995 (to 31 Dec 1997)	16 per cent (minimum, taking 1990 imports as base)	6.96 per cent *per annum*
Step 2 1 Jan. 1998 (to 31 Dec. 2001)	17 per cent	8.7 per cent *per annum*
Step 3 1 Jan. 2002 (to 31 Dec. 2004)	18 per cent	11.05 per cent
Step 4 1 Jan. 2005 Full integration into GATT (and final elimination of quotas)	49 per cent (maximum)	No quotas left

Source: WTO Trading into Future.

Regarding growth of quotas, the ten-year period starting from January 1995 is divided into three stages of 3, 4 and 3 years respectively. Article 2.13 of the ATC Agreement says- *'during stage 1 of this Agreement (from the date of entry into force of the WTO Agreement to the 36th month that it is in effect, inclusive) the level of each restriction under the MFA bilateral agreements in force for the 12 month period shall be increased annually by not less than the growth rate established for restrictions, increased by 16 per cent'*. This did not mean quotas were allowed to grow by 16 per cent. It means that quotas otherwise growing by 6 per cent (see Table 5.1) were allowed to grow by 6.96 per cent. During the second phase starting Ist January 1998, the rate of growth of quotas was to be 25 per cent of 6.96 per cent, at a rate of 8.7 per cent. The third phase starting 1st January 2002 initiated growth of quotas at a rate of 27 per cent of 8.7 per cent, i.e. at a rate of 11.05 per cent per year.

During transitional phase, although there was supposed to be relaxation of existing quotas, some categories in which India had no restrictions earlier faced the threat of restrictions nonetheless. This is because importing countries were practising restrictions according to the formula cited above, but these restrictions were to be applied uniformly to all countries. The rationale behind carrying out the process in four phases is to give sufficient adjustment time both to exporting and importing nations.

Quotas in the Last Stages of the Transitional Period

Indian apparel export faced major quantitative restrictions in the USA, European Union and Canada. Earlier, Indian exports faced quota restrictions in Norway, but by the beginning of January 1997 that restriction had ceased to exist. While the USA has already announced its integration programme it was noticed that more than 90 per cent of the quota restriction that was there in the US, would remain till January 1st, 2005. The European Union announced only the first two stages of integration programme with very few products of India's interest integrated into the WTO framework. During the first phase of ATC, EU integrated a few handloom garment products. The EU did not integrate any more products during the entire phaseout period. Therefore, barring a few products, the integration programme was of little relevance to India. Practically all the existing quotas on Indian cloth export continued till 2005. In short, the integration programme was severely backloaded.

India and MFA Phase-Out

Although dismantling of MFA trade quotas after almost four decades of restrictions posed fresh challenges to all the developing countries as they adjusted to the needs of a free trade regime, there were some positive sides of it, too. In fact, major changes already taking place in the global textile trade justified the idea. Some of the observable trends were (and are):

- A gradual shift of production from developed to developing countries,
- A steady fall in international prices as new suppliers enter the market,
- Growing preference for "outward processing" by manufacturers in advanced countries with a view to "delocalising production processes to nearby countries,
- Expansion of regional arrangements like NAFTA, enlargement of the European Union, Africa Growth & Opportunity Act,
- Growing retail power, with major implications for supply sources, prices, quality and response-times,
- Consolidation of manufacturing operations in a single country so as to provide easy access to required inputs by assembly operations, and
- Vertical integration of units in order to cater to large volumes of uniform quality.

India's commitment to honour the ATC under WTO has already led to a gradual opening up of the domestic market, protected from external competition since independence. Almost all textile and clothing items have been brought under OGL and can be imported freely. The net result is a rise in imports which has started happening, *albeit* slowly. In addition, India will have to bring down its tariffs as part of the Doha Mandate, at least to the level of other developing Asian Countries. In this connection, the developed countries like USA have already mooted a proposal for a "zero for zero" tariff regime by the year 2015 for seven sectors including textiles & clothing. The proposal seeks to reduce all tariffs worldwide on textiles and clothing to a level of "zero". While the proposal appears to be attractive as an instrument to halt the indiscriminate proliferation of regional trading arrangements and growing bilateralism, India needs to tread the path with caution given the structure of the textile industry in India, lack of comprehensive reforms in the domestic tariff and taxation structure, infrastructure bottlenecks, and the impact on the livelihood of millions employed in the sector.

Moreover, the question that whether removing quota restriction will benefit India depends upon binding nature of quota for any specified product category. Removing quotas is essential, especially when it is binding. It harms both the exporting and importing nations; with consumers of the latter paying higher prices and producers from the former cannot export to their full potential.

A study carried out by Martin and Supachalasai (1990) showed that developing nations incur a loss of US $2 billion or 10 per cent the value of their total clothing exports as a result of quota restriction. Therefore, lifting quota restrictions is supposed to benefit India in those markets in which it has a binding export function. Martin (1996) in his paper focused on estimating quota rent and Export Tax Equivalent (ETE) for Indian garments and textile exports. ETE is the rent that exporters collect in way of selling their quotas. It is defined as value of quota divided by prices received by a producer not having quota for any given product. The higher the quota rent, greater is overall welfare loss for India.

A more restricted market also causes efficiency loss, diverting trade from efficient to inefficient producers. With more restrictive markets, values of ETE are large. For example, in terms of market access the US is more restrictive for Indian textile products than EU. In the US, the average ETE for textile products was 28 per cent in 1996, for EU it was 19 per cent during the same year (Kathuria *et al.*, 1998).

However, in most instances, MFA has gone against the interest of developing nations, by restricting their exports to big markets like the US and EU. But the MFA has also helped to guarantee to the developing nations that they are assured a fixed quota for supplying products to some niche markets. Since MFA is a bilateral agreement, quantum of trade is given, irrespective of how competitive any nation are *vis-à-vis* competitors. Hence, greater market access (with MFA phase-out) will become a gainful proposition only for the most competitive industries. So, it is useful to examine how competitive India is in the textile sector.

This study measures India's competitiveness by calculating RCA of textile products, including cotton textiles, wool, silk and synthetic textiles and textile products (all at a three-digit level). RCA is ratio of the share of a product in country's export to its share in the world export. If the ratio is greater than one it implies Indian exports are competitive. Secondly, we measure REC, defined as the ratio of share of India's textile exports to the world's textile exports to the share of India's textile exports to its own total exports. The idea behind calibrating competitiveness using two different methods is to check for insistency. The results are outlined in Table 5.2.

Table 5.2

Competitiveness of Indian Textile Exports

	RCA		*REC*		*World*
Commodity (SITC)	*1990*	*1997*	*1990*	*1997*	*Exports*
Cotton 263	7.85	4.22	6.12	2.74	Decreasing
Textile Yarn 651	3.10	5.66	3.96	2.74	Stagnant
Cotton Fabric Woven 652	6.25	8.52	6.11	6.84	Increasing
Woven Man-Made Fibre Fabrics 653	1.22	3.00	1.69	2.59	Increasing
Other Woven Textile Fabrics 654	4.23	4.19	2.44	2.03	Increasing
Knitted etc. Fabrics 655	1.89	1.23	0.65	0.52	Decreasing
Textile Articles not elsewhere classified (658)	7.24	8.35	4.20	5.97	Increasing

Source: UNCTAD database.

Except for certain products, namely cotton, other woven textile fabrics, and knitted fabrics, in all other categories competitiveness has increased for Indian products. In both methods the trends are similar, reflecting robustness of the result.

The Framework: Conceptualising Effective Rate of Protection

The rate of effective protection is defined as the proportionate increase in value addition for any industry, possible as a result of giving tariffs protection to both its inputs and outputs. The rationale behind its estimation is to calibrate resource allocation effects of tariffs, besides gauging actual protection that any industry enjoys. When tariffs are imposed, it not only protects the domestic industries (by enabling them to raise the output price) but also raises their manufacturing cost by raising prices of inputs (as prices of inputs rises because of tariff). So, it is essential to gauge actual protection (benefit less cost) and hence the need to calculate the ERP.

The basic formula for measuring the rate of effective protection, T_e, is as follows:

$$T_e = (T_1 - wT_2)/(1-w)$$

Where, T_1= tariff rate on output

T_2= tariff rate on input

w = proportion of total price accounted for by inputs

Any given industry will usually face a variety of tariff rates on its output and certainly the several inputs that it purchases, so that both T_1 and T_2 are measured as weighted averages rather than simple average in tariff regulations. The import weight and the value added weight used for calculating ERP are specified as follows:

Table 5.3

Import Weight and Value Added Weight

Group	*Import Weight*	*Value-Added Weight*
Cotton Textiles	0.10	1.20
Woollen Textiles	0.14	1.08
Art, Silk and Synthetic Textiles	0.14	1.08
Jute, Hemp, Mesta Textiles	0.44	0.73
Other Textiles	0.01	1.08

Source: Paper presented by Pooja Sharma and Rajesh Mehta, at ICRIER sponsored Seminar on Trade and Development, New Delhi (1993).

Certain observations are important in this context. When inputs are supplied locally, their prices may not rise by the full amount of tariff. This is true when there is not enough demand for given inputs. On the other hand, a higher tariff rate does not necessarily increase production of domestic input since the inflation may dampen the demand for domestic input supply. Therefore, price inflation in the input market is also included as a factor.

Assumptions

The theory of effective protection makes several assumptions. First, the country imposing tariffs is a small economy, i.e., a price taker. Hence domestic prices are nothing but world prices plus tariff for the imports. Second, imports are assumed perfect substitutes for the imports competing sector in which ERPs are calculated. Finally, there is a fixed co-efficient relationship between final outputs and inputs, i.e., the production function is of Leontief type.

Methodology

In our study, we estimated the effective rate of protection in the following way:

$ERP_j = (V_j / V_j^*) - 1$

Here, $V_j = 1 - \Sigma a_{ij}$

And $V_j^* = (1+t_j) - \Sigma a_{ij} \times (1+t_i)$

Substituting the values for value added, in the original equation yields,

$ERPj = (t_j - \Sigma a_{ij} \times (1+t_i))/ (1 - \Sigma a_{ij})$

Where, V_j^* = value added in jth industry in presence of tariff

V_j = value added jth industry in the absence of tariff

a_{ij} = amount of ith input used for producing one unit of jth output

t_i = tariff imposed on i th (input) commodity

In this form, we estimated ERP for Indian cotton textile industries from 1993-94 till 2004-05, marking the termination of MFA phaseout. To forecast ERP, the model structure included only growth of final stage output, growth of intermediate input and wage share. In this process, different growth scenarios are estimated by taking into account time series data for related variables. Total duties are calculated by summing up excise duties and import duties.

Data Source

The data regarding input is taken from a 60 sector input-output table constructed by the Planning Commission as a Technical Note to the Eighth Five-Year Plan. Regarding production data, different issues of Annual Survey of Industries (2002-03), published by Ministry of Statistics and Programme Implementation have been consulted. The tariff rates for various input-output sectors have been derived from the Public Finance data published by the Centre for Monitoring Indian Economy. Data regarding foreign exports is taken from the International Trade Statistics, United Nation. Data regarding Wholesale Price Index, used for deflating tariff figures, is sourced from Index Numbers of the Wholesale Prices in India, Ministry of Industry, Government of India.

Statistical Analysis

The basic equations are linear in regressors. The number of observations is for a period of 23 years, starting from 1980-81 to 2003-04. Due to non-availability of input figures we made use of trend analysis adjusting the inflation rate to get the numbers for the missing years. Tariff figures are deflated with the Wholesale Price Index. Based on this assumption, growth of final stage output is estimated for following three sectors.

The basic equations are:

For cotton textiles, $Y(CT) = 12.34 + 29.18IN + 65.28\,WS$; $R^2 = 0.86$;

(1.69) (**) (2.84) (**) (2.65) (**)

$DW = 1.89$

For woollen textiles, $Y(WT) = 23.65 - 2.69IN + 74.62\,WS$; $R^2 = 0.81$;

(0.233) (-) (0.431) (-) (1.99) (**)

$DW = 1.97$

For textile products, $Y(TP) = 12.68 - 69.08IN + 58.67WS$; $R^2 = 0.88$;

(3.41) (**) (2.97) (**) (3.12) (**)

$DW = 2.24$

Here, CT stands for cotton textile, WT stands for woollen textile, TP stands for textile products, IN stands for Intermediate Inputs and WS stands for wage share.

Regression Results and Methodology

The parentheses below each variable give value of t statistics and significance level of each variable. Note, (**) implies the respective variable is statistically significant at 10 per cent level of significance, while (-) indicates that the variable concerned is not statistically significant. Durbin-Watson (DW) statistic in all the cases is well above their lower limits, suggesting absence of first order serial correlation in the model. This holds true at 5 per cent level of significance. Also, moderately high R^2, significant t statistics, points to the absence of multicollinearity in the system. The method of estimation is OLS. From estimated equations, it becomes apparent that wage share has a positive impact in all product segment while impact of intermediate input is different in different sets of textile products. The impact is positive for cotton textiles, while it is negative for textile products. The variable is not statistically significant in woollen textiles.

Results

Calculation of effective rate of protection for different segments of textile industries is given in Table 5.4:

Table 5.4

Effective Rate of Protection for the Different Segments of Textiles Products

Year	*Products*		
	Cotton Textiles	*Wool, Silk and Synthetic Textiles*	*Textiles Products*
1993-94	19.0	38.7	59.4
1994-95	34.2	28.6	31.2
1995-96	29.2	35.3	41.3
1996-97	17.9	33.3	48.7
1997-98	10.5	30.6	50.7
1998-99	11.4	22.3	33.2
1999-00	9.2	19.8	20.0
2000-01	8.2	17.6	26.9
2001-02	7.2	15.6	23.9
2002-03	6.3	13.9	21.3
2003-04	5.6	12.4	19.0
2004-05	4.9	10.5	16.9

Source: Calculation based on 60-sector I-O table prepared by Planning Commission (1991) and CMIE data on commodity trade.

The above table shows ERP has fallen for the Indian textile industry. The result is pertinent when taking into account the ongoing process of trade liberalisation and India's commitment at the WTO to bring down its tariff rates.

Limitation of the Study

Theoretically speaking, calculation of ERP should include other forms of non-tariff barriers, like effect of quotas, licensing and subsidies. Also, technology as a factor effecting growth of intermediate input usage could not be captured. As secondary data is hard to come by and given the constraints at collecting primary data, we have not included their effects while calculating ERP. Another limitation of the study is that it corresponds to input data at a higher level of aggregation. This has been done, as tariffs on input at a higher disaggregated level are not available.

Inferences

From the estimation, it is found that there exists an inverse relation between tariff cost of protection and production of output. The correlation co-efficient between output and tariff cost in case of cotton textiles is -0.41, for woollen textile it is -0.52 and for silk textiles is -0.43. Negative sign indicates that a progressive reduction in duty of fibres is expected to generate demand, as there will be a fall in their prices. An inverse relation has also been observed between production and ERP, implying that with rise in competitiveness, output will increase. The correlation coefficient between production and ERP in case of cotton textiles is -0.57, for a woollen textile it is -0.86 and for silk-textiles it is -0.75. Therefore, with a more protective regime both competitiveness and production will fall.

The result is more prominent for cotton, implying the sector is protected and hence less competitive. This becomes evident from the fact that between 1991 and 1998, both China and India registered a negative growth in exports of cotton textile. However, while India's growth rate declined by 51 per cent, China had a fall of only 18 per cent. On the other hand, South Korea and Hong Kong recorded a growth of 5 per cent and 20 per cent respectively. India could not maintain price competitiveness in international market. Therefore, the hypothesis, a greater ERP for a sector makes it inefficient, holds true.

However, such a proposition of giving long-term protection to inefficient units may not be a viable option. Presently, India possesses comparative advantage in production of cotton yarn, woven manmade fabrics, textile yarn and knitted textile articles not elsewhere specified. Unfortunately, the government policies at present are not congenial for the development of these sectors. For example, excise duty on viscose and synthetics adversely affected competitiveness in the woven manmade fabrics. Here, share of Indian exports has fallen despite an increase in world exports share of this commodity. It is important to examine factors that have lead to the poor plight of the Indian textile sector. This has been done in the next section.

India and Its Competitors

India's main competitors in textile exports are and will be China, Korea, Taiwan and Hong Kong. This is true under the assumption that developed nations are unable to come with enough labour saving technologies to outweigh labour cost advantage that developing nations enjoy at present. The success of the Indian garment industry in international arena is because of its ability to handle small and detailed orders, wealthy craftsmanship and availability of indigenous skill at a low price. The present structure does not permit to undertake any large-scale operation. This is due to rigid labour laws. The existing law does not permit retrenching workers even after paying them adequate compensation. The amendment to the Industrial Disputes Act, 1947 made it difficult for the loss making firms employing more than 100 workers to close down. As a result garment manufacturers prefer sub-contracting smalltime producers who do their jobs, instead of hiring labours in their factory. Even if do they hire, they prefer to keep the size of the labour force less than 100.

Unfortunately, the problem with the Indian knitting garment sector originates from its greater dependence on unorganised sector. Being small-scale in nature, it is characterised by poor infrastructure, low capitalisation, outdated technologies, inadequate presence of market research in spotting new market, lesser fund availability to add on existing capacity, and a little or no investment in research and development.

The unorganised nature of the Indian export has prevented growth in this sector. There are very few factories, which can be called world class, either in the type or in numbers of machinery installed. The small-scale structure, otherwise suitable for handling orders in small quantities, may prove to be binding once scope of selling increases with MFA phaseout. With world fashion market demands changing with every season, export production has to keep up with the changes in the fashion world. In India, most of the textile and garment trade takes place through retailers, who do not always keep pace with the changing tastes and preferences in the international fashion scene. As a result, they fail to cater to world demand. It is hardly surprising therefore that Indian exports never feature in any major international fashion shows in the EU or in the US.

Regrettably, requisite investment necessary to rebuild this sector is not forthcoming. A crosscountry survey conducted by Khanna (1993) points out, India is way behind in terms of carrying out investment in this sector. Table 5.5 points this out:

Table 5.5

Machinery and Investment Levels by Apparel Exports Firms (Unit Nos.)

Country	*Total Machines*	*Manual Machines*	*Power Machines*	*Investment ('000)*	*Investment ('000) per Machines*
South Korea	258.08	6.14	240.33	722.19	2.79
Taiwan	264.62	0.15	264.46	579.21	2.18
Hong Kong	698.12	4.35	688.76	2456.64	3.51
China	605.15	1.50	603.65	943.86	1.50
India	119.28	37.26	75.39	29.76	0.25
Thailand	572.32	0	572.32	722.25	1.26

Source: Individual country surveys by Khanna (1993).

The above highlights the low level of investment in Indian garment industries. The average investment in machines per textile firm in India is $ 27690 compared to an initial average investment of $ 2.5 million in Hong Kong and nearly $ 1 million in China. This in turn reflects smaller size of the Indian firm, with an average of

119 machines per firm as against 698 in Hong Kong and 605 in China. It also reflects lower levels of investment per machine, with investment in India being only $ 250 per machine *versus* $ 3510 in Hong Kong and $ 1500 in China. Even because of the average number of machines per firm, India loses out. This is due to Indian firms having a much higher proportion of manual machines, as well as the fact that even their power machines are less sophisticated. In South Korea, Taiwan, Hong Kong and China, average number of processing machines in any apparel export firm is 31, 13, 28 and 35 respectively, against 5 in India. Table 5.6 demonstrates this:

Table 5.6

Type of Machines Installed Per Firm (average) in the Apparel Industries

Country	*Pre-cutting Machines*	*Cutting Machines*	*Sewing Machines*	*Special Machines*	*Processing Machines*
South Korea	2.9	12.3	134.3	77.5	31.0
Taiwan	2.6	7.5	185.1	49.5	12.8
Hong Kong	2.3	13.2	455.4	112.7	27.9
China	2.3	13.2	450.5	104.8	34.4
India	0.0	2.3	103.7	8.6	4.6
Thailand	2.0	12.8	460.8	72.4	21.9

Note: Estimated on basis of data from Textiles Committee, Mumbai for India. For other countries, from individual country surveys.

Source: Khanna (1993).

The same applies in the case of the number of special machines any apparel firm possesses. While in India, on average, only 9 special machines are in place, it is around 78 in Korea, 50 in Taiwan, 113 in Hong Kong and 105 in China. Most investments in India are made for installing sewing machines, while special and processing machines form a meagre share of total investment, unlike its competitors. Low cost of labour is not going to help India balance out inefficiencies. While India's labour is cheaper than most countries, it is not cheaper than in China; which is its main competitor. According to a cost comparison carried out by New York based Weiner International Incorporated, in 1993 the wage cost per hour in China was 40 cents, while in India it was 60 cents. The problem becomes serious considering that most of Indian production comes from the unorganised sector. Since unorganised sector pay less wage than the organised mill sector, therefore labours working in mills have wages more than 60 cents. It implies production in the organised sector is less competitive *vis-à-vis* their Chinese counterparts. The worrisome aspect of the Indian textile industry is the falling labour productivity during the period following liberalisation. In case of the textile group as a whole, four out of seven industries, namely cotton garments and clothing; handloom cotton textiles; cotton khadi, and power-loom cotton textile, witnessed fall in total factor productivity by 0.67 per cent, 1.88 per cent, 3.87 per cent and 0.01 per cent, respectively (Das, 1999).

India's industrial policy also contributes to the decline in India's competitiveness. Garment manufacturing in India is at present reserved for the smallscale industry (SSI) sector. This has been a discouraging factor as units willing to invest above Rs. 3 crore have to obtain permission from the government. There is an export obligation also, that requires 50 per cent of the output produced (in value terms) to be exported.

On the other hand, the nations we compete with have no barrier for investment. Investment is high even in low wage countries. Hence the argument, more investment in capital will drive out labour does not stand strong. Higher investment by reaping higher economies of scale can result in more labour employment, than merely operating under veil of smallscale enterprises with labourintensive mode of production. Therefore, what is necessary is higher investment in Indian textile units and removal of factors such as reservation policy and rigid labour laws.

The Indian garment industry is also less diversified. Although China outweighs India in terms of cotton production, it has taken appropriate steps to increase variety of its textile products. In a world of rapidly changing tastes, such variability and flexibility in production is essential for acquiring any competitive edge. Interestingly, with the phasing out of MFA, major markets will emerge in the higher segments, where China already has a competitive advantage.

For diversifying the fabric base, it will be necessary to ensure availability of manmade fabrics in sufficient quantities to apparel manufacturer at a competitive price. The readymade garments sector is the most important segment, talking about textile exports from India. In value terms it account more than 40 per cent of our textile exports. Indian readymade garment industry mainly manufactures cotton-made apparel. For instance, during 1997, cotton-made garments constituted 83 per cent by volume and 75 per cent by value of Indian garments exports. Unfortunately, the world preference is for synthetic-made garments. Percentage-wise, 80 per cent of the world trade in apparel is done in manmade fibres and synthetic fibres. India predominantly produces cotton-made garments because of higher domestic demand. However, if it wants to look beyond domestic market, diversification is necessary. Table 5.7 shows synthetic consumption as a proportion of total consumption of different fibres during 1992 was roughly 70 per cent in Korea, 66 per cent in Germany, 62 per cent in Japan, 56 per cent in the US, 44 per cent in Indonesia, 42 per cent in Thailand, but only 18 per cent in India.

Table 5.7

Consumption of Textiles in 1992

(per cent)

Country	*Cotton*	*Wool*	*Cellulosics*	*Synthetics*
India	72	2	8	18
China	60	5	4	31
Pakistan	88	2	1	9
Indonesia	43	1	12	44
Malaysia	35	4	–	61
Thailand	50	1	7	42
Korea	22	4	4	70
US	37	2	5	56
Germany	17	6	11	66
Japan	26	6	6	62

Source: World Bank (1997).

There are reasons for greater cotton consumption here. Indian agro-climatic condition favours cotton production and availability of cheap labour does the rest. Although India is a major producer of cotton (accounting for 1.2 per cent of the total world production in 1993), yet its yield per hectare at 294 kgs. is one of the lowest in the world (only 49 per cent of the world average), showing some sign of inefficiency (Gangopadhyay *et al.*, 1996).

The situation is a bit different in the world market. Looking at the international demand structure, rapid industrialisation after World War II and presence of temperate climate in the developed part has increased demand for synthetic products relative to cotton. In a previous table (Table 5.2) we have seen that Indian export of cotton has declined, though cotton received the substantial part of protection and export incentives, as far as the textiles and garment industry is concerned. This reality calls for the diversification of the industry in favour of technical textile area. Currently, only 10 per cent of India's textile export is attributable to synthetics, implying tremendous scope for India to increase its export in synthetics. So far as synthetic inputs are concerned, India possesses competitive advantage in their production. For example, naphtha and natural gas, the main ingredients for producing synthetic fibre, are abundantly available in India. Hence, the reason for India to look beyond cottonmade garments and concentrate more on manmade and synthetic fibre (in compliance with the world demand) is merited.

Talking about the endogenous problem, there is need to revive the Indian mill sector. Presently, India imports a considerable amount of fabrics needed for our garment industry. However, this cannot be a longterm solution. It is necessary to strengthen the mill sector and remove all policy distortions going against its operation. Measures like capping restrictions on firm size and requirement for licences to produce synthetic items has gone against the mill sector.

The gain of distorted policy in favour of handloom and against the mill sector was taken by the powerloom sector. The powerloom did not have any government support that the handloom sector had; however, it did not have any restrictions placed on the organised mill sector. Gradual decline in importance of the mill sector is also reflected in its declining contribution in our export share. Table 5.8 illustrates this:

Table 5.8

Contribution of Mill Sector in Apparel Exports

Year	*Cotton*			*Total (percentage value)*		
	Mill	*Powerloom*	*Handloom*	*Mill*	*Powerloom*	*Handloom*
1985-86	58.5	33.5	8.0	52.4	40.4	7.2
1986-87	50.2	43.9	5.9	44.0	50.8	5.2
1987-88	43.7	51.0	5.3	39.0	56.3	4.8
1988-89	38.1	56.5	5.4	33.1	62.2	4.7
1989-90	38.3	57.3	4.4	30.5	66.0	3.5
1990-91	38.2	58.6	3.2	28.6	69.0	2.4
1991-92	28.5	68.2	3.2	22.1	75.4	2.5
1992-93	25.2	71.5	3.3	20.4	76.9	2.7
1993-94	23.6	73.9	2.5	19.6	78.3	2.1
1994-95	21.0	76.9	2.0	17.1	81.2	1.6
1995-96	22.9	75.5	1.6	18.5	80.3	1.3

Source: ICMF Annual Report, 1997-98.

The increased importance of the powerloom *vis-à-vis* the mill sectors is quite apparent. The production of fabrics irrespective of where they are produced and for the purposes they are produced requires weaving and knitting treatment. The logic behind such treatment is enhance durability and colour fastness of the fabric. Before the advent of the powerloom sector, composite mills carried out such treatment themselves. Now, in 85 per cent of cases, powerloom sector carries out such an operation. In the light of the above, the steps taken in the 2004 Annual Budget (specifically those that did away with the discriminatory system of duties that militated against the mill sector) has to be welcomed. The same has to be done now for the man-made and synthetic fibre sector as well. While the government has indicated that it will move in this direction, distortions remain - government policy ensures higher incidence of taxes on man made and synthetic fibres. For example, during 1997-98, the excise duty on cotton yarn was only 5.75 per cent as against 20.7 per cent for blended yarn and 34.5 per cent for polypropylene filament yarn (PFY). Removal of such policy distortion is necessary. The Indian yarn has been a typical example of discriminated commodity. The government protected downward weaving by restricting export of cotton yarn. Moreover, imported inputs for production of polyester staple fibre (PSF) and PFY are still subject to high duties (Roy, 1998).

Government Action

To find ways and means of revamping the textile sector the government of late has taken various steps. Understanding the declining competitiveness of the textile sector, the government formed a committee headed by the former Textile Secretary, Mr. S. Satyam. The Satyam Committee Report made some important recommendations. They include:

- Deregulate the textile sector. In this regard the report says, "it will be incongruous to talk about its revival in the current context of liberalisation, especially in the backdrop of globalisation, without dismantling the regulatory regime". Government henceforth should stop operating as a regulator and instead become a facilitator.
- Labour laws should be made more flexible. Companies should have the right to retrench excess labour without seeking government approvals as long as they pay 60 days average wages for every completed years of service instead of the present practice of 15 days.
- Modernisation of the textile sector. The fear that modernisation is harmful to labour is wrong. Quotes the report- *"Such developments in other sectors have not been harmful to labour interests; they only benefit them There is, therefore, no reason why textile industry labour should become an impediment to the development process,"*
- Diversification of the textile sector. For instance, there is a large scope to enter the technical textile area. In this context, the report says, *"it is mind boggling to realise that textile can actually covers fields like agriculture, automobiles, aviation, environmental protect furniture, medical, mining, pharmaceuticals and transportation.'*
- About fiscal measures the report states, *"the fiscal policy the textile sector should be aimed at stimulating demand .. and lower tax*

structure, resulting in reduction of prices of fabrics and garments and making them cost effective".

The National Textile Policy was announced in November 2000, based on Satyam Committee Report. One of the main objectives of the policy is to '*..facilitate the textile industry to attain and sustain a pre-eminent global standing in the manufacture and export of clothing.*' The policy aims to raise the existing apparel export to US $ 50 billion by 2010, from its existing level of export.

The government initiated some export promotion measures to strengthen the domestic textiles industry. Prominent among them have been the setting up of a Technology Upgradation Fund Scheme (TUFS) in order to provide impetus to the modernisation of textiles and jute industry and the new export entitlement (quota) policy for the period 2000-04 beforehand so as to minimise rent seeking activities in the quota market. The abolition of Additional Excise Duty on Textiles and Textiles articles and the Additional Excise Duty Act, reduction of Basic custom duty on various textile machinery items and spare parts etc. were some of the favourable steps announced in the Union Budget 2004-05. Added to the flavour, the Union Budget 2005-06 has come up with several notable announcements in favour of the industry. Excise duty on Polyester Filament Yarn and Polyester Texturised Yarn has been reduced to 16 per cent from 24 per cent. Creation of a Special Purpose Vehicle has been announced to improve the infrastructure in manufacturing, with an initial investment of Rs 10000 crore. In order to financially strengthen the TUFS, an enhanced resource allocation has been decided upon. In addition to these, the Foreign Trade Policy has also been re-designed to be quite compatible with the matters related to the export of Textile products. Regarding the FDI policy, foreign equity participation, in the textiles sector, has been allowed upto 100 per cent, through automatic route. Moreover, some schemes like Export Promotion Capital Goods Scheme, Textile Centres Infrastructure Development Scheme, Advance Licensing Scheme, Duty Exemption Pass Book Scheme, Duty Drawback Scheme have been launched. All these government actions are aimed at pushing the country to a platform where she would be able to reap the full advantages of world-wide opening of the textiles sector.

Concluding Observations

However, though the aforesaid government initiatives are quite appreciable, to put the situation in economic terms, they are only 'necessary but not sufficient'. According to a WTO study (Nordås, 2004), the 'welfare gains to India from the elimination of the ATC quotas would be three times as high if combined with domestic reforms.' Taking full advantage from complete phaseout of market-restriction requires not only increasing competitiveness through the removal of distortion arising out of incorrect government policy but also calls for better marketing network (that India presently lack). Besides removing reservation for smallscale industry in the garment segment, it is needed to remove restrictions on raw material imports and rationalise existing excise rates on different types of fibres and fabrics.

To sum up, the following policy options can help Indian garment industry to face new challenges in a better way. First, to make labour laws more flexible, where it is possible to retrench a labour after giving him adequate compensation. Second, abolish the reservation in favour of small-scale industry in the garment sector. Third, remove policy bias against production of synthetic fibre. Fourth, to reduce transaction cost like delays in shipment and clearance involved in importing fabrics. Fifth, developing brand equity if possible through foreign tieup, as the countries like Thailand, Indonesia and others are doing. And last, the Government on its part should provide policy support to make the industry more competitive and efficient. The government should keep it in mind that 'it is a sector where relatively modern technology can be adopted even in poor countries at relatively low investment costs'. A roadmap for development of the industry is pre-requisite. Efforts should be made to ensure easy availability of funds for modernisation at internationally competitive rates. A favourable environment for setting up large capacities with world class technology is urgent need of the hour to reap the benefit of the phase out. Only then India can truly emerge as an 'alternative source of supply to China'.

References

Arpan, DeLaTore, Jose and B. Toyne (1982). "The US Apparel Industry," Georgia State University, *Research Monograph No. 88.*

Alam, Ghayur (1991). "Impact of NonEconomic Factors on Choice of Technology and Organisation of Production: A Study on Small Industrial Firms in India," *Mimeo* for the ILO, New Delhi.

Bagchi, Sanjoy (1990). "Textiles in the Uruguay Round: Alternative Modalities for Integration into GATT" in C.B. Hamilton (1990) edited, World Bank Publication.

Das, Deb Kusum (1999). "Trade Liberalisation and Productivity Growth: Disaggregated Analysis of the Indian Manufacturing Sector", Institute of Economic Growth *Working Paper.*

Debroy, Bibek (1996). *Beyond the Uruguay Round: The Indian Perspective on GATT*, Sage Publication.

Gangopadhyay, Subhashis; Debroy, Bibek and Wadhwa, Willima (1996). "India and the WTO," *Mimeo*, Asian Development Bank, Manila.

Government of India (1990). *The Textile Industry in the 1990s Restructuring With A Human Face,"* New Delhi.

———. (2000). Parliamentary Question Answer Session, Q No. 529.

———. (2000). Parliamentary Question Answer Session, Q No. 534.

Hildegunn Kyvik Nordás,1 ERSD, (2004). *The Global Textile and Clothing Industry post the Agreement on Textiles and Clothing,* WTO.

Kathuria S. and Bharadwaj A. (1998). "Export Quotas and Policy Constraints in the Indian Textile and Garment Industries," *Policy Research Working Paper* 2012 World Bank.

Khanna, S.R. (1991). *International Trade in Textiles: MFA Quotas and a Developing Exporting Country*, ICRIER and Sage Publications, New Delhi.

———. (1993). "The Challenge of Global Competition in the 1990s: An Agenda for Enhancing the Competitive Position of Indian Textiles and Clothing," *Mimeo*, ICRIER, New Delhi.

Martin, Will and Suphat Suphachalasai (1990). "Effects of the Multi-Fibre Arrangement on Developing Country Exporters: A Simple Theoretical Framework in C.B. Hamilton (1990) edited, World Bank Publication.

National Council of Applied Economic Research (NCAER) (1989). *Future Fibre Mix for Textile Industry.*

Satyam Committee (1999). *Report of the Expert Committee on Indian Cotton Textile Industry*, Chairman S. Satyam.

Sharma, Pooja and Mehta, Rajesh (1996). *Trade Reforms and Changes in Effective Protection of Indian Industries*, paper presented at the seminar organised by ICRIER, New Delhi and International Centre for Economic Growth, San Francisco.

Venkatesan, R. and Katti, Vijaya (1999). "Indian Textile Policy for the 21st Century," *Mimeo*, NCAER, New Delhi.

Reports, Ministry of Textiles, Government of India, http://texmin.nic.in/reports.htm.

6

TRIPS and India: Crux of the Patent Controversy

SUBHODIP GHOSH

"Chaos" is a mathematical notion, and is known to be a particularly difficult branch of mathematics. What is, however, interesting is that chaos does not confine itself to mathematics, but manifests itself in almost all walks of life, including business. What is equally intriguing is that some of the most organised sectors in industry can be subjected to chaos. Perhaps, there could be no other better example than the Indian pharmaceutical sector. It is not that the Indian pharmaceutical industry is not organised or is in its nascent stage. In fact, it ranks very high in the third world, in terms of technology, quality and range of medicines manufactured. From simple headache pills to sophisticated antibiotics and complex cardiac compounds, almost every type of medicines is now made in India. It has quality producers and many units are approved by regulatory authorities in USA and UK.[1] India has a highly efficient pharmaceutical industry, which started blossoming thanks to the virtual absence of (product) patent protection of medical drugs.[2] It produces, for example, its own AIDS drugs, which are sold much more cheaply than the original products from abroad. This is where the problem starts.

In fact, to be truthful, what has played havoc in the seemingly placid waters of the Indian pharma sector is the aspect of Intellectual

1. In 1999-00, capital investments in the Indian pharmaceutical industry stood at Rs. 25 billion (from a level of Rs. 11 billion in 1993), with production figures (for formulations standing at Rs. 160 billion and that of bulk drugs at Rs. 38 billion. (The Organisation of Pharmaceutical Producers of India).
2. The Indian Patent Act was enacted with the prime objective of removing the monopoly of information relating to technological know-how that big firms enjoyed over the smaller units. To give a brief outline of the Act it must be pointed out that the criteria for patentability as laid down by the Act is that to qualify for patent protection, inventions should be new and useful to the industry in question. Moreover it only allowed for process patents in inventions relating to food, pharmaceuticals, agricultural chemicals and chemicals.

Property Rights (IPRs), which, to most Indian policymakers, even a decade back, was just another grandiloquent concept. To state simply, intellectual property is generally the name given to that category of property, which is the product of an invention and which does not exist in physical form.[3] The Agreement on Trade Related Aspects of Intellectual Property Rights, commonly known a TRIPS to all and sundry was a consequence of the Uruguay Round of Discussions of the General Agreement of Tariffs and Trade (GATT), which culminated in the formation of the World Trade Organisation (WTO). The TRIPS Agreement covers substantive intellectual property rights and measures for their enforcement. It develops rules to protect intellectual property rights to all participating countries. The TRIPS Agreement lays down norms and standards for seven types of intellectual property, *viz.*, Copyright and Related Rights, Trademarks, Geographical Indications, Industrial Designs, Patents, Undisclosed Information and Layout Designs of Integrated Circuits. The manner of legal compliance is left to each individual WTO member.

In order to trace the aspects of intellectual property protection in India in the post-WTO and particularly post-Doha scenario (since the controversy begins thereafter), one has to look back a bit. When the Paris Convention of 1883 (one of the oldest treaties governing the protection of industrial intellectual property) came into force, member countries were free to determine the standards of protection, the subject matter of protection and the period of protection and maximum divergence were observed in the case of protection of innovations in the pharmaceutical sector. Several countries fearing that patent protection in pharmaceuticals would limit the spread of knowledge and thus prevent the scientific innovations reaching the general and the needy public, neither protected the processes of manufacturing a drug nor the final drug. The logic is, once a product is patented (product patents), the same product cannot be produced by an alternate method or process during the protection period. However, if the process alone is protected (process patents), then an alternative process which is mostly 'invented' around the earlier process could be used to

3. Intellectual property, as a subject, is growing in importance as the numerous exploitable ideas are becoming more sophisticated as the hopes of nations for a successful economic future in a multilateral trading regime are becoming increasingly dependant upon their superior corpus of new knowledge.

produce a similar product, since in pharmaceuticals, a product can be produced by more than one method.

While many of the industrially developed resource rich countries chose to reward the innovators and adopted product patents to promote further innovations, some of the developing countries realised the potential of the process patents in developing the domestic industry and adopted the same. Thus, the developing countries with process patent protection were able to take advantage of the innovations made by early innovators. When a subsequent product is based on an innovation made earlier, the late entrant enjoys the reduction in the cost of developing the product without of course sharing the benefits/profits derived by the new product with the early innovator. But the capacity to exploit the earlier innovations to its advantage depends on the technological development of the country, capacity of the domestic industry, the market size and the type of technology that is used in developing the product. Of the many countries that adopted process patents, developing countries like India, China, Korea and Brazil have developed expertise to develop new products, which were mostly around the earlier innovations of the developed countries. It is assessed that the deficiencies in India's intellectual property system alone are estimated to cost US companies around $500 million a year (Scrip's Year Book, Vol 2, 2000:316).

TRIPS and its Implications for the Indian Pharmaceutical Sector

It is in the area of patents that the greatest deviations existed between TRIPS and the Indian laws.[4] At least three aspects of the

4. Indian laws in general did not require too many changes except in the area of patents. Article 15 of TRIPS says that any sign or combination of signs that can distinguish one good from another can constitute a trademark. Moreover signs such as words, letters, numerals, figurative elements and combination of colours and signs shall be eligible for registration as trademarks. Although Indian jurisprudence protects a distinctive sign or combination of signs as a trademark, the Trade and Merchandise Marks Act, 1958 needed amendments to allow for registration of trademarks to comply with Article 15 of TRIPS. Again, Indian laws are already in tune with TRIPS on conditions imposed on patent applications. Section 10(4) b of the Patents Act of 1970 requires the patentee to disclose the best method of performing the invention, which is identical to what Article 29.1 of TRIPS says. Similarly there is no great change required in the matter of revocation of patents. To comply with TRIPS only an opportunity for judicial review would have to be made available.

Patent Act of 1970 required to be changed. The first pertained to the term of patents, the second was with respect to the nature of rights the patent owner would enjoy and the third area related to patentable subject matter. This again brings into focus the matter of product and process patents. Article 27 of TRIPS says that patents shall be available for any inventions, whether products or processes, in all fields of technology. India allowed only process patents in inventions relating to food, pharmaceuticals, agricultural chemicals and chemicals. According to Article 33 of TRIPS, the term of patents in all fields of technology must be twenty years from the date of filing. However the original Act of 1970 said that the term of patents in the case of processes or methods of manufacture of a substance intended to be used or capable of being used as food or as a medicine or drug should be for a period of seven years from the date of filing or five years from the date of sealing the patent, whichever is less. Patents relating to all other inventions are granted for a period of 14 years from the date of filing the patent, unless shown to be invalid.

There are also two major differences concerning the rights of patentees defined in Section 48 of the Act and Article 28 of TRIPS. Under the Indian law, process patentees only had the exclusive right of using and exercising the patented process. They could not exclude third parties from using, selling or distributing the patented product. The entire debate regarding patenting of products in India began when it was being pointed out in the political circles that it is not right that something for wide public use should be controlled by a secret formula known to only a few large firms. Thus followed the Indian Patent Act of 1970, the main objective of which was to ensure that the benefits of technological development reached the people. The Act allowed for process patents, which meant that the same product could be manufactured following a slightly different process.

The implications of TRIPS for the Indian pharmaceutical sector are: Patents will be granted for products for inventions in all fields of technology; the patent term will be twenty years from the date of the application, which is applicable to all the member countries and thus rules out all the differences in the protection terms prevailed in different countries; patents will be granted irrespective of the fact whether the drugs are produced locally or imported from another country; though the grant of the patent excludes unauthorised use, sale or manufacture of the patented item, yet there are clauses which provide manufacturing or other such rights of the patented item to a person other than the patent holder. In the case of a dispute on infringement the responsibility (to prove that a process other than the one used in the patented product has actually been used in the disputed product) lies with the accused rather than with the patent holder (in the 1970 Act, the responsibility is with the patent holder). This is the broad framework, which will guide the Indian pharmaceutical industry in the WTO regime.

The Problem for India

The lack of protection for product patents in pharmaceuticals had a significant impact on the Indian pharmaceutical industry and resulted in the development of considerable expertise in reverse engineering of drugs that are patentable as products throughout the industrial world but unprotectable in India.[5]

India, more importantly its people, has gained in the bargain. Millions of people are estimated to be HIV-positive in India. In less than two decades, India already is among countries with the highest number of HIV-positive people in the world. Ignorance and poverty are the most important causes of this. Often, AIDS patients die of tuberculosis, an illness still prevalent in India, because they lack the necessary resistance.[6]

There is no cure (yet) for HIV/AIDS. The number of HIV/AIDS deaths has, however, dramatically decreased in the USA and in Europe.[7] This must be attributed in the first place to the revolutionary drug combination therapy, which disturbs the life cycle of the HI-Virus. In India, however, only a minute fraction of HIV/AIDS patients are getting medical treatment.[8]

5. Patents & the Indian Pharmaceutical Industry, Nilesh Zacharias & Sandeep Farias, Business Briefing, Pharmatech 02.
6. Gerster, Richard (2000), 'How WTO/TRIPS threatens the Indian pharmaceutical industry,' http://www.twnside.org.sg/title/twr120h.htm
7. In Switzerland, the number of AIDS deaths annually has dropped from a peak of 686 (1994) to far below 100 (1999). Gerster, op. cit.
8. One billion Indians spend the same amount on medical drugs per year as seven million Swiss men and women.

There is a widespread lack of hospitals and clinics, of personnel, of medical equipment and medicines. The cost of individual AIDS-combination therapy, at more than US$300 per month, is prohibitively high. Yet, it would perhaps not be an exaggeration to conclude that in India, compared to the general price index, drug prices have risen much less in the last 15 years and remain far below average. Self-sufficiency with regard to pharmaceuticals is the guiding principle. The secret of this success is the Indian patent law of 1970.

The argument is principally on the lines of restricting monopolistic practices and making medicines (even the super-specialty drugs) affordable. India had done without product patents for pharmaceuticals till 1995, with the exception of production processes that have been allowed to be patented. In addition, the law allowed for Compulsory Licenses (CL) granted by the State, in the case of a patent holder's not granting voluntary licenses on fair conditions. As an example, the decision to produce the AIDS drug Zidovudine locally (and sell at a lower price), may be spoken about. This in turn provoked the lowering of prices by the international competitors on the Indian market. Today, a packet of ten 100-mg capsules of Zidovudine in India costs less than US$5. The original product is sold for more than double the price in India, Pakistan and Indonesia - and costs five to six times more in the USA and Great Britain. More than 95 per cent of all HIV-infected people - 34 million worldwide - live in developing countries. It could be attractive for other countries to buy high-quality imitation products from India at reasonable prices. But free trade is hampered by national and international patent rules. For a patent constitutes the sole right not only to produce a product but also to import it.

Although the Doha Declaration on the TRIPS Agreement and Public Health in Paragraph 6 directed the TRIPS Council to find an expeditious solution by December 2002 to the problem of countries with insufficient or no manufacturing capacities in the pharmaceutical sector in making effective use of the flexibility of compulsory licenses, there were numerous problems, which had cropped up during the meetings after December 2002.

Availability, accessibility and affordability of medicines are the three most contentious issues on which much of the criticism of TRIPS rests. As the concept of "Access to Medicines" and the right to health become emotive issues, questions are being raised about the viability of a system, which supposedly confers on a handful of corporations the right to deprive millions of poor people access to medicines they desperately need, on the grounds of lack of affordability. As far as the Indian pharmaceutical industry is concerned, after years of being accused of patent piracy, it was an irony of sorts when it was an Indian company, which offered high-cost anti-retroviral (ARV) medicine for AIDS patients in South Africa at lower prices.[9] Such "core competencies" need to be harnessed; and the "autonomy" to manufacture such "generic" drugs encouraged within industry.

The confusion (and cross currents) of differing agenda of member countries and the developed and the developing world has manifested itself in the Indian pharmaceutical sector, which is still very much unclear about the aspect of Compulsory Licenses (CLs) and questions like whether 20 drug manufacturers manufacturing 1 drug will all be eligible for Compulsory Licenses still do the rounds in industry circles. Similarly the "Mail Box" system[10] is also not very clear to industry in India.

Increased problems pertaining to legal aspects especially after the TRIPS Agreement came into being; a rise in patent fees (for filing and maintenance) and the fact that the time period from filing of the application to the granting of the patent is 8-10 years, which is half the total time of the validity of patents — are issues playing in the minds of industry. To get over this problem, patent holders often go for patent extensions, by which the patent holder attempts to extend the life of the patent for another 20 years by bringing out a new indication for the same drug.

9. Raizada, B.K. and Sayed, Javed (2001), "IPR and Drugs and the Pharmaceutical Industry - Concerns for Developing Countries" in *Salvaging the WTO's Future: Doha and Beyond*, Amit Dasgupta and Bibek Debroy (Ed.), Konark Publishers, New Delhi, pp. 274 – 289.

10. For accepting the patent applications from January 1, 1995, which will be processed in 2005.

The purpose of this chapter will be to provide a birds-eye-view of the progress of the controversy surrounding TRIPS and its implications for India and highlight the grey areas for the Indian industry and address the aspects of concern. Further, the paper will also dwell on the TRIPS Agreement very briefly and provide a synopsis of the Indian Patent Act, its principal areas of focus, the divergence with TRIPS and the possible areas of reconciliation as well as the utility of a strong patent regime. Separately, the paper will attempt to provide a picture of the industry's position in India and attempt to provide a critique along with a look into the future and a suggested action plan. Additionally, the paper also includes a section on industry feedback.

The Indian Pharmaceutical Sector

The Indian pharma industry is a successful, high-technology based industry that has witnessed consistent growth over the past three decades. India's pharmaceutical industry in 1996 was valued at between $2.6 and $3.4 billion.[11] Investments in the pharmaceutical industry grew by a compounded annual growth rate (CAGR) of 15.4 per cent from 1993-94 to 1999-00. Production of formulations and bulk drugs grew at a CAGR of 17.2 per cent and 20 per cent respectively between 1990-91 and 1999-00. Even R&D Expenditure, an aspect for which Indian companies have been constantly criticised, grew at a CAGR of 16.2 per cent between 1993-94 and 1999-00. The number of pharmaceutical firms in India multiplied dramatically from 3,000 in 1977 to over 24,000 in 1997.[12] Figure 6.1 below shows the trend of the key indicators of the pharmaceutical industry in India:

Foreign Trade

As can be seen from Table 6.1 and Table 6.2, Indian export figures for pharmaceutical products have improved a great deal over the last thirty odd years with a positive Balance of Payments situation in 1999-00.

---

11. World Country Analyst 1997, Gayle Research. "Repositioning Ranbaxy, Harvard Business School Case, Revised February 18, 1998, p. 1.

12. Tancer, Robert and Srinivas Josyula (1999), *Investing in the Indian Pharmaceutical Industry*, The American Graduate School of International Management.

Figure 6.1

The Indian Pharmaceutical Sector

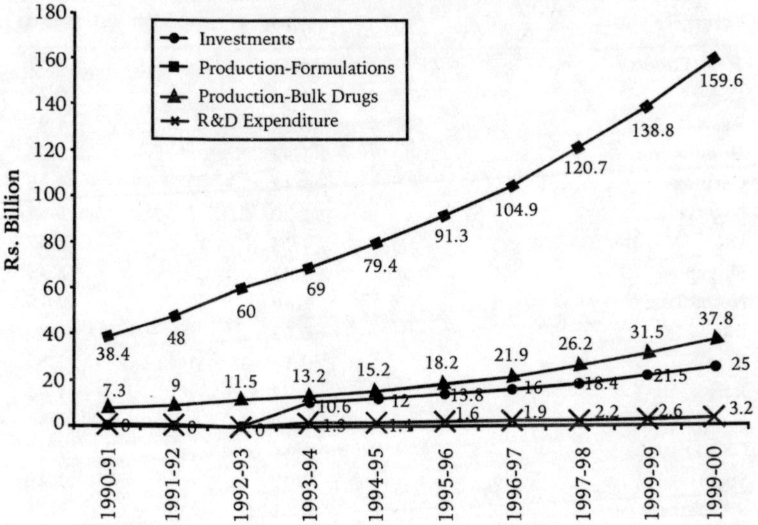

Source: Organisation of Pharmaceutical Producers of India.

Table 6.1

Balance of Trade in Pharmaceutical Sector (Rs. Billion)

Year	*Exports of Drugs*	*Imports of Drugs*	*Balance of Trade*
1960-61	0.02	0.18	-0.16
1970-71	0.08	0.24	-0.16
1980-81	0.76	1.13	-0.37
1990-91	12.55	6.04	6.51
1991-92	14.9	8.07	6.83
1992-93	15.42	11.37	4.05
1993-94	19.92	14.4	5.52
1994-95	24.65	15.37	9.28
1995-96	34.43	18.67	15.76
1996-97	43.4	10.39	33.01
1997-98	53.53	14.47	39.06
1998-99	61.53	14.47	47.06
1999-00	66.31	15.02	51.29

Source: IDMA Annual Publication 2001.

Table 6.2

Exports of Pharmaceutical Products from India (Rs. Billion)

Country	1995-96	1999-00
Total Exports	34.43	66.31
USA	4.24	6.72
Russia	3.04	4.93
Hong Kong	1.92	3.56
Germany	3.42	3.25
Nigeria	1.20	2.58
UK	1.14	2.57
Singapore	0.87	2.45
Netherlands	1.44	2.19
Iran	0.63	1.80
Brazil	0.17	1.63
Italy	0.72	1.51
Vietnam	0.89	1.41
China	0.36	1.37
Spain	0.77	1.29
Sri Lanka	0.83	1.24
Total Exports to top 15 countries	21.64	38.50

Source: 39th IDMA Annual Publication, 2001.

A look at the major export destinations would reveal that not only there is a substantial rise in the value of exports for all destinations except Germany (a very marginal fall); the destinations also include both developing and developed countries.

The Indian Market

A major part of the market is controlled by around 50 companies and while the share of Indian firms is around 62 per cent of industry sales, the share of MNCs in industry sales is around 38 per cent.[13] Multinational firms are much more active in formulations (or branded products) as compared to Indian firms, which concentrate more on bulk drugs and generic pharmaceutical products. Indian companies market their own brands and manufactured drugs in virtually every therapeutic category of the market. What this ultimately results in is the lowering of prices.

13. Tancer and Josyula, *op. cit.*

Leading Therapeutic Classes

Dominant drug sales in India include antibiotics, antibacterials, vitamins, and medicines for tropical diseases. The five therapeutic classes in terms of sales, which are worth mentioning, are antibiotics, cardiovascular products, anti-inflammatory products, and tropical disease products.[14]

Indian Drug Prices

Another significant factor characterising India's pharmaceutical market is its extremely low drug prices, among the lowest in the world. A price comparison of certain blockbuster drugs is illustrated in the following table:

Table 6.3

Blockbuster Drugs Price Comparison of Certain Drugs in U.S. and India

Brand Name	*Generic Name*	*Dosage*	*US Price Per Tablet ($)*	*Indian Price Per Tablet ($)*
Prilosec/Astra Merck	Omeprazole	20 mg	3.76	0.09
Prozac/Eli Lilly	Fluoxetine	10 mg	2.28	0.63
Zocor/Merck	Simvastatin	10 mg	2.07	0.21
Zantac/Glaxo-Wellcome	Ranitidine	150 mg	1.72	0.02

Source: Investing in the Indian Pharmaceutical Industry, The American Graduate School of International Management, 1999, Robert Tancer and Srinivas Josyula.

Due to the lack of drug patent protection and the existing drug price controls, many of the world's latest formulation discoveries were not available in India. Out of 400 recent formulations developed worldwide and available in the global market place, only 33 were available in India.[15] However, most of the multinational and pharmaceutical firms are marketing products that have already reached maturity and were in the public domain in other markets.

14. *World Country Analyst*, 1997, Gale Research.

15. "Pfizer to Invest in India if 'Proper' New Patent Law," *AAP Newsfeed*, January 8, 1998.

Drug Price Control Order

The Government, in order to provide protection to the consumers had introduced the Drug Price Control Order (DPCO).[16] It is believed that drug price controls would remain in some form. The Government used the DPCO to protect against drastic price increases, which affect the affordability of drugs. Experience of successively reducing drugs under prior price fixation in the last three DPCOs has shown that market forces are more than adequate to control the prices. In fact, the Pharmaceutical Policy 2002 indicated a drastic reduction in the number of drugs under price control. According to the industry sources, the new DPCO would cover about 34 bulk drugs and their formulations.

Absence of Product Patents — India is Not Alone

The Indian pharmaceutical industry is a prime example of an industry that is being forced to revisit its long-term strategies and business models as India opens its markets to global trade. In addition to the reasons that made foreign investment in India difficult and unpopular for private firms prior to 1991, the pharmaceutical industry faced the additional problem that India did not offer (product) patent protection for pharmaceutical products.

Global pharmaceutical firms watched developments in India closely after 1991. In 1995 India became a signatory of the Uruguay Round Agreement, TRIPS, thereby showing willingness to accept one of its requirements, the issuance of pharmaceutical product patents. India's adherence to TRIPS would become effective in 2005 as a

---

16. The Central Government played a vital role in controlling drug prices and helped the local industry to develop. The aim was to promote the domestic sector to achieve self-sufficiency. The DPCO in 1985 put a cap on prices of 143 basic drugs, as well as on products formulated by domestic companies considered to be essential, at 75 to 100 per cent markups over their manufacturing costs. In a country of almost one billion people, price controls served as a means of ensuring that even the poorest had access to drugs. A drug would be controlled if its overall annual turnover exceeded $1.05 million or if there were less than five bulk drug manufacturers or ten formulation manufacturers of that specific drug. However, with the liberalisation of the industry, the Government felt strongly encouraged to dissolve the price controls in favour of natural market economic pricing. The main argument against the DPCO is that it has not left any scope for sufficient returns to be reinvested in research and development. Domestic firms argued that unless the permissible profit margins increased, they would be unable to be competitive in 2005 when product patent legislation took effect and they could no longer produce copies of existing drugs.

result of a provision of the Agreement granting developing countries an additional period if it is required "to extend patent protection to areas of technology not so protectable in its territory. Some important issues need to be kept in mind:

1. In many industrial countries, the protection of inventions through patents was only developed in the last 30 years. The Swiss pharmaceutical industry, in particular, fought the enactment of a patent law at the end of the 19th century, in order to be able to imitate foreign drugs, such as Aspirin. In the German Reichstag, Switzerland was considered a 'state of robber barons'.[17] Product patents for medical drugs have only been known in Switzerland since 1978.
2. Until recently, there was no patent system for pharmaceuticals in Brazil, a developing nation like India. The new patent law of 1999 provides the possibility of issuing compulsory licenses. On this basis, Brazil plans to buy raw material for AIDS drugs from abroad.
3. The threat that AIDS poses is well-known. Two-thirds of all HIV/AIDS patients, i.e. 23 million, live in Africa south of the Sahara. To combat this menace, South Africa wants to facilitate the import of reasonably priced, good-quality AIDS drugs and to stimulate production of AIDS drugs inside the country.

With this background, it will be easier to focus on the evolving world intellectual property standards and the pharmaceutical industry, the setting up of TRIPS, the history behind the current debate, a background of the Indian Patents Act and its subsequent amendments, a critique of India's present position and recommendations.

The Debate

The controversy surrounding the current issue of contention has its roots in two separate aspects of India's negotiation agenda in the WTO — the pre-Cancun resolution of some of the outstanding issues on TRIPS and the agenda for Cancun and beyond. The original TRIPS Agreement said that weighing the interests between intellectual property protection and public health considerations, countries, which have adequate manufacturing capacity in medicine can produce

17. Gerster, *op cit.*

predominantly for their own use those medicines which are required for various public health considerations. The dispute was regarding those countries without any adequate manufacturing capacity and which do require cheaper medicines and can also issue compulsory licenses for their own use.

Background to the Current Debates

In November 2001, when Trade Ministers in Doha agreed on a special Declaration recognising the right of countries to take measures to protect public health and promote access to medicines, over and above the obligation to protect intellectual property rights, it was widely acclaimed. The Doha Declaration had confirmed, among others, the right of developing countries to use compulsory licenses to override patents on medicines, in order to allow generic drug manufacturers to produce cheaper versions of patented medicines.

The "Paragraph 6" Problem

- The TRIPS Agreement allows the grant of compulsory licenses (CL)[18] to override patents, so that generic manufacturers may produce their cheaper versions of patented drugs. Countries with insufficient or no domestic manufacturing capacity in pharmaceuticals are faced with a problem because there are no generic manufacturers to produce the drugs domestically. This became popularly known as the "Paragraph 6" problem, named after that paragraph dealing with this issue in the Doha Declaration.[19]

---

18. A compulsory licensing (CL) system is incorporated in the patents, whereby a person other than the patentee or the Government is authorised to produce a patented product. The TRIPS agreement does provide certain grounds (though not limited to them) for a country to exercise the CL option. One of the most interesting questions raised in the TRIPS negotiations has been the State setting limits to the absolute rights of the patent holders through compulsory licenses. The CL Provision gives the Government the right to grant licenses to produce a good to any company even if another company has got the patent and the Exclusive Marketing Right (EMR) for the drug.

19. "We recognise that WTO members with insufficient or no manufacturing capacities in the pharmaceutical sector could face difficulties in making effective use of compulsory licensing under the TRIPS Agreement. We instruct the Council for TRIPS to find an expeditious solution to this problem and to report to the General Council before the end of 2002." (Paragraph 6 of the Doha Declaration on TRIPS Agreement and Public Health).

- An option for these countries is to import such drugs through the CL route. However the constraints placed by the TRIPS Agreement on the countries that have the capacity to produce and export the generic versions may prevent them to export such drugs. The reason is that the TRIPS Agreement (Article 31(f)) requires that the production of generic drugs under a CL is "predominantly for the supply of the domestic market". This restriction would mean that exports of drugs produced under a compulsory license are possible only if the "predominant" portion of the production output has been supplied to the domestic market. This raises the concern that the non-predominant portion may not be sufficient for the needs of the importing countries.
- The Declaration instructed WTO Members to find "an expeditious solution" to this problem by December 2002. On 16th December, the Chair of the TRIPS Council came up with a text containing a proposed solution, which was accepted as a compromise by almost all Members except the US, which insisted that the solution would only apply to HIV/AIDS, malaria, tuberculosis and other infectious diseases. The deadline was thus missed.

The Solution

In Geneva on 30th August WTO Members finally adopted the 16th December text, together with an accompanying Statement by the Chair of the WTO General Council.

As per the revised Cancun Ministerial Draft (Second Revision), the "Decision on Implementation of Paragraph 6 of the Doha Declaration on the TRIPS Agreement and Public Health set out in document WT/L/540" has been welcomed. Yet, there has been doubt in some quarters, particularly the NGOs that the Decision and the Chair's Statement represent a compromise that may have the potential of pushing back the gains made at Doha.

This is basically a waiver of the Article 31(f) limitation on exports, which lifts the requirement of Article 31(f) that pharmaceutical products produced under a CL shall be "predominantly for the supply of the domestic market". With this waiver in force, it means that a predominant portion or even the total amount of production under a CL could be exported to a country wishing to import. The Statement confirms the common understanding of Members that the Decision should be used in good faith to protect public health purposes, and not for industrial or commercial policy objectives. It also emphasises the need to prevent diversion of medicines from the markets for which they are intended — elaborating on the trade diversion prevention measures that are required to be taken by countries using the Decision.

What This Means

Where a patent is in force in the importing country on the drug in question, the importing country Government will have to issue a CL to enable the import of the generic version of the patented drug. In the exporting country, the patent status of the drug is also relevant — if a patent is in force, then the generic manufacturer would have to obtain a CL to produce the drug and export it.

Therefore, in many cases, two CLs will have to be issued. Under the TRIPS Agreement and confirmed by the Doha Declaration, WTO Members have the right to determine the grounds for the grant of compulsory licenses. The standard procedural conditions for the grant of CL are set out in the TRIPS Agreement (Article 31), which includes the conditions that an application for a CL should be preceded by a failed attempt to obtain a voluntary license from the patent holder and the payment of compensation to the patent holder.[20] The Decision now modifies some of these requirements and sets out another set of procedures to be complied with, when the waiver of Article 31(f) is required to allow for generic medicines made in one country to be exported to another.

So, when a developing country wishes to import generic medicines (and the said medicine is under patent protection in the country), the importing country will have to do the following:

---

20. Article 31(b) mentions that any other use (without authorization of the right holder) may only be permitted if, prior to such use, the proposed user has made efforts to obtain authorization from the right holder on reasonable commercial terms and conditions and that such efforts have not been successful within a reasonable period of time. This requirement might be waived by a Party in the case of national emergency or other circumstances of extreme urgency or in cases of public non-commercial use.

a. **Notify the WTO** of its intention to use the solution as an importer (LDCs are not required to notify); the names and expected quantities of product(s) needed and its grant or intention to grant a CL.[21]

b. **Establish insufficient or no manufacturing capacity:** LDCs are automatically eligible, while other developing countries have to qualify to use the solution. Developing countries have to establish either that:

   1. They have no manufacturing capacity in the pharmaceutical sector, or
   2. The capacity is currently insufficient for the purpose of meeting its needs.

   The Decision suggests that countries make this determination themselves; i.e., it is a self-determination test.

c. **Take measures against trade diversion:** All importing countries will have to take "reasonable measures within their means" to prevent re-exportation, as "proportionate to their administrative capacities and to the risk of trade diversion". This appears to be an obligation but it is unclear what the consequences of non-compliance or insufficient compliance will be.

The Procedure of Granting a Compulsory License

The link between IPR and high domestic prices (which shall be discussed in details later) provided the main justifications for weakening the level of protection for drugs by means of comprehensive compulsory licensing practices. CL in the US has more often been used to restrict the anti competitive practices and as a remedy in numerous antitrust case settlements.[22]

---

21. When a Government decides to grant a CL, it must notify the WTO of this decision and its conditions, including the name and address of generic manufacturer, the product, the importing countries and the duration of the CL, as well as, address of website on which information regarding product has been posted.

22. The US's own patent legislation is far more liberal. Under the US law, if the Government wants to use a patent, it can do so without the need for a CL and without negotiating with the patent holder. The patent holder can ask for compensation but has no other rights. In fact, in the US, many compulsory licenses have also been granted in order to remedy anti-competitive practices. In some cases, the licenses have been granted royalty free. Lalitha, N (2002).

The CL must also be subject to the following conditions:

1. It is only for the amount required by the importing Member and must be exported in total to the importing country.
2. The products produced under CL must be clearly identifiable through labeling or marking (e.g., special packaging, colouring or marking)
3. The generic manufacturer is obliged, prior to shipment, to post on the website information on the quantities supplied to each importing country and the distinguishing features of product.[23]

Procedural Deterrents to Compulsory Licensing

a. The producer would also have to satisfy the conditions of having had unsuccessful negotiations with the patent holder for a voluntary license and pay the compensation amount.

b. If granted a CL, the generic manufacturer would be subject to the conditions of the CL as stated above. It would appear that the requirements have to be fulfilled anew for each batch of medicines produced under a CL, and for each and every country of export.

c. There may also be other product registration and drug safety (such as proof of bio-equivalence of the generic product) requirements that may have to be satisfied.

d. Competition from the introduction of generics would also bring down prices of patented medicines. However, the generic manufacturers would have to be able to achieve economies of scale or cost efficiencies to remain viable. This would be dependent on large production runs and large enough orders. The trade diversion prevention measures — in requiring each batch of medicines to be manufactured in different shapes or colours — may be a deterrent.

---

23. The new "deal" on TRIPS and drugs: What does it mean for access to medicines? Cecilia Oh, Third World Network Briefings for Cancun, 2003.

TRIPS and the Indian Legal and Pharmaceutical Set-Up — Where does India Stand?

While for two years after Doha, the pharma companies, the Indian negotiators and the legislators struggled to come to terms with TRIPS, it was only in 2003 that the "hard work" paid off to some extent. India played a proactive role in the August decision in the WTO regarding export of generic medicines. However, on the home front, there are still a lot of unanswered questions. Most of these concern the Indian Patent Act 1970 and its subsequent amendments, the latest being the Patents Amendment Bill 2003.

The Indian Patent Act 1970 and the Need for its Amendment Following TRIPS

Patent rights were introduced in India for the first time in 1856 and in 1970, the Patents Act was passed. India is also a signatory to the Paris Convention 1883 and the Patent Cooperation Treaty 1970. With regard to pharmaceuticals, in the case of substances intended for use or capable of being used as food, drugs or medicines produced by chemical processes, patents were granted only for the processes of manufacture and not for the substances themselves. This exclusion of pharmaceuticals from eligibility for product patents was introduced to break away India's dependence on bulk drugs and formulations and provide for the development of a self-reliant indigenous pharmaceutical industry.

Developing country members were given time till 1st January, 2000 to implement TRIPS. Article 65.4 of TRIPS further says that those countries which fail to provide product patent protection by the general date of application of the TRIPS Agreement for that particular member country, the application may be delayed for an additional period of five years. Moreover Article 70.8 instructs all those countries who have not provided product patents as on the "prescribed" date, to provide a means for acceptance of applications for product patents. Article 70.9 states that during this transition period Exclusive Marketing Rights (EMRs) are to be granted for a period of five years or till the patent is granted or rejected, whichever period is shorter.

India decided to avail itself of the full transition period for developing countries and had till 1st January, 2005 to extend patent protection to pharmaceutical products. In keeping with the TRIPS commitments,[24] India had started on a process of amending the Patents Act culminating with the Patents (Amendment) Ordnance, 2004.

The Amendments

The deadline for the Indian Government to come up with some concrete steps to improve the patent law as per the clauses of the TRIPS Agreement was 14th January, 1999. The Patents (Amendment) Act 1999 introduced the following measures:

a. It provides for Exclusive Marketing Rights (EMRs) to foreign pharmaceutical and agro-chemical companies. EMRs enable a company to market any product exclusively in a country even though it may not have the patent rights. EMRs granted since 1995 have had their share of controversy and debate within the industry itself. As per the provisions in the law, these were to be kept unexamined till 31st December 2004.

b. It provided for a mailbox facility for receipt of patent applications in the area of drugs and agro-chemicals.[25]

c. The Act also provided for compulsory license for the EMR on the same lines as patents.

The Need for More Amendments

Even after resolving (to a great extent) the controversy surrounding Article 31(f), more remained to be done, especially when the issue of granting product patents was still pending. The 1970 Act had many provisions similar to TRIPS. For example Article 31(a) TRIPS says that licenses should be given on the basis of merit

24. Article 70.8, read with Article 65.2 and 65.4 of TRIPS obligates developing countries to provide for a mailbox mechanism for depositing applications and an exclusive rights regime.

25. The Act granted the inventors what is known as "pipeline protection". If the applicant has already filed an application for his or her invention in any convention country and a patent or an EMR has been granted in that country on or after 1st January 1995, the applicant would be eligible to file for patent of pharmaceutical and agrochemical products in India. These patent applications will be kept pending. When India changes its patent law as per WTO recommendations, the pending application will be eligible for product patent. Until such patent is granted or rejected, the applicant will be granted EMRs in India if the application is found eligible.

and over a reasonable time period (Articles 31(c)). A similar provision could be found in Section 88(1) of the Patent Act of 1970. Yet there were numerous areas, which needed to be looked at, and given the changes that have taken place in the patents world in recent times, the Act itself required further amendments.

Third Amendment to the Patents Act, 1970

The Patents Act, 1970 was again amended in June, 2002 to meet the obligations under the TRIPS Agreement which came into force from 1st January, 2000. This amendment related to modifications in the provisions concerning rights of patentee, term of patent protection, compulsory licensing, reversal of burden of proof, etc. Certain provisions were also made in the law to simplify and rationalise the procedural aspects so as to achieve greater user satisfaction.

The Act was again required to be amended to meet the obligations under the TRIPS Agreement, which have been due from 1st January 2005. This is mainly related to introduction of product patent protection for pharmaceuticals. A Bill to amend the Act, namely, the Patents (Amendment) Bill, 2003 was introduced in Parliament (Lok Sabha) on 22nd December, 2003.

Some of the salient features of the Bill were:

a. To introduce product patent protection in all fields of technology as per Article 27 of the TRIPS Agreement.

b. To delete the provisions relating to EMRs and to introduce a transitional provision for safeguarding EMRs already granted.

c. To introduce a provision for enabling grant of compulsory license for export of medicines to countries which have insufficient or no manufacturing capacity to meet emergent public health situations. This provision is in accordance with the agreement reached on 30th August, 2003 for implementation of Para 6 of the Doha Declaration on TRIPS and Public Health.

d. To amend and strengthen the provisions relating to national security.

e. To amend the provisions relating to Appellate Board with a view to extending its jurisdiction to revocation of patents also.

f. To amend the provisions relating to opposition procedures.

g. To amend certain provisions with a view to harmonising them with the Patent Cooperation Treaty to which India is a signatory.

h. To amend the provisions relating to time lines for different activities with a view to introducing flexibility and reducing the processing time for patent application.

i. To amend provisions of the Act with a view to simplifying and rationalizing the procedure aimed at benefiting the users.

The Indian Pharmaceutical Industry and Specific Parameters[26]

Price Issues

- Prices decline with the expiry of patent and with generic competition.
- The number of pharma manufacturers has increased from some hundreds in the 1950s to more than 20,000 in the late-1990s, employing millions. Of such units there are numerous SMEs. The ensuing high competion is an important reason for the relatively lower prices of the medicines.
- Furthermore, because of the socio-welfare implication of pharmaceutical prices, the prices of medicines the world over are subject to Government regulations.
- While some may argue that stronger protection would result in increase in the prices of the drugs, a counter argument is that developing countries may not be affected by the increase in the price of drugs due to low participation of patented drugs (and due to quick appearance of substitutes).

26. Refers to some of the arguments in the paper on TRIPS and Pharmaceutical Industry: Issues and Prospects. Lalitha (2002), *op. cit.*

- Pharmacists in some countries in the West are authorised to dispense generic drugs (priced lower) in the place of prescription drugs. However, if the doctor writes it as 'Dispense as Written' then the pharmacist cannot change the drug. In India, there are only a few such 'common' medicines and prescriptions bearing the generic name are also uncommon. It is totally up to the physicians in choosing between a patented and a generic drug, in cases where alternatives are available.

Research and Development

- It is argued that product patents would facilitate academia-industry interface and enable technical knowledge flows more readily from university laboratories.
- Patents are important for pharmaceuticals because of the huge R&D costs incurred by the firms.
- The higher cost of the R&D (running into hundred million dollars or more) proves to be an effective entry barrier for new firms. Estimates indicate that of 100 drugs that enter the clinical testing phase I,[27] about 70 complete Phase I, 33 complete Phase II, and 25-30 clear Phase III. Only two-thirds of the drugs that enter phase III is ultimately marketed. However, as phase III is the more costly R&D stage, one failure out of three produce may still imply a considerable loss of resources.
- As the following figure shows, R&D investment in India has been very low and started picking up only in the early-90s as evident from the following Figure 6.2.
- Most of the R&D investments have perhaps been directed towards process improvements. For example a drug like Viagra may take more than a decade and several million dollars to develop. However, utilising the information that was available on the internet, US patent records and industry

27. Phase I is for the evaluation of drug safety in human volunteers. Phase II is for the clinical investigation for treatment effect and Phase III is the full-scale evaluation of treatment. Phase 4 is for elucidating uncommon side effects.

literature, some firms may make available indigenous versions of Viagra, within a very short time of the formal launch of drug.

Figure 6.2

Investment in R&D by Public and Private Sector (Rs. Mn)

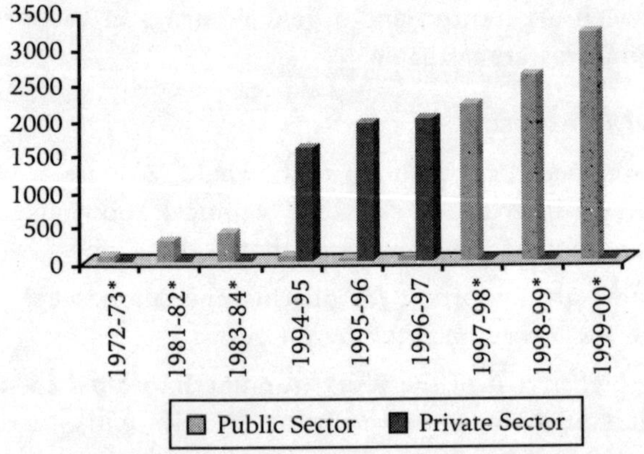

Note: * Break-ups for public and private sector are not available.

Source: Indian Pharmaceutical Industry: An Overview; IDMA (2001), and Handbook of Industrial Policy and Statistics 2000, P. 505.

- At the same time, with the change in scenario, domestic companies, which had invested in biotechnology or in traditional/herbal medicine sector, may be finding the lack of protection as a problem to commercialize their innovations.
- Since it is difficult for each unit to invest in R&D, to economise on scarce R&D resources and to avoid the probable duplication, pooling of R&D resources and mergers of firms have been identified as possible solutions. In India too, several mergers started taking place from 1995 onwards.
- It can also be said that the number of patents filed and granted also indicates the level of R&D capabilities. The Figures below present the number of patents filed by Indians and others in the Patent Office of India. While the trend for the number of patents granted has been declining, the gap

between the number of applications and the number of patents filed increases. Furthermore, for both patents filed and granted, non-residents score much higher than Indians. Probably, a large number of applications are turned down because such inventions already exist or the inventions lack non-obviousness or industrial applicability.

Figure 6.3

Patents Applied for and Granted

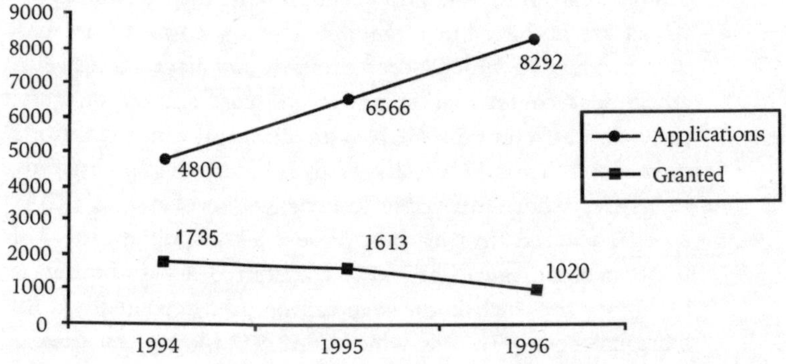

Source: World Intellectual Property Organisation, Industrial Statistics, 1997.

Figure 6.4

Applications for Patents Filed

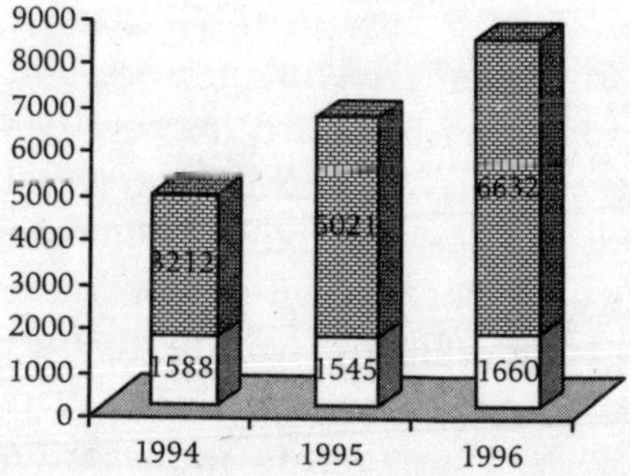

Figure 6.5

Patents Granted

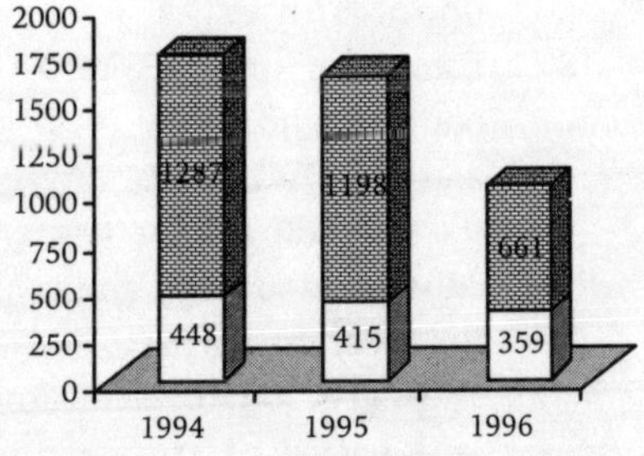

Source: World Intellectual Property Organisation, Industrial Statistics, 1997.

Foreign Direct Investment and Technology Transfer

- FDI embodies two distinct assets — capital and technology. While capital for financing FDI can be raised from financial markets or local capital markets of recipient country, FDI also manifests itself through the transfer of technology to the subsidiary in the recipient country.
- In both horizontal and vertical FDI, MNCs must be characterised by some cost advantages to overcome the disadvantages they face while operating away from home. Such advantages are known as "ownership advantages", which are nothing but intangible assets such as a trademark or a product to which other firms do not have access. Such advantages confer market power and cost effectiveness that provide sufficient incentives to undertake multinational operations. Thus FDI is likely to be more evident in those industries where intangible Knowledge Based Assets (KBAs) specific to each firm in those industries are significant. This is because KBAs can be easily transferred across borders at low costs and such knowledge can be used repeatedly at low marginal costs. That is why strong IPRs are often deemed important determinants of inward FDI.
- However, when a firm serves a foreign market through FDI, IPRs should take on different levels of significance in different sectors. Investment in low technology goods such as textiles or electronic assembly, etc. depends relatively little on the strength of IPRs and more on input costs and market opportunities. A firm could also choose to license or franchise its KBA to an unrelated firm in the recipient country and allow local production in return for royalties and fees. While the original firm may be unwilling to reveal its technology (for fear that the licensee could decline the contract and copy the technology for its own purpose), the licensee, on its part, would be unwilling to sign the contract and agree on royalty terms unless it knows the particulars and value of the technology. Due to this information asymmetry, as long as IPRs are weaker, it will be impossible to develop a satisfactory contract forcing the original firm to acquire a subsidiary, to which it transfers the KBA. Therefore,

FDI will probably be the right strategy when IPRs are weaker. This is a contradiction to the general view that FDI occurs when IPRs are stronger. Then again, FDI only results in actual transfer of technology when the foreign investors are allowed controlling stake in the firms they want to invest in.

- Therefore, perceived inadequacies of intellectual property protection did not hinder FDI inflows in global terms. Thus FDI increased substantially in Brazil since 1970 until the debt crisis exploded in 1985, while in Thailand FDI boomed during the eighties.
- In the case of India after the adoption of process patents in the pharmaceutical sector, the number of foreign collaborations increased from 183 in 1970 to 1041 in 1985.

- In the case of India, total FDI flow has been stagnating, due to various forms of regulatory framework and the Government control over production that was prevalent for a long time. These regulations have been relaxed as part of the liberalisation measures and currently 100 per cent foreign equity is allowed in the pharmaceutical industry. The following Table 6.4 provides information on the total FDI and FDI in the pharma industry.

Table 6.4

FDI in India (Rs. Million)

Year	*Amount Approved*	*Actual Inflow*	*FDI Approved in Pharma*	*Percent of Pharma FDI to Total Approvals*
1993	88590	17870	299	0.34
1994	141870	32890	1630	1.15
1995	320720	68200	1858	0.58
1996	301470	103890	1182	0.39
1997	548910	164250	1829	0.33
1998	308140	133400	911	0.3
1999	283670	168680	798	0.28
2000	370430	127630	16146	4.36
Total	2363800	816810	24653	1

Source: Handbook of Industrial Policy and Statistics, 2000, Foreign Trade and Balance of Payments, CMIE, July 2001.

- Vast differences are observed between the amount approved and the actual inflow, which suggests that a large number of proposed investments do not materialise and perhaps wither away due to the bottlenecks encountered at the time of implementation. In pharmaceutical industry till 1999, the percentage of FDI to total approvals has been around 0.50 per cent or lower. However, with the measures towards adopting stronger patents and increasing the FDI limit in the pharmaceutical industry, the figures improved somewhat in 2000.

The following section consists of feedback received from the Indian pharmaceutical industry on TRIPS and its ramifications in India. The views of the two largest pharmaceutical industry associations in India were sought and are provided below. Some of the responses will, by themselves, answer a lot of questions pertaining to TRIPS and would also probably address some of the misconceptions as well.

Industry Feedback

a. On the aspect of TRIPS encouraging R&D on its own, industry opinion is divided.

   1. Most of the respondents devote 0-5 per cent of their budget on R&D.
   2. Most also agree that funds for R&D will be availed from the market and drug sales.
   3. They are also unanimous in their thinking that although R&D should be encouraged in the post-TRIPS scenario, the focus should always be on generic drugs and on those, whose patents are close to the expiry date.
   4. What is most encouraging is that all are for increasing R&D in the days after the Doha declaration. This puts to rest the fear that the CL route might be misused by developing countries on the grounds of public health.
   5. On the same grounds, most are not inclined to use the compulsory licensing route to produce patented drugs. This is probably because, most of the drugs produced in

India are already out-of-patent or their patents are close to expiry. The fluid state in which the present 3rd Amendment to the Patents Act exists has also made matters not too good. The questions from industry are more with respect to product patents and their introduction, not regarding EMRs or CLs and their applicability.

6. What is confusing is that on the aspect of TRIPS encouraging R&D on its own, most have replied in the negative. The general feeling is that TRIPS is not an overnight phenomenon and it could have resulted in high R&D activities even a long time back. But that has not happened. Also, maintaining a patent is costly as well.

b. Interestingly, the drugs that producers say they would be manufacturing, especially after the Doha Declaration are those which are specific to ailments that are spread throughout the developed and the developing world and are not limited to specific countries. In other words, the world demand (and of course the demand in India) is what governs the drugs that Indian companies want to manufacture. These are:

1. Anti-diabetic drugs
2. Drugs for cardiovascular diseases
3. Drugs for pulmonary diseases
4. Anti obesity drugs
5. Pain killers
6. Vaccines
7. Anti-retroviral
8. Anti-malarial
9. Anti-tuberculosis drugs.

c. While most of them feel that EMRs are good for industry in India (before product patents are introduced), the fact of the matter is that EMRs may have lost their significance to a great extent since product patents are to be introduced in 2005. In fact, some of them feel that product patents could have been introduced in India much before 2005.

d. Yet all of them feel that after the new declaration, it will not be easier to introduce new drugs. What can be inferred from this is that with every relaxation in legislation come more complications. Industry feels that patents in the "new" era will be difficult to obtain and litigations will increase (as many will attempt to go by the CL route).

e. Probable price rise may be an aspect of apprehension for most people. But as far as the industry is concerned, it is widely felt that depending upon the nature of the drug, prices may rise at most by 5-10 per cent. Some even feel that overall, there may be declining trend in prices.

   1. Furthermore, even drug price rises are not a direct fallout of TRIPS or introduction of product patents, but reflect "regular" demand-supply economics.
   2. In any case, the prices of life-saving drugs will probably not see much change post-2005.

f. What the industry cannot pin-point is the price difference between generic substitutes and patented originals. While the general consensus is that drugs produced under the CL route will be around 20-25 per cent cheaper than prices of patented originals (even including royalty, price of the former should be lower), specific forecasts cannot be made due to the following reasons:

   1. A tablet priced at Re. 1/- in India, may cost 20 cents (Rs. 9/-) in USA. Although the value of Re. 1 in India may be compared to 20 cents in USA; yet there is a price difference of Rs. 8/- between the generic substitute and the patented original.
   2. The aspect of affordability also should be looked at. A manufacturer may have to price a drug such that poorer consumers may be able to afford the medicine. Similarly, the cost of labour (which is a key aspect to the cost of production) would also vary from country to country.

A Critique

The process of liberalisation initiated in 1991 has helped develop policies that are focused on attracting capital from overseas and making India a global industrial base. "*The current revenues of the Indian pharmaceutical industry are estimated at US$ 5.5 billion and it is expected to grow at a compounded annual growth rate of 19 per cent and touch US$ 25 billion in revenue by 2010.*" (The Economic Times, 1st May, 2001) As much as India would like to view this as reality, TRIPS is a reality too. India is slowly moving into global markets and competing with international quality standards and prices. Although R&D is an important factor to ensure a competitive edge in the international arena, the future of Indian pharmaceutical industry hinges on patent protection.

Compulsory Licensing and recognising public health issues are all very well for developing countries. However, product patents would also have to be introduced in India in 2005 (as they have been). Will the Indian pharmaceutical industry be able to withstand a head-on collision with foreign pharmaceutical majors post-2005, when product and not process patents rule the roost? Secondly, whether at all the third amendment to the Indian Patents Act will be able to balance the issue of product patents with the aspect of public health and public interest issues articulated in the Doha Declaration, remains to be seen. More importantly, whether the industry itself is as worried as intellectuals about product patents, price rise, R&D, FDI and technology transfer remains to be looked at.

Addressing the "Myths"

The scepticism regarding the access by the developing countries to important breakthroughs in medicine made by the developed countries however linger on. Hence it is feared that it will have adverse effects on trade and may impede the transfer of technology and know-how. As far as India may be concerned, this fear probably does not exist.

- The absence of product patents may have enabled the Indian firms, especially in the pharmaceutical sector to change the process by reverse engineering route and produce the same product. This was important in the initial stages of development of certain sectors, but in the liberal environment now, there is a need for much more concentrated efforts on R&D by our companies. As the feedback from industry suggests, firms do appreciate this fact and are perhaps better placed than ever to utilise product patents to their advantages.

- Yet the focus is on generic drugs. Is it bad for the industry? Definitely not. A document, forthcoming from the United Nations, says:

  "In three and a half years, the prices (for AIDS medicines) have plummeted...generic producers are now empowered to produce fixed-dose combinations endorsed by the World Health Organisation that permit patients to take one pill twice a day rather than two dozen at widely different times, therefore facilitating patient compliance and reducing drug resistance... (This happened) because people imagined and believed that people in developing countries are worth saving and fighting for. As a result with the same amount of money that could buy branded and patented medicines for 20000 rich people in Africa, the world can now buy generic ARVs for two million Africans living with AIDS by the year 2005."

India is to be thanked for this and also for its unique triple anti-retroviral that is an affordable and innovative combination of the life-prolonging AIDS medicines that had been combined into one tablet taken twice a day replacing the complicated regime for AIDS therapy. Many believe this combination is one of the most effective of the AIDS medicines. Although the triple has been legally produced under Indian law, MNCs had targeted this drug. WHO later strongly recommended the triple saying that with this, countries can quickly expand access to anti-retroviral medicines. Today, the price of an Indian triple is not US$ 12000-15000 a year, but around US$ 140 per year.

- Replacement of the Accelerated Access Medicines programme in the Latin American nations[28] meant an open transparent bidding for supply of medicines to Latin American countries. When the bidding ended, apart from only one MNC all other successful bids were generic, most from India. It was reported that the bidding had saved the countries US$ 170 million, and as a result an additional 150000 people could be treated.

---

28. Accelerated Access to Medicines is a programme in which an exclusive market is created for pharmaceutical products from USA, Caribbean and Latin American Countries and the companies producing generic drugs are excluded. However, upon an endorsement by leading NGOs and to some extent, even the US Government, for lower priced Indian medicines, the nine Andean nations and Mexico replaced their planned Accelerated Access by open transparent bidding.

- It is widely believed that after the introduction of the Patents Act in compliance with TRIPS provisions, the prices of medicines will accelerate and medicines will become unaffordable for people. However, truth is, patents can never be awarded retrospectively. Patents can only apply to new discoveries. The transition provisions of TRIPS ensure that patents in India will only be granted for totally new discoveries, post-1st January, 1995. Only items for which no patent has ever been granted in any other WTO country before 1st January, 1995 or for which no application was pending for a patent in any other WTO country as on 1st January 1995 will ever be patentable in India. This means that any medicinal product already available in the Indian market on the date of coming into force of the new law, cannot, and will not, ever be patented in India.
- It should be noted that it takes anywhere between 8-12 years for a new drug to be granted registration by Drug Authorities of any country after which marketing permission is given. This registration period comes out of the overall patent life of the medicines, which is now almost universally 20 years from the date of application. A discoverer thus enjoys at best only 8-12 years of Exclusive Marketing for recovering the cost of research. The number of new drugs registered worldwide each year is between 25 and 35.
- What this essentially means is:

a. Within the transition period (1995-2004) allowed for India, not more than a handful of new drugs will actually qualify for any form of exclusivity.

b. Even after India commences granting patents, by the time patented products become a significant proportion of those already available locally; it will be another 10-15 years i.e. 2015-2020.

c. It is not correct to believe that Multinational Corporations (MNCs) have only one price for a product everywhere in the world and as such the price charged in India will be exorbitant. Even when the product is unique, it may be introduced in India at a price significantly lower than in

Western countries. Most international manufacturers will base their pricing strategy for countries, like India, on "affordability criteria".

- Despite the price controls, monitoring and enforcing such prices has not been commendable. Differences may have persisted between the prices charged by different manufacturers for the same formulation. The applicability of present price controls on patented products should be looked at more so since such controls would definitely benefit the customers. However, costs of establishing and maintaining an effective price control over all patented drugs may be very high.
- The bottlenecks in the DPCO and the aspect of price fixation *vis-à-vis* price monitoring also need a look-in, especially in the context of whether market forces can control the prices.
- The feedback from industry only ascertains the view that on the key parameters of price, R&D and technology transfers, the forecasts of manufacturers in India are good.

TRIPS and its Flexibilities

At the same time, TRIPS has to be accepted as something, which has come to stay. There are some in-built flexibilities, which often go unnoticed. Article 7 of the Agreement states the objectives of IPRs. The protection and enforcement of IPRs should contribute to the promotion of technological innovation and to the transfer and dissemination of technology to the mutual advantage of producers and users of technological knowledge and in a manner conducive to social and economic welfare and to a balance of rights and obligations. As per this, flexibility to define the national laws within the TRIPS framework is available under the clauses of compulsory licensing, exceptions to exclusive rights and the principle of exhaustion. Apart from CL, the other two aspects are discussed briefly below in order to highlight that all member nations including developing countries have been provided with several "breathers" of sorts before TRIPS is implemented fully in 2005.

- As per the TRIPS agreement, during the transitional period, developing countries like India will also have to provide

'Exclusive Marketing Rights' for products patented elsewhere (any other member country) till the patent application for that product is approved or rejected in India. EMRs and patent rights go together and cannot be separated. Although there is a provision for EMRs in the Patents Act (after amendment), without a clear patent right, there cannot be any product marketing exclusivity. Before a patent is granted, it has to be examined in accordance with the provisions of the Indian Patents Act, which provide for legitimate opposition to eliminate invalid and frivolous claims. Granting an EMR without fully ensuring the clear validity of the relevant patent is not fair to manufacturers in terms of denial of their rights, but to the consumers as well, who have to pay the higher price. Therefore, all EMRs and connected patent applications should be examined fully and concurrently after December 2004.

- Article 30 states that "Parties may provide limited exceptions to the exclusive rights conferred by a patent, provided that such exceptions do not unreasonably conflict with a normal exploitation of the patent and do not unreasonably prejudice the legitimate interests of the patent owner, taking account of the legitimate interests of third parties." Accordingly, the following types of exceptions may be provided: 'Acts done privately and on a non-commercial scale or for a non-commercial purpose; Use of the invention for research or teaching purposes; Experimentation on the invention to test or improve on it; Preparation of medicines under individual prescriptions; Experiments made for the purpose of seeking regulatory approval for marketing of a product after the expiration of a patent; Use of the invention by a third party that had used it before the date of application of the patent and importation of patented product that has been marketed in another country with the consent of the patent owner'. The Bolar exception also permits the pre-market testing of generic products during the patent term, so that they can be marketed immediately upon expiration of the patent.
- The other important aspect that is gaining attention is parallel trade. Objectively, the patent owner loses his rights

once the product is on the market or when the patent owner has sold his innovations. This principle is known as the principle of exhaustion of rights or commonly known as parallel trade. TRIPS leaves the decision on rights of national or international exhaustion to national laws. The US adopts a national exhaustion principle whereby the patent owner will have no control over the product once it is placed in the domestic market. But he can exercise his rights outside the US market regarding the price and quantity of the product. International exhaustion gives no right to the patent owner once he has sold his product. The advantage of international exhaustion is that developing countries such as India can scout for cost advantages of the patented product. However, while international exhaustion disallows the exclusive rights of the patent owner globally, a patent owner/ manufacturer can always restrict the supply of the product that is exported. In those cases exercising the compulsory license option can lead to getting the patented product in required quantity.

All these provisions suggest that patented product can be manufactured, traded and used for experimental purposes, within the provisions of the TRIPS Agreement. The national laws will have to clearly define the cases in which such provisions could be used to benefit the people and the industry. TRIPS is not a necessary evil; nor is it a blessing in disguise. It is a system of the new international economic order and is a means to promote trade and commerce. It has its positives and negatives. As far as the Indian industry is concerned — TRIPS has brought it out of its closet.

What the Future Holds

"*...Because the AIDS diagnosis is considered a death sentence, many do not seek treatment...almost all who do, are turned away...many hospitals tell people, 'You've got to go home and die'...In our age of miraculous medicines, no person should have to hear those words.*" George W Bush, President, USA

One can only hope that the future is brighter than the picture painted above. As far as the pharmaceutical sector and TRIPS are concerned, India is on the world stage, playing a role, which is vital not only for its own people, but for nations in the developing world, which have needed medicines, but could not afford them and whose people, like most Indians have suffered from the want of affordable treatments.

It does not seem, at first glance, that the Doha Declaration having been "passed" there would be any fresh debate on the aspect of compulsory licensing. However, as the next section will show, there might be numerous areas within TRIPS, which should be looked at in great details for at least benchmarking the national IPR legislation, if not for anything else.

But there may be more to the story. Post-Doha, after lengthy negotiations, it was decided that nations could decide what constituted a medical emergency (in order to take refuge of the TRIPS flexibilities introduced at Doha), provided the WTO would permit them to design the method under which a nation could obtain its importing rights. It has been argued by certain critics that such a process could be halted quite easily. A nation desiring to import from India on a CL would first have to justify it was unable to manufacture on its own and then pass a national law allowing itself to import via the CL route. This would open up the process of legal challenge, which would take the case to the WTO, thereby initiating a fresh round of controversy and debate.

The Future Focus Areas

What is interesting is that new research in India corresponds to the world trend.

- In the area of biotechnology, significant breakthroughs have already been made in the area of stem cells and cloning which have potential cure for some diseases like cancer, Parkinsons, Alzheimer's and nervous disorders. In contrast to this, in India biotech research is concentrated in the areas of vaccines, diagnostics, molecular and cellular biology, etc. However, DNA research is only at a basic level since patenting of living organisms is still under a scanner. This area is also highly research and resource intensive.
- In the sphere of outsourcing, R&D, manufacturing and marketing rights could be segregated, with each being "outsourced" to firms in different countries.

- There is another interesting development in the realm of Bolar Provision and Data Exclusivity:
    - The Drug Price and Competition Act, the law that opened the market to generics in the USA, the "Bolar" provision explicitly allows the import of a small amount of the raw material before patent expiry so that consumers can have the competitive product available when the patent expires. Naturally, industry lobbies attempted to prevent the export of raw materials until a patent expired, potentially adding three to four years to market exclusivity after a patent expired.
    - Data exclusivity is all about generic "copies" being manufactured without duplicating clinical trials. In the US, data exclusivity lasts for five years and there have been attempts to prolong the protection.
    - These have implications for India as the strength of the Indian pharmaceutical industry is in reverse engineering.
    - The target should be aimed at producing the generic version of the products that are nearing patent expiry. Stress should also be on research leading to new drug delivery mechanisms and in identifying new uses of existing drugs.
    - In order to develop domestic innovations, developing countries require utility models or petty patents. These petty patents can be available for a shorter period of time for process innovations made over an existing product. The TRIPS agreement leaves members to introduce such legislation, as there are no specific rules on this subject.
- There is a growing need for more collaboration between industry and academic institutes as in the West. The following example of Merck (a US based company)[29] can be cited. Between 1972 and 1974, two scientists Michael S Brown and Joseph L Goldstein of the University of Texas identified the key steps in the production of Cholesterol, for which they were awarded the Nobel Prize in 1985. Their

---

29. Lalitha (2002), *op. cit.*

findings motivated Merck's scientists to launch research on cell culture assays for cholesterol inhibitors as early as 1975. In 1978, Merck isolated Lovastatin, the Mevacor compound from a microorganism of the soil. Mevacors NDA was approved for marketing in August 1987. The product reached $260 million sales in 1988, the first full year of marketing and it reached $ 1 billion sales in 1991. As soon as Brown and Goldstein's discovery was made, it was publicly available. Yet Merck was the only company that effectively exploited their findings.

Options Available to India

- India will have to strengthen the patent examination process and speed up the processing procedures. This will help in checking the products that may enter the country utilising the import monopoly route provided by the EMR. As far as India's pharmaceutical industry is concerned, various options are possible in the WTO regime. These are to:
  - (a) Manufacture out-of-patent generic drugs/Produce patented drugs through the CL route,
  - (b) Invest more in R&D,
  - (c) Explore possibilities of new drug delivery mechanisms and alternative use of existing drugs.

The Patents (Amendment) Ordinance, 2004

In order to meet the 1st January 2005 deadline to make its intellectual property regime WTO-compliant, in late December 2004, the Indian Government issued an ordinance — an executive decree not debated in Parliament — that made several amendments to the country's patent regime. The ordinance now tabled in parliament proposes

- To remove the bar on patentability of pharmaceuticals and agro-chemicals from 1st January, 2005. Thus, product patents can now be granted in India.
- To remove the provisions for EMRs. The applications for patent in respect of which EMRs were granted would have to

be examined for the grant of patent immediately on the commencement of the Ordinance.

- New provisions that allow both pre-grant and post-grant opposition. The pre-grant opposition can be filed anytime after the publication of the patent application but before a patent is granted. The post-grant opposition can be filed within a period of one year from the date of publication of the granted patent. Furthermore, in the interim period between post-publication of the application and grant of a patent, the applicant would still enjoy the rights as if a patent for the invention had been already granted. However, the applicant would not be entitled to institute any proceedings for infringement until grant of the patent.
- A new provision that provides for grant of license to manufacture and export the patented product to any country having insufficient or no manufacturing capacity in the pharmaceutical sector to address public health problems provided a compulsory license has been granted in that country. This is in keeping with Para 6 of Doha Declaration.
- Heavy penalties for offences under the Act.

However, there are controversies as well. The grant of CLs, even before the Ordinance came into force, was an issue, which was often debated. An application for the grant of CL can be made to the Controller of Patents only after the expiration of three years from the date of the grant of a patent. It is argued that in a world where diseases spread freely beyond all geographic barriers, a monopoly to manufacture and market a life saving drug for three years can result in colossal loss of human lives.[30]

---

30. In case a patent is not worked in India for three years after its grant, the Controller General of Patents can issue a CL to any one interested in exploiting the patent. Three other conditions are to be satisfied in this regard: (i) "reasonable requirements of the public" are not satisfied, (ii) the patented invention is not worked in the country and (iii) the patented invention is not available to the public at a reasonably affordable price. Using CLs for "working" the patents in the country of grant may be constrained by the terms of the licences that the patent holder may demand. According to Article 31(h) of TRIPS, the right holder needs to be paid adequate remuneration. However, the matter of concern is that it has the potential of making the cost of the licence prohibitive for the developing country firms since the average cost of introducing a new medicine to the market runs into millions.

The price of a patented drug would normally be much higher than other (generic) drugs. There are only a few drugs in the Indian pharma market, which are under patent protection. The number is likely to go up. With new drugs slated to be introduced in the Indian market, the share of patented drugs is expected to rise. But there would be patent expiries too, which would mean that the market for generics will expand.

Recommendations

TRIPS has come of age; and so has the Indian pharmaceutical industry. The confusion regarding compulsory licenses or product patents, the legal provisions of the Third Amendment to the Patents Act, the future of EMRs, etc. notwithstanding, it may be safely concluded that Indian industry can use TRIPS to its benefits. The real challenge is, however, to find an alternative system in which medicines neglected by the market are developed and essential medicines are not subject to the market mechanism. The importance of TRIPS cannot be overemphasised. IPRs constitute the most important assets of a corporation and an environment that fosters research and innovation is a necessity. In a scenario where the controversy over TRIPS has been fuelled by the unwillingness of some nations and corporations to interpret these provisions generously, the basic question pertains to the genuine choices that policymakers in India now have following the link between the trade regime and pharmaceuticals.

Some Basic Suggestions

1. In order to benefit from the new directions consequent upon the TRIPS Agreement, developing countries need to improve their regulatory framework, laws and service, which will help to increase inventive activity.
2. TRIPS can open new horizons for a country's industry and can ensure success through competition. IPRs cannot remain static and have to be abreast of the emerging new technologies and of international developments. The legislation therefore needs to evolve as well.
3. To address the issue of abuse of IPRs by right holders or the resort to practices, which restrain trade or technology

transfer, competition laws and not IPR legislation should be focused on. The mere use of the protection of intellectual property to secure exclusivity in the market place for a new product is in itself not an abuse; but intellectual property can sometimes be involved in the abuse of a dominant market position or in restrictive trade practices. Such situations should be investigated with the aid of an appropriate competition law. Intellectual property laws provide for intellectual property to be valued and exchanged. Competition laws ensure that the market assigns a fair and efficient value to this property.

4. Article 40 of TRIPS accepts that some licensing practices and conditions may have adverse effects on trade and competition. The legislation should be sufficiently flexible to deal with such issues. India should study these possibilities of abuse in details while taking up the necessary amendments to the Statutes.
5. There is, at present, a provision that a country, which is issuing a CL, will have to intimate the TRIPS Council and there will be a separate packaging so that the products meant for the poorer countries do not get diverted to developed country markets. By agreeing this clause, India may well be disadvantaged to a great extent and there is no reason to accept such a stipulation. The strategy should be to build up a consensus on this issue and approach the negotiating table.

Domestic Patent Law Reform

1. Removal of all procedural bottlenecks that might hamper export of generic drugs to the developing/least developed countries.
2. Bringing suitable flexibility in legislation for addressing the probable adverse effects of some licensing practices and conditions have on trade and competition.[31]
3. Facilitating grant of CLs through proper regulatory framework. There are nine possibilities of structuring the

31. These relate to the provisions of Article 40 of TRIPS.

grant of CLs, incorporation of which in the national patent laws would help to develop a competitive environment about the availability of drugs.[32] Effective contingency measures in case of national emergency or other circumstances of extreme urgency should also be drafted.

4. The restrictions on Indians from patenting abroad have been limited only to patent applications for defense and atomic energy purposes. However, the Indian inventor/applicant had to first file an application in India and wait for six weeks to file an application outside India. Alternatively an Indian applicant has to apply for a permit to make an application outside India and wait for such a permit to be granted before making a patent application outside India. An Indian can file a PCT application at an Indian Patent Office. The option of filing an Indian application first, wait for six weeks and file foreign applications is better than the option of filing for a permit due to the element of uncertainty, which is involved.[33]
5. Incorporation of a clear provision in the Patents Act so that no constraint is raised when parallel imports[34] are

32. These nine provisions are embodied in Articles 8 and 31 of TRIPS and include the following: Voluntary licenses registered by patent holder; authorization for meeting the Government requirements (authorized by the Government), A31; CL due to abuse of patent rights by the patent holder, A8; CL for reason of unsuccessful attempt by an enterprise to obtain voluntary license directly from the patent holder, A31(b); CL due to National Emergency, A 31(b); due to circumstances of extreme urgency (health/emergency), A31(b); due to public non-commercial use, A31(b); to remedy anti-competitive practices, A 31(k); second patent for an invention involving important technical advance of considerable economic significance over the existing patents, A31(l). Keyala (2004), p. 8.

33. The Patent Cooperation Treaty (PCT) is an agreement for international cooperation in the field of patents. This treaty is largely a treaty for rationalization and simplification of the procedure with respect to the filing, searching and examination of patent applications and dissemination of the technical information. The PCT system establishes an international system which enables the filing, with a single patent office (the "receiving office"), of a single application (the "international application") in one language having effect in each of the countries, who are party to the PCT and which the applicant names ("designates") in his application. PCT provides for centralized international publication of international applications with the related International Search Reports, as well as their communication to the designated offices. However it is up to the local patent office of each country whether to grant a patent or not. This is called the international phase of the PCT procedure. The national phase follows the international phase.

34. The need for such imports arises when the availability of patented products is not sufficient to meet the domestic demand. However, the patented products available in foreign markets may be priced at a lower level than that at home.

authorised, once the pricing behaviour of the patent holder or supply aspects justify the ground for it.

Trade negotiations are based on a *quid pro quo* rule. In any agenda, India cannot hope to score perfect tens in all issues. There are interesting opportunities and there is a need to decide on the specific path that India will take while proceeding with the negotiations. The last few years at the negotiating table have helped India and the developing world take their stand on core areas of debate. If media flashes have to be believed, even the USA is about to allow generic producers to sell generic ARVs to combat AIDS within the United States. The future is, therefore, for consolidation and seeking out newer benefits.

The need is to raise awareness about patents, their applicability and related legislation within the industry (especially SMEs) and amongst consumers. All attempts to change or improve patenting scenario in India is at legislative level or in legal circles. The fact that patenting is first and foremost about technology is often lost on inventors and legislators alike. The result is that patenting is reduced to procedural matters. Many inventors/scientists may not know what is patentable, particularly given that much of the patenting is about 'incremental' inventions. This leads to confusion about whether their own research is patentable or whether what they are doing is in fact an infringement.

References

Cecilia Oh, "The New Deal on TRIPS and Drugs: What Does It Mean for Access to Medicines?," Third World Network, *Briefings for Cancun*, www.twnside.org.sg

Chakravarthy, S. (2003). "Intellectual Property Rights and Cancun — A Perspective," Rajiv Gandhi Institute of Contemporary Studies (RGICS) *Working Paper Series No. 42*, June.

Deardoff, Alan V. (1992) "Welfare Effects of Global Patent Protection," *Econometrica*, February.

Ghosh, Subhodip (1999). "Agreement on Trade Related Aspects of Intellectual Property Rights — The Impact on Indian SMEs," *Working Paper* for Confederation of Indian Industry, New Delhi.

Gerster, Richard (2000). "How WTO/TRIPS Tthreatens the Indian Pharmaceutical Industry," Third World Network www.twnside.org.sg, Aug-Sep.

Indian Drug Manufacturers' Association (2003). *Bulletin No. 48* Vol. XXXIV, 31st December Pg 9 - 22.

Keayla, B.K. (2004). "TRIPS Patent System and Doha Declaration — Implementation Process by India," *RGICS Working Paper Series* No. 45, January.

Lalitha, N. (2002). "TRIPS and Pharmaceutical Industry: Issues and Prospects," Gujarat Institute of Development Research, Ahmedabad, Paper for National Conference on *TRIPS-Next Agenda for Developing Countries*, held at Hyderabad during October.

Maskus, Keith E. (1997). "The International Regulation of Intellectual Property," Paper prepared for IESG Conference, *Regulation of International Trade and Investment*, University of Nottingham, UK, 12th-14th September.

Maskus, Keith E. (1997). "The Role of Intellectual Property Rights in Encouraging Foreign Direct Investment and Technology Transfer," prepared for the Conference *Public-Private Initiatives after TRIPS: Designing a Global Agenda*, Brussels, 16th-19th July.

Ministry of Commerce and Industry, *India and the WTO*, Monthly Newsletter, December 2003, October - November 2003, September 2003, August 2003.

Raizada, B.K. and Sayed, Javed (2001). "IPR and Drugs and the Pharmaceutical Industry — Concerns for Developing Countries" in *Salvaging the WTO's Future: Doha and Beyond*, in Amit Dasgupta and Bibek Debroy (Ed.), Konark Publishers, New Delhi, Pg 271 - 289.

RIS Policy Brief (2003). *Cancun Agenda, TRIPS and Development — Implications and an Agenda for Action*, July.

Savirimuthu, Joseph (2003). *TRIPS and Public Health — Ways Forward for South Asia*, Cuts Centre for International Trade, Economics & Environment, CUTS.

Scherer, F.M. (2000). "The Pharmaceutical Industry and World Intellectual Property Standards," *Vanderbilt Law Review* Vol. 53:6:2245, Pg 2245 - 2254.

Tancer, Robert and Srinivas Josyula (1999) *Investing in the Indian Pharmaceutical Industry*, The American Grauate School of International Management.

TRIPS, Public Health (2003). "Traditional Knowledge and Geographical Indications," *World Trade and Development Report, Cancun and Beyond, 2003*, RIS-Academic Foundation, Research and Information System for the Non Aligned and Other Developing Countries (RIS), New Delhi Pg 87 - 98.

Website of Organisation of Pharmaceutical Producers of India, www.indiaoppi.com.

Zacharias, Nilesh and Farias, Sandeep (2002). "Patents and the Indian Pharmaceutical Industry" *Business Briefing*, Pharmatech.

7

Reviewing Contingency Measures

NILANJAN BANIK

Introduction

The beneficial effect of free and fair trade is well known. It creates income for the community by reallocating jobs and capital from low productivity to high productivity sectors of the economy. This holds true both in the static and in the dynamic sense. In the static sense we think of benefit accruing to countries trading on the basis of comparative advantage (Ricardian theory), or on the basis of different factor endowments (Hecksher-Ohlin-Vanek model). The dynamic effects of trade on growth depend crucially on the extent of technology transfers or knowledge spillovers, across countries (endogenous growth models and recently, Helpman-Grossman models).[1] In other words, trade plays an important role on economic growth of a region.

Unfortunately over time, numerous barriers have been created to restrict free and fair trade. In the thirties, protectionism became popular, as governments blocked trade with regulations and high tariffs. This was practiced despite protection being a lose-lose policy. The consumer ends up paying more and inefficient industries survived on the basis of infant industry argument. Human resources that could be much more productive in other industries are used in unproductive ones. Successful industries end up bearing the burden of protectionism.

These days subtler forms of protectionism are in place. Most of these protections come in the nature of non-tariff barriers (henceforth, NTB/s).[2] Examples of NTBs include, anti-dumping

1. Current research on endogenous growth theory focuses on quantifying the extent of knowledge spillovers. The two important channels for knowledge spillovers are trade and FDI flow.
2. The difference between tariff and non-tariff barriers is that the latter is non-quantifiable and discriminatory in application.

measures, countervailing measures, sanitary and phyto-sanitary measures, pre-shipment inspection indices, technical barrier to trade, etc. These measures are codified in the "rules" section of General Agreement on Tariffs and Trade (GATT).

World Trade Organisation (WTO) member countries can use these measures to restrict market access but have to use them with cause.[3] For example, using sanitary and phyto-sanitary measures, a country can restrict market access to export originating from other countries on the ground that such exports are not safe for consumption in the importing country. However, sanitary and phyto-sanitary measures becomes a NTB when it is used for restricting market access and not with the intention it was codified in GATT.

The prominent measure among NTBs is anti-dumping duties. Anti-dumping duties are "product" specific or "source" specific duties, imposed on dumped import causing harm to the domestic industry. Under WTO rule, a country can impose anti-dumping duties if the price difference between export price and normal value (price of the good in the domestic market of the exporting country) is more than 2 per cent. Volume-wise, amount of import should be more than 3 per cent of the total import. The rationale with which Anti-dumping Agreement was codified during Tokyo Round of GATT negotiation (1973-79) was to stop "predatory" pricing.[4]

Presently, anti-dumping measures are used more as a NTB rather than stopping predatory pricing rule. Dumping is now seen more as a "state" subject than as a strategy followed by any individual firm. Most recent literatures focus on the NTB aspect of dumping. Ethier and Fischer (1987), Messerlin (1989), Finger (1993), Prusa (1996), Knetter and Prusa (2000) and Clark (1999) mainly focused on NTB aspects of dumping theory. These works mainly look at the anti-dumping measures as practiced by the developed countries/economic

3. WTO was formed during January 1995 as a successor to GATT. It deals with the global rules of trade between member nations. Presently, WTO has more than 145 members, accounting for over 98 per cent of the world trade.

4. Predatory pricing refers to the practice of selling a product far below the costs of production, with the intention of driving the domestic producers out of the market. However, once the low price charged by the incumbents start to serve as an entry barrier, in the long run they raise the prices to make up for the early losses.

groups, like European Union (EU), the US, and Organisation of Economic Cooperation and Development (OECD) group of countries, to restrict market access to export originating from other countries. There now seems to be a consensus that anti-dumping measures are used to promote protectionism and not to prevent predatory pricing policy.

Evidence

Efficient Producers and Anti-Dumping Duty

Looking at the sectors on which most numbers of anti-dumping investigations have been initiated one finds raw materials and intermediate products, i.e. items that are mostly produced by the developing countries. The developed economies, namely, Japan, US and EU mainly specialises in the production of finished goods, and surprisingly, none of the finished goods feature among the most affected items in terms of imposition of anti-dumping duties (Table 7.1).

The five most affected sectors include basic metals, chemicals, machinery and electrical equipment, plastics and textiles. Looking at the leading producers of these items for the year 1998-99, one finds China, Chinese Taipei and Korea, as the world leaders in terms of their export shares in these items. Incidentally, these are also the countries on whose exports maximum numbers of anti-dumping investigations were initiated during 1999 (Table 7.2).

Does this imply that efficient producers are facing maximum numbers of anti-dumping investigations? Given their export share (the bracketed terms) in the world trade one can argue the aforesaid countries are efficient producers of these items. It will be quite irrational on their part to dump products. Given the fact that they are themselves efficient, there is little reason for them to sell at a price lower than their domestic market price, which in any case is low because of their efficient production. Most of these items are low technology items where price plays a more important role in determining the market share than any other factors. And when the domestic prices are themselves low, further lowering the price is rather irrational.

Table 7.1

Initiations of Anti-Dumping Investigations by Sector, 1987-1999

HS Section	*1987*	*1988*	*1989*	*1990*	*1991*	*1992*	*1993*	*1994*	*1995*	*1996*	*1997*	*1998*	*1999*	*Total 1987-99*	*Percentage*
Base metals	20	22	6	42	36	135	78	83	41	39	62	103	107	774	27.5
Chemicals	32	16	19	35	27	52	64	34	31	38	22	26	68	464	16.5
Machinery and electrical equipment	24	37	18	20	41	28	20	13	26	34	34	10	25	330	11.7
Plastics	6	13	13	27	28	40	21	19	19	25	36	30	38	315	11.2
Textiles	6	2	12	17	8	11	30	34	1	23	8	31	34	217	7.7
Pulp and paper	20	2	1	4	14	3	13	4	3	14	34	4	18	134	4.8
Glass and ceramics	2		2	1	4	16	18	7	3	11	11	12	8	95	3.4
Prepared foodstuffs		9	1	4	18	4	2	1	13	5	4	8	3	72	2.6
Other manufactures	2	7	1	4	1	3	17	4	6	5	4	5	10	69	2.5
Minerals	1	4	6	3	17	6	2	4	1	4	3	4	9	64	2.3

Source: WTO Secretariat, Rules Division Anti-dumping Measures Database.

Table 7.2

Five Most Affected Items and the Five Most Affected Countries During the Year 1999

CountriesCommodities	*EU*	*China*	*Chinese Taipei*	*Korea*	*US*
Base Metals	n.a.	21.12 (2)	29.40 (1)	5.66 (4)	n.a.
Chemicals	n.a.	13.16 (2)	12.06 (4)	10.24 (5)	n.a.
Machinery and Electrical Equipments	n.a.	18.28 (2)	14.60 (3)	8.27 (4)	n.a.
Plastics	n.a.	30.09 (1)	23.69 (2)	6.10 (4)	n.a.
Textiles	n.a.	15.05 (2)	15.87 (1)	11.23 (4)	n.a.

Addendum Table: Number of Anti-Dumping Investigations Initiated During 1997

62	*Base Metals*	EU	59
22	Chemicals	China	31
34	Machinery and Electrical Equipments	Chinese Taipei	16
36	Plastics	Korea	16
8	Textiles	US	15

Source: WTO Secretariat, Rules Division Anti-dumping Measures Database and UNCTAD Handbook of Statistics, 2001, United Nation.

Gross Domestic Product (GDP), Exchange Rates and Anti-Dumping Duties

Under normal circumstances, one would expect industry association urging more protection at a time of recession. Governments often reciprocate, as it becomes easier for them to establish dumping during recession. A slump in economic activity increases the chances of domestic industry in the importing country being prone to material injury. It is quite natural to have lower production, shrinking profit and retrenching factors of production during recession. The investigating authority which in most instances is hand in glove with the industry association utilises these evidences as a cause of dumping and imposes duties.

Foreign firms can also get caught because of their strategic response to recession (better known as sporadic dumping in the literature). The firms perceiving a weak domestic demand might offer a lower price. Such an action can also invite foreign authority to impose anti-dumping duties.

Appreciating value of real exchange rate in the investigating country can also help the domestic authority clamp anti-dumping duties. An appreciating domestic currency *vis-à-vis* the foreign producer's currency will mean a lower price of foreign products in domestic market of the investigating country. A significant level of appreciation during the period of investigation makes the task easier for the domestic authority to clamp anti-dumping duties.

Cross-country evidence involving four major users of anti-dumping duties, namely EU, Australia, US and Canada, supports these facts (Knetter, *et al.*, 2000). The study examining anti-dumping filing patterns (of the aforesaid regions) during the period 1980-98, found that both the real exchange rates and domestic real GDP growth have statistically significant impacts on anti-dumping filings.

On exchange rates the study says, *"a 100 per cent real appreciation of the filing country's currency would be expected to generate an additional 45 to 55 anti-dumping filings in the following years"*. And mentioning the effect of GDP growth in explaining anti-dumping investigations, the study says, "a one percentage point decline in the real GDP growth figure of the filing country leads to a 5 to 10 per cent increase in the numbers of filings".

Therefore it is apparent imposition of anti-dumping duties has to do with other factors than with the intention it was introduced during the Tokyo Round of GATT negotiation. Dumping can become successful only if the market of the exporting country is closed or restricted. According to Greg Mastel, formerly a trade policy analyst with the Economic Strategy Institute, "if a company engages in dumping in foreign markets and its home market is open, the price differential will induce the company's competitors or other resellers to re-export dumped products to the dumper's home market. These re-exports would quickly pull the home market price to the dumped price and erase home market profits. Thus, a closed or restricted home market is a virtual pre-condition to a successful dumping strategy" (Lindsey, 1999).

Because of current Agreements in WTO for lowering tariff barriers and phasing-out some important NTB, like quotas, not many countries are now that protected by high tariff barriers or quota restrictions. Hence the basic condition under which anti-dumping duties would have thrived most i.e. under prohibitive tariff and non-tariff barriers, does not exist. There are very few cases where anti-dumping duties have been imposed to stop predatory pricing. In most others, the anti-dumping mechanism is used with the sole objective of preventing market access. Even one of the predominant user of anti-dumping duties, the US, in one of its official submission to the WTO argued, "the anti-dumping rules are not intended as a remedy for predatory pricing practices for firms".

In effect, anti-dumping measures encourage domestic and foreign producers to collude to raise the prices. Evidence shows that firms under anti-dumping investigations prefer to pay anti-dumping duties rather than losing the market share (Gupta, 1999). An estimate by Patrick Messerlin, an economist at the Institute d'Etudes Politiques, in Paris, estimates that because of this pro-cartel effect, anti-dumping duties are generally twice as costly to the economy as equivalent import tariffs (Messerlin, 2000). Only 3 per cent of the anti-dumping cases in the EU and 4 per cent in the US, are because of predatory pricing, in most other cases it is used for preventing market access (Economist, 1998). For instance, the US Department of Commerce assisted tomato growers in Florida by imposing anti-dumping duty against their Mexican counterparts (See Banik, 1998). Instances like these are numerous and as J. Michael Finger, a prominent critic of anti-dumping duties rightly put it, "anti-dumping, as practiced today, is a witches brew of policy-making: power politics, bad economics, and shameful public administration" (Finger, 1993).

Objective of the Study

The present analysis reasons out the NTB aspect of dumping and India's stances for fresh negotiation on the anti-dumping Agreement. The reason why anti-dumping duty has become the most widely used type of NTB owes to its ease of application and effectiveness in its usage. In a period, when raising tariff barriers is prohibitive and resorting to other mechanisms like safeguards calls for compensation to trading partners, it is hardly surprising to see anti-dumping duties being so frequently used.

First, there is no requirement for compensation to the trading partners on whose exports the duty is imposed. Second, under WTO regime clamping of anti-dumping duties is permissible. They are also very flexible. Only some firms in an industry need complain for an investigation to be launched; it can be directed at specific firms and countries and they can be hit with differing duties. Third, it meets the most desired objective of restricting market access. For instance, because of imposition of anti-dumping duties import quantities on average fall by almost 70 per cent and import prices rise by more than 30 per cent (Prusa, 1999). Fourth, with considerable amount of trade liberalisation during nineties, the market opened up, and one way of restricting the sudden surge in imports was to impose anti-dumping duties. There is a direct correlation between surge in imports and imposition of anti-dumping duties. Fifth, imposing anti-dumping duties has some retaliatory effect. For example two-third of the anti-dumping complaint are lodged against countries which are frequent users of anti-dumping duties. And lastly loopholes in the WTO Agreement in anti-dumping has even made the task easier for the members to impose anti-dumping duty at their will.

Loopholes in the Anti-Dumping Agreement

Problems with Interpreting the New Code

The new Code is not yet perfect in the sense that there are still many loopholes in it. The negotiations witnessed a tussle between victims and the users, producers and consumers, where each group tried to shape and interpret the Code to preserve its own interest.

The Code does not take into account the problem arising out of the price comparison. In determining the 'margin' of dumping, it is essential to compare foreign prices with domestic ones. The guidelines regarding this are set out in the Agreement. However, there are some lacunae in the process of price comparison, which are examined in the following section.

Problem in the Average Pricing Principle

In a situation involving a large number of small transactions, the investigating authorities often use the average pricing principle to determine the margin of dumping. Under this system, prices are compared on an 'apple to apple' basis, where comparisons are based on:

a. Either, by comparing the weighted average 'normal values' with the weighted average prices for all comparable export transactions;

b. Or, by comparing the home market prices and export prices, on a transaction to transaction basis.

But this rule is seldom followed. The Agreement permits an exception to this general rule when export prices differ significantly among purchasers, regions or periods. In such instances, a weighted average home market price may be compared with the price of an individual export transaction ('apple to orange' basis). The problem lies in this kind of comparison, where the process is often manipulated to suit imposition of anti-dumping duties. For example, the manner in which US Department of Commerce compare importer's prices charged in the United States with prices in its home country, is questionable. The Department computes average home market price by using the sales data. This average price is then compared with individual sales transactions (not the average) in the United States. Any US sales that are above the average home market value are disregarded. But if any sales are found to be below the average home market value, the Department concludes the imported product has been dumped, and a 'dumping margin' is calculated on the basis of the price differences between the two countries. Moreover, foreign producers can be found guilty of dumping if their selling price in the United States is less than the average world wide selling price.

The process of comparing 'prices' to 'value' is not a simple exercise because the calculations are not simple. It is to be noted, 'value' is based on the producer's cost accounting data according to statutory rules, and it is the area where arbitrary, unfair results can be mandated either by law or can be administratively imposed by the government, favouring a domestic industry. Cost accounting depends far more on judgmental factors than accounting for financial reports because of different ways a producer's general fixed costs might be allocated to individual products.

Problem in the Way of Currency Conversion

Comparing the home consumption price with the export price normally involves the conversion of later into exporting country's currency. As currencies often fluctuate, the rate used for currency conversion could greatly influence the margin of dumping. In order to ensure consistency in the methods used by investigating authorities, the Agreement provides that the exchange rate prevalent on the date of sale should be used for conversion purposes. Despite this, sometimes margin of 'dumping' may become 'significant' because of appreciation in the value of home currency, on the date of transaction.

Problem in Computing 'Constructed Value'

Problems may arise in constructing prices for the 'dumped' products. 'Constructed value' are used as a proxy of 'normal value' when, (1) calculation of normal value is not possible due to small size of the exporting country's domestic market and (2) information regarding price charged by the exporting nation to a representative third country is not available.

The process involving construction of normal value is not that innocuous. Normally the construction is done by taking into account exporter's production costs, other expenses like advertisement cost, distribution cost, marketing cost, etc. and normal profit margins. A problem may arise, in constructing prices for the non-market economies where it is difficult to get data on advertisement cost, distribution cost, marketing cost, etc. Under such a circumstance the extent of dumping depends upon the figure taken by the domestic dumping authority as a proxy for advertisement cost, distribution cost and marketing cost, in these non-market economies.

Problem with Charging Low Prices when it is Rational

The Agreement does not take into account factors, like effect of cross-subsidisation and existence of perishable products. A producer can be alleged of dumping his products, even if he does so by making use of sales from other products to cross-subsidise.

Producers of 'perishable' commodities sometimes may be forced to sell their products at a low price because of the perishable nature of their products. The fresh flower market is a perfect example. These imports arrive fresh, but after some time they started to wilt. When that happens, the flower sellers sell them for whatever they can get. It is rational to sell a wilting flower for something rather than getting nothing. But when they sell them by giving deep discounts, it takes the form of dumping. The new anti-dumping Agreement does not take these factors into consideration.

Hence it is quite debatable whether the pricing methodology is a proper one. There is no special clause to restrict arbitrary and biased construction of 'normal value'. This has sometime resulted in imposition of duties that are based on a 'tainted' version of normal price.

Some Other Issues

The newly introduced Sunset Clause, mentioning the termination period for anti-dumping duties, is not that meaningful. The clause does nothing to bind a time limit for the cases under review. As a result, imposition of anti-dumping duties can continue for more than five years. Moreover, there is no time limit regarding the number of times an anti-dumping duty can be reviewed and extended.

The Committee on anti-dumping formed with the objective to oversee the activities of the member nations, in practice possesses very little power. In case the committee wants to discuss any issue, it has to obtain permission from the concerned member or a company from the member country. The committee can only look at the matters of procedure and evaluation, but possesses no powers to overturn dumping findings. Coupled with this, the panel established by the Dispute Settlement Body, at times, functions in a biased manner. Normally, the panel interprets the relevant provision of the agreement in line with interpreting the public international law. But Article 17.6 of the Agreement specifies, "where the panel finds that a relevant provision of the Agreement admits of more than one permissible interpretation, the panel shall find the authorities' measures to be in conformity with the Agreement if it rests upon one of those permissible interpretations." Therefore, the panel cannot operate wholly independently.

The Agreement is quite ambiguous about the lesser duty rule. Under a lesser duty rule, the authorities impose duties at a level lower than the margin of dumping but adequate to remove injury. The present Code on anti-dumping is unclear about this.

Finally, the consumers are ignored. The new Agreement for the first time necessitates consultation with representative consumer bodies during the time of investigation. The objective is to involve both industrial users and private consumers in investigation of the dumping process. But unfortunately in most of the cases, consultations are not sought from these representative consumer bodies. Even when they are consulted, they are supposed to comment only on the issues related to dumping, the injury element and the causal relation between the two. The wider implications of the dumping action for the consumers, or the effects of an anti-dumping duty on general economic welfare are not addressed. Thus to make the system more efficient and transparent, future trade negotiations should focus on these problems.

India's Negotiating Agenda

From an Indian perspective, the Anti-dumping Agreement has two angles. First, Indian exporters face anti-dumping investigations abroad. More than the imposition of anti-dumping duties, the process of investigations constitutes a NTB and impedes Indian exports. For example, in recent months, Indian exporters of stainless steel bright bars, ropes and cables, wires, unbleached cotton fabrics and potassium permanganate have faced anti-dumping investigations overseas. This aspect of anti-dumping has always been important. Second, products may be dumped into India. Historically, with high import duties and quantitative restrictions (QRs) on imports, this aspect of dumping was not that important for India. But with reforms, import duties have been brought down and QRs are in the process of being phased-out. Therefore, dumping into India has also become important. In recent months, imports in chemicals, rubber, steel, acrylic fibre and industrial sewing-machine needles have faced anti-dumping duties in India.

In the following section, however, we analyse India's negotiating stance from the perspective of being an affected nation.[5] In the appendix we have done a statistical analysis showing how anti-dumping measures are affecting Indian exports. It makes sense, to formulate our negotiating stance in a way so that the exports are harmed less. Some of the recommendations are:

5. This section draws heavily on the earlier work of Debroy and Banik (2000).

a) A *de minimis* dumping margin limit of 2 per cent of export price has been prescribed and no anti-dumping duty can be imposed if the dumping margin is below this threshold limit. This *de minimis* limit is the same for exports from developing as well as from developed countries. Many of the export products of developing countries are produced by labour intensive small and medium enterprises. Imposition of anti-dumping duties, or even the threat of imposition of such duties has a serious adverse effect on the functioning of such units. As a consequence, there is fall in production, heavy unemployment, decline in incomes and increase in poverty levels. In view of the high sensitivity of these sectors to any export disruption, the *de minimis* dumping margin of 2 per cent should be enhanced. The level of enhancement in respect of each developing and least developed country should reflect the disadvantage that the industry in such country suffers vis-à-vis comparable production in developed countries. For instance, the Federation of Indian Chambers of Commerce and Industry has estimated that the disadvantage suffered by Indian industry by way of differential costs of working capital, financing cost of refund of excise duty, intangible infrastructure costs sales tax on local bought outs and octroi amounts to approximately 17 per cent. The inherently high prices sometimes maintainable in the domestic market are not sustainable in exports, and the prices of the latter often represent reduced levels of profitability for the exporters. The price differential of 2 per cent presently constituting the *de minimis* dumping margin is unrealistically low. However, the extent of disadvantage would vary from country to country and its assessment could be a cumbersome, contentious issue. Hence it is better to have an across-the-board *de minimis* level which could be prescribed *vis-à-vis* all developing countries to adequately reflect the higher price levels which prevail in such countries.

b) Article 5.8 of the anti-dumping Agreement presently provides that the volume of dumped imports shall normally be regarded as negligible, if the volume of dumped imports from a particular country is found to account for less than

3 per cent of imports of the like product, unless countries which individually account for less than 3 per cent of the imports of the like product collectively account for more than 7 per cent of the imports into the importing Members. In view of the liberalisation of global trade and in view of the fact that more and more developing countries are entering into what were earlier untapped markets for them; it is necessary to increase these percentages with a view to help developing countries. These percentages should be increased respectively to 7 per cent and 15 per cent in the case of imports from a developing country into a developed country.

c) Since anti-dumping investigations are against specific exporters, the impact of investigations and the resulting duties, if any, are felt by the exporters from developing countries who, more often than not, are very small in size and operations. The cost of defending the interests of the exporters of the developing country Members is also prohibitive and a matter of concern. It is, therefore, important and that investigations should be initiated against developing country member's only if the petition has the support of at least 50 per cent of the domestic industry of the developed country Member. Further, no investigation should be initiated for a period of 365 days from the date of finalisation of previous investigation for the same product resulting in non-imposition of duties. However, if it is established by the complainants that the circumstances have changed drastically subsequently to the finalisation of a case, such investigation should be initiated only if it has the support of at least 75 per cent of the domestic industry of the developed country Member. Further, stricter criteria should be applied for such repeated investigation. Guidelines should be established to define the parameters of 'establishing', 'drastic' change of circumstances and the 'stricter criteria' to be applied in such cases.

d) Article 9.1 of the Agreement allows the investigating authorities to impose anti-dumping duties where all requirements for imposition have been fulfilled. This Article further states that it is desirable that the duty be less than the margin of dumping if such lesser duty would be adequate to remove the injury to the domestic industry. It is a matter of concern that a large number of developed countries, who also happen to be active users of the mechanism, apply duties to the full extent of the margin of dumping. While the Agreements does not make it obligatory for the investigating authorities to follow the 'lesser duty rule' the application of duties to the full extent of dumping margins invariably leads to higher level of protection to the domestic industry which is in excess of the duty required to negate the injury caused to their domestic industry. It would be appropriate, therefore, to have a special provision that the application of the lesser duty rule be made mandatory when a developed country Member is investigating the alleged dumped imports from a developing country Member. In addition, norms and criteria should be established to operationalise the 'lesser duty' route in terms of 'adequacy' to remove 'injury'.

e) The Agreement of anti-dumping has severely limited the role of panels in disputes relating to anti-dumping. Article 17.6 lays down that if the panel finds that the authorities have established and evaluated facts properly, objectively and without bias, it shall not overturn the conclusion reached by the authorities even though, on the basis of same facts, the panel itself would have decided differently. Since developed countries are increasingly resorting to the use of anti-dumping duties against developing countries, it is necessary that dispute-settlement-mechanisms relating to other covered agreements is made applicable to disputes relating to anti-dumping.

In sum, the arguments are the following. Developed countries have been restoring to protectionism and this surfaces through anti-dumping investigations, often through a fresh round of anti-dumping investigations on the same product. Consider for example, Table 7.3, which shows that during the eighties, most anti-dumping investigations were undertaken by developed countries.[6] There must

6. Table from Finger (1993, p. 13). Legal provisions on anti-dumping did not exist in India till September 2, 1985.

be special and different treatment for developing countries. The *de minimis* margin must be increased (for developing countries) and so must the figure for 'negligible' imports from developing countries. If investigations are launched against developing country, the percentage of domestic industry that supports the application must be increased. The lesser duty rule must be followed. If a dispute settlement panel arrives at a conclusion that is different from the conclusion arrived at by the country imposing anti-dumping duties, the panel must be allowed to overturn the imposition of anti-dumping duties. The anti-dumping agreement is not necessarily slated to be reviewed in the course of the Millennium Round of negotiations, due to begin next year. But if there is such a review, these set out the parameters of the Government of India's negotiating position, predicated on special and differential treatment to developing countries. But beyond this special and differential treatment clause, there are problems with the anti-dumping agreements and it is necessary to appreciate these problems.[7]

Table 7.3

Anti-Dumping Case by Source

Year	*USA*	*EU*	*Canada*	*Australia*	*Other Developed Countries*	*Developing Countries*
1980-81	24	37	48	61	3	0
1981-82	51	39	64	54	2	0
1982-83	19	26	34	71	0	0
1983-84	16	33	26	70	1	0
1984-85	61	34	35	63	0	0
1985-86	63	23	27	54	2	3
1986-87	41	17	24	40	5	4
1987-88	31	30	20	20	9	13
1988-89	25	29	14	19	12	14
Total	361	268	292	452	34	34

Source: WTO Secretariat, Rules Division Anti-dumping Measures Database.

First, there is quite a bit of arbitrariness in determining what is a 'like' product. If an exported product is not identical to a product

7. Some of these procedural problems are highlighted in R.K. Gupta (1996) and Nilanjan Banik (1998).

sold in the domestic market, case-by-case cost-based adjustments are made to the sales price in the domestic market and this offers scope for further arbitrariness.

Second, the domestic sales price can be considered if it is 'in the ordinary course of trade'. Thus, low prices charged for sales in the domestic market can be ignored on grounds of these not being arm's length transactions and therefore not in the ordinary course of trade. This serves to jack up the domestic sales price and makes it easier to prove dumping. Alternatively, it can be argued that such sales are below the per-unit average cost of production and should be disregarded.

Third, if the normal value is constructed, there are complicated cost calculations and allocations to be made, for instance, between sales in the domestic market and the export market. If there is a conflict between accounting practices in the exporting country and the importing country, investigating authorities typically follow accounting practices in the importing country. Apart from the fact that Indian exporters often do not maintain accounts book at all, or do not maintain account for exports and domestic sales, the inefficient and non-transparent indirect tax structure makes it difficult to allocate costs appropriately. If such account books are not available, normal value can be constructed on the basis of cost for the same general category of products, those for other exporters or producers or 'any other reasonable method[8]'. Each of these offers further scope for arbitrariness. Incidentally, if required information on costs is not forthcoming from exporters, investigations can be undertaken on the basis of 'best available information'.

Fourth, comparison of the export price and sales price in the domestic market requires exchange rate conversions, and exchange rate fluctuations can influence the comparison. The agreement stipulates that the exchange rate on the date of sales should be considered. But the date of sale can be the date of contract, purchase order, order confirmation or date of invoice, and depending on which it is chosen, comparisons may differ.

Fifth, to obtain the margin of dumping, the weighted average normal value should be compared with a weighted average of export

8. Article 2 of ADA.

prices, or normal value should be compared with the export price on transaction-to-transaction basis. But under certain circumstances, the weighted average normal value can also be compared to the export price for a specific transaction and this can result in higher dumping margins. In addition, in computing a weighted average dumping margin, the agreement is unclear about how negative dumping should be treated.

Sixth, if preliminary investigations establish dumping and injury, exporters may give voluntary price undertakings to revise prices or cease exports at dumped prices. In practice, such price undertakings are any thing but voluntary.

Seventh, the agreement is unclear (a point made in the Ministry of Commerce quote) about whether the amount of anti-dumping duty should be equal to the margin of dumping or less (margin of injury, say). Anti-dumping duties cannot however exceed the margin of dumping.

Eighth, anti-dumping duties are product and source specific. They can therefore be circumvented by changing the customs tariff classification, slightly altering the goods or completing a part of the production process in the country of import or a third country. The anti-dumping agreement has virtually nothing to say on such circumvention.[9]

Ninth, in instances of dumping, users of the dumped product (industrial users or final consumers) benefit from lower prices.[10] These represent welfare gains from dumping. The Uruguay Round anti-dumping agreement, for the first time, stipulates that such users should be consulted. But this evidence is only on dumping, injury and causality, not in terms of welfare gains that accrue to consumers. There are some figures available for the United States.[11] A US International Trade Commission (ITC) study conducted in 1993 and

9. In principle, anti-dumping duties can thus artificially trigger foreign direct investments in a tariff jumping sense. Originally, anti-circumvention was supposed to be part of the Uruguay Round agenda. But all one has is a vague decision of Anti-circumvention and the issue has been referred to the Committee on Anti-dumping.

10. Rather paradoxically, low prices can add to determination of injury. But ceteris paribus, any increase in imports leads to a shift in the supply curve to the right and lower prices.

11. Johnson and Quinin (1995), Matthew P.McCullough (1998).

published in 1995 found that anti-dumping and countervailing duty protection cost the US economy $1.59 billion in lost gross domestic product (GDP). Moreover, the study concluded that when anti-dumping and countervailing duties are imposed on imports, prices for those products, and for their domestically produced counterparts, increase. As a result, the US consumer has to pay more for all these goods, regardless of whether they are imported into or produced in the US. For example, solid urea fertiliser prices increased by 19 per cent, lamb meat prices went up by 10 per cent, and domestic steel pipe and tube prices rose by 10 per cent. In 1987, US consumers paid $23 million more for brass sheet and strip and in the 1984-85 crop year, paid $ 11 million in higher prices for frozen orange juice concentrate. The welfare principles are no different for any other country.

Apart from such welfare losses, given the present provisions of the anti-dumping agreement, it is the easiest thing in the world to prove dumping.[12] But interpreted literally, since all other relevant factors must be excluded, it is virtually impossible to demonstrate injury or causality. In operational term's, most countries therefore establish dumping and have a perfunctory proof of injury or causality. The arguments of this section can be used to contend that the anti-dumping agreement requires further modifications and refinements. But there is an alternative tack to take.

12. Between 1980 and 1988, 89 per cent of cases before the US Department of Commerce found that dumping or subsidisation had taken place, Evans (1995).

APPENDIX

Anti-Dumping Measures *vis-à-vis* Anti-Dumping Duties

Basic Assumptions of the Model

1. The objective of the study is to find out whether it is anti-dumping procedures, or is it the anti-dumping duty that has a more important role for restricting Indian exports.[13]
2. The model is a log linear one. The idea is to determine price elasticity demand for the Indian exports facing anti-dumping duties.
3. Commodities chosen for analysis meet the twin criteria of facing anti-dumping duties abroad and competing with exports originating from four of our main competitor namely, China, Korea, Malaysia and Thailand. This identification is done on the basis of market shares of these economies' exports in world's export.
4. Looking at Indian exports facing anti-dumping duties abroad, they primarily fall under two broad categories, namely, minerals (steel and iron ores) and chemicals. For the present analysis (based on the aforesaid criteria) we select four commodities. First include two chemicals, Amoxycillin and Ampicillin, on which South Africa initiated anti-dumping proceeding on October 1996 and later imposed anti-dumping duties ranging from 8.3 per cent to 12.5 per cent, a year later. Second is when the US imposed anti-dumping duties ranging from 3.87 per cent to 21.02 per cent on Indian Steel Bars. This happened during December 1994. In this case the proceeding was initiated just a year earlier. Third refers to anti-dumping duties varying from 26 per cent to 38 per cent imposed on Indian Hot Rolled Coil and Plate by the Indonesian government. The period was during July 1997. Here, the preliminary anti-dumping investigations got started on December 1996. And the last case refers to anti-dumping

13. Anti-dumping procedures as oppose to anti-dumping duties indicates the procedural formalities that a firm has to fulfill when a case of anti-dumping investigation is initiated against it.

duties varying from 18.56 per cent to 21 per cent imposed on Steel Fanges by the US government during December 1993. Anti-dumping proceeding got started just a year earlier.

5. The effect of anti-dumping duties in restricting our export is captured using a dummy variable, referred as NTB in the model. The NTB dummy is zero before start of anti-dumping investigation and one from the time when anti-dumping proceeding gets started.
6. The exercise capturing importance of anti-dumping procedure *vis-à-vis* anti-dumping duties is done only when the coefficient of the NTB dummy is significant. In case when it is significant, a fresh set of regression is run. This time incorporating data only from the period when anti-dumping duties are imposed. A significant coefficient dummy under newer sets of regressions implies anti-dumping duties as important for restricting Indian exports, whereas an insignificant coefficient dummy implies the procedures as an important factor.
7. The nature of data is a time series one, the period of reference being January 1991 to December 1998. Regressions are based on quarterly instead of annual data to increase the number of observations.
8. The method of estimation is basically OLS (Ordinary Least Squares), but under conditions of auto-correlation, ARMA is used.
9. There is an assumption of absence of money illusion in the export demand functions. That is, export demand will remain unchanged when relative prices remain constant.
10. While estimating, disaggregation is done at a three-digit level for our competing economies and at an eight-digit level for Indian exports. As data for the Wholesale Price Index (WPI) at an eight-digit level is not available, data for the same is taken at a three-digit level.
11. Goods traded at each disaggregated level are assumed to be homogenous in quality. The validity of this assumption is a function of the level of disaggregation.

12. The model specification is the following:

$$\mathrm{Log}X_D = A + \alpha \mathrm{Log}\left(\frac{P_i / E_i}{Pcc}\right) + \beta \mathrm{Log}(GDP) + \gamma(NTB)$$

Where, P_i = Unit value of Indian exports in local currency,

P_{cc} = Weighted average of whole sale price index of India's competitors with 1990 as base year,

E_i = Nominal value of Indian currency per unit U.S. dollar at constant price with 1990 as base year,

X_d = Quantity of Indian exports,

A = Constant term,

NTB = Non-Tariff Barriers, in this case Anti-Dumping Duties,

And, GDP = Gross Domestic Product of the importing nations at constant price in US dollar with 1990 as the base year.

The term $((P_i)/(P_{cc} \times Ei))$ in the given demand function is the inverse of Indian competitiveness *vis-à-vis* our competitors' exports. The nature of its relationship with the regressand (X_d), is negative. When the former rises, Indian exports become dearer relative to competitor's exports and consequently demand falls.

The coefficient α captures price elasticity demand of Indian export *vis-à-vis* our competitors. Therefore, after running the regression, if α turns out to be greater than unity, this implies our exports are competitive. The opposite implies for α having values lesser than one.

The variable GDP affects both Indian and competitor's exports in the same way. With a rise in GDP one can expect an upward shift in export demand function. Hence the relation is positive in this case. The coefficient β reflects income elasticity of demand for Indian exports.

The constant term A in the demand function captures mean residual effect of all other variables affecting demand for Indian exports.

The term γ captures the effect of NTB on Indian exports. The nature of its relationship with dependent variable is negative, as it restricts exports.

Data

Prices of Indian exports have been proxied by unit values of these commodities. Data on Indian exports are taken from Foreign Trade Statistics of India, Principle Commodities and Countries, Directorate General of Commercial Intelligence and Statistics, Ministry of Commerce (MoC)., Government of India. WPI Quarterly data of our competitors are source from International Financial Statistics, IMF publications. Same source is used for getting GDP data. Data on Anti-dumping Duties are obtained from MoC.

Regression Results

The regression results regarding Indian export demand function are as follows:

Table 7.4

Commodities	*Constant*	*Price Elasticity*	*NTB Coefficient*	*Income Elasticity*	R^2	*Adj.* R^2	*D-W*	*Method of Estimation*
Amoxycillin and Ampicillin	12.03 (-)	-1.06 (**)	-0.45 (-)	1.26 (*)	0.742	0.705	1.85	OLS
Stainless Steel Fanges	10.09 (*)	-2.33 (***)	-1.26 (**)	3.21 (**)	0.61	0.56	1.54	AR(1)
Stainless Steel Bars	1.36 (**)	-0.45 (-)	-3.83 (***)	1.95 (-)	0.53	0.48	1.67	AR(1)
Hot Rolled Coil	18.96 (**)	-1.87 (**)	-4.26 (*)	1.27 (**)	0.56	0.52	1.96	OLS

Table 7.5

Commodities	*Constant*	*Price Elasticity*	*NTB Coefficient*	*Income Elasticity*	R^2	*Adj.* R^2	*D-W*	*Method of Estimation*
Stainless Steel Fanges	19.36 (-)	-1.88 (*)	-3.22 (-)	3.21 (**)	0.58	0.54	1.82	AR(1)
Stainless Steel Bars	16.96 (*)	-0.45 (-)	-0.86 (-)	1.98 (-)	0.43	0.39	1.58	AR(1)
Hot Rolled Coil	1.69 (*)	-1.87 (**)	-1.61 (-)	1.27 (**)	0.56	0.52	1.96	OLS

Note: (*)⇒ the given coefficient is significant at 1 per cent level; (**)⇒ the coefficient is significant at 5 per cent level of significance; (***)⇒the coefficient is significant at 10 per cent level of significance; And (-)⇒ the coefficient is not significant.

Table 7.5 reflects carry forward exercise of Table 7.4 and consists of commodities having significant NTB coefficient in Table 7.4.

Inferences

1. Anti-dumping procedures and not the duties are more important in restricting Indian exports. This becomes evident from Table 15 reflecting insignificant dummy coefficient in all the cases.
2. New set of regression is not run for Amoxycillin and Ampicillin as the NTB coefficient is not significant. Here the price and income factors seem to play a more important role in determining its export performance.
3. Almost all the chosen products are price and income elastic, implying there is a demand for the same from our buyers.
4. Barring Stainless Steel Bars, in all other products we are price competitive relative to our competitors'.
5. Some data in the samples shows the presence of lag correlation in the series. This has been taken care by estimating the coefficient using ARMA process.
6. In all cases Durbin Watson "d" statistics is well above their lower limits, suggesting absence of positive first order serial correlation in the estimation process. This holds true at all the three (1 per cent, 5 per cent and 10 per cent) level of significance.

Reference

Banik, Nilanjan (1998). "Anti-dumping Measures – An Indian Perspective," *RGICS International Economic Relations Series* Number 1. New Delhi.

Clark, D.P. (1999). "Non-Tariff Barriers and US Imports from Western Hemisphere Developing Countries." *Journal of Social and Economic Studies*. Volume 48.

Debroy, Bibek and Banik, Nilanjan (2000). *Dumping Issue*. Global Business Review. Sage Publication. Volume 1. International Management Institute. New Delhi.

Eithier, W.J., and R.D. Fischer (1987). "The New Protectionism." *Journal of International Economic Integration*. Volume 2.

Evans, Phillip (1995). *Unpacking the GATT: A Step by Step Guide to the Uruguay Round*. Washington D.C. Consumers International.

Finger, Michael J. (1993). "Anti-dumping is Where the Action Is" in J. Michael Finger (ed.), *Anti-dumping: How it Works and Who Gets Hurts*. Ann Arbor: University of Michigan Press.

Gupta, Poonam (1999). "Why Do Firms Pay Anti-dumping Duty?" *IMF Working Paper* Number 99/166.

Gupta, R.K. (1996). *Anti-dumping and Countervailing Measures: The Complete Reference*. New Delhi: Response Books.

Johnson, Brayan T. and Robert P. Quinn. 3 October (1995). "Abolish America's Costly Anti-dumping Laws." The Heritage Foundation, *Backgrounder Update* No. 261. USA: The Heritage Foundation.

Knetter, M.M., and T.J., Prusa (2000). "Macroeconomic Factors and Anti-dumping Filings: Evidence from Four Countries." National Bureau of Economic Research. *Working Paper Number W8010*.

Lindsey, Brink (1999). *The U.S. Anti-dumping Law: Rhetoric versus Reality*. CATO Institute. Trade Policy Analysis Number 7.

Messerlin, P. (1989) *GATT Inconsistent Outcomes of GATT Consistent Laws: The Long Term Evolution of the EC Anti-dumping Laws*. Mimeo.

McCullough, Mathew P. 18 September (1998). "Protectionism by Any Other Name," Washington Post.

T., Prusa (1996). "The Trade Effects of U.S. Anti-dumping Actions," National Bureau of Economic Research. *Working Paper Number W5440*.

8

Export Performance in the Non-Agriculture Sector

PAVEL CHAKRAVARTY

Introduction

The non-agricultural sector comprises the bulk of the trade items amongst all the items that are traded. The textile and clothing sector has been excluded from this discussion of non-agricultural exports, as there is a chapter dedicated to it specifically. This chapter deals with manufacturing items, pharmaceutical goods, fertilisers, jewellery, mineral fuels and host of other items. The non- agricultural sector mainly constitutes the industrial goods.

Table 8.1

Non-agricultural Exports Before and After WTO

Year	*Non-agricultural Exports (US $ Million)*	*Non-agricultural Imports (US $ Million)*	*Export-surplus (US $ Million)*
1990-91	6364.26	20761.06	-14396.8
1991-92	7137.03	17319.15	-10182.1
1992-93	7858.21	18812.27	-10954.1
1993-94	10842.14	21929.44	-11087.3
1994-95	14908.94	26892.59	-11983.7
1995-96	17535.08	35095.01	-17559.9
1996-97	17886.03	37242.43	-19356.4
1997-98	19787.36	39332.58	-19545.2
1998-99	18702.69	38970.77	-20268.1
1999-00	21910.49	43782.45	-21872.0
2000-01	27935.44	48394.79	-20459.4
2001-02	28495.26	48762.24	-20267.0
2002-03	35259.85	58243.75	-22983.9

Table 8.2

List of Major Export Items at 2-Digit Level in the Post-Reform Period

Code	Name	Average Percentage Share (Post-reform)
71	Natural or cultured pearls, precious or semi-precious stones, precious metals, metals clad with precious metal and articles thereof; imitation jewellery; coin.	17.44
26	Ores, slag and ash.	9.62
42	Articles of leather, saddlery and harness; travel goods, handbags and similar containers articles of animal gut (other than silk-worm gut).	7.66
84	Nuclear reactors, boilers, machinery and mechanical appliances; parts thereof.	6.06
64	Footwear, gaiters and the like; parts of such articles.	5.46
87	Vehicles other than railway or tramway rolling stock, and parts and accessories thereof.	5.40
41	Raw hides and skins (other than furs, skins) and leather.	5.01
30	Pharmaceutical products.	4.14
63	Other made up textile articles; sets; worn clothing and worn textile articles; rags.	3.93
99	Miscellaneous goods.	3.60

Table 8.3

List of Major Export Items at 2-Digit Level in the Pre-Reform Period

Code	Name	Average Percentage Share (Pre-WTO)
71	Natural or cultured pearls, precious or semi-precious stones, precious metals, metals clad with precious metal and articles thereof; imitation jewellery; coin.	24.32
42	Articles of leather, saddlery and harness; travel goods, handbags and similar containers articles of animal gut (other than silk-worm gut).	5.93
84	Nuclear reactors, boilers, machinery and mechanical appliances; parts thereof.	5.37

Contd...

...Contd...

Code	*Name*	*Average Percentage Share (Pre-WTO)*
87	Vehicles other than railway or tramway rolling stock, and parts and accessories thereof.	5.29
72	Iron and steel.	5.07
26	Ores, slag and ash.	4.33
64	Footwear, gaiters and the like; parts of such articles.	4.30
29	Organic Chemicals	3.93
63	Other made up textie articles; sets; worn clothing and worn textile articles; rags.	3.89
30	Pharmaceutical products.	3.63

Table 8.4

List of Major Export Items at 2-Digit Level in the Pre-WTO Period

Code	*Name*	*Average Percentage Share (Post-WTO)*
71	Natural or cultured pearls, precious or semi-precious stones, precious metals, metals clad with precious metal and articles thereof; imitation jewellery; coin.	28.85
27	Mineral fuels, mineral oils and products or their distillation; bituminous substances; mineral waxes.	10.84
29	Organic Chemicals	5.63
84	Nuclear reactors, boilers, machinery and mechanical appliances; parts thereof.	5.41
72	Iron and steel.	4.55
85	Electrical machinery and equipment and parts thereof; sound recorders and reproducers, television image and sound recorders and reproducers, and parts and accessories of articles.	4.44
99	Miscellaneous goods.	3.03
30	Pharmaceutical products.	3.77
63	Other textile articles; sets; worn clothing and worn textile articles; rags.	4.07
73	Articles of iron or steel	3.02

Table 8.5

Identification of Sensitive Non-agricultural Exports at the 6-Digit Level on the Basis of Average Percentage Share

Code	*Name*	*Average Percentage Share*	*Rank*
710239	Other non-industrial diamonds	54.19	1
711319	Articles of jewellery and parts thereof of other precious metal, whether or not plated or clad with precious metal.	9.83	2
300490	Other medicaments (excluding goods of heading 3002,3005,3006) consisting of mixed or unmixed products for therapeutic or prophylactic uses, put up in measured doses or in forms of packings for retail UNIT	4.90	3
999300	Special transactions and commodities not classified according to kind.	4.73	4
294200	Other organic compounds.	4.30	5
999190	Other handicraft goods, as artware.	4.16	6
630492	Other furnishing articles, not knitted or crocheted, of cotton	3.84	7
630790	Other madeup articles	2.48	8
73239300	Other household articles of stainless steel	1.46	9
72104100	Corrugated products of iron or non-alloy steel, otherwise plated/coated with zinc, of a width of 600 mm or more	1.23	10
		100	

Table 8.6

India's Major Export Destinations of the Items in Non-agricultural Category Identified on the Basis of Average Percentage Share

Exporting Country	*Importing Country*	*Code*	*Name*	*Average Percentage Share*
India	USA	294200	Other organic compounds.	9.35
India	Germany	294200	Other organic compounds.	4.77
India	Canada	294200	Other organic compounds.	2.10
Total				**100**

Contd...

...Contd...

Exporting Country	*Importing Country*	*Code*	*Name*	*Average Percentage Share*
India	USA	300490	Other medicaments (excluding goods of heading 3002,3005,3006) consisting of mixed or unmixed products for therapeutic or prophylactic uses, put up in measured doses or in forms of packing for retail UNIT	6.52
India	Russia	300490	Other medicaments (excluding goods of heading 3002,3005,3006) consisting of mixed or unmixed products for therapeutic or prophylactic uses, put up in measured doses or in forms of packing for retail UNIT	4.95
Total				**100**
India	USA	630492	Other furnishing articles, not knitted or crocheted, of cotton	22.77
India	UK	630492	Other furnishing articles, not knitted or crocheted, of cotton	4.53
				100
India	USA	630790	Other madeup articles	17.61
India	UK	630790	Other madeup articles	4.16
India	Germany	630790	Other madeup articles	3.42
Total				**100**
India	USA	710239	Other non-industrial diamonds	16.33
India	Hong Kong	710239	Other non-industrial diamonds	13.01
India	Belgium	710239	Other non-industrial diamonds	6.94
Total				**100**
India	USA	711319	Articles of jewellery and parts thereof of other precious metal, whether or not plated or clad with precious metal.	28.32

Contd...

...Contd...

Exporting Country	*Importing Country*	*Code*	*Name*	*Average Percentage Share*
India	UAE	711319	Articles of jewellery and parts thereof of other precious metal, whether or not plated or clad with precious metal.	8.97
India	UK	711319	Articles of jewellery and parts thereof of other precious metal, whether or not plated or clad with precious metal.	4.91
Total				100
India	USA	999190	Other handicraft goods, as artware.	21.73
India	UK	999190	Other handicraft goods, as artware.	4.92
India	Germany	999190	Other handicraft goods, as artware.	3.21
Total				100
India	Egypt	999300	Special transactions and commodities not classified according to kind.	6.82
India	Singapore	999300	Special transactions and commodities not classified according to kind.	6.73
India	UAE	999300	Special transactions and commodities not classified according to kind.	5.72
Total				100
India	UAE	72104100	Corrugated products of iron or non-alloy steel, otherwise plated/coated with zinc, of a width of 600 mm or more	9.15
India	USA	72104100	Corrugated products of iron or non-alloy steel, otherwise plated/coated with zinc, of a width of 600 mm or more	8.03
India	China	72104100	Corrugated products of iron or non-alloy steel, otherwise plated/coated with zinc, of a width of 600 mm or more	7.93
India	Ethiopia	72104100	Corrugated products of iron or non-alloy steel, otherwise plated/coated with zinc, of a width of 600 mm or more	5.21
Total				100

Contd...

...Contd...

Exporting Country	*Importing Country*	*Code*	*Name*	*Average Percentage Share*
India	USA	73239300	Other household articles of stainless steel	9.11
India	UAE	73239300	Other household articles of stainless steel	7.85
India	UK	73239300	Other household articles of stainless steel	3.10
India	Nigeria	73239300	Other household articles of stainless steel	3.04
India	Bangladesh	73239300	Other household articles of stainless steel	2.03
Total				**100**

Table 8.7

List of Selected Non-agricultural Sensitive Import Commodities at the 6-Digit Level on the Basis of Average Percentage Share

Code	*Name*	*Average Percentage Share*	*Rank*
71023100	Non-industrial diamonds unworked/ simply sawn cleaved or bruted	33.00	1
71081200	Other non-monetary unwrought forms of gold	25.55	2
271000	Petroleum oils and oils obtained from bituminous minerals, other than crude; preparations not elsewhere specified or included, containing by weight 70 per cent or more of petroleum oils or of oils obtained fUNIT	9.12	3
270119	Other coal	6.82	4
847330	Parts and accessories of the machines of heading No. 84.71.	4.45	5
852520	Transmission apparatus incorporating reception apparatus	3.67	6
710239	Other non-industrial diamonds	2.83	7
71081300	Other non-monetary semi manufactured forms of gold	2.31	8
852453	Other magnetic tapes of a width exceeding 6.5 mm	1.96	9
847170	Storage units	1.88	10

Table 8.8

India's Import Destinations of the Selected Items on the Basis of Average Percentage Share

Exporting Country	*Code*	*Name*	*Average Percentage Share*
Australia	270119	Other coal	33.05
South Africa	270119	Other coal	5.82
Indonesia	270119	Other coal	5.53
China	270119	Other coal	3.78
Total			**100**
Unknown	271000	Petroleum oils and oils obtained from bituminous minerals, other than crude; preparations not elsewhere specified or included, containing by weight 70 per cent or more of petroleum oils or of oils obtained fUNIT	50
Total			**100**
Hong Kong	710239	Other non-industrial diamonds	17.18
UAE	710239	Other non-industrial diamonds	12.40
USA	710239	Other non-industrial diamonds	12.26
Total			**100**
Singapore	847170	Storage units	16.12
Korea Republic (South)	847170	Storage units	9.36
China	847170	Storage units	8.72
USA	847170	Storage units	4.76
Total			**100**
Malaysia	847330	Parts and accessories of the machines of heading No. 84.71.	10.24
Singapore	847330	Parts and accessories of the machines of heading No. 84.71.	9.59
USA	847330	Parts and accessories of the machines of heading No. 84.71.	7.61
China	847330	Parts and accessories of the machines of heading No. 84.71.	6.38
Total			**100**

Contd...

...Contd...

Exporting Country	*Code*	*Name*	*Average Percentage Share*
USA	852453	Other magnetic tapes of a width exceeding 6.5 mm	20.07
Sweden	852453	Other magnetic tapes of a width exceeding 6.5 mm	9.24
Germany	852453	Other magnetic tapes of a width exceeding 6.5 mm	4.05
Total			**100**
China	852520	Transmission apparatus incorporating reception apparatus	15.63
Korea Republic (South)	852520	Transmission apparatus incorporating reception apparatus	14.31
Sweden	852520	Transmission apparatus incorporating reception apparatus	5.87
USA	852520	Transmission apparatus incorporating reception apparatus	5.80
Total			**100**
Belgium	71023100	Non-industrial diamonds unworked/simply sawn cleaved or bruted	28.99
UK	71023100	Non-industrial diamonds unworked/simply sawn cleaved or bruted	11.96
Hong Kong	71023100	Non-industrial diamonds unworked/simply sawn cleaved or bruted	3.13
Total			**100**
South Africa	71081200	Other non-monetary unwrought forms of gold	22.80
Switzerland	71081200	Other non-monetary unwrought forms of gold	20.27
Total			**100**
Switzerland	71081300	Other non-monetary semi manufactured forms of gold	20.83
South Africa	71081300	Other non-monetary semi manufactured forms of gold	16.28
UAE	71081300	Other non-monetary semi manufactured forms of gold	6.27
			100

Performance of Imports After Removal of Quantitative Restrictions:

One of the most important policy instruments to control trade had been the system of quotas, which limit the volume of imports to some specified quantity in a specified time period, that volume being less than the usual volume of trade. The effect of quota is of course to raise the domestic price once it restricts the supply to the domestic market and in many ways the welfare effects of a quota are identical to those of a tariff. While the exporting countries may agree to join a Voluntary Export Restraints (VER) scheme rather than a to face a tariff or a quota, it is so not clear from a purely economic point of view why the government of the importing country might favor some form of quantitative restriction rather than a tariff. There was however the important difference that with a tariff there is redistribution from consumers to the government (tax payers) whereas with a quota the redistribution is from consumers to holders of the import licenses. On these grounds one would probably rank tariff as preferable to quota, since it is likely that the quota will lead to a more unequal distribution of income within the economy.

But currently as a consequence of the trade liberalisation policy in 1991, the government has gradually moved away from quantitative restrictions on imports, to make the Indian market equally competitive with the global market and because of growing confidence about the competitiveness of Indian products. In this section we examine how certain products have fared after the removal of quantitative restrictions The total number of tariff lines as on April 1,1996 was 10202. But out of these 10202 tariff lines, the number of tariff lines that were freed as on April 1996 was 6161. Then in the aftermath of WTO, India started to remove its Quantity Restrictions from various products. In 1997-98 391 tariff lines were freed. But on August 1,1998 1429 tariff lines were preferentially freed for imports from the SAARC countries due to signing of some regional trade agreements. In recent years as in 1998-99 the Indian government has removed quantitative restriction from 894 items. In 2000 and 2001, the government withdrew quota protection from 715 items.

The removal of quotas and the cutting down of tariffs have not led to the realisation of fears that India would be de-industrialised.

Nor for that matter have hopes of sustained growth been vindicated. Some of what has been discussed is along lines that could be predicted. Indian exports in labour–intensive goods have done well. But exports of pharmaceuticals have done well too. In the same vein the removal of quantitative restrictions have first seen a sudden rise of imports of certain goods accompanied by a tapering off growth. Sustained rise of imports have been seen for only those commodities that are related to infrastructure.

We end by presenting a table that gives the growth rate of exports of the top 10 exported items (by value).

Table 8.9

Average Percentage Share and Annual Average Growth Rate of the Leading Non-Agricultural Export Items According to Average Percentage Share

Code	*Name*	*Average Per cent Share*	*Annual Average GR*
71	Natural or cultured pearls, precious or semi-precious stones, precious metals, metals clad with precious metal and articles thereof; imitation jewellery; coin.	25.85	22.45
27	Mineral fuels, mineral oils and products or their distillation; bituminous substances; mineral waxes.	7.69	298.25
29	Organic Chemicals	5.83	26.48
84	Nuclear reactors, boilers, machinery and mechanical appliances; parts thereof.	5.21	13.74
72	Iron and steel.	4.37	26.65
85	Electrical machinery and equipment and parts thereof; sound recorders and reproducers, television image and sound recorders and reproducers, and parts and accessories of articles.	4.29	22.11
99	Miscellaneous goods.	3.90	14.69
30	Pharmaceutical products.	3.85	15.95
63	Other made up textile articles; sets; worn clothing and worn textile articles; rags.	3.74	15.15
73	Articles of iron or steel	3.41	14.67

Source: WTO Secretariat, Rules Division Anti-dumping Measures Database.

Section III

Barriers to Trade: A Topical Analysis

This section deals with explicit and non-explicit barriers to trade.

Els Reynaers states that tensions between two equally legitimate goals of liberalised trade and environmental protection have existed for at least a century. Since then, environmental concerns have expanded from occupational health and public safety concerns to a broad range of ecological and global concerns. Although trade agreements and international environmental agreements have long been negotiated, adopted, implemented and studied in their respective realms, the last decade has seen an intensified focus on how these otherwise separately operating regimes may at times not only cooperate but also be in conflict with one another. Indeed, until the 1990s the conflict between trade and the environment did not become a prominent issue within the GATT/WTO setting. Reynaers focuses on one of the three trade and environment negotiating items that has been included in current WTO trade round, to know, the relationship between existing WTO rules and specific trade obligations set out in Multilateral Environmental Agreements and concludes that, "environment" is actually entering through the backdoor of the WTO – not in any WTO agreement but via its dispute settlement mechanism.

Although the developed country attempt to bring labour standard related issues under the WTO purview did not bear fruit in the Seattle ministerial, the issue has surfaced occasionally afterwards. K. D. Raju, focusing on the core labour standard issues and Indian perspectives, has concluded that any attempt to link labour standards with the WTO is objectionable as it is not the right forum to deal this issue. On the other hand, the paper argues in favour of ratification of the core labour standard conventions of the ILO by the Government of India.

The protection of environment had been a major concern area under the WTO, right from the beginning, and sanction on the environmentally hazardous products was permissible under its directive. However, from time to time, it has been proved that several countries are using this provision as a disguised non-tariff barrier. Nivedita Dutta, Mayank Sinha and Upasna Gaur have focused on the international concerns, and identified certain key areas, where India needs to focus and adopt a proactive strategy in future. The authors have pointed that lack of information is a major source of barriers of this kind, and ensuring transparency would be instrumental in eliminating this problem. In order to negotiate properly in future, the authors have recommended that India should bring own house in order first by upgrading the national system for testing, certification and laboratory accreditation, and improve the environmental safety of its exports.

9

Non-Tariff Barriers to Exports and Imports in India

SAON RAY

Introduction

The most important achievement of the Uruguay Round of multilateral trade negotiation has been the reduction of tariffs and the non-tariff barriers (NTBs). The institutional constraints in the WTO rules limit the use of tariffs and there has been substantial reduction of tariffs in most countries. However the incidence of sectoral peaks of protection in NTBs in most countries in specific sectors like textiles and clothing even after the Uruguay Round has caused concern. This has also led to the revival of interest in NTBs as it is perceived that non-tariff barriers still remain important trade barriers.[1] One of the concern in this regard is the changing nature of such NTBs, since non-discriminatory trading policies are being replaced by discriminatory arrangements. This is of utmost importance since the cornerstone of GATT and the WTO is the principle of Most Favoured Nations (MFN) and the incidence of NTBs erodes this basic principle of the WTO.

This chapter examines the sources of NTBs in the case of India with the objective of enumerating such NTBs. While this survey is intended to reveal the nature of such barriers encountered by India in its trade with other countries; it does not provide a comprehensive list of all such barriers faced by India. We also discuss the incidence of such barriers in India. The chapter is organised in

1. The GATT does not ban the use of all NTMs like ERAs, the MFA, export subsidies and farm production support. For a discussion on this point see Bora *et al.*, (2002). MFA is to be phased-out by 2005 and VERs are prohibited (Bachetta and Bora 2001). They also point out that certain contingent protection instruments have been used increasingly; in 1995 the number of anti-dumping investigations were 156 and have increased to 340 of which developing countries are responsible for 50 per cent of the initiations.

the following manner: in the next section we present the issues involved in defining and measuring NTBs and the problems faced therein. In section III we discuss some of the NTBs faced by India in some of the countries it trades with and the NTBs in India. The final section offers policy prescriptions to counter these barriers and sums up the paper.

Overview of Issues

There is ambiguity in the literature as to how to define and quantify these barriers (Deardorff and Stern 1997, Bora *et al.*, 2002): they are referred to as NTMs or as barriers and even distortions in the literature. Thus the first issue that has to be addressed in this connection is the definition of such measures. Baldwin (1970) has defined them as "any measure that causes internationally traded goods and services or resources devoted to the production of these goods and services, to be allocated in such a way as to reduce potential world income". The problem with this definition is that it requires an estimate of 'potential real world income' or the knowledge of directional movements in income under alternative arrangements (Laird and Yeats 1990). Alternatively Walter (1972) proposed that NTBs encompass all private and government polices that distort the volume, commodity composition and direction of goods and services. One problem that arises in this case is what constitutes a trade distortion: some practices followed by firms and governments may not be considered as NTBs although they may distort trade e.g. measures to affect product differentiation through advertising. Lloyd (1974) has defined non-tariff barriers as set of government policy instruments and practices which directly or indirectly restrain imports or distort exports. Lloyd says that it is conventional to exclude from such measures exchange rate changes and other monetary and fiscal measures that are used to maintain external balance.

The next question that needs to be asked is why are such measures applied? The objective is usually some long term measure like promotion of industrial and regional development (Bora *et al.*, 2002). In considering NTBs, it is interesting to ask why governments may prefer them over tariffs. While there may not be a single answer to this, Deardorff (1987) suggests some possible explanations that include: institutional constraints that are built into the GATT/WTO rules and into national constitutions that limit the use of tariffs; the roles of firms and workers in influencing the choice of policies; considerations of reaction to or retaliation against the policies of trading partners; and uncertainty about the ways in which different policies may perform. Deardorff argues that the last of these explanations is the most plausible in so far as governments perceive that tariffs will not work effectively in reducing imports. If the objective is to assist firms and workers who purportedly are being injured by imports, he shows that only an explicit quantitative (non-tariff) restriction can be relied on in an uncertain world.

Models of trade barriers explain such barriers through political and economic reasons. Baldwin (1982) analyses political motivations for trade protection while Magee, Brock and Young (1989) present a survey of models where political factors affect trade policy. The central idea in these models is that the structure of the political system is an important determinant of trade protection with the consumers and producers in the economy having different interests. This is due to the fact that the benefits of trade protection accrue to a small group in the protected industry while the costs are spread to larger group of consumers in the economy. Hillman (1982) captures an aspect of this behaviour through the welfare of consumers who suffer from protection against the interest of an industry seeking protection. Grossman and Helpman (1992) model the process through which interest groups bid for protection. The structure of protection depends on the elasticity of import demand and the ratio of the imports to domestic output. While the first factor captures the extent to which trade barriers distort welfare, the second factor indicates the political importance of the domestic industry.

The empirical literature has examined the causes of such trade distortions through examination of the political and economic characteristics of an industry. Lee and Swagel (1994) use cross country, cross industry data to examine the determinants of trade barriers and find that nations tend to protect weak industries and industries in decline. They argue that industries that are politically important receive protection in the form of NTBs and such barriers as well as exchange controls were more significant as trade barriers than tariffs for trade in manufactures. They find that protection is not specific to particular countries or industries but rather the structure of non-tariff barriers across countries and industries can be explained by sectoral conditions. Ray (1981) estimates equations for the simultaneous determination of imports and trade barriers in the US. Trade barriers are determined by the industry characteristics such as capital intensity, proportion of skilled labour, the domestic supply elasticity and the concentration ratio. NTBs in the US were mainly in the capital intensive and low skill industries. Trefler (1993) estimates trade and NTB equations for the US and find that political factors and proxies for industrial structure like measures of union density and industry concentration have positive impact on the level of protection in the US. Ray and Marvel (1985) estimate tariff and NTB equations for the US, Canada, Japan and the EC as a whole. They find broad similarities in the structure of protection in these countries and although tariff rates were generally low, NTBs undermine this, particularly in the EC.

Non-tariff measures (NTMs) have been defined as export restraints and production and export subsidies and import restraints (Bora *et al.*, 2002). There are a wide variety of such measures and UNCTAD (1994) uses a classification of 100 such trade measures. UNCTAD distinguishes non-tariff measures from non-tariff barriers. The term "measures" is broader than "barriers" since it encompasses all trade instruments that may be used as barriers. The Table A.1 in the Appendix A lists the UNCTAD classification scheme for non-tariff trade control measure of a product specific nature and is categorised into five groups according to the method of operation into fiscal measures, volume restraining measures, import authorisations, measure to control price levels and miscellaneous groups of measures.

The following Table 9.1 from Deardorff and Stern classifies these barriers according to the intent of these measures.[2] Some studies that

2. An alternative scheme presented in Bora *et al.*, (2002) classifies these measures according to the impact of these measures (1) measures that control the volume of imports and include prohibitions and quantitative restrictions on imports and export restraint measures such as VERs, (2) measures that control the price of the imported good like variable levies, anti-dumping duties and countervailing measures. (3) monitoring measures like price and volume investigations and surveillance which are often associated with unfair trading practices and include licenses (4) production and export measures like subsidies either direct or indirect (5) technical barriers which are imposed at the frontier and are standards for health and safety reasons. However most of these classifications are arbitrary as the technical barriers include both price and quantity measures.

focus on the quantification of NTMs are Laird and Yeats (1990), Deardorff and Stern (1988) and PECC (2001).

Table 9.1

Classification of NTBs

Category of Measures	*Kinds of Measures*
1 Quantitative restrictions - measures that control the volume of imports	1. Import quotas 2. Export limitations 3. Licensing 4. Voluntary export restraints 5. Exchange and other financial controls 6. Prohibitions 7. Domestic content and mixing requirements 8. Discriminatory bilateral agreements 9. Countertrade
2 Non-tariff charges and related policies affecting imports	1. Variable levies 2. Advance deposit requirement 3. Anti-dumping duties 4. Countervailing duties 5. Border tax adjustments
3 Government participation in trade, restrictive practices and more general government policies	1. Subsidies and other aids 2. Government procurement policies 3. State trading, government monopolies, and exclusive franchises 4. Government industrial policy and regional development measures 5. Government financed research and development and other technology policies 6. National system of taxation and social insurance 7. Other policies like macroeconomic policies, competition policies, foreign investment policies, foreign corruption policies, immigration policies.
4 Customs procedures and administrative practices	1. Customs valuation procedures 2. Customs classification procedures 3. Customs clearance procedures
5 Technical barriers to trade	1. Health and sanitary regulations and quality standards 2. Safety and industrial standards and regulations 3. Packaging and labeling regulations, including trademarks 4. Advertising and media regulations

Source: Deardorff and Stern (1997).

Two different approaches have been used to quantify these measures: the inventory approach and the estimation of their *ad valorem* equivalents. We briefly describe each of these methods used in enumeration of NTMs and some studies that are based on these methods. The most significant aspect of NTMs is that they are discriminatory and have differential effect on different overseas suppliers. Thus the impact of these measures have to be analysed to assess the nature and magnitude of the distortion created.

The Inventory Approach

NTBs are an important issue in market access since by restricting market access, these trade barriers affect the multilateral trading system. Several indices have been used for empirical analysis of these measures based on the inventory approach. Studies based on the inventory approach include Nogues *et al* (1985), UNCTAD (1983) (developed and developing countries), and Walter (1972) (major industrialised countries). The first measure is the frequency or the transaction index that shows the percentage of import transactions covered by a selected group of NTMs for an exporting country. The measure is

$$F_{jt} = \left[\frac{\sum (D_{it} . M_{iT})}{\sum M_{iT}} \right] * 100$$

where D reflects the presence of an NTM on the tariff line item, M indicates whether there are imports from the exporting country *j* of good *i* in *t* the year of measurement while T is the year of import weights.

Another measure known as the trade coverage ratio, measures the per cent of trade that is subject to NTM for a country at a level of product aggregation. While this measure suffers from the endogeneity of the import value weights; the frequency measure does not reflect the relative value of the affected products and thus cannot give any indication of the importance of NTMs among export items. The trade coverage ratio is given by

$$C_{jt} = \left[\frac{\sum (D_{it} . V_{iT})}{\sum V_{iT}} \right] * 100$$

where D is a dummy variable that takes the value of one if an NTM is applied to the tariff line and zero if there no NTM. V is the value of imports in the item, t is the year of measurement and T is the year of import weights.

The most comprehensive database on NTBs is the UNCTAD Trade Analysis and Information System (TRAINS) including the World Integrated Trade Solution (WITS). The data in this database measure the incidence of NTM and are frequency data. The NTM incidence indicates to what extent the national tariff lines within a Harmonised System (HS) 6 digit classification are affected by 'core' NTMs which include quantity control measures, excluding tariff quota measures and enterprise specific restrictions, finance measures excluding regulations concerning terms of payment and transfer delay and price control measures. It is possible to calculate the trade coverage of NTMs or the value of trade subject to NTMs using this database. Based on this database Bora *et al.*, (2002) calculate that the sectors with highest level of NTM incidence are textiles, clothing and iron and steel while the country with the highest incidence is India and the Taiwan, Province of China (for the latest year for which data is available). Table 9.2 shows the incidence of NTMs as calculated by Bachetta and Bora (2001). They compute NTBs from the exporters perspective for 155 countries using the UNCTAD (TRAINS) database for the major exporters of manufactures (13 countries), major petroleum exporters (11 countries), other developing countries (61 countries), least developed countries (46 countries) and the developed countries (24 countries). The measurement of NTMs in the study indicates the frequency in which at least one NTM was applied at HS 06 digit level to a product aggregation exported by a country or a group to a particular region. Table 9.2 presented below is actually a summary of the tables presented in Bachetta and Bora and it is evident from the table that the frequency of these measures across countries as well as products is broadly similar. While there are variations across the subsectors of industries for the different groups of countries as shown in Bachetta and Bora, at the aggregate sectoral level, no such differences exist. It becomes evident that estimates based on the frequency based measures do not reveal more than being a rough guide to the extent of NTMs in various countries and hence an assessment of the impact of such measures becomes imperative.

Modelling Approaches

One of the problems associated with the inventory based approach, is that they do not provide an estimate of the impact of such measures

Table 9.2

NTBs Faced by Different Regions of the World

	Developed Countries	South Asia	Middle East and North Africa	LAC	Europe and Central Asia	East Asia and the Pacific	Sub-Saharan Africa	Quad*
LDC Exports								
Agricultural and fishery products	48.24	14.87	57.69	34.24	32.93	24.42	18.58	41.98
Minerals and fuels	6.72	3.29	5.73	6.64	6.72	4.52	0.16	6.53
Manufactures	10.67	7.20	10.96	11.68	7.15	5.57	1.74	16.78
Developing Countries								
Agricultural and fishery products	48.24	14.87	57.69	34.24	32.93	24.42	18.58	41.98
Minerals and fuels	6.72	3.29	5.73	6.64	6.72	4.52	0.16	6.53
Manufactures	10.67	7.20	10.96	11.68	7.15	5.57	1.74	16.78
Developed Countries								
Agricultural and fishery products	48.24	14.87	57.69	34.24	32.93	24.42	18.58	41.98
Minerals and fuels	6.72	3.29	5.73	6.64	6.72	4.52	0.16	6.53
Manufactures	10.67	7.20	10.96	11.68	7.15	5.57	1.74	16.78
Major Petroleum Exporters								
Agricultural and fishery products	48.24	14.87	57.69	34.24	32.93	24.42	18.58	41.98
Minerals and fuels	6.72	3.29	5.73	6.64	6.72	4.52	0.16	6.53
Manufactures	10.67	7.20	10.96	11.68	7.15	5.57	1.74	16.78

* refers to European Union, United States, Canada and Japan.

Source: Bachetta and Bora (2001).

on prices, production and consumption. We discuss some of the alternative approaches that try to assess the impact of NTBs. Deardorff and Stern (1997) argue that no typology of NTBs can be complete, since they include a potentially unlimited plethora of policies, some yet uninvented, that alter the price and/or quantity of trade. It is difficult to devise a measure for each of them. Some of the barriers are formal and some are informal. There may be informal barriers arising from (1) administrative procedures and unpublished government regulations and policies; (2) market structure; and (3) political, social, and cultural institutions. The impediments associated with informal barriers may be the result of a conscious effort by a government to favor domestic over foreign interests, or they may be the byproduct of practices and policies that are rooted in domestic institutions. With regard to market structure, the differences between nations in public ownership, monopolisation, the regulation of economic activity, competition/antitrust policies assume significance as they affect the interest of foreign producers.

The trade barrier that occurs due to a NTB depends on many factors which make it difficult to state a single way of measuring the size of such barriers (Deardorff and Stern 1997). In order to fully characterise a NTB, the following factors have to be considered: (1) reduction in quantity of imports (2) increase in the price of imports (3) change in the elasticity of the demand for imports (4) the effect of time (5) welfare cost (6) resource cost and (7) uncertainty.

The reduction in the quantity of imports can be defined in at least two ways: first as a change or actual decline in the quantity imported which depends on the supply behaviour and alternatively by considering the amount of the demand reduced by the NTB if the price paid to foreigners for the import were to remain unchanged (usually in comparison with a free trade price). The increase in the price of imports due to the NTB may raise the actual or the shadow price of imports to demanders. This has further implications for the economy especially if the input is an intermediate input. NTBs often alter the responsiveness of imports in a particular sector to price changes.

For simulation modelling, an important input is the price effect or the price wedge associated with each NTM. This is often called the tariff equivalent of the NTM and is the difference between the free world price of a product and the domestic price which is protected by an NTM. If world prices are genuinely free and not influenced by widespread use of subsidies - they can be obtained from customs invoices or from commodity markets. These can then be compared directly with the domestic ex-factory or wholesale prices of identical products. Sometimes it may be necessary to identify representative products and find comparable domestic products and imports. There is a substantial literature on the tariff equivalence of a quota (Corden 1971, Bhagwati and Srinivasan 1975). Depending on the nature of the NTB, several measures have been devised. Deardorff and Stern (1997) discuss each of these measures and the problems associated with each. The general approach is to estimate the quantity effects of NTBs using cross commodity and cross country regression models to explain trade. This suffers from the problem that the residuals are attributed to NTBs and this overestimates such measures. Deardorff and Stern have suggested alternatives based on elasticity estimation, determinants of variation in elasticity estimates, variations in effects of NTBs over time and the binding of NTBs. Studies based on these approaches have been discussed in Laird and Yeats (1990).

India and NTBs

NTBs Against Indian Exports

A study carried out by the Ministry of Commerce, Government of India based on the UNCTAD TRAINS database on the NTBs faced by India in 2001 examines various aspects of the issue. It lists the various NTBs faced by India from its major trade partners the US, EU and Japan. In 1999, 44 per cent of US imports from India faced NTBs. In value terms, the bulk of these NTBs arose from technical requirements (safety) and labelling requirements (25 per cent and 19 per cent respectively). The other important NTBs were Authorisation (Plants), Technical Requirements (Health) and Inspection Quarantine. The study reveals that the major NTBs faced by world exports to the USA were Inspection (safety) and Technical Requirements (environment), which was mainly on account of automobile exports, which was very low in the Indian case. The commodities from India that faced NTBs in the US were textile items (like woven apparel, miscellaneous textile fabrics, cotton yarn and fabrics, knit apparel), iron and steel, vehicles (not railway), edible fruits and nuts and marine products. However the products from the world that faced the US NTBs were vehicles, machinery like nuclear reactors, boilers and electrical machinery, textile items and pharmaceutical products.

Table 9.3 summarises the NTBs faced by India in terms of commodities.[3] It is clear from Table 9.3 that India faces NTBs on

3. The table was prepared by the Ministry of Commerce in consultation with Export Promotion Councils, Commodity Boards, State governments, information from Indian missions abroad and other international and national sources. The use of business surveys to obtain information on NTBs provide an indication of what traders perceive to be the greatest impediment to their business. WTO (2002b) provides an overview of such surveys.

many agricultural and manufactured items. While the NTMs in the case of agriculture take the form of SPS mainly, it is necessary to quantify the impact of these measures on the Indian economy. Some studies like Mehta and George (2004) have examined this issue in the context of livestock products. More studies are needed to assess the impact on the manufacturing sector.[4]

Table 9.3

NTBs Faced by India

Commodity	*Type of NTBs*	*Country*	*Per cent Share in India's Exports 2000-01*
Agricultural Items			
Spices	TBT/SPS	Most developed counties like USA, some EU countries and Australia	0.80
Tea	SPS/TBT, social clauses	EU, Egypt, Russia, Iran	0.80
Tobacco	TBT	Japan, EU	—
Meat	SPS	Indonesia, Jordan, Lebanon, USA, EU and Philippines.	0.98
Lamb Meat	Tariff rate quota	USA	—
Ground Nut	SPS	EU	0.16
Floriculture	SPS/TBT, procedural issues	Japan	0.07
Cereals	Import policy and TBT	USA	1.68
Mushroom	Tariff rate quota	EU	—
Liquor	TBT	EU	—
Fresh Fruits	SPS and TBT	USA, Kenya, Japan, Australia, China	0.19
Rice (*non Basmati*)	MFN violation	Indonesia	0.39
Milk and Milk Products	SPS/TBT	EU	0.05
Processed Cheese	Circumventing commitments under export subsidies	EU	

Contd...

4. Laird and Yeats (1990) survey some studies especially relating to textiles and clothing for Britain, Australia, EEC, Canada etc. and studies relating to ferrous metals for the US.

...Table 9.3 Contd...

Commodity	*Type of NTBs*	*Country*	*Per cent Share in India's Exports 2000-01*
Poultry Products	SPS/TBT, inspection	Korea, Australia, New Zealand, EU, Latin American countries, Russia, Malaysia, USA	0.11
Agricultural Products (general)	Export subsidies	USA	8.72
Marine Products	SPS and other environmental clauses	USA, EU, Japan, Korea, New Zealand, Saudi Arabia.	3.14
Textiles and Other Related Items			
Synthetic fibre ropes, unbleached cotton fabrics, polyester yarns, synthetic fibres of polyester	Anti-dumping duties, unnecessary procedures	EU, USA	24.35
Cotton bed linen	Anti-dumping duties	EU	
Cotton fabrics	SPS	Germany	
Coir products	Social and environment clauses, TBT	EU	0.11
Chemicals and Related Products			
Pharmaceuticals	Strict registration procedure	Jordan, Lebanon, Bahrain, Azerbaijan.	—
Woven sacks/ bags (plastic)	Quantitative restrictions	USA	—
Plastics	Anti dumping, anti subsidy proceedings	EU, USA, Canada	2.05
Tyres	TBT	Brazil, Mexico, Saudi Arabia, some African countries	—
Glassware and hand cut crystal ware	Certification and registration	Egypt, Saudi Arabia, UAE	—
Engineering Goods			
Steel and wire rod	Tariff rate quota	USA	—
Welded carbon quality line pipes	Safeguard duty	USA	
Hot rolled lead and bismuth	Countervailing duties	USA	
Automobile	TBT/Local content requirement	USA, Malaysia	

Contd...

...Contd...

Commodity	*Type of NTBs*	*Country*	*Per cent Share in India's Exports 2000-01*
Iron and steel inlet grating and iron related products, manhole covers and rings, frames	Government procurement	USA	0.80
Quartz analogue clocks/ time pieces	Certification, Rules of origin	Bangladesh, USA, Tanzania	
Electronic Products	Anti dumping duties	EU, USA	2.52
Leather and Footwear			
Leather products	SPS/TBT, labour issues, procedural delays	Germany, other developed countries, Latin American countries	1.0
Footwear	Provisional safeguard measures	Argentina	0.86

Source: Ministry of Commerce, Government of India.

NTBs Against Imports in India[5]

As is well known, Indian trade policy was very restrictive till the 1980s. In the 1990s, major changes were introduced with significant lowering of tariffs and removal of quantitative restrictions. Several studies have quantified the NTBs in India. Aksoy (1991) has examined the Indian trade regime and the structure of the import licensing regime. Aksoy mapped individual items in the 1988-91 import export policy document into corresponding HS codes at the 6 digit level by matching the product description in the different licensing lists with the individual HS codes for the year 1987-88. He argues that the existing system with multiple tariffs, taxes, quantitative restrictions and controls is very complex and leads to inefficiency. Mehta (1997) quantified the changes in NTBs or quotas using the frequency ratio (per centage of products covered by NTBs using the HS classification for the year 1995). No distinction has been made between the various forms of restrictions. He notes that the extent of NTBs in the pre-reform period (prior to 1991) is

5. The Trade Policy Review of India by the WTO provides in detail the NTBs that remain in its trade policy.

difficult to measure since the government has started publishing the items subject to any NTBs based on HS classification only from October 1995. The estimated index of NTB is 44 for the year 1995. The frequency indices of India's NTB has been calculated for 52 manufacturing groups. For a group of 12 sectors the index is higher than 71 per cent while for a group of 17 sectors it is less than 30 per cent. The index is highest for primary agro based intermediate (76 per cent) goods while it is lowest for other primary intermediate goods (11 per cent). Textile and other primary consumer goods also show a high incidence of more than 60 per cent.

Nouroz (2001) says that India has used quantitative restrictions extensively to reduce imports and proceeds to quantify the same. She uses the frequency and the import coverage measures to trace the movement of commodities under different regimes of licensing for the years 1987-88, 1992-93, 1994-95, and 1997-98. She has followed the procedure used by Aksoy (1991) for the four years under consideration. She observes that substantial reduction in quantitative restrictions have taken place. While 13 per cent of the items were under the Open General License (OGL) in 1987-88, as much as 57 per cent of HS codes were under this category in 1997-98. In terms of the per centage of imports the figures for the two years are 16 and 64 per cent respectively. Items under the canalized category declined from 7 per cent in 1987-88 to 2 per cent in 1997-98. She has also compared the para tariffs for India with that of South America and Asia for the year 1992-93 and concludes that the Indian figures are higher except in agricultural raw materials and fuels.

Das (2003) quantifies the extent of NTBs in Indian three digit industries for the period 1980-81 to 1999-00 using the import coverage ratio. The period was divided into four phases and the industries were broadly classified into the intermediate goods sector, the capital goods sector and the consumer goods sector. The intermediate goods sector witnessed major changes in NTBs in the third phase i.e. 1991-95 with industries where the import coverage declined from 100 per cent to zero per cent (coke oven products, other coal tar products, iron and steel and ferro alloys; aluminum and metal scraps with higher NTBs). Other industries with significant reduction in NTBs with import coverage declining from 100 per cent to around 30 per cent include copper manufacturing, tyres and tubes, refined petroleum n.e.c., plastic products n.e.c. For the group as a whole, NTBs came down from 98.31 *per cent* in 1980-85 to 27.60 *per cent* in 1996-00. For the capital goods sector, the decline was even sharper from 95.11 *per cent* in 1980-85 to 8.15 *per cent* in 1990-96. In this sector import policy in the eighties consisted of banned items and items under the OGL. During the nineties more and more items were placed under the OGL; and substantial reduction of NTBs was undertaken in construction/mining machinery, prime movers and boilers, food and textile machinery, other machinery, general purpose machinery, machine tools and accessories, office and computing machinery, electrical machinery and X-ray machinery. The consumer goods sector has more restrictions than the other sectors and the sectoral average is still high at 33.43 per cent in 1996-00, though it has declined from 98.69 per cent of imports subject to restrictions in 1980-85. Drugs and pharmaceuticals, rubber and plastic footwear and the cotton textile group are the only industries that have a zero per cent of imports subject to restrictions while the sectors that have 100 per cent restrictions are varieties of cotton fabrics, other cotton fabrics, knitted or crocheted finished products, carpets, rugs and floor coverings, leather footwear, leather apparel, leather articles, metal products such as heating equipment, cutlery, ladles, skinners, stoves, cookers, airconditioners, refrigerators, and motorcycles.

Bora *et al* (2002), as discussed above have found that India has one of the highest incidence of NTBs among the countries that they have studied. The highest NTM coverage for India is in textile and clothing (80.58 *per cent*) while the lowest is in iron and steel (0.0); other consumer goods also have high NTM coverage of 61 per cent. However they point out certain problems with the method of measuring NTM; a zero incidence may reflect the absence of data rather than the lack of NTMs. This clearly indicates the limitations of studies based on the frequency method and studies that have assessed the impact of NTBs would provide a better understanding of the issues involved.

Policy Prescriptions and Conclusion

This chapter has examined the issues involved in quantifying NTBs. The evidence on the incidence of NTBs in India and the NTBs faced by India was also reviewed. One important consideration in the analysis of NTBs is that the impact of such measures vary according to the country and the sector. We have seen how the studies based on the frequency based measure suffer from limitations due to the fact that they fail to examine the effect of these measures on the price, quantity or the welfare of a country. What does this mean for the multilateral trading system? Amjadi and Yeats (1995) argue that what the Uruguay Round achieved was the liberalisation of these measures particularly the OECD trade barriers with respect to sub-Saharan Africa. Africa receives important tariff concessions under the Lome Convention. They conclude that the profile of the OECD non-tariff protection facing Africa has changed due to the Uruguay Round. This was dramatic for some countries like Mauritius and Reunion while less so for other countries like Angola, Congo, and Nigeria. The phasing out of the Multi-Fibre Agreement will subject the African exports to aggressive international competition. The tariffication of NTBs in agriculture could also have an adverse effect on the Africa which is a net food importer. Hence an analysis of NTBs, examining one sector or a group of countries alone may not provide the accurate picture for the rest of the world.

While most of the literature dealing with non-tariff barriers have examined the issue of quantification and measurement of these barriers, some have examined the issue from the viewpoint of disputes arising from these barriers in the GATT/WTO. This literature can in fact provide some estimate of how such trade barriers are affecting the multilateral trading system. This is important since apart from an assessment of the impact of such barriers on an economy or a group of economies, it is also important to understand the effect of such measures on world trade and the effect that the removal of such measures can have on the global trading system. Only then measures could be devised to reduce the incidence of such measures from the world.

References

Aksoy, M.A. (1991). "The Indian Trade Regime," *Policy Research Working Paper*, World Bank, Washington.

Amjadi, A. and A. Yeats (1995). "Non-tariff Barriers Africa Faces," *Policy Research Working Paper*, World Bank, Washington.

Bachetta, M., and B., Bora (2001). "Post Uruguay Round Market Access Barriers for Industrial Products," UNCTAD, Policy Issues in International Trade and Commodities, *Study Series No 12*.

Baldwin, R.E. (1970). *Non-tariff Distortions of International Trade*, Washington, The Brookings Institution.

———. (1982). "The Political Economy of Protectionism," in J. Bhagwati, (ed.) *Import Competition and Response*, pp. 263-286.

Bhagwati, J. and T.N. Srinivasan (1975). *Foreign Trade Regimes and Economic Development: India*, New York, Columbia University Press.

Bora, B., Kuwahara, A., and S. Laird (2002). "Quantification of Non-tariff Measures, UNCTAD, Policy Issues in International Trade and Commodities," *Study Series No. 18*.

Corden, W.M. (1971). *The Theory of Protection*, Clarendon Press, Oxford.

Das, D.K. (2003). "Quantifying Trade Barriers: Has Protection Declined Substantially in Indian Manufacturing," *ICRIER Working Paper*, New Delhi.

Deardorff, A.V. (1987). "Why do Governments Prefer Non-Tariff Barriers," Carnegie-Rochester Conference Series on Public Policy, 26, 191-216.

Deardorff, A. V., and R. M., Stern (1997). "Measurement of Non-Tariff Barriers," OECD Economics Department, *Working Paper No. 179*, OECD, Paris.

Grossman, G. and E. Helpman (1992). "Protection for Sale," *NBER Working Paper 4149*, August.

Hillman, A. (1982). "Declining Industries and Political Support Protectionist Motives," *American Economic Review*, Vol. 72, No. 5, 1180-1187.

Laird, S., and A. Yeats (1990). *Quantitative Methods for Trade Barrier Analysis*, Macmillan, London and New York.

Lee, J.H., and P. Swagel (1994). "Trade Barriers and Trade Flows across Countries and Industries," *NBER Working Paper # 4799*, July.

Lloyd, P., (1974). "Strategies for Modifying Non-Tariff Distortions," in H. Corbet and R. Jackson, (eds.) *In Search of a New World Economic Order*, London, Croom Helm, pp. 199-209.

Magee, S., Brock, W., and L. Young (1989). *Black Hole Tariffs and Endogenous Policy Theory*, Cambridge, Cambridge University Press.

Ministry of Commerce and Industry (2001). *Non-tariff Barriers Faced by India and Policy Measures: A Study*, "Interim Findings," Department of Commerce, Government of India, New Delhi.

Mehta, R. (1997). "Trade Policy Reforms During 1991-92 to 1995-96: Impact on India's External Trade," *Economic and Political Weekly*, Vol. XXXII, No. 15, 779-784.

Mehta, R., and J. George (2004). "SPS Measures and Non-tariff Barriers: Perspectives of Small Holder Livestock Producers in Developing Countries," in V. Ahuja (ed.) *Livestock and Livelihood: Challenges and Opportunities in the Emerging Market Environment*, NDDB Board, India.

Neufeld, I.N. (2001). "Anti Dumping and Countervailing Procedures – Use or Abuse? Implications for Developing Countries," UNCTAD, Policy Issues in International Trade and Commodities, *Study Series No 9*.

Nogues, J., A. Olechowski and L.A. Winters (1985). *The Extent of Non-tariff barriers to Industrial Countries' Imports (Report No. DRD115)*, Washington, Development Research Department of the World Bank.

Nouroz, H. (2001). *Protection in Indian Manufacturing: An Empirical Study*, Macmillan, India.

Olechowski, A. and A. Yeats (1982). "The Incidence of Non-tariff Barriers on Socialist Country Exports," *Economia Internazionale*, 35, 2, 3-21.

Pacific Economic Cooperation Council, (PECC), (2001). *Impediments to Trade and Investment in the APEC Region*, PECC Secretariat, Singapore.

Ray, E. (1981). "The Determinants of Tariffs and Non-Tariffs Trade Restrictions in the US," *Journal of Political Economy*, Vol. 89, 105-121.

Ray, E. and H. Marvel (1985). "The Pattern of Protection in the Industrialised World," *The Review of Economics and Statistics*, 452-458.

Trefler, D. (1993). Trade Liberalisation and the theory of Endogenous Protection, An Econometric Study of the US Import Policy, *Journal of Political Economy*, Vol. 101, no. 1, 138-160.

UNCTAD (1983). "Non-Tariff Barriers Affecting the Trade of Developing Countries and Transparency in World Trading Conditions," *TD/B/940*, Geneva, UNCTAD.

———. (1994). *Directory of Import Regimes, Part I Monitoring Import Regimes* (UNCTAD/DMS/2(PART1)/Rev. 1, Sales No. E94.II.D.6), United Nations, New York.

Walter, I. (1972). "Non-Tariff Protection Among Industrial Economies: Some Preliminary Empirical Evidence," *Economia Internazionale*, 55, 335-54.

WTO (2002a). *Trade Policy Review*: India, Geneva.

———. (2002b). *Overview of Non-Tariff Barriers: Findings from Existing Business Surveys*, Geneva.

Appendix Table A.1

Classification of NTBs

1. *Fiscal Measure*	2. *Volume Restraining Measures*	3. *Import Authorizations*	4. *Control of Price Level*	5. *Other Measures*
1.1 Import Specific Charges 1.1.1 Tariffs 1.1.1.1 Tariffs with quotas 1.1.1.2 Seasonal tariffs 1.1.1.3 *Ad valorem* tariffs with specific minimum	*2.1 Prohibitions* 2.1.1 Total Prohibitions 2.1.1.1 Prohibitions of a general nature 2.1.1.2 Health and safety prohibitions 2.1.1.3 Wildlife prohibitions 2.1.1.4 Prohibitions (censorship) 2.1.1.5 Seasonal prohibitions	*3.1 Non-Automatic authorisations* 3.1.1 Authorisations to control entry 3.1.1.1 Discretionary authorisations 3.1.1.2 Conditional import authorisations	*4.1 Minimum Price Systems* 4.1.1 Minimum general import price requirement	*5.1 Technical Requirements* 5.1.1 Health and safety regulations
1.1.2 Charges applied on the basis of declared value 1.1.2.1 *Ad valorem* charges 1.1.2.2 Specific charges 1.1.2.3 Combined charges	2.1.2 Conditional prohibitions 2.1.2.1 General conditional prohibitions 2.1.2.2 Prohibitions on basis or origin 2.1.2.3 Prohibition (except certain purchasers) 2.1.2.4 Prohibition for certain use	3.1.2 Authorization to control standards on compliance 3.1.2.1 Health and safety authorization required 3.12.2 Technical standard authorization 3.1.2.3 Censorship authorization required	4.1.2 Reference import price requirement	5.1.2 Technical Standards
1.1.3 Charges applied on the basis of decreed value 1.1.3.1 Variable import duties 1.1.3.2 Transaction specific charges	2.1.3 Quotas 2.1.3.1 General quotas 2.1.3.2 Global quota 2.1.3.3 Quotas by country		4.1.3 Basic import price requirement	5.1.3 Marking and packaging requirements

Contd...

...Table A.1 Contd...

1. Fiscal Measure	*2. Volume Restraining Measures*	*3. Import Authorizations*	*4. Control of Price Level*	*5. Other Measures*
	2.1.3.4 Seasonal quotas 2.1.3.5 Voluntary export restraints			
			4.1.4 Trigger price system	
1.2 Product Specific Taxes		*3.2 Automatic Authorisations*	*4.2 Price Investigations*	*5.2 Measures to Assist Import Competing Production*
1.2.1 *Ad valorem* taxes		3.2.1 License for surveillance	4.2.1 Anti dumping investigation	5.2.1 Production subsidies 5.2.1.1 Subsidies to material inputs
1.2.2 Specific taxes		3.2.2 Liberal licensing	4.2.2 Countervailing duty investigation	5.2.2 Subsidies to labour
1.2.3 Combined taxes		3.2.3 Automatic licensing		5.2.3 Subsidies to capital 5.2.3.1 Investment grants 5.2.3.2 Research and development grants 5.2.3.3 Product specific accelerated depreciation
		3.2.4 Declaration without visa requirement 3.2.5 Intra community surveillance		
			4.3 Price Surveillance 4.3.1 Price surveillance system	*5.9 Other Import Measures* 5.9.1 Multifibre Arrangement 5.9.1.1 MFA quota 5.9.1.2 MFA consultation level 5.9.1.3 MFA export control
				5.9.2 Additional customs formalities 5.9.3 Import deposits

10

Multilateral Environmental Agreements and the WTO

ELS REYNAERS

Introduction

Tensions between two equally legitimate goals of liberalised trade and environmental protection have existed for at least a century. For instance, the first recorded use of international trade restrictions to protect human health can be traced back to 1906, when an international conference convened by Switzerland adopted a treaty to end the production and importation of white phosphorus matches, believed to cause a "loathsome occupational disease"[1]. Since then, environmental concerns have expanded from occupational health and public safety concerns to a broad range of ecological and global concerns. And as of today around 250 multilateral environmental agreements (MEAs) have been adopted.[2]

Although trade agreements and international environmental agreements have long been negotiated, adopted, implemented and studied in their respective realms, the last decade has seen an intensified focus on how these otherwise separately operating regimes may at times not only cooperate but also conflict with one another. Indeed, until the 1990s the conflict between trade and the environment did not become a prominent issue within the GATT/WTO setting.

---

1. Fletcher, Charles R. "Greening World Trade: Reconciling GATT and Multilateral Environmental Agreements Within the Existing World Trade Regime", *Journal of Transnational Law & Policy*, Spring 1996.
2. See UNEP, The Register of International Treaties and Other Agreements in the Field of the Environment, Nairobi, 1999.

This paper focuses on one of the three trade and environment negotiating items that has been included in the current WTO trade round, to know, the relationship between existing WTO rules and specific trade obligations set out in Multilateral Environmental Agreements. To cover the various facets of this interface, we will first provide a general background on the single undertaking type negotiations, the specific mandate, and put the Fifth Ministerial meeting at Cancun in perspective. The second part provides an overview of the submissions made so far in the Special Sessions of the Committee on Trade and Environment. The third part is aimed at introducing the reader to some of the basic tenets of the WTO 'jurisprudence' pertaining to trade and environment, thereby depicting how a dispute could be approached were it to occur now (independently of the negotiating outcome). This part will also illustrate some of the concerns with the current interpretation of trade and environment disputes by contrasting it with findings of the *US Court of Appeals* judgment in the domestic 'shrimp turtle' case. The fourth part brings forward a crucial piece of the puzzle: the interplay of the negotiating topic with public international law. The fifth and sixth part offer respectively some views on what may lie in store for this negotiating item and some concluding remarks.

Environment as Part of the WTO Negotiations

Included for the First Time

If one were to capture the essential trait that distinguishes the current environment-related discussions within the WTO, as opposed to a decade ago, it would be its absorption within the negotiating agenda of the current round of negotiations. Indeed, for the first time in the history of the GATT/WTO selected environment-related topics have been elevated from mere interesting topics deliberated upon in the Committee on Trade and Environment to full-fledged negotiating items and bargaining chips. What is even more particular about the current round of negotiations, launched at the Doha Ministerial Conference in

November 2001, is that most negotiating items[3] form part of a so-called "single undertaking" negotiations. As under the long-drawn and comprehensive negotiations under the Third UN Conference on the Law of the Sea (1973-1982), the practice of "single undertaking" negotiations or "package deal negotiations"[4] has been adopted within the GATT/WTO regime since the Uruguay Round of negotiations (1986-1992) as well.[5] Single undertaking negotiations entail that WTO Members must agree on all issues as a single undivided package, in this trade round: from agriculture, services, market access for non-agricultural products, WTO rules (such as anti-dumping and subsidies) to trade and environment. Linking of numerous, and even unrelated, negotiating aspects is used to leverage an overall solution between all WTO Members since it creates ample room for 'give-and-take' negotiations between parties. It essentially seeks to avoid negotiations coming to a standstill due

---

3. Doha Ministerial Declaration (DMD), adopted 14 November 2001, directed that the conduct, conclusion and entry into force of the outcome of the negotiations would be treated as part of a single undertaking, with the exception of the mandate to improve and clarify the Dispute Settlement Understanding (see para 47 DMD). See at: "Ministerial Declaration – Adopted on 14 November 2001," WT/MIN(01)/DEC/1, 20 November 2001.

   It must be pointed out that there have been diverging views on the exact breadth of negotiations on Implementation-Related Issues and Special and Differential Treatment, both items for which developing countries are the demandeurs. Implementation-related issues, in the current context, refer to the demand by developing countries to redress the imbalances in the Uruguay Round Agreements (e.g extension of transition periods) that have hindered the realisation of meaningful gains, for which they would not have to offer other concessions under the current round. Developing countries insist that all implementation issues brought forward form part of the current round of negotiations. In contrast, many developed countries bifurcate paragraph 12 of the DMD into a category of implementation issues with a negotiating mandate under the DMD and another category of outstanding implementation issues that must merely be treated as a matter of priority.

   With regard to the so-called four Singapore issues (trade and investment; trade and competition; transparency in government procurement; and trade facilitation) Members agreed in the DMD that negotiations will take place after the Fifth Ministerial Conference "on the basis of a decision to be taken, by explicit consensus" at the Fifth Ministerial Conference (see paras. 20, 23, 26 and 27 DMD respectively). During the Fifth Ministerial Conference it became all too clear that the EC's position according to which the four Singapore issues ipso facto formed part and parcel of the single undertaking was no longer tenable.

4. See Gurdip Singh, *International Law, 2003*, Macmillan India Ltd., p. 241.

5. See e.g. Chandrakant Patel, "Single Undertaking: A Straitjacket or Variable Geometry?," Trade-Related Agenda, Development and Equity (T.R.A.D.E), *Working Paper No. 15*, South Centre, May 2003.

to disagreement on a few topics only, or between certain WTO Members only. Hence, the trade and environment negotiations must be seen against this background: it is one of the many -and also new- negotiating items, and its final outcome will to a large extent be coloured by the 'trade-offs' that will take place throughout the Doha round of negotiations between other (admittedly from a WTO-perspective also more weighty) topics, such as agriculture, where, so it is expected, the EU in particular will have to make considerable concessions.

The Limited 'Environmental' Mandate

Stating that 'environmental concerns' have been included in the current round of negotiations is certainly not precise enough, for the "trade and environment" heading in the Doha Ministerial Declaration (DMD) – that outlines the four corners within which negotiations must take place- only lists three narrowly circumscribed topics. The relevant part of paragraph 31 DMD reads as follows:

"With a view to enhancing the mutual supportiveness of trade and environment, we agree to negotiations, without prejudging their outcome, on:

(i) the relationship between existing WTO rules and specific trade obligations set out in multilateral environmental agreements (MEAs). The negotiations shall be limited in scope to the applicability of such existing WTO rules as among parties to the MEA in question. The negotiations shall not prejudice the WTO rights of any Member that is not a party to the MEA in question;

(ii) procedures for regular information exchange between MEA Secretariats and the relevant WTO committees, and the criteria for the granting of observer status;

(iii) the reduction or, as appropriate, elimination of tariff and non-tariff barriers to environmental goods and services. (...)".

The negotiations identified under para. 31(iii) pertaining to the reduction and elimination of tariffs on environmental goods and services forms is in many respects a more 'classic' GATT/WTO negotiating topic, given that the eight previous negotiating rounds were always dedicated to ever-expanding reductions in tariffs of non-agricultural goods, and that 'services' were included during the Uruguay round as well.

Paragraph 31(ii) is a rather practical negotiating item aimed at strengthening the institutional interactions between international environmental organisations and the WTO. Although there have been very few submissions by WTO Members under this topic,[6] the issue of granting observer status to, for instance, the Convention on Biological Diversity in the TRIPS Council, Committee on Agriculture, TBT Committee and SPS Committee does turn out to be rather contentious.[7] Also, the observer status of international organisations is from a strategic political angle linked to the granting of observer status to certain nations which are not WTO Members. In practice, six MEA Secretariats and UNEP have been invited on an *ad hoc* basis to attend the CTE Special Session meetings (the negotiating meetings).[8]

The focus of this paper, however, is on the negotiating mandate spelled out in paragraph 31(i) on the relationship between WTO rules and specific trade obligations (hereinafter: STOs) set out in Multilateral Environmental Agreements (MEAs), as between Parties to both international instruments.

It essentially addresses the difficulty that may arise when a Party to both international instruments (the WTO Agreements on the one hand and a MEA on the other hand) is faced with conflicting obligations, and where compliance with one treaty may entail infringement of the other international treaty.[9] For instance, under

---

6. WTO, "List of Committee on Trade and Environment Special Session (CTESS) Document", Note by the Secretariat – Revision, TN/TE/INF/4/Rev.1, 21 July 2003.
7. WTO, "Observer Status", Note by the Secretariat, TN/TE/S/4, 31 January 2003.
8. WTO, "Summary Report on the Seventh Meeting of the Committee on Trade and Environment in Special Session – 8 July 2003", Note by the Secretariat, TN/TE/R/7, 1 August 2003. The six international organisations, apart from UNEP, are: Basel Convention on the Control of Transboundary Movements of Hazardous Wastes and their Disposal; the Convention on Biological Diversity; the Convention on International Trade in Endangered Species; the International Tropical Timber Organisation (arguably not an MEA *strictu sensu*); the Montreal Protcol on Substances that Deplete the ozone Layer; and the United Nations Framework Convention on Climate Change.
9. Note that the exact definition of conflict in international law is unclear. For the purpose of this paper the various notions and nuances of "conflict" will not be taken up. See e.g. Joost Pauwelyn, "The Role of Public International Law in the WTO: How Far Can We Go?", 95 *American Journal of International Law* 535-78 (2001), at pp.550-552.

the Convention on International Trade in Endangered Species (CITES) Parties have adopted a practice of "split listing" whereby populations of a species found in certain countries are not permitted to be traded, whereas the same species found in other countries would be allowed to be traded. This distinction from a CITES perspective is based on whether the population of the species is endangered or not. However, from a WTO perspective this may be viewed as submitting different countries to different trade treatment, although the products appear to be identical (or in WTO jargon 'like products').[10] This may violate the Most Favoured Nation principle, a core WTO principle, contained in the General Agreements on Tariff and Trade (GATT, 1994, – Article I), according to which a WTO Member can not discriminate among products on the basis of their national origin (and should extend immediately and unconditionally its most favoured trade regime to all other WTO Members).

Given that MEAs and WTO Agreements are equal instruments of international law, one can not state that a MEA will always prevail over a WTO Agreement, or vice versa. It is a question that necessarily must be scrutinised through the public international law lens (what are the sources of public international law? what does the lack of hierarchy of sources of international law entail? how are international treaties interpreted?), and is in this respect a rather unusual WTO negotiating topic.

From the outset one should point out three relevant facets to the paragraph 31(i) DMD negotiations. First, MEAs often have a large international membership, and may at times be signed or ratified by more countries than the number of WTO Members (currently 146). Second, of the 250 or more MEAs only a few -the CTE identified 32 MEAs[11]- further its objectives via trade measures. Third, the term "specific trade obligations" is a neologism created within the Doha round, and is not found in the general public international law discourse. Third and importantly, no such dispute between MEAs and WTO Agreements has so far actually arisen.

10. See extensively: Wold, Chris "Multilateral Environmental Agreements and the GATT: Conflict and Resolution?", *26 Envtl. L. 841*, Fall 1996, p. 848 and 888.

11. WTO, "Matrix on Trade Measures Pursuant to Selected MEAs – Note by the Secretariat – Revision," WT/CTE/W/160/Rev.1, 14 June 2001. It must be noted that of these 32 MEAs, 17 are regional agreements and that 1 is no longer in force.

Quite aptly Van Calster observes that this negotiating item carries a rather symbolic value as it tests the WTO on how it will be able to relate to other international regimes.[12]

Although trade and environment-related issues have been included for the first time within GATT/WTO negotiations, they were being discussed within the WTO well before that. Indeed, the WTO Committee on Trade and Environment had been set up pursuant to a Decision taken at the Marrakesh Ministerial Meeting in April 1994.[13] Its set-up had largely been influenced by the UN Conference on Environment and Development held in 1992 to which the GATT Contracting Parties made a contribution.[14]

The CTE's overarching tasks were to identify the relationship between trade measures and environmental measures in order to promote sustainable development, as well as to make appropriate recommendations on whether any modifications of the provisions of the multilateral trading system are required.[15] The Marrakesh Decision further listed ten items, encompassing all areas of the multilateral trading system: goods, services and intellectual property that would define the regular 10-point work programme of the CTE. It included, *inter alia*, the relationship between the provisions of the multilateral trading system and trade measures for environmental purposes, including those pursuant to MEAs; as well as the relationship between WTO provisions and environmental taxes, eco-labels, requirements for packaging, recycling; and the effect of environmental measures on market access, especially in relation to developing countries; and Trade-Related Aspects of Intellectual Property Rights (TRIPS).

---

12. Calster, Geert Van "Groen en Poen in de Wereldhandelsorganisatie (WTO) – Model voor de Succesvolle Intergratie van Vrijhandel en Leefmilieu", Tijdschrift voor Milieurecht 2000, p. 294. Reference may also be made to his work in English: J. Cameron, J. Jacobs, G. Van Calster, Trade and the Environment: Law and Policy, London, Cameron, 2000.

13. WTO, Trade and Environment – Decision of 14 April 1994, MTN/NC/45(MIN).

14. It also proved more successful than earlier attempts (a Group on Environmental Measures and International Trade had namely been established in 1971 on the eve of the 1972 Stockholm Conference on the Human Environment, but had remained inactive for almost 20 years). See extensively Hakan Nordstrom and Scott Vaughan, WTO Special Studies, Trade and Environment, 1999 (Annex I – Background Note by the Secretariat).

15. *Ibidem*.

In line with the CTE's broader agenda, the Doha Ministerial Declaration in its paragraph 32 also instructed the CTE (without launching negotiations as such), in pursuing work on all items on its agenda within its current terms of reference, to give particular attention to: (1) the effect of environmental measures on market access; (2) the relevant provisions of the Agreement on Trade-Related Aspects of Intellectual Property Rights; (3) and labelling requirements for environmental purposes.[16] Furthermore, the CTE was asked to report to the Fifth Session of the Ministerial Conference, and make recommendations, where appropriate, with respect to future action, including the desirability of negotiations.

This indicates another important aspect: agenda topics for discussions within specialised WTO Committees are often included with the ambition of integrating them in a more binding manner within the WTO regime, with its exact terms to be agreed upon during negotiating rounds. India, for instance, has always been of the view that existing WTO provisions are "adequate to deal with trade measures taken pursuant to legitimate environmental objectives in existing MEAs", and was –unlike the EC- not in favour of including this regular agenda item in the negotiating mandate.[17]

Putting Cancun in Perspective

After having identified the three specific negotiating topics pertaining to environment within the current round of negotiations, and having touched upon the regular work programme of the CTE (created in 1994), it is worth putting the Fifth Ministerial Meeting held at Cancun (10-14 September 2003) in perspective *vis-à-vis* the environmental negotiating mandate.

Paragraph 45 of the Doha Ministerial Declaration states clearly that the Fifth Session of the Ministerial Conference will take stock of progress in the negotiations, provide any necessary political

16. Paragraph 32 of the Ministerial Declaration – Adopted on 14 November 2001, WT/MIN(01)/DEC/1, 20 November 2001.

17. India, Non-Paper, 23 July 1996; also referred to in: "Multilateral Environmental Agreements (MEAs) and WTO Rules: Proposals Made in the Committee on Trade and Environment (CTE) from 1995-2002," TN/TE/S/1, 23 May 2002. See also: Jha, Veena "Trade and Environment: Doha and Beyond" in *India and the WTO*, Edited by Aaditya Mattoo and Robert M Stern, co-publication of the World Bank and Oxford University Press (2003), p. 303-305, 307-309 and 315.

guidance, and take decisions as necessary. This, as we now know, was far from being achieved. Responding to doomsday-speakers (predicting the end of the WTO) Mr Luis Ernesto Derbez, Mexico's Foreign Minister and Chair of the Ministerial Conference, had to reiterate that the Cancun Ministerial Conference is not about launching or concluding a round, but rather providing the necessary framework and political guidance to allow Geneva negotiators to continue their work towards completing the round by 1 January, 2005. Nevertheless, the set-back experienced at Cancun may not have marked the beginning of the end for the WTO but did entail the work of the negotiating bodies in Geneva to be discontinued during the period of October 2003 to March 2004.[18]

With regard to trade and environment, the Draft Ministerial Text (24 August 2003) forwarded to the Fifth Ministerial succinctly stated that the Members "take note of the progress made" by the Special Session of the Committee on Trade and Environment (CTE) in developing a common understanding of the concepts mandated in paragraph 31(i) DMD and "reaffirm" the commitment to the negotiations.[19]

On the widening of the negotiating mandate on trade and environment issues – with as potential areas: market access, TRIPS, and eco-labels - the Draft Ministerial Text limited itself to taking note of the CTE report and instructing the General Council to report to the Sixth Ministerial.[20] During the first days of the Cancun Ministerial Conference some countries did attempt to include eco-labels as an additional negotiating item, but this proved to be contentious and ultimately premature.

Given the inability of the WTO Members to find a consensus on a Ministerial Text towards the end of the Fifth Ministerial, a mere six-paragraph long Ministerial Statement[21] was adopted requesting officials "to continue working on outstanding issues with a renewed

18. With the exception of the DSU (Dispute Settlement Understanding) negotiations that are on a separate track. See DMD para. 47.

19. See par. 9 of the 24 August 2003 Draft Ministerial Declaration, JOB(03)/15/Rev.1.

20. See par. 20 of the 24 August 2003 Draft Ministerial Declaration, JOB(03)/15/Rev.1.

21. See "Ministerial Statement – Adopted on 14 September 2003," WT/MIN(03)/20, 23 September 2003.

sense of urgency and purpose", taking fully into account all the views expressed during the Conference.

Hence, there was no expectation that a final solution would be brokered at Cancun on the existing trade and environment negotiating items. The only possibility was that some *additional* negotiating topics such as market access, TRIPs and eco-labels could have been included. However, given the overall impasse over crucial areas such as agriculture, overshadowed by the Singapore issues, even this possibility seemed very slim.

What are the Negotiating Positions?

Relevant WTO Rules

Let us first recall that the WTO Members are asked to agree on how the relationship between existing WTO rules and specific trade obligations set out in MEAs should be approached, as between parties to both regimes. This question implies a potential conflict between both international treaties. For instance, what should the outcome be if a WTO Member/MEA Party banned the import of certain products originating from another WTO Member/MEA Party based on its obligations under an MEA, but would still allow trade with third WTO Members/MEA Parties that would for instance, have incorporated certain environmental management practices prescribed by the MEA? Should the obligation under WTO Agreements not to discriminate between like products of the WTO Members prevail or should the environmental concerns contained in the MEA prevail? Also, should there be a one-size-fits-all answer to this conflict?

The interpretation rules of public international law, which will be discussed later, do not allow us to conclude uniformly and unambiguously that in such a situation WTO Agreements would always prevail over MEAs, nor can the reverse be said. Within the Special Sessions of the CTE this issue has mainly been taken up from a WTO-centric point of view and only incidentally been scrutinized from a public international law perspective.

The core WTO rules embedded in the overall principle of non-discrimination between WTO Members and the relevant exceptions that one must be familiar with for the purpose of this topic are: (1) the Most-Favoured Nation principle; (2) the National Treatment principle; (3) the general elimination of quantitative restrictions; and (4) the General Exceptions clause of GATT, 1994.

1. The Most-Favoured-Nation Principle

The Most-Favoured-Nation (MFN) treatment embedded in GATT Article I requires that each WTO Member, with respect to customs duties, charges of any kind, all rules and formalities imposed on or in connection with import or export, provides immediately and unconditionally any advantage, favour, privilege or immunity granted to a product originating from one WTO Member to like products imported from, or exported to, all other WTO Members. In short, a Member cannot discriminate among like products on the basis of their national origin.[22]

2. The National Treatment Principle

Once products have met tariff and other import requirements, and entered the market, the National Treatment (NT) principle of article III of GATT requires parties to treat foreign products the same as "like" domestic products. It directs Member States not to apply internal laws and taxes "to imported or domestic products so as to afford protection to domestic production". Hence, the NT obligation permits parties to impose domestic regulatory requirements on imported products at the point of import provided that the imported product is treated no less favourably than the like domestic product.[23]

3. Elimination of Quantitative Restrictions

The goal of the GATT was to remove all border restrictions and have the remaining trade barriers reflected in the form of tariffs, and subsequently to reduce these tariffs through successive, binding multilateral negotiations.[24] It is in this light that one must read the obligation that no prohibition or restriction (other than duties, taxes or other charges) made effective through quotas, import or export licenses or other measures may be introduced or maintained by a contracting party on the import or export of any product.

22. See e.g. WTO, "Understanding the WTO," 3rd edition, August 2003, p.9, available at: http://www.wto.org/english/thewto_e/whatis_e/tif_e/understanding_e.pdf

23. *Ibidem*

24. Trebilcock, Michael J. & Robert Howse, *The Regulation of International Trade*, Routledge, 1995, p. 30.

4. General Exceptions

If a measure violates a core GATT obligation, a WTO Member may be able to justify it under any of the ten paragraphs of the General Exceptions clause, GATT article XX.[25] The "chapeau" (WTO jargon for 'headnote' that is based on the French word for 'hat') of article XX provides that:

> "Subject to the requirement that such measures are not applied in a manner which would constitute a means of arbitrary or unjustifiable discrimination between countries where the same conditions prevail, or a disguised restriction on international trade, nothing in this Agreement shall be construed to prevent the adoption or enforcement by any contracting party of measures:"

Three such sub-paragraphs of article XX are relevant in environmental cases:

a) "necessary to protect human, animal or plant life or health";

b) "necessary to secure compliance with laws or regulations which are not inconsistent with the provisions of this Agreement, including those relating to (...) the protection of patents, trade marks and copyrights";

c) "relating to the conservation of exhaustible natural resources if such measures are made effective in conjunction with restrictions on domestic production or consumption".

The WTO Member invoking Article XX bears the burden of proving that the contested measure meets the requirements contained in that provision.[26] This is an important aspect for the WTO rules-MEA negotiations as some WTO Members suggest altering this burden of proof (see below).

Furthermore, the Appellate Body of the WTO has explicitly developed a two-tiered test to scrutinise whether a measure can genuinely be justified under article XX: first, the measure must be identified as falling under any of the sub-paragraphs of article XX and only subsequently will the measure be benchmarked against the

25. Other sub-provisions are: (a) necessary to protect public morals; (c) relating to the importations or exportations of gold or silver; (e) relating to the products of prison labour etc.

26. See excellent work by WTO Secretariat, "GATT/WTO Dispute Settlement Practice Relating to GATT Article XX, Paragraphs (b), (d) and (g)," WT/CTE/W/203, 8 March 2002, para. 6-8, 12.

chapeau.[27] This is a logical order since one would first want to identify the type of measure that lays at the essence of the dispute prior to analysing whether it is being applied in a discriminatory manner.

The reason these disputes pertaining to GATT article XX are particularly relevant is because the global trade in goods is largely governed by the GATT. As a consequence, the debate on the relationship between the provisions of the multilateral trading system and trade measures for environmental purposes, including those pursuant to MEAs, as debated within the CTE mainly focussed on the general exception contained within this prime agreement.

WTO Members' General Positions

Since the launch of the Doha round there have been seven meetings of the Special Session of the Committee on Trade and Environment (CTESS),[28] during which a total of 22 submissions were received from 15 WTO Members on this negotiating topic.[29] We will provide an overview of the main negotiating positions.[30] Broadly

27. United States – Standards for Reformulated and Conventional Gasoline (hereinafter US – Gasoline), Appellate Body Report and Panel Report, adopted on 20 May 1996, WT/DS2/R and WT/DS2/AB/R, Appellate Body Report, p. 20-21; United States – Import Prohibition of Certain Shrimp and Shrimp Products, Recourse to Article 21.5 by Malaysia (hereinafter US – Shrimp (Article 21.5)), Appellate Body Report and Panel Report, adopted on 21 November 2001, WT/DS58/RW and WT/DS58/AB/RW, Panel Report, paras. 5.27-5.28, as well as European Communities – Measures Affecting Asbestos and Asbestos-Containing Products (hereinafter EC – Asbestos), Appellate Body Report and Panel Report, adopted on 5 April 2001, WT/DS135, and WT/DS135/AB/R, Panel Report, para. 8.167. For a succinct overview see at: "GATT/WTO Dispute Settlement Practice Relating to GATT Article XX, Paragraphs (b), (d) and (g)", WT/CTE/W/203, 8 March 2002, paras. 9-15.

28. March, June and October 2002; and February, April, May and July 2003.

29. Argentina, Australia, Canada; China, 2 submissions by the European Communities; 2 submissions by Hong Kong, China; India; 2 submissions by Japan; Republic of Korea; Malaysia; New Zealand; Norway; 2 submissions by the Separate Customs Territory of Taiwan, Penghu, Kinmen and Matsu; 4 submissions by Switzerland; and the United States. This does not include Saudi Arabia's submission (TN/TE/W/9) as an Observer to the WTO. See also: WTO, "List of Committee on Trade and Environment Special Session (CTESS) Documents"– Note by the Secretariat, TN/TE/INF/4, 30 June 2003.

30. Excellent background papers are: WTO, "Multilateral Environmental Agreements and WTO Rules: Proposals Made in the Committee on Trade and Environment (CTE) from 1995-2002"– Note by the Secretariat, TN/TE/S/1, 23 May 2002; and WTO, "Compilation of Submissions Under Paragraph 31(i) of the Doha Declaration"– Note by the Secretariat – Revision, TN/TE/S/3/rev.1, 24 April 2003.

speaking, in terms of *outcome*, the 'demandeurs' (WTO jargon for 'pushers') of the trade-environment linkage, to know, the EC, Switzerland and Japan, propose that in the event of a dispute involving a MEA, the environmental trade measure would be accommodated within the WTO regime. Suggestions pre-Doha and post-Doha have ranged from the amendment of GATT Article XX,[31] adopting a waiver,[32] adopting a coherence clause,[33] allowing for a presumption of WTO conformity (by alleviating the burden of proof),[34] introducing a rebuttable presumption of WTO conformity,[35] or a more far-fetched reversal of the burden of proof,[36] to adopting an interpretative decision[37] (which is just short of an amendment but provides for a binding interpretation of an existing provision in a WTO Agreement). In contrast, most other Members, including India, oppose any solution that would confer an automatic or unconditional presumption of WTO-conformity on trade measures[38] or specific trade obligations taken pursuant to MEAs.[39]

31. Submission by Switzerland, "Multilateral Environmental Agreements (MEAs): Implementation of the Doha Development Agenda", TN/TE/W/4, 6 June 2002, paras. 12-13. See pre-Doha also: Non-paper by the European Communities, 19 February 1996.

32. Pre-Doha: Non-Paper by Hong Kong, 22 July 1996; and Submission by ASEAN, WT/CTE/W/39, 24 July 1996.

33. Pre-Doha, Switzerland suggested in its Non-Paper of 20 May 1996, that a Coherence Clause would provide that in case of conflict between WTO rules and a specific trade provision of an MEA, the WTO would limit its scrutiny to whether the measure has been applied in a manner which constitutes arbitrary or unjustifiable discrimination between counties where the same conditions prevail.

34. Pre-Doha submission by Switzerland, WT/CTE/W/168, 19 October 2000. Post-Doha submission by Switzerland TN/TE/W/4, para. 8.

35. Submission by Japan, TN/TE/W/10, paras. 13-14; and submission by Switzerland, TN/TE/W/16, 6 November 2002, p. 3.

36. Pre-Doha submission by the European Communities, WT/CTE/W/170, 19 October 2000; and post-Doha submission by Switzerland, TN/TE/W/16, 6 November 2002, p. 3.

37. Pre-Doha submission by Switzerland, WT/CTE/W/139, 8 June 2000. Post-Doha submission by Switzerland TN/TE/W/4, paras. 14-16; and submission by Japan, TN/TE/W/10, para. 16.

38. Pre-Doha Non-Paper by India, 23 July 1996.

39. Post-Doha submission by the Separate Customs Territory of Taiwan, Penghu, Kinmen and Matsu, "Contribution on Paragraph 31(i) of the Doha Ministerial Declaration," TN/TE/W/11, particularly footnote 5 that includes a reference to meeting reports reflecting this opposition by WTO Members that have not made formal submissions; as well as its submission, TN/TE/W/36, 3 July 2003, para. 4. See also post-Doha submission by the United States, "Sub-paragraph 31(i) of the Doha Declaration," TN/TE/W/20, 10 February 2003, paras. 4-6.

The third sentence of paragraph 31(i) DMD stating that "[t]he negotiations shall not prejudice the WTO rights of any Member that is not a party to the MEA in question" and paragraph 32 DMD providing that the outcome of the paragraph 31(i) negotiations shall not add to or diminish the rights and obligations of Members under existing WTO agreements, nor alter the balance of these rights and obligations, will have a dampening effect on the post-Doha submissions of the demandeurs. That is, an amendment of a GATT Article or a reversal of the burden of proof arguably would affect the WTO rights of WTO Members that are not Parties to a given MEA (remember that quite frequently the US is a signatory to an MEA but not a Party in the absence of ratification). Hence, such far-reaching outcomes that are not only being opposed by many WTO Members but that could be considered as moving beyond the Doha mandate[40] seem unlikely.

Additionally, most WTO Members,[41] including India, have been in favour of structuring the negotiations in a 'bottom-up' manner, where attention is paid to the interpretation of the terms "specific trade obligations", "MEAs" and "set out in MEAs". This 'bottom-up' or step-by-step approach, is in contrast with the 'top-down' approach, suggested by the EC, Switzerland, Norway and Japan that favours developing general definitions first and quickly moving to the possible outcomes of the mandate.[42] Although both approaches have been acknowledged, the bottom-up approach is predominantly followed.[43] As a consequence, the current submissions and

40. See e.g. , WTO, "Summary Report on the Sixth Meeting of the Committee on Trade and Environment Special Session – 1-2May, 2003," Note by the Secretariat, TN/TE/R/6, 12 June 2003, paras. 19-20, 24, 26, 30, 32, and 40.

41. See: Submission by Australia, "Suggested Procedure for the Negotiations under Paragraph 31(i) of the Doha Declaration"; TN/TE/W/7, 7 June 2002. See also: TN/TE/W/11, footnote 2, indicating that Members supporting this approach were: the Philippines, Singapore, Brazil, Thailand, Indonesia, Malaysia, Mexico, Chile, New Zealand, Canada, India, Hong Kong, China, Peru, Cuba, Egypt, Kenya, Uruguay, Bolivia, Korea, Pakistan, and Colombia, as listed at paragraph 59, TN/TE/R/2.

42. See also WTO, "Summary Report of the Sixth Meeting of the Committee on Trade and Environment Special Session, 1-2 May 2003," Note by the Secretariat, TN/TE/R/6, paras. 3-6.

43. These diverging approaches also illustrate the constellation of the two main negotiating blocks on para. 31(i). As 'proponents', the EC, Switzerland, Norway and Japan in favour of a far-reaching outcome on the trade-environment linkage and the 'opponents', de facto headed by the US, and comprising of Argentina, Australia, Canada, Chinese Taipei, Hong Kong, China, India, Korea, Malaysia, New Zealand and several other WTO members that have not made a formal submissions.

discussions pertain to the interpretation of the specific terms used in paragraph 31(i) DMD, the contours of the mandate and the country experiences with MEAs, but have not really touched upon the aspect that lies at the centre of the mandate: how should ultimately the *relationship* between WTO Agreements and MEAs, equal instruments of international law, be governed?

What are Specific Trade Obligations?

Coming to one of the key terms of the negotiating mandate that has also received most attention so far within the Special Sessions of the CTE: what type of trade measures set out in MEAs could qualify as specific trade obligations (STOs) - admittedly a term not used in other international fora or instruments? For clearly, not all 'trade measures' contained in MEAs are STOs.

The EC, which favours a 'top-down' approach tabled four, rather ambitious, conceptual categories of measures 'arising from trade obligations'[44]. The four categories are:

i. Trade measures explicitly provided for and mandatory under MEAs;

ii. Trade measures not explicitly provided for nor mandatory under the MEA itself but consequential of the *"obligation de résultat"* of the MEA. This category covers cases where a MEA identifies a list of potential policies and measures that Parties could implement to meet their obligations.[45]

iii. Trade measures not identified in the MEA which has only an *"obligation de résultat"* but that Parties could decide to implement in order to comply with their obligations. In contrast to the previous category, the MEA does not list potential policies and measures so countries have greater scope as regards the exact nature of the measures they might decide to deploy to reach the objectives of the MEA.

---

44. Submission by the European Communities, "Multilateral Environmental Agreements (MEAs): Implementation of the Doha Development Agenda," TN/TE/W/1, 21 March 2002, para. 25.

45. Note that the term "obligation de résultat" (French for result-oriented obligation) stems from contract law in civil law countries indicating a liability to achieve an agreed result, for which only limited exceptions can be invoked in the event of failure to achieve the said result.

iv. Trade measures not required in the MEA but which Parties can decide to implement if the MEA contains a general provision stating that parties can adopt stringent measures in accordance with international law.

Japan echoed this four-pronged categorisation in its submission by submitting four similar categories,[46] and Switzerland explicitly supported EC's submission.[47] Since the EC's third and fourth category will easily be dismissed as not covering trade obligations that are specific, the main attention has been drawn to the second and first categories. Indeed, as a trained negotiator, the EC tabled four categories, knowing that at least two categories would outrightly be rejected, one possibly rejected, and one most likely agreed upon. A consensus seems to be emerging on the first category (trade measures explicitly provided for and mandatory under MEAs) that could qualify as an STO.[48] However, most WTO Members, including India, find the second EC category too broadly defined to qualify as a 'specific trade obligation'[49]. Their rationale is that as soon as any discretion is provided, the trade measure no longer remains specific enough to qualify as an STO.[50] In this regard, India's submission stated that "the term "*specific trade obligation*" has three elements that must be considered together i.e. the provision must be *specific* with a *trade* element and should be in the nature of an *obligation*." In its view, to qualify as an STO the provision in a MEA must be specific and mandatory in character, and so precise in its direction that there can be no doubt about the action or restraint that a party to the MEA must adopt.[51] Furthermore, the WTO Members in favour of a

46. Submission by Japan, "The Relationship Between Existing WTO Rules and Specific Trade Obligations Set Out in Multilateral Environmental Agreements (MEAs)," TN/TE/W/10, 3 October 2002, para. 11

47. Submission by Switzerland, "Multilateral Environmental Agreements (MEAs): Implementation of the Doha Development Agenda," TN/TE/W/4, 6 June 2002, paras. 3-4.

48. WTO, "Summary Report on the Sixth Meeting of the Committee on Trade and Environment Special Session – 1-2 May, 2003", Note by the Secretariat, TN/TE/R/6, 12 June 2003, paras. 6, 8, 14, 19, 38 and 40.

49. Ibidem, paras. 8, 9, 19, 22, 26, 30, 36, 38 and 40.

50. For instance, Submission by Argentina, TN/TE/W/2, 23 May 2002, para. 7; Submission by the Republic of Korea, TN/TE/W/13, 8 October 2002; para. 4; and Submission by the United States, TN/TE/W/20, 10 February 2003, para. 3.

51. Submission by India, "Relationship Between Specific Trade Obligations Set Out in MEAs and WTO Rules", TN/TE/W/23, 20 February 2003, para. 7. Supported by e.g. submission by Malaysia, TN/TE/W/29, 30 April 2003, paras. 8-10.

"bottom-up" approach, including India, have submitted detailed analyses of the provisions of several MEAs that would or would not qualify as an STO to further the negotiations in this respect.[52]

When are STOs "set out" in MEAs?

The next issue that has attracted the attention of the negotiators within the Special Session of the CTE is the exact meaning of the words in paragraph 31(i) according to which specific trade obligations must be "set out" in MEAs. All agree that an STO explicitly mentioned in the text of the treaty would be "set out" in an MEA. The debate, however, moves beyond this minimum threshold and revolves around the more contentious issue of whether STOs contained in Conference of the Parties (COP) decisions, recommendations, resolutions, etc. would also qualify as being "set out" in a MEA.

That is, numerous MEAs have established institutional arrangements to govern a treaty, such as the creation of Secretariat, setting-up specialist subsidiary bodies, holding regular meetings in the form of Conference or Meeting of the Parties (COP or MOP). The COP has various tasks that may be different for each MEA and can range from:[53]

i. Administrating internal matters (e.g establishing subsidiary bodies, deciding on arrangements for meetings, adopting rules of procedure for itself and subsidiary bodies, providing guidance to those bodies and the Secretariat).

ii. Supervising parties' implementation of and compliance with MEAs and deciding on the consequences of non-compliance with the MEAs.

iii. Acting at the external level adopting arrangements with international organisations with international organisations and states.

---

52. See: WTO, "Compilation of Submissions Under Paragraph 31(i) of the Doha Declaration", TN/TE/S/3/Rev.1, 24 April 2003.

53. Based on the excellent work by Robin R. Churchill and Geir Ulfstein, "Autonomous Institutional Arrangements in Multilateral Environmental Agreements: A Little-Noticed Phenomenon in International Law", *American Journal of International Law*, Vol 94, No. 4, October 2000, pp. 623-660.

iv. Contributing to the development of new substantive obligations by the parties by amending an MEA or adopting new Protocols.

Hence, the issue is blurred by the fact that such COP decisions generally tend to relate to the administration of the MEA, but may at times also have genuine law-making powers.

The EC has identified three broad categories of COP decisions to which it attaches different consequences:[54]

i. COP decisions introducing amendments to the MEAs, such as decisions to amend the MEA and decisions adopting or modifying technical annexes. The EC concludes that these COP decisions "being legally binding, can therefore qualify as STOs".

ii. COP decisions aimed at interpreting or at further specifying the concrete implementation by Parties of certain provisions of the original MEA or subsequent COP decisions. The EC finds that these COP decisions even if not legally binding, can nevertheless have an important role to play in the interpretation of MEA provisions, including that of STOs contained in the MEA.

iii. COP decisions of a purely general and political nature, which are not legally binding and therefore do *not* contain "obligations".

Numerous WTO Members, including India, find that the EC stretches the language of paragraph 31(i) DMD too far. Rather, they agree that STOs which are contained in Annexes, Protocols and amendments to MEAs that have been adopted by Parties of the MEAs could qualify as being "set out" in the MEA,[55] but refute the linkage according to which all COP decisions which are legally binding would automatically be covered by the mandate.[56] They point out that

54. Submission by the EC, "The Relationship Between MEAs and WTO Agreements: 'Set Out in MEAs'," TN/TE/W/31, 14 May 2003, paras. 6-10.

55. Submission by Malaysia, "Paragraph 31(i) of the Doha Ministerial Declaration," TN/TE/W/29, 30 April 2003, para. 14.

56. WTO, "Summary Report on the Sixth Meeting of the Committee on Trade and Environment Special Session – 1-2 May, 2003," Note by the Secretariat, TN/TE/R/6, 12 June 2003, paras. 8,9,10.

in such situations it is actually the amended treaty, once the amendment entered into force, which was legally binding, not the COP decision itself.[57]

Environmental 'Jurisprudence' within the GATT/WTO Regimes

Were a Dispute to Arise Now

As mentioned earlier, India has indicated throughout the regular CTE meetings pre-Doha that the existing WTO provisions would be adequate enough to deal with trade measures taken pursuant to MEAs. Pending any outcome of the current round of negotiations where WTO Members will ultimately have to strike a compromise on the relationship between existing WTO rules on the one hand and specific trade obligations set out in MEAs on the other, it is opportune to outline the major tenets of the WTO 'jurisprudence' based on the ten trade and environment disputes brought before the GATT/WTO dispute settlement mechanism that involved the interpretation of the exception clause, Article XX of GATT.[58] One must bear in mind that all these cases related to unilateral environmental measures and not measures taken in pursuance of a MEA. Nevertheless, were a dispute to arise now between WTO Members that are also Parties to a MEA regarding the infringement

57. WTO, "Summary Report on the Seventh Meeting of the Committee on Trade and Environment Special Session – 8 July, 2003," Note by the Secretariat, TN/TE/R/7, 12 June 2003, paras. 23-25 and 41.

58. The six cases brought under the GATT are: United States – Prohibition of Imports of Tuna and Tuna Products from Canada ("US-Canadian Tuna") adopted 22 February 1982; Canada – Measures Affecting Exports of Unprocessed Herring and Salmon ("Canada-Salmon and Herring") adopted 22 March 1988; Thailand – Restrictions on Importation of and Internal Taxes on Cigarettes ("Thailand-Cigarettes") adopted on 7 November 1990; United States – Restrictions on Imports of Tuna ("US-Tuna, Mexico") circulated but not adopted 3 September 1991; United States – Restrictions on Imports of Tuna ("US-Tuna, EEC") circulated but not adopted 16 June 1994; United States – Taxes on Automobiles ("US-Automobiles") circulated but not adopted 11 October 1994; whereas the 4 cases brought under the WTO regime are: United States – Standards for Reformulated and Conventional Gasoline ("US-Gasoline") adopted on 20 May 1996; United States – Import Prohibition of Certain Shrimp and Shrimp Products ("US-Shrimp") adopted on 6 November 1998; United States – Import Prohibition of Certain Shrimp and Shrimp Products, Recourse to Article 21.5 of the DSU by Malaysia ("US Shrimp-Article 21.5") adopted on 21 November 2001; and European Communities – Measures Affecting Asbestos and Asbestos-Containing Products ("EC-Asbestos") adopted on 5 April 2001.

of a core WTO obligation caused by the WTO Member to conform with a specific trade obligation set out in a MEA (assuming that they would agree on the jurisdiction of the WTO Dispute Settlement Body), the approaches evolved by the dispute settlement Panels and Appellate Body would be pertinent.

Unlike in India's jurisprudence, the *stare decisis* principle according to which precedent decisions are to be adhered to by the courts in subsequent cases is not followed by the WTO dispute settlement regime.[59] Adopted Panel and Appellate Body reports are not binding, except with respect to resolving the particular dispute between parties to that dispute. Nevertheless the findings of these environmental disputes remain relevant because the Appellate Body has explicitly held that adopted reports are an important part of the GATT *acquis*. It further held that they are often considered by subsequent panels and that they create legitimate expectations among WTO Members and should therefore be taken into account where they are relevant to any dispute.[60]

As mentioned above, the Appellate Body of the WTO has explicitly developed a two-tiered test to scrutinise whether a measure can genuinely be justified under GATT article XX: first, the measure must be identified as falling under any of the sub-paragraphs of the exception clause, and only subsequently will the measure be benchmarked against the chapeau (the headnote or overarching paragraph covering all sub-paragraphs). We mentioned earlier as well that GATT Article XX has three sub-paragraphs of relevance for environmental concerns. For the purpose of this paper, however, we will restrict ourselves to some of the main aspects of Article XX(b) pertaining to measures that are "necessary" to protect human, animal or plant life or health. The headnote requires that such measures are not applied in a manner which would constitute a means of arbitrary or unjustifiable discrimination.

---

59. Peter C Maki, "Interpreting GATT Using the Vienna Convention on the Law of Treaties: A Method to Increase the legitimacy of the Dispute Settlement System", 9 Minn. J. Global Trade 343 (Winter 2000) at p. 348, referring also to Ramon R Gupta, "Comment – Appellate Body Interpretation of the WTO Agreement: A Critique in Light of Japan-Taxes on Alcoholic Beverages", 6 Pac. Rim. L. & Pol'y J., 683 (1997).

60. See: Japan – Taxes on Alcoholic Beverages, Appellate Body Report adopted on 1 November 1996, WT/DS8,10,11/AB/R, p. 15.

Whereas, the first part of the two-tiered test has been passed by several "environmental trade measures", the second part (the headnote) was only successfully passed in one case so far, the '*EC-Asbestos*' case where France banned the manufacture, processing, sale, import, placing on the domestic market, etc., of asbestos and products containing asbestos fibres.[61]

Necessity Test Under Article XX(b)

The examination of whether or not a measure taken by a WTO Member is "necessary" under paragraph (b) has proved to be a crucial step in panel practice. Initially, the "necessity test" was equated with a "least-trade restrictiveness" requirement. That is, a contracting party could not justify a measure inconsistent with another GATT provision as "necessary" if an alternative measure, which it could reasonably be expected to employ and which was not inconsistent with other GATT provisions, was available to it.[62] For instance, in the *Thailand-Cigarettes* case it was held that instead of an import ban on foreign cigarettes, a ban on cigarette advertising could curb the demand of cigarettes (including foreign cigarettes).[63] In cases where no alternative measures consistent with the GATT are available, a contracting party must use the one which entails the least degree of inconsistency with other GATT provisions.[64]

More recently there has been an evolution in the interpretation of the necessity requirement. In the *Korea-Various Measures on Beef* case, adopted in 2001, the Appellate Body introduced additional considerations. It observed that the term "necessary" should not be limited to what was "indispensable". Nevertheless, a "necessary" measure is located significantly closer to the pole of "indispensable" than to the opposite pole of simply "making a contribution to"[65]. The Appellate Body further bifurcated the necessity test as follows:

---

61. EC – Measures Affecting Asbestos and Asbestos-Containing Products, Appellate Body Report and Panel Report adopted on 5 April 2001, WT/DS135.
62. US-Section 337 of the Tariff Act of 1930, Panel Report adopted on 7 Nov. 1989, para. 5.26.
63. Thailand-Cigarettes, Panel Report, para. 78.
64. See US-Section 337, para. 5.26, Thailand-Cigarettes, para. 75, United States-Measures Affecting Alcoholic and Malt Beverages case, Panel report adopted on 19 June 1992, para. 5.52.
65. Korea-Measures Affecting Imports of Fresh, Chilled and Frozen Beef, Appellate Body Report, adopted 10 January 2001, WT/DS169/AB/R, para. 157.

i. Situations where the measure is indispensable, i.e. the only available; and

ii. Situations where a Member may be able to justify its measure as "necessary" even if there would be other measures available. It added that a measure with a relatively slight impact on imported products might more easily be considered as "necessary" than a measure with intense or broader restrictive effects. Most significantly, the Appellate Body stated that this analysis involved in every case a process of weighing and balancing a series of factors, such as the contribution made to the enforcement of the law or regulation at issue, the importance of the common interests or values protected by that law or regulation, and the accompanying impact of the law or regulation on imports or exports.[66]

In the *EC-Asbestos* case the Appellate Body considered that the preservation of human life and health, pursued by the ban on asbestos and products containing asbestos, was a value both "vital" and "important in the highest degree".[67]

Hence it must be observed that the necessity requirement has evolved from a least-trade restrictive approach to a less-trade restrictive one, supplemented with a proportionality test ("a process of weighing and balancing a series of factors").[68]

Based on these interpretation of Article XX(b), and other considerations, several authors are of the opinion that the measure taken pursuant to a MEA with a large number of Parties could be considered as "necessary" for the protection of human health.[69]

Headnote of Article XX

1. Components of Headnote Article XX

Once a measure satisfies the conditions set by one of the paragraphs of article XX, the Panel or Appellate Body must turn to

---

66. Korea-Various Measures on Beef, paras. 163 and 164.

67. EC-Asbestos, AB Report, para. 172.

68. Also: "GATT/WTO Dispute Settlement Practice", WT/CTE/W/203, p. 18.

69. See e.g. Joost Pauwelyn, "The Role of Public International Law in the WTO: How Far Can We Go?", 95 *American Journal of International Law*, 535-78 (2001), at p. 572, and references.

the introductionary clause or chapeau of Article XX. It requires that measures must not be "applied in a manner which would constitute a means of arbitrary or unjustifiable discrimination between countries where the same conditions prevail, or a disguised restriction on international trade".

The Appellate Body has underscored that the function of the Article XX chapeau is the prevention of "abuse of the exceptions" of Article XX[70] and that it embodies the recognition on part of the WTO Members to maintain a balance of rights and obligations, between the right to invoke an exception on the one hand and the substantive rights of the other Members under GATT 1994 on the other hand.[71]

The main characteristics of the chapeau requirements are best exemplified based on the *US-Shrimp* case and the subsequent *US-Shrimp (Article 21.5)* case.[72]

2. Facts of US-Shrimp Case

Since 1987, US regulations require that shrimp trawlers install turtle excluder devices (TEDs) when operating in US waters.[73] Section 609 of Public Law 101-162[74] pursuant to which the regulations were adopted contains two parts: (a) directing the Secretary of the State to initiate *international negotiations* to protect the five sea turtle species protected by the US Endangered Species Act of 1973 (ESA);[75] (b) *prohibiting the import* of shrimp harvested with fishing technology that may harm sea turtles (i.e. excluding from the outset aquaculture-grown shrimp, hand-caught shrimp, etc.). The import ban shall not be imposed if the *government of the harvesting nation* has provided evidence of the adoption of a programme on the incidental taking of sea turtles *comparable to* the one of the US.

---

70. See US-Gasoline, *AB Report*, p. 21.
71. See US-Shrimp, *AB Report*, para. 156.
72. Article 21.5 Dispute Settlement Understanding (DSU) Agreement refers to a case where the implementation of recommendations and rulings by Panels or the Appellate Body is challenged.
73. TEDs prevent sea turtles from being retained in the harvesting nets by means of a metal grid barring entry to the closed end of the net.
74. 16 United States Code (U.S.C.) §1537 (hereinafter section 609).
75. In 1998, all species of sea turtles were included in Appendix I of CITES.

The Department of State initially held that section 609 only applied to the Caribbean and Western Atlantic Region. This triggered the first case filed by environmental and animal rights groups (Turtle Island & others) before the US Court of International Trade (1st CIT case). The CIT ruled in December 1995 that section 609 should be applied on a world-wide basis.

The world-wide application of the shrimp import prohibition in turn triggered the first "shrimp turtle case" in the WTO setting, filed by Malaysia, Thailand, Pakistan and India. The Panel had found that the ban imposed by the United States was inconsistent with GATT Article XI on the elimination of quantitative restrictions.[76] The Appellate Body further ruled that the measure could qualify for provisional justification under Article XX(g), but failed to meet the requirements of the chapeau of Article XX. In light of the Panel and Appellate Body findings and recommendations the US administration had to make sure the certification procedure for shrimp imports was made more "flexible".

In a case filed subsequently, Malaysia questioned the compliance by the US with the recommendations of the Appellate Body.[77] In particular it claimed that the US was not entitled to impose any prohibition in the absence of an international agreement on the matter.

3. A Means of Arbitrary or Unjustifiable Discrimination

The Appellate Body identified two major aspects that hindered the US measure from passing the chapeau test.[78]

First, the serious, across-the-board effort to negotiate with the objective of concluding bilateral and multilateral agreements for the achievement of a certain policy goal, was absent.[79] It was noted that

---

76. US-Shrimp, *Panel Report*, para. 7.17.

77. United States – Import Prohibition of Certain Shrimp and Shrimp Products, Recourse to Article 21.5 by Malaysia (hereinafter US – Shrimp (Article 21.5)), Appellate Body Report and Panel Report, adopted on 21 November 2001, WT/DS58/RW and WT/DS58/AB/RW.

78. Several other criteria to interpret the headnote of Article XX have been distilled from other panel and AB reports as well, see more at: "GATT/WTO Dispute Settlement Practice Relating to GATT Article XX, Paragraphs (b), (d) and (g)", WT/CTE/W/203, 8 March 2002, pp. 20-28.

79. US-Shrimp, *AB Report*, para. 166.

the US did not undertake across-the-board negotiations since it only negotiated with some but not all interested parties and the effect was found to be plainly discriminatory. In the implementation case filed by Malaysia, the *US-Shrimp (Article 21.5)* case, the Appellate Body clarified that the duty to undertake good faith negotiations did however not entail the duty to *conclude* an agreement.[80]

Second, the flexibility of the measure plays an important role in the assessment of the discriminatory nature of the application of the measure. Thus, the Appellate Body indicated in the *US-Shrimp* case that the lack of flexibility in the certification process, which did not take into account the different situations in different countries, amounted to unjustifiable discrimination.[81] However, in *US-Shrimp (Article 21.5)* case the Appellate Body found that the 1999 US Revised Guidelines did incorporate the recommendations on "flexibility" and "comparable in effect" of the first *US-Shrimp* case,[82] and could remain in force as is.

The US Court of Appeals Differs

Having touched upon the main characteristics of how the exception clause GATT Article XX (b) –covering environmental measures- and the headnote of Article XX have been interpreted by the Panel and the Appellate Body, it is worth turning to how the US courts have interpreted the shrimp-turtle case domestically. For although an impressive amount of analyses has taken place on the US-Shrimp case *per se* and its ramifications for WTO-dispute settlement practice,[83] surprisingly little attention has been paid to the jurisprudential developments in the US. This is particularly interesting as the US Court of Appeals concludes that the US Section

80. US-Shrimp (Article 21.5), *Panel Report*, para. 5.67.

81. US-Shrimp, *AB Report*, para. 161.

82. US-Shrimp (Article 21.5), *Appellate Body Report*, para. 144.

83. E.g. Robert Howse, "The Appellate Body Rulings in the Shrimp/Turtle Case: A New Legal Baseline for the Trade and Environment Debate", 27 Colum. J. Envtl. L. 491; B.S. Chimni, "WTO and Environment – Shrimp-Turtle and EC-Hormones Cases", Economic and Political Weekly, May 13, 2000; Petros C. Mavroidis, "Amicus Curiae Briefs Before the WTO: Much Ado About Nothing", Jean Monnet Working Paper, No. 2/01; Jayati Srivastava and Rajeev Ahuja, "Mainstreaming Environment Through Jurisprudence – Implications of the Shrimp-Turtle Decisions in the WTO for Indian and Other Developing Countries", *ICRIER, Working Paper* No. 78 (April 2002), to name but a few.

609 of Public Law is purely protectionist in nature. We will first summarise the subsequent domestic cases filed before the CIT.

After the 1st CIT case, the State Department issued its revised Guidelines in 1996 and interpreted the "certification procedure" pertaining to TED requirements less literally by shifting away from the so-called *nation-by-nation* scrutiny (is their a comparable programme imposing TEDs adopted by exporting nations?) to the *shipment-by-shipment basis* (can the exporter attest it has used TEDs, independently of whether such domestic programme has been adopted?). This *shipment-by-shipment* approach was challenged by Turtle Island and led to the 2nd CIT case.

In December 1996, the CIT confirmed Turtle Island's position and held that the embargo should be applied on a nation-by-nation basis rather than a shipment-by-shipment one. In 1998 the *US Court of Appeals* vacated the orders by the CIT to the State Department to enforce section 609 on a nation-by-nation basis based on procedural arguments.[84] From then on, and in all its subsequent Guidelines, the State Department confirmed the *shipment-by-shipment* approach.

Thereafter, Turtle Island filed suit to challenge the 1998 Guidelines of the State Department (3rd CIT case). In 1999, the CIT confirmed its earlier judgement and entered a final declaratory judgement in 2000 in favour of Turtle Island.

The *US Court of Appeals*, in its March 2002 judgment,[85] scrutinised the legislative history of section 609 that mainly consisted of speeches on the Senate floor, for further guidance as to whether or not a *shipment-by-shipment* or *nation-by-nation* certification approach was intended by the legislator. Its major findings are worth quoting:

> *"But what is unmistakingly clear from the discussion on the Senate floor is that the primary purpose of the bill was to protect the domestic shrimping industry, and not the sea turtle. The advocates of the bill were Senators from Gulf states who had long opposed the domestic TED regulations because they*

---

84. Earth Island's withdrawal was to preserve its right to gather additional evidence and to challenge the government's revised guidelines in a separate action. The CIT denied permission to withdraw based on the public interest at stake. The US Court of Appeals held that Turtle Island did not request the permission to withdraw by unilaterally did so by which it terminated the CIT's jurisdiction over the case except for the matter of attorney fees.

85. Turtle Island Restoration Network vs. Evans, 00-1569, -1581, -1582 (Fed. Cir., March 21, 2002, see in particular part B of the judgment

believed that TEDs reduced shrimp catches. (...) The Senators who spoke in favour (none spoke against) feared that American shrimpers would be at a disadvantage competing in the domestic market with foreign shrimpers, who were not burdened with TED regulations. By imposing TED requirements on foreign shrimpers exporting to the United States, the sponsors of section 609 hoped to provide American shrimpers with a level playing field."[86]

It further observed that many of the comments made on the Senate floor reflected deep skepticism about the effectiveness of TED requirements and about the wisdom of placing sea turtle conservation above the economic well-being of domestic shrimpers.[87] It respected Turtle Island's long struggle on behalf of the Earth's endangered sea turtles but concluded that Congress did not share Turtle Island's position and confirmed the government's current implementation of section 609.

Thus, as such the US Appellate Court went much further than the WTO panels and Appellate Body and unequivocally found the US measure not related to the conservation of a natural resource. Pushing these arguments hypothetically forward to the WTO scene, the US measure may not even have provisionally qualified under GATT Article XX(g) requiring that a measure would relate to the conservation of a natural resource. Hence, the measure would have failed to pass the first threshold of the two-pronged test under GATT Article XX, and the measure would have simply been found to infringe core WTO rules, for which no exceptions would be available.

Some Observations

It is worth noting that the panels and Appellate Body do attempt to "pierce the environmental veil" by screening whether measures are genuine environmental measures that can pass the two-tiered test or mere protectionist measures cloaked in environmental arguments. Though, as the judgement of the *US Court of Appeals* related to the US-Shrimp case illustrated, the DSB may not always be able to pierce the veil well enough (true, the scope of jurisdiction, rules of

86. *Ibidem.*

87. Judge Newman dissented: "I do not agree with the majority that if there is a commercial aspect to legislation, the humanitarian purpose becomes irrelevant." Also: "a shipment-by-shipment approach not only weakens the incentive for countries to impose TED requirements, but it removes the anticipated "level playing field: for domestic interests (...)."

interpretation, substantive law to be interpreted, etc. of the domestic courts and the international WTO dispute settlement mechanism vastly differ). However, in the eyes of the countries affected these legal technical differences may be a meagre solace given the sharply different outcomes. It should also be clear that the *US Court of Appeals* decision has been included here to better illustrate the difficulty of separating the wheat from the chaff – sifting the genuine environmental measures from the predominantly protectionist measures.

Originally the panels and the Appellate Body interpreted Article XX narrowly, whereas the evolution of the least-trade-restrictive test to a proportionality test in its latest cases, originally developed in non-environmental cases, do indicate that a "greener" light will be shed on future cases. The practice of the DSB and the rules one tends to distil from the cases remain, by the inherent design of the DSB, mainly coloured by the particular facts of the cases. Differing future approaches are thus never excluded. Although only one case passed the two-tiered test of Article XX so far, the dispute settlement bodies have absorbed unilateral trade measures with environment objectives to a significant degree. One may agree with Chimni that the WTO is far from being the anti-environment organisation as portrayed by northern ngos and academics. Or, put differently, "environment" is actually entering through the backdoor of the WTO – not in any WTO agreement but via its dispute settlement mechanism.[88]

Interplay with Public International Law

Vienna Convention on the Law of Treaties

In the previous parts we have given an overview of the current status of submissions pertaining to paragraph 31 (i) of the Doha Mandate, indicated some of the major tests developed by the Panels and the Appellate Body of the WTO for GATT Article XX that could be invoked by a WTO Member to justify environmental measures. To fully comprehend the WTO rules and MEA negotiations - and its core issue: which treaty would prevail in the event of conflict?- one must be familiar with some aspects of public international law. For, as

---

88. Chimni, B.S. "WTO and Environment – Shrimp-Turtle and EC-Hormones Cases", *Economic and Political Weekly*, May 13, 2000.

Pauwelyn observes, WTO rules are part of the wider corpus of public international law – even though this may come as a "surprise" to many WTO negotiators.[89]

Both the WTO Agreements and MEAs are international treaties. Moreover, public international law is typified by the absence of hierarchy between sources of international law, and hence, the inherent equality of international treaties. As a consequence, the public international law rules pertaining to treaty application and interpretation are relevant. These in turn have been codified in the *Vienna Convention on the Law of Treaties, 1969* (Vienna Convention). The rules adopted in the Vienna Convention are generally accepted as representing "customary rules of interpretation of public international law" – which are binding on all States by way of 'international custom' independently of whether a State ratifies the Treaty.[90] This is important, since India, for instance, has not ratified the Vienna Convention.

Although these customary rules of interpretation apply automatically to WTO Agreements as well, Article 3.2 of the WTO Understanding on Rules and Procedures Governing the Settlement of Disputes (Dispute Settlement Understanding or DSU) explicitly provides that the dispute settlement system of the WTO will clarify the existing provisions of WTO Agreements "in accordance with customary rules of interpretation of public international law".[91] The Appellate Body confirmed that the GATT "is not to be read in clinical isolation from public international law".[92]

We will turn to two cardinal principles of treaty application and interpretation: (1) *lex posterior* rule or later in time rule, and (2) the rule according to which the more specific treaty or provision takes precedence over the more general one (*lex specialis generalia specialibus non derogant* or in short *lex specialis*).

89. Joost Pauwelyn, "The Role of Public International Law in the WTO: How Far Can We Go?", *95 American Journal of International Law 535-78 (2001)*, at p. 538.

90. See: Lennard, Michael "Navigating by the Stars: Interpreting the WTO Agreements", *Journal of International Economic Law (2002)*, pp. 17-89, at p. 18.

91. See: Joost Pauwelyn, "The Role of Public International Law in the WTO: How Far Can We Go?", *95 American Journal of International Law 535-78 (2001)*, at p. 542 (supporting the thesis that the WTO is not a "self-contained regime" but forms an integral part of public international law).

92. "United States – Standards for Reformulated and Conventional Gasoline", *Appellate Body Report*, adopted on 20 May 1996, WT/DS2/AB/R, p. 17.

Later in Time Rule

Article 30 of the Vienna Convention on the application of successive treaties relating to the same subject-matter states in essence that the more recent treaty will prevail over the earlier treaty.[93] In a situation with just a few Parties this rule may work just fine. However, its limitations are felt when applied to treaties which not only have a large number of parties, such as the WTO Agreements and MEAs , but where Parties would also have ratified the treaties at different moments in time.[94] Broadly speaking, for a country A that joined the WTO in 2002 but ratified a MEA in 1992, the MEA would prevail; whereas for country B who joined the WTO in 1999 and only ratified the MEA in 2004, the WTO rules would prevail. This rule would clearly fall short in offering clarity when countries A and B would have a dispute over which treaty prevails.

An additional difficulty with the *lex posterior* rule is that WTO Agreements and MEAs may, in the terms of Pauwlyn, constitute "continuing treaties", for which the date of its conclusion or adoption would be an imperfect demarcation in time, as these are continuously being confirmed, implemented, adapted and expanded, for instance, by means of judicial decisions, interpretations or new norms.[95]

Lex Specialis? Lex Generalis?

Given the above difficulties with the *lex posterior* rule set out in the Vienna Convention, commentators tend to turn to another principle for guidance when trying to solve the issue of which international treaty (in our case: WTO Agreements or MEAs) will prevail over the other in the event of conflict.

The rule according to which the more specific provisions or legislation will prevail is widely applied in domestic statutory

93. Article 30(3) of the Vienna Convention rather formulates is as "when all parties to the earlier treaty are also parties to the latter treaty, but the earlier treaty is not terminated or suspended (...), the earlier treaty applies only to the extent its provisions are compatible with the latter treaty."

94. See comprehensively: Joost Pauwelyn, "The Role of Public International Law in the WTO: How Far Can We Go?", *95 American Journal of International Law 535-78 (2001)*, at p. 545-547.

95. *Ibidem*, at 545. Also: Joost Pauwelyn, "The Nature of WTO Obligations", *Jean Monnet Working Paper* 1/02 (2002), p. 40-42.

interpretation, and has a large support in public international law too (although it is not included in the Vienna Convention)[96] and is to a certain extent reflected in the WTO Agreement (but solely in relation to other WTO Agreements).[97]

When applying this rule to WTO Agreements and MEAs one would have to decide which one of them is the "more specific" one? The difficulty here is then that one could argue either way. For, in many ways WTO rules are *lex specialis* vis-à-vis general international law rules.[98] At the same time, given the all-pervasiveness of WTO rules it could be considered as *lex generalis* as well.[99]

These interpretational difficulties indicate that the task of the WTO Members that are asked to negotiate on the relationship between existing WTO rules and specific trade obligations set out in MEAs is certainly a challenge.

It also exposes quite clearly that WTO negotiators are actually asked to solve an intricate legal technical issue that must be seen through a public international law lens, not merely a trade-prism. This is why, Steve Charnovitz proposes that this legal issue be taken up extensively by the International Law Commission,[100] a body set up in 1947 to promote the progressive development of international law and its codification.

What lies Ahead..

In the short-term, that is, as part of the current trade round, WTO negotiators would still have to address the possible outcomes of the paragraph 31(i) negotiations.

---

96. Lennard, Michael "Navigating by the Stars: Interpreting the WTO Agreements", *Journal of International Economic Law, (2002)*, pp. 17-89, at p. 70-71.

97. See: Interpretative Note to Annex 1A of the WTO providing that: "In the event of conflict between a provision of the General Agreement on Tariffs and Trade 1994 and a provision of another agreement in Annex 1A, the provision of the other agreement shall take precedence to the extent of the conflict".

98. Joost Pauwelyn, "The Role of Public International Law in the WTO: How Far Can We Go?", *95 American Journal of International Law, 535-78 (2001)*, at p. 539.

99. *Ibidem*, at p. 540.

100. Charnovitz, Steve "Expanding the MEA Mandate in the Doha Agenda", *Global Environment & Trade Study* (GETS), 2003, available at: http://www.ongomcmexico.org.mx/WebPage/web/doctos/GETS7.pdf

As seen, a substantial number of WTO Members, including India, are opposed to far-reaching negotiating outcomes, such as amending Article XX, providing automatic WTO-conformity, altering the burden of proof, since it would prejudice the WTO rights and alter the balance of rights and obligations of WTO Members not party to an MEA – something which is explicitly excluded by the wordings of paragraph 31(i) DMD and para. 32 DMD.

Also, in the absence of an actual dispute between WTO rules and a trade measure taken pursuant to a specific trade obligation set out in a MEA, that would help visualising the consequences of any form of accommodation of such measures, WTO Members would be reluctant to simply agree to any form of WTO-conformity of such domestic trade measures. For giving up certain rights – without knowing what it may entail in the future – is never an easy admission. Also, a WTO Member's interest may vary from case to case, thereby not making that choice easier.

Even 'environmental jurisprudence' within the WTO has seen a considerable interpretational evolution and one can observe a tilt in favor of taking into account environmental concerns. Although merely relying on the outcome of dispute settlement Panels and the Appellate Body may not offer absolute certainty of where the balance would fall (in favour of WTO Agreements or a MEA), but the dispute settlement route at least gives the opportunity on a case by case basis for a WTO Member to be heard and defend its case.

These aspects taken together do indicate that a likely outcome would be that WTO Members agree on a general statement on the mutual supportiveness of both the WTO and the MEA regimes.[101]

In the longer run, there is a high possibility of other items of the 10-point regular work programme of the CTE to be 'levelled up' to negotiating items in a next round of negotiations with the aim of absorbing it in firm WTO rules (for instance, the issue of the relationship between WTO provisions and environmental taxes, eco-labels, requirements for packaging and recycling).

---

101. Charnovitz, Steve "Expanding the MEA Mandate in the Doha Agenda," *Global Environment & Trade Study (GETS)*, 2003. See also: Submission by the United States, TN/TE/W/20, 10 February 2003, para. 4; and Submission by the Separate Customs Territory of Taiwan, Penghu, Kinmen and Matsu, TN/TE/W/36, 3 July 2003, para. 14.

One of the main tasks of the CTE is indeed to make appropriate recommendations on whether any modifications of the provisions of the multilateral trading system are required.[102]

This is also clear from the reading of paragraph 32 of the DMD requesting that the CTE pay particular attention to: (1) the effect of environmental measures on market access; (2) the relevant provisions of the Agreement on Trade-Related Aspects of Intellectual Property Rights; (3) and labelling requirements for environmental purposes.[103] Although the necessary support could not be mustered at Cancun, it is not all together excluded that it may in the future.

Conclusion

That environment is even being discussed today within the WTO regime must be attributed to the growing importance of international environmental fora and treaties. For instance, the creation of the CTE was largely in response to the global attention paid to the Rio Conference in 1992.

Trade and environment regimes have very different objectives all together. This does not mean that at times there may not be overlaps or explicit cross-references (for instance the inclusion of "sustainable development" in the preamble of the WTO agreement).[104] Some of these overlaps may be deliberate and yet others are not. Pursuing environmental objectives set out in MEAs via trade measures are not adopted with the intent to infringe WTO rules, yet the domestic applications of such measures may.

The separate regimes however are, by now, aware of this potential conflict and also try to address this issue. In the CTE

102. *Ibidem.*

103. Paragraph 32 of the Ministerial Declaration – Adopted on 14 November 2001, WT/MIN(01)/DEC/1, 20 November 2001.

104. Relevant excerpt of the Preamble of the Agreement Establishing the WTO reads as follows: "Recognising that their relations in the field of trade and economic endeavour should be conducted with a view to raising standards of living, ensuring full employment and a large and steadily growing volume of real income and effective demand, and expanding the production of and trade in goods and services, while allowing for the optimal use of the world's resources in accordance with the objective of sustainable development, seeking both to protect and preserve the environment and to enhance the means for doing so in a manner consistent with their respective needs and concerns at different levels of economic development (...)".

regular meetings, WTO Members have for almost a decade been pondering on the relationship between WTO rules and trade measures. The World Summit on Sustainable Development's Plan of Implementation adopted at Johannesburg in 2002, calls for mutual supportiveness between the multilateral trading system and the multilateral environmental agreements.[105]

The Doha Ministerial Declaration narrowed down the scope of this debate considerably by specifying that the negotiations would be focused on the relationship between existing WTO rules and 'specific trade obligations' –not the entire range of trade measures - set out in MEAs.

The paragraph 31(i) negotiations have mainly been structured in a 'bottom-up' manner that has made room for a step-by-step analyses of the various terms used. Another important restriction of the current mandate is its limitation to "as among parties" to both the WTO Agreement and the MEAs, excluding any Party/non-Party discussion. Furthermore, the DMD also specifies that the negotiations shall not prejudice the rights of any Member that is not a Party to the MEA in question and that the outcome shall not add or diminish the rights and obligations of WTO Members, nor alter the balance of these rights and obligations.

WTO Members in the CTE Special Session have predominantly tabled views on what a MEA is, what the newly coined term STO could cover, while scrutinising the numerous provisions of the selected MEAs.

They have, however, not yet addressed the 'relationship' part of the negotiations – how should these equal instruments of international law, WTO rules on the one hand and MEAs on the other, relate to one another given the identified potential conflict. To answer this question, rules of public international law must necessarily be taken into account. This is why some suggest that this work be continued in a comprehensive manner by the International Law Commission, and not merely left up to the WTO, which in light of the single undertaking type negotiations may have other considerations in mind than the mere solving of this challenging international legal issue.

---

105. United Nations, *Report of the World Summit on Sustainable Development*, Johannesburg, South Africa, 26 August-4 September 2002, A/CONF.199/20

References

Journal Articles

Chimni, B.S. (2000). "WTO and Environment – Shrimp-Turtle and EC-Hormones Cases," *Economic and Political Weekly*, May 13, 2000, pp. 1752-1761.

Churchill, Robin R., and Ulfstein Geir (2000). "Autonomous Institutional Arrangements in Multilateral Environmental Agreements: A Little-Noticed Phenomenon in International Law," *94 American Journal of International Law 623*, pp. 623-660.

Fletcher, Charles R. (1996). "Greening World Trade: Reconciling GATT and Multilateral Environmental Agreements Within the Existing World Trade Regime," *5 Journal of Transnational Law & Policy 341*, pp. 341-372.

Howse Robert (2002). "The Appellate Body Rulings in the Shrimp/Turtle Case: A New Legal Baseline for the Trade and Environment Debate," *27 Colum. J. Envtl. L. 491*; (23 pgs.), available at: http://www.worldtradelaw.net/articles/howseshrimp.pdf

Lennard, Michael (2002). "Navigating by the Stars: Interpreting the WTO Agreements," *Journal of International Economic Law (2002)*, pp. 17-89.

Maki, Peter C. (2000). "Interpreting GATT Using the Vienna Convention on the Law of Treaties: A Method to Increase the legitimacy of the Dispute Settlement System," *9 Minn. J. Global Trade 343*, pp. 343-360.

Pauwelyn, Joost (2001). "The Role of Public International Law in the WTO: How Far Can We Go?," *95 American Journal of International Law 535-78*.

Van Calster, Geert, "Groen en Poen in de Werehldhandelsorganisatie (WTO) – Model voor de Succesvolle Intergratie van Vrijhandel en Leefmilieu," *Tijdschrift voor Milieurecht* 2000, p. 288-299.

Wold, Chris (1996). "Multilateral Environmental Agreements and the GATT: Conflict and Resolution?," *26 Envtl. L. 841*, p. 841-919.

Books

Jha, Veena (2003). "Trade and Environment: Doha and Beyond" in "*India and the WTO*," Edited by Aaditya Mattoo and Robert M Stern, co-publication of the World Bank and Oxford University Press, pp. 388.

Singh, Gurdip, *International Law*, 2003, Macmillan India Ltd., pp. 585.

Trebilcock Michael J. and Howse Robert (1995). "*The Regulation of International Trade*," Routledge, 1995, pp. 510.

Working Papers

Charnovitz, Steve (2003). "Expanding the MEA Mandate in the Doha Agenda," *Global Environment & Trade Study (GETS)*, available at: http://www.ongomcmexico.org. mx/WebPage/web/doctos/GETS7.pdf

Mavroidis, Petros C., "Amicus Curiae Briefs Before the WTO: Much Ado About Nothing," *Jean Monnet Working Paper*, No. 2/01.

Nordstrom Hakan and Scott Vaughan Scott (1999). *WTO Special Studies*, "Trade and Environment".

Patel, Chandrakant (2003). "Single Undertaking: A Straitjacket or Variable Geometry?," Trade-Related Agenda, Development and Equity (T.R.A.D.E), *Working Paper* No. 15.

Pauwelyn, Joost (2002). "The Nature of WTO Obligations," *Jean Monnet Working Paper* 1/02, pp. 49.

Srivastava Jayati and Ahuja Rajeev (2002). "Mainstreaming Environment Through Jurisprudence – Implications of the Shrimp-Turtle Decisions in the WTO for Indian and Other Developing Countries," *ICRIER, Working Paper* No. 78.

WTO (2003). "*Understanding the WTO*," 3rd edition, pp. 112

Official Documents International Institutions

United Nations, *Report of the World Summit on Sustainable Development*, Johannesburg, South Africa, 26 August-4 September 2002, A/CONF.199/20.

WTO, *Trade and Environment – Decision of 14 April 1994*, MTN/NC/45(MIN).

WTO, *Matrix on Trade Measures Pursuant to Selected MEAs – Note by the Secretariat – Revision*, WT/CTE/W/160/Rev.1, 14 June 2001.

WTO, *Ministerial Declaration – Adopted on 14 November 2001*, WT/MIN(01)/DEC/1, 20 November 2001.

WTO, "GATT/WTO Dispute Settlement Practice Relating to GATT Article XX, Paragraphs (b), (d) and (g)," WT/CTE/W/203, *Note by the Secretariat*, 8 March 2002.

WTO, *Multilateral Environmental Agreements (MEAs) and WTO Rules: Proposals Made in the Committee on Trade and Environment (CTE) from 1995-2002*, TN/TE/S/1, 23 May 2002.

WTO, "Observer Status," Note by the Secretariat, TN/TE/S/4, 31 January 2003.

WTO, "Compilation of Submissions Under Paragraph 31(i) of the Doha Declaration," TN/TE/S/3/Rev.1, 24 April 2003.

WTO, "List of Committee on Trade and Environment Special Session (CTESS) Document," *Note by the Secretariat* – Revision, TN/TE/INF/4/Rev.1, 21 July 2003.

WTO, "Summary Report on the Sixth Meeting of the Committee on Trade and Environment Special Session – 1-2 May, 2003," *Note by the Secretariat*, TN/TE/R/6, 12 June 2003.

WTO, "Summary Report on the Seventh Meeting of the Committee on Trade and Environment in Special Session – 8 July 2003," *Note by the Secretariat*, TN/TE/R/7, 1 August 2003.

WTO, *Draft Ministerial Declaration*, JOB(03)/15/Rev.1., 24 August 2003.

WTO, *Ministerial Statement* – Adopted on 14 September 2003, WT/MIN(03)/20, 23 September 2003.

Submissions made by WTO Members

a) *Submission by ASEAN*, WT/CTE/W/39, 24 July 1996.

b) WTO, *Submission by Switzerland*, "Multilateral Environmental Agreements (MEAs): Implementation of the Doha Development Agenda," TN/TE/W/4, 6 June 2002.

c) WTO, *Submission by Switzerland*, WT/CTE/W/139, 8 June 2000.

d) WTO, *Submission by Switzerland*, WT/CTE/W/168, 19 October 2000.

e) WTO, *Submission by the European Communities*, WT/CTE/W/170, 19 October 2000;

f) WTO, *Submission by the European Communities*, "Multilateral Environmental Agreements (MEAs): Implementation of the Doha Development Agenda," TN/TE/W/1, 21 March 2002.

g) WTO, *Submission by Argentina*, TN/TE/W/2, 23 May 2002

h) WTO, *Submission by Switzerland* TN/TE/W/4, 6 June 2002.

i) WTO, *Submission by Australia*, "Suggested Procedure for the Negotiations under Paragraph 31(i) of the Doha Declaration"; TN/TE/W/7, 7 June 2002.

j) WTO, Submission by Japan, TN/TE/W/10, 2 October 2002.

k) WTO, *Submission by the Separate Customs Territory of Taiwan, Penghu, Kinmen and Matsu*, "Contribution on Paragraph 31(i) of the Doha Ministerial Declaration," TN/TE/W/11, 2 October 2002.

l) WTO, *Submission by the Republic of Korea*, TN/TE/W/13, 8 October 2002.

m) WTO, *Submission by Switzerland*, TN/TE/W/16, 6 November 2002.

n) WTO, *Submission by the United States*, "Sub-paragraph 31(i) of the Doha Declaration," TN/TE/W/20, 10 February 2003.

o) WTO, *Submission by India*, "Relationship Between Specific Trade Obligations Set Out in MEAs and WTO Rules," TN/TE/W/23, 20 February 2003.

p) *Submission by Malaysia*, "Paragraph 31(i) of the Doha Ministerial Declaration," TN/TE/W/29, 30 April 2003.

q) WTO, *Submission by the EC*, "The Relationship Between MEAs and WTO Agreements: 'Set Out in MEAs'," TN/TE/W/31, 14 May 2003.

r) WTO, *Submission by the Separate Customs Territory of Taiwan, Penghu, Kinmen and Matsu*, TN/TE/W/36, 3 July 2003.

Panel and Appellate Body Reports

Thailand – Restrictions on Importation of and Internal Taxes on Cigarettes (hereinafter *Thailand – Cigarettes*), adopted on 7 November 1990, BISD 37S/200.

United States-Measures Affecting Alcoholic and Malt Beverages case, Panel report adopted on 19 June 1992.

United States – Standards for Reformulated and Conventional Gasoline (hereinafter *US – Gasoline*), Appellate Body Report and Panel Report, adopted on 20 May 1996, WT/DS2/R and WT/DS2/AB/R.

Japan – Taxes on Alcoholic Beverages, Appellate Body Report adopted on 1 November 1996, WT/DS8,10,11/AB/R.

Korea-Measures Affecting Imports of Fresh, Chilled and Frozen Beef, Appellate Body Report, adopted 10 January 2001, WT/DS169/AB/R,

United States – Import Prohibition of Certain Shrimp and Shrimp Products, Recourse to Article 21.5 by Malaysia (hereinafter *US – Shrimp (Article 21.5)*), Appellate Body Report and Panel Report, adopted on 21 November 2001, WT/DS58/RW and WT/DS58/AB/RW.

European Communities – Measures Affecting Asbestos and Asbestos-Containing Products (hereinafter *EC – Asbestos*), Appellate Body Report and Panel Report, adopted on 5 April 2001, WT/DS135, and WT/DS135/AB/R.

Domestic Judgments

Turtle Island Restoration Network versus Evans, 00-1569, -1581, -1582 (Fed. Cir., March 21, 2002.

11

Social Clause in WTO and Core ILO Labour Standards: Concerns of India and Other Developing Countries

K.D. RAJU

Introduction

While the recently concluded Fourth World Trade Organisation (WTO) Ministerial Conference in Doha in 2001 reaffirmed their 1996 Singapore Declaration[1] that International Labour Organisation (ILO) is the competent body to set and deal with the issue of core labour standards, it cannot however be taken for granted that the issue of the relationship between trade and labour standards has been put to rest. The countries like EU and US are pushing the agenda of linking trade with labour standards through various regional agreements. The developing countries argue that there is a hidden agenda of protectionism behind the rhetoric.

The emergence of the World Trade Organisation in 1994 marked a new era in the multilateral trading system. The core principles of the system are:

- Reduction of tariffs;
- Most favoured nation treatment (MFN);
- National treatment; and
- Elimination of quantitative restrictions.

Gradually non-trade concerns like environmental issues, labour standards, and even national laws and policies which directly or indirectly affect trade also came into the agendas of the multilateral system for discussion. The debate on this subject is mainly based on the feeling that the countries with lower labour standards will gain

1. http://www.wto.org/english/thewto_e/minst_e/min96_e/min96_e.htm

an unfair advantage in the international market when compared with labour intensive products of the developed countries. Hence the developed countries want a social clause in the rule based multilateral trading system. The developing countries are opposing this move as a barrier and burden on them, which denies market access for their goods and services. Whether there is any real economic advantage for these countries is a moot question. The core labour standards are provided in the ILO Conventions. The ILO paper says, *'The International labour standards, which have been proposed for the social clause, are not about setting international wage levels or benefits. Rather, the social clause will only contain core labour standards that embody human rights, as defined by the United Nations Universal Declaration and Covenants on Human Rights'*.[2] Therefore it is sufficiently clear that the idea is not one of fixing global minimum wages.

What is a Social Clause?

A social clause refers to a legal provision in a trade agreement aimed at removing the most extreme forms of labour exploitation in exporting countries by allowing importing countries to take trade measures against the exporting countries which fail to conform to a set of internationally agreed minimum labour standards.

The idea is simply to permit WTO member-states to deviate from the normal principle of non-discrimination among trading partners by allowing them to prohibit (or prohibitively tax) the importation of goods from countries that do not observe 'core labour standards'. This idea is pushed by the trade powers like US and the EU in the multilateral forum. These countries are pushing these ideas ever since the pre – Tokyo round of trade negotiations. The US legislations, Section 301 and Special 301 threatened counter measures against denial of internationally recognised worker's rights. Recently, the EU and the US are using core labour standards as a criterion for granting trade preferences to developing countries under the Generalised System of Preferences (GSP).[3] The idea of introducing universal labour standards was envisaged with the ILO. But in the absence of

2. Hoe Lim, *The Social Clause: Issues and Challenges,* ILO at p.2.
3. Chaulia Sreeram, "Social Clause in WTO – Cases For and Against," *Economic and Political Weekly,* February 16, 2002, end notes.

a compelling mechanism with the ILO to implement these standards in the domestic level, these countries are vigorously arguing for incorporating these ideas into the WTO.

Who are the Proponents of the Social Clause?

In the above backdrop, it is observed that in developed countries unemployment and income disparities in their domestic market is increasing and they are linking this to cheap labour standards in the South. Therefore they want to protect their industries from cheap imports through a social clause in WTO and can take advantage of rising third world wages. Chaulia Sreeram comments *"A social clause is seen as a political desideratum by policy-makers in Europe and America to construct broad consensual support for multilateral trade liberalisation among labour unions and the productive workforce"*.

The developing countries see this move as a hidden agenda of the developed world for trade protectionism and denial of market access for their goods in the Western markets. They also argue that a forum like WTO, constituted for trade facilitation should not handle issues like labour and environmental standards. That will undermine the mandate of the ILO and will result in a cleavage of interests between the South and the North. There is no consensus on this matter among the members. While developing countries have firmly resisted efforts to introduce a social clause into multilateral trade matters, they are not at all opposed to the endeavour to construct a 'social floor' under globalisation. After all, the whole purpose of development is to raise the security and well being of the entire population in developing countries. The pertinent question is how best to achieve this.

The current initiatives of the advanced countries intending to make core labour standards compulsory by threatening sanctions are regarded by developing countries as being protectionist. "They question why a country like the US, which has not ratified many of the core ILO conventions and whose own degree of unionisation is barely above the average for developing countries, should push so hard for using trade measures as a weapon to enforce labour standards including the right to unionise".[4] Similar division can be

4. Singh, Ajit and Ann, Zammit, *The Global Labour Standards Controversy: Critical Issues for Developing Countries*, South Centre 2000, p.6.

seen within the community of non-governmental organisations. International agencies are also divided on this issue. World Bank is very critical of the social clause proposal and the ILO does not want to separate trade from human rights standards.[5]

The Link between Trade and Labour Standards in the Multilateral Trading System

The proposal to link labour standards with international trade is not new. During the UN Conference on Trade and Employment of 1946-48, it was proposed that a social clause be included in the Havana charter, which was meant to create the International Trade Organisation (ITO), the predecessor of General Agreement on Tariff and Trade (GATT). The provision on labour standards in the Havana Charter (CH, Art.7) reads:

> The members recognise that all countries have a common interest in the achievement and maintenance of fair labour standards related to productivity and thus in the improvement of wages and working conditions as productivity in the production for export, create difficulties in international trade and, accordingly, each Member shall take whatever action may be appropriate and feasible to eliminate such conditions within its territory.

The Havana Charter was not ratified by the US and as a result ITO was not established. But in 1995, when the WTO came into existence these provisions were dropped. It included just a single provision, i.e. Article XX (e), which permits governments to ban goods produced by prison labour.

At the WTO Ministerial Conference in Singapore in late-1996, the ministers discussed the issue of labour standards extensively and in their declaration held that:

> *We renew our commitment to the observance of internationally recognised core labour standards. The International labour Organisation (ILO) is the competent body to set and deal with these standards, and we affirm our support for its work in promoting them. We believe that economic growth and development fostered by increased trade and further trade liberalisation contribute to the promotion of these standards for protectionist purposes, and agree that the comparative advantage of countries, particularly low-wage developing countries, must in no way be put into question. In this regard, we note that the WTO and ILO Secretariats will continue their existing collaboration.*[6]

5. ILO, The social dimensions of the liberalisation of world trade, ILO, Geneva, 1994.
6. WTO, Singapore Ministerial Declaration (1996), WT/MIN(96) DEC, 18 December, WTO, Geneva.

The ministers committed themselves to the implementation of core labour standards for the first time and maintained that the ILO is the competent organisation to deal the issue of labour standards. They rejected the use of these standards for protectionist purposes and reiterated the need for collaboration between the ILO and the WTO Secretariats.

A Report by the United Nations Conference on Trade and Development (UNCTAD 1999, Trade and Development Report), pointed out that in almost all developing countries that have undertaken rapid trade liberalisation, wage inequality had increased. Industrial employment of unskilled workers had declined and real wages have fallen drastically, by 20-30 per cent in some Latin American countries.

The North is always preaching that the social clause will enable the multilateral system to monitor the inhuman treatment of workers at the domestic level and will enhance labour standards in the developing countries. It is true that protecting the basic human rights of workers is a necessary and vital thing in all countries. But whether these labour standards are to be imposed compulsorily with punitive action is the real question.

Other Arguments For and Against Minimum Labour Standards

Generally it can be said that the developed nations are advocating minimum standards while the developing nations have flatly rejected the idea. The industrialised countries argued that the lack of universal standards lead to exploitation and asymmetry in international trade. The ILO argued that the standards could not be separated from human rights. The export-oriented firms are employing children for their cost competitive advantage in the global market. A study conducted by the ILO reveals that increase in the costs for replacing child labour with adult labour is only 4 per cent and these can be easily absorbed by the industry. The former Director General of the WTO Mike Moore opined, "labour standards would damage the poor.[7]"

7. Mike Moore, Labour Issue is "false debate", obscures underlying consensus, http://www.wto.org/wto/press 152.htm, 28.11.99, p1.

Hence in order to reduce child labour, children should be replaced by the estimated 800 million unemployed youth freeing the children to go to school and get knowledge and work for the future. More importantly the question is whether only those exporting countries have the moral obligation to implement the standards or these importers have a contributory obligation to support those countries willing to implement these standards in their industries.

Labour Standards and Effect on Trade

The Organisation of Economic Co-operation and Development (OECD, 1996) study found that the high and low standards in the labour sector appear to have little impact on international trade or performance. It also found that liberal labour policies have been accompanied by better productivity in the long run. Supporting this view an ILO study revealed that a number of complaints occurred in the sectors of the countries have better standards. Hence there is no justification for linking trade and social clause. In the case of child labour, developing countries argue that child labour is essentially a domestic problem - for example only 8 *per cent* of India's child labour force is engaged in the export sector.[8]

Industrialised countries enjoy a comparative advantage through huge capital and technological powers. Social clause can become a tool for developed countries to impose their social standards on developing countries and distort international trade to the detriment of consumer welfare within the developed world itself. The developed countries are trying to insert a social clause whose definition itself has not been established. The apprehension of the developing countries is well founded in such a situation that this will be used as a protectionist tool to shield uncompetitive sectors and they therefore are strongly arguing against the inclusion of the social clause in the WTO.

The ILO Core Labour Standard Conventions

It can be said that all aspects of labour standards involve the International Labour Organisation (ILO). Its tripartite structure, allows governments, trade unions and employer associations to meet on an equal footing under the auspices of the specialised body of

8. Free the Children International, the Myth Underlying Child Labour? http://freechildren.org/hdro/oc32.c.htm, 23.12.99,p.3.

United Nations. The ILO defines labour standards that are to be adopted by the member countries. Since its establishment in 1919, ILO has adopted 174 conventions and 181 recommendations on different subjects. The core standards are contained in these ILO conventions. Once these conventions are ratified by the members it becomes obligatory on the part of the members to abide by them. The ILO will supervise the implementation of the mechanism at the domestic level.

The proposals for a social clause are based on the following ILO conventions:

1. Convention 29: Forced Labour Convention (1930);
2. Convention 87, Freedom of Association and Protection of the Right to Organise (1948);
3. Convention 98: Right to Organise and Collective Bargaining (1949)
4. Convention 100: Equal Remuneration Convention (1951);
5. Convention 105: on the Abolition of Forced Labour (1957).
6. Convention 111: Discrimination (Employment and Occupation) Convention (1958).
7. Convention 138: Minimum Age Convention (1973);
8. Convention 182: on the Worst Forms of Child Labour (1999).

Many countries including India are yet to ratify these conventions. India has not ratified the conventions dealing with freedom of association and collective bargaining: Conventions 87 and 98 and Conventions 138 and 182 pertaining to child labour (Table 11.1).

As mentioned before the WTO Ministerial Conference held in Doha reaffirmed their earlier commitment made in the Singapore Conference, that ILO will deal the issue of labour standards. Once again the responsibility of maintaining core labour standards all over the world has been entrusted to the ILO. But the developing countries argue that they cannot afford to implement higher labour standards because of political constraints, economic problems and of course the fear of losing competitive advantages in the international market. But the high level of ratifications of these conventions suggests that the underlying principles in these conventions are widely accepted. These core labour standard conventions are basic Human Right

Conventions which are supported by three parties of the ILO structure and have achieved more than 50 per cent ratification.

Table 11.1

ILO Core Conventions

Sl. No.	Convention	Year	Convention No.	Number of Countries Ratified
1	Forced Labour	1930	No.29	163
2	Freedom of Association and Protection of the Right to Organise	1948	No.87	142
3	Right to Organise and Collective Bargaining (1949)	1949	No.98	154
4.	Equal Remuneration	1951	No.100	161
5.	Abolition of Forced Labour	1957	No.105	161
6.	Discrimination (Employment and Occupation) Convention	1958	No.111	160
7.	Minimum Age Convention	1973	No.138	134
8.	Worst Forms of Child Labour	1999	No.182	150

Source: ILO dated 19.05.2004.

Figure 11.1

ILO Core Conventions Ratifications As On 19.05.2005

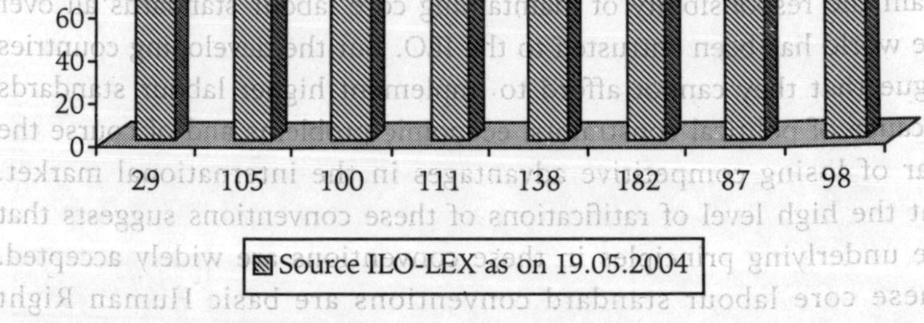

Towards Social Clause

Presently there is a greater consensus on globalisation and world trade, which was not there in the past. Therefore the question arises as to whether the ILO can enforce these labour standards throughout the world with its current structure and the philosophy of voluntarism, in the context of the entrustment of this task, in the Doha Ministerial Conference of the WTO. The whole question is whether non-compliance of these standards should be followed by punitive actions like trade sanctions or special tariffs on the products coming from such countries and there is no unanimity in this issue among the ILO Members. Among the above conventions India has ratified 38 ILO Conventions of which 36 are active, including Convention 29, 100 and 111. For the other conventions the Indian government claims that national laws are enacted and Constitutional provisions are sufficient for tackling the problem. There appears to be a lack of interest within the Government circles to ratify these conventions despite the transformed international scenario.

The developed countries are keen on the social clause under the WTO discipline. They are paying renewed attention to the standards and world trade. These are reflected in some of their regional integration agreements and trade agreements like the development of a social clause in the European Union and in the negotiation of a North American Agreement on Labour Co-operation in conjunction with the North Atlantic Free Trade Agreement (NAFTA). But the studies conducted in these countries show that these countries never supported various rights, including the right to strike.

The Core Labour Standards

The core labour standard conventions mentioned above contain the basic rights of workers. The freedom of association and collective bargaining convention (Convention No. 87 and 98) protects the right of workers to form trade unions and engage in collective bargaining. The freedom of workers to organise themselves will give them the feeling that other abuses, like child and forced labour, discrimination and unsafe conditions in the work place can be prevented. Ultimately the object of implementing all these standards is the welfare of the workers. But unfortunately globalisation in the current pattern is in the reverse direction that is eroding even these existing benefits. Article 2 of the Convention No. 87 provides:

"Workers and employers, without distinction whatsoever, shall have the right to establish and, subject only to the rules of the organisation concerned, to join organisations of their own choosing without previous authorization". But this right is denied in the Economic Zones all over the world.

There are serious difficulties from a developing country perspective in the case of Conventions 87 and 98 concerning the freedom of association. The conventions are talking about a picture of unlimited freedom of association. It does not take into account the fact that unlimited bargaining power will disrupt the industry and will lead to social chaos. The government also should have a say and control in the case of unemployment, small-scale sectors and other social obligations. The convention says nothing about small [9]scale and un-organised workers, which form a majority of the entire labour force in most of the developing countries. It is correctly opined by Ajit Singh and Ann Zammit that *"It would appear that human rights defined and interpreted in terms of these two core conventions are destined only for a small part of the working population, benefiting mainly those who are already relatively privileged"*.

Forced Labour

Convention No. 29, the Forced Labour Convention (1930), and Convention No.105, the Abolition of Forced Labour Convention (1957) focuses on the issue of forced labour. Forced labour is defined as work required under threat of penalty and extracted without a voluntary offer by the worker. They condemn slavery and bonded labour and also (Convention No.105) exhort that compulsory labour is not to be used for purposes of political coercion or education, forced economic development, or as disciplinary devices against strikes. The conventions contain a broad range of prohibitions against prison labour. Certain exceptions are made allowing compulsory labour. Work may be mandated by the government if it is in public interest and in response to "imminent necessity" (e.g., impending war), or for normal civic obligations, or

9. Singh, Ajit, and Ann Zammit, *The Global Labour Standards Controversy: Critical Issues for Developing Countries*, South Center, 2000, p.41.

for compulsory military service. Work may be required also of convicted prisoners in the public interest. Prison work is disallowed if it is contracted privately, unless the work is performed under public supervision or is voluntary on the part of the prisoners.

As of 30 September 2002, 162 countries had ratified Convention No.29 and 156 countries had ratified Convention No. 105. The United States has ratified only Convention No. 105; among the OECD nations Canada has chosen not to ratify Convention No .29. Japan has ratified Convention No. 29 but not Convention No.105. China has not ratified either of the conventions, but is "meticulously studying" them for potential ratification in the future. The list of countries which have not ratified both the conventions include Armenia, Vietnam, Republic of Korea, Sao Tome and Principe and Mongolia. The United States continues to reject ratification of Convention No. 29 because its state laws conflict with the provisions on prison labour. In particular, the growing trend toward private sub-contracting of the operation of prison facilities could well be found to conflict with the prohibition of private supervision of prison labour. The Philippines objects to several of the categories of exemptions from forced labour and refuses to ratify Convention No. 29, however it argues that its ratification of Convention No. 105 requires it to abolish compulsory labour more broadly. Mozambique takes an interesting position: because it has already done what it can do to eliminate forced labour within the institutional capacities of the country,[10] therefore they see no particular need to ratify Convention No. 29 (presumably because of political opposition to doing so). Singapore and Malaysia have formally denounced Convention No.105 as it interferes with their political and developmental processes.

Discrimination

Freedom from discrimination is also considered as a basic right by the ILO and is promoted by two fundamental conventions, Convention No. 100, Equal Remuneration (1950) and Convention No. 111, Discrimination in Employment and Occupation (1958). Convention No. 100 calls for equal pay for work of equal value, without discrimination on the basis of gender. This provision may be

---

10. *Ibid.*, (ILO) 1995b, p. 4.

given effect by a combination of laws and regulations, wage determination devices, and collective bargaining. "Objective appraisal" of jobs is suggested as a means of determining the meaning of "work of equal value." Convention No.111 mandates the elimination of discrimination in employment, training, and access to particular occupations on the basis of race, colour, sex, religion, political opinion or social origin. Discrimination could arise from any "distinction, exclusion or preference" made on the basis of any of these personal characteristics.

As of September 2002, Convention No. 100 had been ratified by 159 nations and Convention No. 111 by 156 nations. The United States has ratified neither convention, again because of concerns about their technical consistency with American laws. For example, it is claimed that the ILO's conception of "equal remuneration for work of equal value" does not match the American legal standard of "equal pay for substantially equal work." Nevertheless, US laws are substantially in compliance with the spirit of the convention, at the same time various provisions are in conflict with laws at the state and federal levels.

Child Labour

Child labour is covered by the core ILO conventions Nos. 138 and 182 on minimum age and worst form of labour. According to a recent ILO survey, the number of working children between the age of 5 and 14 in developing countries is 250 million and out of this about 120 million of them are full timers. In India alone, it has estimated 70 – 80 million-child workers.[11] This does not however mean that child workers are found only in developing countries. In 1990 an inspection by the United States Department of Labour found more than 11,000 children working illegally.[12]

Therefore it is apparent that child labour is not only a problem of developing countries but also of the industrialised countries. The Convention No. 182 compels the countries to work with ILO to fix time bound phase-out periods to eliminate the worst forms of child

---

11. Free the Children International, the myth underlying child labour? http://www.freechildren.org/factsmyths.htm, 21.03.00,p1.

12. Committee on Labour Standards, *Model WTO 2000*, p.7.

labour. The reasons for the continuing existence of child labour may vary from country to country, but in many countries the main reason is poverty and high costs of education which compel parents to send their children to the factories for earning their daily bread. It is more a social problem than an economic one, one that can only be eradicated by increasing the social status and income of the poor. Without proper projects for compensating the parents for loss of income from their children the imposition of mere standards will lead to many children resorting to illegal activities where they will become a burden on society than when they were working a earning. It is very clear that without such projects for eradication of poverty the objective of promoting the welfare of children will not be fruitful. Such schemes for example are found to be very successful in Brazil.

In June 1998 the ILO discussed new international standards on child labour. The new standards call for the immediate suppression of extreme forms of child labour including:

- Slavery and slavery-like practices;
- Forced labour, debt bondage and serfdom;
- Use of children in illegal activities, prostitution and pornography;
- Any work or activity which is likely to jeopardise the health, safety or morale of children.

Besides the ILO Convention, there is another convention to protect children: The United Nations Convention on the Rights of the Child. This convention has been signed by 191 members of the UN except USA and Somalia.

The final basic right is freedom from the exploitation of child labour. The ILO has approached this issue indirectly, by establishing Convention No. 138, Minimum Age (1973). It calls for setting a minimum age for entry into employment (15 years or the end of compulsory education, whichever is later). If the work is dangerous or immoral, the minimum age should be 18 (reflecting some notion of what constitutes the age of majority), though definitions of what is dangerous or immoral are left to national choice. Exceptions from these rules are provided. A minimum age of 13 or 14 is acceptable for light work if it is "not prejudicial" to educational attainment.

Poor countries can set a minimum age of 14 (12 for light work) in general and of 16 for dangerous work. Child labour is acceptable if it is an "integral part" of a course of education or training approved by worker and employer groups and by competent authorities. Finally, exemptions exist for children working on family farms.

Only 117 countries had ratified Convention No. 138 as of September 2002 and several countries have not ratified this vital convention including rich countries like Canada, New Zealand, Australia, the United States, and Switzerland. They object to various provisions of the convention and simply refuse to ratify it. For example, Canadian law (federal and provincial) does not provide for prohibition of work for persons under school-leaving age, nor does it prohibit night work for children under the age of 13. New Zealand has numerous restrictions on child employment, but in ways that are somewhat inconsistent with the provisions of the convention. Switzerland has wide sectoral exemptions from its minimum-age laws and has no legislation covering work outside a formal employment relationship. The United States notes several inconsistencies of the convention with its federal and state laws. Mexico objects to the provisions on minimum ages for dangerous work, citing their inconsistencies with its law, while Mozambique admits that it lacks the educational infrastructure that could support the ratification of the convention (ILO, 1995). India has not ratified both conventions Nos. 138 and 182. In general, it is clear that specifying a minimum working age of 15 (or 18 for hazardous jobs) remains unrealistic in many developing countries, given the low frequencies of young people completing primary schooling. On a more conceptual level, several nations object to the Minimum Age Convention for its indirect approach to the issue of child labour exploitation. It can be argued that some kinds of work undertaken by young people are neither detrimental to their development nor is it coerced. On the other hand, prohibiting the employment of young persons may force them into worse situations in uncovered sectors or in other areas where these standards were not enforced. In short, the minimum-age approach does not distinguish work from exploitation. The convention is also criticised for not setting out safeguards against exploitation of child labour.

Freedom of Association

The ILO also considered the right of workers to associate freely and to engage in unobstructed collective bargaining with employers and these rights are included in Convention No. 87, Freedom of Association and Protection of the Right to Organise (1948) and Convention No. 98, Right to Organise and Collective Bargaining (1949) in its core conventions. Convention No. 87 guarantees freedom of association. It calls for free rights to establish and join trade unions, with no formalities such as prior authorization requirements, minimum membership requirements, or limits on the number of unions by enterprise or sector. Trade unions are supposed to be free to hold elections and pursue their interests without governmental interference. Right to strike is inherent in the convention, except with regard to the military and police, whose rights in this regard are subject to national laws. Convention No. 98 extends the scope of protection for labour organisation, calling for no discrimination in employment decisions against union members, protection of organisations from interference by employers, and an exhortation to governments to promote collective bargaining. These conventions are among the most widely ratified. Convention No. 87 has been ratified by 141 countries and convention No. 98 by 152 countries as of September 2002. India has not ratified any of the two conventions till date. Some of the countries have ratified the conventions while many of the provisions are reserved. For example, Mexico has adopted Convention No. 87 but retains governmental rights to declare strikes illegal and limits the number of unions per state enterprise. Indonesia and Malaysia have ratified Convention No. 98 (not number 87) but place significant restrictions on rights to organise (e.g., unions are disallowed in the Malaysian electronic sector) and onerous registration and size requirements on trade unions. At the same time, despite having strong national labour laws, Canada, New Zealand, Switzerland, and the United States have refused to ratify one or both of the conventions (both in the case of the United States). Again, the issue is incompatibility of laws with the conventions. Canadian and American laws allow wider exclusions of collective bargaining rights or the right to strike, while numerous states in the United States allow the hiring of replacement workers, which practice could be construed as a restriction on the right to strike without interference. Switzerland claims that the language in the conventions precluding anti-union discrimination is inconsistent with provisions of its labour law. Indeed, rights to strike are typically limited to some degree even in developed nations. These limitations, such as right-to-work laws and the ability to lock out and fire workers and to replace them at will, are the subject of significant debate. Such rights vary by country and even by sub-regional authorities within countries, without much attention paid to the prescriptions of the ILO conventions. At the other extreme, rights to strike can be very heavily protected through closed-shop rules, in which labour unions have nearly unlimited rights, perhaps coming at the expense of employee rights.

These different angles regarding problems of ratification point to difficulties with the ILO conventions. Ratification of an ILO convention by a country is a commitment to make its laws consistent with the convention (although it is more accurate to state that most countries which ratify conventions do so after their labour laws are already consistent). However, this does not mean that actual labour practices will meet stipulations in the conventions. A primary explanation is that the conventions have no binding powers of enforcement. Indeed, the ILO has resisted the notion of international enforcement of its conventions on grounds that doing so could severely limit ratification and push many countries out of the organisation altogether. On the other hand, non-ratification is not a meaningful indicator of weak labour protection. For one thing, those countries that consider their laws to be in conformity with conventions may choose not to undergo the cost of ratification. For another, numerous countries with strong labour laws, such as Canada, Switzerland, and the United States, find their laws incompatible with convention requirements, both for minor technical reasons and for substantive reasons. This situation makes questionable the notion that existing ILO conventions can serve as a meaningful basis for an enforceable international social clause on minimum labour protection.

Summing Up

The issue of implementing labour standards throughout the world in the context of increasing international trade has been the subject of heated discussion at national and international forum like

WTO. The developed countries are pushing this agenda in the WTO and at the same time the developing countries are opposing the move to link labour standards with trade.

The workforce in India is estimated to be around 315 million according to the 1991 census, that is 37.6 per cent of the total population. Out of these 249.3 million are rural workers and 65.6 million are urban workers.[13] The labour welfare clause is provided in our constitution in Part IV. While it was made non-enforceable, it is however mandatory that every state, while making laws, should keep these goals in mind. The Supreme Court while interpreting the directive principles has played an activist role to translate the spirit of Part IV in the Constitution.

India's Stand on Linking Labour Standards With the Social Clause in the WTO

The Delhi Declaration of January 1995 at the Fifth Labour Ministers' Conference of Non-Aligned and Other Developing Countries expressed deep concern regarding efforts to link international trade and enforcement of labour standards through the imposition of the social clause. The WTO, Singapore Declaration of December 1996 also reiterated its commitment to entrust the matter to the ILO rather than the WTO and the ministers also agreed that labour standards should not be used for protectionist purposes and that the comparative advantage of the developing countries should not be questioned. India also played an active role in Seattle in 1999 to prevent linking trade with labour and environmental issues. All the stakeholders in India including the trade unions and Government are in favour of upgrading labour standards, but are against the linking of labour standards with trade and also against enforcing it under the threat of trade sanctions.

India's Adherence to Core Labour Standards and Important Legislations

As in most other countries, the ILO conventions and recommendations have influenced India also in enacting the

13. *Indian Labour at a Glance, A Dossier on Labour Standards,* Centre for Education and Communication, New Delhi, 1995.

legislations on wages, working conditions, welfare and social security, protection of the vulnerable sections of the society, non-discrimination etc. The Constitution of India and its labour legislations uphold all the fundamental principles contained in the eight core international labour standards. India has also ratified four out of the eight core conventions that constitute the fundamental principles. India's record is better than that of US, which has ratified only two of the eight core conventions.

The issue of labour is a concurrent subject in the Indian Constitution. Article 246(4) of the Constitution provides for joint legislation with regard to trade unions, industrial disputes, social security, conditions of work, employer's work workmen's compensation, maternity benefit etc. The labour law in India contains a number of legislations at the central as well as state levels. The beginning of labour laws in India can be traced back to the Fatal Accidents Act, 1885, Factories Act, Mines Act and other legislations. Over time the number of legislations increased to more than hundred, many of them have been replaced and now there are forty laws in force. At present, the Government of India is planning to amend many labour laws in accordance with the spirit of globalisation. This position was reiterated by the Prime Minister of India while addressing a labour conference held at New Delhi in the month of September 2002.

The problem with labour laws in India is that the multiplicity of them leads to different interpretations and complexities. Hence there is an urgent need for a comprehensive Indian Labour Standards Act, which would come under a single authority, 'The Indian Labour Authority' to enforce laws with greater ease and efficiency. The multiplicity of enforcement agencies and lack of co-ordination between them aid defaulters in avoiding implementation of these laws. Dr. Roberto Zagha of World Bank, found in his study that there are a host of conflicts in the Indian labour laws. For example the concept of "wage" is defined in eleven different ways in eleven different laws![14]

14. Swamy, Subramanyam (2000), *India's Labour Standards under the WTO Frame Work*, Konark Publishers, New Delhi, p.46.

The Freedom of Association

The Indian Constitution guarantees the freedom of Association in Article 19. Workers are guaranteed the right to form and join trade unions of their own choice without prior authorisation. This fundamental right is not unrestricted and like other fundamental rights it is subject to restrictions. The trade unions have the legally protected right to strike. But the notice is required in the public sector and in certain special industries. The Trade Union Act of 1926 prohibits employers from retribution against striking workers. India has not ratified Conventions Nos. 87 and 98 concerning the freedom of association and the right to collective bargaining due to technical difficulties in granting trade union rights to civil servants. But the main reservation of the government can be seen in the opinion of the former Chief Labour Commissioner of the Government of India, S.Nath (1997) that "*these conventions have not been ratified by India because the policy of the government has been to restrict the freedom of association to only manual workers (workmen) and exclude supervisory and managerial workers.*"[15] The ratification of the conventions would involve granting the following rights to Government servants:

- To strike;
- To openly criticise Government policies;
- To freely join foreign organisations.

Obviously these rights cannot be granted to Government servants on many grounds. The Constitution, however guarantees these rights and further the right of collective bargaining was included in the Industrial Disputes Act, 1947.

The important legislations pertaining to core labour standards are the following:

1. *The Child Labour (Prohibition and Regulation) Act, 1986*

The objective of the Act says "An Act to prohibit the engagement of children in certain employments and to regulate the conditions of work of children in certain employments and to regulate the conditions of work of children in certain other employments". The

15. C.S. Venkitaratnam (1998), Globalisation and Labour-Management Relations, India and International Labour Standards, p.292.

Act forbids employment of children below the age of 14 years and regulates the following areas of child labour:

- Health and safety at workplaces
- Hours and period of work
- Weekly holidays
- Maintenance of registers of children in employment

The use of child labour is banned especially in hazardous industries. Under the schedule Part A (Section 3), the following activities are prohibited:

- Occupation connected with transportation of goods or passengers or mails by railways;
- Jobs created in moving trains or requiring changing of platforms;
- Railway construction done in the proximity of railway lines;
- Works in ports or within the limits of the port.

Part B of the Schedule prohibits the employment of children in certain processes of work, basically, which are harmful to children like:

- *Bidi* making;
- Carpet weaving;
- Cement manufacturing;
- Cloth printing, weaving and dyeing;
- Manufacture of matches, explosives and fireworks;
- Mica cutting and splitting;
- Soap manufacturing;
- Tanning;
- Building and construction etc.

While legally child labour is prohibited in India, according to the available statistics, out of the total 250 million child labourers all over the world, 70 to 80 million are in India itself.[16] The Constitution (Articles 24, 39 and 45) prohibits the employment of

16. http://www.freechildren.org/factsmyths.htm, 21.03.00, P1.

children in hazardous industries and also has eight legislations containing provisions for protecting children. This Act incorporates fourteen Conventions of the ILO. India has not ratified the ILO conventions relating to child labour, Conventions No. 138 and 182, but provides for ban in hazardous industries.

2. *Bonded Labour System (Abolition) Act, 1976 as Amended in 1985*

This Act prohibits bonded labour or forced labour in any form. Article 23 of the Indian Constitution upholds this prohibition. The Act is comprehensive and takes into account all the debt-related forced labour that exists in various regional and social customs.

The Act provides for:

- Extinguishments of liability to repay bonded debt;
- Property of bonded labourers to be freed from mortgage.;
- Protection against eviction of freed bonded labour from his home;
- Creditor not to accept payment against extinguished debt.

The Act also provides for the constitution of Vigilance Committees to implement and monitor the laws and also to facilitate the rehabilitation of bonded labourers. The Vigilance Committees are authorised to act as defendants for legal suits filed against the bonded labourer. The Constitution also prohibits forced labour. According to Article 2 of Convention No. 29, forced or compulsory labour means any service or work taken "involuntarily." According to a Supreme Court decision forced labour is defined as work at less than the minimum wage. This type of system is prevalent throughout the country despite the fact that such violations are punishable by imprisonment up to three years. India ratified the concerned ILO convention No. 29 on 30.11.1954 itself and Convention No. 105 on 18.05.2000.

3. *The Contract Labour (Regulation and Abolition) Act, 1970*

This Act aims at abolition of contract labour with respect to such categories as may be notified by the government and at regulating the service conditions of contract labour where abolition is not possible. This Act protects contract labourers from the exploitation of employers by treating contract workers as always "temporary" and denying all their rights.

This Act advocates the abolition of contract labour in areas where the work is of a continuous nature and therefore requires permanent employees or workers. It also lay down proper regulation of contract labour in some areas. They include:

- Prohibition of contract labour;
- Registration and licensing of contractors;
- Welfare and health of contract Labour;
- Regulation of wages;
- Maintenance of labour registers, muster rolls and employment cards to workers;
- Constitution of a Central Advisory Board and State Boards to advise the concerned governments on the implementation of the Act.

4. Equal Remuneration Act, 1976

The principle of equal pay for equal work is contained in Clause (d) of Article 39 of the Indian Constitution which is an accompaniment of the equality clause enshrined in Article 14 and 16 of the Constitution. This directive envisages that the State shall, in particular, direct its policy towards securing equal pay for equal work for both men and women. This principle implies that persons holding identical posts may not be treated differently.

This Act provides for wages for equal work and also that gender bias does not exist in wages paid to men and women for the same nature of work. It firmly lays down that a woman worker should get wages equal to men workers for jobs of equal labour weight under the same establishment. This is inconsistent with Article 1 of the Convention No.100 which guarantees equal remuneration irrespective of whether or not the employment is under the same employer. In the unorganised sector like agriculture and garment production, grass root implementation is difficult. Further this Act provides for equal treatment in recruitment on the basis of gender, except in cases where women are restricted from being employed. India has ratified conventions, Nos. 100 and 111 in the area of equality of opportunity and discrimination in respect of employment and occupation. The Act also provides for the Government to appoint authorities for hearing and deciding claims and complaints. In India certain states like Gujarat, Rajasthan, Punjab, Karnataka and Pondicherry follow certain restrictive practices like confining employment strictly to local people. Such restrictions are violative of Article 16 of the Constitution itself.

5. *Industrial Disputes Act, (1947), Amended in 1984*

The objects of the Act can be summarised as follows:

- Promotion of measures for maintaining security, amity and good relation between the employer and workmen;
- The settlement of disputes;
- The prevention of illegal strikes and lock-outs;
- Relief to workmen in the case of lay-off, retrenchment and closure of an undertaking;
- Provide for collective bargaining.

This Act provides for the settlement of industrial disputes through proper enquiry and procedures. Special provisions are laid down to approach redressal forums in the case of lay-offs, retrenchment, and closure and other unfair labour practices on the part of the employer. It not only covers factory workers as a collective, but also the worker as an individual. That means those who are not members of the worker unions can also approach the Tribunals for redressal of their grievances. India has not ratified the ILO convention relating to the right to organise and collective bargaining, Convention No. 98. In the context of economic growth, as a developing country India cannot afford legal sanctity for collective bargaining and the right to strike only to its comparatively highly paid middle class, as this would ultimately lead to paralysis of the service sector and the economy as a whole.

6. *The Factories Act, (1948), Amended in 1976*

This Act provides for the health, safety and other welfare safeguards of workers in factories. It was amended in 1976 to include the provisions for the appointment of safety inspectors and Statutory health surveys of the workers. To protect the health of the workers, the Act provides for the following stipulations:

- Provision for drainage of effluents;
- Maintenance of hygiene and cleanliness of factory premises;
- Provision for proper disposal of wastes and effluents;
- To provide ventilation and temperature control;
- Proper management of dust and fumes;
- To provide artificial humidification;
- To prevent overcrowding of factory premises;
- Provision of sufficient lighting;
- Provision of drinking water;
- Provision of elevators;
- Provision of spittoons etc.

In terms of safety, in the factory premises, the following stipulations are provided:

- Fencing of machinery specially those that can be dangerous if not enclosed properly.
- Special protective dresses for workers handling moving machines or parts of machinery in motion.
- Young persons should be discouraged from using moving machinery.
- Emergency gears and devices for cutting off power during emergencies are to be provided.
- No worker is to be allowed to carry excessive weights.
- Protection to eyes to be provided.
- Precautions against fumes and gases to be provided.

Special provisions are also included to handle hazardous processes in factories which include:

- Constitution of Site Appraisal Committee – the main function of the Committee is to inspect and approve sites for the location of factories involving hazardous substances.
- Compulsory disclosure of information by the occupier.
- Permissible limit of exposure to toxic and hazardous substances.
- Workers participation in safety management.

Indian Trade Unions and the Social Clause

Labour unions have played a critical role in the formation of the international labour standards by the ILO. The history of trade unionism in India can be traced back to the year 1890, when for the first time an association of mill workers was formed in the name and style of "Bombay Millhands Associations". The Indian Trade Union Act, 1926 laid down the procedure for the registration of trade unions and their duties and privileges. Now the government is also planning to amend the various labour laws in tune with the requirement of globalisation. The role of trade unions in the collective bargaining process is important in the changed international trade scenario. The unions render service to their members like negotiating on their behalf, for better working conditions, protecting them from unfair treatment and so on. It is time for the trade unions to train their members in accordance with international requirements and increase their efficiency.

During the Uruguay Round of negotiations the International Confederation of Free Trade Unions (ICFTU), the World Confederation of Labour (WCL), and the European Trade Union Confederation (ETUC) prepared a joint statement on the social clause and they prepared a proposal supporting the formation of a Joint Advisory Committee of the ILO and the WTO for the implementation of core labour standards. But the Indian counterpart Indian National Trade Union Congress (INTUC), of the ICFU, Mr. Sanjeeva Reddy publicly voiced his union's opposition to the ICFTU's proposal.[17]

Indian trade unions are generally of the view that the underlying motive of the developed countries[18] in linking the social clause with international trade, was yet another attempt to introduce unilateral and arbitrary non-tariff protectionist barriers to the multilateral free trade regime, although the function of the WTO is to make international trade fair and free. On the other hand all trade unions are supporting the ratification of ILO core conventions.

17. *The Times of India*, November 25, 1994.

18. The author personally interviewed and collected the opinions from various persons and organisations mentioned above.

The Secretary of the Centre of Indian Trade Unions (CITU), W.R. Warada Rajan opined that "*nobody is against the social clause in principle and the concerned ILO Conventions to be ratified by the Government of India, but we are against the linking of trade and social clause in WTO. ILO is the right forum to deal the matter*". Ms. Amarjit Kaur of All India Trade Union Committee (AITUC) asked "*what is the right of US and other developed countries to talk about social clause when most of the Indian companies in the Economic Zones have collaboration with the developed country companies and they are not only reluctant to implement these core labour standards but banning the trade union activities and collective bargaining in these areas. They didn't have the moral background for preaching the compulsory labour standards when they are not implementing in their own countries.*"

The Hind Mazdoor Sabha (HMS) is of the view that there is much need for improving the working and living conditions of workers and it would like to see more equitable distribution of gains from economic growth. The Government should adopt measures that ensure progressively increasing labour and social standards. On one hand they argue for the improvement of social standards and at the same time they are against policing of implementation by the developed world.

Conclusion and Suggestions

The formation of the WTO provides a threat as well as an opportunity for labour movements and their working conditions. Economic integration has dramatically altered the terrain in which labour endeavours to pursue its interests and defend its achievements. Any decision-making at the international level has its own disadvantages for local workers mainly because economic and working conditions vary from country to country. Local struggles are better than taking a substantial decision in the international level affecting different stakeholders in the different context and problems. Lobbying with international organisations like the ILO, World Bank and IMF should be for the betterment of the worker community rather than for employment cuts and lowering of wages. In many structural adjustment aid to poor countries, the conditionality of the IMF and the World Bank stipulates, reduction in government employment or wage cuts etc.

There is no dispute in the fact that international trade has been one of the pillars of growth for developing countries. It is recognised that the objective of improving the standards of living of its workers is the prime consideration of every country. But the developed countries' attempt to combat child and forced labour, to encourage the freedom of trade unions and the freedom to engage in collective bargaining on the basis of the ILO conventions are seen by developing countries with a doubtful eye. They fear that the linking of labour standards with a social clause in the WTO system will hamper their competitiveness in the international market. We saw the main arguments of the proponents of the social clause, like the US and the EU and those who are opposing linking trade with labour standards, the developing countries and jurists. The developed countries are still arguing for a social clause in the WTO to monitor the implementation of labour standards and punitive actions for non-compliance.

The task was entrusted with the ILO early in the 1996 WTO Ministerial Conference held at Singapore and the decision was reaffirmed in the Doha Ministerial Conference in 2001 also. Thus the ILO has a greater role to play in the implementation of core labour standards in the member countries. In ratifying core labour conventions the developing countries are in a better position than the developed world. Every country has problems in implementation at the domestic level. The OECD study (1996) suggests, that the incorporation of the social clause would not harm the economic performance of developing countries. The developing countries fear that this clause would be used against them as a protectionist measure by the developed world without making any effort for improving the social condition in their societies. Even though the exact figure of goods produced by child, prisoner or exploited labour is not available it would be a very small per centage of world trade. It is therefore difficult to agree to the argument of the inclusion of a social clause that will govern the entire range of international trade on the pretext of eradicating exploitation by controlling exports of an extremely small number of goods produced by the so-called exploited class as termed by the developed countries.

Even prior to the 1996 Singapore Ministerial Conference, organisations like ICFTU lobbied for linking labour standards with the WTO. Even after Singapore Ministerial also they launched a massive campaign for convincing the south affiliates about the necessity of linking the trade with labour standards. Before taking a stand on an important issue such as this, it would be appropriate to hold consultations in order to analyse the problems of the South in the interpretation of core standards at the domestic level. The OECD studies reveal that there is no additional economic burden due to the implementation of core labour standards. At the same time the ILO studies discovered that more complaints about the violation of the standards are from the developed countries itself. Before considering the implementation of the social clause, the following questions remain to be answered.

- How will trade be linked with the WTO? Will it be linked through the existing WTO Agreements or through a separate agreement on social clause?
- Whether compulsory implementation is needed?
- Who will decide if a certain country is violating labour standards?
- Who will be affected? The entire country or a particular sector or a particular industry?
- How will one measure the violation of the core labour rights, and what will be done to rectify a violation?
- Will there be any technical and financial support from the developed world for implementation in developing countries?
- If a violation is not rectified, will there be sanctions?
- Whether alternatives are available instead of sanctions?
- Who will decide on the violation? the ILO or the WTO Dispute Settlement System (DSU)?
- How do we ensure that the social clause efficiently achieves the desired results?
- Whether the social clause has a link to poverty alleviation?
- Whether there is a separate standard for developing countries?

In the Doha Ministerial Conference the proponents of this issue tried to put it on the agenda but failed due to the threat from the developing world that this would derail the negotiations itself. It is expected that fresh attempts would be made by the proponents to re-launch this issue in the next round of negotiations. Now the developed world has started including countries under the Generalised System of Preferences (GSP) dependent on whether a country has been complying with core labour standards or not. Therefore, it would be a mistake for developing countries to think that the issue has been settled.[19]

The aim of this paper was to highlight the major issues that have arisen in the on-going debate on linking trade with labour standards. It is not possible for developing countries to implement core labour standards without sufficient economic reform. The real question is whether the developed countries will help the developing world in terms of resources.

Suggestions

- The trade should be for the development and for alleviating the poverty in developing countries.
- Forcing compliance with ILO core labour standards will not achieve the declared objective of raising labour standards in the developing countries.
- ILO convention Nos. 87 and 98 on freedom of association and on free collective bargaining are too narrow and exclusive as far as the developing countries are concerned.
- Right to livelihood should be added as a basic right.
- The basic labour standards cannot be maintained without proper technical and financial assistance from the developed and international organisations.
- Any attempt to enforce labour standards through trade sanctions has negative repercussions in the exporting developing countries.
- The improvement of labour standards in the developing countries would require faster economic growth and due attention to reduce poverty and inequalities.

---

19. Kofi Addo, "The Correlation Between Labour Standards and International Trade: Which Way Forward", *Journal of World Trade*, 36(2) 2002, p.30.

- Implementation of these standards through regional trade agreements is also objectionable.
- WTO should disassociate from efforts to make labour standards compulsory, including by means of trade sanctions.
- The ILO can help the developing countries by conducting some basic studies like estimating the cost of implementation of core labour standards and providing support to these countries and act as a nodal agency for chanelising technical as well as financial support to these countries.
- The list of core labour standards is to be expanded to include other standards like right of livelihood for all workers.
- The WTO can play a level playing field only when they can understand and implement special and differential treatment provisions concerning the developing countries.
- The IMF and World Bank should desist from imposing conditionality stipulating particular labour standards, when granting developmental aid to developing and least developed countries.
- The developed countries should include policies that are favourable for the economic development of poor countries, because they are the major beneficiaries of globalisation.

National Level Concerns

- Government of India has to initiate proceedings for the ratification of the remaining core ILO labour standard conventions.
- If the government is not willing to ratify these conventions in the present form, then they should argue for changes and make efforts for consensus on this issue among the developing countries.
- The ratification of these conventions should increase the credibility of the Government of India and can argue against linking of trade with labour standards in the multilateral forum like WTO.

- The proposed amendments to the Industrial Disputes Act, 1947 and Contract Labour (Regulation and Abolition) Act should not be for closing down the industries rather it would be in tune with the realities of globalisation and without hurting the interests of labours.
- The Second National Labour Commission reported that the proportion of the workforce in the organised sector had dipped from over 11 *per cent* to below 8 *per cent* during the period 1980-81 and 1996-96. This reflects the consequences of liberalisation.
- All the laws should be made applicable to the unorganised sector also, which constitute the major segment of the Indian workforce.
- In India there are sufficient laws on the labour management field. But there is lot of conflicts and lack of co-ordination between the implementing agencies at the Centre as well as at the State level. Hence there is an urgent need to codify all these laws into a single law, may be in the name of Indian Labour Management Relations Act and the administration of this law should be under a single agency constituted under the Ministry of Labour may be named as Indian Labour Management Authority.
- The monitoring mechanism should be strengthened throughout the country in an integrated way and there should be a meaningful co-ordination between the central and state agencies.
- The amendment to all present legislation should be done only after consulting the trade unions and the industry.
- The national labour policy should address all these issues and take decisions only after consulting all stakeholders.
- There is an unusual unanimity among the Indian trade unions with regard to the linking of trade with labour standards and they are against that movement and the Government of India also supporting the view of the trade unions.
- The trade unions are for the ratification of all core labour standard conventions.

- The Government of India's position on this matter is reflected in the second National Labour Commission Report (para 8.97). It says "*The Study Group of Social Security constituted under the commission felt that it might not be possible to ratify all the conventions of the ILO immediately, but it is desirable to plan for their eventual ratification by upgrading laws and practices, beginning with the Minimum Standard convention. The commission endorses the view of the Study group*". The government should prescribe a time frame for the ratification of the remaining four core ILO conventions.
- Awareness among the trade unions and workers are very important in the issue and the role of industry is also crucial for the success of implementation of these standards.

References

Singh, Ajit and Ann Zammit (2000). *The Global Standards Controversy: Critical Issues for Developing Countries*, South Centre.

Hoe Lim, *The Social Clause: Issues and Challenges*, ILO, Bureau for Workers Activities.

ILO, *The Social Clause: Issues and Challenges*, downloaded from ilo.org.

ILO (2001). *Trade Liberalisation and Employment*, GB.282/WP/SDG/2.

Jenkins, Rob (2001). "India and the Trade-and-Labour – Standards Controversy," prepared for the seminar, *India in the Beginning of the 21st Century*, Instituto do Oriente, Lisbon, March.

WTO (2000). Labour Standards, WTO Quo Vadis?.

Howard, James *Core Labour Standards and Human Rights in the Workplace*, International Institute for Environment and Development, *www.iied.org*.

CEC (1995). *Social Clause in Multilateral Trade Agreements*, A Dossier on Labour Standards.

Mishra, L. (2000). "Child Labour at the WTO", *PTI Economic Service* 2000 Jan.15;33(4) 17-30.

Chaulia, Sreeram (2000). "Social Clause in WTO- Cases For and Against," *EPW 2002* Feb.16; 613-616.

Torres, Raymond (1996). "Labour Standards and Trade," *The OECD Observer* No.22 October/November 1996.

IFWEA (1998). "Workers Rights and Human Rights," *IFWEA Journal* December 1998, http://solidar@compuserce.com.

Khor, Martin (1997). "The WTO and the Battle Over Labour Standards," *Third World Network Features*, January 1997.

OECD (2000). "International Trade and Core Labour Standards," *OECD Observer 2000*, www.oecd.org.publications/Pol_brief/

Mayne, Ruth and Caroline le Quesne (1999). *Calls for a Social Clause, Global Trade and Global Social Issues* Edited by Annies Taylor and Caroline Thomas, Routledge, London.

Addo, Kofi "The Correlation Between Labour Standards and International Trade," *Journal of World Trade* 36(2): 285-303.

Venkitaratnam, C.S. (1998). "Globalisation and Labour Management Relations-Dynamics of Change," *Indian Journal of Labour Economics*, December 1998.

Raynauld, Andre and Jean-Pierre Vidal (1998). *Labour Standards and International Competitiveness: A Comparative Analysis of Developing and Industrialised Countries*, Edward Elgar Publications, USA.

Swamy, Subramanyam (2000). *India's Labour Standards and the WTO Framework*, Konark Publishers, New Delhi.

Madhavi, A.D. and M. Vijayalakshmi, *Freedom of Association and Promotion of Social Dialogue in EPZs of India, Labour issues in EPZ's in South Asia-role of Social Dialogue*, Edited by A.S. Oberai, A. Sivanathiran ad C.S. Venkitaratnam, Indian Industrial Association.

12

Environmental Standards as Non-Tariff Barriers and the Problem of Market Access

NIVEDITA DUTTA, MAYANK SINHA
UPASNA GAUR

Environmental standards are the responses and outcomes of society's increasing consciousness against the inappropriate usage of resources and the resulting adverse environmental impact. These environmental impacts are often manifested as adverse impacts on animal-plant life, and human health. Hence, environmental standards could also be interpreted as health-related standards. However, developing countries have faced certain standards which, although are clubbed as environmental norms, have really turned out to be Non-tariff barriers (NTBs) in disguise. This brings us to the issue of market access.

Market access concerns are crucial as trade liberalisation and improved access to the world markets lies at the heart of the sustainable development paradigm. Improved market access invariably results in increased export earnings, generation of additional resources, which can be utilised for reducing poverty and protecting the environment. However, there are increasing apprehensions that these benefits, in the future, might be offset by the imposition of new environmental requirements that may take the form of indirect trade barriers. These measures could affect market access opportunities for developing countries and, hamper their growth process and efforts to eradicate poverty.

For India and other developing countries, there are four prime concerns on market access issues. *Firstly,* simply an imposition of trade sanctions or environmental requirements will not serve as the most efficient devices to protect the environment. Hence efforts for environment protection should be undertaken as part of national legislation, based on the developmental concerns of the nation.

Secondly, environmental regulations could be used as non-tariff barriers to trade thereby limiting market access for the export products of the developing countries. *Thirdly*, the technical and financial capacity of firms in developing countries, especially small- and medium-sized enterprises, to conform to environmental regulations set by developed countries is limited. *Lastly*, in case of local environmental effects, using the same standard across countries, or even different regions within a country, may be wholly inappropriate. Such standards would be more effective and efficient if they took cognisance of specific environment and development conditions of individual countries and regions.

The other area of concern relates to market access barriers created on account of non-product-related production processes and methods. There is concern that these would increasingly be used as non-tariff barriers and would impinge on the autonomy of individual nations to set environmental standards according to national imperatives.

This paper attempts to analyse the several environmental and health-related standards in India, particularly in the context of increasing adherence to international standards. Attempting a review of Indian standards for specific sectors, notably agro-products like tea, marine products, textiles, leather and leather products, the paper will draw inferences on the various impacts and concerns for Indian exports. In this context the 2002 Doha Ministerial Declaration instructs the Committee on Trade and Environment (CTE) to take an in-depth look into "...*the effect of environmental measures on market access, especially in relation to developing countries, in particular the least-developed among them and those situations in which the elimination or reduction of trade restrictions and distortions would benefit trade, the environment and development*".[1]

Hence it is important that the various environmental measures like health and safety regulations, packaging, labelling and recycling requirements, environmental charges and taxes etc. meet genuine environmental concerns and do not pose barriers to market access opportunities of developing countries. As tariffs and quantitative

1. Doha Ministerial Declaration, adopted on 14th Nov, 2001; WT/MIN (01)/DEC/1, 20 November 2001.

restrictions on trade have decreased, more attention is paid on non-tariff barriers such as technical measures, food safety regulations, labelling requirements and quality standards. The Agreement on Sanitary and Phyto-sanitary (SPS) measures seeks to protect consumers by providing rules for food safety and health of plants and animals. The Agreement on Technical Barriers to Trade (TBT) aims to ensure that technical regulations, standards and conformity assessment procedures do not create unnecessary obstacles to trade. In the process, however, it also recognises that each country has the right to set the level of protection that it deems appropriate in these areas.

Concerns for Developing Countries

Given the nature and depth of the existing regulatory structures in case of SPS and TBT agreements in the developed countries, the developing countries often find it difficult to comply with such standards. SPS measures potentially act as significant barriers to trade in agricultural and food products since in many instances they are incompatible with prevailing systems of production and marketing in developing countries. Further, the developing countries often lack appropriate scientific and technical expertise to deal with such standards and as a result have lost export opportunities. Also, the multiplicity of standards in developed country markets has further compounded the problems being faced by developing country exporters. Consequently, the impact of environmental measures on market access and trade assumes enormous importance. This is magnified in light of the fact that the past decade has seen a global proliferation of environment and health-related standards along with a rise in the trade in environmentally friendly goods. Since the inception of the WTO, more than 2,300 notifications have been received and approximately 11 per cent thereof are related to environmental standards (Nordstrom and Vaughan, 1999). The total number of notifications issued by the EU itself in 2002, based on product category is 1,515 (EIC[2]).

---

2. EIC : The Export Inspection Council was set up by the Government of India under Section 3 of the Export (Quality Control and Inspection) Act, 1963 (22 of 1963), in order to ensure sound development of export trade of India through Quality Control and Inspection and for matters connected thereof. EIC is an advisory body to the Central Government.

For instance, the regulation of aflatoxins in food products has gained considerable attention in recent years. In 1997, the European Commission (EC) proposed a harmonisation of maximum acceptable level of aflatoxins in certain foodstuffs. The standard ranged from 4ppb[3] in cereals, edible nuts, and dried fruit, to 10ppb for nuts that are subject to further processing. Henson *et al.*, (1999) noted that the EC proposal had led to concerns among food exporters about the new and more restrictive standards' effect on trade patterns. Several exporting countries feared losses in their exports as a result of the more restrictive standard. Countries such as Bolivia, Brazil, Peru, India, Argentina, Canada, Mexico, Uruguay, Australia, and Pakistan requested detailed risk assessment norms used by the European Union in designing the new standard. As a consequence, the EC relaxed the proposed aflatoxin standard in cereals, dried fruits and nuts. The revised aflatoxin standard in groundnuts subject to further processing was set at 15 ppb (8 ppb for B1) and 10 ppb (5 ppb for B1) for other nuts and dried fruits subject to further processing. For cereals, dried fruits, and nuts intended for direct human consumption, the standard was much more stringent and was set at 4 ppb (2 ppb for B1).[4] The aflatoxin standards suggested by the Codex Alimentarius, however, is significantly more relaxed than the EC standards. The overall Codex standard is approximately 9ppb (Otsuki and Wilson (2001)).

These varied and high levels of standards increase the cost of meeting these standards prohibitively. In a study conducted by the World Bank[5] it was predicted that the implementation of a new aflatoxin standard in the EU will have a negative impact on African exports of cereals, dried fruits and nuts. An econometric analysis shows that the EU standard, which would reduce health risks by approximately 1.4 deaths per billion a year, will decrease African exports of these products to the EU by 64 per cent or US $670 million (Otsukti, Wilson & Sewadeh 1998).

---

3. parts per billion.
4. Otsuki, Wilson and Sewadeh (2001a) provide a more detailed discussion of aflatoxin standards.
5. As cited in Otsukti, Wilson & Sewadeh (1998).

The Indian Experience

Background

Food standards, strict limitations on the use of certain substances, and SPS measures seem to be having an adverse impact on the market access for the developing countries. A report by UNCTAD,[6] 1998, on Least Developed Countries (LDCs) provides a series of examples of LDCs (Bangladesh, Nepal, Sri Lanka etc.) already having suffered significant export losses because of their inability to respond to the environmental standards, health and sanitary requirements in the developed markets (Veena Jha 2002[7]).

At the global level about 185 products have been identified which face environment-related trade barriers in at least one importing nation (Chaturvedi and Nagpal 2003). In the case of India, these products comprise primarily agricultural goods, constituting 62 per cent of India's total agricultural exports (ITC[8]/2001). The SPS measures have been used excessively as protective measures especially against the Indian food and the agro-product exports. India has voiced its concerns about the SPS measures functioning as market access barriers at ministerial meetings, particularly with regard to Article 10.1 of the SPS Agreement which states that "...in the preparation and application of sanitary or phyto-sanitary measures, Members shall take into account the special needs of developing country Members..."; however, no such concern seems to have been incorporated into the implementation of the agreement. India has also suggested that only those standards developed by relevant international bodies with the involvement of developing countries should be treated as international standards for the purposes of SPS as well as TBT Agreements.

Concerns for India

Indian exporters have expressed serious concerns regarding the use of SPS and TBT measures as non-tariff barriers. The potential

6. United Nations Conference on Trade and Development.
7. Veena Jha (April 2002) A Scoping Paper for South Asia: Strengthening Developing Countries' Capacities to Respond to Health, Sanitary and Environmental Requirements.
8. International Trade Centre.

problems that could arise are primarily because of lack of timely and accurate information, simultaneous application of multiple standards and regulations, costs and difficulties of testing and verification procedures, and lack of scientific data for specific thresholds or limit values. Regulations and standards on food may create market access problems on account of lack of transparency and inconsistent application of procedures (Veena Jha 2002).

Importing countries have at different points of time continued to use SPS measures as non-tariff barriers. Some of these cases are discussed below:

- The European Union had banned frozen fishery products from India in 1997. The ban was imposed on the grounds of health & hygiene and SPS measures. It was stated that the products from India might be contaminated with micro-organisms, which may constitute a hazard to human health.
- A German ban on products containing pentachlorophenol (PCP) resulted in a short-term setback for Indian leather exports in 1989-90. The costs involved in substituting this chemical were exorbitant (Veena Jha 2002).[9]
- The Netherlands, Austria and Germany have adopted national legislation banning the *use, import and sale* of carcinogenic azo-colourants. At present, there are 24 amines, which fall under this ban.
- China imposed a ban on Indian grapes for Mediterranean fruit fly. This fly does not even exist in India (Chaturvedi and Nagpal 2003).
- India's tea exports have also been affected by concerns from importing countries regarding the pesticide residue level in Indian tea (Veena Jha 2002).
- Japan has imposed a zero tolerance clause on certain insects and also with regard to quarantine of flowers. The Quarantine Authority in Japan takes a lot of time for clearance due to elaborate fumigation process it imposes. Also, Indian roses are brought to auction platforms towards the end of the auction process after all the domestic supply

9. See footnote 7 for reference.

is auctioned leading to low price realisation for Indian flowers. Moreover, auctions do not provide sale reports to the exporters from India as in the case of Dutch auctions. The Japanese importers provide their own sale reports instead of the original reports from the auction agency. These kind of measures act as non-tariff barriers with regard to market access on flowers (BIS[10] and APEDA,[11] 2003).

- Italy and Germany had detained Indian spice consignments on the ground of pesticides residue.
- More stringent limits on DDT residues in tobacco prescribed by Japan of 0.4ppm[12] against the international allowable levels of 1-2 ppm that India was complying with, restricted India's exports to Japan.
- India exports *Basmati* rice and *papad*s, based on cereals, to the US. According to the US regulations, each exporter and their products are required to be registered with the US Department of Agriculture (USDA) before these can be allowed to be imported into the US. Each consignment is examined thoroughly for impurities like sand particles, human hair, rodent excreta, etc. The level of presence of these contaminants in the products is very low and poses severe difficulties in complying with the requirements. If any consignment is found to be contaminated with slightly higher levels, the entire consignment is rejected and causes a total loss to the exporter. The procedures followed by USDA are unreasonable and uneconomical, thereby, being trade restrictive (APEDA 2003).
- There has been a large number of rejections of consignments from Spain and Italy taken place due to the presence of *Bacterial Inhibitors*. However, bacteriological inhibitors can be any of the permitted additives/preservatives, permitted antibiotics used in the seafood industry. There is no clear scientific justification for the rejections of these consignments (EIC/2003).

---

10. Bureau of Indian Standards, New Delhi.
11. Agricultural and Processed Food Products Export Development Authority (APEDA); Website: www.apeda.com/scripts/newscentremodule.html
12. parts per million.

A case study conducted by Research and Information System (RIS) shows various hurdles faced by the exporters. A case in point is the experience of an Indian company exporting seedless grapes, to a large chain of departmental stores in Europe. Prior to exporting, this company had to fill in an elaborate questionnaire, which covered issues like the status of their employees, working environment facilities, etc. The exporters were supposed to meet certain social standards before they could start exporting what the importing company terms as, '*Socially Responsible Trading*'. This departmental chain has actually come out with a code for its exporters which covers apart from social issues, the building of health centres and acquiring of new sets of imported instruments for fire extinguishing and evacuation belts, etc. The RIS survey also shows that the production cost would go up by 35 to 40 per cent because of compliance with this code.[13] Apart from this, the grape exporters have to meet various standards prescribed by *Eurepgap*, such as pesticide record keeping, disposal and post harvest preparation, etc. Additionally, the European countries levy an import duty of additional 12.5 per cent on Indian grapes as against a number of supplies from African countries (Chaturvedi and Nagpal 2003).

The hurdles faced by the exporters in India have resulted in several serious implications. India's export of agriculture and allied products was approximately Rs. 29,312 crore[14] during 2001-02, which constituted 14.0 per cent of the total exports. The share of export of this sector has gradually come down over the years; i.e. from 19.5 per cent in 1997-98, to 18.6 per cent in 1998-99, and 15.6 per cent in 1999-2000 and 14.01 per cent in 2000-01. Some of the important reasons for this are the higher quality standards and multiple standards imposed by the importing countries.[15]

One case of concern is the level of aflatoxin. The permitted levels of aflatoxin and the multiple standards across countries are a major problem faced by the Indian chilli exporters to Europe.[16] An

13. Based on primary survey of Industries conducted by RIS (2001-02).

14. All the relevant figures have been taken from the Economic Survey, 2002-03 and the previous years. Reference to other sources has been clearly specified.

15. This problem has been highlighted in Issues on SPS and Environmental Standards for India C.J. Kithu.

16. For eg: B1& B2+G1+G2 should be less than 4 ppb in Germany whereas it is <5 ppb in Sweden & Finland and 10 ppb in Spain.)

additional burden for exporters is the fact that all EU standards are very high. The variability in standards among countries within Europe has caused great difficulty for exports from India (Kithu 2001[17]).

A similar scenario emerges for standards on pesticide residues followed by different European countries. There exists a wide range of variability in the maximum pesticide residue limits across different countries. For instance, the MRL for malathion is 0.05 ppm in Germany and Netherlands, while in UK it is 8 ppm. Similarly, for Parathion it is 0.1 in Netherlands and 1 in UK. This multiplicity of standards across these three countries (i.e. Germany, the Netherlands and the United Kingdom) for few important pesticides is clearly depicted in Figure 12.1

Figure 12.1

Multiplicity of Standards Across Three EU Countries

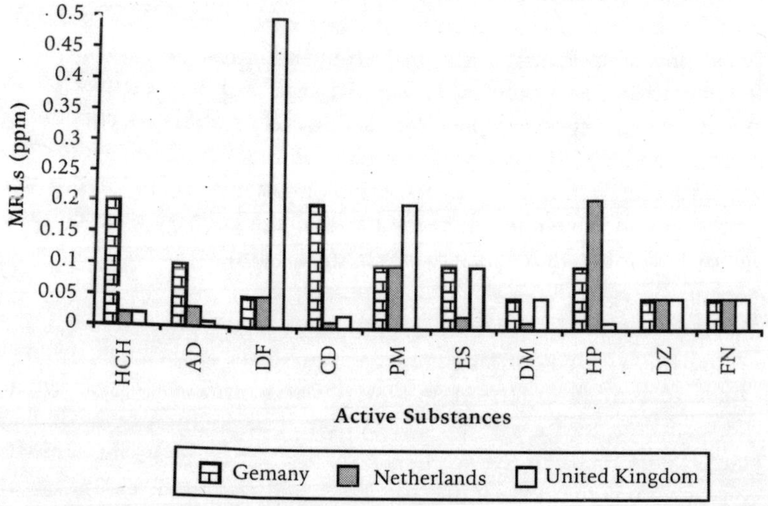

Source: EU Draft Legislation, Issues on SPS and Environmental Standards for India, (Kithu 2001).

17. Kithu,.C., Deputy Director, Spices Board, Issues on SPS and Environmental Standards for India paper presented at the UNCTAD/World Bank Conference on 11-13 January 2001.

The stringent measures put forward hike the hidden cost on analysis, investment for processing units and upgrading technical competence of technicians. India is not adequately equipped to meet these requirements. Hence a detailed analysis of the impacts and adequate coping mechanisms need to be devised, to mitigate the negative impact of these standards on Indian exporters.

Sector Specific Analysis

The subsequent sections of the paper will focus on the experiences of few selected sectors (tea, fisheries and marine products, textile, leather and leather products) in India with SPS Standards developed by other countries. The choice of the products is deliberate. Tea is one of the oldest and prominent export commodities from India. It is highly dependent on land and water and hence is affected by environmental regulations. Similarly, marine and leather products are major foreign exchange earners of the country. The marine industry has attracted legislation on environment in India as it did have some harmful effects on the environment. Leather and leather product sector is based on tanning which is known to be one of the most water polluting industrial activity. Leather manufacturing and tanning is a multistage activity. Each of these stages of production involves the letting-out of effluents containing heavy chemicals like chrome, sodium sulphide, calcium hydroxide, etc. These effluents have led to serious problems of land and water pollution and have affected many parts of the country's agricultural sector and other industries that rely on natural resources.

1. Tea

India is widely known as the largest producer as well as consumer of tea. Indian tea exports have typically been around 17 per cent of the world tea trade, with Sri Lanka, Kenya and China being India's chief export rivals in the world tea market. The Indian tea industry employs more than one million workers and the total tea exports in 2001 were US $ 548.11 million with the chief export destinations being United Kingdom, US, Canada, Commonwealth of Independent States (CIS), etc.

In recent times Indian tea has been losing out primarily because of the plunging world average auction prices. At the same time, factors attributable to external stipulations and value judgements on issues of environment, and attempts at inclusion of norms against use of child labour have aggravated the situation for the Indian tea exporter. Lately, there have been growing reports of pesticide residues in Indian tea, which has impacted its market access significantly. Many complaints have been faced by Indian tea exporting firms on account of high levels of a chemical namely bicofol in Assam, Terai, and Booras tea, which is seen to have some health impacts on consumers. Germany has banned Indian tea at different points of time on the basis of the presence of high residue levels of ethion in Darjeeling tea. However, in most cases no sound scientific justification has been given for the complaints made.

Consequently, tea manufacturing and exporting units have increasingly reported noticeable levels of arbitrariness in the bans imposed by the importing countries. In 1995 the German limit of 0.01 mg of tetradifon and 2 mg of ethion per kg of tea were arbitrarily imposed because of the lack of data from India on its pesticide safety limits for tea. The Teekanne Darjeeling Gold brand of tea was rejected because it contained 0.24 mg of tetrafidon per kg that was 24 times the limit set by Germany soon after the German Institute of Environment Analytics, Messzelle, denounced the brand as unsafe because of the high residue levels of ethion, tetrafidon and heptachlor in Indian tea. However, there were no rejections from other European markets. This is an instance of how non-standardised and arbitrary norms stipulated by a country hinder market access (Kaushik and Saqib 2001).

Apart from arbitrariness in the bans, Indian exporters face the problem of multiplicity of standards across countries. MRLs of pesticides are used as regulatory instruments to protect human health and the environment from harmful consequences of excessive pesticide use by tea producers. In 1962, the Codex Alimentarius was set up under the aegis of FAO (Food and Agricultural Organisation) to develop global benchmarks for food additives, pesticides, chemicals and contaminants in all agricultural commodities, including tea. However, there is great variation in the levels fixed for different pesticides across countries as observed in the Figure 12.2.[18]

18. Source: Tea Board: Kolkata 1999; www.fao.org; Gopal K. Kadekodi (2002) "Trade and Environment: Conflicts & Prospects".

The standards set by most of these countries tend to diverge widely from the international levels. As is seen from Figure 12.2 below, in the case of Deltamethrin the MRL set by the Codex is 10 mg per kg, while for Germany, UK and the Netherlands is 5. Similarly, for Dicofol the level set by the Codex is 50 and that by EC is less than half its value.

Figure 12.2

A Comparison of Maximum Residue Limit in Various Countries

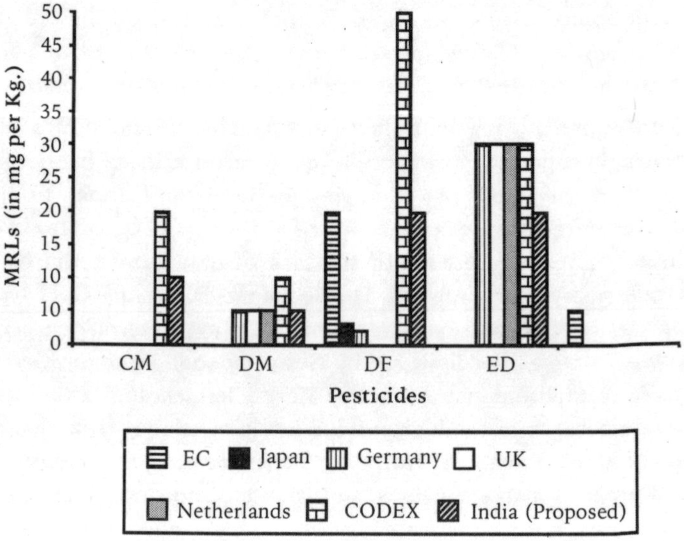

The Indian tea producers, with help from the Government of India, have taken several remedial steps to meet these standards. They have adopted ISO norms and are also stringently abiding by the government-initiated scheme of adopting the HACCP[19] standards. The industry is facing high costs of compliance as the cost of testing, verification and certification for the presence of residue levels is highly prohibitive. In a study conducted by TERI,[20] it was reported that the tests for clearing a consignment to Germany could cost as high as US $234 per analysis. Therefore, the industry is facing difficulties in adopting such measures imposed by importers.

19. Hazard Analysis and Critical Control Point.

20. The Energy and Resources Institute, New Delhi, India, 2003.

The Indian government, on its part, has been adopting various measures to make its products environment-friendly. It has banned the use of many pesticides for use in the tea industry. It has also laid down guidelines limiting the usage of certain chemicals during the plucking season by the tea manufacturers. In spite of the efforts made by the Indian government there still are cases where environment is used as a barrier to trade.

2. Fisheries and Marine Products

The fisheries sector in India plays an important role by contributing to national income, exports, food and nutritional security and employment generation. The economic reforms initiated in 1990s helped fisheries attain higher growth in exports; the value of marine product exports was Rs. 8,730 million in 1990-91 and rose to Rs. 63,180 million in the year 2000-01.[21] Of the total global fisheries exports, the Asian countries account for an overwhelming 84 per cent, of which as much as 30 per cent is from India, making it a key marine products exporter ranking only second to China among the Asian countries.[22] Domestic de-regulation, accompanied by the "blue revolution" helped the fisheries sector to graduate to exports of high value added frozen and canned items destined to more sophisticated markets like the United States (US), European Union (EU), France, Australia, Canada and Japan.

India is fairly competitive in fisheries exports, and the reduction of tariffs under the WTO regime offered it significant opportunities for economic growth and poverty alleviation, given that over 90 per cent of units fall in the small-scale sector. The new trade regime calls upon countries to lower domestic and export subsidies and import tariffs, thus providing larger market access to imports. However, tariff barriers in developed countries have now given way to non-tariff barriers, often in the form of environmental, hygiene, sanitation, and packaging regulation.

There have been several instances when India's seafood exports have been banned on grounds of environment and health concerns by

21. Economic Survey (2001-02), Ministry of Finance, Government of India, New Delhi.
22. World Review of Fisheries and Aquaculture: Fisheries Resources — Trends in Production, Utilisation and Trade; http://www.fao.org/docrep/w9900e/w9900e02.htm

taking recourse to the WTO Agreements on Sanitary and Phyto-sanitary (SPS) and Technical Barriers to Trade (TBT), most of which have been imposed by the developed countries. For instance, India has lost market access as some consignments of India's marine exports attracted automatic detention in the US. The US stipulated that marine products must be sampled and tested before it gained entry in to the country, meaning that procedurally there would be long delivery delays, storage costs and possibly a substantial refusal rate. In another instance, US restricted the imports of shrimps from countries not using Turtle Excluder Devices (TEDs) justifying it as a measure towards conservation of endangered species of sea turtles. This, however, was opposed by India, Pakistan and Thailand who argued that the embargo on shrimps by the US was inconsistent with Article XI of the GATT prohibiting quantitative restrictions that are not duties, taxes or charges.

Compliance with these standards has resulted in significant increase in the production costs. According to exporters (and confirmed by Marine Products Exports Development Authority (MPEDA)), the compliance costs for meeting these existing EU norms is 15-40 per cent of the Free-on-Board (FoB) value, with costs being higher for the existing units.[23] According to MPEDA it is expected that while about two-thirds of the units would be able to upgrade themselves to the EU norms, the rest might perish. These would impose unavoidable financial and social costs on the marine sector in India with the small players being the hardest hit, given that 95 per cent of the units are in the small-scale sector. For example, the costs of upgrading sanitary conditions in the Bangladesh frozen shrimp industry to satisfy EU and US hygiene requirements is estimated to be $17.6 million in 1997-98.[24] The total industry cost required for maintaining Hazard Analysis Critical Control Point (HACCP) is $2.2 million per annum. European standards are even more stringent than HACCP methods. In the case of marine products, EU regulations concerning implementation of food safety systems, additive requirements and other process controls are of a very high order. As a result, many Indian companies were required to upgrade their facilities, which entailed a huge expenditure and a number of

23. Kaushik and Saqib (2001).

24. Cato and Santos (1998); also see Cato (1998).

companies were forced to close down their factories for a long duration to enable them to upgrade their facilities with heavy investments. Currently, only 90 out of 404 plants in India are approved for fishery exports to the EU.[25]

Thus, it can be observed that in these sectors, existing market access is being eroded on account of environmental measures; and more importantly, environmental measures in the making have the potential to restrict developing countries' access to foreign markets. This may be because of high compliance costs as well as different specifications in these norms. For example, the HACCP requirements assume that there is only one standard both for exported and domestic food. It does not take in to account the fact that in India, the standard and regulatory agencies are different for imported and domestic food products.

3. Textiles

Textile exports account for 55 per cent of India's export earnings.[26] The share of ready-made garments in the export basket has hovered around 12 per cent. In 1999-2000, it was 12.9 per cent and in 2000-01 it was 12.5 per cent. This proportion went up marginally to 13 per cent in 2000-01 but then came down to 11 per cent in 2001-02. It is also a net foreign exchange earner as the import content in textiles is very little compared with other major export products. This sector takes up 4 per cent of GDP and 14 per cent of industrial products. It provides employment to 15 million people. Although the Indian textile industry is characterised as powerloom, handloom and mill sector a majority of the ready-made garments exports come from SMEs, which account for as much as 63 per cent of total exports.

Around 40 per cent of India's textiles are directed to the European Union, but the stringent environment conditions in developed countries have adverse consequences for India's export performance. In 1993, the Germany textile industry introduced two eco-labels, one which gave norms for consumer goods and indicated a lower content of pollutants, and another which sets norms for production processes. It indicated that all processing conditions were

25. Jha *et al.*, (2000).

26. Economic Survey (2002) Ministry of Finance, Government of India.

analysed with reference to the degree of pollution of air, water and soil. Apart from this, other national and private labels were also developed in Europe. For example, the Ostereichisches Textil-Forschungsinstitut has developed the 'Oekotex' label relating to both raw material and final product. In the textile and clothing sector, Germany has recently introduced the 'Eco-Tex' Standard – 100, which lists various criteria for evaluating textiles from an ecological perspective. Eco-tex standard 100 has been developed by the International Association for Research in Eco-Textiles that offers manufacturers for garments and textiles the opportunity for certification of eco-friendly products.

Pilot studies undertaken to analyse the impact of eco-labelling on the textile sector have shown that the exporters are not aware about eco-labelling schemes that might emerge as one of the prominent NTBs in the textile sector post-2004. Neither the export councils, nor a majority of the general exporters are aware of the problems that can emerge in the future. Although the Indian government had taken a step to introduce eco-labelling in India through "Eco-Mark", this label has gained no credibility in the international markets and therefore has become completely useless. The important factor remains that the Indian exporters supply to a single buyer abroad, and as a result, try to comply with the norms that the particular buyer asks for. If there is no immediate demand for such norms or labels, the exporters, do not, voluntarily switch to environment-friendly production processes. This attitude needs to be changed and a more pragmatic approach would be to slowly shift to producing environmentally friendly goods so that when such norms are imposed, a switchover would be possible without incurring huge compliance costs at one particular point of time, thus retaining the existing market share.

India should learn from its past experiences, espacially those pertaining to the ban of dyestuffs like cobalt blue and sulphur black in the international market. There was a severe loss of market share and it took the textile as well as the leather industry several years before they could stabilise their position. Though viable substitutes have been explored since then, switching over to them entailed investments of over US$13 million, mainly for upgrading of technology and new treatment plants in order to obtain the requisite quality. Likewise opting for non-benzidine dyes, such as direct black 38 dye and direct black 22, also costs $8-10 per kg. Though small and medium enterprises' (SMEs) contributions to the export basket are not available, one study estimates that over 60 per cent of production are by small-scale enterprises. One can therefore extrapolate that an important part of exports comes from small-scale units.

4. Leather Industry

India, which has largest holding of livestock in the world is expected to play a dominant role in the leather industry, which is spread over the organised as well as unorganised sector. Small-scale enterprises account for over 75 per cent of the total production. This industry has been identified as one of the thrust areas of exports. Traditionally, the Indian leather industry has been an exporter of tanned hides and skins. Currently, leather footwear, footwear uppers, leather goods and garments are among the fastest growing export items in India. The footwear sector has been identified as an area of extreme focus. Export from the leather sector today accounts for about 4.3 per cent of India's total exports. The export performance of the leather sector has improved considerably during the past decade. The value of exports went up from Rs. 3,036 crore during 1991-92 to Rs. 6,436 crore in 1998-99. Germany is the largest single export market for Indian leather goods. The other important markets are France, UK and Italy. The composition of the Indian leather industry is vast, employing about 1.4 million people. There are about 2,000 tanneries in Tamil Nadu, West Bengal, Maharashtra, Uttar Pradesh, Karnataka and Rajasthan. Of these 75 per cent are SMEs.

On environmental standards the leather industry faces problems on both the domestic and external front. Restrictions on the use of certain chemical dyestuffs and several other mandatory regulations in major export markets pose serious problems for the leather sector. Germany, along with other European countries, has already restricted benzidine-containing dyes and openly demands benzidine-free leather imports. Germany has banned all imported leather products containing pentachlorophenol (PCP), with the aim to protect its consumers from the possible incidence of cancer. PCP has been in use as a preservative for raw hides and skins. It also restricts the use of formaldehyde. Only products treated with environment-friendly chemicals are accepted in Germany and other developed country markets. The EC standards for PCP in this regard are high at around 1,000 ppm or 10mg/kg. The stringent environmental standards imposed by EC have been criticised not only by the developing countries but also certain EU member countries themselves, such as Italy and France. It is also to be noted that Italy has a big leather industry and France is itself a major producer of PCP. Therefore, it is reasonable to believe that the protest from these two countries on the PCP ban is to protect their domestic industries. The increasingly stringent export standards have contributed to a rise in the cost of production, especially in the leather sector, where costs using the more environmentally friendly methods are nearly three times higher.[27] Most of the studies on competitiveness and environmental standards are based on environmental capital costs.

However, India, in its efforts to increase its leather exports, banned the production of PCP and its use in the processing of leather. According to some recent estimates, the price of this substitute is around 10 times higher than the existing price of PCP. For the easy availability of the substitutes, government reduced the import duty from 150 to 50 per cent on these chemicals. Further, the Centre Leather Research Institute (CLRI) has also indigenously developed technology to enable local production of TCMTB, which is a substitute for PCP. A large number of alternatives of PCP exist such as 'Busan 30', which is acceptable to the international market. PCP was manufactured locally at a cheaper price in India, whereas 'Busan 30' needs to be imported from Germany or the US.

Conclusion

Typically, most developed countries at the WTO, notably the European Union, Australia, Norway and others have supported the usage of trade as a means to address environmental issues. Other countries, such as Japan, Indonesia, Thailand, Brazil along with India have recognised the need to address issues relating to the environment but do not fully agree with the notion of using trade as

27. Parikh *et al.*, (1994).

an instrument to achieve environmental goals. India's position at the WTO has been that environmental requirements should be developed and applied in a manner that will minimise the adverse effects on market access for developing countries.

It is imperative to have greater transparency in mechanisms, which enable the implementation of the SPS and TBT agreements as well as environmental requirements such as eco-labels, eco-taxes, product related-PPMs, packaging etc. This would ensure that the agreements themselves do not become instruments that impede fair trade and hinder market access opportunities of developing countries. In this respect, there is a need for greater information exchange between the trading partners on environmental requirements in the importing country, the ways and means to meet these requirements as well as the possibility of harmonisation and mutual recognition of 'equivalent' measures and 'special and differential treatment' to developing countries. Also to the extent possible developed countries should take the developing countries on board in evolving the environmental criteria, standards and requirements from the outset, which would go a long way in reducing hardships to the complying party and also minimise trade distortions.

As is clear from various studies, exporting countries are facing a number of institutional constraints in meeting the international standards. Besides, the lack of timely and precise information about these standards is also a great obstacle for exports. In this regard, small and medium enterprises face several problems. While large firms obtain timely and accurate information directly from importers in developed-country markets and various other sources, SMEs tend to depend on secondary sources, basically government sources, often implying considerable time delays. Creating awareness of regulations voluntary labels and eco-friendly technology would require government intervention.

India should also have to upgrade the national system for testing, certification and laboratory accreditation in order to meet trade demands. In textiles, some such agencies do exist, (for example, NITRA[28]) though they are not enough. In this regard, it is important to focus on ability of the private sector to meet such demands.

---

28. Northern India Textile Research Association, Ghaziabad, Uttar Pradesh.

Collaboration should be made with international private institutes that undertake such testing, to open centres in our own country (for e.g. a quality certification trademark for woollen products known as 'Woolmark' –an Australian company, has its office in New Delhi, India). India should undertake mutual recognition agreements with their trade partners, so that duplicative testing can be avoided and certification requirements can be obtained in a number of product sectors.

India needs to face this challenge and improve the environmental safety of its exports. Some steps should also be taken by the Indian industries, with the assistance of the government to make Indian exports environment-friendly. One possible way is to tighten control over the export of infringing products, by tracking down the exporters who ship such products. An intensive exercise should be undertaken to study indigenous processes and their effectiveness for product quality, safety and standards, and the process standards 'imported' for adoption here should be tested against these standards and modified appropriately for application: domestically. Thereafter, if the exporters face market access problems, 'equivalence' should be negotiated with the trading partner(s) in that market. India should also upgrade the national system for testing and certification. This will in turn reduce the costs of international accreditation for certification of Indian products for their exporters. Lastly, there is also an immediate and pressing need to develop international mechanisms to develop channels to provide market information and analysis about these products and strengthen capacity building initiatives. Pooling of micro level data available to individual industries to facilitate and develop a macro-vision is extremely essential in this regard. Once a sizeable set of data is available, it will easier to quantify trade distortion effects of these environment measures, if any and create a base for strengthening our position in the international negotiations.

References

Cato, J.C. (1998). *Economic Issues Associated with Seafood Safety and Implementation of Seafood HACCP Programmes*, FAO, Rome.

Cato, J.C. and C.A. Lima dos Santos (1998). "European Union 1997 Seafood Safety Ban: The Economic Impact on Bangladesh Shrimp Processing". *Marine Resource Economics*, 13(3):215-227.

Chaturvedi, S. and G. Nagpal (Jan, 2003). "WTO and Product Related Environmental Standard: Emerging Issues and Policy Options," *EPW* Special Article, http://www.epw.org.in/showArticles.php?root=2003&leaf=01&filename=5341&filetype=html

Henson, S.J. and J.A. Caswell (1999). "Food Safety Regulation: An Overview of Contemporary Issues," *Food Policy*. 24(6):589-603.

ITC (2001). "Environmental Trade Barriers: Who Wins, Who Loses, What is the Score?" *International Trade Forum*, August 3.

Jha, Veena (ed.) (2003). *Trade and Environment Issues and Options for India*, UNCTAD, Geneva.

Jha, Veena (2002). "Environmental Regulation and the WTO" in Hoekman, B., A. Mattoo and P. English (eds.) *Development, Trade and the WTO: A Handbook*, Washington, DC: World Bank, pp. 472-481.

Jha, Veena *et al.*, (2000). *Achieving Objectives of Multilateral Environment Agreements: A Package of Trade Measures and Positive Measures*, United Nations Publication.

Kaushik, A. and Mohammed Saqib (2001). "Environment Requirements and India's Exports: an Impact Analysis," *RGICS Working Paper Series* No. 25.

Kithu, C. (2001). *"Issues on SPS and Environmental Standards for India"* Paper Presented at the UNCTAD/World Bank Conference on 11-13 January 2001.

Nordstrom, H. and S. Vaughan (1999). "Trade and Environment," *WTO Special Studies 4*, WTO, Geneva.

Otsuki, T. and J.S. Wilson (2001a). "Global Trade and Food Safety: Winners and Losers in a Fragmented System," *World Bank Working Paper* 2689.

Otsuki T., J.S. Wilson and M. Sewadeh (2001). *A Race to the Top? A Case Study of Food Safety Standards and African Exports*, World Bank - Country Economics Department

Otsukti, T., J.S. Wilson and M. Sewadeh (1998). *Saving Two in a Billion: A Case Study to Quantify the Trade Effect of European Food Safety Standards on African Exports*. Development Research Group (DECRG), The World Bank.

Parikh, J.K., V.K. Sharma, U. Ghosh and M.K. Panda (1994). *Trade and Environment Linkages: A Case Study of India*, Report Prepared for United Nations Conference on Trade and Development, August.

Section IV

Services and E-commerce: The Emerging Sectors

India's export potential in the service sector has been subject to a number of barriers. Arguably, a major reason for this constraint is India's excessive reliance on across-the-board reform potential of the GATS. However, unlike the trade in goods, bilateral arrangements have a special role to play in case of trade in services. India needs to adopt a proactive stance in trade diplomacy to achieve increased market access. Through an analysis of India's trade potential, trade diplomacy and the barriers it faces, Pritam Banerjee strongly argues in favour of initiating bilateral GATS+ initiatives with the Industrialised economies, namely the G3 (US, EU and Japan). Banerji argues the move is a must for ensuring employment growth, FDI inflow, and increased export earning. Since sequence of liberalisation is most important in the case of trade in services, bilateral GATS+ initiatives agreed is capable of guaranteeing India an edge in G3 markets for the next two to three decades.

Suparna Karmakar looks at the treatment of infrastructural services at the WTO and GATS focussing on the transport and telecom sectors. On the issue of telecom services it is pointed out that India has made considerable concessions under Modes 3 and 4. These concessions, Karmakar stresses have been made unilaterally as domestically the need for opening up this sector to receive the latest technologies have been felt by domestic players. This proactive appraoch is however not present in the area of transport even though the benefits that would accrue from such a liberalisation would be immense.

While there is an urgent need for negotiating market access for services for Indian export, the domestic sector also has to be opened gradually for the partner countries. Presently, the negotiations are in the request-offer phase. So far India has not committed to open up the education sector. But it is expected that pressure from the developed countries will ultimately lead to the opening of the sector very soon. K.D. Raju focuses on the Indian scenario and the ongoing GATS negotiations and competitiveness of Indian higher education sector. He comes out with a set of recommendations for Indian negotiating strategy on opening up of education sector in future, as well as for introducing a comprehensive domestic education policy. In addition, Raju also gauges the implications on the recent Supreme Court ruling on the operation of private universities, which bears an immense consequence on the future of education services in India.

With regard to e-commerce, Dipankar Sengupta points out that historical circumstances and aspects of government policy has given India a tremendous advantage in certain services that are knowledge-intensive in nature and can be transferred over the wire making it just right for e-commerce. However, Sengupta argues that if Indian-owned businesses are to make a headway, India must not just seek liberalisation of those services with concessions on Modes 1 and 2, but also relevant concessions on Modes 3 and 4.

13

Towards an Appropriate Approach to Trade Diplomacy in Services

PRITAM BANERJEE

Introduction

International trade in services has become a key factor driving structural change in the world economy. Total exports of services quadrupled, growing from US$ 400 billion in 1980 to about US$ 1.6 trillion in 2002, while the share of services in total trade grew from 16.2 per cent to 19.4 per cent. International trade in services is dominated by industrialised countries, which account for the bulk of services imports and exports and run a surplus in their balances of trade in services *vis-à-vis* emerging economies and Least Developing Countries (LDC). However, the role of some emerging economies in international trade in services has been increasing, and leading the pack of such emerging economies is India. The dynamism shown by India in global services trade is of immense importance, it has the potential to make India into a leading global economy in the next two decades. The reasons for this are simple; The 21st Century will belong to service industries as work processes become more technical, as communications becomes cheap and as digital technology carries images and sounds instantly across the world.

For India to take advantage of its dynamic comparative advantage in services and emerge as a global economic powerhouse, it will have to negotiate and access the global market in services as efficiently and as quickly as possible. Unfortunately, the experience of past negotiations in the GATS does not provide cause for optimism. The challenge for India is to devise proactive strategies for international trade negotiations, so that they can be harnessed to deliver improved access to foreign markets. One such strategy would involve moving beyond the rather limited framework of the GATS to proactive trade diplomacy at the bilateral level. The purpose of this article to bring out the problems that India is facing in negotiating market access in services and provide the strategic framework for a GATS+ (i.e. beyond GATS) bilateral approach for seeking market access. This article shall also touch briefly on the Indian trade diplomacy at GATS, the current state of play in services trade and the barriers that India faces at the global level in services trade. The chapter is organised as follows; the first section deals with India's Services Sector, the second with India's trade diplomacy in the GATS, the third deals with the issue of Barriers and the fourth with India's Trade diplomacy in services: Multilateral *versus* Bilateral GATS 'plus'. The chapter them turns its attention to the problems that might arise with respect to Bilateral GATS 'plus' before concluding.

Before proceeding further, it is important to define some important terms used in GATS jargon.

Modes: The four modes of supply in GATS define the way a service is delivered by the service provider to the final consumer of that service. The different modes are:

Mode 1: Cross border supply of services i.e. services delivered by provider based in one country to consumer in another. Best example is BPO, where the service provider is in India and the consumer in the USA.

Mode 2: Consumption abroad i.e. services consumed abroad by national of another country. Best examples are in tourism where a British tourist stays in an Indian hotel, she consumes hospitality services 'abroad' from the Indian hotelier.

Mode 3: Commercial Presence i.e. services provided by an operator based abroad to consumers of that country. Best example is US banks based in India providing banking services to Indian consumers.

Mode 4: Movement of Natural Person (MNP) or Movement of skilled personnel i.e. services provided by nationals of one country by traveling to and working in another country. Best example is Indian software professionals working in US offices.

SECTION 1

INDIA AS A GLOBAL FORCE IN SERVICES TRADE

The emergence of India as one of the fastest growing economies in the world during the 1990s is attributable in significant part to the rapid growth of its services sector. During the 1990s, Indian service sector grew at an average annual rate of 9 per cent, contributing to nearly 60 per cent of the overall growth rate of the economy. At the same time, India's exports of services displayed among the fastest rates of growth in the world, over 17 per cent per annum in the 1990s, and grew two and a half times faster than the domestically focused part of the services sector.[1]

Table 13.1

Exports Growth of Services in the 90's

Country	*Exports Growth of Services in the 90's (Annual Average)*
India	17.5 %
China	15.8 %
Korea	12.3 %
Malaysia	12.0 %
Turkey	9.0 %
Taiwan	8.0 %
United States	6.0 %
World	5.6 %

Source: WTO Tables and calculations.

While the most visible growth has been in information technology and business process outsourcing services, other sectors, including telecommunications, financial services, community services and hotels and restaurants, have also grown considerably faster than GDP over time.

Unlike its experience in trade in goods, India, in a short span of time, has emerged as one of the most dynamic suppliers of services in the world. India today accounts for 1.4 per cent of global exports

1. E-Commerce Development Report: UNCTAD 2003.

in services, compared to 0.7 per cent in goods. In recent years, services exports have increased at an annual average rate of 23 per cent compared to only 5.4 per cent in the case of goods, while world exports of goods and services have grown at an average annual rate of 3.9 and 3.7 per cent, respectively. India's position of strength in trade in services *vis-à-vis* goods is also apparent when export performance of individual items within the two sectors is compared: textile and apparel, one of India's leading export items in goods, and software, a major service export.[2]

The increased specialisation of India's exports of services in a selected set of sub-sectors within the services sector is also reflected in the changing composition of its exports. Between 1995-2002, the relative shares of travel and transportation services have fallen from 31 and 19 per cent to 14 and 10 per cent, respectively, while the share of software exports increased from 19 per cent to 34 per cent. In dollar terms, software exports have expanded from $1.8 billion in 1997-98 to over $7 billion in 2001-02, at an average annual rate of 46.3 per cent per year, and now account for almost half of miscellaneous business, professional, and technical services.

There appears to be a major shift underway in the exports of IT and business process outsourcing (BPO) services in terms of the composition and mode of delivery of exports. As recently as 1997-98, nearly 96 per cent of all software exports from India were in the form of information technology services (ITS), like custom application development, application outsourcing, packaged software installation and support, network infrastructure management, IT training and education, network consulting and integration, and hardware installation and support. On the other hand, BPO services, comprising data entry, data conversions, medical transcriptions, insurance claims, call centres, database services, etc., were only 4 per cent of total exports. In a short-span of four years, the BPO services category has grown to 24 per cent of total software exports, registering an average annual growth rate of more than 100 per cent in the last five years.[3]

---

2. World Development Report: World Bank, 2002.
3. Weighing the Benefits of Offshore Outsourcing: Lorraine Cosgrove Ware, CIO Research Report, 2003.

As the bulk of BPO services are processed in India, unlike ITS which involve some visits to clients' sites, this has had a major impact on the mode of delivery of software exports. In 1993-94, nearly 62 per cent of all software exports from India were carried out at the clients' location, i.e. "on-site." Only one out of every five dollars of export orders were carried out within India, i.e. "off-shore". By 2002-03, off-shoring became the dominant mode of delivery of software exports, accounting for almost 58 per cent of total exports.[4] The rising share of BPO services in total exports and the off-shore delivery model have led to increased employment opportunities in India and have also raised the prospects of sustaining the high growth rate of software exports in the future.

There are no signs that this growth will slow down. Exports of information technology related services from India are expected to increase from US$ 7.9 billion in 2001-02 to US$ 57 billion by 2008-09, growing at an average annual rate of 38 per cent A study by Deloitte Research shows that the global market in offshore financial services could be as large as US$ 356 billion by 2008-09 of which a large share would go to India.

Knowledge Process Outsourcing or KPO: Potential and Prospects

India has been quickly moving up the value chain in Mode 1 (cross border) services and traditional BPO activities are giving way to more knowledge intensive activities that involve greater amounts of value addition. Activities like Research and development in pharmaceuticals, biotechnology and product innovation are being outsourced to India.[5] Recently, activities centred on films and filmmaking, i.e. animation, editing, etc. are being outsourced.[6] It is expected that a lot of routine lab work, such as testing and quality control etc will move from US and Europe to India in a big way in the coming decades. Such trends are changing the face of the world and the very concept of trade. It is obvious that India will have to

4. NASSCOM-McKinsey Report 2002.
5. Lords of the Labs: Indian Scientists are turning the Country into a High-Productivity Laboratory for the World, Subir Roy, *Business Standard*, Published: December 31, 2003.
6. BPO: It's Not Call Centres, Stupid, *Economic Times*, January 30, 2003.

aggressively negotiate at multilateral as well as bilateral levels to maximise the possibilities that arise out of such new trends in globalisation. Since KPO will involve complicated issues like Intellectual Property Rights regimes, data disclosure and protection norms, Mutual Recognitions of qualification and training (MRA) and of course Government Procurement, it makes infinite sense to deal with such issues with major trading partners bilaterally first, before going the tougher and slower multilateral route that is bound to get bogged down by inconvergent interests of different WTO members. Before we elaborate on negotiating strategies in services for India, it is important to look at India's record and current focus in trade diplomacy for trade in services.

SECTION 2

A BRIEF OVERVIEW OF INDIAN TRADE DIPLOMACY AT THE GATS

GATT negotiation in the early-1970's and 1980's reflected the agenda of the NIEO (New International Economic Order) that had become the clarion call for all developing countries at that period. Till the Tokyo Round of negotiations (1973-79), an informal group of ten developing nations provided leadership to the 'South' countries. This group was often referred to as the G-10, and its members were Argentina, Brazil, Egypt, India, Indonesia, Chile, Jamaica, Pakistan, Peru and Uruguay. A sub-group within this 10 nations was referred to as the BIG 5, that is Argentina, Brazil, Egypt, India and Indonesia and these five nations often did the agenda setting for almost all G-77 countries (i.e. all member states of the GATT who were from the developing world).[7] The voting patterns in this period of GATT trade diplomacy clearly indicate that most developing nations followed the BIG 5. What was true for the GATT framework in its entirety was true also for GATS. In the context of the GATS, India was in fact the leader even within the BIG 5, stalling any moves for market liberalisation services. The basic position of the BIG 5 and thus of the developing world was that the northern

7. Kumar, R, *"Developing Country Coalitions in World Trade Negotiations,"* Lynne Rienner Publishers and International Development Research Centre, Ottawa, 1995.

countries had a huge comparative advantage in the services industry. These Northern countries dominated logistical, financial and technical services across the world, and it was impossible for the 'South' service industries to survive the competition with their Northern counterparts in a liberalised international market for services. The South position consistently opposed the inclusion of services as a part of the GATT negotiations till the end of the Tokyo Round.

Things changed drastically at the Uruguay Round that started in 1986. The Southern unity on GATS broke down, while the BIG 5 was still opposed to the inclusion of services in the negotiations, South Korea, Chile, and the ASEAN countries disagreed with the BIG 5. In fact, GATS become the catalyst issue at Punta Del Este in Uruguay for the break up of the celebrated 'south position' at the GATS. The two acknowledged leaders of the South in the GATT negotiations, India and Argentina looked increasingly isolated. By the 1990 ministerial conference in Brussels, India and Argentina slowly emerged again as the unofficial representatives on an issue that has again provided a remarkable platform of unity to the G-77 nations in the GATS negotiation. This issue was that of MNP.* India and Argentina are now seen as leaders (with increasing support of two major blocs, the ASEAN and the three east European countries of Czech Republic, Hungary, Poland), leading the southern argument on MNP at the GATS, but they are also forming coalitions with developed countries on MNP to gain maximum benefits out of a future MNP structure.[8] India's recent, mostly post-Doha, emphasis on Mode 1 is a fall out of its ongoing BPO-ITES revolution. The growing importance of ITES has forced the Indian Government to look for new ways and new alliances that broad based and not 'South' centric to get maximum benefits.

Summary of India's main negotiating aims at Doha were[9] the following:

1. Take full market access and national treatment commitments in Modes 1, 2, 3 & 4.

---

* Movement of Natural Persons.

8. GATS 2000 Negotiations and the Options for Developing Countries, Mina Mashayekhi, South Centre Publications, Geneva, 1999.

9. India Schedules of Offer and Requests: Summary Paper. Ministry of Commerce, Government of India.

2. Institute a visa system to fulfil these commitments.
3. Allow inter-firm mobility for professionals.
4. Delink independent professional from commercial presence.
5. Recognise the educational qualifications, training and experience of Indian professionals.
6. Exempt temporary service providers from host country's social security taxes and contribution.
7. Permit majority shareholding of foreign companies with respect to commercial presence.
8. Remove the condition of wage parity in horizontal commitments.

SECTION 3

INDIAN SERVICE SECTOR EXPORTS: BARRIERS AND CONSTRAINTS

As mentioned earlier, the biggest failure of the GATS has been its inability to push for substantial and comprehensive liberalisation for trade in services. This does not augur well for countries like India, which over the years have attained substantial comparative advantage in services. The causes of failure of the GATS in this regard are the topics of discussion in subsequent sections. This section briefly analyses the type and magnitude of barriers facing Indian service sector exporters in the different modes of supply and in different countries.

There are five primary types of barriers to services, these are:

(1) Quantitative-Restriction: QR type policies are commonly applied to service providers. Two prominent examples are the bilateral agreements regulating international air transportation services, which are usually reciprocal and company specific, and ocean-cargo-sharing arrangements, which also often rely on reciprocity in providing shipping services in mutual trade. In many countries, there are outright prohibitions directed against foreign providers of such services as domestic transportation, basic telecommunications, and legal, insurance, education, surveying, and investment advising services. Restrictions on trans-border data flows

are also prevalent and may impede market access by foreign providers.

(2) Price-Based Instruments: These may take the form of visa fees and entry or exit taxes, discriminatory airline landing fees, and port taxes. Tariffs can be significant barriers to trade in goods that embody services (e.g., films, television programmes, and computer software) or goods that are used in producing services (e.g., computers, telecommunications equipment, advertising material). Further, many service sectors are subject to government-sanctioned or monitored price controls, examples including air transportation, financial services, and telecommunications. Government subsidies are commonly used in such service sectors as construction, communications, and road and rail transport.

(3) Licensing or Certification Requirements: This type of barriers are typically imposed on foreign providers of professional and business services. Environmental standards may also impact on service providers, particularly in transportation and tourism.

(4) Government Procurement Policies: These are often designed to favour domestic over foreign providers of services as well as goods by means of preference margins and outright prohibitions.

(5) Discriminatory Access to Distribution and Communications Systems: Such barriers are common in many countries in such sectors as telecommunications, air transport, advertising, insurance, and dealer networks.

Barriers to Trade in Services from an Indian Perspective: Modes and Major Markets

India needs to secure access to foreign markets and counter current and potential protection. Cross border supply (GATS Mode 1) and the presence of natural persons (GATS Mode 4) are the two key Modes of service delivery in which India has a comparative advantage. In these Modes, it is natural to think of India's interest on a horizontal basis because exports are not confined to a closed list of sectors but span the whole breadth of services sectors, especially if we take a dynamic view of India's evolving comparative advantage.

This is not to deny the significance of other modes: consumption abroad (GATS Mode 2) is relevant for certain services like education and health, and commercial presence (GATS Mode 3) is increasingly important in IT and banking services.

Securing access to foreign markets through Modes 1 and 4 presents contrasting challenges. The presence of providers in foreign markets is highly restricted, facing a range of barriers, including burdensome visa formalities, stringent quotas, and discriminatory taxes and standards. Cross-border supply faces few explicit restrictions. But the dramatic expansion of Indian exports and the perceived exodus of white-collar jobs from importing countries are beginning to provoke protection. Measures proposed so far have sought only to prevent governments from procuring Indian services. But as the pain of adjustment grows, so will the temptation to introduce barriers in larger non-government markets.

In a world where technology increasingly allows the spatial fragmentation of goods and services production and where off-shoring to operational units abroad or even outsourcing to foreign third party service providers is increasingly popular with multinational enterprises, India has managed to secure a leading position in the export of a number of services. As we saw in Section I, in addition to being a leading supplier of IT Services, India is now witnessing striking growth of exports of so-called Business Process Outsourcing (BPO) services. The latter service activity arises from the outsourcing (or out-location) of non-core business processes throughout the value chains of both manufacturing and services industries. Even within BPO activities, India has moved from providing only low-end back-office services (data entry, etc.) to more integrated and higher-end service bundles in fields like customer care, human resource management and product development. Every day the boundary between hitherto non-tradable and currently tradable services shifts somewhat. There are no obvious limits to the range of services (and not just BPO services) that could be exported by India. It is not unrealistic to assume that technology, the Indian skill set and business practices will evolve further to make possible and profitable cross-border trade in ever more sophisticated services (R&D, engineering services, etc.).

Unfortunately, the well-publicised creation of jobs in India's service economy, and the potentially broader emergence of developing countries as offshore service providers for the industrialised world, has created fears in the North that may translate into protectionism. Because the job creation process in countries like India is perceived as an exodus of white-collar jobs by industrialised countries labour unions and politicians, concerns have increasingly been voiced about this relocation of work. Much attention has been given to the fact that in several U.S. States, for example, legislation is pending that will introduce an outsourcing ban with respect to government contracts. But there are many less blatant measures that could be introduced to create barriers to the cross-border trade in services. In Europe, for example, legal norms designed to protect workers in outsourced deals, known as TUPE (Transfer of Undertakings and Protection of Employees),[10] as well as recent privacy directives, could have an inhibiting effect on trade. India and other developing countries must, therefore, address the question of how liberal cross-border trade of services can be secured.

There is little doubt that despite the dramatic development in technologies for electronic delivery, Mode 4 will remain important for a range of services. The movement of service-supplying personnel remains a crucial means of delivery even for the Indian software industry, with close to half of Indian exports still supplied through the temporary movement of programmers to the client's site overseas.[11] Given its current and potential endowments of both professionals and less skilled service providers, India has an interest in Mode 4 well beyond IT-related services. In fact, as their populations age and their average levels of training and education rise, developed countries will face an increasing scarcity, in particular, of moderately and less skilled labour. Given that there is really no substitute for human labour, at least in some occupations (e.g., the caring occupations, personal services, and a range of professional services), the demand for Mode 4 is likely to increase over time.[12] But Mode 4 faces a range of barriers in all countries. A major problem is that the temporary movement of service providers invariably comes under the purview, not of international trade policy,

10. Stern, R.M., "Quantifying Barriers to Trade in Services," *Research Seminar in International Economics*, University of Michigan, Discussion Paper No. 470, 2000.

11. NASSCOM-McKinsey Report: 2002.

12. Mashayekhi, Mina, GATS 2000 Negotiations and the Options for Developing Countries, Southcentre Publications, Geneva, 1999.

but of immigration legislation and labour market policy. Visa formalities are in themselves a significant obstacle, and the conditions attached are used to implement a range of restrictions. These include prohibitions and quotas either explicitly or through a variety of economic needs tests. Wage-parity conditions tend to erode the cost advantage of hiring foreigners and have the same restrictive impact as quotas. Discriminatory treatment is implemented through a variety of fiscal and regulatory means. Non-recognition of professional qualifications poses a particular challenge because of the difficulty in distinguishing between legitimate and protectionist denial of recognition.

The elimination of impediments would generate gains not just for India and other exporting countries but also for the importing countries. Recent estimates suggest that there are huge returns to even relatively small movements of labour. For example, it is estimated that an increase in developed countries' quotas on the inward movements of both skilled and unskilled temporary workers equivalent to 3 per cent of their work forces would generate an increase in world welfare of over US$150 billion a year.[13] Both developed and developing countries would share in these gains, and they would be largest if both high-skilled mobility and low-skilled mobility were permitted. However, it is also true that fears about cultural identity, problems of assimilation, and the drain on the public purse, are much more acute with regard to the movement of less skilled workers than the movement of skilled professionals.

India has an interest in the export of health services by attracting foreign patients to domestic hospitals and doctors. Cost savings for patients and health insurers can be significant. For example, the cost of coronary bypass surgery could be as low as Rs. 70,000 to Rs. 100, 000 in India, about 5 per cent of the cost in developed countries.[14] Similarly, the cost of a liver transplant is one-tenth of that in the United States.[15] But a major barrier to

---

13. Trade in Services and Development Implications: UNCTAD Report 2004.
14. Nielson, Julia and Daria Taglioni, "Services Trade Liberalisation: Identifying Opportunities and Gains". *OECD Trade Policy Working Paper*, 2004.
15. NASSCOM-McKinsey Report 2002.

consumption abroad (Mode 2) of medical services is the lack of portability of health insurance. For example, US federal or state government reimbursement of medical expenses is limited to licensed, certified facilities in the United States or in a specific U.S. state. In EU countries also, public insurance does not cover elective care received abroad, and Canada only makes an exception for cancer treatment in some neighboring US states. The lack of long-term portability of health coverage for retirees from OECD countries is also one of the major constraints to trade. In the United States for instance, Medicare covers virtually no services delivered abroad. Other nations may extend coverage abroad, but only for limited periods such as two or three months. This constraint is significant because it tends to deter some elderly persons from traveling or retiring abroad. Those who do retire abroad are often forced to return home to obtain affordable medical care. The potential impact of permitting portability could be substantial. If only 3 per cent of the 100 million elderly persons living in OECD countries retired to developing countries, they would bring with them possibly US$30 to 50 billion annually in personal consumption and $10 to 15 billion in medical expenditures.

At this point it might be interesting to have a look at some trade protection data across countries, in different sectors. Though trade protection data in services is hard to come by, Bernard Hoekman prepared a Table in 1995,[16] that captures the situation adequately. While the numbers are dated, they are good indicators of general state of affairs because not much as happened in terms of services trade liberalisation since the end of the Uruguay Round.

Table 13.3 provides a more detailed explanation the kinds of economic activity the mentioned services sectors (in Table 13.2) cover.

It is quite apparent from the Table 13.3 that protection is highest in those sectors (Financials Services and Communication Services, Business Services and Research and Development) where

16. Hoekman, Bernard. 1995. "Assessing the General Agreement on Trade in Services," in Will Martin and L. Alan Winters (eds.), The *Uruguay Round and the Developing Countries*, World Bank Discussion Paper No. 307. Washington, D.C.: The World Bank. Revised version published in Martin and Winters (eds.), Cambridge University Press, 1996.

Table 13.2

Ad Valorem Tariff Equivalents by Services Sectors for Selected Countries

Country	*Construction*	*Distribution*	*Financial Services*	*Social and Personal Services*	*Communication Services, Business Services and Research and Development*
Australia	12	7	25	26	185
Austria	5	5	20	13	100
Canada	6	9	26	40	120
Chile	40	34	45	42	180
European Union	10	10	30	23	180
Finland	19	15	25	31	180
Hong Kong	32	32	39	42	150
Japan	5	5	29	32	160
Korea	16	21	37	40	150
Mexico	24	21	40	29	180
New Zealand	5	13	30	36	120
Norway	5	13	25	24	120
Singapore	12	34	36	33	138
Sweden	12	13	23	26	185
Switzerland	5	8	28	32	178
Turkey	5	34	35	35	32
United States	5	5	25	32	110

Source: Hoekman (1995).

Table 13.3

Sector Classification

Sector Classification	*Some Specific Activities Covered*
Construction	Architecture and consulting, engineering and planning services, project management
Distribution	Wholesale, Retail and warehousing
Financial Services	Banking, Insurance and brokerage (includes Financial BPO's)
Communication Services, Business Services and Research and Development	All BPO's (except Financial BPO's), Legal and ac counting services (including BPO's in this sector), research, analysis design services, telecommunications.
Social and Personal Services	Sanitation, environmental and sewerage, cultural and entertainment services, sports and recreation services.

Source: United Nations Statistical Division (Sector Classification Registry Tables).

India has an comparative advantage and export interest. Moreover, such protection is substantial in countries that are the major importers (or potentially major importers) of such services from India, i.e. USA, EU, Japan and other Industrialised economies. Given this background, it becomes imperative that India comes with proactive strategies to negotiate market access in services trade and it does by looking beyond the GATS as a framework.

SECTION 4

STRATEGIC SHIFT IN SERVICES TRADE NEGOTIATION: GATS+ BILATERAL ENGAGEMENT

Liberalisation of services trade under the multilateral framework of WTO-GATS has been extremely slow. India itself must shoulder some of the blame for lack dynamism of GATS as a liberaliser of the global market for services; it has never quite adopted a proactive agenda to the GATS.[17] India is not alone; most countries are unwilling to push for an ambitious liberalisation programme under the GATS framework. While some countries, mostly developed states, showed some initiative to try and open up their areas of comparative advantage i.e. Telecommunications and financial services, globally through GATS, the developing country agenda of movement of skilled labour (Mode 4) has been floundered.[18] It is the structure of the GATS framework that is itself to blame for this slow movement in real liberalisation. The biggest weakness is that GATS operates on a request-offer, positive list approach to scheduling liberalisation commitments. Under such an approach, countries retain the full right to undertake no commitments and they are under no legal obligation to supply information to their trading partners on the nature of discriminatory or access-impeding regulations maintained at the domestic level. Furthermore, with the 'request and offer' principle, each member draws up a wish list of what kind of market access it would like from each of the other members and this 'request' is submitted to the services council. After some

17. "Stop Being Defensive in WTO", Says T N Srinivasan, *Cancun Briefing Series, Financial Express*, 2003.

18. Mashayekhi *op cit*.

negotiations, each member comes up with an 'offer' list that provides the maximum market access it can provide to all other members. It is important to note, that in most cases the requests have no bearing on the offers, as most countries decide before hand how much they will liberalise after each round of negotiations. It is also important to note that since MFN operates, these offers are not member specific, but multilateral. This entire system has several flaws that negate any constructive movement towards successful market liberalisation.

To begin with, there is a very large transaction cost involved, as commitments are bartered sector-by-sector, and then mode-by-mode in each sector. Even in a bilateral set up, such negotiations will have much higher transaction costs relative to the usual formula based negotiation in goods that are oriented towards tariff cuts and are uniform for all members. Given a multilateral framework, the transaction costs for such sector/mode oriented give and take is phenomenal, and takes away a lot of the incentive for many countries to pursue a proactive approach in the GATS. There is tremendous difficulty in accomplishing an exchange and balance of concessions in the GATS between countries in this sort of a multilateral framework, as often many of the member countries do not share a reciprocal interest in each other's markets.

The second, and the far bigger problem, is that of the free rider. Under the GATS framework, any market concession is for ALL members by the virtue of the MFN principle in WTO. Thus, the problem that arises in such a system is that most members are tempted to understate their willingness to pay for any concession from a trading partner. Each member hopes that reciprocal concessions from other members will be sufficient to induce that trading partner to make the concessions it itself desires from it. Thus, the concessions on market access negotiated at the GATS are almost always less than optimal.[19]

Given this scenario, the effectiveness of the GATS, as a platform where India can engage in negotiations for trade in the area of its

---

19. Mattoo, Aaditya and Marcelo Olarreaga, *Reciprocity Across Modes of Supply in the World Trade Organisation: A Negotiating Formula*, Development Research Group (DECRG), World Bank, 2001.

comparative advantage, i.e. services, is questionable. It becomes apparent that India should adopt a GATS+ bilateral approach with target markets for its services, i.e. US, EU and Japan (G3). Such a GATS+ approach does not in any way mean that India does not use the GATS and further its interests in global services trade in a multilateral framework. Both the GATS and the bilateral approaches should be used in conjunction to extract the maximum gains for India's services industry.

There are several strategic reasons why a GATS+ approach might be very useful for India's engagement in the global negotiations for services market access:

1. The G3 are more likely to liberalise trade in services under Mode 1 (Cross border supply) and Mode 4 (movement of skilled personnel) from a preferred source like India rather than extend such market access on a MFN basis under the multilateral framework of WTO-GATS.
2. The existing GATS Service Sectoral Classification list (W 120) does not provide an adequate description of the range of services that India has acquired a strong interest in. Many of the listed "input" or "support services" (for example payroll or customer care services) do not have fully corresponding entries in the W 120. Furthermore, it is not possible to "infer" commitments on input services from commitments on main service classifications (e.g. commitment on insurance claims processing cannot be inferred with certainty from a commitment on non-life insurance services)[3]. Yet again, the costs of negotiating any amendment or reform of the W 120 will be prohibitive and beset with opposition. Given India's deep economic engagement with G3 countries in business and professional services, especially with the US, a GATS+ bilateral engagement will be much more fruitful and conducive to Indian interests in this area.
3. It will be easier for G3 and India to remove regulatory barriers on the trade in skilled services in a bilateral framework rather than a multilateral one. As mentioned earlier, the transaction costs of negotiating such complicated

regulatory barriers, as they exist in the services sector, in the request-offer multilateral framework of the GATS is so high that it will be next to impossible to achieve anything fruitful. It also must be remembered that Mutual Recognitions Agreements (MRA) is far easier to negotiate bilaterally and is the most efficient mechanism to eradicate regulatory barriers. MRA's are essential for India's growth as an exporter of professional services in both Mode 1 and Mode 4.

4. The G3 and India GATS+ bilateral can remove the impediments to such knowledge-based trade through comprehensive agreements on intellectual property right protection and data exclusivity. Such an alliance will bring down costs of research for G3 companies and make G3 high technology more competitive in the world market. Yet again, the transaction costs involved in arriving at any semblance of an agreement at the multilateral GATS framework in such issues is next to impossible. Also, the G3 will be far more comfortable working with India on a stand alone basis on technology based services rather than extending such concessions to all countries for various political, security and strategic reasons.

5. A GATS+ approach can deal with India's long-standing demand for greater and freer movement of skilled personnel (Mode 4) to industrialised economies. A good example is that U.S. employers, large and small alike, struggle to find enough skilled professionals, particularly in the high-tech sector. Unnecessary and inadequate H-1B quotas have put this vital immigration status in jeopardy and threaten to undermine the competitiveness of U.S. companies in the global marketplace. (While the H-1B global quota is a GATS commitment by the US in Mode 4, for understandable reasons, US will like to maintain a cap on it, at the same time it would like to hire skilled labour, especially from India for the sake of its own productivity. A 1997 report by the National Research Council of the National Academy of Sciences found that skilled immigrants (46 per cent of which

came from India) raise the incomes of U.S.-born workers by at least $10 billion per year[20]). Some people believe that those estimates are understated because they do not account for the domestic economic impact of highly skilled foreign national workers on overall U.S. productivity. Thus the best way is to bypass the GATS and have a bilateral GATS+ agreement with India, whereby Indians are granted a special GATS+ E-visa outside the purview of the GATS committed H-1B programme.

6. G3 MNC's in services such as insurance, finance and banking, utilities and telecommunications are eager to enter a huge (with the future potential of being colossal) Indian market. India will be far more comfortable granting a GATS+ market access exclusively to the G3 on Mode 3 (supply of services through commercial presence) rather than do so on a multilateral basis under WTO-GATS, as that would mean extending to all countries, some of whom might not be desirable in the Indian market for political or security reasons.

7. In particular, the GATS+ bilateral route can provide India the ability to pursue policy approaches differing from those emerging from the incipient multilateral framework under the GATS. Because the GATS itself remains incomplete, with negotiations pending in a number of key areas (e.g. emergency safeguards, subsidies, government procurement, domestic regulation), The proliferation of RTA's that have a strong services component in recent years has shown that GATS+ approaches are possible and are indeed desirable, as they tend to liberalise services much further. Such regional experimentation has generated a number of useful policy lessons in comparative negotiating and rule-making dynamics, and India should keep and open mind in its approach to get market access in services and incorporate such ideas in negotiations for GATS bilateral services engagement.

---

20. National Research Council, *The New Americans: Economic, Demographic, and Fiscal Effects of Immigration* (Washington: National Academy Press, 1997).

Theoretical Support for GATS+ Approaches

Preferential Trading Arrangements (PTA) with US, EU and Japan on Services Only

Theoretically, gains from preferential trade in services are more than that in goods. This is due to the fact that there are a very few tariff barriers in services, protection being in the form of regulatory barriers. Thus, there is lesser chance of trade diversion. This idea has been firmly asserted by many experts including Mattoo and Fink.[21]

Furthermore, there is great complimentarity between G3 and India in the services sector. While India has made great strides in production and delivery of services that require skilled human resources, the US leads the world in several services sectors such as insurance, banking and environmental services.

Demographic changes also give strong theoretic support for an India-G3 PTA in services. Ageing populations in countries such as the US demand that these economies look for alternative skill labour supply chains, and India is ideally placed be in such a supply chain. India will have 17 per cent of global working age population by 2050, while US will have only 4.10 per cent and EU 6 per cent.[22]

There is also a strong convergence between India and the US as partners in research and development oriented services, and this can be deepened to India's advantage through a GATS+ PTA. A growing body of work argues that flow of knowledge and skills are expedited through preferential trade agreements, especially those in services. This will be especially true for a North-South PTA.[23] Given the high skilled scientific manpower India, the US-India PTA can become the cornerstone for an important technological/scientific alliance of the future. US companies are already keen to outsource laboratory research and testing to India.

---

21. Mattoo, Aaditya and Carsten Fink, "Regional Agreements and Trade in Services: Policy Issues," *World Bank Research Working Paper* 2852, 2002.
22. *Long-term Global Demographic Trends: Reshaping the Global Landscape*, CIA Publication, 2001.
23. "North-South R&D Spillovers" by Coe, Helpman and Hoffmaister, *Economic Journal* No.107, 1997.

Strategies for GATS+ Negotiations: Alternatives to the Request and Offer Approach

The 'Negative List' Approach

The alternative, "top-down" approach to services trade and investment liberalisation is based upon the concept of negative listing, whereby ALL sectors and non-conforming measures are to be liberalised unless otherwise specified in a transparent manner in reservation lists appended to an agreement. Non-conforming measures contained in reservation lists are then usually liberalised through consultations or, as in the GATS, periodic negotiations.

A number of distinguishing features of negative listing can be identified. For one, such an approach enshrines and affirms the up-front commitment of signatories (subject to reservations) to an overarching set of general obligations. This is currently the case under the GATS solely with respect to the Agreement's provisions on MFN treatment (Article II, with scope for one-time exceptions) and transparency (Article III), with all other disciplines applying in a piecemeal manner to sectors and modes of supply on those terms inscribed in members' schedules of commitments. A second, and perhaps more immediately operational, defining characteristic of negative listing lies in its ability to generate a standstill, i.e. to establish a stronger floor of liberalisation by locking-in the statutory or regulatory *status quo*. An important governance-enhancing feature arising from the adoption of a negative list approach is the greater level of transparency it generates. The information contained in reservation lists will be important to prospective investors, who value the one-stop shopping attributes of a comprehensive inventory of potential restrictions in foreign markets. They are also likely to benefit home country negotiators, assisting them in establishing a hierarchy of impediments to tackle in future negotiations.[24] Such information can in turn lend itself more easily to formula-based liberalisation, for instance by encouraging members to agree to reduce or progressively phase-out "revealed" non-conforming measures that may be similar across countries (e.g. quantitative

---

24. Sauvé, Pierre (1996), "Services and the International Contestability of Markets", in *Transnational Corporations*, Vol. 5, No. 1.

limitations on foreign ownership in airlines). The production of a negative list may also help to generate a useful domestic policy dialogue between the trade negotiating and regulatory communities, thereby encouraging countries to perform a comprehensive audit of existing trade- and investment-restrictive measures, benchmark domestic regulatory regimes against best international practices, and revisit the rationale for, and most efficient means of satisfying, domestic policy objectives.

Zero for Zero (Reciprocity) Formula and Harmonising Regulatory Principles

Another approach is to use the philosophy of zero for zero used in liberalisation of the trade in goods. Under this system, all partners agree to liberalise sectors reciprocally and harmonise all regulatory principles (through MRA's) for such sectors. The main advantage of such an approach is that the partners can chose the exact sectors they are all comfortable with liberalising, agree upon a final list of sectors and modes, and then go ahead with rapid liberalisation. The reciprocity clause (i.e. zero for zero) eliminates any free rider problem, forcing all parties to liberalise equally. Though the negative list approach is likely to be a more comprehensive mechanism of liberalisation, the zero for zero approach may be easier to negotiate and more focused sectorally, picking those for the PTA that will guarantee maximum gains for all partners.

The Special and Differential (SDT) Clause in North-South PTA

India will have to use the 'special and differential treatment' card strategically in any negotiations with the G3 for a GATS+ PTA. The main areas for SDT will be in longer implementation periods to meet market access commitments in mode 3 (commercial presence) in certain areas like banking, insurance, distribution etc. and meeting certain regulatory and quality standards for some areas. Given such SDT clauses are a part of any such GATS+ PTA with the G3 countries, India should have little to fear.

The case for GATS+ PTA remain strong.

Potential Hurdles to GATS+ Bilateral Engagement: Sectoral Issues

Like any aspect of trade negotiation, a GATS+ approach that is bilateral in nature will be met with some domestic opposition. Such opposition will arise predominantly from those sectors of the domestic services economy that have been long protected, and some of them rendered uncompetitive due to faulty domestic policy. Since many of such sectors are represented by powerful lobby groups comprising of educated and articulate members of professional services, such opposition has the potential to be a major hurdle in India's attempts for proactive GATS+ bilateral engagement in services. Since India's potential partners for successful GATS+ engagement will be precisely interested in opening up these sectors, as a trade-off in such GATS+ diplomacy, it is the one issue that needs resolution before India embarks on any GATS+ initiative. At this point it is useful to look briefly at some such sectors that will oppose GATS+ approaches and the issues governing them.

Note: In the following Tables, the GATS commitments are taken from India's sectoral offers made to the services council in WTO in 2003. The GATS+ offers are based on the summary of sectoral requests received by the Ministry of Commerce, India, from USA, EU and Japan in the services council, WTO in 2003.[25]

Table 13.4

Telecommunications

GATS Commitment	*Potential GATS+ Offer*	*Domestic Policy Issues Applicable to Foreign Service Providers*
Foreign equity restricted to 25 per cent in most categories. Restrictions on number of providers.	Foreign stake allowed over and above 51 per cent in most (or all) categories. Restrictions based on economic needs test remain.	Some policy uncertainty on tariff, inter-connect regimes. Regulator is gradually establishing credibility.

25. India Schedules of Offer and Requests: Summary Paper. Ministry of Commerce, Government of India.

Telecommunications has long been a sector that has been protected in India, and till recently was a public sector monopoly. Here the private sector, though displaying enormous dynamism, is yet to mature. Regulatory issues are still being debated, and operational tariffs remain high compared to international standards. Liberalisation in this sector is important, as new technologies will bring down costs in this key infrastructure input of the economy. This sector also needs to expand rapidly given India's low communication penetration as well as to fructify India's ambition to become an Information Technology (IT) superpower. Despite this background, vested interests abound, and strong pressures against liberalisation is expected, both from the less than efficient public sector stake holders, as well as the nascent private sector interests.

Table 13.5

Insurance

GATS Commitment	*Potential GATS+ Offer*	*Domestic Policy Issues Applicable to Foreign Service Providers*
Limited commitments only on reinsurance and overseas brokers.	Full mode 3 commitments on all sectors i.e. 75 per cent to 100 per cent foreign equity allowed in all segments.	Minimum capitalisation norms; Funds of policyholders to be retained within the country; Compulsory exposure to rural and social sectors and backward classes.

Like telecommunications, Insurance has long been protected from foreign competition and has until recently been a Public sector monopoly. Privatisation is a recent phenomenon and domestic providers are yet to get the experience and reach the scale of operations that will make them robust and competitive relative to the large-scale multinational Insurance firms. Thus, opposition from both Public sector as well as the nascent Private sector operators is expected to be high for any moves to GATS+ liberalisation.

The domestic banking sector in India has been entirely dominated by the public sector. It is only recently that some private players have come into the market. If the banking sector is liberalised, the most virulent opposition will come from the vested interests in the large public sector banks. The private sector has shown tremendous dynamism and is expected to meet any challenge from international players head on (CII Sectoral Survey).

Table 13.6

Banking

GATS Commitment	*Potential GATS+ Offer*	*Domestic Policy Issues Applicable to Foreign Service Providers*
Commercial presence through licensed branches; Cap on the number of licenses and limit on share of total banking system assets requirements.	Licensing regime made more transparent. All caps removed on number of licenses and limit on share of total banking system assets is raised substantially.	Mandatory priority sector lending and rural branch requirements for domestic banks. This can be extended to Foreign players in a more liberalised regime, as otherwise it will be inequitable framework for domestic players.

Table 13.7

Distribution Services

GATS Commitment	*Potential GATS+ Offer*	*Domestic Policy Issues Applicable to Foreign Service Providers*
No GATS commitment	100 per cent FDI (mode 3) allowed in wholesale, and 75 per cent to 100 per cent FDI with some region specific restrictions allowed in retail.	Land market distortions.

India has a large unorganised distribution sector with low tax compliance. It has never been exposed to foreign competition, and until recently, large retail outlets were never the norm. How much of a challenge can foreign players be, even with deep pockets, remains to be seen as the Indian market is highly fragmented and price conscious. Since this sector remains highly unorganised, save a few local commercial associations, the real nature of the domestic opposition to liberalisation is yet to be gauged.

Table 13.8

Legal Services

GATS Commitment	*Potential GATS+ Offer*	*Domestic Policy Issues Applicable to Foreign Service Providers*
No GATS commitment	Full commitment on mode 2 and 3, limited commitments on Mode 4.	Limitations on partnership norms, operational flexibility.

The legal sector, long protected and with its true growth limited by archaic bar council rules and policy distortions, is strongly opposed to any liberalisation in this sector (CII Sectoral Survey). On the flip side, the legal services industry has the potential to grow through by providing Mode 1 services on legal consultation. It also has potential to cater to a large export market for Mode 1 and 2 legal arbitration.

Table 13.9

Accountancy

GATS Commitment	*Potential GATS+ Offer*	*Domestic Policy Issues Applicable to Foreign Service Providers*
No GATS commitment. Also, Foreign service providers not allowed to undertake Statutory Audits	Full market access to foreign operators in Mode 1, 2, 3 and 4.	Only partnership firms allowed with number of partners limited to 20.

Protected from global competition and stunted by domestic policy, the domestic players, like their counterparts in legal services, are strongly opposed to liberalisation (CII sectoral Survey). Ironically, just like legal services, the accountancy sector has tremendous potential for growth as global providers of accountancy services, especially in Mode 1 and 2. Limited mobility for Indian professionals in Mode 4 will also help.

The rail and air services have long been protected from and foreign competition and until recently the air was a public sector monopoly, rail remains one. Foreign participation in road transport is hampered by local state level policies, corruption in regulatory bodies and a highly fragmented, unorganised market. Public sector companies in rail and air, as well as truckers associations will probably make a strong case against liberalisation.

Table 13.10

Transportation Services

GATS Commitment	*Potential GATS+ Offer*	*Domestic Policy Issues Applicable to Foreign Service Providers*
No GATS commitment	Full market access to foreign operators in Mode 1,3 and 4.	Restrictions on inter-state movement of goods; Overlapping responsibilities and coordination issues between government departments (e.g., multi-modal transport).

SECTION 5

POTENTIAL HURDLES TO GATS+ BILATERAL ENGAGEMENT: NON-SECTORAL ISSUES

While the most virulent opposition to any GATS+ bilateral engagement by India is likely to come from certain sectors that are challenged by foreign competition, there are some reservations to such a GATS+ approach that is entirely independent of sectoral opposition and is based on experience of PTA's that have a substantial services component. If US, EU or Japan undertake a Preferential Trade Agreement in Services with India, it will be the first of its kind in the world. While there are no pure services PTA, some PTA's have a strong services component. This section investigates the main issues in three other major North-South services oriented Preferential Trade Agreements. The PTA's investigated here are;

1. **US-Singapore Free Trade Agreement**. This agreement has been passed by US House of Representatives on July 2003. The date of entry into force is yet to be arrived at.
2. **US-Chile Free Trade agreement**. This agreement has been passed by the US House of Representatives on July 2003. The date of entry into force is yet to be arrived at.

3. **EU-Czech Republic Free Trade Agreement**. This agreement was signed on 1st February, 1995 and entered into force on 9th October, 1996.

Unless otherwise mentioned, the points and features discussed in this section are common to all the three PTA's. It is important to analyse in some detail the modalities and norms of such North-South services oriented PTA's as they have strong implications for India. It is important to understand the economic impact of the norms discussed below and think ahead in terms of strategy *vis-à-vis* India's rules of engagement in services GATS+ PTA's.

Labour Standards

The PTA mandates the right of each partner to establish its own domestic labour standards, and to adopt or modify its labour laws. It enjoins each partner to ensure that its laws provide for labour standards consistent with the internationally recognised labour rights under the ILO Declaration on Fundamental Principles and Rights at Work and its Follow-up (1998), of which India is already a signatory.

The PTA also recognises that each partner retains the right to exercise discretion with respect to investigatory, prosecutorial, regulatory, and compliance matters in ALL aspect of labour laws and standards.

This implies that there is nothing in the PTA that should have cause for concern for India, as the PTA grants complete sovereignty over the framing and implementation of labour laws. The only reference framework, i.e. the ILO declaration, is a shared value system between India and the other main countries i.e. EU, US and Japan, and Indian laws are compliant with the principles of ILO.

The PTA recognises that it is inappropriate to encourage trade or investment by weakening or reducing the protections afforded in domestic labour laws. Thus, each partner is ***expected*** (not explicitly prohibited) to ensure that it does not waive or otherwise derogate from domestic laws in a manner that weakens or reduces adherence to the internationally recognised labour rights. This aspect of the PTA is troublesome from an Indian point of as nothing explicitly prevents the US/EU/Japan from using labour standards as a protectionist policy. The above clause is not subject to dispute settlement and does not explicitly prohibit the use of labour standards as barrier to trade. This is especially of concern to sectors like ITES and nursing services.

Environmental Standards

The PTA's recognises the right of both PTA partners to establish its own levels of domestic environmental protection and environmental development policies and priorities. Most importantly,

1. The PTA recognises the sovereignty of individual partners in matters of regulation and enforcement.
2. It does not empower a partner's authorities to undertake environmental law enforcement activities in the territory of the other partner. Each partner is under obligation to ensure that its laws provide for high levels of environmental protection and shall strive to continue to improve those laws.

This implies that the PTA does not specify what 'high level of environmental protection' mean and can lead to disputes. Since the high level protection is open ended, it is open to abuse as trade protectionist measures. The problem with environment standards within the PTA is same as labour standards. While it dispels any fears of interference on India's labour and environmental policy or implementation by assuring the sovereignty of individual partners in these issues, it does nothing to allay fears that excessively high labour or environmental standards will not be used as trade barriers. This is an area that India will have to aggressively address in any GATS+ PTA framework.

Conclusion

The growth of a dynamic services sector for domestic consumption is crucial for the Indian economy. India needs a dynamic services sector to support growth in Agriculture and Industry. FDI in the different services sectors will bring innovation and spur reforms in the economy. Such FDI will also become an important source of new technology flows. Liberalised services sectors that have attracted significant FDI, such as telecommunications, are among the fastest growing sectors in the economy and contributing to the transformation of the India.

The growth of the services sector is also important for creating rapid employment for India's educated youth in the private sector.

Such growth will be helpful towards implementing structural reforms in India's public sector that has traditionally employed a large bulk of India's educated labour force.

In this context, the importance of market access for India's service sector producers cannot be emphasised more. India will have to take a proactive stance in trade diplomacy to achieve such market access. To this end, it must seriously consider bilateral GATS+ initiatives with the Industrialised economies, namely the G3 (US, EU and Japan). India just cannot take a 'wait and watch' gradualist policy for services trade, waiting for consensus at a multilateral level. The urgency of the matter arises from a very crucial aspect of services trade i.e. the sequence of liberalisation is most important in the case of services. Due to considerable search and sunk costs, benefits of preferential trade liberalisation will dominate eventual global trade liberalisation. In other words, a temporary privileged access to markets will tend to translate into a long-term advantage in that market. Nothing could suit India better; bilateral GATS+ initiatives NOW will guarantee India an edge in G3 markets for the next two to three decades. It is time India and Indians lived up to their destiny, as a global economic power and pre-eminent knowledge economy.

References

CIA Publication (2001). *Long-term Global Demographic Trends: Reshaping the Global Landscape.*

Economic Times (2004). "BPO: It's Not Call Centres, Stupid," January 2004.

Financial Express (2003). *'Stop Being Defensive in WTO*, Says TN Srinivasan,' *Cancun Briefing Series.*

Government of India, *India Schedules of Offer and Requests: Summary Paper* Ministry of Commerce.

Kumar, R. (1995). *Developing Country Coalitions in World Trade Negotiations* Lynne Rienner Publishers and International Development Research Centre, Ottawa.

Mashayekhi, Mina (1999). *GATS 2000 Negotiations and the Options for Developing Countries*, South Centre Publications, Geneva.

Mattoo, Aaditya and Carsten Fink (2002). "Regional Agreements and Trade in Services: Policy Issues," *World Bank Policy Research Working Paper* 2852, June 2002.

Mattoo, Aaditya and Marcelo Olarreaga (2001). "Reciprocity Across Modes of Supply in the World Trade Organisation: A Negotiating Formula," Development Research Group (DECRG), World Bank.

NASSCOM-McKinsey Report: 2002

Nielson, Julia and Daria Taglioni (2004). "Services Trade Liberalisation: Identifying Opportunities and Gains," *OECD Trade Policy Working Paper.*

Roy, Subir (2003). "Lords of the Labs: Indian Scientists are Turning the Country into a High-Productivity Laboratory for the World," *Business Standard*, Published : December 31, 2003.

Stern, Robert M. (2000). "Quantifying Barriers to Trade in Services," Research Seminar in International Economics, University of Michigan, *Discussion Paper No. 470.*

UNCTAD (2003). *E-Commerce Development Report.*

———. (2004). "Trade in Services and Development Implications" *UNCTAD Report.*

Ware, Lorraine Cosgrove (2003). "Weighing the Benefits of Offshore Outsourcing," *CIO Research Report.*

World Bank (2002). *World Development Report.*

WTO (2002). *Communication from India. Negotiating Proposal for Computer and Related Services*, WTO Document S/CSS/W/141.

———. (2003). *Developing Country (incl India) Submission to Services Council.* WTO Document TN/S/W/16.

———. (2000). Indian Proposal for Movement of Natural Persons in GATS: WTO Document S/CSS/W/12, November 2000.

———. (1998). *Services Council Draft on MNP*: WTO Document No. S/C/W/758, December 1998.

14

Infrastructure Concerns Under GATS Trade in the Telecom and Transport Services

SUPARNA KARMAKAR

Introduction

Infrastructure is a key requirement in any country or region that wishes to create and retain its national and international competitive edge. The impact of adequate provisioning of infrastructure facilities in any country is not only seen on the economy of the country under consideration, but also impacts the region's income growth and development. In fact, provisioning of adequate and complementary infrastructural facilities is very important, even for retaining political power in a country like India, and the voter's mandate in the 2004 general elections can arguably be interpreted as a demand for improved social and physical infrastructure in the country. It is no secret that the lack of adequate and commensurate infrastructural facilities is what sets India apart from China in the mind of the investor (both foreign and domestic firms). Thus, the significance of the sector in a country's economy is multi-dimensional.

The concern about infrastructure in the context of WTO, however, is slightly different from domestic policy imperatives. For while at home, the concerns mainly relate to adequate provisioning and creating amenable policies that foster development and growth of the sector, in the international policy context the concerns shift focus into compatibility of WTO Members' domestic policies of such service provision amongst the Member countries in the multilateral trading bloc, and also to fair and liberal market access for Members that is facilitated by framing proper trade rules and designing acceptable conventions. Commensurate development of infrastructure services in particular, viz. transport, telecommunications, power, and financial services, are now deemed critical for sustaining growth in developing economies.

It should be remembered that the World Trade Organisation (WTO) is the only global international organisation that deals with the rules of trade between nations. At its heart are the WTO agreements, negotiated and signed by the bulk of the world's trading nations and ratified by their national parliaments. The goal is to help producers of goods and services, exporters and importers, to conduct their business in a free and fair manner. Under the WTO, special focus and importance has been accorded to the services sector, under which category the infrastructural sub-sectors feature, and the issues pertaining to liberalisation thereof are discussed under the General Agreement on Trade in Services (GATS).

At the time when GATT was reborn as WTO in 1995, trade in services under GATS was incorporated in the agenda of the WTO as a part of the 'single undertaking'. As a signatory to WTO, India therefore is committed to liberalise progressively the trade in services in the different designated sectors by December 2006, when the Uruguay Round Negotiations under the Doha Work Programme is expected to be completed. Discussions and negotiations of services sector liberalisation are held at the Special Sessions of the Council for Trade in Services (CTS).

The Uruguay Round identified 12 services areas where liberalisation is mandated. Infrastructure does not figure as a special service, but there are services featuring in GATS that come under the ambit of infrastructure. This chapter will discuss the impact of liberalisation of two such services, namely telecom (communication services) and transport (including road, rail, aviation and maritime). This chapter limits discussion on a specific issue, *viz*. the treatment of infrastructure in WTO and GATS, and the implication for the sector's development (and policy flexibility) in developing countries like India. The sections that follow contain brief discussions on the importance of the services sector, and the manner of negotiations on these key sub-sectors related to infrastructure, and finally, conclude with a critical analysis of the future prospects and negotiation imperatives necessary to ensure the development of a dynamic and world class infrastructure sector in India.

Why are Services Important?

Services account for a large share of production and employment in most economies, the developed and increasingly also the developing countries. At the end of the last millennium, services represented the fastest growing sector of the global economy and accounted for 60 per cent of global output, 30 per cent of global employment and nearly 20 per cent of global trade. Countries like the US and UK, and several other OECD countries, have a services-to-GDP ratio of over 75 per cent. In India, the sector has accounted for over 50 per cent of GDP since mid-1990s, growing at an average annual rate of 9 per cent per annum. Business services have been the fastest growing sector in the 1990s, attaining a growth rate of about 20 per cent per annum.

In the fiscal year 2003-04, the sector remained the principal driver of the Indian economy, contributing 57 per cent to GDP. In particular, in the last year, the infrastructure sectors have grown handsomely; the structural shifts in the economy has boosted growth in 'trade, hotels, transport and communication', and has seen a phenomenal expansion in the number of subscribers of the cellular services (current teledensity is 9.37 per cent). The average length of roads laid down in the last few years has shot up sharply due to the so called 'Golden Quadrilateral' Project. The railways and other transport sectors have also grown at a very rapid pace in 2004.

The dollar value of world trade in commercial services[1] increased to US$ 2.10 trillion (16% year-on-year) in 2004, out of which India's share was about 1.5 per cent. According to International Trade Statistics 2004, the share of commercial services in India's total trade was 27 per cent in 2002. Incidentally, the share of the IT & ITeS (the BPO and telecom sector) services is much less than that could be justified by the recent hullabaloo; nevertheless, in terms of importance in the recent phase of decelerating employment opportunities in the country, this sector assumed significance.

The key service sectors for India other than IT & Telecom are: health services and social sectors, tourism and related services (viz

1. IMF - Balance of Payments Statistics, 2004. Note here that commercial services trade as measured by the IMF BoP Statistics cover mainly trade under modes 1 & 2, as defined by GATS.

transport), education and training services, engineering services, among others. In this chapter, we will concentrate on the telecom and the transport services and try to determine the impact of the ongoing negotiations in WTO on the development of the said sectors. Not surprisingly, these are also the areas where the country has an aggressive interest (for further liberalisation) in the ongoing negotiations.

GATS in Brief

It would not be out of order to first discuss briefly the system and modalities for services negotiations under WTO before proceeding to discuss specifically the infrastrucutral services negotiations and implications thereof. As discussed earlier, the General Agreement on Trade in Services (GATS) is the first and only set of international rules governing the international trade in services. First negotiated in the Uruguay Round, it was developed in response to the huge growth of the services economy over the past 30 years and the greater potential for trading services brought about by the communications revolution. India has been a signatory to this Agreement since its entry into force in 1995. The GATS rules apply in principle to all service sectors except "services supplied in the exercise of governmental authority", these being services that are supplied neither on a commercial basis nor in competition with other suppliers.

GATS sets out a framework of legally binding obligations and commitments governing the conduct of world trade in services. It is supported by a number of schedules of specific commitments undertaken by individual WTO Members.[2] These commitments bind Members *not* to introduce more restrictive rules, which could have an adverse effect on trade flows and volumes. GATS also gives the flexibility to each member country to decide the service sectors in which it will undertake and schedule commitments, i.e. it follows the 'positive list' approach for liberalisation. India made initial commitments at the time of entry of GATS into force. These have now come up for review. Further, to allay fears, an annex to the GATS makes it clear that the agreement has nothing to do with

2. Also see http://www.wto.org/english/thewto_e/whatis_e/tif_e/agrm6_e.htm

individuals looking for employment in another country, viz. immigration, or with citizenship, residence or employment requirements. Negotiations are targeted merely at market access for temporary movement of professionals, or laws governing market access of service providers in foreign countries, and members still have the right to regulate the entry and stay of the persons concerned by requiring visas. GATS, like the GATT, recognises the sovereign right of WTO Member governments to regulate, and to introduce new regulations on, the supply of services within their territories in order to meet national policy objectives.

The WTO-mandated negotiations under GATS to work out the rules and a framework for further liberalisation of trade in services are currently underway. For, written into the GATS is a commitment by WTO member governments that the negotiations shall aim to achieve 'progressively higher levels of liberalisation of trade in services through the reduction or elimination of the adverse effects on trade in services of measures as a means of providing effective market access, and with a view to promoting the interests of all participants on a mutually advantageous basis and to securing an overall balance of rights and obligations'. In that sense this Agreement is still a 'work-in-progress'.

The service sectors which are under negotiation are based on the W/120 Classification of sectors and sub-sectors[3]. These classifications cross-refer to the United Nations Central Product Classification (CPC). The commitments so far have been based on the UN Provisional CPC, which was the basis for the negotiations during the Uruguay Round.

The services negotiations which began on January 1, 2000, have been structured so as to finalise the new Agreement under the 'single undertaking' model adopted at Doha[4] (under the Doha Development Agenda), which was earlier targeted for conclusion by Januray 1, 2005. As per the revised targets post-Cancun, the Doha Work Programme negotiations, of which services are a part of the single-undertaking, negotiations were scheduled to conclude in December

3. The full list is available at http://www.wto.org/english/tratop_e/serv_e/mtn_gns_w_120_e.doc
4. Also refer to http://www.wto.org/english/tratop_e/dda_e/dohaexplained_e.htm#services & http://www.wto.org/english/tratop_e/serv_e/s_negs_e.htm

2005, at the 6th Ministerial Meeting of WTO at Hong Kong, but the timeline has now been extended by another year.

The main objective of these negotiations is to liberalise commitments in all the service sectors and all the 'modes' of supply of services and to improve the multilateral rules for trade in services. As per the decision taken in the Doha Ministerial Conference in 2001, each member country will have to take commitments for progressive liberalisation under each of the 'supply modes' according to the needs and developmental status of the economy and the concerned services under a positive list approach.

There are four identified modes of supplying services under GATS:[5]

Mode 1: *Cross-border trade.*

Mode 2: *Consumption abroad.*

Mode 3: *Commercial presence.*

Mode 4: *Presence of natural persons.*

An Annex to the GATS makes it clear, however, that the agreement has nothing to do with individuals looking for employment in another country, or with citizenship, residence or employment requirements. The members still have a right to regulate the entry and stay of the persons concerned, for instance by requiring visas.

Members, however, are also at liberty to schedule their commitments (MFN treatment, Transparency, National Treatment and Market Access) in any one of the following ways:

(i) *Full commitment*: 'none' or 'no limitations', which implies that the Member does not seek in any way to limit market access or national treatment through measures inconsistent with Articles XVI or XVII of GATS.

(ii) *Commitment with limitations*: the Member details the measures maintained which are inconsistent with market access or national

5. These modes are defined in the previous chapter. But for further details go to http://www.wto.org/english/tratop_e/serv_e/serv_e.htm & http://www.wto.org/english/thewto_e/whatis_e/tif_e/agrm6_e.htm; also see the *Guidelines and Procedures For The Negotiations On Trade In Services*, at http://docsonline.wto.org/DDFDocuments/t/S/L/93.doc for modalities and procedures of GATS negotiations and scheduling of commitments.

treatment, and implicitly commits itself to take no other inconsistent measures.

(iii) *No commitment*: 'unbound' indicates that the Member remains free to maintain or introduce measures inconsistent with market access or national treatment.

(iv) *No commitment technically feasible*: 'unbound' indicates that in the sector in question, a particular mode of supply cannot be used.

"Commitments" generally involve the following obligations:

1) General Obligations:

MFN: The 'most favoured nation' obligation applies across all sectors and all modes of supply, unless otherwise indicated through an exemption. This obligation forces all members to give the most favourable treatment that it has accorded to any of its trading partners to all other WTO members. In short, it obliges each country not to discriminate against any of its fellow members in the WTO.

Transparency: This principle obliges all members to identify and publicise all rules and regulations affecting trade in services. Any change in the regulations must also be made public. Information about any particular regulation must be readily available through national enquiry points.

2) Specific Obligations:

National Treatment: This obligation requires non-discrimination between foreign and domestic services and service suppliers once they have entered the market.

Market Access: This obligation means that there can be no discrimination among services and service suppliers and that the only restrictions that can be enforced by members, provided they are scheduled, are quantitative and legal restrictions on :

- the number of service operations;
- the value of service transactions or assets;
- the number of operations or quantity of output;
- the number of natural persons supplying a service;
- the participation of foreign capital;
- the type of legal entity.

It has also been mandated that the negotiations shall aim to increase the participation of developing countries in the trade in services. There shall be appropriate flexibility for individual developing country Members. Special priority shall also be granted to least-developed country Members.

The Present Status of Negotiations, and the Domestic Policy Stance

Under successive rounds of negotiations of GATS, aimed at progressive liberalisation, Members individually choose the sectors in which binding commitments are to be made, and those in which commitments are not to be made. This is known as a 'positive listing', or 'bottoms-up', approach. Negotiations are to proceed on the basis of requests and offers; that is, countries request each other to consider liberalisation in particular sectors, and respond with offers. Agreement to liberalise is not reached until all participating Members – including developing countries – are satisfied with the total package being offered.

As per the decision taken in the Doha Ministerial Conference, it was decided that each member country must submit initial requests by June 2002 and initial offers by March 2003. This request-offer process is underway. However, most countries, including India have, interpreted these deadlines as indicative only.

In India, the Cabinet Committee on the WTO has already put in place a roadmap for services negotiations, and mandated the Commerce Ministry to request opening up on nine services. The list cleared includes financial services, construction and engineering, computer and related services, architecture, telecommunications, health, accounting, tourism and maritime services. But the audio-visual, educational, distribution, professional and other business services also merit attention and liberalisation, as we have substantial stake as well as export potential in these sectors.

The WTO Committee also maintained that a more aggressive stance should taken during the negotiations and leverage the country's inherent strength in the sectors like IT & telecom, education, entertainment and audio-visual, accounting, health, travel & tourism, construction and architecture, etc, to garner benefits in other sectors as well as greater market access in these sectors.

However, it must be remembered that since there exist convergence among sectors, one needs to be careful while making offers since there exist many cross-cutting issues. A second important issue on which the House saw broad agreement was on the need to institute and implement a sound domestic regulatory system, and on the need for having it in place and functioning before the GATS commitments become operational. It was also observed that there is no need for linking this latter to the GATS commitments that the country might undertake.

Internationally, the liberalisation focus has been on the first three Modes of service provision listed under GATS, and of the three, more stress has been put on the Modes 2 & 3, *viz.* consumption abroad and commercial presence. However India has long clamoured for Mode 4, or the movement of natural persons, believing it to be of more relevance. Unfortunately the existing level of liberalisation here is extremely unsatisfactory, and the general commitments under Mode 4 of GATS mostly pertain to business travellers and intra-corporate transferees who must be managers, executives or specialists, in other words, skilled professionals. This is an area of opportunity for India, and greater liberalisation under Mode 4 would bring in even higher gains.

The existing commitments are of limited interest to countries that are not significant foreign investors and whose comparative advantage lies in relatively unskilled, labour-intensive services. Moreover, commitments are often qualified by other restrictions: prior employment, relevant experience, numerical quotas, economic needs tests, and residency requirements. While it is true that the current Mode 4 commitments do not reflect the actual entry conditions for natural persons, what with the members having bound less than the access granted in practice, locking-in a greater liberalisation in the present round of negotiations would reduce uncertainties for companies and lead to better planning of efficient supply-modes of key services. Consequently India's proposal for the 'model schedule' in the current round of negotiations have been focused on facilitation of exchange of market access commitments and defining an acceptable set of multilateral rules that are transparent and less burdensome for members.

Discussions and Commitments Under Telecom Services

Under *telecom services* in GATS, negotiations are mandated under classifications of UNCPC 752 and 752, viz. telecommunications and telecommunications related services. In addition, some countries have sought commitments on telecom related services such as cable network services, satellite based navigation, positioning and timing services provided through global navigation satellite system.

The mandate of the negotiating group on the principles[6] of the basic regulatory framework is to ensure that

- Competition safeguards are instituted to prevent anti-competitive practices such as cross-subsidisation, misuse of information, etc.;
- Ensuring non-discriminatory, transparent, fair and cost-based interconnection with national networks;
- Transparent licensing processes ;
- Independence of regulators, who are not accountable to any of the suppliers and are impartial with respect to all market participants;
- Non-discriminatory and transparent procedures for allocation of scarce resources, including frequencies, numbers and rights of way, etc.

As of Early 2005, the Commitments from India are as follows:[7]

- In Modes 1 and 2, India has not taken any commitments.
- In Mode 3, commitments have been taken in -
  - In voice telephone service for public use, service permitted subject to licence;
  - In wire-based service, quantitative restrictions are imposed. Also, total foreign equity in the private operator cannot exceed 25 per cent. The resale of voice telephone services is not permitted;

6. Highlights of the Reference Paper on Basic Telecommunications available at http://www.wto.org/english/tratop_e/serv_e/telecom_e/tel23_e.htm
7. Details in Government of India – Ministry of Commerce website hosted by Trade Policy Division at http://commerce.nic.in/wto_counsel_paper.htm & http://commerce.nic.in/IndiaSchedules.doc

- In circuit switched data transmission services, Private leased circuit services and Facsimile services, limitation of service area and licensing requirements exist;
- Data and message transmission services permitted only through incorporation with a foreign equity ceiling of 51 per cent;
- Cellular mobile services are subject to licensing and quantitative restrictions. Foreign equity in private operators cannot exceed 25 per cent;
- In Mode 4, the horizontal commitments given cover the entry and temporary stay of business visitors, ICTs and professionals.

The Summary of Requests made to India are:

- Eliminate existing limitations and take full commitments in Basic Telecom & Value Added Services and telex & telegraph services;
- Allow wireless transmission technologies including WLL;
- Make full commitment on EDI and code and protocol conversion;
- Eliminate restrictions on the number of operators and on geographical coverage for wire-based public voice services, private leased circuit services, cellular telephones etc.;
- Eliminate the prohibition on resale for wire-based public voice services and private leased circuit services;
- Eliminate the limit of 25 per cent on total foreign equity for wire-based public voice and cellular mobile telephone services;
- Remove the restriction on equity of 51 per cent for Electronic mail, Voice Mail, on-line information and data base retrieval, enhanced/value-added facsimile services;
- Commit fully to the reference paper of the Basic Telecommunications negotiations relating to interconnection, independence of regulator, dispute resolution machinery, transparency and competitive safeguards and objective allocation of scarce resources;

- Remove MFN exemptions relating to accounting rates.

It needs to be recalled here that in the telecom sector, India's liberalisation has been undertaken unilaterally well before the committed dates, which imply that the GATS liberalisation is unlikely to pose any special danger to the domestic industry. The entry of private and foreign players has led to significant expansion in the telecommunication network, introduction of new technologies and a striking improvements in productivity and welfare in the country. In fact, domestic constituents in the private sector do feel the necessity for more aggressive and greater opening up of the domestic market to foreign capital and technology, which will bring in higher cost- and technology-efficiency for companies and welfare gains for the consumers in this knowledge-based and capital-intensive sector. The consistent rise in teledensity in the reform era is proof that the rapid deepening of consumer base in India is correlated with the reduced prices made possible by the liberalisation in the sector. It is undeniable that the desired expansion in the sector will be contingent on concentrated and high levels of investment in projects that have fairly long gestation periods. By locking-in the current changes permanently in place, the negotiations will dispel fears of potential investors of future policy reversals by adverse and politically motivated government fiats.

Discussions and Commitments under Transport Services

The *transport services* negotiations under GATS cover UNCPC 71 (Land, transport services), UNCPC 72 (Water transport services), UNCPC 73 (Air transport services) and UNCPC 74 (Supporting and auxiliary services). Thus, a major chunk of physical infrastructure, as is commonly understood, comes under the transport services.

As of early 2005, *India has made no firm commitments in this sector*. However, MFN exemption has been scheduled on cargo sharing between bilateral partners insofar as Bulgaria, Pakistan and the UAE are concerned and on cargo reservations for all countries in line with UN liner code. Given that the WTO Committee of the Union Cabinet considers maritime services to be an area of aggressive interest for the country, it is to be expected that further commitments could be on 'offer' when they are finally undertaken.

However, India has *received a large number of requests for liberalisation* of the transport sector, especially the *Maritime Transport* sector. In brief, India has been requested to:

- Take full market access and national treatment commitments in Mode 1, 3 & 4;
- Remove discrimination between foreign and national flag vessels in payment of charges, access to provisions etc.;
- Remove requirement of citizenship for operating as customs broker/agents and freight forwarding agents;
- Eliminate restriction on foreign capital in international shipping companies.;
- Eliminate preference to Indian vessels i.e. Export CIF/ import FOB basis;
- Remove reservation for national flag vessels in Government and Aid cargo;
- In maritime freight forwarding, remove restrictions on capital, setting up of branch offices and of joint ventures;
- Allow foreign companies to set up 100 per cent owned subsidiary companies in the maritime agencies and customs brokers service.

Under *Auxiliary Services*, requests are to:

- Take market access and national treatment commitments on Maritime agency and freight forwarding services and on Towing services;
- Eliminate Obligations to use public facilities in respect of cargo handling services. ;
- Take commitments on Rental and lease services without operators;
- Remove restrictions on storage and warehousing services and customs clearance services;
- Take additional commitments for access to and use of port facilities;
- Further, full commitments are requested for Ship broking services, Classification societies, General sales agent services;

Maintenance & Repair of vessels; and handling of cargo by ships and restrictions related thereto.

For *Air Transport,* requests are to:

- Take full market access and national treatment commitments in Mode 2 & 3 and horizontal commitments in Mode 4 on maintenance & repair of aircraft & parts thereof and on Ground Handling Services;
- Take full market access and national treatment commitments in Mode 1, 2 & 3 and horizontal commitments in Mode 4 on selling and marketing, computer reservation systems;
- Take full market access and national treatment commitments in Mode 3 and horizontal commitments in Mode 4 on Air port Management Services .

Under *Rail Transport,* requests are to:

- Take full market access and national treatment commitments in Mode 3 and horizontal commitments in Mode 4.;
- Take full market access and national treatment commitments in Modes 1,2 & 3 and horizontal commitments in Mode 4 in Maintenance & Repair of Rail Transport Equipment.

For *Space Transport,* India has been requested to take commitments in the sector.

Road Transport requests are for:

- Take full market access and national treatment commitments in Mode 3 and horizontal commitments in Mode 4 on Freight transport ;
- Take full market access and national treatment commitments in Mode 1,2 & 3 and horizontal commitments in Mode 4 on Maintenance & Repair of Road Transport Equipment..

For *Multimodal activities,* requests are for:

- On inland forwarding of cargoes, commit the ability to rent or lease or to have access to and use of multimodal facilities;
- Offer binding commitments on road and rail cabotage transport of cargo where an international; sea leg is involved;
- Take commitments as per definitions in model schedule to

allow repositioning/moving equipment (i.e. empty containers, flatbeds) on their vessels between ports of India. Allow feedering of cargoes between main ports and way ports for multinational cargo between ports of India through vessels of any flag;

- Take full market access and national treatment commitments in Modes 1, 2 & 3 and horizontal commitments in Mode 4 on maintenance & repair of vessels.

Under the classification *Services - Auxiliary to All Modes of Transport*, requests have come in for:

- Take full market access and national treatment commitments in Modes 2 & 3 and horizontal commitments in Mode 4 in Storage & Warehouse services;
- Take full market access and national treatment commitments in Modes 1,2 & 3 and horizontal commitments in Mode 4 in freight transport agency & pre–shipment inspection, Cargo Handling services and other auxiliary transport services ;
- In customs clearance agent services, take commitments to be taken and eliminate nationality and residency requirements.

In *Logistics & related services*, requests are for India to take liberalisation commitments in the sub-sectors identified as follows:

- freight transportation services;
- cargo-handling services;
- storage and warehousing services;
- custom clearances services;
- transport agency services;
- container station and depot services;
- inventory management services;
- order processing services;
- production planning services; and
- production control services.

Again, like in the telecom sector, the transportation sector needs heavy and long-gestation investments, and while recognising the security concerns of the domestic economy, rapid expansion of the transportation sector (physical infrastructure) will call for participation by foreign investors in the sector in development and maintenance of the key transportation services that come under this heading. Again, as before, there is a strong feeling among many experts in the sector that gains from greater and more rapid liberalisation will more than compensate for the losses or discomforts to be suffered by domestic players (largely the public sector utility behemoths) consequent to the competition that would be generated in the sector by private sector. However, as in the telecom sector, the potential consumer gains are immense and liberalisation will enable rapid development of the physical infrastructure of the country, the latter being widely referred to as the main stumbling block for rapid economic growth and higher investments in the sector, both by domestic and foreign investors. Autonomous liberalisation along with growth of multimodal transport (which requires effective coordination between different modes of transport) indicates that there is significant scope for widening the coverage and extent of commitments in transport services during the DDA negotiations.

In Conclusion...

Having discussed the implications of deeper liberalisation in the two sectors under discussion, and the general modalities of liberalisation strategies by the government, it is clear that in the aggressive pursuit of national interest, unilateral and aweeping liberalisation has been undertaken in certain sectors, which if formalised and sealed-in in the current GATS round will enable the country to trade-off concessions in other areas in order to effect a package that is more balanced and in favour of India's domestic interests. For, contrary to the expectations emanating from India's current level of development, clearly with the services being the main-stay of sources of domestic growth and international comparative- and competitive-advantage, gains from the ongoing multilateral trading negotiations should also emanate from more liberal commitments in the services sector. The GoI therefore has decided to open up certain sectors, in particular the telecom services and maritime services, for there is expectation and belief in an aggressive interest of the country in these two areas.

Unfortunately, while there has been great focus on movement of goods and capital, particularly from markets in the developed world to developing countries, hardly any attention has been paid to market access to professionals in business services from developing countries e.g. engineers, doctors, technicians *etc*. The fear expressed in the developed countries that there will be transfer of job opportunities from the North to the South pays scant regard to the fact that the free inflow of goods and services into developing countries can likewise lead to displacement of industry, unemployment, decline in effective demand, fall in incomes and the deprivation of the globally underprivileged. This is however a natural fallout of international trade policy and negotiations where success hinges on carving out reciprocal 'gives' and take and thought-out negotiating strategies in order to benefit the domestic constituency. India has fortunately come a long way from the Uruguay Round in terms of developing negotiation acumen and strategising.

Hence, India will necessarily have to take the lead in the WTO deliberations for ensuring that the comparative advantage of our professionals is allowed to be exploited in full measure, even while acceding to open markets to goods and services in which the developed world has had a decisively comparative advantage. Developing countries, including India, are still net importers of the globally traded services. Related are issues of bilateral Mutual Recognition Agreements and Free Trade Agreements that look into possibilities of faster liberalisation in trade in services that might better serve Indian interests than a multilateral forum. India will therefore have to continue and persist in exploring the different issues in the GATS negotiation more aggressively, in an attempt to ultimately effect a win-win situation for the country and its huge pool of skilled and semi skilled professionals and service providers.

15

Trade in Education Services Under the WTO-GATS Regime: An Indian Outlook

K.D. RAJU

Introduction

Education is vital for social and economic growth of every country. In the 'Golden Age' of India, universities like Nalanda and Takshashila were famous all over the world, attracting students from foreign lands. Education is largely a governmental activity in India, but it is fast becoming a worldwide service industry under the WTO.

The last decade has witnessed a sea change in the international and national education scene. India signed the World Trade Organisation (WTO) Agreement in 1994 along with General Agreement on Trade in Services (GATS) as a part of single undertaking, which came into force in 1995. It was for the first time that the services had come up to the agenda of multilateral trade negotiations under the General Agreement on Tariffs and Trade (GATT). Services represent the fastest growing sector of the global economy and account for 60 per cent of global output, 30 per cent of global employment and nearly 20 per cent of global trade.[1] The WTO will complete ten years of its existence on 31 December 2004; this will also mark the end of the transitional phase allowed to the developing countries including India. As Scott Sinclair rightly said, "Essentially unknown to the public, the agreement is designed to facilitate international business by constraining democratic governance. The talks are taking place behind closed doors in close consultation with international corporate lobbyists".[2]

1. WTO, Understanding the WTO-Services: Rules for Growth and Investment, http://www.wto.org.
2. Scott Sinclair, GATS – How the World Trade Organisation's New 'Services' Negotiations Threaten Democracy, Canadian Centre for Policy Alternatives, (2000), p. 1.

The GATS established a multilateral framework of principles and rules for trade in services with the objective of expansion and progressive liberalisation of such trade as a means of promoting economic growth of all trading partners and the further development of developing countries. It provides for disciplines on transparency, most favoured nation (MFN) treatment, market access and national treatment. Education is one of the twelve services included in the Uruguay Round. The categories are:

- Business services, including R&D, computer, real estate, rental/leasing, advertising, marketing etc;
- Communication services, including telecom, postal, audio-visual;
- Construction and related engineering services;
- Distribution services;
- Education services;
- Environmental services, including environmental protection, refuse disposal etc;
- Financial services, including insurance, banking, asset management and financial information;
- Health and social services;
- Tourism and travel services;
- Recreational, cultural and sporting services;
- Transport services, including sea, air, rail, and road; and
- Other category.[3]

The first section of the study explains the GATS provisions with regard to education. The second section analyses Indian scene and various implications and competitiveness of the sector in the light of the Supreme Court judgment scraping more than 100 private universities in the country. The third part concludes by suggesting some strategies for national policy framework for the better functioning of the Indian education system.

3. See http://www.dti.gov.uk.

SECTION I

EDUCATION SERVICES UNDER THE GATS

GATS and Education Services under Article 1.2 of GATS[4] classify four modes of supply in educational service trade. They are:

- *Cross border supply:* Under this mode services are supplied across the borders without moving students and service providers. It includes courses through distance education, online courses, educational testing services and educational materials that are provided overseas. It also includes sale of books, educational materials and CDs, service provided through satellite transmission, and audio video conferencing, which can cross national boundaries.[5]
- *Consumption abroad:* This includes students or consumers travelling from one country to another. Under this category India is one of the largest *importers* of education services i.e., sending students abroad like US and other countries. It exports services when students come to India for study.
- *Commercial presence:* It means an actual presence of an education provider through the establishment of offshore campuses or facilities or partnership agreement with institutions in the host country.
- *Presence or movement of natural persons.* As the title suggests, it means the movement of teachers or researchers travelling to another country in order to provide educational services to the foreign students. For example - visiting lecturers.

According to Article 1.3 of GATS, government services remain outside the purview of GATS, provided that they are neither supplied

4. Article 1.2 of GATS provides that:
   (a) from the territory of one Member in to the territory of any other Member;
   (b) in the territory of one Member to the service consumer of any other Member;
   (c) by a service supplier of one Member, through commercial presence in the territory of any other Member;
   (d) by a service supplier of one Member, through presence of natural persons of a Member in the territory of any other Member.

5. Duc Nguyen-Hong & Robert Wells, "Restrictions on Trade in Education Services: some Basic Indexes," *Productivity Commission Staff Working Paper*, Canberra, October 2003.

on a commercial basis nor in competition with one or more service suppliers. Under the GATS, education services are classified into five categories[6], which include:

Primary Education Services: These include services related to primary and pre-school education but excludes child day-care and adult literacy programmes.

Secondary Education Services: These cover high school, vocational education and technical training.

Higher Education Services: These include two areas. The first relates to teaching of practical skills (training) after 10+2 level and also includes pre-degree, technical and vocational training institutes like (polytechnics). The second category relates to conventional education provided by Universities and colleges in the country including professional institutions.

Adult and Continuing Education Services: These include adult learning and continuing education programmes in general and vocational subjects and also refresher and training programmes.

Other Education Services: These cover all other services not mentioned or defined above but ultimately fall under the purview of learning and training.

Higher Education: A Comparative Analysis

The impact of British rule has a wider influence on Indian higher education system. The system of courses, examinations, affiliations and universities all are remnants of the colonial era.[7] It has been estimated that in the 1990s 1.5 million students were studying abroad. Out of the 5,14,000 foreign students who were studying in US, more than 54 per cent were from Asia. U.K, Germany, Australia and France are the other leading exporters. In 1995 a global market for international higher education was estimated at $ 27 billion.[8] In

6. The Classification of Educational Services Under United Nations Central Product Classification System (UNCPC) 1991 includes all these categories.
7. David Arnold Institute of International Education, Globalisation of Higher Education: What it Means for India, Paper prepared for Roundtable on Internationalisation of Higher Education in India, Association of Indian Universities, Mysore, Karnataka, 2001.
8. Sharma, G.D. *Trade in Education Service Under WTO Regime – An Indian Response*, (New Delhi: 2001).

1996, education and training services generated $7.5 billion in export. This proves the US interest in the liberalisation of this sector. In many countries, service sector contributes the main export earner. Education services were the third largest service in 2000-01. In New Zealand also it was the fourth largest service sector in 2000.[9]

Some of the regional groupings like OECD countries are targeting international student mobility as a focal point of revenue, which came to $30 billion in 1999. 1.5 million foreign students were in OECD countries, of which 56 per cent are from non-OECD countries. Most of the international trade in higher education services takes place within the OECD countries, which received 85 per cent of the world's foreign students. Out of which 45 per cent are from Asia especially India which had sent 48,515 students which contribute 3 per cent of the total.[10]

SECTION II

THE INDIAN SCENARIO AND GATS

The liberalisation of Indian economy started in 1991 prompted more and more students to go abroad for higher education. India has the second largest higher education sector in the world with 8.8 million students, which constitutes, seven per cent of the total population. The number of universities increased from a level of 18 at the time of independence to 306 (including 18 Central Universities, 186 state Universities, 5 Institutions established under State Legislature Act, 84 Deemed Universities and 13 Institutes of national importance) under the government and about 150 private universities (most of them are in the state of Chhattisgarh). The Open Universities are nine in number and that of Women Universities are five and employ a total force of more than four hundred thousand teachers.[11]

---

9. OECD Centre for Educational Research and Innovation, Indicators on Internationalisation and Trade of Post-secondary Education, (Washington, D.C. USA: Department of Commerce, 2002).

10. Larsen, Kurt and Stephen Vincent – Lancrin, *The Learning Business: Can Trade in International Education Work*, Centre for Educational Research and Innovation (CERI), 2003.

11. *India 2004*, A Reference Manual, Ministry of Information and Broadcasting, Government of India.

Government is the principal provider of higher education in the country. But the per centage is decreasing gradually. The per capita total government expenditure on education in 1995 was less than $10 per year in India as against $1,400 in the US.[12] The share of higher education in total planned resources has decreased from 1.2 per cent in the Fourth Five Year Plan to 0.35 per cent in the Eighth Five Year Plan. The expenditure on higher education per student fell from Rs. 7676 in 1990-01 to Rs. 5692 in 1998-99 (a fall of about 25 per cent).[13]

Consumption Abroad

Every year nearly 66,000 Indian students are going abroad and the figure reached one hundred thousand in 2002 and the total expenditure was nearly $ 1.5 billion. More than 66 per cent of Indian students are studying in the US and pursuing post-graduate degrees; only 22 per cent are undergraduate students. Business, management, engineering and computer science students account for more than 75 per cent of all Indian students in the US. On the other hand, only 6000 foreign students are coming to India for pursuing higher education, mostly from other developing or least developed countries. The flows of students from the developed countries are meagre.

Commercial Presence

At present, there are no foreign University campuses in India, but nearly 27 franchise institutions (mainly 10 from the UK and 12 from the US) are opened in the area of management and engineering. The UK based Wigan & Leigh, has established campuses in a number of Indian cities. The University of Illinois-linked Quantum Institute has also opened its branch in New Delhi.[14] The franchise partners are not affiliated to any Indian University. Distressingly, most of the institutions franchised in India are not recognised or accredited in their own countries.

12. UNESCO-1998.
13. Powar, K.B. "Indian Higher Education in a GATS-Controlled Regime: Looking for a Pathway in the Haze of Uncertainty," *Higher Education Policy and Practices*, Vol.1, No. 1 & 2, July - September, 2003, p. 3.
14. Thomas, Binu S. *Deccan Herald*, Bangalore, 23 May 2003.

Very few Indian institutions have used the opportunity of liberalisation under the GATS. The Birla Institute of Technology and Science, Pilani and Ranchi have opened institutions in Dubai and Oman respectively. The Universal Group in Nepal and the Central Institute for Languages, Hyderabad opened centers in Kyrgizstan. Incidentally, all are Deemed Universities and privately financed except the last one. The Indira Gandhi National Open University (IGNOU) focuses on distance education and is planning to spread its operations to many countries. Movement of faculty and researchers to foreign countries are small in number and the foreign teachers in India are negligible.

Negotiating Positions in WTO after Doha

According to the GATS commitments, member governments will have to undertake negotiations on specific issues and enter into successive rounds of negotiations in order to progressively liberalise trade in services. The first round had to start not later than five years from 1995.[15]

The service negotiations started officially in early-2000 under the Council for Trade in Services. In March 2001, the Services Council fulfilled a key element in the negotiating mandate by establishing the negotiating guidelines and procedures. The Doha Declaration proposed the deadlines for the conclusion of the negotiations as part of a single undertaking.

The stipulated time frame under the Doha declaration was:

- Started in: 2000.
- Negotiation guidelines and procedures: March 2001.
- Requests for market access: by 30 June 2002.
- Initial offers of market access: by 31 March 2003.
- Stocktaking: 5th Ministerial Conference (Cancun), 2003.
- Deadline: by *1 January 2005* as a part of single undertaking.

In response to the deadlines prescribed in the Doha Development Agenda, till April 2003 only 30 Members had submitted their requests and 16 countries had submitted their offers which includes

15. See GATS Article XIX. http://www.wto.org.

US, Canada, Japan, Australia, New Zealand and Norway. Even the time period over the process is still in progress. The draft Cancun Ministerial Declaration circulated to the Members by the Director-General Supachi Panitchpakdi on 31 August 2003 proposed that:

> *We stress the importance of full engagement by all participants, inter alia through the continuous exchange of requests and offers. With a view to providing effective market access to all Members, due regard shall be given to the quality of offers, particularly in sectors and modes of supply of export interest to developing countries. We call upon those participants who have not yet submitted their initial offers to do so as soon as possible.*
>
> ... the Special Session of the Council for Trade in Services shall review progress in these negotiations by 31 March 2004. ...we note that the interest of developing countries, as well as other Members, in Mode 4. In accordance with GATS provisions, there shall be due respect for the right of Members to regulate and to introduce new regulations in pursuance of national policy objectives.[16]

The WTO Cancun Ministerial failed and the stocktaking has not happened within the stipulated time. India submitted its offer to the Council for Trade in Services (12 January 2004)[17] in which it offered to liberalise many sectors like accounting and book-keeping services, engineering services, computer services, medical and dental services, services provided by midwives, nurses, physiotherapists and para-medical personnel; construction and engineering services; financial services, tourism services, and maritime transport services. Fortunately, education is out of the list for the time being. But it is clear that in future India has to open its educational services also. In view of India's social and economic commitments it is not advisable to open educational services except the higher education sector, which the other countries also want to open up. The delay in the submission of requests and offers may affect the final negotiation and it seems that, meeting the deadline of 31 December 2005 is unlikely to happen.

Competitiveness of Indian Higher Education

In India, the education system is mostly controlled by the government, based on social needs and values, for disseminating knowledge among various sectors in the society. The government is

16. See http://www.wto.org.
17. World Trade Organisation Council for Trade in Services Special Session, Conditional Indian Offer, TN/S/O/IND, 12 January 2004.

controlling the private sector for the implementation of its social obligations through the regulators like University Grants Commission (UGC), All India Council for Technical Education (AICTE) and Distance Education Council (DCE). Recently, the government directed the prestigious management institutions (IIMs) in the country to slash the fee structure up to 80 per cent[18] for the implementation of its social policies.

Being a WTO member India is committed to progressive liberalisation of the sector. The entry of foreign operators without any control will put public as well as private sectors in a disadvantageous position. It is often said that, "if you want to destroy a country, destroy its education systems." India cannot commodify its higher education sector. The foreign providers coming to India for capital investment in the sector will be looking for business and profit. The quality education provided by the reputed foreign institutions will be costly and can be affordable only to the elite class of the society. This may lead to categorisation of students and disadvantageous to the underprivileged and the middle class sections of the society, which will be harmful for the social set up of the country in the long run.

But in the meantime, it is better to take stock of the things in the country for meeting the challenges. The Indian Universities have been established many years back and are starving for sufficient infrastructure and facilities. The quality of education varies widely from one institution to another especially in the professional level. Several universities in India do not have a flexible academic structure and the degrees from these universities will have a lower value in the job market than foreign universities. The syllabi are obsolete; there is a lack of multidisciplinary courses, teachers' apathy, excessive examination orientation, poor infrastructure, little research to speak of, bureaucratic meddling, etc. are among the problems. These maladies have been identified by a series of education commissions as the ills that plague the system. It is true that Indian universities have many problems with regard to fund raising to match up with the quality of foreign institutions. But the apathy cannot be excused at the cost of development of the country.

---

18. *The Economic Times*, New Delhi, 6 February 2003, p. 1.

In this background the foreign universities consider India as a potential market with a large English speaking and affluent middle class society. But one way it is better for Indians to avail quality education from these institutions without going to foreign countries and spending half of the amount presently. It is relevant in the context that India is presently spending $ 1.5 billion a year. At the same time some of the Indian institutions like IITs and IIMs can establish their presence in other countries and take advantage of the liberalisation of the market. The opening of institutions will open a job market for the highly qualified professionals and researchers in the country.

The real question is whether the Indian universities are prepared to compete in a $2.2 trillion education market in the world and the world trade in 1996 was approximately $50 billion annually.[19]

Towards Commercialisation

Education is already a big business, but the potential to spread its market will depend upon the competitiveness of institutions to utilise the untapped public education market.[20] The trade in education service is a huge and potential growth area in today's economy. According to European Commission, the GATS agreement is "first and foremost an instrument for the benefit of business"[21]. The US government's recent (March 2003) offer on GATS negotiations includes education also. At the same time the US Trade Representative made it clear that, "no intention to promote the privatisation of public educational institutions"[22]. On the one hand there are initiatives for internationalisation and comodification of education and on the other there is a major risk that the WTO's initiatives that will clash head-on with the principles upheld by all those who value a quality public education system.[23]

19. The APEC study (2001) revealed that the global market for consumption abroad in higher, secondary and vocational education would exceed $50 billion in 1996. 2002 study by Larsen, Martin and Morris estimated that the consumption abroad market for OECD countries alone accounted for $30 billion in 1999.
20. Educational International, The Threat to Higher Education, A Briefing on Current World Trade Organisation Negotiations, p. 11.
21. *Ibid.*
22. Ruth Flower, Director of Public Policy and Communications, AAUP. http://www.aaup.org
23. Educational International, The WTO and the Millennium Round: What is at Stake for Public Education? – Common Concerns for Workers in Education and the Public Sector (1999), http://www.ei-ie-org.

The most popular argument in the country is that, education is a public good and should not be commercialised. But the reality is that the government is cutting grants to the universities and force them to fees hike. Another argument in the country is that, the entry of foreign institutions will hamper the poor to access the higher education. But studies show that 80 per cent of those who avail the higher education in the country is not the poor.

In the ancient India, *"gurukul"* education was considered as sacred rather than a profit making activity. Since independence the sector is completely controlled and owned by the government. But the spread of private players in the sector led to the present "comodification" of education, from the primary level to the higher and professional education.

In the liberalisation process, we should also be in the main stream selling our "products" and "brands" in the international market. The Indian government through its regulator, the University Grants Commission (UGC) constituted a committee to study the options to export Indian education abroad. This is a paradigm shift in the education policy ever since. Outlining a three-pronged strategy, the Commission's Tenth Plan profile states that it will for the first time be encouraging universities to set up campuses abroad apart form regulating collaborations between Indian and foreign universities[24]. This programme is now named as "Promotion of Indian Higher Education Abroad" (PIHEAD) aimed at attracting foreign students. 25 Indian universities are selected for promoting Indian education abroad, includes University or Hyderabad, Cochin University of Science and Technology, Delhi University, Madras University, Jamia Milia, Symbiosis Society and Manipal Academy of Higher Education; a Deemed University among others. The UGC standing committee convenor for PIHEAD Mr. Bhushan Patwardhan opines that these institutions would be taken to premier education fares abroad for attracting students to India and will be allowed to set up campuses abroad. The committee also recommended for setting up special economic zones (SEZs) which provide an internationally competitive and hassle-free environment for providing knowledge-based services. The idea is to create an

24. See http://www.prayatna.typepad.com.

infrastructure where both Indian as well as foreign universities and other educational institutions can set up "shops" and offer a wide "menu" of courses both in science and humanities.[25] The committee has earlier recommended that IITs and IIMs be allowed to set up "shops" in the global shores. The trend is clear that Indians have also started thinking in terms of "shops" and "menu" for the comodification of the sector. But it is not clear how they are going to "attract" students from abroad.

Prof. Yashpal & Another versus the *State of Chhattisgarh & Others*

The matter of establishing private universities all over the country without complying with the existing rules and regulations came to the apex judiciary and it issued notices to concerned authorities including these universities working in Chhattisgarh. Public interest litigation was filed by the former UGC Chairman Prof. Yashpal, challenging the Constitutional validity of the state legislations allowing registration of private universities without providing for even basic educational facilities.[26]

The main contention of the petitioner was that Section 5 of the Chhattisgarh Act[27] which permits the establishment of private universities by notification in the Gazette. Section 6 permits affiliation of colleges or other institutions to such universities. The petitioner alleged that the State Government has simply issued notifications in the official Gazette and established universities in a discriminate manner without checking the infrastructure, teaching facility, laboratories, libraries or the financial sources. Within a short span of one year as many as 112 universities were established. Some of them were worked from single rooms and extended their business all over India. The Act completely avoided the control of the statutory bodies like the University Grants Commission, All India

25. *The Times of India*, 28 January 2004.

26. Supreme Court Writ Petition (civil) 19 of 2004.

27. Section 5(1) of the Act states "the State Government may by notification in the Gazette establish a University by such name and with such jurisdiction and location of campus as may be specified therein having regard to (a) the desirability to establish a University, (b) recognition or authorisation as may be required under any other law for the time being in force to conduct the syllabus and to grant degrees or diplomas or awards.

Council of Technical Education (AICTE), Medical Council of India, Dental Council of India etc. These universities were awarding degrees and offering courses never heard known to people. There was no mechanism to check the compliance of facilities after establishment of the universities. The working of these universities will affect the standard maintained in the Indian universities for years.

The State of Chhattisgarh, the respondent in this case mainly took the plea that education is in the Entry 32 List II of Seventh Schedule to the Constitution[28] and the state government is competent to establish a university in accordance with the University Grants Commission Act, 1956.

However, the petitioner pointed out that incorporation of a University is a state subject in accordance with Entry 32 List II, but under Entry 66 of List I is co-ordination and determination of standards in institutions for higher education or research and scientific and technical institutions. This was confirmed in many cases decided by the Supreme Court.[29] It was held that "item 11 of List II and item 66 of List I must be harmoniously construed. The two entries undoubtedly overlap; but to the extent of overlapping, the power conferred by item 66 List I must prevail over the poser of the State under item 11 of List II." It means the validity of State legislation would depend upon whether it prejudicially affects the standards sets in accordance with item 66 List I.

The Supreme Court in *State of Tamilnadu & Anr. versus. Adhiyaman Educational and Research Institute*[30], held the view that "*the state legislation is in conflict with the Central legislation though the former is purported to have been made under Entry 25 of the Concurrent List but in effect encroaches upon Legislation including subordinate legislation made by the Centre under Entry 25 of the Concurrent List or to give effect to Entry 66 of the Union List, it would be void and inoperative.*" In *Osmania University Teachers Association v. State of Andhra Pradesh & Anr.*[31], the Supreme Court categorically reiterated that it was the exclusive responsibility of the Central

28. List II, Seventh Schedule to the Indian Constitution deals with State List which includes education and universities.

29. *Gujarat University versus.* Sri Krishna, AIR 1963 SC 703.

30. 1995 (4) SCC 104.

31. 1987 (4) SCC 671.

government to determine the standards for higher education and the same should not be lowered at the hands of any particular State as it was of great importance to national progress. All these decisions upheld the role of Central Government in maintaining the standards in education.[32] All these universities had not complied with the regulation issued by the UGC named *UGC (Establishment and Maintenance of Standards in Private Universities) Regulations, 2003.*

The Court observed that under the provisions of the impugned Act, a project report is sufficient to establish a university without checking the infrastructure facilities or teaching facilities in accordance with the UGC Act. It was of the view that "the manner in which a University is notified by issuance of a Gazette notification under Section 5 and conferment of a juristic personality under Section 6 of the Act is clearly contrary to the Constitutional scheme and is not contemplated by Article 246 of the Constitution.[33]"

Section 2 (f) provides that "University" means a University established or incorporated by or under a Central Act, a Provincial Act or a State Act, and includes any such institution as may, in consultation with the University concerned, be recognised by the Commission in accordance with the regulations made in this behalf under this Act. It is clear that states are free to establish universities, subject to the regulations of the UGC. The Co-ordination and maintenance of standards in higher education is absolutely vested in the UGC in the country. Hence, the so-called "universities" established in the State of Chhattisgarh were flouting the UGC Act and constituted sheer abuse of the Constitutional provisions for dubious and vexatious objectives.

There are no two opinions that the 112 universities established in the State of Chhattisgarh were exploiting the students and the society by offering unknown courses and working without the basic facilities. Even some of them were working from single shop rooms. Addressing the graduates of the Allahabad University in 1947, Jawaharlal Nehru, the first Prime Minister of India, said: *"A university stands for humanism, for tolerance, for reason, for the adventure of ideas and for the search for truth.*

32. See also the Constitutional Bench decision in Kerala State Electricity Board versus. Indian Aluminium Co., 1976 (1) SCC 466.

33. The Supreme Court Judgment, para. 28. Yashpal & Others *versus* the State of Chhattisgarh.

It stands for the onward march of the human race toward higher objectives. Universities are places of ideals and idealism. If the universities discharge their duties adequately, then, it is well with the nation and the people."

However, it seems that the establishment of these frivolous institutions will damage the heritage and culture of university system in India. To that extent the Supreme Court correctly held that the establishments of these universities are a "fraud on the Constitution." On the other hand, most of these universities were opened off-campus centers and even off-shore campuses in which nearly 30,000 students were pursuing various courses. The Supreme Court directed these universities to affiliate themselves to the existing two universities in the State. However, technically only the students studying in the State of Chhattisgarh can register to these universities and the illegal off-campus centres cannot be affiliated to any universities. Consequently, most of the students' future were under a cloud. Neither the Court nor the State Government is concerned about these students or their future. There is an urgent need to regulate the working of the private sector educational providers in the country at the Central level.

Policy Options

The prospect and liberalisation of the education services in order to compete more efficiently and profitably in the global marketplace raises critical concerns about quality, affordability and more fundamentally, the role of governments to provide a quality public education system for the benefit of the society. Hence before making any policy, which affects the entire education system in the country, it should be debated properly among the academicians, students, policy-makers and the society at large.

The possible options, which could be considered for making the national policy and commitments in the GATS negotiations, are:

- India should analyse the possible opportunities available under different modes of service.
- The competitiveness, strength and weakness of Indian institutions and sectors should be taken into consideration.
- The consideration of economic, social and sovereign functions of the country should be protected.

When considering the fact that India is the second largest provider of higher education in the world, it should be able to exploit the possible markets all over the world. India can open institutions abroad targeting wherever the Indian Diaspora are widespread all over the world (Powar: 2003). Indians are champions in the sectors like Bio-technology and information technology. It would be appropriate to support the US proposal that the training services should be included in the negotiations because India has a strong experience in conducting the Common Admission Test (CAT) for the Indian Institute of Management, the Joint Entrance Examination (JEE) of the Indian Institute of Technology, the National Eligibility Test (NET) of the University Grants Commission etc. India can provide training through e-learning all over the world and make advantage out of the liberalisation. But proper guidelines should be issued to the private sector and give a transition period of at least 6 years to the players for the proper arrangement and upgradation of technology and facilities (Deodhar: 2002).

India can make use of its strength in traditional areas like Ayurvedic Medicines, Arts and Culture, Yoga and English language. It should also be noted that some of the best management institutes in Asia like IIMs and some of the private institutes keeping good excellence are located in India.

When liberalising the sector India has to make use of the exceptions permitted under the GATS for protecting the interests of the country. Article II.1 provides for Most Favoured Nation (MFN) treatment, which stipulates the countries, not to treat less favourable than that it accord to like service suppliers of any other country. At the same time Article II.2 allows countries to negotiate exemptions from this commitment and include it in the individual schedules.

The national treatment principle stipulates that India cannot discriminate between foreign institutions and Indian institutions in the case of policy matters. For example, in India graduate degree course is for three years whereas in most of the foreign countries it is two years. Post-graduation is one year abroad and in India it is for two years. Hence, India has to streamline its courses and syllabi in accordance with the international standards. Otherwise, it will be difficult for the Indian universities to get students from the developed world.

Article XI I.1 allows countries to control or put restrictions on trade in services in the event of balance of payment problems (BoP) or economic development reasons. In future, if it is found that there is an excess flow of foreign exchange outside country, India can use this provision and restrict the trade in education services. Article IX allows members to impose restrictions to protect public order or morality, prevention of deceptive and fraudulent practices or deal with the effects of a default on service contracts. This provision could be used if the Indian authorities find that any educational institution is indulging in fraudulent practices and exploitation of Indian teachers and researchers going abroad for services. Emergency safeguard mechanisms are provided in Article X. Article XIV bis. provides for security exceptions.

Article XV provides that "subsidies have distortive on trade in services. Members shall enter into negotiations with a view to developing the necessary multilateral disciplines to avoid such trade-distortive effects." India cannot withdraw the subsidies to the higher education sector for the time being. It will have a devastating effect on the higher education system and the free and compulsory education in the primary level will be hampered in that case.

In India the private education co-exist with the public domain and it will be to supplement rather displace the public education systems. The recently published UGC "Model Act for Universities of the twenty first century" also reflects the same feeling. It recognises the globalisation of higher education and entry of foreign Universities to the country as a reality and how to meet the challenges, through re-orientation and better management. For maintaining better quality administration in the education system in the country, an independent authority that can be named, "National Education Regulatory Authority" may be established with statutory powers and independent existence.

A Suggested Way Ahead

What follows are some suggestions that may be used as guidelines for making the Indian commitments in the GATS as well as for a comprehensive domestic education policy.

- India should ask for gradual liberalisation and insist for a transitional period of five years for upgradation of Indian institutions.

- For a smooth transition, more exchange programmes of students between WTO Members should be encouraged.
- Quality and accessibility of higher education must be prioritised before profitability.
- India may commit for all modes of trade in higher education, provided it should take massive advertisement programmes abroad.
- India may include specific proposals to other countries to commit in the areas of commercial presence of Indian institutions.
- The inclusion of teachers and researchers may be included under Mode 4 with the increasing demand for Indian teachers at the secondary and higher education level.
- India should support the US view for including educational testing and training services to be included in the country commitments.
- The protectionist measures like imposition of entry barriers in the movement of persons and emigration rules should be opposed. Otherwise incidents like the recent arrest of IT professionals in Malaysia and Singapore will again happen in the future.
- India should take help from international bodies like UNESCO and other developed countries for modernising the Indian education system.
- India should develop a strong communication and technology network for Cross-border supply of education through e-learning method. This can be implemented through the well-known open universities like IGNOU and nine other open universities.
- The cross-border e-learning is an ambitious proposal of many countries including the US. But the un-controlled e-learning will raise the question of quality as well as flow of foreign exchange.
- The foreign providers should be permitted only if they can conform to the norms of regulators like UGC, AICTE, Distance Education Council (DEC), Indian Nursing Council, Medical Council of India and Indian Bar Council etc.

- Action taken by the Governments for the provision of higher education must not be considered as a restriction on trade in services.
- Government grants and payment of tuition fees on behalf of students must not be considered as subsidies.
- There should be unification of regulators and regulations in the country and to set up a "National Education Regulatory Authority" for this purpose.
- The accreditation and recognition of foreign degrees and professionals can be entrusted to the proposed "Authority."
- The franchising of foreign institutions to the Indian counterparts should not be allowed to operate from rented buildings and without required permissions from the concerned statutory bodies.
- Presently not even a single foreign university has established its campuses in India. Setting up of campuses in India should be promoted in view of imparting quality education in the country.
- India should take stock of the domestic situations and try to upgrade the whole education system especially the higher education sector to compete at the international level.
- Provide adequate financial facilities to universities that are already identified by the government as of national importance.
- Implement the academic reforms especially in teaching research and syllabi.
- Formulate a realistic national education policy in view of GATS implementation.
- A clear policy for private education sector in the country is a necessity. So far various states and central government have different policies and the judiciary is intervened a number of times to interpret the same.
- Undertake innovative ideas like Education Zones as recommended by the UGC committee.

- Setting up of a "National Fund for Education." This fund can be used for the upgradation of the selected universities and Institutions in the country and the underprivileged can make use of the fund for pursuing their education.
- Allow the centres of excellence in the country to make more resources through consultancy and take up specialised research.
- Complete autonomy in institutional, academic and conditions of employment are to be given to the institutions, provided the government could fix the minimum qualifications and rules.
- Encourage institutions interested in this area to undertake the in-depth research required to fully understand the implications of GATS.

16

E-Commerce and the WTO: Towards an Appropriate Indian Position

DIPANKAR SENGUPTA

Introduction

The Information-Communication-Technology (ICT) Revolution through its impact on the dissemination and organisation of information had promised to be the ultimate economic equalizer greatly reducing barriers to entry, increasing competition, lowering prices and in the process greatly increasing social welfare. Such an analysis, even if containing elements of wishful thinking was also grounded in economic theory.

For example, with reference to the Theory of the Firm[1], the ICT Revolution had two aspects one internal to the firm and the other external to it. The component of the ICT Revolution internal to the firm ensured that smoother flows of information that came about helped to eliminate tiers from the organisational pyramid and gave rise to a flatter organisation eliminating costs while giving rise to nimbler organisations. Secondly by reducing transactions costs, it reduced the need for vertically integrated operations and made sub-contracting economical. It was therefore not necessary to achieve a critical minimum size to undertake the production of any commodity. Thus transactions costs that had given rise to the firm itself now threatened to give rise to the 'virtual' firm by its lowering.

The external component that affected all agents was how cheaply information could be disseminated to all economic agents. Combined with the first impact, it meant that barriers to entry were being lowered dramatically as any economic agent could undertake the production of a range of commodities and sell to markets that

1. Coase, R. "The Nature of the Firm," *Economica*, 1937.

could be penetrated with the help of the ICT Revolution. Thus monopolies would give way to more competitive structures, prices would fall and welfare increase.

The ICT Revolution also held out hope to the Less Developed Countries (LDCs) by the possibility of entrepreneurs from the these countries penetrating developed country markets in the field of labour-intensive goods like garments boosting growth and employment.[2]

Sadly many of these promises have been belied. The role of goodwill and branding has stood by established players (and almost by definition monopolists) in good stead.[3] The consumer, it seems is willing to pay a premium for a product in whose quality he has confidence, from a firm he knows rather risk buying a product of uncertain quality from an unknown firm. Given limited time searching for 'good deals' even with the ICT Revolution is time-consuming and competes with his time for other things. Thus even as online buying has taken off, it is established brand-names who have reaped the rewards of long years of goodwill.[4] This is not to say that the ICT Revolution had failed.

The Promise of the ICT Revolution

The promise of the ICT Revolution lies in its role as a mode of delivery. Its role as a transmission belt of information *par excellence*, makes it a delivery mode of information-intensive services *par excellence*. It follows therefore that any economy that has an advantage in delivering a service that has a high component of economically generated information and can take advantage of the modern telecommunications to export this service wherever this service is required will gain from the ICT Revolution.

But what are the services that are being referred to? Obviously, knowledge intensive services that can be transferred (most preferably

2. Sengupta, D. "Exporting through E-commerce: How Indian Exporters have Harnessed the IT Revolution" *Occasional Paper IX*, Centre de Science Humaines, New Delhi.
3. Sengupta *op cit*.
4. For a more realistic view on e-business in general, see Coltman, T, A. Latukefu, D.F. Midgley, "E-business: Revolution, Evolution or Hype?" www.ccc.agsm.edu.au/papers/researchBriefings/A01_Paper_RB001_eBizRevolutEH.pdf. 2001.

over the wire) cheaply and speedily. For example the preparation of a firm's accounts (after raw data has been sent by the firm over the net to an outfit/entity in India) is a service that can be done anywhere and sent anywhere. Similarly, customer care services that call-centres provide, i.e. instant information relevant to customers of a particular product. At a higher level of technology, on-line interactivity with variety of machines (not just computers) enables services like maintenance contracts to be fulfilled from afar. Software design too can be done in one place and delivered to another over the wire. The ICT Revolution has made services considered hitherto non-tradable into tradable services.

Clearly a range of services is being implied with each service differing from the other in terms of technical content, time requirement of delivery (i.e. whether the service has to be delivered in real time as by call-centres, or may be delivered later as in software design), etc each characteristic having an impact on the cost at which any economy can deliver this service. For example, a calculation of the costs involved in running a call centre (or any business operation) would involve the hardware costs (same in any country plus tariff and transportation charges), payment to employees (significantly lower in India and other LDCs) the size of the labour pool for scaling up operations (vast in the case of India). If the operation in question is labour-intensive in question, then an economy with cheap labour has a definite advantage.[5] However, if the service so demanded is particularly sophisticated (e.g. computer support), then the cost of labour may be very high especially in an LDC where institutes for training such people may be rare or non-existent. Certainly not any LDC would have a comparative advantage on this field. Even if IT specialists existed and drew lower salaries than their Western counterparts, their absolute numbers, number of institutions that train them are also of importance when it comes to scaling up operations. The cost of imparting education, i.e. the cost of setting up such institutions, the costs of running them and the salaries drawn by teachers are also important. Clearly, this is one area where India has considerable advantage with low costs all along the chain and it is in precisely this area where Indian firms have delivered spectacularly in terms of export in recent times.

5. Sengupta *op cit.*

This chapter argues that India's successes have taken place despite the lack of progress on GATS because of certain historical reasons and it is likely that Indian exports in this sector will grow despite a lack of progress in GATS. This chapter argues that contrary to received wisdom that holds that concessions in modes 1 and 2 will secure e-commerce, India's peculiar factor conditions as well as the manner in which this sector is organised in India, some concessions in Modes 3 and 4 are imperative as well.

The chapter is organised as follows; the section below describes India's IT and ITES export profile and the circumstances that led to India's success in this field. The is followed by a discussion on the nature of ownership of IT and ITES companies and its implication for India's dynamic comparative advantage in this field. This is further followed by a discussion on what concessions India could ask from potential trading partners that could enable Indian IT and ITES firms to find a larger bridgehead in countries that import services electronically. The paper concludes with a brief discussion on the possibility of trade diversion on account on the WTO decision not to tax digitised trade.

A Brief Profile of Indian IT Exports: Explaining India's Successes[6]

The Indian IT sector has been the star performer of the Indian economy growing from a $5 billion sector in 1997-98 to a $ 16.5 billion sector in 2002-03. The extent to which this sector is export-driven can be gauged by the fact that exports grew in the same period from $ 2.9 billion to $ 12.5 billion. Exports of IT services grew from $ 1.76 billion to $9.9 billion in the same period while ITES (IT enabled services) were coming to their own contributing $ 1.47 billion in 2001-02.

In the IT sector e-commerce penetration is not as high as one would think it may be with 'on site' services contributing 58 per cent of the IT exports as late as 1999.[7] On-site services are said to have been rendered when 'factors move to the site of the receiver' and

6. This section borrows heavily from Sengupta *op cit.*

7. See Parthasarathi, A. and K.J. Joseph (2002) "Limits to Innovation with Strong Export Orientation: The Experience of India's Information Communication Technology Sector", *Science, Technology and Society,* Vol 7, No.1

clearly not the sign of e-commerce penetration. Off-shoring, where 'services are developed domestically and sent over the wire' contributed only 34 per cent to IT exports in the same year. ITES by contrast comprises entirely of activities of the customers that have been 'off-shored.'

It has become clear recently, that it is ITES that will drive exports and not IT *per se* for the reasons stated herewith.[8] For one the industry has long been warning of a coming massive shortage of IT professionals, which will put a sudden brake on the growth of this sector.[9] Secondly, it has become apparent for sometime that China has been making considerable headway in this sector and coupled with the considerable hardware skills that she possesses, the synergies that she will be able to draw coupling hardware with the upcoming software skills that she will catch up and even surpass India.[10] Thus India will in all probability have to learn to live with China as a formidable competitor.

What is it about this apparently high technology sector that gives India such a comparative advantage over other economies? In particular, why did India succeed in this area when her performance in exporting goods has not been nearly as spectacularly? The key to India's successes lies not only in the nature of the sector, but also certain historical factors such as India's colonial heritage as well as certain investments made by the Indian state when it implemented the Mahalanobis Model of growth in order to industrialise rapidly.

While the Mahalanobis Model of Industrial growth may not have led to rapid economic growth like the kind seen in East Asia, its emphasis on technology necessitated a parallel building up of capacities in development of technical skills. The Indian Institutes of Technology as well as the numerous state-run engineering colleges are the result of that capacity creation which did not flag even when the Mahalanobis Model did. Thus even when India remained a largely illiterate country, it had high quality institutions that produced trained technical personnel who could not be gainfully absorbed by an industrial sector, which by the mid-sixties had run out of steam.

8. See Strategic Review 2003, The IT Industry in India, Nasscom, New Delhi, 2003.
9. India's Software Firms to Reap Outsourcing Windfall, http://itmatters.com.ph/news/news_05102002b.html
10. Statement by M.R. Narayana Murthy of INFOSYS quoted in Basu, I, "China Gaining on India's Lead," www.atimes.com/atimes/South_Asia/FH28Df01.html

This was compounded by the fact that the state also continued to set up colleges that imparted education in the liberal arts and commerce even when supply of such graduates far exceeded demand. This practice common to many Less Developed Countries was sought to be explained by Todaro as a device to help unemployed youth to 'mark time' while searching for employment. The fact that India had been Britain's colony ensured that education in many of India's educational institutions was imparted in English. All these factors that came into motion long before India's tryst with IT became a reality demonstrate the role of circumstance in India's comparative advantage in this sector. They ensured a large stock of technically proficient as well as ordinary graduates conversant in English who could supply the labour in producing services that were skill-intensive.

The technological factors that were crucial in India's success in this field were the massive advances in communications technology which ensured that data and information could be sent at very little cost and increasingly in real time. Thus the high cost of power and its erratic supply prevalent in India as well as the absence of good port infrastructure were not as inhibiting as they have proven to be in the case of exports of goods.

In short, the Indian state otherwise known for its planning did nothing deliberate to promote the export of IT and IT enabled services whose growth rate far outstrips the growth rate of export of goods. But what it did was to endow India with a massive stock of graduates conversant with English and with enough institutions to ensure that this stock if anything would be augmented. Moreover a large per centage of these graduates had technical skills.

Thus in a skill-intensive sector where India's labour costs were cheap and where the telecommunications revolution itself became a cheap and instant mode of delivery of skill-intensive services, services hitherto non-tradable became tradable. India with her enormous endowment of educated labour was among the first beneficiaries.

The nature of this sector and India's success makes at least one thing clear. Here India's ability to export does not depend on the ability of Indian labour to be on-site, *i.e.* near the customer to deliver the service. Nor does the customer have to travel to India to take advantage of India's cheap educated labour pool. This service can be rendered without either the customer or the service provider having to move. Therefore this service comes under the category of 'cross-border services'. *Thus it is obviously in India's interest to see that as few restrictions as possible are placed on services that come under this category.* While it is tempting to conclude that this goal more or less sews up this sector for India, this chapter will argue further to show that this is not so.

It must also be mentioned that given the fact that the future of E-commerce will largely be determined by GATS India's successes in this area have despite their being little progress in talks on services. This in no small measure is due to the fact that India exports these services to developed countries which are liberalised to begin with and where entry into sector like services is open even without the economy (the service importer) having made any formal commitment or concession. Secondly, as many of these services are intra-firm with displacement of local firms not evident, opposition to such imports are not organised or as coherent (as Japanese imports of cars were in the 1980s). Thirdly in the case of ITES, it is by and large firms located in the recipient country itself that have facilitated the import of services and a high proportion of these imports are intra-firm. So even while formal commitments under GATS are limited, exports of services to these countries have taken off. But this state of affairs too should not make Indian policy-makers sanguine and an appropriate agreement under GATS does away with the uncertainty and makes long term planning for economic agents in this field easier hopefully leading to more optimal decisions and cutting down of costs.

The Nature of Ownership in the IT Sector: Explaining a Paradox and its Implications

The paradox that prevails in the IT sector is as follows; while 78 per cent of the IT firms that design software and are in the business of maintaining systems are Indian owned whereas in the relatively low-tech ITES sector Indian ownership falls below 50 per cent with Multinational Corporations (like GE itself a technology company) dominating the field.[11] This in actual fact is a reflection of the

11. NASSCOM-McKinsey Report 2002.

manner in which communications technology itself has evolved coupled with the existing global outreach of these companies. For example transnational companies which had a presence in India for a considerable period have been acquainted with the fact that India had a large class of educated pool of professionals who were as good as their Western counterparts with tasks like preparing financials statements, keeping accounts etc. In general, these corporations knew of a large stock of English speaking college-educated people that existed in India. However, the services that this class of people could render were by and large non-tradable. Like the services of the barber, the service of an accountant had to be delivered *in situ* and not from a distance that is till the advent of the ICT revolution.

The transnational firms at first started to outsource labour-intensive service operations from sites where such labour was expensive to India initially as an in-house process and then extended to other commercial enterprises for a fee. It is thus only natural that foreign transnationals with established global outreach and knowledge conditions of potential costs and savings globally should steal a march over their Indian counterparts.[12] Thus it is imperative that India seeks and be prepared to give concessions on services where India has an advantage.

This would include sectors like Financial Services, Audit and Accounts, indeed any service elements of which can be delivered electronically and whose production can be produced with the professionals that India possesses in large numbers. Equally importantly, it must be insisted that while granting this concession, technological neutrality of the delivery of service must be guaranteed so as to prevent electronic delivery from being prohibited and thus neutralizing India's advantage in this field. However shortsightedness in this area, especially among Indian firms in the field of accountancy still persists. Indian firms given limitations on their activities and size[13] '*remained stunted in size as well as in outlook. Sadly enough given their outlook and government policy they have been unable to evolve into an entity more sophisticated than what they are...*[14]'. Far from reorganising

12. Sengupta *op cit.*

13. The Indian Company Act of 1970.

14. Interview with Employee of an Audit Major, name withheld.

themselves and marrying technology to take advantage of the vast opportunity presented to them, Indian firms still seek protection from foreign firms till they grow stronger.

What Should India Not Do?

Before undertaking a discussion on what should India's objectives should be to secure India's e-commerce advantages, it is worth discussing what not to do, i.e. let Indian accountancy firms get protection form their foreign counterparts. This is especially important as there is a body of opinion that tilts in this direction.

Indian auditing firms led by the middle-sized firms have lobbied with the government to put restrictions on entry by foreign firms. The committee set up by the government under Sunil Bhargav (a representative of the Middle sized audit firms) to gauge the effects of liberalising entry has submitted its report but this is not yet been made public. However if public comments[15] are anything to go by, then Indian Audit firms far from welcoming the opportunity offered to them by the potential liberalisation of this service fear the future.

Industry representatives echo calls in the West that have shown concern at the nature of the audit industry especially after the Enron scandal and the role of auditors Arthur Anderson. They say that given the extraordinary market power of the Big Four free trade in services is a misnomer and will lead to trade distortions. They claim (not unreasonably) that there is *de facto* discrimination against Indian firms and professionals and that professional standards are used as a trade barrier. They ask not for the negotiation for the mutual removal of such barriers but calls for the effective exclusion of foreign firms for a period of 8 years *after* India attains 3.5 per cent share of the world market for accountancy services for two consecutive years[16]!

This by any account seems to be a drastic remedy which if implemented will effectively shut out Indian firms from the financial markets in the rest of the world as the necessary certification by one

---

15. Bhargav, S. "WTO GATS Regime: Implications for the Accountancy Sector," *The Chartered Accountant*, Vol. 51 No. 5 2002.

16. Bhargav *op cit.*

of the big four will not be forthcoming. However, as our interviews with representatives of the big four in Delhi have confirmed, this is not the intention of the Indian firms.[17] They seek to force the Big Four to be represented by Indian middle size accountancy firms such that their certification becomes *de facto* certification by the big four. It is however extremely unlikely that this position will be accepted in full or in part by the developed countries at any future GATS negotiations and may lead to the closure to Indian firms of the very sectors where India has a cost advantage. Moreover, it would be foolish to deny MNCs key players with global outreach a presence in India. Given India's factor abundance in this area there is enough room for both and obstructing entry in an area where India has a cost advantage (so that only domestic firms benefit from it) would surely slowdown Indian exports of services in this potentially large sector.

However credence must be given to complaints of *de facto* and at times *de jure* discrimination and these must be tackled. A situation must be created whereby Indian BPO outfits are able to set up offices anywhere to market their services and compete with the MNCs are actually allowed to do so. It is here that concessions on Commercial Presence are relevant.

Indeed, Indian BPO outfits if they are to increase their presence in this sector it is extremely important that they have the right to set up offices in countries with high wages for professionals in the fields where they have expertise. The implications for a negotiating objective will be stated in the following section.

While these are early days for BPOs, it is likely the initial conditions from which this sector evolves will have an impact on India's dynamic advantage in this sector. This point needs to be elucidated further.

If we believe in Arrovian 'learning-by-doing', then it may be argued that the efficiency and cost at which BPO firms can offer a service would depend on the scale of operations of the firm which itself is a function of the time in which the firm has been in business. Thus Indian firms need to get in as early as possible.

17. Interviews of Employees of Audit Majors, names withheld.

Secondly, the quality and breadth of services offered will also depend on the number of years the BPO firm has been in operation. Thus from a firm that simply prepares payrolls and other financial statements, it may evolve into entity which can offer firm diagnostics like offering advice on how to re-arrange production to minimise costs. For that a firm needs to evolve into an entity that processes data with a more sophisticated purpose to generate more sophisticated information. This cannot happen overnight and the sooner Indian firms get into high gear the better.

What is its impact for local labour? What is the guarantee that even Indian firms will not look out of India once other sources of educated professionals are revealed to be as inexpensive as India's? It may be argued those determinants of supply of factors of production (in this case educational institutions like colleges that train such professionals) as well as their quality and up-gradation (as exemplified by design of syllabi and its frequency of being updated) depends on demand on these factors. Thus a head-start in this sector should induce educational institutions in India to shape their strategies accordingly. It may be further argued that Indian BPO firms being based in India will have a greater urgency to participate or urge the upgradation of syllabi than foreign BPOs who have a greater field to source professionals given their global outreach. Thus even if nominally cheaper source of professionals are made available, the scale, quality and range of professionals that an entrenched incumbent should be able to provide cheap and quality outsourcing services even if wage rate of professionals rise.

What should be the stance then that India adopt at WTO negotiations? Before we delve into that it would not be out of place to look at a general discussion that discusses ways and means to strengthen E-commerce at the WTO.

E-commerce and the WTO

Can e-commerce be strengthened by appropriate e-commerce initiatives at the WTO? Before we answer this question, it would not be out of place to ask what the WTO agreements have done for e-commerce *per se*. There is a body of opinion that holds that the WTO has to be given some credit for the growth in e-commerce worldwide.

---

* For example, INFOSYS's Campus Connect Programme.

Hauser and Wunsch-Vincent[18] contend that the explosion in e-commerce that has been seen can be (at least in part) be credited to the WTO and the current under-utilisation of e-commerce potential can be laid down at the door of unresolved issues within the WTO itself. They point out that the explosive growth in e-commerce has commenced only after the completion of the Uruguay Round and thus is not referred in the WTO treaties specifically save the Ministerial declaration exempting electronically delivered transactions from duties. But there are some specific clauses that affect e-commerce.

For example it is argued that in so far as goods are delivered in the traditional physical mode they are subject to GATT-commitments and the country-specific tariff concessions. Thus in so far as goods have been electronically searched and ordered, e-commerce (of which a significant proportion is normal goods trade) benefits from the WTO. However of far greater importance is the Information Technology Agreement (ITA) arrived at the 1996 Ministerial with regard to trade in IT goods where tariff cuts leading to a tariff free policy by 2000 was agreed upon. Given the fact 50 countries who were signatories to this agreement account for 95 per cent of trade in IT goods this agreement helped to lay the foundation of an IT infrastructure that is indispensable for e-commerce.

In the same vein the less than dramatic progress of so-called ITA II have seen to it that a number of goods required for the better functioning of the internet have not been given the boost by way of concessions as in 1996. This possibly detracts from technological progress required by modern telecommunications. Thus the ITAs when followed up have boosted e-commerce by laying the foundations for modern communications, and when not, have detracted from it. In so far as e-commerce depends on this infrastructure, e-commerce, it is claimed is accordingly affected.

Hauser and Wunsch-Vincent further argue that it is GATS that is of particular significance to e-commerce in a variety of ways. They point out that electronic transactions necessitates infrastructure services (payments etc.) whose liberalisation falls as much under

---

18. Hauser, Heinz & Sacha Wunsch-Vincent, "A Call for a WTO E-Commerce Initiative," *International Journal of Communications Law and Policy*, Issue 6, Winter 2000-2001.

GATS. More importantly, e-commerce takes place mainly in services from which it follows that the liberalisation of such services (medical, legal, consulting, finance etc.) is crucial for e-commerce to realise its full potential.

Hauser and Wunsch-Vincent however point out that certain clauses that forbid suppliers with monopolistic rights from impairing the use of specific concessions in other sectors. Thus for example no matter how much the synergy, the telephone monopoly may not inconvenience the internet services provided from other countries) afforded by Article VIII. Similarly the Basic Telecommunications Agreement that seeks to liberalise the telecommunications sector by calling for market access as setting down competition policy principles the signatory countries seek to impose and competitive and coherent playing field in this area. In such a milieu, e-commerce can only do better.

Hauser and Wunsch-Vincent call for specific e-commerce initiative of the WTO to strengthen e-commerce. Elements of this initiative include the conversion of the Moratorium on duties on e-commerce into a permanent formal agreement and the categorisation of digitised tradables into goods and services so as to determine which treaty should be competent to deal with them, GATT or GATS. Further liberalisation of trade is called for *via* expansion of the ITA towards more WTO and non-WTO members. In the area of services, they call for the strengthening of the Basic Telecom Agreement, more market entry and National treatment commitments in Mode 1 and Mode 2 with stress on labour-intensive services exports (from LDCs to DCs) and knowledge-intensive services (from DCs to LDCs), the strengthening of TRIPS etc.

In light of the arguments offered above, it has to be pointed out that e-commerce is by and large a phenomenon that has been driven by technology and organisational learning rather than the WTO. It is true that liberalisation of trade (which is what the WTO sets out to do) leads to its enhancement and thus increase in e-commerce. It is also true that the ITA enhances the level and quality of telecommunications infrastructure and thus boosts e-commerce. But e-commerce has a presence of its own as evidenced by the fact that even domestic trade has been so dramatically penetrated by it. It may even be added additionally, contrary to Hauser *et al.*, the direction of trade when it comes to knowledge-intensive services need not be from DCs to LDCs but could be in either direction.

In so far as it is the trade in tradable services where e-commerce is important, the relatively un-advanced nature of GATS shows that it has not been a major impediment to e-commerce. Indeed estimates that show this sector expanding with India, by one estimate, gaining $ 250 billion do not assume any dramatic advance in GATS (for example with member-countries giving concessions in areas that Hauser *et al.*, propose). This is because e-commerce in services have in part the look of corporates reallocating functions to various international subsidiaries taking advantage of locally cheap inputs, in many cases educated labour. The next step (as earlier sections have pointed out) was offering these services to other firms followed by independent third-party service providers. By and large these developments were autonomous of developments at the WTO negotiations.

More significantly, the stress that Hauser *et al.*, put on IT infrastructure misses a key point. This is the fact; that the nature of organisations that use IT and e-commerce is the key to understanding the potential of e-commerce as organisational skills and innovative e-strategies can and have transcended shortcomings in IT infrastructure. Indeed in some cases the presence of adequate infrastructure has not boosted e-commerce as firms attempting to forge e-strategies were not sophisticated to forge viable ones. The success on the other hand of ITC's e-*chaupals* in rural India (where power connections are rare not to speak of telecom infrastructure) *versus* the failure of garment exporters around the national capital region to use e-commerce to boost exports is a testimony to organisational skills trumping IT shortcomings.[19]

This is not to say that the outline of the action plan that Hauser *et al.*, lay out are unnecessary; indeed they would go a long way in *securing* the gains made by e-commerce but they cannot be given the credit for its *existence and growth*.

Moreover as Mattoo and Schuknecht[20] point out that it is not enough to call for the liberalisation of the services that can be

19. For a comparison of strategies see Sengupta *op cit*

20. Mattoo, Aaditya and Ludger Schuknecht, "Trade Policies for Electronic Commerce" http://econ.worldbank.org/docs/1133.pdf, 2000.

rendered through modern telecommunications; *confirming the principle of technological neutrality in the GATS they opine is the single most step to ensure that the rules of the GATS apply to e-commerce*. The importance of the Mattoo-Schuknecht argument cannot be overemphasised. As they point out that a prohibition on the electronic delivery of a service does not amount to a quota on the total volume or value of the service if there are other means of delivering this service. It may of course be argued that if a member country bars electronic delivery and keeps other means of delivery open, that means of delivery is likely to be Mode 4 (movement of natural persons) which means that the services may be delivered anyway but at a higher cost with the added result of the importing country hosting a large number of immigrants. But the importance of the Mattoo-Schuknecht must be conceded if the purpose is to avoid disruptions to e-commerce.

However the magnitude of the overall task in reforming the GATS to secure the gains and fully realise the potential of e-commerce as Mattoo-Schuknecht reveal is huge. Firstly three differences between the legal framework of GATS and GATT (that have crucial bearing on e-commerce) are pointed out. Firstly, unlike in GATT, national treatment in GATS is not a general obligation; while it applies to all measures affecting the supply of a service, it only applies to sectors that a member has explicitly scheduled and may be subject to limitations. From this follows the second difference- GATS has little to say about custom duties or taxes in general except these be consistent with national commitments. Lastly, where GATT generally prohibits (except for emergencies) quantitative restrictions, GATS only prohibits this in sectors where the member country has made commitments to provide market access without limitations. Given these differences the classification of a tradable item as a good or a service can make a difference to the way it is treated and the protectionist measures that it would face. Clearly, classification as a good makes trading easier. Classification as a service creates numerous potential and actual obstructions.

From here Mattoo-Schuknecht argue that the logical solution is to negotiate fully liberal commitments under GATS on market access (thus eliminating quantitative restrictions) and on national treatment (eliminating discriminatory taxation). Specifically with regard to e-commerce-compatible services (e.g. financial services, customer care-related services etc) focus is placed on cross-border supply (Mode 1) with the provisio that supply abroad (Mode 2) may also be relevant as the two modes are not always distinguishable and the latter is subject to less restrictions. They also point out that very few members have made unrestricted commitments in e-commerce compatible services.

How then can GATS be clarified and strengthened? Apart from technological neutrality that needs to be enshrined, Mattoo and Schuknecht also stress (like Hauser *et al.*) on the need to classify traded products into goods and services, *e.g.*. Should trade in all tangibles be classified as services? In the same vein modes of supply need to be distinguished as the differences between Modes 1 and 2 are not always clear. More significantly, it is domestic regulations (which act as explicit barriers) that have to be addressed. Domestic regulatory objectives (it should be ensured) are not used to discriminate or protect against imports. Indeed Article XIV (which allows members to take measures that in specified circumstances violate GATS obligations *e.g.* on grounds of public morality, health, public order etc) enjoins members not to apply the safety measures contained in it as a protectionist device. Mattoo-Schuknecht also hold that Article VI of GATS has provisions that can be used to ensure that legislation that 'obstructs commerce' for ostensibly legitimately reasons (information failure) be administered in a manner that is reasonable, objective and impartial. How as Mattoo and Schuknecht point out that it does not lay down guidelines that ensure the laws enacted are not more burdensome than necessary. They rightly point out that this a removable shortcoming (as evidenced in Agreement on Technical Barriers to Trade).

While the inclusion and liberalisation of Mode 1 and 2 services in the plan set out by Hauser *et al.*, as well Mattoo-Schuknecht cannot be faulted, such a strategy does not optimally serve India's e-commerce interests. As we have said it is in India's interests not only to promote e-commerce but also to see that Indian firms have a presence in the sectors where India has a comparative advantage. Given this objective, neglecting to include mode 3 and Mode 4 could prove to be a serious shortcoming for Indian interests, i.e. the right of commercial presence (Mode 3). Equally important is the right to have limited Mode 4 access for professionals for which outsourcing has become the norm. This is not necessary for delivering the service *per se* but more for marketing purposes, i.e. a bridgehead in the country importing the service. As we have pointed out that Indian BPO outfits who do not have the global outreach of most MNCs that dominate this field need to market themselves globally; setting up offices for this purpose in potential markets is an integral part of such strategies, if not for actual delivery of the service but for the marketing of such services and business-related communications. In the same vein concessions on Mode 4 may also be required even if the bulk of the services are to be delivered online. The Indian government has been mindful of this and indeed its submissions have stressed on this point focusing on the movement of professionals and the recognition of educational qualifications while accepting the need for adequate safeguards to prevent people coming in on temporary work permits from entering the permament labour market. India has stressed on the need to minimise discretion discrimination.[21] Indeed what is also commendable is India's offer in this regard where it has made commitments under Modes 1 and 4 which are of course '*conditional on other WTO Members making substantive and satisfactory offers in sectors and modes of supply where India has indicated its interests*'[22]. This is an appropriate 'give and take' approach where India's previous concessions include '*substantially improved access in critical service sectors such as Accounting and Book Keeping services, Engineering services, Computer & related services, Medical and Dental services, Services provided by Midwives, Nurses, Physiotherapists and para-medical personnel, Construction and related Engineering services, Financial services, Health services, Tourism services and Maritime Transport services*'[23]. Moreover this is a far cry from India's near silence in Geneva in 1998 when the Global E-commerce Agreement was signed. This silence was not unnatural as the potential of export of IT enabled services was not obvious to many. Luckily nothing in this agreement has gone against India's interests so far.

---

21. Communication from India to the Council for Trade in Services, Proposed Liberalisation of Movement of Professionals under General Agreement on Trade in Services (GATS) 24 November 2000, S/CSS/W/12

22. India, Conditional Initial Offer to the Council for Trade in Services, TN/S/O/IND, 12 January 2004.

23. *ibid.*

This, it may be argued consists of a more complete and comprehensive solution; i.e. one that liberalises services that are tradable while ensuring neutrality on the mode of delivery, ensures Mode 1, mode 2 comprehensively, mode 3 and Mode 4 selectively. The ITAs, while welcome are not crucial (from India's point of view) in the sense India would have to undertake telecom reform in self interest while destination countries have a higher level of telecom infrastructure to begin with.

Fears of Protectionism

Towards the end of the first term of George W. Bush's Presidency, the outcry created over lost jobs due to outsourcing seemed to reach a crescendo. The fact that job creation during George W. Bush's first term was actually negative compared to impressive record of sustained job creation during the Clinton Presidency made this controversy even more emotive. Thus not surprisingly, there were attempts by U.S. law makers to introduce Bills in the U.S. Congress that would curb outsourcing. While many observers have taken serious note of such efforts, Mattoo and Wunsch-Vincent[24] opine that these movements show that it would be prudent to initiate a bold move in GATS that secures current openness and pre-empts protectionism particularly in those areas where India has a comparative advantage. They opine that negotiations relating to GATS of the Doha Development Agenda are an ideal opportunity to secure this.

Mattoo and Wunsch-Vincent point out to the disturbing fact that many of the services that are traded electronically and where the Indian IT and BPO sectors have an enormous cost advantage do not have a corresponding entry in the GATS Services Sectoral Classification List (the so-called W/120). When this is seen in the context of the unsatisfactory nature of the structure of GATS commitments made by Members in mode 1, there is clearly an uncomfortably large potential for trade disruption especially as existing commitments do not match current structure of cross-border trade in services and thus obviously cannot capture potential exports.

24. Mattoo, Aaditya and Sacha Wunsch-Vincent, "Pre-empting Protectionism in Services: The GATS and Outsourcing." *Journal of International Economic Law*, Vol. 7, No. 4, 2004.

To remedy this situation Mattoo and Wunsch-Vincent suggest a formula-based approach as in the context of the severely unequal bargaining powers that different Members have this approach is more equitable, efficient and more biased towards the weaker party. Secondly the transactions costs of this approach (as compared to one where commitments are bartered sector-by-sector, country-by-country) is significantly lower. Thirdly it reduces free-riding that arises under an MFN-based negotiations. Lastly, it is credible way of granting credit to unilateral liberalisers.

Thus Mattoo and Wunsch-Vincent outline two approaches.

The first option presents a targeted approach to ensure free cross-border trade in selected set of IT and BPO services. Members would be expected to make full market access and national treatment commitments on the positive list of services so chosen that it covers/matches existing trade. The service categories are specified in their most aggregative form to include all possible sub-activities. Care should be taken when services that imply capital account convertibility are considered.

Evaluating this approach, Mattoo and Wunsch-Vincent point out that this approach covers a range of existing service activities and has an incremental approach that most Members are comfortable with. Additionally they hold that this option can serve as a model for consultation with the service industries for further refinement and re-classification and addition that may be required such that business activity may be planned in a climate of legal security.

But Matto and Wunsch-Vincent also admit that this approach leaves out certain swathes that are being traded today. Moreover the static nature of the classification scheme will be an impediment in the future given the dynamism and innovation inherent in these services and thus would in all possibility leave the GATS structure permanently lagging behind reality. Lastly, this option focuses only on BPO and IT services to the exclusion of other areas where cross-border trade is possible and where India could have or develop expertise.

The second option proposed by Mattoo and Wunsch-Vincent is more coherent and bold. This entails a horizontal commitment to liberalise (i.e. provide market access and national treatment) cross-border trade in all services supplied on a cross-border basis (as compared to the first where only services listed in an agreed upon schedule were considered). This commitment would also apply to any new services that may be introduced in the future. The exception that they propose has to deal with any service that has implications for and/or may require capital account convertibility or require movement of freight and personnel. Mattoo and Wunsch-Vincent also propose variants on this option. If this option as it is remains too bold to act upon they suggest that either there be a 'prudential carve-out' of the other financial services that still remain (after those affecting the movement of capital have been omitted) or limit the scope of horizontal commitment to situations where businesses are consumers.

The reason for including a 'carve-out' in the first variant has much to do with precautionary reasons. GATS being new, few Members if any are sure about whether their desired optimal mix between national autonomy and commitment to multilateral disciplines will coincide with eventual legal interpretation.

The second variant captures the situation as it exists today but makes it secure. Mattoo and Wunsch-Vincent opine that this approach leaves out private consumers (leading to potential distortions). To that it limits the extent of liberalisation.

How Justified are Fears? An Evaluation

How justified are the fears of protectionism against import of cross-border services in the USA as expressed by some observers? It must be first realised that the bulk of trade in cross-border services is business-to-business (B2B) trade. The saving that US businesses generate when they outsource non-core operations to countries like India have already been discussed. Thus US business forms a very strong lobby against protectionist tendencies in this sector. This may be contrasted to the treatment meted out to Japanese Car imports in the 1980s where the Reagan Administration forced Japan to accept Voluntary Export Restraints (VERs). In this case the consumers happened to be American private customers. Thus such car imports affected the bottomlines of the American companies. It was not surprising then that protectionist measures followed.

Secondly, new data on job losses in the USA have shown that job losses due to outsourcing[25] have been considerably less that feared. Furthermore some have argued that upto 75 *per cent* of the employees whose tasks are outsourced are redeployed in other functions[26] which increases firm flexibility. All these findings coined with the lobbying power of Corporate America make significant protectionist developments unlikely.

This of course is not to argue against Mattoo and Wunsch-Vincent's contention that there needs to be movement in the negotiations in GATS such that India's interests in this sector are secured. But the implied urgency of this approach may lead India to take steps that may secure India's interest only inoptimally.

The first option proposed by Mattoo and Wunsch-Vincent is too limited and complicated and is not discussed further. The second option that Mattoo and Wunsch-Vincent propose while breathtakingly simple is too bold given (as the proposers themselves point out) that given the relatively under-developed nature of GATS Members perceive themselves in areas of legal uncertainty as to contours of their national power to legislate and their GATS commitments. Thus an approach that secures the present situation and incorporates all requirements for its continuance is the one that Members are most likely to agree to. This is obviously Mattoo and Wunsch-Vincent's second variant of their second option.

But there are more things responsible for the current structure of services traded electronically like IT services and BPO than this second variation of the second option. While Mattoo and Wunsch-Vincent have restricted their analysis to liberalisation of Modes 1 and 2, as pointed earlier, the *de facto* presence of aspects of commercial presence and movement of natural persons (especially some types of skilled labour) have also contributed to this trade. This is all the more needed as has been pointed earlier if Indian firms are to have an increasing presence in this sector. Thus an agreement to secure or at least preserve the current volume and structure of cross-border trade in services especially BPO and IT

25. *Extended Mass Layoffs Associated with Domestic and Overseas Relocations, First Quarter 2004*, http://www.bls.gov/news.release/reloc.toc.htm

26. See Hoffman, Thomas, "Sidebar: Researcher Says Offshore Moves Don't Lead to Big U.S. Job Losses," *Computerworld*, December 22, 2003.

services must include these non-cross-border aspects as well. The negotiating strategy of the government of India reflects this as well.

Is this variant of the second option trade distorting in so far as consumers are not covered? While *de jure* this may be so, the non-inclusion of consumers may turn out to be *de facto* irrelevant. This is because in most developed countries it would be difficult for countries to set up an economic regime that allows business to avail of a service from abroad at fraction of a cost while consumers pay up to several times that amount for the same service. Thus in spite of the absence of a commitment in an international treaty the ability to discriminate against consumers may not be availed of!

Trade Diversion *Versus* Trade Creation

Recently, there have been arguments that how the WTO's decision not to tax e-commerce may end in diversion rather than trade creation. Mattoo *et al.*, use a simple but illuminative example where the price of an imported good, imported both electronically and through conventional means is given by

$$p_e = p_o + d_e + t_e$$

$$p_a = p_o + d_a + t_a$$

where p_o is the price in the exporting country, d_e and d_a is the cost of delivery through electronic and conventional means and t_a and t_e is the tax imposed on goods.

Given that t_e is 0, trade diversion would take place if d_e is greater than d_a. While Mattoo and Schuknecht agree that this unlikely to be the case for most goods they opine that for items like films it may not be true and thus trade may be diverted instead of being created the decision not to tax digitized trade.

It may be opined that even for items like films, the cost of delivery can only fall. Given the rate of technical progress and the rate of innovation in telecommunications sector, the improvements in the format and development of new more efficient format will probably ensure that even films and books will be transferred to end-users quickly and efficiently electronically. Even if the quality of certain services like legal advice is dependent on the proximity between the lawyer (the service provider) and client (the customer) and the technological substitute for legal proximity (i.e. video conferencing) expensive, it is only a matter of time before technological developments ensure that costs fall sufficiently low.

The point of this section is simple; any information-intensive service that is currently embedded in a physical commodity (i.e. films and music on polyester and tape, works of fiction and non-fiction on paper) or currently requires physical proximity (legal advice) lends itself to electronic delivery and given the swiftness of technological progress in the field of telecommunications it is likely that electronic delivery will prevail even if this mode of delivery is subject to the same level of taxation as conventional trade. Thus the problem of trade diversion if any is likely to be transient (as Mattoo and Schuknecht also hint).

Conclusion

Because e-commerce cuts across many other key WTO issues such as services, and intellectual property rights, it is not expected that an international trade regime that governs Global e-commerce will be in place any time soon. Yet given its undoubted integrality in global commerce the WTO has begun to apply its mind as to how e-commerce fits into the multi-lateral trade framework and the appropriate regulatory regime that should be put in place.

India's successes in exploiting e-commerce especially in the field of services that can either be digitized or be rendered over modern lines of communication in real time or otherwise has come in spite of their being no agreement governing trade in services on the scale of that which has been achieved in the case of goods. They have come as a result of historical circumstances, i.e. the factor building exercise that the Indian state put in to supply manpower to man the aborted Nehru-Mahalanobis model which was taken advantage of by Indian and foreign IT and ITES firms which by and large operated outside the ambit of the state. Additionally, it has also occurred given the unsatisfactory state of GATS. What India needs to do is more in the nature of safeguarding what it possesses and ensuring that the sector or at least its driving forces are rooted in India and give rise to a process that ensures that India retains dynamic advantage so as to neutralise the effects of a rise in the cost of manpower. Given the difficulties of getting a global agreement on services, India should try the PTA track *en route* to a more inclusive/global agreement.

A protectionist attitude that seeks to protect the very areas where India has or is acquiring an advantage is self-defeating. This as has been shown is no longer the case. There is a spirit or at least a realisation of give and take. But by and large the key to unlocking India's strengths lies in policy-making in India. Although this is changing, the policies aimed at controlling the economy have hobbled Indian presence in this sector. It with the overhauling of these policies that the way ahead in unlocking India's potential in e-commerce lies.

Section V

Some Future Concerns

The sudden rise in the number of Regional Trading Agrements (RTA), especially after the formation of WTO is indicative of the dissatisfaction that exists among the member countries over the slow pace of multilateral trade liberalisation. The substitution of multilateral liberalisation by RTAs is indeed a worrying trend. Moreover, the lack of clarity in the WTO agreement to stop trade-diversion is an area of major concern. Analysing the RTAs India has entered into in the recent years, Anirudh Shingal and Julien Chaisse note that there is hardly any substantial impact on the country's trading opportunities. Looking over the global scenario of RTA formation, the authors conclude that the most important use of an RTA could be to enforce reduction in the MFN tariff. The authors conclude by expressing faith on the multilateral trade liberalisation for trade expansion, instead of overlapping RTAs ('Bhagwati's Spaghetti bowl'), which only add to confusion and disputes over rules of origin.

Julien Chaisse points out that the Dispute Settlement Mechanism (DSM) is a central feature of the WTO agreement, which acts as a safety valve in the system. The compulsory enforcement of the final Dispute Settlement Body (DSB) verdict also strengthens the efficiency of multilateral trading system to a great extent. However it has been observed that a number of developing country members are dissatisfied with certain procedural, legal and enforcement-related impediments, during and after a dispute, namely – permanent panellists, remand, *amicus curiae* submissions, legal cost, cross-retaliation etc. Analysing various reform proposals submitted by the developing countries, Chaisse points out developing countries believe that the DSM should be modified at the earliest in order to effectively protect their interests.

While the Precautionary Principles (PP) as of now lies outside the purview of WTO, there has been a debate on its incorporation within the multilateral forum. However, it finds its way through exception clause of Article XX of GATT 1994 especially section (b) & (g), and under the SPS provisions in a limited sense. The issue has come to forefront in a number of occasions such as GMO products and other environment-related disputes. Swapan Bhattacharya notes that the Indian business community believes that PP may emerge as a new form of NTB on Indian agricultural exports like dairy products, edible products of animal origin and GMO-based, some fruits, coffee, tea, groundnuts and some tobacco products. Quoting earlier panel results he notes that existing SPS agreement is sufficient to address a country's health, safety and environmental standards when trade challenges are initiated and settles against incorporation of PP provisions under WTO.

Sachin Chaturvedi and S.R. Rao analyse the various dimensions of international negotiations that concern biotechnology from a developing country viewpoint. Starting with an overview of the sector they look at the regimes aimed at ensuring Biosafety and the tension that these regimes have with the WTO as well as the efforts made by Developing countries to put into place a regime that prevents Bio-piracy and ensures the wide and safe application of this technology given the current IPR regime.

17

A Burden or An Incentive: Developing World Trade and the Role of RTAs

ANIRUDH SHINGAL
JULIEN CHAISSE

Multilateralism to Regionalism

The multilateral trading system existed first as the GATT from 1947 to 1994 and then as the WTO since 1995. Regional Trade Agreements ("RTAs"), defined as "a free-trade agreement, customs union or common market consisting of two or more countries[1]", however, began coming into their own only in the 1990s. Before that, there were virtually no such agreements until 1970 and less than 50 in 1990. This suggests that greater reduction in trade barriers (both tariff and non-tariff) was achieved in the earlier rounds of the GATT, which precluded the need for countries to resort to RTAs. Once, however, this initial thrust *via* the multilateral route was saturated, countries had to look at other ways of expanding their trading opportunities and this phenomenon was further propelled by the lack of substantial progress in successive Trade Rounds.

Scope of RTAs

Regional cooperation has indeed been adopted as a means of expanding the process of economic development by many countries across the world. RTAs can enable a broader coverage of economic issues than what is available multilaterally, for instance, in terms of competition, investment and movement of natural persons. Politically, an increase in the bargaining power, which creates a necessity for economic reforms and precludes the reneging on such commitments, would be one of the benefits emanating from an RTA.

---

1. "Regional Trade Agreement," in: Goode Walter: *Dictionary of Trade Policy Terms*, Cambridge University Press, Cambridge 2003, p. 292.

Thus, in addition to expansion of trading opportunities, there are other reasons, both economic and political, for which a country might negotiate a RTA.

RTAs: The Phenomenon

RTAs have been proliferating at an alarming rate and this has significant implications for a country's market access in the major markets of the world (Figure 17.1).

Figure 17.1

Evolution of Regional Trade Agreements in the World (1948-2002)

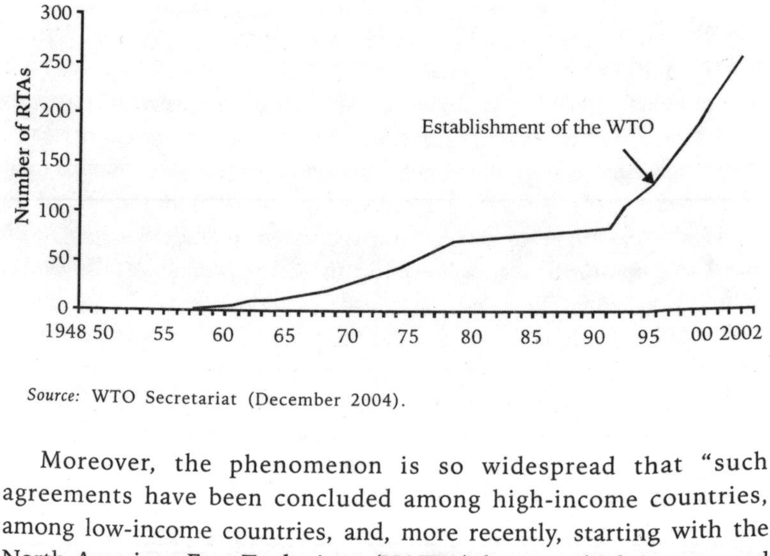

Source: WTO Secretariat (December 2004).

Moreover, the phenomenon is so widespread that "such agreements have been concluded among high-income countries, among low-income countries, and, more recently, starting with the North American Free Trade Area (NAFTA) between high-income and developing countries"[2]. Nevertheless, "the South Asian region (has) lagged behind in terms of regional cooperation under the economic integration scheme in comparison to North America, Western Europe and South East Asia"[3].

---

2. Cherunilam, Francis: "Economic Integration of Developing Countries with Special Reference to SAPTA and ISFTA," in: Basavaraja M.G.: *World Trade Organisation, Regional Trading Arrangements and India,* Serials Publications, New Delhi 2003, p. 257.
3. Gupta, Anshuman: *SAARC – SAPTA to SAFTA,* Maulana Abdul Kalam Azad Institute of Asian Studies (Kolkata), Shipra Publications, New Delhi 2002, p. 71.

What is at Stake for India?

An answer to the question of the magnitude of intra-regional trade in South Asia lays down the broad parameters of what is at stake. Of course, it must be mentioned here that this could be endogenous i.e. the actual trade in the region could well reflect the impediments to trade or the ineffective trade liberalisation in this region as opposed to being a realistic measure of what is actually trade-able. Having said that, the reality would be a combination of both these factors including the supply-side capacities of these countries. But what remains unchanged is that irrespective of the magnitude of this trade, removal of tariff and non-trade barriers would definitely increase the volume of intra-South Asian trade.

South Asian intra-regional trade as a proportion of world trade declined from a high of 20 per cent in 1948 to as low as 2 per cent two decades later. While the generally low proportions indicate the magnitude of trade in this region, what is interesting to note is the slight upward trend in this per centage since the coming into existence of the SAPTA in 1993, indicating that whatever reduction in barriers has been attained, has had some impact.

Disciplines on RTAs in the WTO: GATT and GATS

Provisions on RTAs in the Legal Texts come primarily in the form of Article XXIV of the GATT and Article V of the GATS, which require *inter alia,* that substantially all trade be covered between the parties forming an RTA and that the latter does not result in making *ex post* conditions more trade-restrictive for non-parties to the Agreement than what they were *ex-ante*. Economic theory refers to the 'trade creating' and the 'trade diverting' effects of an RTA, while analysing the welfare effects on both parties and non-parties to an Agreement. As a result, the necessary economic test then for an RTA to have a positive net welfare effect is for trade creation to exceed trade diversion. However, consensus on the conformity of the RTAs with the provisions of the GATT was reached in only one case – the Czech-Slovak Customs Union! Examinations of RTA issues have been plagued by divergences of view on a series of systemic lacunae both in the substantive rules of the WTO and in the very process of examination. Moreover, the WTO Understanding on the

Interpretation of Article XXIV, adopted as part of the Final Act of the Uruguay Round, has done little to resolve the more difficult issues.

I. *Legitimisation of a Certain Kind of Regional Integration*

The legitimisation of a certain kind of regional integration consists in reality in the analysis of the *ratione materiae* scope of the exception regime of the economic regional integration. The fundamental principle of the international trading system lies in the most favoured nation principle, which guarantees the equality of treatment of all Member nations of the WTO. The MFN principle obligates each Member to extend any tariff (or related) concession granted to one Member to all other Members. "The MFN rule should have the effect of accelerating the process of trade barriers elimination since it requires a wide dispersion of concessions among GATT members"[4]. The MFN principle is thus the *key* multilateralism provision in the GATT 1947. However an RTA has as its main aim, the establishment of a zone of preferential exchange and is *ipso facto* discriminatory. Indeed "as far as multilateralism is concerned, the speed and depth of trade openness that can be achieved at a multilateral level are limited, whereas preferential or regional agreements make it possible to take advantage of the economies of scale offered by a broad market and to incorporate more employment, technology and innovation, which are central elements in economic development, provided that the rules of origin are simple and are aimed at the creation and not the diversion of trade. The rationale for the inclusion of Article XXIV of the GATT supports this argument. This Article is an exception to the multilateral institution that is based on the MFN principle of most-favoured-nation (MFN) and this exception is permitted in cases

4. "However, there was a core political motive for adoption of an unconditional MFN rule. In the pre-war environment, trade concessions were widely used as an instrument of diplomacy. Political alliances were created and maintained through economic preferences. Since diplomatic decisions were often made for reasons apart from improving world prosperity, an economic system in which trade concessions were used as political instruments would be unlikely to generate a global welfare-optimising result. The MFN principle is intended to de-politicise the trading system so as to reduce the chances of breakdown into a system of diplomacy-based alliances. The net effect should be to distribute the benefits of trade widely". Abbott Frederick: "North American Economic Integration: Implications for the WTO, the EU and Asia," Snyder Francis (Ed.): *Regional and Global Regulation of International Trade*, Hart Publishing 2002, p. 79.

where it is difficult to reduce the trade barriers. Moreover, it may act as a supplemental practical route to universal free trade"[5].

A. GATT and GATS Regime for RTAs

The Uruguay Round brought trade in services within the purview of the WTO, and the General Agreement on Trade in Services (GATS) established an additional mechanism for the review of regional services arrangements (RSAs). Article V of the GATS permits Members of RSAs to eliminate barriers on trade in services among themselves without extending these concessions to non-Members, provided that such RSAs involve substantial "sectoral" coverage, involve the elimination of substantially all discrimination in covered sectors, and do not raise barriers to non-Members within covered sectors. The inclusion of a provision requiring that the benefits of an RSA be extended to businesses with commercial presence within the RSA significantly ameliorates the potential discriminatory impact of these arrangements on non-party national service providers"[6].

What Article V of the GATS regulates is generally similar to its GATT counterpart in Article XXIV. However, there are two important differences between the two. First, provisions in Article V of the GATS apply to individual sectors and sub-sectors, whereas provisions in Article XXIV of the GATT explicitly require that newly introduced tariffs and non-tariffs barriers be "not on the whole higher or more restrictive". Secondly, the rules for RIAs to be found in Article V of the GATS seem, as a whole, to be weaker than those in the GATT, considering the fact that, in the GATS, no liberalisation in services is explicitly required for an agreement to be acceptable. Rather, a simple standstill on existing measures is sufficient according to Article I:b of the GATS[7]. An RTA under Article V of the GATS should have substantial sectoral coverage, in terms of the number of sectors, volume of trade and modes of supply. The "substantially all trade" ambiguity is slightly abated *vis-à-vis* Article XXIV of the GATT. The

5. Ramachandran Lija: "SAARC: Where Does It Stand?," in: Basavaraja M.G. : *World Trade Organisation, Regional Trading Arrangements and India*, Serials Publications, New Delhi 2003, pp. 293-294.
6. Abbott Frederick: "North American Economic Integration: Implications for the WTO, the EU and Asia," in Snyder Francis (Ed.): *Regional and Global Regulation of International Trade*, Hart Publishing 2002, p. 80.
7. See: Park Sung-Hoon: "Regionalism, Open Regionalism and Article XXIV GATT," in Snyder Francis (Ed.): *Regional and Global Regulation of International Trade*, Hart Publishing 2002, p. 277.

debate on the meaning of these matters as well as on any inter-linkage between Article V of the GATS and Article XXIV of the GATT is much less advanced than the debate on systemic issues related to trade in goods even as Article V of the GATS is limited in terms when compared to Article XXIV of the GATT.

B. Distinction Between the Agreements of Cooperation and Agreements of Economic Integration

Economic regionalism can have the following two aspects:

1. *Simple Agreements of Economic Cooperation*

On the one hand, economic regionalism could be concretised by simple agreements of economic cooperation like the ones establishing the OECD, ASEAN etc. Their aim is to establish a better coordination of the national economic policies with just few obligations accepted on a case-by-case basis. As those agreements do not affect in a large way the orientations taken by the WTO, they are not concerned by the status of RTAs in the WTO.

2. *Regional Trade Agreements having the Aim to Create an Integration*

On the other hand, certain agreements primarily aim at building an integration of the national member countries. Those agreements are of particular importance for the WTO as they proceed to the withdrawal of trade barriers or they institute common policies for their members.[8] On account of their consistent impact on world

8. For example, the objective of the EEC Treaty was to establish a common market between the Member States of the Community in which goods, people, services and capital could move freely. In order to achieve this, a 12-year transitional period up to 31st December 1969 was introduced. For the sake of cohesion, liberalisation at the internal level had to be in tune with that at the external level and the Community, therefore, has had sole competence for common commercial policy since the transitional period ended. Up to 1970, it was for Member States to coordinate their trade relations with non-Community countries. Gradually, the expansion of international trade made common commercial policy into one of the Community's most important policies. The common commercial policy, established by European Community Treaty, is then one the main foundations of that Community, for if the internal mechanisms of the common market were to work effectively, coordinated action in external trade was also essential. The most important Article of the Treaty is the 133EC, which laid down operating principles for the common commercial policy, in particular requiring it to be based on "uniform principles", giving the Commission exclusive rights to make proposals under this policy, and conferring on the Commission exclusive competence to conduct trade negotiations with third countries on behalf of the Community. See Chaisse Julien: "The European Common Commercial Policy facing the Challenges of the Globalisation," in: Aggarwal Manmohan *et al.*, (eds): *The Future of the Global Economy: Regional Trajectories and Global Institutions. (forthcoming January 2005).*

trade, such agreements are identified by the WTO and they could take the following two forms:

The Customs Union, defined as *"the substitution of a single customs territory for two or more customs territories"* (Art XXIV 8 i)), under the condition that "duties and other restrictive regulations of commerce [...] are eliminated with respect to substantially all the trade between the constituent territories of the union or at least with respect to substantially all the trade in products originating in such territories" (Art XXIV 8 i).

The Free Trade Area, defined as *"a group of two or more customs territories in which the duties and other restrictive regulations of commerce [...] are eliminated on substantially all the trade between the constituent territories in products originating in such territories"* (Art XXIV 8 b).

Both free trade areas and customs unions however share a common goal: elimination of tariffs and non-tariffs barriers "on substantially all the trade between the constituent territories". The principal source of disagreement regards the interpretation of the phrase "substantially all trade." Different readings of the term are basically linked to two distinct schools of thought – the quantitative, which necessitates that a substantial volume of the trade be liberalised[9] and the qualitative, according to which no major sector of economic activity should be excluded from the coverage of the agreement.[10] In this regard, it is suggested that parties to RTAs should be made to comply with a higher threshold that could be the Australian proposal of liberalisation of at least 95 per cent of the trade or alternatively, all the trade. Other interpretative problems relate to unilateral preference (reciprocity under Article XXIV: 8) and the Exceptions Clause, and within the latter, questions of whether the list is exhaustive, the treatment of the Safeguards Measures under Article XXIX and if the principle of non-discrimination ought to be observed.[11] In this regard, it may be

9. Hence, a requirement to liberalise all trade would deprive the word "substantial" of its meaning.

10. The exclusion of agriculture or textiles and clothing, for instance, would therefore fail to meet the "substantially all trade" test.

11. About how GATT article XXIV regulate RTA regulation of national TBTSPS measures. Trachtman Joel: "Towards Open Recognition? Standardisation and Regional Integration under Article XXIV of GATT," *Journal of International Economic Law* 2003 Volume 6 No. 2, p.470.

argued that the list of exceptions is not exhaustive and Articles XIX ("Emergency Action on Imports of Particular Products") and XXI ("Security Exceptions") of the GATT could be relied upon by parties to RTAs to restrict each other's trade, provided the conditions specified in these Articles are met. On the issue of non-discriminatory imposition of such measures, it would be more consistent with the spirit of Article XXIV, if parties to RTAs excluded imports of their partners from the application of trade-restrictive measures.[12]

C. Trade Creating Integrations (for World Trade): Acceptance of Regional Integration Under the WTO

"The basic idea behind provisions in Article XXIV is that the GATT will, in principle, permit discrimination but only in return for full fledged liberalisation among the members of an FTA or a CU"[13]. To that extent, Article XXIV: 4 states that the purpose of an RTA 'should be to facilitate trade' among parties and 'not to raise barriers to the trade' of third parties. One of the most intractable issues that have arisen in connection with the interpretation of this Article concerns its scope and its relationship with other provisions of Article XXIV. Is it a general statement of principle or a separate obligation that needs to be complied with by the parties to the RTA? The Understanding on the Interpretation of Article XXIV ("the Understanding") could not resolve the issue but the Appellate Body in the Turkey-Textiles case[14] concluded that "Paragraph 4 contains purposive, and not operative, language. It does not set forth a separate obligation itself but, rather, sets forth the overriding and pervasive purpose for Article XXIV which is manifested in operative language in the specific obligations that are found elsewhere in Article XXIV." It is proposed that the Committee on RTAs ("CRTA[15]") should formally adopt the views of the Appellate Body in this matter as it would be extremely difficult to insist that the

12. A view implicitly shared by the Panel in the Argentina safeguards case.

13. Park Sung-Hoon: "Regionalism, Open Regionalism and Article XXIV GATT," in: Snyder Francis (Ed.): *Regional and Global Regulation of International Trade*, Hart Publishing 2002, p. 276.

14. Report of the Appellate Body, *Turkey - Restrictions on Imports of Textile and Clothing Products*, WT/DS34/AB/R, 22 October 1999.

15. The CRTA was established by the General Council of the WTO in February 1996 to carry out the examination of agreements referred to it by the Council for Trade in Goods, the Council for Trade in Services and the Committee on Trade and Development.

formation of a free trade area ("FTA") or customs union ("CU") should not result in a rise in the barriers facing any of the products of any of the WTO Members. Hence, a global approach would be far more realistic and would adequately protect the interests of third countries given that it incorporates certain elements.

Article XXIV: 5, which was intended to safeguard and promote the interests of third countries from the RTAs formed by WTO Members, is one of the most controversial provisions in the GATT, based on a set of assumptions. Interpretative problems have been experienced regarding the meaning of the phrases "as between the territories of contracting parties" and "duties and other regulations of commerce", amongst others. In particular, it results in inadequate focus on non-tariff barriers ("NTBs") like rules of origin and quantitative restrictions. In this regard, it is proposed that the CRTA should specify that the phrase "regulations of commerce" includes quantitative restrictions and rules of origin so that these qualify within the meaning of Article XXIV: 5. However, this should not mean that the parties to a RTA could introduce these NTBs arbitrarily. Hence, with respect to quantitative restrictions, parties to RTAs should not be allowed to circumvent other GATT obligations as laid out in Article XI of the GATT merely by invoking the provisions of Article XXIV. In particular the "necessity test[16]", as laid down by the Appellate Body in the *Turkey – India Textiles Case*[17], should be formally endorsed by the CRTA. As for rules of origin, since these could be used by parties to RTAs to divert trade from more competitive third-country sources, harmonisation of preferential rules of origin is proposed.[18] In the interim, the WTO should insist on adopting the least distorting rules of origin by parties to FTAs. Moreover, the rules of origin applied by WTO Members forming a FTA should not be

---

16. The Appellate Body stated that the adoption of quantitative restrictions upon the formation of a CU will only be allowed where it can be demonstrated by the parties to the agreement that in the absence of the imposition of those measures, it would not be possible to establish the CU. Thus, in effect, parties to the agreement have the burden of proof if they wish to introduce measures generally prohibited under the GATT.

17. Report of the Appellate Body, *Turkey - Restrictions on Imports of Textile and Clothing Products*, WT/DS34/AB/R, 22 October 1999.

18. The point has been made in the CRTA that an FTA 'could be just as significant in its trade impact as a CU, but faces significantly less stringent rules.' This is because there exist no explicit WTO disciplines on the use of preferential rules of origin that are a feature of FTAs.

"more restrictive than the *status-quo ante* regional content of exports." On whether the general incidence of duties and regulations of commerce has become more or less restrictive following the formation of a CU, it may be pointed out that the Understanding clarified that the applied rate of duty needs to be considered in carrying out the evaluation, but even the clarifications here are not without their limitations. Furthermore, to ensure the adequate protection of third country rights, parties to RTAs should be obliged to extend their preferences to all Members of the WTO within a 10-year period. However, given the possible enormous political backlash associated with this, it is proposed that parties to CUs should be required to adopt the lowest MFN tariff on every product which was being applied by any of the parties to the RTA before the formation of the CU. Regarding the issue of a transitional period for the formation of FTAs, the conditions under which Members could obtain an extension of the time period, need to be specified.

II. WTO Conditions on the Legal Validity of Regional Economic Integrations

Because only the good economic integrations have to be encouraged, the WTO imposes some conditions on the procedure and on the substance of the RTAs. The fundamental aim is to ensure that those integrations will be good not only for the contracting parties but also for the third parties! To that extent, the central role in the process of validation of any RTA is handled by the Committee of Regional Trade Agreements (CRTA). On 6th February 1996, the WTO General Council created the Regional Trade Agreements Committee. Its purpose is to examine regional groups and to assess whether they are consistent with WTO rules. The committee is also examining how regional arrangements might affect the multilateral trading system, and what might the relationship be between regional and multilateral arrangements. The process of validation depends on procedural conditions (A) and substantial conditions (B).

A. Procedural Conditions

1. Obligation of Notification of the RTA

Any WTO Member that wants to initiate one of the two kinds of economic integration must inform the Council for Trade in Goods

(Art XXIV: 7 and paragraph 7 Understanding on the Interpretation of Article XXIV of the General Agreement on Tariffs and Trade 1994). Further, this notification has to be made before the entry into force of the agreements. The Council for Trade in Goods adopts the terms of reference and transfers the trade agreement to the Committee on Regional Trade Agreements (CRTA) for examination. Such a notification is compulsory in the field of services too (Art V.7 (a) of the GATS). Then the Council on Trade in Services may decide to pass the agreement to the CRTA for examination. Such an examination is then optional and not mandatory as it is in the case of the GATT (Art V.7 (b) of the GATS).

According to Article XXIV: 7(a), the CRTA can make any recommendation it deems appropriate and § 7 to 10 of Understanding on the Interpretation of Article XXIV of the General Agreement on Tariffs and Trade 1994. It may deem the RTA to be inconsistent with the reference agreement (GATT or GATS). These recommendations are compulsory and "the parties shall not maintain or put into force, as the case may be, such an agreement if they are not prepared to modify it in accordance with these recommendations" (Art XXIV: 7 ii) is fine.

Article XXIV: 7 is one of the most abused provisions of Article XXIV routinely ignored by WTO Members. Under this, WTO Members entering into RTAs are required to notify their agreements to the CRTA before implementation but in practice it works the other way round. A case in point is the CU between EU and Turkey. The purpose of prior notification was to allow the CRTA to conduct a quick examination of the RTA in order to determine the creation of trade between parties without raising barriers to the trade of third countries. In this regard, therefore, incentives need to be created to convince Members of the necessity of such an examination.

This system of examination has never worked in a proper way. Indeed, only in a few cases have the parties reached an agreement on the validity of the FTA. In fact, the FTA has been explicitly declared valid only 5 times out of 106!

In the period 1948-1994, the GATT received 124 notifications of RTAs (relating to trade in goods), and since the creation of the WTO in 1995, over 130 additional arrangements covering trade in goods or services have been notified.

Table 17.1

Notifications of RTAs in Force to GATT/WTO
As of December 1, 2004

	Accessions	*New RTAs*	*Total*
GATT Art. XXIV (FTA)	5	136	**141**
GATT Art. XXIV (CU)	5	9	**14**
Enabling Clause	0	19	**19**
GATS Art. V	2	32	**34**
Total	12	196	208

Examination Process

Status	*WTO Provision*			*Grand Total*
	Enabling Clause	*GATS Art. V*	*GATT Art XXIV*	
Examination not requested	16	2	2	20
Factual examination not started	0	9	28	37
Under factual examination	1	15	23	39
Factual examination concluded	0	4	70	74
Consultations on draft report	0	4	8	12
Report adopted	2	0	24	26
Grand Total	19	34	155	208

Source: WTO Secretariat (December 2004).

As a result, it must be stressed that neither the Contracting Parties in the GATT era, nor the Council for Trade in Goods today can block the entry into force of an RTA. Consequently, these regional agreements benefit from a presumption of validity as long as they have not been declared otherwise.

Furthermore, "any interim agreement referred to in sub-paragraphs (*a*) and (*b*) shall include a plan and schedule for the formation of such a customs union or of such a free-trade area within a reasonable length of time" (art XXIV 5(c)). The plan or schedules are elements examined (Art XXIV 7). But the "reasonable length of time" has always been a very controversial point. Now, the Understanding on the Interpretation of Article XXIV of the General

Agreement on Tariffs and Trade 1994 gives a very clear indication by saying that it should be 10 years.[19]

This time period could be quite short, especially if we consider that the transitional period at the time of the establishment of the EEC was 12 years. Furthermore, there can be some differences in the case of developing countries, like the Enabling Clause.

The Enabling Clause, introduced in 1979 as part of the results of the Tokyo Round, covers RTAs in the area of trade in goods between developing countries. The parties to such an agreement are to notify the agreement to the WTO Committee on Trade and Development, including action to introduce modification or withdrawal of their mutual preferences. However, such agreements are not subject to the same examination process as agreements notified under Article XXIV. It thus significantly relaxes the conditions for creating RTAs that include only developing countries and thus dilutes even the weak discipline imposed by Article XXIV of the GATT.

2. *Periodic Examination of the RTAs*

Theoretically, a periodical examination of all RTAs should be made. But once again, the practice of GATT 1947 has renounced this point. However the Understanding on the Interpretation of Article XXIV of the General Agreement on Tariffs and Trade 1994 plans some regular reports (without any indications of length): "Customs unions and constituents of free-trade areas shall report periodically to the Council for Trade in Goods, as envisaged by the CONTRACTING PARTIES to GATT 1947 in their instruction to the GATT 1947 Council concerning reports on regional agreements (BISD 18S/38), on the operation of the relevant agreement. Any significant changes and/or developments in the agreements should be reported as they occur".

B. Examination of Substantial Compatibility with GATT/GATS Provisions

Two conditions are put forward to validate RTAs and to ensure so that they are really "trade creating".

---

19. The "reasonable length of time" referred to in paragraph 5(c) of Article XXIV should exceed 10 years only in exceptional cases. In cases where Members party to an interim agreement believe that 10 years would be insufficient they shall provide a full explanation to the Council for Trade in Goods of the need for a longer period. Understanding on the Interpretation of Article XXIV of the General Agreement on Tariffs and Trade 1994, §3.

1. Essential of the Exchanges or the Internal Trade Requirement

First, duties and other restrictive regulations of commerce must be eliminated between the constituent territories of the union or between the constituent territories but only "with respect to substantially all the trade" (Art XXIV 8 (i) and (ii)) in the case of a free-trade area as well as a customs union. Some quantitative criteria have at times been proposed, but none has been used and there is no clear legal definition of this "substantially all the trade". In fact, the phrase has never been defined even in the Understanding on the Interpretation of Article XXIV of the General Agreement on Tariffs and Trade 1994.

Moreover the Appellate Body itself noticed that "Neither the GATT CONTRACTING PARTIES nor the WTO Members have ever reached an agreement on the interpretation of the term "substantially" in this provision.[20] It is clear, though, that "substantially all the trade" is not the same as *all* the trade, and also that "substantially all the trade" is something considerably more than merely *some* of the trade. We note also that the terms of sub-paragraph 8(a)(i) provide that members of a customs union may maintain, where necessary, in their internal trade, certain restrictive regulations of commerce that are otherwise permitted under Articles XI through XV and under Article XX of the GATT 1994. Thus, we agree with the Panel that the terms of sub-paragraph 8(a)(i) offer "some flexibility" to the constituent members of a customs union when liberalising their internal trade in accordance with this sub-paragraph.[21] Yet we caution that the degree of "flexibility" that sub-paragraph 8(a)(i) allows is limited by the requirement that "duties and other restrictive regulations of commerce" be "eliminated with respect to substantially all" internal trade".[22]

Besides, this rule is very smoothly applied to developing countries through the Enabling Clause 79.[23]

20. Report of the Appellate Body, *Turkey - Restrictions on Imports of Textile and Clothing Products*, WT/DS34/AB/R, 22 October 1999, para. 9.148.

21. Report of the Appellate Body, *Turkey - Restrictions on Imports of Textile and Clothing Products*, WT/DS34/AB/R, 22 October 1999, para. 9.146.

22. Report of the Appellate Body, *Turkey - Restrictions on Imports of Textile and Clothing Products*, WT/DS34/AB/R 22 October 1999, paragraph 48. For a comment of this report; See: Mathis James: WTO, *Turkey – Restrictions on Imports of Textile and Clothing Products*, Legal Issues of European Integration Volume 27 2000 n°1, pp. 103-114.

23. See supra II) A) 1).

2. The External Trade Requirement

Pursuant to Article XXIV 4 and 5 (i) and (ii), there is a general obligation "not to raise barriers to the trade of other contracting parties with such territories". As a result, the duties and commercial regulations must not be more restrictive or higher than before the establishment of the economic integration. This one could be realising either as a free-trade area or as a customs union. In addition, while the GATS does not deal with external protection, Article V:5 GATS "makes it plain that compensation analogous to that offered in the GATT context under GATT article XXIV:6 will be offered in the GATS context if a WTO Member entering into an PTA has to modify its schedule."[24]

a) In the Case of a Customs Union

The first case is that of a customs union that pre-supposes the existence of a Common External tariff itself defined as "the uniform tariff rates applied by the members of a customs union against non-members. Members of a customs union agree to eliminate or phase-out all tariffs among themselves. At the same time, they replace their individual tariffs with a single (tariff) applied to third countries. Membership of a customs union may, therefore, entail an unchanged, higher or lower tariff by individual members on a given product. Under WTO rules, the resulting changes may not be used to increase the level of protection overall. Free-trade areas do not have a common external tariff."[25]

In this case, *"the duties and other regulations of commerce imposed at the institution of any such union or interim agreement in respect of trade with contracting parties not parties to such union or agreement shall not* ***on the whole be higher*** *or more restrictive than* ***the general incidence*** *of the duties and regulations of commerce applicable in the constituent territories prior to the formation of such union or the adoption of such interim agreement"* (Art XXIV 5 (i)). There are consequently two obligations for the external trade requirement: not to raise the overall level of protection above a certain threshold and a specific obligation to compensate in cases

24. Matsushita Mitsuo, Mavroidis Petros C. and Schoenbaum Thomas J. : *The World Trade Organisation - Law, Practice, and Policy*, Oxford University Press, Oxford 2003, p. 356.

25. "Common External Tariff," in: Goode Walter: *Dictionary of Trade Policy Terms*, Cambridge University Press, Cambridge 2003, p. 69.

where customs duties in some constituents of a CU had to be raised to match the CU-level.

Once again, this has been a very controversial provision, difficult to comprehend. On this point, the Understanding on the Interpretation of Article XXIV of the General Agreement on Tariffs and Trade 1994 attempts to bring a clarification: "The evaluation under paragraph 5(a) of Article XXIV of the general incidence of the duties and other regulations of commerce applicable before and after the formation of a customs union shall in respect of duties and charges be based upon an overall assessment of weighted average tariff rates and of customs duties collected" §2. "The Secretariat shall compute the weighted average tariff rates and customs duties collected in accordance with the methodology used in the assessment of tariff offers in the Uruguay Round of Multilateral Trade Negotiations".

b) In the Case of Free-Trade Areas

Pursuant to article XXIV: 5 (ii) "the duties and other regulations of commerce maintained in each of the constituent territories and applicable at the formation of such freetrade area or the adoption of such interim agreement to the trade of contracting parties not included in such area or not parties to such agreement shall not be higher or more restrictive than the corresponding duties and other regulations of commerce existing in the same constituent territories prior to the formation of the free-trade area". As in the case of a free-trade area, there is, of course, no common external tariff. Article XXIV concerns itself with internal regulations such as rules of origin, which can affect external protection. Indeed, "rules of origin are particularly appropriate in an FTA context: unless goods circulating through an FTA are accompanied by a certificate of origin, exporters will have an incentive to the cheapest port of entry (because external protection remains an issue of national sovereignty, and it could very well be the case that there are asymmetries as to the level of customs duties among members of an FTA). The first best would be that the national systems conferring origin at the pre-FTA stage remain in force unchanged post-FTA. This is almost never the case, however. Members of the FTA negotiate regional rules of origin that, from an empirical perspective, are, more often than not, stricter after the creation of an FTA. In the absence of a WTO Agreement on Rules of

Origin, regionalization of rules of origin can be challenged only under GATT Article XXIV:5(b)."[26]

3. Protection of Third-Countries: Renegotiation of Compensation after the Establishment of an RTA

According to Article XXIV: 6: "If, in fulfilling the requirements of subparagraph 5 (*a*), a contracting party proposes to increase any rate of duty inconsistently with the provisions of Article II, the procedure set forth in Article XXVIII shall apply. In providing for compensatory adjustment, due account shall be taken of the compensation already afforded by the reduction brought about in the corresponding duty of the other constituents of the union".

While most issues of interpretation *vis-à-vis* Paragraph 6 have been resolved by the Understanding, one persistent matter pertains to the calculation of the compensation in respect of increased NTBs subsequent to the formation of a RTA. The Understanding notes that for the overall assessment of the incidence of other regulations of commerce that cannot be quantified and aggregated easily, "the examination of individual measures, regulations, products covered and trade flows may be required."[27]

III. Panorama of Indian Participation in RTAs

India is a party to the following major Agreements:

A. India-Bangladesh

A trade agreement signed with Bangladesh, which came into force on 4 October 1980 and could be extended by further periods of three years, was valid up to 3 October 2001.[28] India then proposed to extend the agreement up to 3 October 2004. In 1997, a transit route of 60 km. through Indian territory was opened for trade between Bangladesh and Nepal. India continues to grant duty exemptions to most goods produced in Nepal. Preferences apply to some basic

26. Matsushita Mitsuo, Mavroidis Petros C. and Schoenbaum Thomas J. : *The World Trade Organisation - Law, Practice, and Policy*, Oxford University Press, Oxford 2003, pp. 351-352.
27. To go further, See: Matsushita Mitsuo, Mavroidis Petros C. and Schoenbaum Thomas J. : *The World Trade Organisation - Law, Practice, and Policy*, Oxford University Press, Oxford 2003, pp. 354-355.
28. Article XIII of the Trade Agreement between India and Bangladesh [Online]. Available at: http://commin.nic.in/doc/trade_agrmnt.htm *[5 July 2001]*.

goods and all manufactured goods other than: alcoholic liquors/ beverages and their concentrates except industrial spirits; perfumes and cosmetics with non-Nepalese/non-Indian brand names; and cigarettes and tobacco. India revised and reviewed certain provisions of the India-Nepal Treaty, which was valid until 5 December 2001, because some Nepali products (e.g. hydrogenated vegetable oil, acrylic yarns, copper wire, iron pipes, and zinc oxide) flooded the Indian market.[29] The agreement was renegotiated on 6 March 2002. Imports from Nepal are exempt from special additional duties (SADs), but are subject to additional duties (ADs) (Chapter III(2)(iii)). A new Transit Treaty between India and Nepal was signed on 5 January 1999. The new Treaty, valid for periods of seven years (until 5 January 2006), can be renewed automatically for further periods of seven years, unless either party gives written notice of its intention to terminate, six months before the date of termination of the treaty.

B. India-Sri Lanka

India and Sri Lanka signed a free-trade agreement (FTA) on 28 December 1998, which came into operation on 1 March 2000. India grants duty-free access to over 1,000 tariff lines and a 50 per cent margin of preference to all other items except those on a negative list. Tariffs are to be reduced to zero over a period of three years. Tariff concessions on textiles are 25 per cent below the MFN rate. India has retained some 400 items in the negative list, including garments, petrochemicals, alcoholic spirits, and coconut oil. Tariff quotas apply to tea and garments under the FTA. India's tariff quota for tea was set at 15 million kg./year at a preferential rate of 50 per cent. The tariff quota for garments should not exceed 8 million pieces/year at a concession of 50 per cent, of which 6 million should be manufactured from fabrics of Indian origin.[30] Imports of tea are allowed only through the ports of Kochi and Kolkata, and garments

29. Reuters, 14 and 19 August 2001.

30. Origin is determined according to domestic content and substantial transformation. Thus, origin is granted when raw materials/inputs originate in countries other than the contracting parties (i.e. Sri Lanka or India) or are of undetermined origin if they do not exceed 65 per cent of the f.o.b. value of the final good. If raw material/ inputs originate in Sri Lanka for production in India (or vice-versa) domestic content can be reduced to 25 per cent. The final good must also undergo substantial transformation at the four-digit level of the Harmonised System.

may be imported only through Chennai and Mumbai. The agreement allows for the use of safeguard and anti-dumping measures. In addition, in case of balance-of-payments difficulties, members may provisionally suspend the preferential treatment. When any such measures are taken, the member that initiates the action has to simultaneously notify the other party. India also participates in the Bangladesh, India, Myanmar, Sri Lanka, Thailand–Economic Cooperation (BIMST–EC), which came into force in 1997 as a forum to facilitate and promote trade, investment, and technical cooperation among the member countries, with the objective of creating a free-trade area. BIMST–EC is designed to act as a link between SAARC and ASEAN.[31]

C. South Asian Preferential Trade Arrangement (SAPTA)[32]

1. From SAARC to SAPTA (Notified to WTO)

The Sixth South Asian Association for Regional Co-operation (SAARC)[33] Summit held in Colombo in 1991 strongly mooted the idea of a SAARC Preferential Trading Arrangement (SAPTA) and the Foreign Ministers of all the member states (India, Pakistan, Bangladesh, Nepal, Sri Lanka, Bhutan and Maldives) signed the Agreement on 2 April 1993 during the Seventh SAARC Summit in Dhaka. SAPTA became effective from 7 December 1995. The basic principles of SAPTA are as follows: overall reciprocity and mutuality of advantages, step-by-step negotiations and extension of preferential trade arrangement in stages, inclusion of all types of products-raw, semi-processed and processed, special and favourable treatment to LDCs. "The first round of negotiations under SAPTA took place in 1995. By December 2000,[34] three trade negotiations (were) completed, under which 5553 items at Harmonised System (HS) six digit levels (were) offered for tariff and non-tariff concessions by the

---

31. Ministry of Commerce and Industry (2000).

32. Bangladesh Bhutan India Maldives Nepal Pakistan Sri Lanka, For an extensive description of this agreement, See: Gupta Anshuman: *SAARC – SAPTA to SAFTA*, Maulana Abdul Kalam Azad Institute of Asian Studies (Kolkata), Shipra Publications, New Delhi 2002, pp. 71-83.

33. On the Objectives of SAARC itself, See: Mangalamurthy S. : *South Asian Association for Regional Co-operation*, Chethana Book House, Mysore 2003, pp. 19-41.

34. To go further in details in the successive stages of negotiations, See: Gupta Anshuman: *SAARC – SAPTA to SAFTA*, Maulana Abdul Kalam Azad Institute of Asian Studies (Kolkata), Shipra Publications, New Delhi 2002, pp. 85-11.

member states. India being the largest economy of the region, offered the maximum number of items (2925 items) for preferential trade."[35]

a) Salient Features of SAPTA

SAPTA provides for the exchange of concessions between its Members on tariffs, para-tariffs, non-tariff measures and direct trade measures. Tariff preferences can be exchanged using any of the following four approaches:

- **Product-by-product,** which implies negotiations at the HS-6 digit tariff line level;
- **Across the board,** which connotes a uniform reduction applicable to all products being negotiated;
- **Sectoral,** construing agreements on specified products or groups thereof closely-related in end use or in production; and
- **Direct trade measures,** which include measures conducive to promoting mutual trade of Contracting States such as long and medium term contracts containing import and supply commitments for specific products, buyback arrangements, state trading operations, and government and public sector procurement.

Additionally, the following provisions are significant from the perspective of the effectiveness of the SAPTA and the extent to which it can be used to increase the region's exports and trading opportunities:

- **Coverage:** All products, manufactures and commodities in their raw, semi-processed and processed forms are covered under the SAPTA.
- **Rules of origin:** SAPTA has stringent and well-defined rules of origin requirements for both LDC and non-LDC SAPTA Members, which must be met for imports to be eligible for tariff preferences. There are rules for both goods "wholly produced or obtained" and for goods "not wholly produced

---

35. Gupta, Anshuman: *SAARC – SAPTA to SAFTA*, Maulana Abdul Kalam Azad Institute of Asian Studies (Kolkata), Shipra Publications, New Delhi 2002, p. 86.

or obtained" in an exporting SAPTA country. The former category includes domestic raw materials, agricultural products, fish, waste and scrap, and products wholly obtained from these inputs.

- **Special and differential treatment for LDCs:** These include, *inter alia,* provisions for deeper and wider tariff preferences, removal of non-tariff and para-tariff barriers, and favourable terms for technical assistance. Interestingly, concessions accorded by a non-LDC to an LDC SAPTA Member do not apply to non-LDC Members of this agreement. This is an exception to the general principle of MFN, which is otherwise applicable to the concessions extended under SAPTA from LDC/non-LDC to all Members and from LDC/non-LDC to LDC Members.

b) Trade Liberalisation under SAPTA:
Tariff Concessions and Product Lines

There have been three rounds of trade liberalisation under SAPTA so far. During the First and Second Round, trade negotiations were conducted on a product-by-product basis. In the Third Round, the negotiations were also conducted chapter-wise. For the Fourth Round, it has been decided that the negotiations would, as far as possible, be conducted on Chapter-wise, Sectoral and Across-the-Board basis. While the first round initiated in December 1995, saw 226 products being put on the table, this number further increased to 1868 and 3456 in the next two rounds. Consequently, by the end of October 1999, close to 5500 products under the HS-6 classification, were liberalised by the Members. As of now, over 5100 products stand liberalised under SAPTA, as can be seen from Table 17.2. However, the distribution of these concessions is lop-sided, with 50 per cent of the coverage being on account of concessions made by India alone and that too, predominantly in favour of LDCs in the South Asian region.

Unfortunately, most of the products that were put on the concessions' list are either not relevant from the perspective of their importance in the trade composition of SAPTA Members or have low trade intensities. As can be seen from the Table 17.2, the margins of preference vary widely from 10 per cent to 100 per cent but broadly

Table 17.2

Tariff Concessions Under SAPTA

Country	No. of Products	%age of Total Products	No. of Products: To LDCs alone:	No. of Products: To non-LDCs alone:	Depth of Tariff Concessions: To LDCs alone:	Depth of Tariff Concessions: To non-LDCs alone:
Bangladesh	572	11.2	116	455	10 % and 15%	10%
Bhutan	266	5.2	159	107	10%, 13%, 15%, 18% and 20%	10% and 15%
India	2565	50.3	2025	500	50%, 60%, 100%	10%, 15%, 20%, 25%, 30%, 40%, 50% and 90%
Maldives	390	7.6	3	368	15%	5% and 10%
Nepal	426	8.4	164	227	10% and 15%	5%, 7.5% and 10%
Pakistan	685	13.4	397	274	10%, 15% and 30%	10% and 20%
Sri Lanka	197	3.9	53	92	10%, 15%, 20%, 30%, 35%, 50%, 60% and 75%	10% and 20%
TOTAL	**5101**	**100**	**2917**	**2023**		

Source: SAPTA Merged Consolidated National Schedule of Concessions.

range from 10 per cent to 20 per cent for most products on which concessions have been offered to non-LDC SAPTA Members. Moreover, as is indicated in the Figure 2 (first panel), 60 per cent of all products on which concessions have been offered pertain only to products of trade interest to LDC SAPTA Members. This, therefore, does not accommodate the export interests of India, Pakistan and Sri Lanka. Further, there exist wide disparities in the coverage of products of export interest to non-LDC SAPTA Members, ranging from about 20 per cent for India to close to 95 per cent for Maldives. Finally, looking at the ratio of concessional tariff lines to the 5300 total HS-6 tariff lines on which each country can potentially trade[36] (second panel), one finds that all SAPTA Members, with the exception of India, have put less than 13 per cent of their total tariff lines on the negotiating table. While the number for India is close to 50 per cent, as also mentioned above, more than 80 per cent of this

36. This again provides an estimate of the likely upper bound as LDC SAPTA Members import a far smaller range of commodities than the 5300 total tariff lines at the HS-6 level recognised by the World Customs Organisation.

Figure 17.2

Product Coverage Under SAPTA

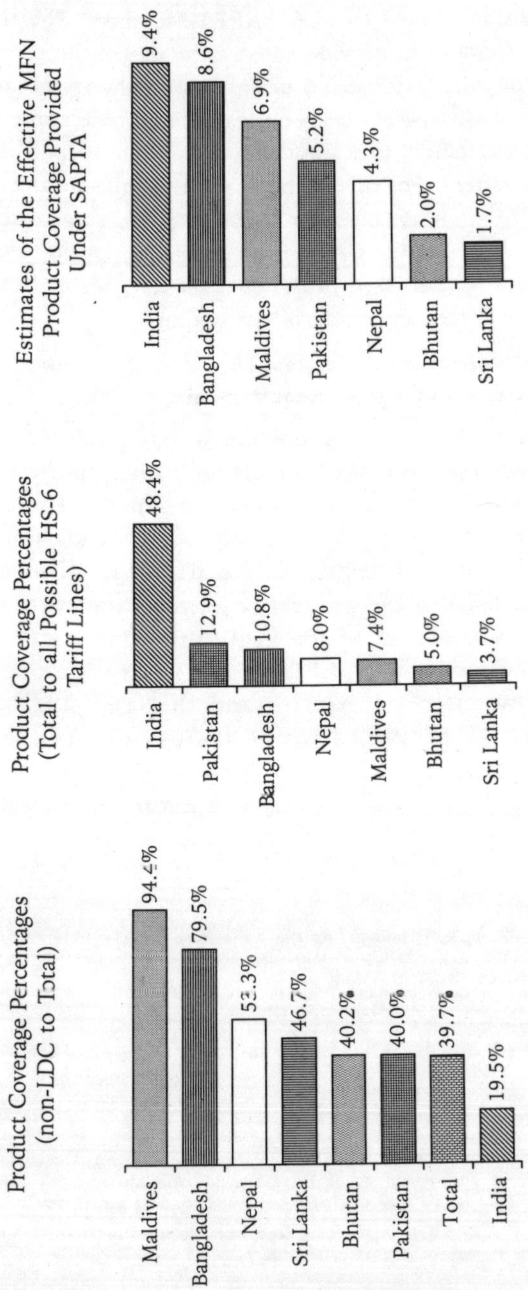

Source: SAPTA Merged Consolidated National Schedule of Concessions.

is concessions offered to LDC SAPTA Members. The third panel therefore attempts to provide some estimates of the effective MFN product coverage[37] provided under SAPTA by its Members as a percentage of all possible HS-6 tariff lines and once again, these turn out to be extremely low numbers, less than 10 per cent for all SAPTA Members. For all of these reasons, the product coverage under SAPTA does not meet the "substantially all trade" requirement in Article XXIV: 8 of the GATT.[38] In addition, stringent rules of origin requirements, as discussed in the next section, further limit SAPTA's potential for increasing trade in the region.

c) Trade Liberalisation Under SAPTA:
Stringent Rules of Origin Requirements

The rules of origin for goods not wholly produced or obtained in the region and those for "cumulative" origin further restrict the scope of SAPTA for liberalising trade in the region. SAPTA provides that the total value of the materials, parts or produce originating from non-contracting states[39] (or of undetermined origin) and used in the production of the exported item, should not exceed 50 per cent of the FOB value (limit raised to 60 per cent after amendment to SAPTA at the Twenty-first Session of the SAARC Council of Ministers) and that the final process of manufacture be performed within the territory of the exporting Member. This is equivalent to a local content requirement of 50 per cent (40 per cent post-amendment) of FOB price. The provisions for cumulative rules of origin require that goods

---

37. This is obtained by multiplying the proportions in the first and second panels, as the former is a measure of MFN product coverage under SAPTA and the latter, a measure of actual to potential trade.

38. Pursell and Sattar (2003) reach a similar conclusion in 'Trade Policies in South Asia: An Overview.' They point out that for all the seven Members of the SAPTA, only 8.4 per cent of the 5300 HS-6 tariff lines for imports from India, Pakistan and Sri Lanka, and 6.2 per cent for imports from LDC SAPTA Members, are actually covered by regional tariff concessions. In fact, the conclusion remains unchanged if the concessions are evaluated in terms of import value in lieu of number of product lines. As an illustration, in 1998, only 15 per cent (US $ 480 mn) of total imports of SAPTA countries from within the region were subject to a SAPTA concession by at least one Member during the three negotiating Rounds. This in no way qualifies as "substantially all trade."

39. The value of the non-originating items is taken either as the CIF value where proven or as the earliest ascertainable price of these items in the territory of the Contracting State where processing occurs.

processed in more than one SAPTA Member state have at least 60 per cent of FOB value (reduced to 50 per cent after the amendment) as value added in SAPTA countries to qualify for preferential treatment. Given that value addition in most SAPTA Members is low in many of their most competitive exports, these requirements further limit the effectiveness of the agreement by acting as a credible non-tariff barrier to trade.

Table 17.3

Rules of Origin Requirements Under SAPTA

SAPTA Provisions for Rules of Origin (maximum permissible % of FOB value of imports)	*Before Amendment*		*After Amendment*	
	For Non-LDCs	*For LDCs*	*For Non-LDCs*	*For LDCs*
Rule 3 (a): Not Wholly Produced or Obtained				
Domestic Value Addition in an Exporting Country	50%	40%	40%	30%
Maximum Input permitted from Non-Contracting States	50%	60%	60%	70%
Rule 4: Cumulative Rules of Origin				
Aggregate Domestic Value Addition in an Exporting Country including inputs sourced from within the SAARC region	60%	50%	50%	40%
Maximum Input permitted from Non-Contracting States	40%	50%	50%	60%

Source: SAPTA

d) Results

Not surprisingly, the results have not been satisfactory: the share of intra regional trade in the total trade of SAARC countries is very insignificant. This has not increased even after the formation of the SAPTA. Today, SAARC countries' share in total world trade is not even one per cent, and their trade among themselves lingers below three per cent of their total foreign trade. This compares poorly with more than 60 per cent for intra-EU trade of their global trade and nearly 40 per cent for North America, and East Asia.

Although some liberalisation measures have been taken following the establishment of SAPTA, some of them are regarded as flawed or inadequate. It is even suspected that the concession exercise is just so much playing to the gallery. Consider, for example the fact that the majority of the products offered concessions by members are not being imported by them at all. It is, therefore, not surprising that preferential imports cover only a very small per centage of the total intra-regional trade."[40]

2. *From SAPTA to SAFTA and a Regional Free-Trade Area (Non-notified)*

The SAPTA was always envisaged as a stepping-stone to a South Asian Free-Trade Area, which would essentially involve abolishing intra-regional trade restrictions and tariffs. The mandate for this would be WTO-plus especially with respect to provisions for trade facilitation and would cover both tariff and non-tariff barriers including tariff eliminations without any import restrictions; removal of "structural impediments" to regional trade; harmonisation of customs procedures and documentation; banking facilitation; port and transport facilitation; and facilitation of trade-related services. While there was no two-opinion that such measures would significantly increase trading opportunities in this region, what remained to be seen was whether the countries could muster the required consensus to formalise such an arrangement.[41]

a) SAFTA's Objectives

This has now finally happened. The SAARC Members signed the Agreement on the South Asian Free Trade Area, the SAFTA, on the 6th of January 2004, at the 12th SAARC Summit in Islamabad. The SAFTA is slated to enter into effect on January 1, 2006 and in the interim the tariff concessions granted under SAPTA would continue to hold sway. As expected, the SAFTA Agreement aims to eliminate tariffs, para-tariffs and non-tariff restrictions on the movement of goods in the region through a well-laid out 'Trade Liberalisation Programme' (Article 7).

It also has an elaborate set of additional measures, detailed in Article 8, including adoption of trade facilitation measures and

---

40. Cherunilam Francis: "Economic Integration of Developing Countries with Special Reference to SAPTA and ISFTA," in: Basavaraja M.G. : *World Trade Organisation, Regional Trading Arrangements and India*, Serials Publications, New Delhi 2003, p. 275 and p. 277 and p. 278. In the same direction, Gupta Anshuman: *SAARC – SAPTA to SAFTA*, Maulana Abdul Kalam Azad Institute of Asian Studies (Kolkata), Shipra Publications, New Delhi 2002, p. 45-50 and Mangalamurthy S. : *South Asian Association for Regional Co-operation*, Chethana Book House, Mysore 2003, pp. 167-168.

41. While the SAFTA was supposed to be formalised by 2001 (and in any case, no later than 2005), the deadline was further extended to 2008 for India, Pakistan and Sri Lanka and to 2010 for the four LDCs in the region.

progressive harmonisation of legislations by Contracting States in relevant areas. Like the SAPTA, special and differential treatment is accorded to LDC Contracting States, which finds a place in Article 11, in the 'Trade Liberalisation Programme,' and under the application of Safeguard Measures in Article 16(8) of the SAFTA Agreement. Both these legal texts have similar provisions with respect to the coverage of goods, MFN treatment, suspension of concessions for BoP reasons, non-application, reservations, amendments, withdrawal from Agreement and notification of a Depository, who is the Secretary General of the SAARC in both cases. The main differences in the two Agreements are presented in Table 17.4.

b) Trade Liberalisation Programme
Under the Agreement on SAFTA

The most significant aspect of the SAFTA Agreement is the trade liberalisation envisaged under Article 7. This requires non-LDC Contracting States to reduce tariffs to 20 per cent (30 per cent for LDCs) within two years from the coming into effect of this Agreement i.e. up to January 1, 2008. If the actual tariff rates at that time are below 20 per cent (30 per cent for LDCs), the Agreement requires an annual reduction on the basis of margin of preference of 10 per cent (5 per cent for LDCs) on actual tariff rates for each of the two years. This means that a basic tariff rate of 10 per cent would be reduced to 8.1 per cent for non-LDCs and to 9 per cent for LDCs over the first two years under the SAFTA Agreement. Further, both LDC and non-LDC Contracting States are required to bring their tariff rates to 0-5 per cent within a second time frame of eight and five years,[42] respectively, beginning from January 1, 2008. The Contracting States are encouraged to adopt these reductions in equal annual installments of at least 15 per cent for non-LDCs and 10 per cent for LDCs.[43] However, for products of export interest to LDCs, non-LDC Contracting States are required to bring down tariffs to 0-5 per cent within three years of coming into effect of the Agreement i.e. by Januray 1, 2009.

42. Sri Lanka has been given a second time frame of six years.

43. However all these reductions in tariff are not applicable to tariff lines included in 'Sensitive Lists,' which would have an upper ceiling, would be mutually agreed and negotiated by the Contracting States and made an integral part of the text of this Agreement. These would be subject to a periodic four-year review (or even earlier) by the SAFTA Ministerial Council, with a view to reducing the number of items.

Table 17.4

A Tale of Two Agreements – SAPTA and SAFTA

Subject	*Treatment under SAPTA*	*Treatment under SAFTA*	*Comments*
Trade liberalisation	Provides for arrangements relating to tariff, para tariff, non-tariff and direct trade measures	Provides for an elaborate *'trade liberalisation programme'* under Article 7	SAPTA plus
Additional measures	These relate to trade facilitation and communication provisions[44]	SAPTA plus harmonisation of standards, mutual recognition of tests and accreditation of testing labs, simplification of banking procedures for import financing, *removal of barriers to intra-SAARC investments, rules for fair competition and promotion of venture capital and simplification of procedures for business visas* (Article 8)	WTO plus
Special and differential treatment to LDCs[45]	Provisions for deeper and wider tariff preferences, removal of non-tariff and para-tariff barriers, special consideration in the application of safeguards, flexibility in use of quantitative restrictions and favorable terms for technical assistance (Article 10 and additional measures in Annex 1)	Longer time frames for tariff reduction and flexibility in derogation for products of export interest (Article 7); consider acceptance of price undertakings in the application of trade remedies, *list of possible areas for technical assistance to be negotiated and incorporated in text, appropriate mechanism for compensation for loss of customs revenue* (Article 11); application of safeguards (Article 16.8)	WTO plus
Proposed methodology for negotiations	Product – by – product, sectorally or across the board	Implicitly "across the board"	SAPTA plus
National treatment	No provision	*Provision under Article 5 a la Article III of the GATT*	SAPTA plus

Contd...

...Contd...

Subject	*Treatment under SAPTA*	*Treatment under SAFTA*	*Comments*
Safeguard measures	Aggrieved Contracting State(s) have the right to withdraw equivalent concessions in the event of non-resolution	Provisions in details for investigation procedures; upper time limit for suspension of concessions at 3 years; provision for emergency safeguards in "critical circumstances;" S&D for LDCs	SAPTA plus
Rules of origin	Detailed in Annex 3	To be negotiated and incorporated into the text of the Agreement	
Modification or withdrawal of concessions	Provided for in Article 17	*No provisions*	SAPTA plus
Dispute settlement	Committee has 120 days to resolve the dispute	Detailed provisions in Article 20. The Committee of Experts and SAFTA Ministerial Council perform the functions of the Panel and the Appellate Body, respectively. Dispute resolution may take from 30 days (min) to 240 days (max)	SAPTA plus
General exceptions	Not provided for	*Provided under Article 14 a la Articles XX, XX(a), XX(c) and XX(f) of the GATT*	SAPTA plus

44. These require transport and transit Contracting States to improve the communication system, transport infrastructure and transit facilities for accelerating the growth of trade within the region.

45. The SAFTA Agreement accords very special status to Maldives under Article 12 as despite its potential or actual graduation from being an LDC, it would continue to receive special and differential treatment accorded to LDCs in this Agreement.

D. General System of Trade Preferences among Developing Countries (GSTP)[46]

"Indian products receive preferential treatment under the Generalised System of Preferences (GSP) schemes of Australia, Bulgaria, Canada, Czech Republic, the European Union, Hungary, Japan, New Zealand, Norway, Republic of Belarus, Republic of Poland, Russian Federation, Slovak Republic, Switzerland, and the United States.[47] India participates in the Global System of Trade Preferences among Developing Countries. India offers tariff concessions ranging from 10per cent to 50per cent on 53 tariff lines at the HS six-digit level.[48] The rules of origin for the GSTP have not changed since the previous Review of India."[49] With more than Euro 5 billion of preferential imports to the EU, India has been ranking 2nd among the users of the EU's GSP Since 1990.

E. Bangkok Agreement[50]

India continues to be a party to the Bangkok Agreement signed in 1975.[51] The agreement provides for liberalisation of both tariff and non-tariff barriers; at present it is limited to tariff concessions. India provides concessional entry on 188 tariff lines (at the HS six-digit level), the duty rates are generally 5 per centage points below the

46. Algeria, Argentina, Bangladesh, Benin, Bolivia, Brazil, Cameroon, Chile, Colombia, Cuba, Democratic People's Republic of Korea, Ecuador, Egypt, Ghana, Guinea, Guyana, India, Indonesia, Islamic Republic of Iran, Iraq, Libya, Malaysia, Mexico, Morocco, Mozambique, Myanmar, Nicaragua, Nigeria, Pakistan, Peru, Philippines, Republic of Korea, Romania, Singapore, Sri Lanka, Sudan, Thailand, Trinidad and Tobago, Tunisia, United Republic of Tanzania, Venezuela, Vietnam, Yugoslavia and Zimbabwe.

47. Information compiled by the WTO Secretariat (Statistics Division). Recently, the United States announced that it would enhance preferential trade access under the GSP for 42 Indian products: Jewellery, Leather Goods, and Carpets. (*Reuters*, 8 August 2001, and *Financial Times*, 9 August 2001).

48. Tariff concessions of 50per cent apply to specific tariff lines (HS 4104.21, 4104.22 and 4104.29) and are available only to Bangladesh, United Republic of Tanzania, Benin, Guinea, Haiti, Mozambique, and Sudan (Government of India, 2001).

49. Trade Policy Review Body, Trade Policy Review – India, Report by the Secretariat, WT/TPR/S/100 22 May 2002, p. 22.

50. Bangladesh, China, India, Republic of Korea, Laos, Sri Lanka.

51. The members of the agreement are: Bangladesh, Republic of Korea, Sri Lanka, India, Lao People's Democratic Republic, and China.

standard rate.[52] The third round of negotiations is expected to be launched shortly.[53]

F. India-Thailand FTA[54]

A Framework Agreement for establishing an FTA between India and Thailand was signed in October, 2003. Its key elements cover an FTA in Goods, Services and Investment and Areas of Economic Cooperation. The Agreement also provides for an Early Harvest Scheme under which common items of export interest would be eligible for tariff elimination on a fast-track basis. The FTA entered into effect on September 1, 2004. The first phase of the FTA involves tariff reduction on 82 agreed items (gearboxes, television picture tubes, wrist watches, parts of seats, compressor type refrigerators, textile spindles, spinning rings, flyers, machinery for moulding, pipes, boiler shells, ball bearings, flywheels, pulleys, signalling equipment and printed circuits) in three years. The Agreement will also cut import duties in each country by 50 per cent in the first year, another 25 per cent the following year, and eliminate them altogether by 2006. The second phase of the Free Trade Agreement would begin from then onwards and the two countries would have a free trade regime by 2010.[55]

G. India-ASEAN CECA[56]

A Framework Agreement on Comprehensive Economic Cooperation Agreement between ASEAN and India was signed on October 8, 2003 in Bali, Indonesia. Its key elements include an FTA in Goods, Services and Investment and Areas of Economic

52. India also provides concessional entry to ten additional products imported from Bangladesh: dried fish, leather of bovine or equine animals, goat or kid-skin leather, composition leather, timber, jute or bamboo pulp, newsprint, printing paper, hand-woven Jamdani sarees, and carpets wholly made of jute (Goyal, 2000; and Notification No. 26/95-Cus, 16 March 1995. Available online at: http://www.cbec.gov.in/cae/customs [23 July 2001]).

53. See: "Trade Policy Review Body, Trade Policy Review – India," *Report by the Secretariat*, WT/TPR/S/100 22 May 2002, p. 21.

54. To see the consult the text of the agreement, see: http://commerce.nic.in/india_thailand_fta.htm

55. See: "Thailand, India to sign FTA on Oct. 9", *The Hindu* 9 August 2003.

56. To see and consult the text of the agreement, see: http://commerce.nic.in/agree_asean.htm

Table 17.5

An Overview of RTAs Signed by India

Agreement	Date of Entry into Force	GATT/WTO Notification				Examination Process	
		Date	Related Provisions	Type of Agreement	Document Series	Status	Ref.
SAPTA	7-Dec-95	22-Sep-93	Enabling Clause	Preferential arrangement	WT/COMTD/10	Examination not requested	...
TRIPARTITE	1-Apr-68	23-Feb-68	Enabling Clause	Preferential arrangement	L/2980 L/2980/Add.1	Report adopted	15S/83 14.11.68
GSTP	19-Apr-89	25-Sep-89	Enabling Clause	Preferential arrangement	L/6564/Add.1	Examination not requested	...
Bangkok Agreement	17-Jun-76	2-Nov-76	Enabling Clause	Preferential arrangement	L/4418 L/4418/Corr.1	Report adopted	25S/109 14.03.78

Compiled from WTO Source (December 2004).

Cooperation. The Agreement also provides for an Early Harvest Programme covering the Areas of Economic Cooperation and a common list of items for exchange of tariff concessions. The ASEAN nations include: Brunei, Laos, Malaysia, Philippines, Thailand, Cambodia, Indonesia, Myanmar, Singapore and Vietnam. India will reduce its tariff for Brunei, Cambodia, Laos, Indonesia, Malaysia, Myanmar, Singapore, Thailand and Vietnam in 2011. Correspondingly while Brunei, Indonesia, Malaysia, Singapore and Thailand will reduce their tariff for India in 2011, the new ASEAN members like Cambodia, Laos, Myanmar and Vietnam (CLMV) will do so in 2016. Philippines which has expressed its reservations to the FTA has agreed to eliminate its tariff on a reciprocal basis for India by 2016. India will unilaterally extend concessions on 11 tariff lines to CLMV.

Conclusion

The absence of substantial reduction in trade barriers in the trade rounds of the WTO has meant that members have increasingly been resorting to regional trade agreements. Economic theory shows that for RTAs to be optimal, their trade-creation effects should outweigh their trade diversion effects. However, neither procedural nor substantive laws in the WTO seem to ensure this. The Legal Texts themselves have enough loopholes for these agreements to be a danger to free trade, and even legal precedents in dispute settlement have not been able to clarify these loopholes completely.[57] RTAs are therefore an imperfect substitute for the multilateral trading system. Even in the case of India, the various RTAs entered into have not had any substantial impact on increasing the country's trading opportunities. Going the WTO way is therefore the optimal and Members would do well to ensure that the system does not run into unrequited delays. Having said that, the most important use of an RTA could be to enforce reduction in the MFN tariff.

---

57. Editor's Note – India has learnt this fact through bitter experience. On 6 June 2003, it submitted a proposal to WTO (Document No. TN/RL/W/114), calling for (i) continuation of 'enabling clause' to help the developing countries, (ii) reduction in the adverse effect of ROO requirement on India's textile and garmet exports and (iii) reduction in the adverse effect of harmonisation of SPS-TBT measures on a fast track, which considerably hurts the primary exports.

References

Articles

Abbott Frederick (2002). "North American Economic Integration: Implications for the WTO, the EU and Asia," in: Snyder Francis (Ed.): *Regional and Global Regulation of International Trade*, Hart Publishing, pp. 71-96.

Von Bogdandy Armin and Makatsch Tilman (2001). "Collision, Co-existence or Co-operation? Prospects for the Relationship Between WTO Law and European Union Law," in: De Burca Graine & Scott Joanne : *EU & the WTO : Legal & Constitutional Aspects*, Hart Publishing, pp. 131-150.

Ramachandran Lija: "SAARC: Where Does It Stand?," in: Basavaraja M.G. : *World Trade Organisation, Regional Trading Arrangements and India*, Serials Publications, New Delhi 2003, pp. 291-301.

Chaisse Julien: "The European Common Commercial Policy Facing the Challenges of the Globalisation," in: Agarwal Manmohan *et al.*, (eds): *The Future of the Global Economy: Regional Trajectories and Global Institutions*. (forthcoming 2005)

Chaisse Julien and Chakraborty Debashis: "The Doha Development Agenda on Disputes Resolution," *Amity Law Review*, Vol. 6 No. 1 pp. 8-20, June 2005.

Cherunilam Francis: "Economic Integration of Developing Countries with Special Reference to SAPTA and ISFTA," in: Basavaraja M.G. : *World Trade Organisation, Regional Trading Arrangements and India*, Serials Publications, New Delhi 2003, pp. 257-281.

Choi Won-Mog : "Regional Economic Integration in East-Asia," *Journal of International Economic Law 2003* Volume 6 No. 1, pp. 49-77.

Cremona Marise: "Rhetoric and Reticence : EU External Commercial Policy in a Multilateral Context," CML Rev. 38 (2001), pp. 359-396.

Cremona Marise : "Neutrality or Discrimination? The WTO, the EU and External Trade," in: De Burca Graine & Scott Joanne : *EU & the WTO : Legal & Constitutional Aspects*, Hart Publishing 2001, pp. 151-184.

Cremona Marise : "The External Dimension of the Single Market: Building (on) the Foundations," in: Barnard Catherine and Scott Joanne : *The Law of the Single European Market : Unpacking the Premises*, Oxford : Hart Publishing, 2002, pp. 269-294.

Debroy Bibek: "India's Approach to the WTO: Cancun and After," in: Debroy Bibek and Saqib Mohammed (eds): *Future Negotiation Issues at World Trade Organisation*, Globus Books, New Delhi 2004, pp 83-122.

Desker B.: "In Defence of FTAs: From Purity to Pragmatism in East Asia," *The Pacific Review*, March 2004, Vol. 17, No. 1, pp. 3-26.

Inama Stefano: "Trade Preferences and the WTO Negotiations on Market Access - Battling for Compensation of Erosion of GSP, ACP and Other Trade Preferences or Assessing and Improving their Utilisation and Value by Addressing Rules of Origin and Graduation?," *Journal of World Trade 2003* Vol. 37 No. 5, pp. 959-976.

Laird, S. "Regional Trade Agreements: Dangerous Liaisons?," *World Economy* Volume 22, December 1999.

Marceau Gabrielle and Reiman Cornelis : "When and How Is a Regional Trade Agreement Compatible with the WTO?," *Legal Issues Economic Integration* 2001, p. 297.

Matambalya Francis A.S.T. and Wolf Susanna: "The Cotonou Agreement and the Challenges of Making the New EU-ACP Trade Regime WTO Compatible," *JWT 35* (2001, No.1), pp. 123-144.

Mathis James: *WTO, Turkey* – "Restrictions on Imports of Textile and Clothing Products," *Legal Issues of European Integration* Volume 27 2000 No. 1, pp. 103-114.

Mavroidis Petros C. : "Judicial Supremacy, Judicial Restraint, and the Issue of Consistency of Preferential Agreements with the WTO : The Apple in the Picture," in : Kennedy Daniel L. and Southwick James D.: *The Political Economy of International Trade Law – Essays in Honor of Robert E. Hudec*, Cambridge University Press, Cambridge 2002, pp. 583-601.

Mukherjee Arpita: "GATS 2000 Negotiations and India: Issues and State of Play," in: Debroy Bibek and Saqib Mohammed (eds): *Future Negotiation Issues at World Trade Organisation*, Globus Books, New Delhi 2004, pp. 233-265.

Park Sung-Hoon: Regionalism, "Open Regionalism and Article XXIV GATT ? Conflicts and Harmony," in: Snyder Francis (Ed.): *Regional and Global Regulation of International Trade*, Hart Publishing 2002, pp. 263-283.

Pauwelyn Joost: "The Puzzle of WTO Safeguards and Regional Trade Agreements," *JIEL 2004*, Vol. 7, No. 1, pp. 109-142.

Sapir André : "Le régionalisme et la nouvelle théorie du commerce international sonnet-ils le glas du GATT ?," *Politique Etrangère* 1993, No. 2, pp. 277-293.

Trachtman Joel: "Towards Open Recognition? Standardisation and Regional Integration under Article XXIV of GATT," *Journal of International Economic Law 2003* Volume 6 No. 2, pp. 459-492.

Books

Basavaraja M.G. : *World Trade Organisation, Regional Trading Arrangements and India*, Serials Publications, New Delhi 2003 (345 p.).

Dam, K. *The GATT: Law and International Economic Organisation*. University of Chicago Press. 1970. pp 274-295.

Debroy Bibek and Saqib Mohammed (eds): *Future Negotiation Issues at World Trade Organisation*, Globus Books, New Delhi 2004 (486 p.).

Geiger Till et Kennedy Dennis: *Regional Trade Blocs, Multilateralism, and the GATT : Complementary Paths to Free Trade?*, London : Pinter, 1996 (183 p.).

Goode Walter : *Dictionary of Trade Policy Terms*, Cambridge University Press, Cambridge 2003 (437 p.).

Gupta Anshuman: *SAARC – SAPTA to SAFTA*, Maulana Abdul Kalam Azad Institute of Asian Studies (Kolkata), Shipra Publications, New Delhi 2002 (136 p.).

Kennedy Daniel L. and Southwick James D.: *The Political Economy of International Trade Law – Essays in Honor of Robert E. Hudec*, Cambridge University Press, Cambridge 2002 (696 p.).

Kessie E.: *The World Trade Organisation and Regional Trade Agreements: An Analysis of the Relevant Rules of the WTO*, SJD Thesis Chapter 7, pp 204-211.

Mangalamurthy S. : *South Asian Association for Regional Co-operation*, Chethana Book House, Mysore 2003 (254 p.).

Matsushita Mitsuo, Mavroidis Petros C. and Schoenbaum Thomas J. : *The World Trade Organisation - Law, Practice, and Policy*, Oxford University Press, Oxford 2003 (770 p.).

Shingal Anirudh: *Examining Possibilities of Expanding Pakistan's Trading Opportunities through Regional Trade Agreements*, Fakhar Law International, March 2004.

Snyder Francis (Ed.): *Regional and Global Regulation of International Trade*, Hart Publishing 2002 (304 p.)

Vasudeva P. K.: *India and World Trade Organisation: Planning and Development*, A. P. H. Publishing Corporation, New Delhi 2000 (345 p.).

Official Documents

Trade Policy Review Body, Trade Policy Review – India, Report by the Secretariat, WT/TPR/S/100 22 May 2002.

Report of the Appellate Body, *Turkey - Restrictions on Imports of Textile and Clothing Products*, WT/DS34/AB/R, 22 October 1999.

Negotiating Group on Rules, compendium of issues related to regional trade agreements (Background Note by the Secretariat), TN/RL/W/8/Rev.1, 1 August 2002.

Committee on Trade and Development - SAARC Preferential Trading Arrangement (SAPTA) - Information submitted by the SAARC Members, 25 april 1997, WT/COMTD/10.

The Decision of the Contracting Parties of November 28, 1979 – the Enabling Clause

Working Papers

Brenton Paul: "Integrating the Least Developed Countries into the World Trading System: The Current Impact of EU Preferences under Everything But Arms," *Working Paper World Bank*, 2003 (31 p.).

World Bank. "Trade Blocs and the World Trading System." *Trade Blocs*. Oxford University Press. 2000. Chapter 5. pp 108 – 120.

18

Dispute Resolution in the WTO: The Experience of India*

JULIEN CHAISSE
DEBASHIS CHAKRABORTY

Introduction

The result of the Uruguay Round of multilateral negotiations (1986–94) comprised of agreements covering many different sectors of international trade.[1] The whole commitments made under WTO Agreements must be implemented by the Member States of the WTO,[2] but obviously at the moment of the implementation,[3] problems arise with regard to the violations or simply to the interpretation of so many dispositions. As a result, a central feature of the WTO is its Dispute Settlement Mechanism (DSM), which has had an enormous impact on the world trade system and trade diplomacy.[4] The WTO/DSM is unique in international law essentially because it is juridical

* An earlier version of the paper has been presented in a conference organised by Rajiv Gandhi Institute for Contemporary Studies and China Association for International Friendly Contacts, November, 2003.

1. These WTO Agreements have been published in India in: Gupta K.R.: *World Trade Organisation: Text – Volume I*, New Delhi, Atlantic Publishers and Distributors 2000 (338 p.) and *World Trade Organisation: Text – Volume II*, New Delhi, Atlantic Publishers and Distributors 2000 (339-716 pp.).
2. Of course the object of any treaty is to impose binding obligations on the states who are parties to it. And States are bound to carry out, in good faith, the obligations they have assumed by treaty. This is the essence of the doctrine of *Pacta Sunt Servanda*, which means that the pledged must be followed. But in addition of this rule of general international law, the legal basis of the implementation of the WTO Agreements stays explicitly in the Article XVI.4 of Agreement Establishing the World Trade Organisation: "Each Member shall ensure the conformity of its laws, regulations and administrative procedures with its obligations as provided in the annexed agreements".
3. Which can be defined by: "putting into effect the undertakings made in trade negotiations". "Implementation", in: Goode Walter: *Dictionary of Trade Policy Terms*, Cambridge University Press 2003, p. 174.
4. See the very interesting article of M. Stoler on the negotiations on the DSM and the results; Stoler Andrew: *The WTO Dispute Settlement Process: Did the Negotiators Get What They Wanted?*, *World Trade Review*, 2004 Volume 3 No. 1, pp. 99-118.

and legalistic system for disputes dedicated to preserve the rights and obligations of WTO Members.[5] This assessment is based on a comparative analysis with other international jurisdictions, but is even more relevant within the frame of a comparison with the very frequent use of arbitration in international private law. Moreover and unlike once again some of the more specialised systems of this type,[6] these attributes are nested in a broad and comprehensive jurisprudence which clarify and develop the law arising from the Agreements. On the whole more than any other international organisation, the WTO is really able to ensure the efficiency of its law. One of the immediate consequences of such a well functioning system is that the developing countries are now making frequent use of the dispute settlement mechanism, bringing cases against developed and developing country members.

I – LEGAL FRAME OF DISPUTE RESOLUTION IN THE WTO

The legal frame of dispute resolution in the WTO can be analysed through the main legal characters and the different steps of the process of the DSM.

A. Main Legal Characters of the WTO Dispute Settlement Mechanism

The need of a jurisdiction or simply of a third party to resolve the litigations can be easily understood if we consider that in a "primitive system" without third party, the parties in litigation are dependant on the power of the other, everybody can suffer of a risk of escalation in the counter-measures and ultimately there will not be any uniformity in the interpretation of the laws. The GATT 47 dispute settlement mechanism already was a progress in the way leading to the intervention of a third-party to solve trade litigations. But with the establishment of the WTO, the resolution of

5. Article 3-Understanding on Rules and Procedures Governing the Settlement of Disputes (DSU): "The Members recognise that it serves to preserve the rights and obligations of Members under the covered agreements in accordance with customary rules and interpretation of public international law".
6. To have an outline of dispute settlement in the international organisations, See: Amersinghe, C.F., "Dispute Settlement by International Organisations", *Indian Journal of International Law*, Volume 43 No. 3, July-September 2003, pp. 409-444.

international trade disputes has entered a new and a highly legalistic era. The efficiency of the GATT dispute settlement was limited,[7] since the consensus of all was required to adopt a report. The foreseeable refusal of the only succumbing party was sufficient to prevent the adoption of the report of a GATT dispute settlement panel. Under the WTO, the GATT consensus requirement is reversed: consensus in the WTO is required to reject (called *"negative consensus"*), rather than to adopt, the report. This change has made WTO dispute settlement into what is the most effective area of adjudicative dispute settlement in the entire arena of public international law.[8]

1. Compulsory Jurisdiction

One of the most notable features of the panel procedures in the WTO is that the latter has a compulsory jurisdiction over a case brought by its members.

In the GATT (the precursor of the WTO), consensus was required for the Contracting Parties to establish a panel. This meant that the consent of the defendant had to be obtained before a panel could be established. In contrast of this weakness, the WTO establishes a panel unless there is a consensus not to do so. Therefore, the consent of the Defendant State to establish a panel is no longer required. If a member requests the establishment of a panel, consensus not to establish a panel is lacking by definition, and the Dispute Settlement Body (DSB) will establish a panel. Thus, a WTO member has a right to request establishment of a panel, and the WTO effectively has compulsory jurisdiction. The WTO is unique having established a universal system of dispute settlement with compulsory jurisdiction and having dealt with numerous interstate disputes.[9]

---

7. To have an overview of the previous GATT Dispute Settlement System (1948-1995), See: Petersmann Ernst-Ulrich: *"The GATT/WTO Dispute Settlement System International Law, International Organisations and Dispute Settlement,"* Nijhoff Law Specials: Volume 23 Kluwer Law International, The Hague, 1997, pp. 66-91.

8. To that extent the first case submitted to the WTO/DSM was illustrative since it pit Venezuela (as plaintiff) against United States of America (as defendant). Such a case would have been unimaginable under GATT-47. See: United States - Standards for Reformulated and Conventional Gasoline - Report of the Panel, WT/DS2/R WT/DS2/R, 29 January 1996.

9. Of course, other conventions that provide for compulsory jurisdiction for a court established in the convention include the UN Convention on the Law of the Sea, the Treaty establishing the European Economic Community, the European Convention on Human Rights and the American Convention on Human Rights. But these courts are limited to specific regions and they have not dealt with many interstate disputes.

2. *Integrated Character of the Dispute Settlement Understanding*

Once again, if we compare to the legally fragmented previous "GATT *à la carte*" system "where GATT contracting parties could choose whether they wanted to adhere to the various Tokyo Round Agreements and to pursue disputes through the general GATT or special Tokyo Round Dispute settlement mechanisms, the new WTO dispute settlement system is an unified system with much broader jurisdiction and less scope for "rule shopping" and "forum shopping"[10].

The DSU is integrated because it deals with any dispute arising from WTO Agreements and there is a single set of rules for all disputes. Consequently, the dispute settlement process covers the WTO Agreement (the Agreement establishing the World Trade Organisation), GATT 1994, other agreements on goods, services, the plurilateral agreements and the DSU itself.[11]

3. *Binding Force of Reports of WTO Panels and the Appellate Body*

As soon as the DSB has adopted the report, the report becomes binding on disputing parties as a matter of international law. And the losing party must bring its legislation into line with the recommendations. The adopted reports of a panel and the Appellate Body do notably bind the parties to the dispute for some reasons expressed clearly in the DSU Agreement[12]:

---

10. Petersmann, Ernst-Ulrich: *"The GATT/WTO Dispute Settlement System International Law, International Organisations and Dispute Settlement," Nijhoff Law Specials*: Volume 23 Kluwer Law International, The Hague, 1997, p. 178.

11. In *Brazil — Desiccated Coconut*, the Appellate Body defined the term "covered agreements" as follows: "The 'covered agreements' include the WTO Agreement, the Agreements in Annexes 1 and 2, as well as any Plurilateral Trade Agreement in Annex 4 where its Committee of signatories has taken a decision to apply the DSU. In a dispute brought to the DSB, a panel may deal with all the relevant provisions of the covered agreements cited by the parties to the dispute in one proceeding". Appellate Body Report, *Brazil - Measures Affecting Desiccated Coconut*, WT/DS22/AB/R, 21 February 1997, p. 13.

12. Professor John Jackson counts at least 11 clauses, which strongly suggest that "the legal effect of an adopted panel report is the international law obligation to perform the recommendation of the panel report". Jackson John: *The WTO Dispute Settlement Understanding: Misunderstandings on the Nature of Legal Obligation*, in: Jackson John: *The Jurisprudence of GATT and the WTO: Insights on Treaty Law and Economic Relations*, Cambridge University Press, Cambridge, United Kingdom, 2000, p. 166.

- The first objective of the dispute settlement mechanism is usually to **secure the withdrawal of the measures concerned** and compensation should be resorted to **only if** the immediate withdrawal is impracticable (DSU Article 3.7),[13]
- and the DSU further provides that an appellate body report **must be unconditionally accepted** by the parties to the dispute (DSU Article 17.14),
- the DSU provides that compensation and the suspension of obligations are available only as **temporary measures** in the event that the recommendations and rulings are not implemented within a reasonable period of time (DSU Article 22.1),
- the DSU provides that only in cases of non-violation complaint there is no obligation to withdraw the measure challenged (DSU Article 26.1.b.).

B. The Process of the Dispute Settlement

A WTO dispute settlement procedure is launched at the request of one or more member governments for a consultation regarding complaints against defending members. This process is entirely government-to-government (what excludes juridical person, Non-Governmental Organisations (NGOs) and other International Organisations). Of course this process is available only to WTO members in procedures against other members. The DSU provides that all members will settle their differences regarding the covered agreements by referring those disputes to the procedures of the WTO as elaborated in the DSU. If more than one country brings a complaint against the same measure, the complaints are consolidated and reviewed by a single panel.

The first stage in the resolution of a dispute consists of consultation. If it is not successful the formation of a panel is almost

13. This basic aim is affirmed elsewhere in the DSU. Article 3.4, for example, stipulates: 'Recommendations or rulings made by the DSB shall be aimed at achieving a satisfactory settlement of the matter in accordance with the rights and obligations under this Understanding and under the covered agreements.' This point was reminded in the report: Appellate Body Report, *United States - Measure Affecting Imports of Woven Wool Shirts and Blouses from India*, WT/DS33/AB/R, 25 April 1997, p. 19.

automatic. If the parties disagree with the panel's findings, they may appeal to the Appellate Body.

1. The Starting of the Process: The Consultations

The first step in dispute settlement is a consultation between the complaining party (or parties) and the responding party (or parties). Before taking any other action the countries in dispute have to talk to each other to see if they can settle their differences by themselves. In that extent, the aim of the consultations is to explore the nature of the complaint in a confidential[14] and bilateral way. It is at the same time used by the respondents to determine the arguments of the complainant or by the complainants to find out the responding party's potential defenses. There can be third parties, but their role is limited. They can be joined unless the party to whom the request for consultations was addressed, objects.

If the parties have failed to settle the dispute by the end of 60 days, then the complaining party may ask the DSB to establish a dispute panel.[15] The request should identify the specific measures in debate, and provide a brief summary of the legal basis of the complaint sufficient to present the problem clearly. Under the new procedures of the DSU, the DSB must automatically approve the request for a panel procedure, although there are some provisions for short delays to that approval.[16]

When the DSB approves the establishment of the panel (normally composed of three members), the secretariat begins the sometimes prolonged process of designating the panelists for the particular procedure, ideally by means of consensus between the parties. If the parties cannot agree within 20 days, the matter is referred to the WTO's Director-General, who then has the authority to impose a panel on the parties.[17]

---

14. Report of the Panel, *Japan - Taxes on Alcoholic Beverages*, WT/DS8/R, WT/DS10/R and WT/DS11/R, 11/07/1996, Point V). 5).3), p. 105.

15. DSU Article 4.7.

16. DSU Article 6.1.

17. DSU Article 8.7.

2. *From the Establishment of a Panel to the Adoption of the Report*

A panel must be established no later than the second meeting after the request for a panel first appears on the DSB's Agenda and its function is notably to "make an objective assessment of the matter before it, including an objective assessment of the facts[18] of the case and the applicability of and conformity with the relevant covered agreements, and make such other findings as will assist the DSB in making the recommendations or in giving the rulings provided for in the covered agreements"[19]. The panel, normally composed of three individuals, then receives oral and written arguments from the parties to the dispute and from third parties. Any WTO member can become a third party in a dispute, usually by simply indicating that it has an interest in the subject matter. This interest may not involve a direct effect of a potential decision on the government; it may be a broader notion of the third-party government's interest in the direction of the jurisprudence concerning the interpretation of the treaty clauses relevant to the case.

The terms of reference determine the subject matter jurisdiction of the panel, and fulfill the due process objective of notifying the responding party of the claims at issue. Unless the parties agree within twenty days to the contrary, panels will proceed under standard terms of reference, as set out in Article 7.1, which instructs them "to examine, in light of the relevant provisions in (name of covered agreement(s) cited by the parties to the dispute), the matter

---

18. For example, in India – *Quantitative Restrictions* on imports of agricultural, textile and industrial products case, India argued in its appeal that the Panel had acted inconsistently with Article 11 of the DSU because it had delegated to the IMF its duty to make an objective assessment. The Appellate Body stated: "The Panel gave considerable weight to the views expressed by the IMF in its reply to these questions. However, nothing in the Panel Report supports India's argument that the Panel delegated to the IMF its judicial function to make an objective assessment of the matter. A careful reading of the Panel Report makes clear that the Panel did not simply accept the views of the IMF. The Panel critically assessed these views and also considered other data and opinions in reaching its conclusions. [...] We conclude that the Panel made an objective assessment of the matter before it. Therefore, we do not agree with India that the Panel acted inconsistently with Article 11 of the DSU." Appellate Body Report, *India – Quantitative Restrictions on Imports of Agricultural, Textile and Industrial Products Case*, WT/DS90/AB/R, 23 August 1999, paragraphs 149 and 151.

19. DSU Article 11.

referred[20] to the DSB by (name of party) in document... and to make such findings as will assist the DSB in making the recommendations or in giving the rulings provided for in that/those agreement(s)".

That document will specify the measures claimed to be inconsistent with WTO obligations and the specific WTO provisions of the WTO obligations that are said to be violated. As the Appellate Body reminded and explained it, terms of reference are important for two reasons: "First, terms of reference fulfill an important due process objective — they give the parties and third parties sufficient information concerning the claims at issue in the dispute in order to allow them an opportunity to respond to the complainant's case. Second, they establish the jurisdiction of the panel by defining the precise claims at issue in the dispute"[21].

The parties must provide their submissions within time limits set by the panel. Oral arguments are presented in hearings, which are closed to the public and to WTO members not participating as complainants, respondents, or third parties.[22] The first hearing before the panel is between the disputing parties (excluding third parties).

---

20. In Guatemala – Cement I, the Appellate Body addressed the term "matter" and held that: "The word 'matter' appears in Article 7 of the DSU, which provides the standard terms of reference for panels [...] when that provision is read together with Article 6.2 of the DSU, the precise meaning of the term 'matter' becomes clear. Article 6.2 specifies the requirements under which a complaining Member may refer a 'matter' to the DSB: in order to establish a panel to hear its complaint, a Member must make, in writing, a 'request for the establishment of a panel' (a 'panel request'). In addition to being the document which enables the DSB to establish a panel, the panel request is also usually identified in the panel's terms of reference as the document setting out 'the matter referred to the DSB'. Thus, 'the matter referred to the DSB' for the purposes of Article 7 of the DSU and Article 17.4 of the Anti-Dumping Agreement must be the 'matter' identified in the request for the establishment of a panel under Article 6.2 of the DSU. That provision requires the complaining Member, in a panel request, to 'identify the specific measures at issue and provide a brief summary of the legal basis of the complaint sufficient to present the problem clearly.' (emphasis added) The 'matter referred to the DSB', therefore, consists of two elements: the specific measures at issue and the legal basis of the complaint (or the claims)". Appellate Body Report, *Guatemala – Anti-Dumping Investigation Regarding Portland Cement from Mexico*, WT/DS60/AB/R, 2 November 1998, paragraph 72.

21. Report of the Appellate Body, *Brazil - Measures Affecting Desiccated Coconut*, WT/DS22/AB/R, 21/02/1997, p. 21.

22. About the practice of third party intervention since 1995, See: Footer Mary E.: *"Some Aspects of Third Party Intervention in GATT/WTO Dispute Settlement Proceedings,"* in: Petersmann Ernst-Ulrich: *International Trade Law and the GATT/WTO Dispute Settlement System*, Studies in Transnational Economic Law, Volume 11, Kluwer Law International 1997, pp. 235 and followings.

If necessary a hearing of the third parties follows the first hearing, but the disputing parties are also present and can actively participate in the discussion. Following the initial hearings and submissions, the parties have the opportunity for replying submissions and a reply hearing, normally limited to the disputing parties. After this, the panel drafts an interim report, which is given to each of the parties. At that time, each of the parties have the opportunity to comment on it (normally within 30 days) or reach a settlement, keeping in mind the likely report of the panel.

Nevertheless panels are not confined to the parties as sources of the information they need. They have the right to seek information and technical advice from any source they deem appropriate.[23]

After the comment period on the interim report has expired, the panel decides whether to revise its report or whether further proceedings (including oral or written submissions by the parties) are necessary. In the absence of further proceedings, the panel completes a final report that goes to the DSB for adoption.

The adoption of the report is a critical step and a significant change from procedures under GATT. Since negative consensus can be broken by parties who feel that the report should be adopted, the DSB is automatically to have adopted the report of the first-level panel unless the report is appealed or there is a consensus of the DSB against adoption.

The adopted report then becomes binding on disputing parties as a matter of international law and where a panel (or the Appellate Body) concludes that "a measure is inconsistent with a covered agreement, it shall recommend that the Member concerned bring the measure into conformity with that agreement"[24]. Moreover this article states that "the panel or Appellate Body may suggest ways in which the Member concerned could implement the recommendations". This provision has been interpreted by panel according to whom

---

23. DSU Article 13.1. And see: *Pauwelyn Joost: "The Use of Experts in WTO Dispute Settlement," International and Comparative Law Quarterly*, 2002 Volume 51 Part 2, pp. 325-364.

24. DSU Article 19.1. Moreover, the panel may suggest a precise way to bring the measure into conformity with that agreement, See for example, Report of the Panel, *United States - Continued Dumping and Subsidy Offset Act of 2000*, WT/DS217/R, WT/DS234/R, 16/09/2002, point No. 8.6.

"Article 19.1 appears to envision suggestions regarding what could be done to a measure to bring it into conformity or, in case of a recommendation under Article 4.7 of the *SCM Agreement*, what could be done to 'withdraw' the prohibited subsidy. It is not clear if Article 19.1 also addresses issues of surveillance of those steps. That said, any agreement that WTO Members might reach among themselves to improve transparency regarding the implementation of WTO obligations can only be encouraged"[25].

3. The Appeal Process: Appeal to the Appellate Body

The parties may appeal the report to the Appellate Body, who may uphold, modify or reverse the legal findings and conclusions of the panel.

The Appellate Body is composed of seven individuals who have been selected by the DSB through a consensus process. These individuals are retained part time for their services, depending on the caseload. The Appellate Body members each hold terms of four years, renewable once. Appeals are heard by a specifically constituted division, composed of three members of the Appellate Body.

An appeal has to be based on points of law such as legal interpretation; it cannot re-examine existing evidence or examine new evidence.[26] The Appellate Body itself explained the difference: "Findings of fact, as distinguished from legal interpretations or legal conclusions, by a panel are, in principle, not subject to review by the Appellate Body. The determination of whether or not a certain event did occur in time and space is typically a question of fact. [...]". Further it said "Determination of credibility and weight properly to be ascribed to (that is, the appreciation of) a given piece of evidence is part and parcel of the fact finding process and is, in principle, left to the discretion of a panel as the trier of the facts. The consistency or inconsistency of a given fact or set of facts with the requirements of a given treaty provision is, however, a legal characterisation. It is

25. Panel Report, *Brazil – Export Financing Programme for Aircraft*, WT/DS46/RW, 9 May 2000, paragraph 7.3.

26. DSU Article 17.6. See, Sacerdoti Giorgio: *Appeal and Judicial Review in International Arbitration and Adjudication: The Case of the WTO Appellate Review*, in: Petersmann Ernst-Ulrich: *International Trade Law and the GATT/WTO Dispute Settlement System*, Studies in Transnational Economic Law, Volume 11, Kluwer Law International 1997, pp. 245 and followings.

a legal question"[27]. In that extent, the Appellate Body performs "a general function of guaranteeing the proper application and interpretation of the law in case of disputes within the organisation in the interest of all its members"[28].

The Appellate Body then goes through a process similar to that of the first-level panel: oral and written submissions, a hearing with discussion and questioning by the division members, and then the preparation of an Appellate Body report. This is supposed to be accomplished within 60 days, and in exceptional cases within 90 days, but more frequently the latter is the case.[29] Indeed, occasionally even that time limit proves inadequate for the Appellate Body to complete its work on an appeal.

Once the Appellate Body has completed its report, it sends the report to the DSB, which adopts the report virtually automatically, through the "reverse consensus" process.

If a country has done something wrong, it should correct its fault. If it continues to break an agreement, it should offer compensation or suffer a suitable penalty that has some bite.

4. *The Implementation of Reports*

The priority at this stage is for the losing "defendant" to bring its legislation into line with the rulings or recommendations.[30] The Dispute Settlement Agreement stresses that "prompt compliance with recommendations or rulings of the DSB is essential in order to ensure effective resolution of disputes to the benefit of all members".

27. Report of the Appellate Body, *Measures Concerning Meat and Meat Products (Hormones)*, WT/DS26/AB/R and WT/DS48/AB/R, 16 January 1998, paragraph 132. About the distinction between the facts and the law, See: Kuyper Pieter-Jan: *"The Appellate Body and the Facts,"* in: Bronckers Marco and Quick Reinhard: *New Directions in International Economic Law – Essays in Honour of John H. Jackson*, The Hague Kluwer Law International, 2000 p. 309.

28. Sacerdoti Giorgio: *"Appeal and Judicial Review in International Arbitration and Adjudication: The Case of the WTO Appellate Review,"* in: Petersmann Ernst-Ulrich: *International Trade Law and the GATT/WTO Dispute Settlement System*, Studies in Transnational Economic Law, Volume 11, Kluwer Law International 1997, p. 274.

29. DSU Article 17.5.

30. DSU Article 19.1. However, in situations involving « non-violation » complaints, the Member is not required to withdraw the measure. See, Chua Adrian: *"Reasonable Expectations and Non-Violation Complaints in GATT/WTO Jurisprudence," Journal of World Trade Volume* 32 No. 2, April 1998, pp. 27-50.

If the Member state that is the target of the complaint loses, it must follow the recommendations of the panel report or appeals against the report, which after their adoption have become those of the DSB itself. The Member State must communicate its intention to do so at a Dispute Settlement Body meeting held within 30 days of the report's adoption.[31] If complying with the recommendation immediately proves impractical, the member will be given a "reasonable period of time" to do so.[32]

If it fails to act within this period, it has to enter into negotiations with the complaining country (or countries) in order to determine mutually acceptable compensation: for instance, tariff reductions in areas of particular interest to the complaining side. But any compensation agreed upon must conform to the requirements of the covered agreements, which includes the most-favored-nation requirements of the agreements.[33]

If after twenty days, no satisfactory compensation is agreed upon, the complaining side may request the DSB for permission to impose limited trade sanctions ("suspend concessions or obligations") against the other side. But if the sanction in case of non-fulfillment is that procedure of counter measures, the amount of trade sanctions must be authorised and open to arbitration. Actually these procedures constitute true matters of new dispute regarding enforcement.[34] The DSB should grant this authorisation within 30 days of the expiry of the "reasonable period of time" unless there is a consensus against this action.

Within this frame, as discussed earlier, disputes have increased even more. Indeed, more than 300 requests for consultations were made and panels were established in more than 100 cases.[35] It is remarkable that the WTO has dealt with so many interstate disputes

31. DSU Article 21.3.

32. On the question of what is a *"reasonable period of time,"* See: Stoll Peter-Tobias and Steinmann Arthur: *WTO Dispute Settlement: The Implementation Stage*, Max Planck Yearbook of United Nations Law 1999, Vol. 3.

33. DSU Article 22.1

34. Professor Ruiz-Fabri develops this growing concept of *"dispute of the enforcement"* in: Ruiz-Fabri Hélène : *Le contentieux de l'exécution dans le règlement des différends de l'organisation mondiale du commerce, Journal du Droit International* No. 3, 2000, pp. 605-645.

35. See, Update of WTO Dispute Settlement Cases, WT/DS/OV/22, 14 October 2004.

in accordance with defined procedures. The DSM is functioning much better than was expected in 1994. Once the DSM was in place during that year, the governments decided to start negotiations to refine the DSM as its present form was considered to be a transitional arrangement. However, no concrete agreement had taken place.

II – TRADE DISPUTES BROUGHT TO THE WTO BY INDIA

The volume of India's external trade has increased quite steadily over the years since the inception of WTO in 1995.[36] However, increased trade at the same time enhances the possibility of a rise in trade disputes. On one hand, Indian products might face barriers in other markets more often. For instance, Indian products have been subject to frequent anti-dumping and countervailing measures in the recent period in various destinations, involving several developing and developed nations. On the other hand, the Indian procedures, applied on imports, might come under fire on the basis of their WTO-compatibility. In particular, the increased use of anti-dumping measures on imports in recent years could be mentioned.[37]

First, before turning our attention to India in particular, the overall participation trends for developing countries should be considered. The scenario has been summerised in Table 18.1. It could be seen that developed countries had lodged 127 cases against other developed countries, while 75 cases have been initiated against developing countries. On the other hand, developing countries have moved to DSB in 70 and 51 cases complaining against developed and developing countries respectively. Only in 6 cases developing and developing countries have jointly moved to DSB complaining against developed countries. However, till date no developed-developing country joint effort has been notified to DSB against any developing country.

---

36. From 1994-95 to 2003-04, India's export and import has more than doubled over this seven year period.

37. The WTO Trade Policy Review, *India* (2002) notes that, 'While import licensing and tariff restrictions are generally declining, there appears to have been an increase in other import measures. India has become one of the major users of anti-dumping measures, with some 250 cases initiated since 1995.'

Table 18.1

Analysis of Complaints by Developed/Developing Members

Complaints by Developed Country Members	
Respondents - Developed	127
Respondents - Developing	75
Complaints by Developing Country Members	
Respondents - Developed	70
Respondents - Developing	51
Complaints by Developed and Developing Country Members	
Respondents -Developed	6
Respondents - Developing	0

Source: Compiled from WTO Documents (April 2005).

A. The Cases: Material and Statistical Aspects

To begin with, India, like the other contracting parties has participated quite actively in the DS forum during the WTO regime, unlike the earlier GATT era. Under the GATT regime, India was involved in only one dispute against Poland in early-nineties regarding a modification in tariff structure on imported cars from outside European Economic Community of the later. India requested consultation and establishment of a panel under Article XXII:1 and XXIII:2 of GATT 1947 respectively. The panel was established in December 1994. However, India withdrew its claims under GATT 1947 to request consultations with Poland under Article 4 of the Understanding of Rules and Procedures Governing the Settlement of Disputes and Article XXIII:1 of GATT 1994 in October 1995. The dispute was mutually settled in 1996.[38]

Therefore, India's participation in dispute settlement is solely a WTO phenomenon. If a focused attention in paid on the pattern of the disputes engaging India, a couple of interesting facts come to forefront.

38. WTO Trade Policy Review, *India* (1998).

Table 18.2

Cases Against India

(updated upto 4th December, 2004)

No.	Case	Year	Complainant	Dispute	Result
1	DS 50	9 July 1996	US	Patent protection for pharmaceutical and agricultural chemical products	Lost
2	DS 79	6 May 1997	EC	Patent protection for pharmaceutical & agricultural chemical products	Lost
3	DS 90	22 July 1997	US	Quantitative restrictions on imports of agricultural, textile and industrial products	Lost
4	DS 91	22 July 1997	Australia	Do	Amicably Settled
5	DS 92	22 July 1997	Canada	Do	Amicably Settled
6	DS 93	22 July 1997	New Zealand	Do	Amicably Settled
7	DS 94	23 July 1997	Switzerland	Do	Amicably Settled
8	DS 96	24 July 1997	EC	Do	Amicably Settled
9	DS 120	23 March 1998	EC	Measures affecting export of certain commodities	Establishment of panel deferred in 2000
10	DS 146	12 October 1998	EC	Measures affecting the automotive sector	Lost
11	DS 149	12 November 1998	EC	Import restrictions maintained by India for reasons other than Articles XVIII B of GATT 1994	No panel formed
12	DS 150	3 November 1998	EC	Measures affecting customs duties	No panel formed
13	DS 175	7 June 1999	US	Measures relating to trade & investment in the motor vehicle sector	Lost

Contd...

...*Table 18.2 Contd...*

No.	Case	Year	Complainant	Dispute	Result
14	DS 279	9 January 2003	EC	Import restrictions maintained under the export and import policy, 2002-2007	No panel formed
15	DS 304	11 December 2003	EC	Anti-dumping measures on imports of certain products from the European Communities and/or Member States	Consultation in progress
16	DS 306	2 February 2004	Bangladesh	Anti-dumping/Article Vi GATT94	Consultation in progress
17	DS 318	1 November 2004	Taiwan	Provisional and definitive anti-dumping measures on chemical and related products	Consultation in progress

Source: Compiled from WTO documents.

First, India's trade policy is increasingly becoming WTO-compatible, as seems from Table 18.2, which shows that over the 8-year period since inception, a total of 17 cases have been filed against India.[39] The fourteenth case, (DS 279) has been filed on 9th January, 2003, whereas the earlier one (the thirteenth, DS 175) was filed way back in June, 1999. The last case has been filed on the 1st November 2004. While increased association with WTO policies is the underlying reason, it has to be highly commended.

Second, throughout this 10-year span, the cases filed by India do not portray any such time trend, and are more or less evenly distributed as seen from Table 18.3, where the cases involving India as complainant has been reported. In total India has lodged 16 cases in WTO. However, agreed solution has not been reached in one case involving EC as the respondent even after the appellate body report, as a result of which India moved to compliance panel to resolve the dispute[40] (DS 141).

39. An analysis of WTO-compatibility of India's trade policy is attempted later.

40. Although reported separately in table 2, DS141 and WT/DS141/RW should be considered as a single case.

Table 18.3

Cases Filed by India

(updated upto 4th December, 2004)

No.	*Case*	*Year*	*Respondent*	*Dispute*	*Result*
1	DS 19	18 October 1995	Poland	Import régime for automobiles	Amicably Settled
2	DS 32	15 March 1996	US	Measures affecting imports of women's and girls' wool coats	Won
3	DS 33	1 April 1996	US	Measures affecting imports of woven wool shirts and blouses	Won
4	DS 34	23 March 1996	Turkey	Restrictions on imports of textile and clothing products	Won
5	DS 58	14 October 1996	US	Import prohibition of shrimp and shrimp products	The panel termed US measure WTO-inconsistent. However, the appellate body reversed certain rulings.
6	DS 134	8 June 1998	EC	Measures affecting import duties on rice	Settled
7	DS 140	7 August 1998	EC	Anti-dumping measures on imports of unbleached cotton fabrics from India	EC did not continue the anti-dumping duty. India is not pursuing.
8	DS 141	7 August 1998	EC	Anti-dumping measures on imports of cotton-type bed-linen from India	Won
9	DS 168	13 April 1999	South Africa	Anti-dumping duties on import of certain pharmaceutical products from India	No panel formed
10	DS 206	12 October 2000	US	Anti-dumping and countervailing measures on steel plate from India	Panel rejected some of India's claims, but ruled certain US procedures to be WTO-in consistent.
11	DS 217	9 January 2001	US	Continued Dumping & Subsidy Offset Act of 2000	Won
12	DS 229	17 April 2001	Brazil	Anti-Dumping Duties on Jute Bags from India	No panel formed
13	DS 233	30 May 2001	Argentina	Measures Affecting the Import of Pharmaceutical Products	No panel formed

Contd...

...Table 18.3 Contd...

No.	Case	Year	Respondent	Dispute	Result
14	DS 243	22 January 2002	US	Rules of origin for textiles and apparel products	Panel rejected India's claims
15	DS 246	12 March 2002	EC	Conditions for the granting of tariff preferences to developing countries	Won, but certain panel rulings were modified by Appellate Body
16	DS 313	8 July 2004	EC	Anti-dumping Duties on Certain Flat Rolled Iron or Non-alloy Steel Products from India	EC has agreed 16 terminate the measure at issue

Source: Compiled from WTO documents.

Third, it is of some interest to investigate whether any developed-developing pattern is reflected through India's participation in the DS process. As far as the cases against India are concerned, the divide is too prominent. Among the 17 cases, 8 have been lodged by EC, followed by US with 3 cases. Switzerland, New Zealand, Canada and Australia have lodged one case each, and those are basically concerned over a single issue. India has till date faced only one case lodged by a developing country, Bangladesh, in 2004. However, a slightly different picture emerges, when the cases filed by India are considered. It could be seen that although the major chunk of cases has been filed against developed countries,[41] in four cases the respondent has been developing nations (Argentina, Brazil, Turkey, Poland).

Fourth, the distribution of cases by subject is also of some importance. While most of the cases filed by India are on imposition of anti-dumping and other type of duties and WTO-incompatibility of import measures on textile products, the same for the cases against India centers on three broad issues, namely, import restrictions, patent regime, and anti-dumping investigations.

Fifth, while participation to DSB, either the move to or being dragged into it has some significance, the ultimate result does matter. When the cases initiated by India are considered, Table 18.3 clearly reveals that it has won 7 cases, out of 16. However, it has lost in a

41. The number of cases being five, six and one against EC, US, and South Africa respectively.

Table 18.4

India Participating in DSB as Third Party (updated upto 4th December, 2004)

Case No.	*Complainant*	*Respondent*	*Dispute*
DS 21	United States	Australia	Measures affecting the importation of salmonids
DS 114	EC and their member States	Canada	Patent protection of pharmaceutical products
DS 136 and DS 162	EC and Japan	United States	Anti-dumping Act of 1916
DS 139 and DS 142	Japan and EC	Canada	Certain measures affecting the automotive industry
DS 152	EC	United States	Sections 301-310 of the Trade Act of 1974
DS 165	EC	United States	Import measures on certain products
DS 192	Pakistan	United States	Transitional safeguard measure on combed cotton yarn from Pakistan
DS 193	EC	Chile	Measures affecting the transit and importation of swordfish
DS 194	Canada	United States	Measures treating export restraints as subsidies
DS 199	United States	Brazil	Measures affecting patent protection
DS 204	United States	Mexico	Measures affecting telecommunications services
DS 210	United States	Belgium	Administration of measures establishing customs duties for rice
DS 212	EC	United States	Countervailing measures concerning certain products from the European Communities
DS 221	Canada	United States	Section 129(c)(1) of the Uruguay Round Agreements Act
DS 222	Brazil	Canada	Export credits and loan guarantees for regional aircraft
DS 234	Canada and Mexico	United States	Continued Dumping and Subsidy Off set Act of 2000
DS 236	Canada	United States	Preliminary determinations with respect to certain softwood lumber from Canada
DS 244	Japan	United States	Sunset review of anti-dumping duties on corrosion-resistant carbon steel flat products from Japan
DS 257	Canada	United States	Final countervailing duty determination with respect to certain softwood lumber from Canada
DS 270	Philippines	Australia	Certain measures affecting the importation of fresh fruit and vegetables
DS 290	Australia	EC	Protection of trademarks & geographical indications for agricultural products and foodstuffs

Source: Compiled from WTO documents.

recent case, namely – the dispute regarding rules of origin for textiles and apparel products. On the other hand, in couple of cases, although the measures of the opponents have been ruled WTO-incompatible, certain claims of India have been rejected by the panel.[42] The other cases are either continuing or settled amicably. On the other hand, it has not won a single case lodged against it, and lost 5 cases out of 17. This in a way suggests the legitimacy in the claims of the appellant countries.

While India was directly involved in a total of 33 cases, it has also participated extensively in a number of cases as interested third parties. A brief account of select cases is provided in Table 18.4. It is observed from this table that no particular trend could be extracted form the complainant/respondent level analysis; the accused defaulters include both developed and developing ones. However, if the cases are considered from the issue-level, a trend emerges, India had participated mostly in cases concerning disputes over TRIPS, textile products, primary products and dumping. Since all these cases concern India's interest areas, it could be concluded that it is fast emerging as quick learner in the WTO dispute resolution process.

B. The Indian Notion Towards DSB: Systemic Aspects

1. The Doha's Reviewing Process of the Dispute Settlement Understanding

At the Doha Ministerial Meeting in November 2001, the Ministers agreed to include the Dispute Settlement Understanding (DSU) as one of the subjects of the Doha Work Programme and to negotiate these improvements.[43] In this respect, paragraph 30 of the Doha Ministerial Declaration provides that: "*We agree to negotiations on improvements and clarifications of the Dispute Settlement Understanding. The negotiations should be based on the work done thus far as well as any additional proposals by Members, and aim to agree on improvements and clarifications not later than May 2003, at which time we will take steps to*

42. For instance, the dispute with US regarding anti-dumping and countervailing measures on steel plate from India could be cited.

43. Chaisse, Julien and Chakraborty Debashis: *The Doha Development Agenda on Disputes Resolution*, Amity Law Review, September 2004.

ensure that the results enter into force as soon as possible thereafter"[44]. But since its commencement, the negotiations have not led to the desired results. Especially the 1994 Ministerial Decision provided dispute settlement rules should be reviewed by 1 January 1999. The review on its own functioning started in the Dispute Settlement Body in 1997. The deadline was extended to 31 July 1999,[45] but there was no agreement.[46] From the Doha's Declaration, not any other new agreement was found. All members, however, expressed a readiness to continue negotiation beyond 31 May 2003 towards an agreement. In this respect, before the Cancun Summit, at its meeting on 24 and 25 July 2003,[47] the General Council agreed to extend negotiations from 31 May 2003 to 31 May 2004.

However, the process of DSU reviewing is still going on[48] and DSU reform will have implications for developing countries. However, it is probable that negotiations concerning other agreements (e.g., Intellectual Property, Textiles, Agriculture) will remain more important. Yet, as the developing countries participate more actively in international trade and the dispute settlement

---

44. Ministerial Declaration, adopted 14 November 2001, WTO Document WT/MIN(01)/DEC/1.

    Paragraph 30 of the Doha Ministerial Declaration has several significant elements:

    - It recognises that the DSU is in need of improvement and clarification,
    - Paragraph 30 provides that negotiations for reform are to take place based on work done, as well as new proposals,
    - It establishes what appeared to be a deadline, May 2003, to complete negotiations on DSU reform,
    - Fourth, it does not contain a guarantee that improvements and clarifications will enter into effect before the end of the negotiations.
    - Paragraph 30's final sentence leaves open the possibility that the "single undertaking" principle of agreeing to the results of the negotiations as a package, thereby eliminating the possibility to "pick and choose" which agreements to sign on to, may be applied to DSU reform,
    - Nevertheless, Paragraph 47 of the Ministerial Declaration leaves open the possibility that DSU reform will be outside of the single undertaking.

45. General Council - *Minutes of Meeting - Held in the Centre William Rappard on 9-11 and 18 December 1998*, WT/GC/M/32, 09 February 1999, page 52.

46. To have a recapitulation of the arguments expressed during the debate, See: General Council - *Minutes of Meeting - Held in the Centre William Rappard on 6 October 1999*, WT/GC/M/48, 27/10/1999, point 7.

47. General Council - *Minutes of Meeting - Held in the Centre William Rappard on 24 - 25 July 2003*, WT/GC/M/81 28 August 2003, p. 20, paragraph 75.

48. See for example, Dispute Settlement Body, *Proposed agenda - Meeting of 25 and 26 November 2004*, TN/DS/W/71, 23 November 2004.

system, the direct implications of the DSU will increase. The growing use of the DSU by India and other developing countries provides a case in point. This means that it is in the long-term interest of India to follow DSU reform while simultaneously participating in the negotiations concerning the other areas.

2. Indian Standpoint

Broadly since the inception in 1995, India has been contented with the working of DSB, as it provides a major balancing tool in the system, i.e., any defaulter is liable to be punished in the forum, subject to establishment of its non-compliance with WTO. However, from time to time Indian government has pointed out that there is ample scope for betterment of the current system. The dissatisfaction generally circles around eight major issues, which are discussed in the following:

a. Need to Protect Developing Country Interests

The Dispute Settlement Understanding (DSU) enshrines special and differential treatment in various clauses, but the lack of clarity in them might often lead to interpretations actually hurting developing countries. In addition, like other developing countries, India also believes that the presence of the words "shall" and "should" in a number of relevant clauses to protect their interest often fail to do so. The reliance should not be on the benevolence of the developed countries. Instead the responsibility should be made binding legally. It is believed by India that, "There is however no way to ensure that such treatment is accorded to these countries in practice. Therefore, there seems to be a need for developing a screening process to check whether such requirements are adhered to[49]."

b. High Legal Costs

Given the fact that dispute settlement proceedings are extremely expensive, and developing and least developed countries do not have requisite legal expertise to handle such cases, they are at a disadvantageous position as compared to their developed counterparts. In this light there is an urgent need to protect the

49. WTO Newsletter, Ministry of Commerce, April 1999, p. 6.

interest of the developing countries so as not to allow developed countries to use DSP as an instrument for harassing developing countries and LDCs. In the DSB, the burden of proof rests on the respondent. Hence, a developed country should not be allowed to initiate a case against a developing country unless it is able to demonstrate that the alleged violation of an agreement by the former causes economic losses to it above *de minimus* level.[50]

c. Implementation during Reasonable Period

Once the dispute settlement body passes its verdict in a case, the findings have to be incorporated by the losing country (if respondent) within a reasonable period of time, usually negotiated among the two sides.

In determining the reasonable period of time, the Arbitrator in EC – Hormones (Article 21.3) defined such a period as the "shortest period possible within the legal system of the Member to implement the recommendations and rulings of the DSB". The Arbitrator held, *inter alia,* that "when implementation can be effected by administrative means, the reasonable period of time should be considerably shorter than 15 months": The ordinary meaning of the terms of Article 21.3(c) indicates that 15 months is a 'guideline for the arbitrator', and not a rule. This guideline is stated expressly to be that 'the reasonable period of time ... should not exceed 15 months from the date of adoption of a panel or Appellate Body report' (emphasis added). In other words, the 15-month guideline is an outer limit or a maximum in the usual case. For example, when implementation can be effected by administrative means, the reasonable period of time should be considerably shorter than 15 months. However, the reasonable period of time could be shorter or longer, depending upon the particular circumstances, as specified in Article 21.3(c).

Article 21.3(c) also should be interpreted in its context and in light of the object and purpose of the DSU. Relevant considerations in this respect include other provisions of the DSU, including, in particular, Articles 21.1 and 3.3. Article 21.1 stipulates that: 'Prompt compliance with recommendations and rulings of the DSB is essential

---

50. For instance, in the EC-banana case, one Latin American Country could not participate in the case due to the high legal cost, although the outcome of the debate was of enormous interest.

in order to ensure effective resolution of disputes to the benefit of all Members' (emphasis added). Article 3.3 states: 'The prompt settlement of situations in which a Member considers that any benefits accruing to it directly or indirectly under the covered agreements are being impaired by measures taken by another Member is essential to the effective functioning of the WTO and the maintenance of a proper balance between the rights and obligations of Members' (emphasis added). The Concise Oxford Dictionary defines the word, 'prompt', as meaning 'a. acting with alacrity; ready. b. made, done, etc. readily or at once'. Read in context, it is clear that the reasonable period of time, as determined under Article 21.3(c), should be the shortest period possible within the legal system of the Member to implement the recommendations and rulings of the DSB. In the usual case, this should not be greater than 15 months, but could also be less"[51].

However, it has been noticed in a couple of cases that the losing side has not implemented any change in its WTO-incompatible policy during the reasonable period of time, thereby causing continued economic losses to the winner. India has experienced this twice, in case of the dispute against Turkey (textile and clothing products) and EC (bed linen).[52] A similar experience was noticed in EU-import regime for banana case, although India was not a disputing party to it. The DSB does not have any power to force the defaulter to implement these provisions at an early date.

d. Suspension of Benefits

The WTO allows the winner party to suspend favourable treatment, i.e. in simple words, retaliate, in case the loser party does not comply with its obligations even at the end of the 'reasonable period of time'. The extent of retaliation depends on the level of estimated trade loss due to continuation of WTO-incompatible measures in force. In *EC – Hormones (US)*,[53] the Arbitrators stated that

51. Award of the Arbitrator, EC Measures Concerning Meat and Meat Products (Hormones), WT/DS26/15, WT/DS48/13, 29 May 1998, paragraphs 25-26.

52. While India ultimately won the case against EU after a long tussle, it was noticed that the biggest exporter firm to EU has stopped exporting, as the transitory phase was too long. The incident reinforces the urgency of incorporating necessary provisions at the earliest.

53. Decision by the Arbitrators, EC – *Measures Concerning Meat and Meat Products (Hormones)*, WT/DS26/ARB, 12 July 1999, paragraph 16.

the minimum requirements attached to a request to suspend concessions or other obligations are: "the request must set out a specific level of suspension, i.e. a level equivalent to the nullification and impairment caused by the WTO inconsistent measure, pursuant to Article 22.4; and (2) the request must specify the agreement and sector(s) under which concessions or other obligations would be suspended, pursuant to Article 22.3".

However, it is actually an inefficient tool, as developing countries are not adequately equipped to impose such a policy measure on their developed counterparts. The proposed policy could be helpful to developing countries, only if all other nations or at least the majority of WTO members jointly suspend concession on the defaulter. For instance, it is highly unlikely that India could extract some tangible market access by adopting a retaliatory strategy against EC or US. In addition, there are no clear guidelines indicating the procedure to determine such compensation or suspension of concession.[54] India strongly believes that this issue should not be left entirely to negotiations between unequal trade partners, and proper guidelines should be laid in this regard.

e. Participation of NGOs

Access to the dispute settlement system is presently limited to WTO Member governments. Other entities or organisations are not eligible to be WTO Members and consequently, are denied formal participation in the dispute settlement process. NGOs have, however, been afforded a limited opportunity to express their views through the submission of *amici curiae* briefs. India strongly believes that there should not be any room for the NGOs to take part in the dispute settlement process. There was a move by US to facilitate NGO participation in the DS process in the late nineties, and India protested against this move with several other countries. The Appellate Body also decided to invite *Amicus Curiae* briefs in one case (involving EC on asbestos and products containing asbestos).[55]

54. This particular point has been stressed by the Commonwealth Business Council (2001) as it suggested elimination of the retaliation option altogether in favour of compensation. p. 67.

55. An *Amicus Curiae* brief is "an opinion offered to the court by a disinterested party (called *amicus curiae* or friend of the court) in the hope that it would assist the judges in arriving at the best possible outcomes", *"Amicus Curiae"*, in: Goode Walter: *Dictionnary of Trade Policy Terms*, Cambridge University Press 2003, p. 18.

First of all, there is a systemic reason not to accept *amicus curiae* and more generally involvement of any entity which would not be a Member States. As M. Martha notices: "without fundamental changes to the current system, an alteration of the rules regarding capacity of non-members to sue or be sued would lack functionality and is likely to increase the current imbalance between the administration of justice in the WTO and the political processes of the WTO"[56].

The involvement of private parties into the dispute resolution process and particularly the submission of *amicus curiae* are not supported by India who feels that this move is untenable primarily due to three reasons. First, the ultimate compliance obligations under WTO are to be fulfilled by the governments, not the NGOs. Therefore, involving NGOs might change the inter-governmental character of it. Secondly, government positions for a case are arrived only after discussions with all domestic stakeholders. If governments are certain that NGOs have a further chance to influence the DSB, then the system loses efficiency. Thirdly, the developing countries would always be in a disadvantageous position *vis-à-vis* their developed counterparts as their NGOs are relatively unprepared to send briefs without being asked for or to respond to invitations to send briefs owing to resource constraint.[57] But we must add another reason as to why developing countries fear the radicalism of NGOs in the field of environment or labour law: what is an advantage in one case could become disadvantageous and uncontrollable in another. Whether the principle of *amicus curiae* will be accepted or not is still one of the subjects of negotiations under the process of DSU review.

---

56. Martha Rutsel Silvestre: *Capacity to Sue and be Sued Under WTO Law*, World Trade Review 2004 Volume 3n No. 1, p. 51. M. Martha identifies many elements opposed to participation of non-member to the dispute resolution process: "the lack of such a "norm-logical" need results primarily from the fact that the WTO does not constitute a supranational legal order, the subjects of which comprise the organisation, the Members and their national. Second, the substantive norms of the WTO are intergovernmental by nature. Third, the remedies available, that is, cessation of the harmful governmental measure, compensatory trade concessions, and ultimately authorised proportional retaliation, are also governmental by nature. Fourth, the WTO disciplines comprise reciprocal rights and obligations for the members. Hence, without fundamental changes to the current system, an alteration of the rules regarding capacity of non-members to sue or be sued would lack functionality and is likely to increase the current imbalance between the administration of justice in the WTO and the political processes of the WTO".
57. WTO Newsletter, Ministry of Commerce, December 2000, p. 18.

f. Structure of DSB

India is in favour of the current system of selection of the panel members by mutual agreement between the parties, and strongly opposes any move to destabilise it. There was a draft proposal from some members several years' back that there should be a permanent seven-member panelists committee, from which three could be selected at random for a particular dispute. India was strongly opposed to this move on the ground that it would lead to increasing uncertainty to the system.

g. Authoritative Interpretation by Panels and AB

The DSB rulings are not supposed to change the obligations of the countries under WTO. However, the Panels and Appellate Bodies often seem to overstep their respective mandate and enter the area of 'authoritative interpretation' or 'amendment', reserved only for the members as per articles IX and X of the WTO agreement. In addition, India is not happy the way certain unilateral trade measures regarding SPS and environmental concerns were partially upheld by the DSB.[58]

h. Transparency in DSB Proceedings

There is no official negotiating history of WTO, on the basis of which cases should be analysed. The WTO Secretariat sometimes provides notes to Panels as official negotiating history in certain disputes as references. However, these papers are strictly confined to the panel members and not even shared with the parties involved in the dispute, thereby hurting their right as members to access information.[59] The system needs to be changed immediately, and there should be complete transparency in the procedure.

The impacts of DSB results have been mixed for India. While on one hand it had to bring its regulations over domestic patent regime

58. For instance, a number of cases could be cited, e.g. US – Shrimps, Turtle and the EC – Hormones cases, as described in WTO Newsletter, Ministry of Commerce, March 2001, p. 2. Chimni (2002) has also raised concern in this regard.

59. For instance, in 'Canada-EC dispute on pharmaceutical patents and generic products, the Panel Report quotes from an 'Informal GATT Secretariat Note' to which WTO Members do not have access.' WTO Newsletter, Ministry of Commerce, March 2001, p. 3.

and import restrictions in line with its obligations under WTO, it has caused EC to change its anti-dumping regulation in the aftermath of the bed-linen case on the other. Indeed the EC, taking into account the facts that the WTO Reports conclude that the "Community acted inconsistently with the WTO Agreement on Implementation of Article VI of the General Agreement on Tariffs and Trade", has changed its legislation and adopted a new regulation.[60]

The future trends in India's participation under DSB in the coming years could be estimated on the basis of the trade policy review reports. There are two WTO Trade Policy Reviews on India, published in 1998 and 2002 respectively. A comparative analysis of the two reports is provided in Table 18.5. While the earlier review (1998) has been critical of India on various accounts like tariff reform, import restriction procedures, absence of full compliance with TRIPS, non-liberalisation of domestic service sectors etc., the later review (2002) has put words of high praise for the reform measures. A comparison of the Tables 18.5 and 18.2 allows the analysis to check the high correlation between the unfinished reform agenda and filing of a case at WTO. As noted earlier, the non-notification of any case against India at DSB for a long time (June 1999 – January 2003) signifies the increasing WTO-compatibility of India's domestic system. The concerns raised over India's unfinished agenda in the 2002 report are too little in number, and a great upsurge in cases involving India, as respondent is therefore not expected barring the exception of anti-dumping. However, no definitive comment could be passed on its participation in DSB either as a complainant or an interested third-party member. It seems contingency measures, and anti-dumping measures in particular, are going to play a major role in India's WTO association, and in DSB participation. The concern raised by the Trade Policy Review (2002)

60. Council Regulation (EC) No 1644/2001 of 7 August 2001 amending Regulation (EC) No 2398/97 imposing a definitive anti-dumping duty on imports of cotton-type bed linen originating in Egypt, India. Article 2 of this regulation saying:

"1. *The application of the anti-dumping duties specified in Article 1 is hereby suspended with regard to imports originating in India.*

2. *The anti-dumping duties specified in Article 1 shall expire six months after the entry into force of this Regulation with regard to India unless a review has been initiated before that date. During such a review, if any, the application of the anti-dumping duty shall remain suspended pursuant to paragraph 1*".

Table 18.5

A Comparative Analysis of Country Reviews: India

Policies Praised	*Policies Where Further Reform Advocated*
Trade Policy Review (1998)	
• Rapid reform in tariff rates over 1993-94 to 1997-98. • Overall economic reform measures. • Amendment in Copyright law in line with TRIPS.	• Complex structure of tariff regime and tariff escalation. • Import restriction on consumer goods. • Restrictive import licenses and other procedural hassles on imports. • Presence of indirect subsidies, export subsidies and other incentives. • Unfinished compliance with TRIPS. • Reform in case of agricultural products. • Transparency in decision making. • Reform in services.
Trade Policy Review (2002)	
• Simplification of tariff structure. • Complete elimination of quantitative restrictions. • Reduction in export restrictions. • Review of FDI policy. • Move towards full conformity with TRIPS. • Significant reform in certain key service sectors e.g. - telecommunication, financial services and to some extent in infrastructural services.	• Increase in use of contingency measures on imports. • Wide range of price and distribution controls in agriculture. • Existence of certain commodity specific entry restrictions.

Source: Compared on the basis of the two reviews.

on increasing trend in anti-dumping measures and the request of EC (and subsequently Bangladesh and Taiwan) for consultation over imposition of anti-dumping measures in India on 27 commodities,[61]

61. The details about the consultation is outlined in WT/DS304/1, Dated 11 December 2003.

Table 18.6

Major Affected Countries by Imposition of Anti-Dumping Duties

Major Countries	*Total Number of Impositions*	*Major Countries*	*Total Number of Impositions*	*Major Countries*	*Total Number of Impositions*
1st July 1999-30th June 2000		*1st January 2001- 30th June 2001*		*1st July 2001-30th June 2002*	
EC	32	China	22	China	46
China	30	Korea	10	EU	39
Korea	23	Taipei	9	Indonesia	15
Taipei	13	India	8	Korea	14
Indonesia	15	Thailand	6	Brazil	13
Thailand	12			Taipei	13
India	11			India	12
Total	**222**	**Total**	**134**	**Total**	**288**

Source: WTO Annual Report (Various Issues).

are indicative of this fact. On the other hand, India had moved to DSB on several occasions complaining about the anti-dumping proceedings in other members, ranging from developed to developing countries. In the light of the increasing trend in usage of contingency measures in recent years, and India's vulnerability to them as seen from Table 18.6, more cases are likely to be lodged in the coming days. It is unfortunate to note that, in spite of the pro-active stance adopted by India in WTO forum in the recent years,[62] proper planning is still lacking and strategic appointments, a major tool, are yet to be considered.[63]

62. The shift in India's negotiating stance in recent times has been discussed in Chakraborty (2003).

63. "It is therefore unfortunate that India has supported the election of a commerce secretary to the Appellate Body with no background in international law.", Chimni (2002).

References

Books and Articles

Amersinghe, C.F., "Dispute Settlement by International Organisations", *Indian Journal of International Law,* Volume 43 No. 3, July-September 2003.

Bourgeois, Jacques, "Some Reflections on the WTO Dispute Settlement System From a Practitioner's Perspective", *Journal of International Economic Law, 2001,* Volume 4, No. 1.

Bronckers, Marco and Quick, Reinhard (Ed.), *New directions in International Economic Law – Essays in Honour of John H. Jackson,* The Hague Kluwer Law International, 2000 (593 p.).

Chaisse, Julien and Chakraborty, Debashis: "The Doha Development Agenda on Disputes Resolution", *Amity Law Review,* Vol. 6, No. 1, pp. 8-20, 2005.

Chakraborty, D., "The Changing Face of Indian Negotiation Strategy in WTO", in Dipankar Sengupta and Sudhir Kumar Singh (Ed.) *NDA Government's Foreign Policy,* Author's Press, New Delhi (forthcoming).

Chimni, B.S., "WTO and Environment: Legitimisation of Unilateral Trade Sanctions", *Economic and Political Weekly,* January 12, 2002.

Chisti, Sumitra, "Dispute Settlement System under World Trade Organisation", *Occasional Paper No. 19,* IIFT, 2001.

Chua, Adrian, "Reasonable Expectations and Non-Violation Complaints in GATT/WTO Jurisprudence", *Journal of World Trade,* Volume 32, No. 2, April 1998.

Commonwealth Business Council, *Developing Countries and the WTO Trade Debate: Compelling Case for Full Participation in the New Round,* 2001.

Das, Abhijit, "Dispute Settlement Procedures", Paper Presented in a Seminar on *The New WTO Round: Is Free Trade Fair Trade?* in 2001, jointly organised by Rajiv Gandhi Institute of Contemporary Studies and Liberty Institute.

Das, Bhagirath-Lal, *The WTO Agreements: Deficiencies, Imbalances and Required Changes,* TWN & Zed Books, 1998 (472 p.).

Goode, Walter, *Dictionary of Trade Policy Terms,* Cambridge University Press, 2003 (437 p.).

Government of India, Ministry of Commerce, Directorate General of Anti-dumping and Allied Duties, *Annual Report* (2001-02).

Government of India, *India and The WTO,* Monthly Newsletter of The Ministry of Commerce and Industry, (various issues).

Gupta, K.R., *World Trade Organisation: Text – Volume I,* New Delhi, Atlantic Publishers and Distributors, 2000 (338 p.).

Gupta, K.R., *World Trade Organisation: Text – Volume II,* New Delhi, Atlantic Publishers and Distributors, 2000 (339-716 pp.).

Jackson, John, *The Jurisprudence of GATT and the WTO: Insights on Treaty Law and Economic Relations,* Cambridge University Press, Cambridge, United Kingdom, 2000 (497 p.).

Martha Rutsel Silvestre: "Capacity to Sue and be Sued Under WTO Law", *World Trade Review 2004,* Volume 3 No. 1, pp. 27-51.

Pauwelyn, Joost, "The Use of Experts in WTO Dispute Settlement", *International and Comparative Law Quarterly,* 2002, Volume 51, Part 2, pp. 325-364.

Petersmann, Ernst-Ulrich, (Ed.), "International Trade Law and the GATT/WTO Dispute Settlement System", *Studies in Transnational Economic Law,* Volume 11, Kluwer Law International, 1997 (704 p.).

Petersmann, Ernst-Ulrich, "The GATT/WTO Dispute Settlement System International Law, International Organisations and Dispute Settlement", *Nijhoff Law Specials:* Volume 23, Kluwer Law International, The Hague, 1997 (368 p.).

Ruiz-Fabri Hélène, "Le contentieux de l'exécution dans le règlement des différends de l'organisation mondiale du commerce", *Journal du Droit International*, No. 3, 2000, pp. 605-645.

Stoler Andrew: "The WTO Dispute Settlement Process: Did the Negotiators Get What They Wanted?", *World Trade Review 2004* Volume 3 No. 1, pp. 99-118.

Stoll Peter-Tobias et Steinmann Arthur, "WTO Dispute Settlement: The Implementation Stage", *Max Planck Yearbook of United Nations Law*, 1999, Volume 3.

World Trade Organisation, *Annual Report* (various issues).

World Trade Organisation, *Trade Policy Review*, India (1998).

World Trade Organisation, *Trade Policy Review*, India (2002).

WTO Secretariat, *The WTO Dispute Settlement Procedures*, Cambridge University Press, 2nd Edition 2003 (146 p.).

WTO Secretariat, *Update of WTO Dispute Settlement Cases*, WT/DS/OV/22, 14 October 2004.

List of Panel, Appeal and Arbitration Rulings

United States - Standards for Reformulated and Conventional Gasoline - Report of the Panel, WT/DS2/R WT/DS2/R, 29 January 1996.

Report of the Panel, Japan - Taxes on Alcoholic Beverages, WT/DS8/R, WT/DS10/R and WT/DS11/R, 11 July 1996.

Report of the Appellate Body, Brazil - Measures Affecting Desiccated Coconut, WT/DS22/AB/R, 21 February 1997.

Appellate Body Report, United States - Measure Affecting Imports of Woven Wool Shirts and Blouses from India, WT/DS33/AB/R, 25 April 1997.

Report of the Appellate Body, Measures Concerning Meat and Meat Products (Hormones), WT/DS26/AB/R and WT/DS48/AB/R, 16 January 1998.

Appellate Body Report, Guatemala – Anti-Dumping Investigation Regarding Portland Cement from Mexico, WT/DS60/AB/R, 2 November 1998.

Decision by the Arbitrators, EC – Measures Concerning Meat and Meat Products (Hormones), WT/DS26/ARB, 12 July 1999.

Appellate Body Report, India – Quantitative Restrictions on Imports of Agricultural, Textile and Industrial Products Case, WT/DS90/AB/R, 23 August 1999.

Panel Report, Brazil – Export Financing Programme for Aircraft, WT/DS46/RW, 9 May 2000.

Report of the Panel, United States - Continued Dumping and Subsidy Offset Act of 2000, WT/DS217/R, WT/DS234/R, 16 September 2002.

Annexes

Table 18.7

Indian Position (A)

Clause	*Current/Proposed Positions*	*Developing Country Proposals*
Mutually Agreed Solutions	Article 3.6 of DSU requires any mutually agreed solutions among the disputing parties to notify to the WTO. However, no time period has been specified.	The terms of settlement should be notified in sufficient details to DSB and other relevant councils within 60 days of such agreement.
Amicus Curiae Briefs	EC and US has proposed modification in Article 13 of DSU, and argued in favour of defining the framework and conditions for allowing *Amicus Curiae* briefs in potentially all cases.	No need to make provisions for accepting *Amicus Curiae* briefs. The purpose could be served by clarifying the meaning of the word 'seek' in Article 13 of DSU.
Terms of Appointment of Appellate Body Members	Currently the system provides for reappointment of Appellate Body members, for a second-year term.	The practice is not in line with the high dignity of the office. The future appointments of the Appellate Body members should be for a non-renewable fixed term of six years.
Inputs provided by the Secretariat	WTO does not have an official negotiating history, and the Secretariat provides notes to Panels as one in certain disputes, which are not passed to the parties even.	It is necessary to ensure that the parties to the dispute promptly receive all the documents, notes, information etc. available to the Secretariat once a panel is established and appendix 3 of paragraph 10 should be amended accordingly.
Sufficiency of notice of appeal	The parties deserve a right to appeal against adoption of the panel report. The notices of appeal normally identify the nature of appeal, and the issues of law in it. However, in a couple of cases, the issues are unclearly stated and the other party, especially developing ones, loses valuable time in responding.	The appellate Body was requested to lay down guidelines on the nature of Notice of appeals, while revising the working procedures.
Third party rights in appeal procedures	The provisions in Article 17.4 give discretion to the Appellate Body to hear or not hear from the third parties.	In order to ensure internal transparency and to enhance participate in the DS process, article 17.4 should be modified along the lines of Article 10.2.

Source: The draft submitted to WTO dated 23rd September 2002 (TN/DS/W/18).

Table 18.8

Indian Position (B)

Clause	*Current/Proposed Positions*	*Developing Country Proposals*
Suspension of Concessions and other Obligations	The developed countries, losing side in a dispute, often do not cooperate with their developing counterparts. However, the only feasible option left with them, i.e., withdrawal of concessions, given the level of dependence is associated with high economic cost.	Cross-retaliation is most effective to tackle a problem in these cases. The complaining developing country should be permitted to seek authorization for suspending concessions and other obligations in the sectors of their choice, bypassing the lengthy process of proving a loss first.
Litigation Costs	The litigating parties have to finance their case.	The increasing cost of legal battles is a major barrier and financial responsibility on developing countries. Therefore, the legal cost to the developing countries, if they win the case against their developed counterpart in violation with the WTO-principle, should be reim bursed by it.
Article 4.10	The Article requires, "During consultations members should give special attention to developing country Members' particular problems and interests."	The word 'should' needs to be replaced by 'shall' and specific attention has to be given according to the status of the developing country. Then the provisions would be mandatory and effective.
Article 12.10	The provision relates to the situation when a developing country is the defending party, while the other party is not necessarily a developed one. The provisions deal with consultation phase and panel proceeding.	The proposal suggested modification in the agreement and seeks to extend the overall, as well as individual, time frame for disputes involving developing countries as defending parties.
Article 21.2	The consideration to developing country interest as a litigant has been described as 'Particular attention should be paid to ..."	The word 'should' needs to be replaced by 'shall' and specific attention has to be given according to the status of the developing country. Then the provisions would be mandatory and effective.

Source: The draft submitted to WTO dated 9th October 2002 (TN/DS/W/19).

19

Precautionary Principle: A Newly Emerging Non-Tariff Barrier to Developing Countries' Trade

SWAPAN K. BHATTACHARYA

Introduction

In the last Cancun Ministerial Conference of the World Trade Organisation, the European Union had been insisting on the adoption of Precautionary Principle as the basis for all environmental related disputes. This was not the first time when the European Union directly asked the relevance of Precautionary Principle for the settlement of environmental-related trade disputes of the WTO. In Shrimp- Turtle Case between India and USA, the Hormones Case between the EU and USA, Salmon Case between Canada and Australia and the Japan-Varietals Case between United States and Japan, the EU clearly indicated the weakness of Sanitary and Phyto-sanitary Standards (SPS) of the WTO in addressing the concern of food safety, environmental damage and health of human beings, plants and animals. In the above-mentioned disputes, the European Union raised the questions whether the SPS Agreement's preference for scientific evidence going far enough in dealing with possible risks for consumers and producers or "safety first" approach should be taken as the basis for future standards where "scientific uncertainty" only aggravates the environment and enhances the health risk.

Several WTO jurisprudence related to trade-environmental disputes prove in no uncertain terms that Precautionary Principle has relevance to the trade regime and secondly, by consciously avoiding ruling on its status as custom, as strongly advocated by the European Union, the Appellate Body implicitly recognises that it will have to revisit the issue in future trade dispute. In the Hormones Case, though Appellate Body upholds the spirit of Article 5.1, 5.2 and 5.7

of SPS of WTO in justifying its applicability in the trade related dispute by ignoring the basic tenet of Precautionary Principle as customary rule, the EU preferred silence on that issue in the expectation of future permanent rule based on further research. The Appellate Body clearly mentioned that "the precautionary principle, whether, or to what extent is relevant in the interpretation of SPS Agreement of the WTO is the subject of debate among academics, law practitioners, regulators and judges." It clearly indicates that the status of precautionary principle in international law is something it should not rule on. Nevertheless, in many areas of US laws, such as system of pharmaceutical approvals, are based on the precautionary principle. If the ruling of the Appellate Body sets the future standards, the potential effect of WTO determination on a range of US laws is immense. If precautionary principle of the Cartegena Protocol on Biosafety becomes customary rule of all environmental related disputes of the WTO, the potential damage of the trade interests of the developing countries would be enormous. The first casualty will be the prospect of agricultural exports to the markets of the developed countries.

Since the onset of the World Trade Organisation (WTO) on 1 January 1995, India has been encountering with the plethora of non-trade related measures in the markets of developed countries that adversely affect its trade potentials. Many of these measures are taken unilaterally and do not pass through the multilateral route. Emergence of labyrinthine environmental standards in the pretext of sustainable development pose serious threat to Indian exporters. Majority of the newly emerging standards are still opaque in nature and their obvious and distinct linkage with the international trade is yet to be ascertained by the scientific proof. Yet, trading communities of the developing countries have been riddled with the proliferation of non-tariff barriers to their trade in the form of "green standards" at the name of environmental protection. In fact, about 200 MEAs (Multilateral Environmental Agreements) have been concluded so far in order to effectively deal with the environmental problem faced by the international community. India has so far signed quite a large number of such MEAs to address the environmental concern in proper perspective and has passed several legislations ensuring environmental protection.

International trade does not affect environment *per se*, nor trade has an transboundary effect either, it is the production and consumption activities of exporting country, which have several negative externalities *viz.* generating more pollution, depleting ozone lair, enhancing global warming and threatening endangered species from extinction. More precisely, it is not the production itself that creates problem to the environment but it is the process of production that have insalubrious consequences to the environment. The emergence of precautionary principle aims to arrest declining environmental quality due to overexploitation of nature. The basic objective of the precautionary principle (PP) is to safeguard the uncertainty, which is tantamount to "No regrets", "Safety first" and "Look before you leap" policies in case of danger that may emerge due to environmental degradation. Environmental measures must anticipate, prevent, and attack the cause of environmental degradation. PP is a tool to combat such degradation and to achieve the objective of sustainable development, where there are threats serious or irreversible damage, lack of full certainty should not be used as a reason for postponing measures to prevent environmental degradation.[1]

PP has been referred most extensively to all disputes related to environment; in some cases (i.e. US pharmaceutical approval) it has been a part of the law over the years. Its original mandate is to take anticipatory measures to protect environment. The major area of concern is the applicability of PP and the loss of biodiversity resulting from the trade in byproducts, and the critical role of time element in resolving environment related trade disputes. The PP got international acceptability at the first International Conference on the Protection of the North Sea in 1984, when the focus was on emissions into the marine environment. The PP played increasingly significant role since its endorsement by the Second International Conference of the North Sea in 1987.

Environmental issue has been in the active agenda of the WTO since Singapore Meet though it is yet to be a part of the system. In order to address environmental related problems, WTO has

1. United Nations Economic Commission for Europe (ECU), *Multilateral Declaration on Sustainable Development in the EEC Region*, May 1990, para. 7.

constituted Committee on Trade and Environment (CTE). Though this issue is yet to be under multilateral rule, WTO has been interpreting environment-related disputes by using Exception Clause of Article XX of GATT and sanitary and phyto-sanitary standards (SPS) of the GATT 1994. In defining its role for protecting environment WTO says,

> *"[We must] recognise that much more progress is needed in the WTO Committee on Trade and Environment. Its work must be revitalized if the trade and environmental agendas are to advance in a mutually supportive way.... Other areas where we need to clarify the relationship between both policy objectives-trade liberalisaion and environmental protection-include among others.... the so-called precautionary principle"*[2]

The emergence of PP in the trade-environment dispute is a recent phenomenon though it has been a part of international convention/treaties related to environment for quite sometimes. More prominently it began to appear in international legal instrument only in the 1980s but has since experienced what has been called as a meteoric rise in the international law.[3] Precautionary principle is commonly called as "statement of commonsense" and its role is to balance the completive concerns of economic development against limited environmental resources. Due to advancement of science and technology and the rapid progress of globalisation, economic development puts increasing pressure on the existing natural resources. The demand for higher economic development coupled with the trade liberalisation lead to extensive exploitation of natural resources, supply of which is limited. In order to balance between the increasing trade and most optimal use of natural resources, environmental lobby has been advocating the use of precautionary approach to minimise environmental damage. Due to its immense importance in environmental related matters, PP has now entered the jurisprudence of the WTO's dispute settlement body through indirect way. It is no longer a remote concept exclusively located in the sphere of environmental law.

---

2. "The Future of the World Trading System," Address by Renato Ruggiero, Director General of the WTO, 15 April 1998, to the Institute for International Economics Conference, Washington DC, reproduced at www. wto.org/speeches/bergen.htm.
3. Cameron and Abouchar, "The Status of the Precautionary Principle," op. cit., p.80 see also James Cameron and Will Wade-Grey, "Addressing Uncertainty: Law, Policy and the Development of the Precautionary Principle," *CSERGE Working Paper*, GEC 92-43, 1992, also in Bruno Dente, ed. Environmental Policy in Search of New Instrument, Dordrecht, Kluwer Academic Publisher, 1994.

The PP is still outside the ambit of the WTO framework but finds its way to enter latter's domain through exception clause of Article XX of GATT 1994 especially section (b) & (g). It also provides a limited application under the provisions of sanitary and phyto-sanitary standards (SPS). Nevertheless, it fails to utilise some of the requisite approaches in other agreements like GATT 1994 and technical barrier to trade (TBT). PP is generally 'risk averse' in nature. This is often adopted in anticipation of probable risk, where, in many cases, sufficient scientific proof is absent and knowledge is limited. Since scientific knowledge is too limited to quantify uncertainties, that's the reason why it cannot establish probability distribution of potential uncertainties.

The Precautionary Principle: History, Origin and Definition

The importance of the precautionary principle was strongly felt during 1960s, when people began to realise that rapid economic development caused enormous damage to environment by cutting trees, building roads, massive deforestation, extensive use of chemicals in the agriculture, large scale use of asbestos in housing, extraction of ground water and natural resources etc. The pressure of economic development on natural resources became so evident that individual countries as well as world bodies started thinking seriously on this issue.

Conceptually, individual countries and organisations such as the EEC and the UN began to take measures to protect environment initially on an *ad hoc* basis. The process was accentuated by two events developed during 1972. First development was the publication of reports *Limits of Growth* by Club of Rome where environmental impact of economic growth was presented and showed how natural resources were encroached upon by the process of rapid economic development. The report warned that if production and consumption activities continued to grow without addressing the environmental concern, there may be catastrophe and it would go beyond the control of human endeavour.

Secondly, the UN Conference on the Human Environment adopted a non-binding set of principles, which, the participating states promised to honour even without any legal binding. Most important feature of the conference is the Principle 21, in which it is affirmed that states are obliged to ensure that activities within their jurisdiction or control do not cause damage in another state of beyond national jurisdiction, such as on the high seas. According to Principle 7, it is urgent that States should prevent pollution of seas. Another significant result of the conference was the creation of UNEP (United Nations Environment Programme).

In 1987, the Brundtland Report was published, which addressed continued degradation of world environment as a result of economic growth. Similar to Club of Rome's report *Limits of Growth* in 1972, the Brundtland Report, *Our Common Future* issued a strong warning against the environment unfriendly production and consumption activities. The Brundtland Report presents an attractive and acceptable solution to the continued slide in environmental quality, namely, a shift towards a sustainable development without quantifying the limit of tolerance and development. The Report prescribes this solution as development that meets the need of the present without compromising the ability of future generations to meet their needs. But the report fails to clarify how much pollution is sustainable, how many fish can be caught without endangering rights of future generations and how exactly production and consumption patterns can be made sustainable without compromising the development process. Nevertheless, the idea of sustainable development was welcomed worldwide in spite of its several flaws. This is because it is the second best solution.

The international treaty, which makes explicit reference of the precautionary approach, was the 1985 Viena Convention on Ozone Depleting Substances (ODS), wherein the parties recongnised "precautionary measures" taken at the national and international levels.[4] The most commonly referenced form of the principle comes from the Bergen Declaration of 1990. During 1990, Economic Commission for Europe (ECE), an UN organ convened a meeting to discuss the modalities of the implementation of the Brundtland Report. The participants made a non-binding declaration, which is as follows:

> *"In order to achieve sustainable development, policies must be based on the precautionary principle. Environmental measures must anticipate, prevent and attack the causes of environmental degradation. Where there are threats of serious irreversible damage, lack of full scientific certainty should not be used as a reason for postponing measures to prevent environmental degradation."*

4. Vienna Convention on Ozone Depleting Substances, 1985, Preamble, n. 179.

In this Declaration, sustainable development is linked to precautionary principle. Though there have been critics of the above Declaration, the principle was finally embraced at the United Nations Conference on Environment and Development (UNCED) in Rio de Janeiro in 1992.[5] Five environmental instruments, two binding (the United Nations Framework Convention on Climate Change and the Convention of Biological Diversity) and three non-binding (Agenda 21, the Rio Declaration on Environment and Development, and Statement of Forest Principles), signed and acceded to virtually by all Heads of States. Though the full acceptance of the principle as universal can be seen as coinciding with this conference, the PP has since reaffirmed in virtually every international agreement on the environment and becomes the lead principle in the European Union's environmental law. Since Europe is the most environment conscious continent in the world, the approach has been applied by all tribunals in disputes relating to environment and becomes a part of the domestic regulation.

In fact, there are plethora of definitions of the precautionary principle, it is worth distinguishing in two broad classes: first the strong PP, which basically says, *take no action unless you are certain that it will do no harm;* and second, weak PP, which says that *lack of full certainty is not a justification for preventing an action that might be harmful.* Both types of definitions have indication for trade measures in case of environmental damage and have seeds of protectionism in international trade.

The genesis of the principle is in Germany, where the principles formed one of the basic principles of environmental policy since mid-1970s. It is to be noted that German equivalent of the PP (the *versorgepvinzip*) is used for specific purposes where a difference is made between human behaviour those causes dangers in one hand and the risks on the other. The government comes out with all possible means (*Gefahrenvorsorge*) in order to prevent dangers pertaining to human health. But if there is a possibility of risk, this is to be investigated and preventive measures can be taken (*Risikovorsorge*) depending upon the magnitude of risk. Outside Germany, precautionary principle was introduced in Europe in the

5. Cameron & Abouchar, " The Status of the Precautionary Principle," op. cit., p. 37.

1980s and became the basis of 1987 Treaty that banned dumping of persistent toxic substance in the North Sea. In Sweden and Germany, increasing number of environmental measures is based on PP. This evidently shows that even without achieving legal status it becomes a guiding principle in the international trade.

Due to its origin, PP is often treated as a German variant. Allen Mazur (1996) shows that PP-like arguments have been in the US system since the 1950s. During that period, groups of political conservatives opposed fluoridation of water on the ground that fluoride was used as rat poisons and the involuntary fluoridation amounted to mass medication. In the 1960s, left wing radicals similarly used PP-like arguments against nuclear power. Both fluoride and radiation have in common known negative effects at high dose and thus pose a risk of widespread damage if they are misused. An early application of this open-ended precautionary approach can be seen in the 1985 decision of the European Commission to ban hormones used for animal growth promotion. The ban was instituted (under EC Directive 81/602) on the basis that their safety has not been conclusively proven.

The PP is subject to twelve different definitions and various other interpretations in international treaties and declarations. Due to its wide coverage and voracity of the problem, this approach is fast becoming a fundamental principle in international environmental law. In the last ten years, this principle has shown a meteoric rise in guiding human activities to prevent harm to the environment and to human health. There may be variation in interpretations, but the Wingspread Statement is the first of this kind to give a much comprehensive definition of the PP. On 23-25 January 1998, a group of scientists, government officials, lawyers, labour unions and grass-root environmentalists met at Wingspread in Racine, Wisconsin to define and discuss the PP. Wingspread Statement on the PP is as follows:

> *"We believe existing environmental regulations and other decisions, particularly those based on risk assessment, have failed to protect adequately human health and the environment -the larger system of which humans are but a part.*
>
> *"We believe there is compelling evidence that damage to humans and the worldwide environment is of such magnitude and seriousness that new principles for conducting human activities are necessary.*

"While we realise that human activities may involve hazards, people must proceed more carefully than has been the case in recent history. Corporations, government entities, organisations, communities, scientists and other individuals must opt a precautionary approach to all human endeavours.

"Therefore, it is necessary to implement the Precautionary Principle: When an activity raises threats of harm to human health or the environment, precautionary measures should be taken even if some cause and effect relationship are not fully established scientifically. In this context the proponent of an activity, rather than the public should bear the burden of proof.

"The process of applying the Precautionary Principle must be open, informed and democratic and must include potentially affected parties. It must also involve an examination of the full range of alternatives including no action".

Therefore, it is always argued in favour of the application of PP in order to prevent environmental related health problems. When activity raises threat to human health or the environment, precautionary measures should be taken even if cause and effect relationships are not fully established scientifically or there exists a considerably time lag to prove the same.

PP has increasingly been referred by environmentalists of the developed countries to address all matters of trade that creates damage to environment since early-1990s; the USA is yet to accept it as binding rule in international trade. At the United Nations Conference on Environment and Development (UNCED) in Rio in 1992, USA expressed its reservations for PP on several grounds. USA might have expected that this might be used against it due to green house effect. USA argues that there is no sufficient scientific evidence for the causal relationship between green house effect and change in human behaviour, which negates the validity of the principle. Other countries, especially European Union, were more inclined to follow this approach because waiting for proof might result in irreversible harm. In the (non-binding) Rio Declaration on Environment and Development, Precautionary Approach (as contained in the Article 15) says:

"In order to protect the environment, the precautionary approach shall be widely applied by states according to their capabilities, where there are threats of serious or irreversible damage, lack of full scientific certainty shall not be used as a reason for postponing cost effective measures to prevent environmental degradation."

There are several problems associated with this definition. First, the term 'threat' is not very clear from the definition. It is to be restricted to events with an actuarially ascertainable probability. Or more precisely, including all manner of hypothetically possible events the probability of occurrence of which, whilst not zero, *cannot* be ascertained? A problem with this second possibility is that 'threats' is so loosely defined that it can include everything from the risk of the Yamuna flooding, which may inundates entire Delhi (which may occur once in a century, i.e. annual probability is 1:100) to volcano eruption in Andaman & Nicobar Islands. Second, it is necessary to define damage, and in particular to distinguish 'damage' from mere 'change'. Third, all changes (and hence all damage) is irreversible in the strict sense that the precise structure of the world that pertained before cannot once again come into being. Attempting to reverse some 'damage' will result in other changes occurring to the state of the world. Fourth, it is then necessary to define 'serious damage'. This is problematic because the notion of seriousness is clearly a subjective one and it is used in relative terms. Fifth, science has not yet, and is unlikely in the future, to provide a full-fledged deterministic theory of the universe from which all particular events can be predicted. In other words, there will always be scientific uncertainty, both with regard to environmental effects and with regard to all other matters, especially concerning the future.

The parties to the UN Framework Convention of Climate Change also corroborate uncertainty in prediction of timing, magnitude, and regional pattern, as these vary from country to country. In this Convention, all the parties are in favour of adopting precautionary measures to anticipate, prevent or minimise the cause of climate change and mitigate its adverse effects. Following the line of Rio Declaration, this Convention also prescribes the similar measures, with emphasis on cost effective criteria;

> *"Where there are threats of serious or irreversible damage, lack of full scientific certainty shall not be used as a reason for postponing cost effective measures to prevent environmental degradation, taking into account that policies and measures to deal with climate change should be cost effective so as to ensure global benefits at the lowest possible costs."*

The precautionary principle also embodied in the Hague Declaration on Principles of Environmental Law. Legal experts from 80 countries gathered in the Hague to talk about the role of principles in environmental policies. At the end of the Conference, a Declaration was adopted. In this Declaration, it is stressed that the

Rio Declaration should be given the fullest possible legal effect. One way of doing so is to incorporate environmental principles into both national legal systems and policies.

The importance of PP at several stages of environment related disputes has been acknowledged in ECE countries on the protection and use of transboundary water resources and international lakes (known as Helsinki Convention 1992). First, the parties are empowered to take all appropriate measures to prevent, control and reduce pollution of waters causing or like to cause transboundary impact (Article 2(2)(a). Secondly, Article 2(5)(a) states while taking the measures, the parties "shall be guided by" a number of principles. It first mentions the precautionary principle. It says, "*by virtue of which action to avoid the potential transboundary impact of the release of hazardous substances shall not be postponed on the ground that scientific research has not fully proved a causal link between those substances, on the one hand, and the potential transboundary impact, on the other hand*". The Helsinki Convention thus extended the definition with a broader scope than the Rio and Bergen Declaration, as it does not limit itself to serious or irreversible damage.

During 1990s host of binding international treaties emerged referring the application of PP. One such treaty is the Treaty of Maastricht, for the European Community. In this treaty. Article 2 calls for an economic growth, which is both sustainable and respects the environmental friendly. Strangely enough, the wording sustainable growth is used instead of the more common expression sustainable development. Another novel feature of the EC Treaty is that in Article 130R, where the term precautionary principle is added to the list of environmental principles, which was introduced in 1987 via the Single European Act.

Precautionary approach became the main guiding principle of the London Dumping Conventions of 1972 and 1991. The parties agreed that "appropriate preventive measures are taken where there is reason to believe that substances or energy introduced into the marine environment are likely to cause harm, even when there is no conclusive evidence to prove a causal relationship between imports and their effects". It can also be noted that one year later, Agenda 21 asked the parties to the Convention for a change of the voluntary moratorium on the dumping of low radioactive wastes into a binding stop in the light of the precautionary principle.

The question of protecting North Sea was discussed at length in a number of international conferences held in Berman (1984), London (1987), The Hague (1990) and Esbjerg (1995). The Germany attracted international attention on PP through these conferences. The conclusion of the first conference was that " damage to the environment can be irreversible or remediable only at considerable expense and over long periods and that, therefore, coastal states and the EEC must not wait for proof of harmful effects before taking action". The word precaution was not used yet. At the second conference in 1987, the London Declaration was adopted. This time a reference to the necessity of a 'precautionary approach' is made. This may require action to control imports of the 'most dangerous substances' even before a causal link has been established by absolutely clear scientific evidence. By1990, at the third conference in the Hague, the parties declared that they '*will continue to apply the precautionary principle to take action in order to avoid potentially damaging impacts of substances that are persistent, toxic and liable to bioaccumulate even when there is no scientific evidence to prove that a causal link between emissions and effects*'. The latest one i.e. Esbjerg Declaration (1995) recommends that the precautionary principle can also be applied in fishery management.

While enforcing PP, the situation is always judged whether the importation involves risk in human health and environment or it is uncertain not having any scientific proof as yet. If there is no uncertainty about the environmental risks, the measure is preventive, not precautionary. In the face of uncertainty, however, the principle wants the state to act in an effort to mitigate the risks. Putting in the best way, "*the precautionary principle stipulates that where the environmental risk being run by regulatory inaction, or in some way, uncertain but non-negligible, regulatory inaction is unjustified*". This definition of the PP leaves three issues undecided. The issues are (a) the meaning and extent of non-negligible risk, (b) the regulatory action that is justified by the principle, and (c) threshold and responses to uncertainty. These issues are subjective in nature and policies relating to these issues are political without having any sound scientific base. Politicians often determine the extent of risk and what should be the policy framework to minimise the risk. In most of the cases, they give priority to the national objectives. The question remains as to how much such political decision supersedes scientific evidence. Again the examples from international law range in degree, from "no scientific evidence to prove a causal link before a causal link has been established by absolutely clean scientific evidence". Science cannot be divorced from the precautionary principle because a scientific view of the risk is an essential ingredient of the evolution of risk that the principle anticipates.

Three observations can be made from the foregoing analysis. First, the PP has been experiencing a meteoric rise in recent times in the developed countries. This may be attributed to the public perception of scientific inadequacy in addressing environmental regulations. Secondly, the fact that science is uncertain at most basic level throws doubt on its adequacy, in theory, in addressing environmental concern. Finally, all scientific assessments of environmental damage are dependent on subjective assumption of what constitutes harm, especially degrees. Therefore, it necessarily involves judgments that have cultural, economic and political dimensions.

The main thrust of the PP is apparently very simple and straightforward. Where an importation raises threats of harm to the environment or human health, precautionary measures should be taken even if certain cause and effect relationships are not established scientifically. Commonsense phrasings capturing the essence include " an ounce of prevention is worth a pound cure", " a stitch in time saves nine", and "if in doubt, don't pump it out". On closer scrutiny, however, the principle is difficult to grasp, providing only "bare bones" and requiring further fleshing out in national and international legal system. Debates continue over what should trigger the principle with words such as "likely harm" or "serious or irreversible harm". Who should "pull the trigger" and make such determinations is open for discussion, as is the question of required precautionary control measures.

Precautionary Principle: The Conceptual Framework

In spite of plethora of definitions given by several diplomatic conventions, the conceptual clarity in the interpretation of the precautionary principle is yet to be ascertained. Preventive standards may be precautionary or non-precautionary in certain degrees, but it is almost certain that precautionary standards cannot be non-preventive though it varies in degree. This is because of the fact that the key element in defining the core of precaution is the lack of unambiguity about the cause-and-effect relationships or the possible extent of a particular environmental harm. If there is no uncertainty about the environmental risks of a situations, then the measure is preventive, not precautionary. The basic characteristic of the PP is its uncertainty whose probability distribution is very small. Therefore, it is also suggested that precautionary approach should be taken with much caution and there should be scientific criteria, which objectively determine the extent of measure and probability distribution of the event. In the face of uncertainty, however, the PP, like *Vorsorgeprinzip* allows the state to act in an effort to mitigate the risks. To put it most meaningful way, " *precautionary principle stipulates that where the environmental risks being run by regulatory inaction, are in some way uncertain but non-negligible , regulatory inaction is unjustified*"[6].

This definition of the conceptual core of the PP does leave three issues undecided. These are: the meaning and extent of non-negligible risk, the regulatory action that is justified by the principle, and the thresholds and responses to uncertainty. It is important to point out that the third issue, of thresholds, is really addressing the question of how to determine answers to the first two issues, and exercise that ultimately relies on politics and incorporation.

Similar to confusion mentioned above, there remains further ambiguity in making distinction between risk and uncertainty. Conceptually, risk is the amalgam of the probability of an event occurring and the seriousness of the event's consequences[7]. Therefore, if the probability of occurrence of an event is high or with higher frequency, the strategy is high risk. At the beginning, the threshold of risk must incorporate the notion that, in order to make the event non-negligible, a given risk must at least in theory, have both of its aspects meet this threshold. In fact, the most common form of

---

6. See Cameron, "The Precautionary Principle," *op. cit.*, and also Cameron and Wade-Gery, "Addressing Uncertainty", *op. cit.*, pp. 26-27.
7. See Cameron and Wade-Gery, "Addressing Uncertainty, *op. cit.*, pp. 9-10.

precaution adopted till to date contains minimum risk severity though it is always alleged that of "serious or irreversible harm"[8]. But risk obviates itself altogether from the PP when its likeliness and severity are known. If both the probability and the magnitude of risks are known, precaution is not a factor because the level of uncertainty involved is relatively low. Risk is inseparable from uncertainty, then, but is not the same as uncertainty.

Now question arises what should be the optimum justifiable regulatory actions that would minimise the risk. The problem is a bit complicated here. Regulation seeks the advancement of particular social ends through legislations instrument is designed through a political process to change behaviour for the public good. The ends sought through precautionary means range from avoidance of irreversible environmental harm to protecting biodiversity "regardless of its worth to man." This range of ends provides a further scaling of the precautionary aspect of any environmental regime, with the degree of precaution increasing as more emphasis is placed on environmental ends. Thus, in cost-benefit of action in such cases.

Now the pertinent question is how the threshold of (a) non-negligible risk and (b) cost of regulatory inaction should be set. A general precautionary answer to this question stipulates that the thresholds should be (a) low and (b) high, though that again begs the question of degree. Since the scientific evidence is uncertain, this determination must be made in a more overtly judgmental forum, namely that of politics, because such institutions are where one must regulate public affairs absent recourse to pure science.

One can make following observations from the above discussion. First, the precautionary principle can attribute much of its rise, national and Internationally to a public perception of scientific inadequacy in addressing environmental concern. Secondly, the fact that science is uncertain at its most basic level throws doubt on its adequacy, in theory in addressing environmental concern.[9] Evidently, science has little ability to answer the questions of law and policy,

---

8. United Nations Economic Commission for Europe (ECE), Ministerial Declaration on Sustainable Development in the ECE Region, Bergen, May 1990.

9. Cameron, "Precautionary Principle," *op. cit.*, pp.15-17.

which ask science to provide answers in yes or no terms, a task it is uniquely designed to avoid. Finally, all scientific assessments of environmental damage are dependent on subjective assumptions of what constitutes harm, especially in degree, and therefore, necessarily involve judgments that have cultural, economic and political bases.

The moment it is established that the threshold of non-negligible risk and justified regulatory action in response to uncertainty depends on political determination, two other points become apparent. The first, is the phenomenon of changing uncertainties and precaution due to a change in physical circumstances and geographic location. This notion of understanding differing ecological, cultural, political and economic needs of differing places and physical circumstances, often found under the rubric of "equity" in international environmental discourse, has many impacts on the implementation of the PP. Of course, different states will define non-negligible risk and justified regulatory acts differently based on differing probability and severity of risk and differing capabilities to regulate.

Finally, novel feature of the precautionary measures is the shifting of the burden of proof away from traditional legal standards, which have said that parties accused of environmental degradation must be "proven wrong" before they are required to stop the activity. The PP determines what the thresholds are for both risks and justifiable regulation, can ease the required burden for what exactly constitutes a likely harm, making it less than scientific proof. In fact, this burden of what must be proven can shift completely, requiring that there should be proof of no harm prior to action, rather than proof of harm prior to halting action. But what must be proven is only one facet of the burden of proof. The party bearing the burden is of legal concern as well, and it has been pointed out that the burden of proof should rest with the party seeking to change the status quo.

Precautionary Principle under Biosafety Protocol: Newly Emerging NTB to International Trade

India has signed Biosafety Protocol to the Conservation of Biological Diversity (CBD), commonly known as Catagena Protocol on 13 February 2001. Biosafety protocol has several pluses and minuses. In a poor country like India, negative spillovers are more than positive outcomes. It has long-term impact on India's trade. Once it gets Parliament's assent, it will get legal status and all provisions of this Protocol are binding to the parties. Still it is not very transparent as to what should be the retaliatory mechanism resulting from possible violation, but obviously exportation of the developing countries in general and India in particular would be much expensive once it follows the circuitous route of testing procedures. This is because of the fact that conformity in testing procedures is yet to be harmonised even among the developed countries.

Conceptually the Protocol has noble objectives to check the transborder movement of living modified organisms, which have harmful effects to environment and human health of the importing countries. But in practice it may emerge as a major non-tariff barrier to trade. The need for an institution/convention was felt since the conclusion of CBD in 1992, which can provide information about the use and safety regulations required by the contracting party in handling LMOs. It also requires information on the potential adverse impact of the movement of living organisms across the border in the environment. Groundwork has been going on since CBD, but the issue of the need and modalities of the "Biosafety Protocol" was taken up by constituting on open-ended Ad Hoc Group of Experts on Biosafety (BSWG) at the insistence of G-77 countries and China. The first Conference of Parties (COP) held in 1994 in Bahamas. Based on the recommendations of the *Ad Hoc* Group, the second COP was held in Jakarta in 1995, decided to negotiate an internationally binding protocol and had set up BSWG. Since 1996, BSWG has several meetings to consolidate the text of several articles dealing with substantial matters and continued till 1999. Though it failed to arrive in a general consensus on some critical issues of the text of the "Biosafety Protocol" the contracting parties does not abandon the hope for a consensus. Finally, in September 1999, a compromised text of the protocol on biosafety got final shape in Viena Meet and formally agreed to in Montreal at 4.45 AM on 29 January 2000.

The Biosafety Protocol which is known as Cartagena Protocol was opened for signature at the UN Office at Nairobi by states and regional economic integration organisations from 15 to 26 May 2000 and remained open at UN Headquarters at New York from 5

June 2000 to 4 June 2001. The protocol shall enter into force on the nineteenth day after the date of deposit of the fiftieth instrument of ratification, acceptance, approval or accession by states and regional economic integration organisations that are parties to the Convention. The ratification is purely on voluntary basis and any country, if it wishes so, may withdraw from the Protocol by giving written notification to the Depository, which takes place upon expiry of one year after the date of its receipt by the same.

The Protocol differs from the CBD in its approach towards environmental needs first and accepting PP as guiding principle for trade in agriculture and pharmaceutical products more precisely GM based products secondly. The Protocol prescribes the application of precautionary principle in ensuring the safe transfer, handling and use of living modified organism resulting from modern biotechnology that may have adverse effects on conservation and sustainable use of biological diversity. Defining living modified organisms, the Protocol says, "any living organism that possesses a novel combination of genetic material obtained though the use of modern biotechnology ", and living organism is defined as "any biological entity capable of transferring or replicating genetic material, including sterile organisms, viruses and viroids. The Protocol has given a comprehensive definition of modern biotechnology. The broad contour of the modern biotechnology is: "in vitro nucleic acid techniques, including recombinant DNA and direct injection of nucleic acid into cells or organelles or fusion of cells beyond the taxonomic family". Risk assessment is one of the important properties of the protocol. The Protocol stipulates risk assessment, includes both human health and environment in a purely scientific manner.

The Protocol has some exclusive provisions. Article 5 excludes the transbounary movement of pharmaceutical LMOs use for human and LMOs which are not like to have adverse effects on conservation and sustainable use of biological diversity of taking also into account risks to human health. Always, by definition, it is not clear to make distinction between various LMOs including agricultural and pharmaceuticals. In practice, unknown risk cannot be ascertained within a stipulated time due to scientific uncertainty and insufficient relevant information. Addressing LMOs, which are pharmaceutical for human is kept out of this Protocol. Considering the importance of pharmaceutical LMOs into human health, these are put under separate international agreements/convention. It is believed that BSP may not have sufficient teeth to control the movement of pharmaceutical LMOs in a particular time frame. Though the pharmaceutical LMOs have been hazardous to environment and health and are known to be incorporated and replicated into the genome for human cells. For example, edible vaccines (i.e. potatoes, bananas), viral vaccines, naked viral genome vaccines, naked viral vectors for gene therapy, naked DNA vaccines and vectors and naked nucleic acids vectors and vaccines, genetically engineered vaccines and vectors are more infectious than intact viruses.

The most trade-distorting component of the biosafety protocol is the acceptance of "precautionary approach" for the future transboundary movement of LMOs. Article 10.6 of the Protocol clearly specifies how measures should be taken in the wake of any scientific uncertainty in order to minimise adverse effects on environment and human health. It precisely says that, "lack of scientific certainty due to insufficient relevant scientific information and knowledge regarding the extent of the potential adverse effects of a LMO in the conservation and sustainable use of biological diversity in party of import, taking into account risks to human health, shall not prevent that party from taking a decision, as appropriate, with regard to the import of the living modified organism in question in order to avoid or minimise such potential adverse effects".

Clarifying the procedure for LMOs intended for direct use as food or feed or food processing, Article 11.1 says, *"a party that makes a final decisions regarding domestic use including placing on the market, of a LMO that may be subject to transboundary movement for direct use as food or feed or for processing shall, within fifteen days of making that decision, inform the parties through Biosafety Clearing House (BDH). The party shall provide copy of the information in writing, to the national focal point of each party that informs the Secretariat in advance that it does not have access to the BCH."* This provision shall not apply to decisions regarding field trials. Countries are given freedom to set their national policies, laws regulations and guidelines for the importation of LMOs meant for direct use of food, or feed, or for processing. A developing country or economy in transition requires to give a declaration to the BCH that it will be guided by the principle prior to its decision to import LMO, for the first time. This is because of the absence of its domestic regulatory framework. The procedures are as follows:

(a) A risk assessment undertaken in accordance with Annex III of the Protocol, and

(b) A decision made within a predictable time frame, not exceeding two hundred and seventy days.

The novelty of the Protocol is that it has replaced the word "commodities" by food, or feed or processing. The Cartagena Protocol excludes LMO-FPP from the Advanced Informed Agreement (AIA) procedure by Article 7.2. Risk assessment procedures under the Protocol are too complicated for exporters to follow. Accordingly to Article 15.1, "risk assessment shall be carried in a scientifically sound manner and taking into account recognised risk assessment techniques. Such risk assessments shall be based at a minimum of information provided in accordance with Article 8 and other available scientific evidence in order to identify and evaluate the possible adverse effects of LMOs on the consideration and sustainable use of biological diversity, taking into account risk to human health".

Prior to the transboundary movement of LMOs meant for export, a clearance from the biosafety clearing house (BCH) is needed certifying that such movement does not cause any harm to the environment of the importing country as well as it does not involve any risk to human health.

BCH requires detailed information on following areas:

(a) Any existing laws, regulations and guidelines for implementation of the Protocol, as well as information required by the parties for the advanced informed agree (AIA) procedure:

(b) Any bilateral, regional and multilateral agreements/ arrangements.

(c) Its final decision regarding the importation or release of living modified organisms, and

(d) Reports submitted by it pursuant to Article 33, including those on implementation of advance informed agreement procedure.

Major area of concern is that this Protocol opens the floodgate of conflicts between the provisions of WTO and provisions contained in the Protocol itself. Since WTO has well-structured dispute settlement mechanism, any member is free to take up any trade dispute to the dispute settlement panel for adjudication. The system is most transparent and juries consist of eminent personalities in the respective areas. Biosafety Protocol (BSP) empowers the members to put embargo on importation if it is found that such importation threatens environment and contains risk to human health, superseding the multilateral rules as embodied in the WTO. Though WTO follows two standards, *viz.* technical barriers to trade (TBT) and sanitary and phyto-sanitary standards (SPS), it is feared that in any dispute related to environmental standards, provisions contained in the Protocol will precede the WTO provisions. Since BSP is an MEA, all disputes relating to environment and human health have to pass through precautionary lens, a major component of the BSP. PP is an essential part of the BSP any importation can be stopped in precaution even in absence of any scientific proof.

The Biosafety Protocol has given much emphasis on precautionary principle. The Protocol refers to or paraphrases the precautionary language five times in the Rio declaration (Preamble, Article 1, 10, 11 and Annex III). Most regulators participating in the drafting of the Biosafety Protocol were environmentalists, whose mandates, domain traditionally have not been very large. They often ignore the progress made by developing countries in the area of biotechnology and its social dimension. The Biosafety Protocol emerges as UN's major regulatory and monitoring tool relating to biotechnology. Such regulatory framework severely compromised the potential of the new technology. BSP is detrimental to the interest of the developing countries in general and India in particular. Under this protocol agricultural technology is much vulnerable because, while innovation is high, market incentives are small and negligible. Here, the regulators remove a very important provision, which is very helpful to crop breeders; ability, readily and rapidly to test large numbers of new varieties in the field trials. Traditionally, each year an individual breeder of corn, soybean, wheat or potato commonly tests in the field as many as 50,000 distinct new genetic variants. But stultifying regulations prevents this level of research actively for genetic varieties developed with the lowest and the most precise techniques, known as genetic modification (GM), recombinant DNA technology, gene-splicing etc. The cost of such regulations is very high. In the USA, at present there are only few 'agbiotech' companies and many have failed over the years because they could not cope with the skyrocketing expenses. Ultimately, consumers will pay inflated prices for over regulated products and higher taxes to support bloated bureaucracies, and they will have fewer options in the market place.

India has sufficient reasons to be worried for the provisions of this protocol. India has successfully come across green revolution in sixties as a result of which she is a food surplus country at present. Furthermore, it has now emerged as one of the leading countries in the world in biotechnology research and genetic manipulation. India has significant contribution in many frontiers of GMO based research and very successful in genetic modification (GM), recombinant DNA technology and gene-splicing methods. India may face upheaval task in implementing biosafety protocol on several counts. First, it has got to surrender its own methods of testing and certification that will be replaced by the stringent certification procedures of the West. Second, due to spectacular advancement of biotechnology research over the years, there have been tremendous progress in GMO based research through recombinant DNA. Any scientific proof of adverse impact of GMO-based products to human health is yet to be ascertained, but sporadic research negates this hypothesis. There is absolutely no evidence that any gene has ever been transferred to human being through food or drinks despite the fact that plant and animal DNA has always been a part of the daily human diet. Research shows (Royal Society 1998) that an estimated 4 per cent of human diet is composed of DNA (Chassy and Sheppard 1999) and an average adult British consumes 1,50,000 K.M. of DNA in an average meal (Lewis and Pelevifz,1999). Third, evidence shows that GM crops are also being engineered to improve nutrition in order to combat disease of affluence afflicting population in developed as well as developing countries. Trend in world food production shows that presently developing countries import 10 per cent of their production. Therefore, if production is not increased through genetic manipulation, developing countries will remain food deficient countries forever in one hand, and the world food prices would sore up in the other. Fourth, thanks to the genetic manipulation , India has created world record in the productivity of "dwarf" variety of wheat, which is the main reason why India is a food surplus country today rather than perennially food deficit country depending heavily on imports. Fifth, a common health concern is that the new genes inserted into GM plants could be incorporated into a consumers' genetic make up. This proves wrong because all the products made from GM crop contain the gene inserted into it. Refined Soya oil made from Rounding Ready Soya does not contain any of the glyphosate resistant gene, although the unrefined oil may have detectable amounts (Royal Society 1998). Sixth, critics say that genes transferred from food to which many people are allergic could trigger allergies in unsuspecting consumers of such GM crop. This concern can be detected during pre-commercialisation tests conducted by Pioneer Hi-Breed, which shows that a soybean, which has been bio-engineered to boost its nutritional quality using a gene from the Brazil nuts, is in fact allergic. This could be eliminated before commercialisation. Seventh, mankind gets enormous benefit from the GM drop due to reduced mortality and improved public health based on the uncertainty and expectation value criteria. We must conclude that the PP also requires the cultivation of GM crops in order to consume the planet's biodiversity, provided due caution is taken with respect to herbicide tolerant and pest resistant GM crops. Finally, PP supports using terminator-type technology which would one way or another, disable-GM plant's ability to reproduce because that would minimise the possibility of gene transfer to weeds and non-GM plants. Such precautionary approach is detrimental to the food security of the developing countries in general and India in particular.

Precautionary Principle and the World Trade Organisation: Areas of Conflict

Precautionary Principle has so far been a customary international law related to environment. This principle has been incorporated in numerous international treaties pertaining to the protection of pollution both at sea, air and in the earth. PP has also incorporated into several non-treaties like: Charter for Nature (1982), Declaration of the Second North Sea Conference (1987), UNEP Governing Council Recommendation (1989), Bergen Declaration (1990), Declaration of the Third International Conference on the Protection of the North Sea (1990), Rio Declaration on Environment and Development (1990), Agenda 21 (1992) etc. Simultaneously, PP is a part of many international treaties, which are binding on the parties that sign and ratify through their national legislations. In such cases, parties, who violate the provisions many face international reactions. Some of the binding treaties are: Montreal Protocol on Substances that Deplete the Ozone Layer (1990), London Convention (1991), Convention on Biological Diversity (1992), UN Framework Convention on Climate Change (1992), Convention of the Protection of the Marine Environment of the Baltic Sea Area.

Precautionary principle has given prime importance to the BSP. In defining its relationship with the other international agreement, Article 31 of the Biosafety Protocol says," the provisions of this protocol shall not affect the rights and obligations of any party to the protocol deriving from any existing international agreement to which it is also a Party, except where the exercise of those rights and obligations would cause serious damage or threat to biological diversity". With such comprehensive definition, the Biosafety Protocol would have been subordinated to the WTO although this comes much late than the formation of WTO.

There are three provisions in the WTO agreement, which if applied, may have entered into direct confrontation with the Biosafety Protocol. These are; (i) Article XX of GATT which is exemption clause especially XX(b) and XX(g), which have permitted stringent measures in order to protect the environment. (ii) Sanitary and phyto-sanitary standards (SPS), and (iii) technical barriers to trade (TBT).

Though the mandate of the WTO is to promote free movement of goods and services across its members, it allows departure from the principle of free trade on environmental ground. It allows members to act on its own to protect environment and human, plant and animal health under three provisions mentioned above.

Exception Clause Under Article XX of GATT

Protection of human, animal and plant health and environment has been embodied in the paragraphs (b), (d) and (g) of Article XX of the General Agreement. Though there are separate international conventions in every area as mentioned above, GATT also has its own provisions to promote free and fair trade. The text of Article XX of GATT reads as follows:

> *" Subject to the requirement that such measures are not applied in a manner which would constitute a means of arbitrary or unjustifiable discrimination between countries where the same conditions prevail, or a disguised restriction on international trade, nothing in this Agreement shall be construed to prevent the adoption or enforcement by any contracting party of measures:*
>
> *(b) necessary to protect human, animal or plant life or health.*
>
> *(d) necessary to secure compliance with laws or regulations, which are not inconsistent with the provisions of this Agreement, including ....*
>
> *(g) relating to the conservation of exhaustible natural resources if such measures are made effective in conjunction with restrictions on domestic production of consumption......."*

Agreement on Technical Barriers to Trade (TBT)

According to provisions contained in the TBT, every individual member of the WTO is empowered to set "technical regulations and standards, including packaging, marking and labeling requirements, and procedures for assessment of conformity with technical regulations and standards" without creating unnecessary barriers to others trade. The TBT is particularly designed in such a manner that it prevents any arbitrary standard that may protect domestic industry from foreign competition. Its basic objective is to promote internationally acceptable quality, which will enable the members to gain access to international markets. The TBT agreement also prescribes for certain obligations to be followed by the members relating to the preparations, adoption and application of technical regulations and standards, and the procedures for assessing whether the products conform to these regulations and standards.

The TBT agreement places obligations on two types of measures: regulations and standards. A regulation establishes mandatory product requirements based on processes and production methods (PPMs), whereas a standard establishes voluntary requirements for products and related PPMs. Harmonisation of different national standards is the basic requirements for pursuing a new standard to fulfill a legitimate objective. The TBT agreement does not explicitly incorporate PP in the text. But the PP is relevant to the application of the TBT to domestic measures in two ways:

- It may be used as a general principle behind the adoption of a specific rule that is classified as a technical barrier;

- It may determine the level of protection a country chooses.

Agreement on Sanitary and Phyto-sanitary Measures (SPS)

The provisions contained in the SPS agreement of GATT are the main safeguard measures to protect environment and human, animal and plant life and health outside of the MEAs (Multilateral Environmental Agreements). The provisions in the SPS agreement, in a way, precautionary measures against all damages mentioned above arise out of trade. SPS measures are quite capable of protecting environment and health and life of human, animal and plant without depending on the precautionary principle as enshrined in the BSP. So far international trade disputes relating to above issues are settled through SPS provisions of GATT without taking reference to precautionary principle as contained in many international agreements and treaties.

Quite a large number of trade disputes had been referred to WTO panel for adjudication where application of precautionary principle appeared, but panel settled all disputes under the spirit of SPS agreement, though it recognised the importance of precautionary principle in settling trade disputes relating the environment. Despite the fact that PP has been embodied in numerous Treaties/Protocols to deal with the environmental problems, the SPS agreement recognises the importance of "the use of harmonised sanitary and phyto-sanitary measures between Members on the basis of international standards, guidelines and recommendations developed by the relevant international organisations , including the Codex Alimentarius Commission, the International Office of Epizootics, and the relevant international and regional organisations operation within the framework of the International Plant Protection Convention, without requiring Members to change their appropriate level of protection of human, animal or plant life or health. The SPS has also detailed rules for "the application of the provisions of GATT 1994 which relate to the use of sanitary and phyto-sanitary measures, in particular the provisions of Article XX(b)."

All the provisions contained in above mentioned three international conventions are not legally-binding standards to its members, but this may clash with the labeling procedures under

Article 18 and procedure outlined for risk assessment under Article 15 of the Biosafety Protocol except in the cases of LMOs-Pharmaceuticals and LMO-FFP (Living Modified Organism-Food, Feed, Process). Article 2(2) of the SPS agreement stipulates that measures should be based on sound scientific evidence, which is quite absent in the PP as contained in the BSP that states that measures can be taken without sufficient scientific evidence if the situation is so warranted. Article 5(7) provides a 'review' mechanism for SPS measures within a reasonable time. These provisions could be invoked against countries that have not applied their biosafety measures on the ground of socio-economic reasons.

After several cases presented to the dispute settlement body of the WTO and its subsequent deliberations, it is amply clear that PP is now implicated in the trade and environment debate. Since the Singapore Meet, the EU has been vigorously trying to include PP in the WTO Agenda where it has "clarification of the application of the precautionary principle". In its official agenda, EU asks for a right balance between prompt, proportional action, where justified, and the avoidance of unjustified precaution, bearing in mind that the basic concept of the precautionary principle is already present in the WTO in several key provisions. The EU has made comprehensive reference to the precautionary principle to prevent imports of US hormone-raised beef.

In the post–WTO regime, first case, which was reported to the dispute settlement body of the WTO on environmental ground was Shrimp-Turtle case between India and USA. Citing Article XX of GATT, the US prohibited the import of shrimp and shrimp products from certain South Asian countries, contending that its shrimp trawl vessels are required to use TEDs at all times when operating in waters where there is a likelihood of intercepting sea turtles, and Section 609 of its Public Law 101-162 applies comparable standards to imported shrimp. India, Malaysia, Pakistan and Thailand asked for a dispute settlement under the WTO.

The panel was constituted for this purpose and they concluded that while the WTO Preamble confirms that environmental considerations are important for the interpretation of the WTO Agreement, "that central focus of that agreement remains the promotion of economic development through trade, and the provisions of GATT are essentially turned towards liberalisation of access to markets on a non-discriminatory basis". With regard to invoking Article XX exceptions, the Panel decided that a member cannot defeat "the purposes and objects of the GATT (1994) and the WTO Agreement or its legal obligations under the substantive rules of GATT by abusing the exception contained in Article XX". The panel reported the US import ban to be unjustified and recommended that the DSB request the US to bring this measure into conformity with its obligations under the WTO agreement. Not satisfied with this, the US requested for an Appellate Body, who reversed the findings of the panel. The Body in its verdict said that the right of a Member to invoke an exception under Article XX and the rights of the other Members under varying substantive provisions (e.g. Article XI, i.e. general elimination of quantitative restrictions) of the GATT 1994, needs to be examined on a case-to-case basis.

The Appellate Body argued that Article XX paragraphs (a) to (j) comprise measures that are recognised as exceptions to substantive obligations established in the GATT 1994, because the domestic policies embodied in such measures have been recognised as important and legitimate in character. Requiring exporting countries to comply with certain policies prescribed by the importing country may not necessarily be unjustified under Article XX. The Body carried out its own analysis about the justifiability of the measures but they did not spare US on several counts for not taking other measures in order to avoid unjustifiable discrimination. These are in way of early negotiations about the harmonisation of domestic policies and followed by other countries, ignoring the differential regulatory regime exist in different countries, differences in socio-economic conditions etc. Finally, the Appellate Body concluded that the measure that was applied in a manner which amounted to a means not just of "unjustifiable discrimination", but also of "arbitrary discrimination" between countries where the same conditions prevail, contrary to the requirements of the Chapeau of Article XX. The measure was not a justified protection under Article XX of the GATT 1994. Consequently, the Appellate Body did not consider examining also whether the US measure applied in a manner that constituted a "disguised restriction on international trade" under the Chapeau of Article XX.

During the deliberations of the Shrimp-Turtle Case between India and USA both at the Panel and the Appellate Body level, the Worldwide Fund for Nature (WWF) insisted that this was a typical case of environmental protection where precautionary principle can be applied because of its positive spillovers to the environmental protection. The WWF urged the Panel that in review of Article XX exceptions, the panel should bear in mind the precautionary principle in that the subject matter of the dispute concerned an endangered resource threatened with extinction. The sanitary and phyto-sanitary agreement (SPS) 1994 adopts a form of precautionary approach safeguarding human or animal life and since the threat of turtle extinction was both serious and irreversible there should be cost-effective measures taken to prevent such damage from occurring.

The Appellate Body upholds the spirit of the SPS agreement in protecting human or animal or plant lives and environment without going into the merits of precautionary principle in settling disputes in which SPS has already established its role. Not satisfying with the decision of the Appellate Body, the WWF again files a supplementary *amicus curiae* brief, in which it alleged that the panel failed to consider customary law in not applying the PP. It claimed that the SPS Agreement required the treaty-GATT 1994 in this case, to be interpreted taking into account relevant rules of international law. Though Appellate Body rejected WWF's argument of the application the PP in the Shrimp-Turtle case, it had given ample indication of its willingness to have more arguments regarding custom and the principle in the Beef-Hormone case between EU and USA, where applicability of PP was much stronger than earlier.

In dispute relating to Shrimp-Turtle, the PP could not supersede the provisions contained in the SPS agreement, but certainly this approach got much relevance in the Hormone case in the interpretation of the SPS agreement. Ultimately, the precautionary principle did not get a berth in the final decision of the Hormone case too, because it overrode the explicit wording of Article 5.1 and 5.2 of the SPS agreement. The Appellate Body pointed out that the essence of the precautionary principle i.e. risk assessment and ban on import in precaution of the environmental damage, virtually incorporated into Article 5.7 of the SPS Agreement. Therefore, SPS is quite sufficient to address the issue of environmental concern. In fact, it supersedes the requirements of GATT Article XX and this is outside of the scope of the TBT agreement. In essence, SPS agreement has two major components. The first is that measures to be based on risk assessment and the second one is the right to take provisional measures where the science is insufficient, which is the essence of the precautionary principle too.

Contradicting the argument of the Body, the EU tried to establish the fact that the precautionary principle had become "a general customary rule of international law" or at least a "general principle", and should be applied to Article 5.1 and Article 5.2. The US further argued that it did not consider the principle to be part of international law but merely "an approach". The US further argued that the SPS agreement does recognise a precautionary approach; indeed, Article 5.7 permits the provisional adoption of SPS measures even where the relevant scientific evidence is insufficient. Thus it argued that there was no need to invoke a "precautionary principle" in order to be risk averse since the SPS agreement recognised the discretion of members to determine their own level of sanitary protection.

Though the Body did not give any distinctive judgment in favour of PP, in deliberation stage it unambiguously recognised the essence of the EU's appeal "whether or to what extent, the precautionary principle is relevant in the interpretation of the SPS agreement." They decided that *"the precautionary principle cannot override our finding*....namely the EC import ban....in accordance with the good practice, is, from a substantive point of view, not based on risk assessment. The Appellate Body did however agree with the EU "that there is no need to assume that Article 5.7 exhausts the relevance of a precautionary principle". In Hormone case too, the Body did not take a decision of the substantive application of the principle, but it was able to "note some aspects of the precautionary principle in the SPS agreement". To some extent the essence of the PP is reflected in the Article 5.7 of the SPS agreement, and to a large extent it is also imbibed in Article 3.3 , which explicitly recognises the right of members to establish their own appropriate level of sanitary protection, which may be higher, or more cautious, than international standards and guidelines.

Another important outcome of the Hormone case is the decision on burden of proof. The Body explicitly confirmed that the burden is on the member challenging an SPS measure to establish *prima facie* evidence that there is lack of risk assessment. Once that burden has been met, the burden then shifts to the defending party to counter the inconsistency. The Body interpreted that 5.1 and 5.2 requirements that measures be "based on" risk assessment were determined by a "rational relationship test between the measure and a risk assessment, which can be established in absence of scientific certainty."

Two conclusions emerged from this deliberations. First, the principle is relevant to the trade regime. Secondly, by avoiding ruling on its status as custom, the Appellate Body ensured that it will have to revisit the issue in future cases. The decisions of two cases have opened new vistas of trade disputes and its possible trade measures. The WTO dispute settlement body took cognizance of the precautionary principle when this was still at the formative stage and yet to be a part of any international Protocol/Treaty/Convention. In such situation, it is legitimate to uphold the essence of the provisions of the SPS agreement, which is already a part of the WTO. Any trade dispute under the jurisdiction of WTO, it is not difficult to resist the applicability of the PP especially when it is yet to be part of any international customary law. Though several countries adopt PP as customary international law in all matters related to environment, it is still part of the domestic law and yet to be a part of the WTO's jurisprudence. BSP came into force in 2003, where PP was an integral part of it and it would get the status of an international law when signatories would pass legislations to give effect to its application in international trade. Afterwards, it will be very difficult to ignore the importance of PP in justifying trade measures related to environment. International trading communities should be much worried about this.

There have been two more cases in the DSB relating to the application of PP in environmental matters. One is the *Australia-Measures Affecting importation of Salmon* and other was the *Japan-Varietals*. The first case was between Australia and Canada, in which Canada challenged an Australian prohibition on the import of uncooked salmon. Both the Panel and Appellate body ruled that Australia was in violation and failed to meet the requirements of Article 5.1 because it was not based on risk assessment. This is for the first time the Body interpreted 'risk assessment' in the light of environment rather than interpreting it in the health context. It defined the elements of a risk assessment to be: (i) identification of the pests or diseases sought to prevent as well as the biological and economic consequences of their entry, (ii) evaluation of the likelihood of entry and the consequences absent of the SPS measures, and (iii) evaluation of the likelihood with the measure in place.

In *Japan-Varietals* case, the US challenged Japan's fumigation and varietal testing requirements on eight orchard crops. The Appellate Body cited Article 2.2 of SPS, pointing out that only 5.7 allows access to SPS measures absent scientific evidence and risk assessment. Japan had violated this by maintaining requirements for four of the crops absent "sufficient" scientific evidence. Further, giving a broad outline to this case, the Appellate Body mentioned four requirements created by 5.7 saying a member could adopt a provisional measure if: (i) the situation was one of insufficient scientific information, (ii) it was adopted based on pertinent available information, (iii) the member sought to obtain the additional information for a risk assessment, and (iv) the member reviews the measure within a reasonable period of time.

Precautionary Principle and Future Potential of India's Exports

Precautionary principle may pose a major threat to Indian exporters through environmental route. Recently host of India's exports are subject to environmental measures of the West. Standards related to environment are so complicated and non-transparent in nature that it is very difficult for India to cope with the newly emerging norms. Most importantly, all the standards, which developed countries have been propagating are not even harmonised. Most of the environmental standards are nationals and vary from country to country. The scapegoat of the growing environmental standards has been the Indian small-scale sector, which finds it difficult to comply with the cost escalation due to newly emerging standards. There has been ample evidence that in some industries cost escalation has gone exorbitantly high, puts enormous burden on producers. Many small and medium scale industries have wiped out in this process.

UNCTAD has conducted two studies in the mid-nineties, showing the extent of India's exports are subject to growing environmental standards of the West. The results show a very grim picture and it leaves no room for complacent. India is the largest exporter of tea in the world. Its export potentiality has been severely eroded due to stringent measures of pesticide content. Germany has made complaint about the high residue levels of Ethion, Tetradifon and Heptachlor in Indian tea. Complaints are also coming from other OECD countries about Assam, Terai and Dooras tea containing high levels of Bicofol. Being bow down the eco-regulations of the West, Indian government has banned 12 hazardous pesticides and has restricted the use of some less hazardous pesticides.

On food processing, both Japan and EU have stringent regulations. In Japan Food Sanitation Law prohibits the import of many citrus from India viz. carambola, pomegranate, passion fruit etc. The Residue Standards of Agro Chemicals Law, applicable to nuts, sets limits to the extent of use of at least 22 pesticides. One state in India attempts to substitute DDT with the more eco-friendly pesticide, viz. Malathion. The resulting cost of adopting the more acceptable pesticide was found to be four times the original cost, thus substantially increasing burden to the producers. A host of horticultural products in which India has comparative advantage in the world market are subject to the rigorous environmental standards in the form of pesticide content.

Marine products are another potential area of our exports, which are in the crossroad of danger due to several standards related to environment. The EU, especially Germany, has taken the lead in defining environmental product standards related to fish and fish products. The most important standards relate to the cadmium, mercury and lead content in fish. The EU directive has also imposed standards on strict hygiene requirements during handling, processing and storage of marine products. Japan's laws with respect to shrimps, a major export from India, pertain mostly to the level of pesticide and antibiotics content in the exported fish. All types of antibiotics and oxolinic acid and oxytetracyclines are banned, even though there is no fixed limit, if traces of the above are detected, the shrimp consignment is liable to be rejected. Similarly, if traces of pesticides including DDT, Aldrin and Heptachlor are detected, the consignment may be rejected. Frozen fish and fishery products are subject to quality control and inspection prior to export, depending upon the stipulations made by the importers . Without a certificate of inspection, the export of frozen marine products is prohibited. There are lot more examples of standards which act as effective barriers to trade.

Indian dyestuffs are also hard-hit by the growing environmental standards. Regulations on dyestuffs have direct impact on the textiles and leather sectors because both these sectors have encountered cost increase in an attempt to conform to eco-standards of this intermediate product. The use of certain dyestuffs such as cobalt blue and sulphur black has been banned in external markets. Complying with stringent standards regarding the toxic content of dyes may be difficult and expensive. Leather is one of the most affected sectors among Indian exports. Besides, stipulations on dyes several other regulations may affect trade. Germany in particular, has banned the use of pentachlorophenol (PCP), while in the EU, the permissible level is 1000 particles per million. Germany and some other countries limit the use of formaldehyde. The use of other environmentally friendly chemicals has also become mandatory, restricting the process by which leather may be manufactured. Textile and garment sectors are also subject to stringent regulations of the OECD countries. Statutory measures also require that compulsory labeling concerning formaldehyde protect consumers. In addition, a ban has been issued on the use of some substances, which have been identified as carcinogenic or allergenic.

1996 ESCAP study shows that approximately 25 per cent of India's total exports to the OECD counties are vulnerable to the environmental measures, though not directly affected by the measures as yet. The study shows that the products that are most sensitive to the US markets are: fruits/vegetables and shrimp. In the Japanese market most environmental sensitive product is shrimp and in the EU market the products that may be affected by these measures are: textiles, footwear and paper/pulp.

Recently, EU has enforced Genetically Modified Organism(GMO)-based restrictions (covered under SPS agreement of WTO) against several food products, fruits and vegetables, meat, fish or crustaceans, molasses or other aquatic invertebrates. Entire group of lobsters and shrimps are under SPS. A host of dairy products like birds eggs, natural honey, edible products of animal origin are under GMO and its use is based on hormonic reason i.e. Special Risk Material (SRM of the mad cow disease) and SPS etc. Some fruits, coffee, coffee husks/skins, coffee substances, tea, groundnuts and some tobacco products are under pesticide residue measures of the EU. Azo dyes used by textiles and yarns are also prohibited in the European market.

In the US market, Indian exports, which are covered under environmental measures are: fruits, vegetables, dairy products, honey, edible products of animal origin, different types of fish aquatic products are under SPS. A wide array of textile products is under eco-labelling arrangement of the US. In the Japanese market, the entire group of fish, crustaceans, molasses and other aquatic invertebrates and tea are subject to SPS restriction. Besides, garlic and ginger are subject to labeling requirements.

Recently, Germany has been emerging as one of the most "green conscious" countries in the world. It has variety of environmental measures, which pose serious threat to Indian exporters. The new environmental measures raise important question about their impact on export and the need to adopt products to new and evolving specification. Major concern to the exporters of this region is not the variety of new environmental measures on their products, but difficult to obtain the necessary information about the environmental requirements and their lack of transparency, which can form significant non-tariff barriers to trade to the exporter of this region. Germany has variety of environmental measures viz. the blue angel, eco-label, MST, MUT, green dot, Dual System etc. The products and product groups that are likely to be seriously affected by German environmental and health related measures are: fishery products, other food and beverage products, coffee and tea, wood and wood products, paper, fibers, yarn, textiles, garments, and especially cotton products, leather products, packaging materials made of leather. (see Christine Wyatt in Veena Jha *et al*, eds., 1997).

Precautionary principle is at the nascent stage and is yet to be ratified by all the countries. Biosafety Protocol in which precautionary principle is a major component, would come into force once it is ratified by all the countries and get legal status by national legislations. All the environmental standards will come under the ambit of the precautionary principle. Many of the measures related to environment are not WTO-consistent and one can approach to the dispute settle body for adjudication. But under the biosafety Protocol, all the environmental measures are legally binding to the signatories. The main domain of the precautionary principle will be the environment and human, animal or plant health. If any dispute arises regarding the justifiability of the PP, WTO forum may not be in a position to shut down their eyes from the precautionary principle, as this is now a legal binding. Presently, Indian exports, which are under environmental standards of the West, will come under the domain of the precautionary principle. There has been sufficient reasons for Indian exporters to be worried because if PP plays its wider role it will be very difficult for India to conform with the newly emerging labyrinthine standards and related measures, which are not even supported by the scientific evidence.

Concluding Observations

First, US beef industry may be happy with the outcome of the DSB ruling, but the jurisprudence established by this case threatens numerous US laws. The panel decisions demonstrate how the SPS agreement is sufficient to address country's health, safety and environmental standards when trade challenges are initiated. By tradition, in many areas of the US law (i.e. the system of pharmaceutical approvals) are based on precautionary principle. The environmental movement as a kind of standard to bear arms against those who threaten environmental damage has recently adopted this approach. Biosafety Protocol confirms this.

Second, main target of precautionary principle is to enforce trade restrictions on GMO-based products. In this area developing countries have comparative advantage because they are having vast pool of biotechnologists and these countries have invested huge resources for food security. It is estimated that 10 per cent of their total food consumption is imported. To be self reliant in food production they have done breakthrough in many GMO-based research, which they do not want to sacrifice at the name of environmental protection. Even before biosafety protocol came into force, the EU has enforced GMO-based restrictions (covered under

SPS) against several food products, fruits and vegetables, meat, fish or crustaceans, molasses and other aquatic invertebrates. Entire group of lobsters and shrimps are under SPS. A host of dairy products like bird's eggs, natural honey, edible products of animal origin are GMO-based and its uses are banned on harmonic reason i.e. special risk material (SRM of the mad cow disease) and SPS etc. Some fruits, coffee, coffee husks/skins, coffee substances, tea, groundnuts and some tobacco products are under pesticide residue measures of the EU. Rather several research findings in the Western countries show that there is absolutely no evidence that GM food is injurious to health. Furthermore, there is not conclusive proof that any genes has ever been transferred to human beings through food or drink despite the act that plant and animal DNA has always been a part of the daily human diet. In fact, an estimated 4 per cent of human diet is composed of DNA and an average British adult consumes 1,50,000 KM of DNA in an average meal.

Third, there has been apprehension among the Indian business community that PP may emerge as a new form of non-tariff barriers to agricultural trade. One glaring example in this context is the Japan's unilateral decision to ban imports of unmanufactured tobacco from India in the pretext of pesticide residue. As against international (Codex) standards of 6 particles per million (PPM), Indian standards is as high as 1-2 PPM, but Japan insists on 0.4 PPM on its imports. Following this stringent rule Japan virtually stops imports of unmanufactured tobacco from India.

Fourth, after signing Cartagena Protocol on Biosafety, roadblock to the application of PP is removed. Members will frequently take recourse to this approach to safeguard their rights to prohibit or regulate trade in the public interest. Debate will continue for "sound science *versus* precaution" in the years ahead. The application of the PP involves scientific argument about risk or irreversibility in a political or legal context and the case against it will be judged in the same context.

Fifth, application of PP depends on subjective judgment. Since degree of "damage" is basically left to the policy-makers, there is little objectivity involved in it. This is purely a national concept and political leaders will determine what should be the actual limit of tolerance of environmental damage. Conversely, if trade restriction is suggested to prevent environmental damage and to protect the lives and health of human, animal and plant without having any scientific proof, there has been a possibility that almost everything on earth in the areas of food, feed and process (FFP) can be brought under the jurisdiction of precautionary approach in expectation. Since application of PP basically depends on political decision, countries having good political equation may remain scot-free but the developing countries and countries in transitional phase may be the actual victim.

Sixth, Precautionary Principle limits the role of WTO. By nature, precautionary principle is much stringent than provisions contained in the SPS and TBT Agreement of the WTO. Once PP comes into force, SPS becomes ineffective. Precautionary approach will virtually determine every trade disputes related to environment and health and life of human, animal and plant. Sound science will take a back seat then. WTO dispute settlement body will become teethless due to lack of suitable mechanism to counter the rampant use of the precautionary approach to address environmental issues.

References

Bhattacharya, S.K. (2002). "Precautionary Principle under Biosafety Protocol: Needs for a Cautious Approach," *Economic and Political Weekly*, 22 June, Mumbai.l

————. (2000). "Trade and Environment Linkage: A threat of Green Protectionism?" *Margin*, Vol.32, No.3, April-June. NCAER, New Delhi.

————. (2001). "Growing Environmental Standards of the West: A Veiled Threat of Non-Tariff Barrier to India's Trade," in R.K. Sen (ed.) *Environment and Economic Development with Reference to India*, Deep and Deep Publisher, New Delhi.

————. (2001). "Interface between Trade and Sustainability: Challenges and Success in the SAARC Region," *South Asian Survey*, Vol.8 No.2 January-March, Sage Publication, New Delhi, London.

————. (2001). "The Entwining of Trade Policies with the Environmental Standards: Options for India", *Annual Volume of the Indian Political Economy Association*, New Delhi.

Carmian Barton (1996). "The Status of the Precautionary Principle in Australia: Its Emergence in Legislation and as a Common Law Doctrine", *Harvard Law Review*.

Chang. H.E. (1995). "An Economic Analysis of Trade Measures to Protect the Global Environment", *Georgetown Law Journal*, 83.6, 2131-213.

Chassy, B., and Sheppard, L. (1999). "GMO Food Safety Risk is Negligible", *ACES News*, University of Illinois.

Cameron and Wessesman, *Amicus Curie*, Brief Submitted by WWF/FIELD, Commissioned by and Submitted on behalf of WWF, International Gland, Switzerland, Para 3.63, on file at FIELD.

Danial Bodansky, "The Status of the Precautionary Principle in US Environmental Law," in O' Riordan and Cameron, *Introduction to Precautionary Principle*.

Esty, D.C. (1994). 'Greening the GATT' – *Trade, Environment, and the Future*, Washington, DC: Institute for International Economics.

Fletcher, C.R. (1996). "Greening World Trade-reconciling GATT and Multilateral Environmental Agreements Within the Existing World Trade Regime", *Journal of Transnational Law and Policy*, 5.2, 341-72.

Gary Sampson and W.B. Chamber, eds, (1999). *Trade, Environment and the New Millennium*, United Nations University Press, Tokyo.

GATT (1988). *Report of the GATT Panel, Canada- Measures Affecting Exports of Unprocessed Herring and Salmon*, GATT Doc. I./6268 (Para 4.6), Adopted 22 March, 1988.

————. (1992). GATT's *Follow-Up to the UN Conference on Environment and Development, GATT Doc. SR.48/1 (2 December 1992) (decision by Contracting Parties)*.

Hey, E. (1992). "The Precautionary Principle in Environmental Policy and Law; Institutionalising Caution", *4, Geo Environmental Legal Review, 303, pp. 308-309*.

Hickey, James E., Jr., and Walkar, Veru R. (1995). "Refining the precautionary Principle in International Environmental Law. *14 Va. Environmental legal Journal, 423, 436*.

James Cameron and Juli Abouchar (1996). "The Status of the Precautionary Principle in International Law", in David Freestone and Ellen Hey, eds, *The Precautionary Principle in International Law: The Challenge of Information*, London, Kluwer law International.

James Cameron (1994). "The Precautionary Principle- Core Meaning, Constitutional Framework and Procedures for Implementation", *Conference Paper*, Institute for Environmental Studies, University of New South Wales.

James Cameron and Will Wade-Grey (1992). "Addressing Uncertainty: Law. Policy and the Development of Precautionary Policy," *CSERGF Working Paper*, GEC 92-13.

James Cameron, Paul Demaret and Damien Gerdin, eds, (1994). *Trade and Environment: The Search for Balance*, Vol. 1, London, Cameron & May.

James Cameron and Abouchar (1991). "The Precautionary Principle" A Fundamental Principle of Law and Policy for the Protection of Global Environment," *Boston College of International and Comparative law Review,* 14n (1) Winter.

James Cameron (1999). "The Precautionary Principle" in Gary Sampson and W.B. Chamber, eds, Trade, Environment and the New Millennium," United Nations University Press, Tokyo.

Julian Morris, (2000). *Rethinking Risk and the Precautionary Principle,* Butterworth – Heinemann Publisher, Oxford.

Jackson, J.H. (1977). "The WTO Dispute Settlement Understanding- Misunderstandings on the Nature of Legal Obligation," *American Journal of International Law,* 91.1, 60-4.

————. (1988a). *The World Trade Organisation – Constitution and Jurisprudence,* London, The Royal Institute of International affairs.

————. (1988b). "Dispute Settlement and the WTO- Emerging Problems" *Journal of International Economic Law,* 1.3, 329-51.

L. Gundling (1999). "The Status in International Law of the Precautionary Principle," *International Journal of Estuarine and Coastal law,* 5(3).

Mazur, Allen (1996). Why Do We Worry About Trace Poisons, www.fplc.edu/ RISK/ vol7/winter/mazur.htm (accessed 4 April).

Montague, P. (1988). The Precautionary Principle, *Rachel's Environment and Health Weekly,* No. 586, 19 February. http://www.monitor.net/rachel/r586.html (accessed 9 April 2000), Wingspread definition is detailed in this Weekly.

Normuha, Federik (1999). "India's High Court Stops Field Trials of Biotech Cotton," *Environmental News Service,* February 23.

Parikh, J., V.K. Sharma, U. Ghosh and Manoj Panda (1994). *Trade and Environment Linkages; A Case Study of India,* Indira Gandhi Institute for Development Research, Mumbai.

P.K. Rao (2000). *The World Trade Organisation and the Environment,* McMillian Press Ltd.

Royal Society (1998). Genetically Modified Plants for Food Use, www.royalsoc.ac.uk/ st_po140.htm 11 January 2000.

Sahwney, Aparna (2000). "GATT/WTO and Environmental Provision", in B. Bhattacharya, ed. *Seattle and Beyond: the Unfinished Agenda,* Indian Institute of Foreign Trade, New Delhi.

Sands, Philippe (1994). "The Greening International Law: Emerging Principles and Rules", *Global Legal Studies Journal,* 293, 301.

Souja Boehmer-Christiansen, "The Precautionary Principle in Germany-Enabling Government" in O' Riordam and Cameron, *The Introduction of the Precautionary Principle.*

Supplementary *Amicus Curie* Brief Submitted by WWF/FIELD, Commissioned by and Submitted on behalf of WWF, International Gland, Switzerland, para 3.63, on file at FIELD, Para 9.4 listing Article 31 (3)(e) of the SPS Agreement 1994.

UNCTAD (1995). *Trade Environment and Development Lessons from Empirical Studies: The Case of India,* UNCTAD, and Geneva.

US Letter on "Precautionary Principle" to Codex Secretariat, January 6, 1999.

UN. *The Rio declaration on Environment and Development,* UN Conference on Environment and Development, UN doc. A/Conf. 151/15/Rev.1(1992).

————. "The Framework Convention on Climatic Change", UN Doc. A/AC.237/18 /Part III/Add.1 (1992).

————. "The Ministerial Declaration of the Second World Climatic Conference", Nov. 7, 1990, reprinted in *International Environmental Law* 473(1998).

————. "The Second International Conference on Protection of the North Sea, Ministerial Declaration 1", (1987) .

———. "The World Charter for Nature", GA Res. 37/7, UNGHAOR 37the Session, Supple. No. 51, UN Doc. A/Res/37/7(1982).

UN, Cartagena Protocol on Biosafety to the Convention on Biological? Diversity, see www. Biodiv. Org/biosafe/index html.

Vasantha Bharucha (1997). "The Impact of Environmental Standards and Regulations Set in Foreign Markets on India's Exports," in Veena Jha *et al.*, eds, *Trade Environment and sustainable Development: A south Asian Perspective,* UNCTAD & UNDP.

Veena Jha *et al*, eds, (1997). *Trade Environment and Sustainable Development: A South Asian Perspective,* UNCTAD & UNDP. Geneva.

WTO (1991). *"EC Approach to Trade and Environment in the New WTO Round"*, WT/GC/W/194, 1 June.

———. (1998). *"EC Measures Concerning Meat and Meat Products (Hormones)"*, Complaint by the United States. AB-1997-4, Report of the Appellate Body, WT/DS26/AB/R,WT/DS 48/AB/R 16 January.

———. (1998). *Trading Into the Future,* Geneva: WTO Secretariat.

———. (1999a). *Director General's Opening Remarks at the WTO High Level Symposium on Trade and Environment,* Geneva; WTO Secretariat.

———. (1999b). *Background Note- High Level Symposium on Trade and Environment,* Geneva: WTO Secretariat.

20

Biotechnology and International Trade Regime: Options Before Developing Countries

SACHIN CHATURVEDI
S. R. RAO

Introduction

In recent past, adoption and diffusion of biotechnology has raised several policy challenges for the governance of this technology especially in the developing countries due to rapid expansion of the biotechnology industry. These countries have been strategically strengthening capacity, infrastructure and expertise in regulation and commercialisation of biotechnology particularly in the areas where rich bioresources are utilised. The applications of this technology, both in pharmaceuticals and agriculture, are finding new vistas of economic growth for developing countries. Illegal introduction of GM products, threat of overexploitation of natural resources (their biomolecules and genes), potential risks to environment and global contention on the technology has confounded the prevailing confusion on some of the intricate issues linked to the trade and biosafety of GMOs. However, the position taken by the civil society organisations and some of the national governments especially from Europe and Africa have highlighted the growing polarization on this issue. These discussions have important implications not only for developed countries which are major exporters of GM goods but also for some of the developing countries which have infused GM goods in the production chain. Developing countries, that are major exporters of non-GM agricultural goods, are also affected due to requirement of GM free certification by some importers. This affects the exports of developing countries adversely.

The related challenge is that the international regulatory arrangements like the Cartagena Protocol on biosafety have yet to become effective international instruments to guide policy frameworks dealing with transboundary movement of GMOs. The development of multilateral, regional and national standards and regulations for the release, safety assessment of food from genetically modified organisms has to be formulated as per the letter and spirit of the Convention on Biological Diversity (CBD). Along with this, the negotiations are taking place in other international organisations such as the WTO, which may have impact on international trade. They include Technical Barriers to Trade (TBT), the Sanitary and Phyto-sanitary Measures (SPS), Trade-related Aspects of Intellectual Property Rights (TRIPs) and Agreement on Agriculture. They also become relevant in the overarching trade issues such as market access and competitiveness.

This chapter makes an effort to critically analyse each of these dimensions of international negotiations and emerging perspectives for developing countries. Section II takes an account of the global status of biotechnology while Section III discusses at length the Cartagena Protocol and different national regulatory regimes. In Section IV, WTO and trade related implications are analysed.

Adoption and Diffusion of Agricultural Biotechnology

In the last one decade or so, the area under commercial cultivation of GM crops has gone up many times. Between 1996 and 2001, the area under transgenic crops in industrial countries increased (5.6 million hectares) compared with developing countries (2.8 million hectares). The per centage growth was higher in the developing countries of the South (26 per cent) than in the industrial countries of the North (17 per cent).[1] The area under GMOs in the developing countries grew at a rate of 14 per cent in 1997 to 16 per cent, in 1998, to 18 per cent by 1999, 24 per cent in 2000 and 26 per cent in 2001. Thus, in 2001 it showed a rise of more than a quarter. Developing countries have almost 19 million hectares under transgenic crop cultivation. Latin American and CIS countries are the leading developing countries which have embarked on the GM adoption path in the last two years. However, no agricultural biotechnology product has yet been approved in the EU. In addition,

1. ISAAA. 2001. "Global Review of Commericalised Transgenic Crops: 2001", No. 24.

several countries including Japan, Korea and temporarily Sri Lanka have already passed or are considering regulations mandating labelling for foods obtained from biotechnology.

In the US, in the year 2001, biotechnology varieties accounted for about 26 per cent of corn, 68 per cent of soybeans and 69 per cent of cotton planted.[2] These crops are the source of various ingredients used extensively in many processed foods, such as corn syrup, soybean oil and cottonseed oil. In Argentina, the main biotechnology crop is soybean while in Canada it is canola. As is clear, the total area under GM crops is 19 per cent of the total cultivated area while 46 per cent of the area under soybean is with GM crops and 7, 20 and 11 per cent under maize, cotton and grape, respectively. Thus, in some areas, concomitant cultivation of GM and non-GM leads to mixed produce. The extant of GM in non-GM produce has become a matter of concern for trade, both for raw and processed produce.

The global market of biotechnology has also grown rapidly in the last few years. In 1995 it was at $75 million while in 1998 it was $1.5 billion. This is now being projected to $6 billion by 2005. This period has also seen a very rapid rise in acquisition, alliances and mergers. There are several factors responsible for these initiatives. James (1998) explains that firms having larger status in pharmaceuticals/biotechnology are now entering in agricultural sector. In the period 1995-98 there were 25 major acquisitions and alliances, which alone were worth $17 billion. Out of them three major mergers were worth $13 billion. In this game of mergers Monsanto has emerged as the biggest player. It has acquired some of the largest firms in this US commodity markets and has got acquisition of important patents. For instance, DeKalb has 11 per cent of US commodity market with lots of important patents. Similarly, Delta & Pineland is the largest US company for cotton seeds. Monsanto has also acquired international seed operations of Cargill for $1.4 billion. Cargill specialised in seeds of corn, sunflower, rapessed, soyabean, alfalfa, sorghum, wheat and hybrid rice in 51 countries. Unilever owned Plant Breeding International Cambridge Ltd. (PBIC), earlier a public research institute has also

2. GAO. 2002. Genetically modified foods: Experts View Regimen of Safety Tests as Adequate, but FDA's Evaluation Process Could Be Enhanced, United States General Accounting Office, May.

been brought by Monsanto. PBIC largely focuses on cereal varieties and potato. Among the mergers, one finds creations of Novartis as a major step towards tapping of synergies in the biotechnology business. Ciba and Sandoz have merged their pesticide and seed business of $5 billion to take form of Novartis. Similarly, the impose of the merger of Hoechst and Rhone Poulenc to form Aventis was to achieve better operational efficiency. Aventis now has an R&D budget of $3 billion and annual sales of $20 billion, all over the world.

Advances in Biotechnology

These growth patterns are likely to go up as technology advances. Now biotechnology offers several ways by which average yield can be directly increased. One is through improvements in the "architecture" of the plant to enable it to absorb more photosynthetic energy or convert a larger portion of that energy into grain rather than stem or leaf. This was, in essence, the "Green Revolution" approach of breeding dwarfing genes into plants, so that the plants could make better use of fertiliser and water and produce more grain. This approach is being pursued in the new rice architecture being studied by the International Rice Research Institute (IRRI), Manila as well as by some private sector industry undertaking research in the fundamental mechanisms that controls plant architecture. Another approach for climates, where it is useful, to modify the plant for a shorter growing season by enhancing its efficiency in the use of fertiliser, pesticides and water. Molecular hybridization has also been demonstrated to increase the productivity of several crops, including rice and wheat, by 15 to 20 per cent.[3] It must be noted that the on-farm yield improvements observed so far have been for transgenic varieties developed to reduce on-farm production costs rather than for the purpose of increasing yields.

However, it is not yet clear whether yield-increasing experiences reflect a one-time advancement, or indicate achievement of a continuing increase in the yield. Considering that there are many new technologies that will, over time, be applicable for plant

3. James, Clive and Anatole Krattiger. 1999. "The Role of the Private Sector." pp. 4-5 in *Biotechnology for Developing-Country Agriculture: Problems and Opportunities, Focus 2*, ed. By Gabrielle J. Persley. Washington, DC: International Food Policy Research Institute.

improvements and/or integrated into plants, the most reasonable conjecture is that the new technologies will continue to provide yield increases. These will be introduced on a regular basis, and that each of the associated yield increase will be somewhat more than historical trends.[4] Similarly, there are possibilities to improve the nutritional value of cereals by enhancing the presence of special nutrients or chemicals. A commercial example is the increase in the levels of biotin (vitamin H) for application in animal and human nutrition and development of golden rice with carotenoid production.

Public sector breeders have also been looking into similar special purpose applications, such as inserting genes so that vitamin A and iron becomes available through the consumption of rice.[5] Among the potentially more important applications for specific markets are those that seek to improve the quality of feed crops. New varieties of transgenic maize that contain higher oil levels to boost energy and improve feeding efficiency or have characteristics to reduce phosphorous in animal waste are examples that are currently under development.[6] In an interesting development that is certainly relevant to feed grains, is a patent covering the insertion of a protein into plants, which when eaten would facilitate control of animal parasites.

Developing crop varieties with many improved traits than single gene based single trait transgenics is also researched. Companies like Garst Seeds, a subsidiary of Advanta, has developed maize hybrids, which can tolerate two different classes of chemical herbicides.[7] In the United States, currently about 20 per cent of the maize production is destined for such markets, with the production of high-fructose corn syrup and of alcohol being the largest with a number of the industrial uses.[8] Maize and sorghum are among the crops that

4. Toenniessen, G. 1991. "Potentially Useful Genes for Rice Genetic Engineering," in G. Khush & G. Toenneissen, *Rice Biotechnology* (CABI).

5. *ibid*

6. USDA 1999. Economic Research Service, "Value-Enhanced Crops: Biotechnology's Next Stage" *Agricultural Outlook*, February 23.

7. Spinney, Laura,"Biotechnology in Crops: Issues for the Developing World" (May 1998) http://www.actionbioscience.org/biotech/oxfam_spinney.html

8. US International Trade Commission, Industry and Trade Summary: Milled Grains, Malts, and Starches, USITC Pub. 3095, March 1998, at p. A-6.

produce a high yield of starch/energy per hectare, and are the leading temperate zone crops for production characteristic of important crop plants within wide bounds, making it possible to use almost any starch producing plant for many industrial purposes.

There are also other non-traditional uses of cereal crops such as production cellulose, clearly available from other sources, but perhaps usefully produced in grain cultivation under certain circumstance. These developments may have significance for rice and other cereals, which are more widely grown in the developing countries. To the extent that imported cereals are priced higher than those domestically grown, using starch and other traits from domestically produced bio-engineered cereals in developing countries industries could lead to costs savings and boost farm incomes. Another important possibility is genetically altering crop plants for the production of proteins of pharmacological significance. Some of the patents in this area have wide applicability to different products, including for example, to the production of maize. One patent has very broad claims, but its example, emphasise production in rice. Several of the patents mention production of specific products not all of which are therapeutic. However, commercial applications of these technologies are not yet widely available. Cartagena Protocol and National Regulatory Regimes in Agricultural Biotechnology are two broad sets of regulatory regimes, which have become part of the system. One set emanates from national regulatory mechanisms evolved during last one decade and the other from the recently enforced Cartagena Protocol. The former, apart from having individual countries, also have groupings like the EU which has proposed to establish regulations requiring documentation to trace the presence of biotechnology products through each step of grain handling and food production processes. In fact, the EU now has also proposed to apply similar regulations for animal feeds.

It would be interesting to take stock of this important protocol. The Cartagena Protocol on Biosafety to the Convention on Biological Diversity was adopted by the Conference of the Parties to the Convention on 29 January 2000. In accordance with its Article 36, the Protocol was opened for signature at the United Nations Office at Nairobi by States and regional economic integration organisations from 15th to 26th May 2000, and remained open for signature at

United Nations Headquarters in New York from June 5, 2000 to June 4, 2001. The Protocol has been signed on behalf of 107 States and regional economic integration organisations while very few have ratified. Ukraine is the 39th country to have ratified the Protocol in December 2002. The Protocol has become effective after the 50th ratification. India has also ratified this and the concerned Cabinet Committee has also cleared the proposal.

After five years of intense negotiations, governments have finalised this legally binding agreement for protecting the environment from risks posed by the transboundary transport of Living Modified Organisms (LMOs) using modern biotechnology.

This international protocol uses the term LMO rather than GMO. It is assumed that this is a more precise term. LMO is defined as, "Any living organism that possess a novel combination of genetic material obtained through the use of modern biotechnology" (Article 3 g). Under the Cartagena Protocol, on Biosafety, governments will signal whether or not they are willing to accept imports of agricultural commodities that include LMOs by communicating their decision to the world community via an Internet-based Biosafety Clearing House. In addition, shipments of these commodities that may contain LMOs are to be clearly labelled. LMOs include various food crops that have been genetically modified for greater productivity or nutritional value, or for resistance to pests or diseases. Common examples include tomatoes, grains, cassava, corn, and soybeans. Seeds for growing crops are particularly important because they are used intentionally to propagate or reproduce LMOs in the environment. Together, these agricultural LMOs form the basis of a multibillion dollar global industry. Pharmaceuticals derived by using LMOs form the basis of an even larger industry (although pharmaceuticals are not covered by this agreement).

Stricter 'Advanced Informed Agreement' (AIA) procedures will apply to seeds, live fish, and other LMOs that are to be intentionally introduced into the environment (Article 7.2). In these cases, the exporter must provide detailed information to each importing country in advance of the first shipment, and the importer must then authorise the shipment. The aim is to ensure that recipient countries have both the opportunity and the capacity to assess risks involving the products of modern biotechnology. Moreover, the information should also include the modifications introduced; the technique used; the resulting characteristics of the LMO; the regulatory status of the LMO in the country of export and the contact details of the importer and the exporter. The notification has to be accompanied by a risk assessment report. Another important feature of the Protocol emanates from the Preamble as well as from the Articles 1, 10 and 11. This is "precautionary approach". This means that if there is a scientific uncertainty about the impact of genetic manipulation on biodiversity and human health, then the importer country may enforce restrictions on imports and this flexibility would remain till importer on its own arrives on scientific certainty about implications.

One of the most contentious issues that negotiators had to resolve involved the relationship between the Protocol and other international agreements, notably those under the WTO. It is important to ensure that the Protocol and the WTO are mutually supportive. The Protocol is not to affect the rights and obligations of governments under any existing international agreements. While at the same time one also has to ensure that the potentially dangerous activities can be restricted or prohibited even before they can be scientifically proven to cause serious damage.

Regulatory Regime at National and Regional Level

Over the years, the regulatory regime in different countries has emerged at different pace and has taken all different directions. The national responses have largely been driven by specific national situations. For instance "mad cow disease" in European situation led to extreme consumer rigidity for genetically modified food. Annex 1 briefly depicts the evolution and current shape of biosafety policy across various countries.

The European Community (EC) introduced an approval system for the deliberate release of GMOs in the environment. In the following years, the labelling of GMOs was made mandatory. This included foodstuffs and food containing additives or flavourings that have been genetically modified. Gradually, now even animal feed has to be mandatorily labelled. These initiatives of the EU have created a large public debate world over. However, the European Commission has reserved the right to support biotechnology research. The

Commission has also acknowledged that Europe's biotechnology industry is lagging behind. In fact, a four-prong strategy has been worked out to catch up in this technology race.[9]

Apart from EU, Japan has also come out with stringent regulations. A committee in charge of developing rules for biotechnology labelling was appointed in 1997 under the Ministry of Agriculture, Forestry and Fishery (MAFF). This ministry has announced to introduce mandatory safety checks to guard against imports of unapproved genetically modified crops for human consumption as well as animal feed.[10] This almost has set in a zero tolerance for food imports containing unapproved gene spliced products.

As the global debate over the benefits and safety of genetically modified food rages on, China has passed regulations that require clearer labelling of these types of products. Now it is being proposed that China would introduce mandatory labelling of food. China's State Council considered and passed the Regulations Concerning the Biotech Safety Management of Agricultural Gene Alteration. In the past, when crops with genetic alterations graduate from the laboratory to the field, they had to be approved by the Ministry of Agriculture. However, when they were transformed into merchandise, there were no such regulations. The new legislation will regulate the biological products with gene alterations requiring the above-mentioned food labelling, for example, so that the issues related to gene alteration can meet international standards.[11]

In India, though biosafety policy evolved in last decade, it has yet to address trade-related issues. The policy was announced in 1990 and then subsequently revised. However, the issues like imports of genetically modified goods are now being further strengthened. One of the recent controversies which highlighted this lacuna was related to import of genetically modified soybean from the US by a donor agency serving food programme for children.[12] India's Biosafety and

9. *Checkbiotech.org*, October 02, 2001

10. *Checkbiotech.org*, April 02, 2001.

11. Genet (2001). Monsanto and Syngenta Monopolise Key Gene Marker Technologies. May 16.

12. Chaturvedi, Sachin. 2001. "Continued Ambiguity on GMOs". *Economic and Political Weekly*, October 20.

Recombinant DNA Guidelines (1990) fall under the Environment (Protection) Act of 1986. In 1994, after India signed the Convention on Biodiversity, the DBT revised its earlier guidelines to accommodate the safe handling of GMOs in research, application and technology transfer. This includes the large scale production and deliberate release of GMOs plants, animals and products into the environment. Guidelines are also provided for the shipment and importation of GMOs for laboratory research.

In India the most important committees are: the Institutional Biosafety Committees (IBSC), responsible for the local implementation of guidelines, the Review Committee on Genetic Manipulations (RCGM) responsible for issuing permits; and the Genetic Engineering Approval Committee (GEAC), responsible for monitoring the large scale and commercial use of transgenic materials. These committees have statutory authority. Most of the committee members are from the scientific community and the staff of Department of Biotechnology (DBT) and the Ministry of Environment and Forestry (MoEF). DBT appoints the members to the committees. The GEAC is supposed to be assisted by the State Biotechnology Coordination Committees (SBCC) and District Level Committees (DLC). However, several states are still in the process of establishing SBCC and DLC committees. Efforts are being made to technically equip the members of these committees with information and literature.

WTO and Trade Implications

The issue of GMO possibly span several WTO agreements, including SPS, Agriculture, Trade-related Aspects of Intellectual Property Rights (TRIPs) and Technical Barriers to Trade (TBT). They GMOs related issues have also been discussed in the Committee on Trade and Environment (CTE). Although member governments have notified a large number of regulations related to GMOs to the SPS Committee, most of the discussion on the subject has been in the TBT Committee with the focus on labelling regulations. In the current agriculture negotiations, some members have called for clarity in the WTO rules as applied to products of new technologies.

The SPS Committee, meeting on October 31 and November 1, 2001, for the first time discussed Genetically Modified Organisms. In considering notifications for the first time in the SPS Committee, the US and Canada enquired about the EU's restrictions on Genetically Modified Organisms (GMOs). They complained that the EU had failed to notify its latest directives on traceability and labelling under SPS, even though these indicate that health protection is one of the objectives. The EU delegate mentioned that any comments on this notification should be sent to its authority handling technical barriers to trade issues. Under "other business", the US also complained about the lack of scientific justification for the EU's continued de facto moratorium on approval of GMO products, and Canada said that the latest EC measures discriminate against products produced by GM technology, even where no trace remains in the final products.

In the TRIPs Committee, it is the Article 27 which has remained at the centre of focus. Article 27 of the TRIPs Agreement defines the types of inventions, which have to be eligible for patent protection and those which can be exempt.These include both products and processes, and they cover all fields of technology.

At the Doha Ministerial the developing countries also joined the debate. As a result, the issues related to indigenous knowledge system (IKS) and access and benefit sharing (ABS) were also included. As a result the Doha Development Agenda (DDA) (Paragraph 19) provides for the relationship between the UN Convention on Biological Diversity (CBD), which explicitly acknowledges IKS and ABS and seeks to look into the relationship between TRIPs Agreement and the CBD.

In this debate several developing countries have contributed through their submissions covering issues like biodiversity and indigenous knowledge system and thus have expanded the scope of the debate itself. In between the WIPO General Assembly also established an Inter-governmental Committee on Intellectual Property and Genetic Resources, Traditional Knowledge and Folklore. The conclusion of International Treaty on Plant Genetic Resources for Food and Agriculture (ITPGRFA) under the aegis of FAO further encouraged protection and promotion of farmers' rights and indigenous knowledge system.

The Article 27.3(b) covers biotechnological inventions. It is currently under review in the TRIPs Council, as required by the TRIPs Agreement. Some countries have broadened the discussion to cover biodiversity and traditional knowledge. India and many other developing countries have been demanding an explicit position on benefit sharing on traditional knowledge system. The Doha Ministerial statement said:

> "We instruct the Council for TRIPs, in pursuing its work programme including under the review of Article 27.3(b), the review of the implementation of the TRIPs Agreement under Article 71.1 and the work foreseen pursuant to paragraph 12 of this declaration, to examine, inter alia, the relationship between the TRIPs Agreement and the Convention on Biological Diversity, the protection of traditional knowledge and folklore, and other relevant new developments raised by members pursuant to Article 71.1. In undertaking this work, the TRIPs Council shall be guided by the objectives and principles set out in Articles 7 and 8 of the TRIPs Agreement and shall take fully into account the development dimension."

Broadly speaking, Article 27.3(b) allows governments to exclude plants, animals and "essentially" biological processes (but micro-organisms, and non-biological and microbiological processes have to be eligible for patents). However, plant varieties have to be eligible either for patent protection or through a system created specifically for the purpose (*sui generis*), or a combination of the two. For example, countries could enact a plant varieties protection law based on a model of the International Union for the Protection of New Varieties of Plants (UPOV). The review of Article 27.3(b) began in 1999 as required by the TRIPS Agreement.

The topics raised in the TRIPs Council's discussions include: the pros and cons of various types of protection for new plant varieties (patents, UPOV, etc); how to handle moral and ethical issues (e.g. whether invented life forms should be eligible for protection); how to deal with traditional knowledge and the rights of the communities where genetic material originates (including benefit sharing when inventors in one country have rights to creations based on material obtained from another country); and whether there is a conflict between the TRIPs Agreement and the UN Convention on Biological Diversity (CBD). At WTO some developing countries including India have also suggested that patent applicants disclose the origin of genetic material used, which would make benefit sharing easier to implement. These countries have also emphasised on benefit sharing through prior agreement between the researchers and the host country where the genetic material originates.

However, one finds that the advances in agricultural biotechnology to some degree are paralleled by enhancement in the IPRs under TRIPs and at times in addition of TRIPs as well. This has brought under sharp focus the optimal patent scope and its coverage. This is now being discussed at length in the TRIPs Committee and the debate is largely around patentability and non-patentability of plant and animal inventions and the protection of plant varieties.

The Checklist of issues submitted to WTO by Brazil, Cuba, India and Peru among others is a recent example of the kind of documents that are needed at this stage to delineate the concept of disclosure requirements and related issues so as to bring out the negotiating process from the current state of '*status quo*'. The Switzerland proposal of making disclosure requirement an optional one under the national legislation rather than a mandatory provision at the international level may be explored for further facilitating the movement of the debate. The African group wants the TRIPs agreement to prohibit patenting of all life forms, including micro-organisms and wants *sui generis* protection for plant varieties to preserve farmers' rights. The US position is closer to that of Switzerland in the sense that the US proposal argues for national legislations to address CBD objectives on access to resources, traditional knowledge, benefit sharing.

In case of India atleast some of these objectives have been included in the national legislations and guidelines. However given the emerging trend of free trade agreements across various countries and the IPR provisions in them, it is important that one looks into the IPR regime beyond the TRIPs framework as well. One may find this trend completely opposed to the spirit and objective of Article 7 of TRIPs. The objective of TRIPs as stated is "the protection and enforcement of intellectual property rights should contribute to the promotion of technological innovation and to the transfer and dissemination of technology, to the mutual advantage of producers and users of technological knowledge and in a manner conducive to social and economic welfare, and to a balance of rights and obligations." Here we briefly mention three broad trends in the patent regime important from the standpoint of the developing countries in context of their access to biotechnology *per se*.

The pertinent question is what agenda developing countries should pursue and to what extent it is technologically tenable.[13] An answer to this should only guide the future course of action for the developing countries, not only with respect to the TRIPs negotiations but also their IPR policy in general. In this context, it needs to be mentioned at the outset that the increasing importance of genetic engineering in agricultural research across the world, a continued increase of Genetically Modified Organisms (GMOs) and the ability to patent plants has actually reduced the importance of plant variety protection and consequently of the *sui generis* system within the IPR regime.

Here it would be interesting to take note of the broad trends in the intellectual property regime at the level of individual developed countries. Till recently, life forms used to be exempted from patenting. However, developments in biotechnology are compelling for revising the approach towards the intellectual property regime. These policy changes have largely been taking place in the USA, but now European Union and Japan are also all set to closely follow in this race despite the fact that EU and Japan are opposed to biotechnology. Accordingly, various national governments are bringing in changes in the national laws in order to protect and encourage investments in biotechnology. These policy changes have further widened the scope of the ongoing debate. Now it covers a wide range of issues such as the range of product patents and the patentability of genes, gene-sequences and parts of gene-sequences derived from humans, animals, plants or microorganisms. The added aspect is of the relationship between the patent system and the plant variety system. Moreover, patenting, especially of human body parts, has posed an ethical limit for biotechnology itself. In the following sections we attempt to analyse some of these prominent trends in the patenting regime.

The Plant Variety Protection (PVP) and the patents are the two important forms of intellectual property rights. In context of developing countries, PVP has been there for some time but patents

13. Chaturvedi, Sachin. 2002. "Agricultural Biotechnology and New Trends in IPR Regime: Challenges before Developing Countries". *Economic and Political Weekly*, Vol XXXVII, No. 13, March 30.

for plants is a recent phenomenon. Both patents and PVP provide exclusive monopoly rights on the creation for commercial purposes over a period of time. A patent is a right granted to an inventor to prevent all others from making, using, and/or selling the patented invention for some years. The criteria for a patent are novelty, inventiveness (non-obviousness), utility, and reproducibility. Although patents were designed for industrial application, with biotechnology patent offices now grant patents on micro-organisms and, in some countries, on all life forms.

The intellectual property regime for plant variety protection emerged with a strong commitment for public interest in mind. The whole provision for compulsory licensing was introduced with this intention only. Under this provision of compulsory licensing, a holder of plant breeders' rights can neither refuse any applicant nor can offer unreasonable terms for this. Plant variety protection has worked well as a mechanism to promote the interests of the plant breeders for developing new varieties through giving them proprietary rights on the one hand and as a custodian of public rights of access and use of genetic material on the other. PVP gives patent-like rights to plant breeders. What gets protected in this case is the genetic make-up of a specific plant variety. The criteria for protection are different: novelty, distinctness, uniformity, and stability. PVP laws can provide exemptions for breeders, allowing them to use protected varieties for further breeding, and for farmers, allowing them to save seeds from their harvest.

In plant breeding, thus, PVP is the weaker sister of patenting mainly because of these exemptions. PVP also encourages cross licensing between a holder of PVP and a holder of a patent. Under the breeders' exemption of plant variety rights, anyone may use protected material for breeding purposes. However, the patent regime does not reciprocate this.

Impact on Trade

As is clear, though international trade regime at WTO has yet to address challenges emanating from advancements in biotechnology, the prohibitive measures have already started affecting the trade. Table 20.1 shows how US export of corn and soybean has declined in several of those countries which have resorted to these prohibitive tactics. In 1997 import of Corn from European Union was 1000 metric tonnes, which declined to 0.07 metric tonnes by 2000. Similarly, import of Soybean from EU has declined from 8000 metric tonnes in 1997 to 6000 metric tonnes by 2000. Apart from this, delays in authorisation to import some Bt corn from the US by France cost US exporters about $300 million in exports to the European Union (Cunningham *et al.*, 2000). Only about 2 million tonnes of the 42 million tonnes of US corn exports went to the EU in 1997. In 1998, only 0.3 million tonnes of the 41 million tonnes went to the EU. Factors that have been used to explain the declines include bans of GM corn by France, Austria and Luxemburg (Cunningham *et al.*, 2000). Similar declines have been documented for soybeans. Only 9 million tonnes (out of 26 million tonnes) of US soybean exports went to the EU in 1997 and only 6 million tonnes (out of 20 million tonnes) were exported to the EU.

Some developing countries like India have recently gone through very tough time in terms of governance of biotechnology.[14] Genetically modified cotton was initially illegally introduced in the production system, which is all set to create problems in those countries where imports of GM variety are banned, a problem similar to what we mentioned in case of US. However, as Table 20.2 shows, total impact on exports of only those crops in which biotechnological applications have been planned, for instance, cotton, corn, soybean and vegetables to only three countries would be $6201 million in case of India. It would nearly be $1700 million to the EU alone. The situation becomes much more challenging when one realises that there are very few equipped laboratories in which GMO testing can be done. Therefore, a clear market strategy and options with technological choices would have to be made with a lot of precaution.

At the Committee on Agriculture this issue came up again in the same context. In a special session of the Committee on Agriculture, the European Union tabled a controversial paper on food safety,

14. Chaturvedi, Sachin. 2003. "GMO Experience in India". *Biotechnology and Development Monitor* (forthcoming).

Table 20.1

US Exports of Corn and Soybeans to Selected Regions/Countries, 1997-2000

Region/ Country	Corn (106 metric tonnes)*			Soyabeans (106 metric tonnes)		
	1997 Jan-Dec	1999 Jan-Dec	2000 Jan-Dec	1997 Jan-Dec	1999 Jan-Dec	2000 Jan-Dec
Africa	3.95	6.69	6.46	0.11	0.28	0.23
Asia	27.68	31.45	26.73	11.68	12.14	14.94
European Union	1.56	0.09	0.07	8.96	6.46	6.10
Japan	15.45	15.33	14.87	3.70	3.68	3.58
South Korea	3.44	6.16	2.29	1.25	1.17	1.34
Canada	1.03	0.97	1.49	0.26	0.33	0.33
China (Taiwan)	5.44	4.73	4.72	2.27	1.95	1.93

* 1 metric tonne = 2,204 pounds.

Source: ERS/ USDA. FATUS Report. Available online at http://www.ers.usda.gov/db/fatus/

Table 20.2

India's Exports of (Potential GM) Crops

(US $ Million)

	Cotton	Corn	Soyabean	Vegetables	Tot Crops Imported by Countries	per cent Share In Total Exports of Crops
EU	1725.64 (28.99)	0.05 (2.27)	0.08 (32.00)	41.44 (16.77)	1767.21	28.50
Japan	161.79 (2.72)	—	0.11 (44.00)	1.36 (0.55)	163.26	2.63
South Korea	189.03 (3.18)	—	—	0.52 (0.21)	189.55	3.06
Total	5951.7	2.2	0.25	247.07	6201.22	100.00

Source: India Trade 2001.

Note: Figures in Parenthesis are percentage share in total exports.

proposing criteria for the application of precaution under the Agreement on Sanitary and Phyto-sanitary Measures (SPS) that would serve as a guideline for panelists in future disputes. According to the EU, the issue needs to be addressed to avoid the public perception that the WTO requires members to force consumers to accept unsafe food. The EU, other European countries, Japan and Korea argued that Article 5.7 of the SPS Agreement should be clarified through an understanding that would send the right signals to consumers.

Article 5.7 allows members to take provisional health measures when relevant scientific evidence is insufficient, and the substance of the discussions revolved around whether the Article was clear enough to maintain the balance between the need for consumer protection on the one hand and the need to avoid disguised protectionism on the other.

To create predictability for members and to prevent Article 5.7 from being abused for protectionist purposes, the EU proposed that precaution be applied according to the following five criteria: (i) the measure should not be discriminatory; (ii) it should be aimed at achieving consistency in the level of protection that the Member has chosen; (iii) the adopted measure should presuppose an examination of the benefits and costs of action and lack of action; (iv) it should be reviewed if new scientific information is obtained; and (v) the measure must be based on scientific evidence provided by qualified and respected sources, but not necessarily by the majority of the scientific community. The US and many developing countries strongly opposed this effort to bring food safety onto the agriculture negotiating agenda. They argued that the EU's version of the precautionary principle was based on political rather than scientific considerations. Suspecting that the EU was chiefly interested in finding another avenue for addressing the controversial precautionary principle in the WTO, the US, the Cairns Group and India took a position that instead of the agriculture negotiations, food safety should be discussed at the SPS and the TBT Committees.

Concluding Remarks

The entry of biotechnology especially in the post-green revolution scenario when agriculture production seems to pose several challenges, the concerns like food security assumes key importance in the context of developing countries. The opinion about biotechnology among the developing countries is mixed. There are experts who actually enlist several factors why biotechnology per se is not the right technology to ensure food security and reduce poverty in the developing countries. They even go up to the extent of saying that biotechnology is a technology that has been shaped by a narrow range of private interests – interests that are incompatible with the demands of an ecologically sound and socially-just agriculture. Thus, the issues that the advent of this technology raises, cover a much wider canvass. The ethical dimension of the Genetically Modified Organisms have further confounded the ongoing confusion on the relevance of biotechnology for the developing countries.

In the last decade or so, the transnational corporations have emerged as a major source of biotechnology products. This trend has, probably, further contributed to the concerns among the developing countries as reports about bio-piracy become galore. These concerns have got reflected in the sharper debate being initiated to assess the relevance of this technology for developing countries.

In such a scenario it may not be entirely misplaced to observe that, since biotechnology is a frontier technology, upcoming in a dynamic international environment, it probably requires an altogether different approach to ensure the growth of the technology along with the desired socio-economic goals. Thus, it poses a two-fold challenge: on one hand, the growth of technology has to be ensured and on the other, policies would have to be evolved not only to restrict its adverse implications but also for ensuring growth in the agricultural sector. Any imbalance between the two may offset the wider developmental impetus, the agricultural sector needs at this point. It is high time that agricultural R&D plans prioritise investment on new technologies so as to rightly balance or rather supplement the traditional techniques with new technologies to serve socio-economic interests.

The emerging trade regime under WTO has influenced international trade to a great extent. These changes have severe implications for the developing countries. More so when they are already struggling with the implementational hurdles of the TRIPs regime. There are many developing countries, which have yet to put in place national legislations to position themselves vis-à-vis the international negotiations at the WTO. Several of them come out with several drafts of biodiversity and patent laws but they have yet to see light of the day. There have been various reasons for this delay but now it seems to be clear that it would not only adversely affect the access to technology but also the patenting of research tools would also exclude the late comers in the technology race from imitation or even from product development in any other form.

The WTO TRIPs regime article 27.3 (b) refers to have either a patent regime or an effective *sui generis* system for protection of plant varieties. In the last decade or so, the developing countries have strongly debated the various aspects of *sui generis* system and what actually constitutes it. However, as is evident from the earlier sections, the varietial protection is being attempted through much more stronger patent regime, which do not allow any kind of exemption and is much narrower in its scope than the plant patents or plant variety protection. There is a continuous growth in what is called the utility patents in the US and the Biotechnology Directive of EU has suggested a similar mechanism for the protection of biotechnological inventions in Europe. Along with this there is also a growing trend of patenting the research tools as well. Thus, in light of the developments in biotechnology, the profile of patent regime is fast changing in the developed countries. Needless to mention that a large part of this research is emanating from the private sector.

The above analysis shows that it is desirable that developing countries would make choices in the biotechnology at selective levels. Even within agricultural biotechnology there are several options which take the horizon far ahead of adoption and diffusion of GMOs alone. This decision should be subject to a critical evaluation of the need assessment of developing countries. In order to obtain benefits and be competitive in biotechnology, developing countries need to access not only the products but, more importantly, to the technology and certainly the tool for it.

In addition, access to genetic resources and the associated traditional knowledge plays a role, highlighting the need for benefit sharing and prior informed consent. At another level, there has to be a multilateral effort to help build capacity related to institutions, infrastructure, policy development and implementation, human resources, local-level ecological data, and research and development in the developing countries in general and in underdeveloped countries in particular. These countries also require support to adopt GM product along with provisions for its safe use and capability to handle its importers and exporters. As far as international negotiations are concerned, a strategy founded on well-informed opinion on technical aspects should be evolved. This includes participation in international negotiations at the WTO and international standard-setting organisations.

As is clear, biotechnology has great potential to be used as commercial technology and thus would be capable of generating a profit exclusively for its owner and others who may be able to access its conditionally at a very high cost. The access is also determined by the terms and conditions set by the IPR Regime. In case of biotechnology, TNCs have a far stronger monopoly than any time before in the history of agriculture science. As biotechnology is an emerging technology, the owners guard the source of their competitive advantage to the core. In some cases they may internalize transfer of technology, within their network of affiliates rather than externalising such a transfer to unaffiliated licensees.

This scenario completely rules out any possibility of deploying conventional instruments for transfer of technology. The developing countries would have to reconsider their technology policy to encourage and support innovation in the field of frontier technologies. For this they may have to improve upon the existing technological base. In fact, the need is to set their own R&D agenda in the realm of biotechnology. As at present R&D plans are not based on the economic requirements of respective developing countries. Since this is highly capital-intensive technology, the developing countries may consider to pool their resources for creating common facilities like Gene Banks, instruments for marker assisted technology, etc.

Select Bibliography

Buckingham E. Donald (2001). "Hot Potato, Hot Potato: Regulating Products of Biotechnology by the International Community". *Journal of World Trade,* Vol. 35 No. 1.

Cunningham, Carrie and Laurian J. Unnevehr (2000). "A Market Segmentation for Genetically Modified Corn and Soyabean Exports" in William H. Lesser (ed.) *Transitions in Agbiotech: Economics of Strategy and Policy, Proceedings of the NE-165 Conference,* June 24-25, 1999, Washington, D.C., including papers presented at the *International Consortium on Agricultural Biotechnology Research Conference,* June 17-19, 1999 in Rome Tor Vergata, Italy. University of Connecticut and the University of Massachusetts. Ch. 34, pp. 638-650.

Ekanem, E. *et al.,* (2001). "Economic Risks of Genetically Engineered Foods in International Trade". Paper presented at the *International Food and Agribusiness Management Association World Food and Agribusiness Symposium* held in Sydney, Australia June 27-28.

Fabi, Randy (2000). "Star Link Impact on US Corn Exports." Archived at *http://www. Plant. uoguelph.ca/safefood/archives/agnet-archives.htm,* November 30.

Nielsen Chantal and Kym Anderson (2000). "GMOs, Trade Policy, and Welfare in Rich and Poor Countries". *Policy Discussion Paper,* No. 21, University of Adelaide.

Perdiks Nicholas (2001). "Reforming the WTO to Defuse Potential Trade Conflicts in Genetically Modified Goods". *Journal of World Trade,* Vol. 35, No. 3.

Zedalis Rex J. (2001). "Labeling of Genetically Modified Foods: The Limits of GATT Rules". *Journal of World Trade,* Vol. 35 No.2.

Section VI

Singapore Issues

Four new issues surfaced in the Singapore Ministerial for future discussion – namely, (1) Government Procurement, (2) Trade and Investment, (3) Trade and Competition Policy and (4) Trade Facilitation – collectively known as Singapore issues. In the current framework, we consider only the first, third and the fourth issues.

In the first paper under this section, Pritam Banerjee and Dipankar Sengupta argue India has much to gain from the process of Trade Facilitation. The key argument is that since India has already opted for an export-led growth strategy, many of the measures required, if any, under the current Trade Facilitation framework are either underway or would be taken anyway. Thus additional obligations that a trade facilitation agreement would entail are unlikely to be considerably expensive. On the other hand benefits obtained through reduced transaction costs are huge as are the potential gains through enhanced exports and FDI. Looking from an Indian perspective the land-locked nature of the North East as well as its India's isolation from energy-rich Central Asia can also be remedied if Article V of GATT is suitablly amended.

Sandwip Das point out that the government of India has no policy regulating government procurement; there are numerous rules and procedures made by central, sub-central and regional authorities at multiple layers of the federal economy, but there is no act passed by the parliament. These rules are non-uniform, outmoded and complex, leaving scope for favouritism, political pressure and corruption. The system cannot guarantee neutrality and fairness in purchase decisions, although regulatory bodies, audits and vigilance pose credible threats to those who intend to engage in corrupt practices. However, the overall impact of the current regulatory framework on corruption is difficult to comment upon. There are also indications that excessive vigilance restricts innovation in purchase. So far as a multilateral agreement on government purchase is concerned, India should have no problem with transparency as well as providing MFN treatment to others. The basic problem would arise in giving National Treatment, as India's concern with certain protected sectors is genuine.

Pradeep Mehta, Nitya Nanda and Alice Pham take cognisance of the challenges posed by cross-border competition issues and attempt to identify the relevant competition problems. They opine that the exisiting bilateral and regional cooperation arrangements to deal with such issues as grossly inadequate and the need for a multilateral framework remains. The proposed competition framework at the WTO also in their opinion fails to pass muster. Mehta *et al.*, suggest that a new agency (under the auspices of the UN) combining the principles and structures of WIPO and Interpol and other multilateral bodies be set up.

21

Economic Growth, Exports and the Issue of Trade Facilitation

PRITAM BANERJEE
DIPANKAR SENGUPTA

Introduction

Trade facilitation covers all the steps that can be taken to smoothen and facilitate the flow of trade. The term has been used widely to cover all sorts of non-tariff barriers, including product testing and impediments to labour mobility, but in the WTO, discussions are limited to "the simplification and harmonisation of international trade procedures" covering the "activities, practices and formalities involved in collecting, presenting, communicating and processing data required for the movement of goods in international trade". It relates to a wide range of activities at the border such as import and export procedures (e.g. procedures relating to customs, licensing and quarantine); transport formalities; payments, insurance and other financial requirements.

The importance of trade facilitation assumes added importance given the current economic regimes of most developing countries, especially India, than it did before 1991. While aggregate demand was driven by government expenditure before 1991, it is exports that have increasingly taken over this role today. Thus any measure that helps export growth including Trade Facilitation measures assumes paramount importance for export-driven economies. This of course was not always so. Prior to 1991, the role of exports was merely to pay for imports. This was necessitated by the fact that no economy could produce all it needed and the imports grew as economies grew. Thus given the limited role of exports, the role of measures that reduce transaction costs of exporters was also not topmost in the minds of policy-makers. Moreover, in a regime of import-substituting-industrialisation, many trade facilitation measures would not just help exporters in exporting goods, they would also help importers in importing goods which in-turn would displace domestic production. In that sense certain trade facilitation measures were perceived to be running counter to government policy of economic growth through import-substitution. Today, given the reversal in government policy, it may be argued that pursuing Trade Facilitation measures is seen as required for the sake of economic growth via expanded trade as well as through supplementation of domestic investment with Foreign Direct Investment (FDI) that would find TF an added attraction to invest in India.

Viewed in this context, the importance of Trade Facilitation is obvious. The plethora of the procedures that have to be gone through at the border when importing or exporting, have increased in recent years, adding to the cost of trading both for governments and business. One reason is the increased trade volumes brought about by the progressive reduction of tariffs and quotas in international trade through successive rounds of trade liberalisation under the General Agreement on Tariffs and Trade (GATT). The volume of international trade has expanded relative to the size of many national economies, making it more difficult for administrations to cope on the basis of unchanged resources. At the same time, the reduction of other types of barriers has brought border-crossing costs to business, such as waiting time and Customs procedures, into new prominence.

At the multilateral level, Trade Facilitation would involve co-operation between several organisations like World Customs Organisation (WCO), Standard setting bodies like OIE (Office Internationale de Èpizooties) and IPPC (International Plant Protection Convention), and logistics related bodies like International Maritime Organisation etc.

At the national level, co-ordination between various authorities dealing with areas such as customs, shipping and ports, airports, warehousing, standard setting and monitoring authorities etc. are required.

A brief outline of existing literature on Trade Facilitation, especially in the Indian and Asian contexts will be discussed in this chapter. The purpose of this exercise is to identify possible approaches towards investigating Trade Facilitation as an issue for India's trade dynamism. The relevance of a WTO agreement on Trade Facilitation for India is a function of the costs and benefits that accrue to India's trade dynamism.

Before delving into the existing literature however, it is important to discuss the reasons behind what are some of the trends that intensify the need for looking at trade facilitation issues and what Trade Facilitation broadly involves.

Trends in International Trade: Pushing the Need for Trade Facilitation

Globalisation of Production: International Supply Chains

The success of many South East Asian economies as manufacturing economies stem from the *endaka* of the 1980s, i.e. the phenomenon of the soaring yen following the Brady Plan. To maintain the competitiveness of Japanese exports, the Japanese factory system was de-localised with the capital-intensive and skill-intensive operations taking place in Japan (where capital was cheap) and the labour-intensive operations like assembly being re-located to the labour-abundant economies of South East Asia. However, it was not cheap labour alone that made this evolution possible. What was critical for the new cross-border factories that intermediate goods/parts crossing borders did so with minimum cost and time making the entire operation cost-effective. Today manufacturers have honed this practice to new heights.

Modern supply chain management techniques and the rapid spread of information technologies and e-commerce have progressively increased the use of just-in-time techniques by manufacturing industry and encouraged the growth of integrated global supply, production and distribution systems. In this environment, where manufacturers rely on the uninterrupted reception of the necessary components to meet production contingencies, business cannot afford to have imported or exported goods tied up for long periods because of unnecessary or over-complicated trade procedures and requirements and thus will not invest in those economies where such procedures and requirements exist.

Increased Complexity of Trade

Goods and Services traded across borders have become increasingly sophisticated, at the same time the rules and regulations that govern tariffs and non-tariff measures have become increasingly complicated over time. Preferential trade agreements have added to this complexity a proliferation of rules of origin. Threats to national security have also increased in recent times. All these factors add up to make the process of goods and services crossing borders far more difficult than they used to be half a century ago. Threats to national health and consumer welfare have also become greater and tend to have global repercussions (a good recent example is the SARS in East and SE Asia).

Given this background, it is important to meet this basic challenge, i.e. to make trade as easy and quick as possible to harmonise global supply chains and production process while ensuring that Governments are able to efficiently administer customs and safeguard national health and security.

Some of the universally accepted general principles to meet this challenge are as follows:

1. Transparency

Procedures and practices are widely recognised as an essential element for ensuring that regulatory objectives are achieved efficiently while at the same time enhancing the benefits expected from trade and investment liberalisation. Transparency underpins the ability of market participants and stakeholders to fully understand the conditions and constraints for entering and operating in a market; to gain an accurate picture of the costs and returns of their involvement; to have the time and flexibility needed to meet requirements and adjust to potential changes; and to be equipped to deal with any discriminatory or arbitrary treatment. Transparency is crucial in making domestic regulations and administrative practices more efficient and in enhancing their integrity. This is achieved by revealing the costs and benefits of policy decisions and administrative practices and ensuring that their purpose is clear and appropriately implemented. It may be argued that aspects of transparency have actually to do more with market access for foreign players (than export promotion) although it also benefits domestic exporters. It is argued that by making transparency selective (i.e. biased in favour of domestic players) can also achieve the latter. However in an era when global advantages and disadvantages are dynamic concepts it is best not to be discretionary when it comes to recipients of information.

2. Consistency

Uncertainty in trade operations translates very quickly into unwarranted transaction costs in the form of warehousing and demurrage expenses, transport and insurance fees and financing charges, as traders need to ward off potential disruptions in their production and logistics chain. Such problems can quickly become a strong disincentive for smaller businesses that lack the necessary logistic support to deal with such constraints. Non-discretionary and uniform administration of applicable requirements allows traders to know what to expect in their everyday dealings with Customs and other border agencies and to make informed decisions about their activities in a market. This requires clear and precise procedural guidance that is based on standard policies and operating procedures and is applied consistently whatever the authority or trader involved. Consistent application of the rules guarantees efficiency and integrity in the administration, shielding it from attempts to obtain illegal advantages.

3. Non-discrimination

It is important to ensure the impartial and uniform application of all border-related regulations, procedures and practices. It goes beyond equal treatment between trading partner countries, to focus on the treatment of individual traders. Impartiality and uniformity does not mean all products have to be treated in an identical manner, but it does call for effective equality of administration where the same circumstances apply. Simplifying border procedures helps achieve Customs and other public policy objectives in the most cost-efficient way, both for the administration and for affected traders. It is an essential path to increasing efficiency for Customs and other border administrations seeking to deploy limited resources to enhance productivity, face increasing budgetary constraints and improve revenue collection through more flexible, risk-based and targeted operations. At the same time, simplifying procedures lifts restrictions and burdens that unnecessarily add to traders' cost of doing business as well as generating undue delays at the border. Measures to simplify border procedures and to avoid unnecessary burdens include doing away with unnecessary or outdated requirements, such as requesting information that is already available to the authorities, or requesting the same information more than once for different departments; Customs, food inspection agencies, health and safety authorities, etc. It also involves updating regulations to take account of changed contexts, technologies and markets; and ensuring that the implementation process is in proportion to the desired result. This means, for example, not introducing measures to improve revenue collection that cost more to implement than is actually gained in revenue. On the other hand, if Customs authorities can partly or totally process shipments before arrival of the goods, based on the transmission of the requested information in advance, or replace border controls by post-clearance audits, it simplifies the whole process. It reduces bottlenecks, which in turn reduces delays and related expenses for traders such as the risk of spoilage of perishable goods and theft, and reduces opportunities for corruption by minimising direct transactions between officials and traders or their agents.

The next obvious question that we need to ask ourselves is whether there is a case for a multilateral framework that can guarantee the above universal principles to be enforced on a worldwide framework.

The Case for WTO Rules for Trade Facilitation

The key advantages of achieving a WTO undertaking in the area of trade facilitation would be renewed political impetus to make border controls more efficient and strengthened international coherence in tackling the issue. The need to enhance efficiency in order to face an increasingly complex international trading environment has been an important driving force behind Customs reforms undertaken at national level around the world in recent years. However, it has frequently not gone far enough to do away with deeply entrenched outdated institutional settings and cumbersome procedures. To be successful, a trade facilitation agenda needs wide political support and the sustained commitment of those involved in the formulation and implementation of trade policy, both within the administration and among the economic actors. It is important that Developing Countries and India in particular, realise that having a global standard as WTO rules would imply means predictability and uniformity of rules across economies. It makes easier the setting up of the global factory system. More importantly for countries desirous of setting up their own trading networks, Trade Facilitation makes such an endeavor easier as networks can adopt a common standard operating procedure at least with respect to some operations as a result of common rules and standards.

Decisively launching the reform process and keeping it on the right track is crucial for achieving well-designed trade facilitation reforms that pay off quickly and end up being self-sustaining. Overcoming resistance to change from vested interests requires considerable political effort that is not easy to muster without a high level of motivation. Trade facilitation rules in the framework of the WTO could offer this missing impetus at the multilateral level, providing an external discipline to ensure continuing domestic political commitment and shield from temptations to backtrack. Coherence is also essential. Trade facilitation efforts, national or international, need to be consistent between different policy areas. Partial approaches that lack coherence appear a sure recipe for failure. Speeding up Customs clearance, for example, will not help move goods faster if there is no road system to carry them. It is also a question of better co-ordination between the narrow area of trade facilitation and the areas of Customs valuation, rules of origin, import licensing or sanitary controls. A coherent multilateral setting would also provide a solid background for designing well-targeted technical assistance and capacity-building projects, overcoming regional divides, ensuring that the projects' different components are mutually supportive and better targeting aspects of co-operation between border agencies of concerned countries.

A Review of the Literature

Brian Staples[1] points out that there are existing Agreements within the WTO that indirectly deal with the idea of Trade

1. Staples, Brian, "Trade Facilitation: Improving the Invisible Infrastructure', in *Development, Trade and WTO* eds. Hoekman, Mattoo and English. World Bank Publication, 2002.

Facilitation. He argues that such agreements have already established a large part of modalities and ground rules that can be used to frame a WTO agreement on Trade Facilitation. Staples uses the WTO agreements on Import Licensing Procedures, Technical Barriers to Trade (TBT) and Sanitary and Phyto-Sanitary measures (SPS) as examples of important steps towards Trade Facilitation.

Staples also points out that GATT articles V (freedom of transit), VIII (simplification of fees and formalities related to trade) and X (requiring timely and adequate publication of all laws and guidelines that might affect trade), already provides for the basic principle of Trade Facilitation in a WTO (i.e. multilateral) context. Staples identifies six major problems with unilateral Customs reform, and uses it reinforce the need for multilateral level initiatives aimed at trade facilitation. These six major problem areas are:

1. Out of date customs procedures
2. Inadequate legislation
3. Belief that computerisation is the answer to the above 2 problems.
4. Inadequate attention to staffing needs and modern administration.
5. Lack of co-ordination between tax, ports, warehousing and customs: Piecemeal reforms
6. Failure to make the connection between transparency and corruption.

"*Transaction Costs of Indian Exports*"[2] presents an Indian perspective of the costs incurred by Indian exporters and importers at different stages of the trading process. Briefly, they can be classified under the following heads:

1. Obtaining different export-import codes.
2. Obtaining different licenses.
3. Revalidation of export/import licenses.
4. Issuance of Trading house category.

2. *Transaction Costs of Indian Exports*: Export-Import Bank of India Publication, October 2002.

5. Obtaining various refunds like duty drawbacks etc.
6. Obtaining adequate and reliable warehousing.
7. Getting remittances through banks.
8. Customs clearances and Port clearances.
9. Final dispatch/release of export/import consignments.

This report also highlights that Leather, Textiles, Chemicals and engineering goods had the biggest problem with custom/port procedures, while Gems and Jewelry had the least. This indicates that a nuanced sectoral approach to trade facilitation that looks at specific needs of different sectors is as important as a holistic reform of the trading infrastructure. Such focus will add to the overall efficiency of the larger trading system.

The report also stated that the average export/import transaction in India took thrice as long as the officially stipulated time, highlighting the serious lack of implementation of official guidelines.

In *"Trade Facilitation: The World Bank Experience"*[3] Jayanta Roy states that the average customs transaction involves 29-30 different parties, over 40 documents and around 200 data elements. Roy classifies the focus of Trade Facilitation measures on three main areas:

1. Transport - Logistics, including improvements in cargo dwell time.
2. Governance - Transparency and management practices. Reduce paper work, move towards EDI (electronic data interchange), provide single window facilities etc.
3. Trade Enhancement - New infrastructure and technology for trade e.g. container transport facility, refrigerated trucks and warehouses, just-in-time warehouse management techniques etc.

Roy highlights two areas within the gamut of trade facilitation that require a multilateral framework in order to be effective. The first is regulatory measures i.e. global harmonisation on product classification, transport liability regimes and insurance practices. The

3. Roy, Jayanta (1998), *Trade Facilitation: The World Bank Experience*, Trade Facilitation Symposium, WTO.

second is operational and transport facilitation measures e.g. harmonisation of customs regulation and documentation and globally enforceable standards in cargo dwell time and port facilities.

In *"Maritime Transport Costs and Port Efficiency"*[4] Containerization (used as a proxy for technological improvement in logistics) has negative and significant impact on transport costs. Since transport costs are shown to have negative and significant impact on trade flows, it follows that development of logistics is an important component of facilitating trade. More pertinently, the coefficient related to port efficiency is negative and significant. Thus greater the efficiency at port level, the lower the transport costs. This result clearly supports two very important aspects of trade facilitation i.e. development of logistics and reform and streamlining of port and customs procedures. This paper provided strong statistical evidence that Trade Facilitation is a key component of increasing trade flows between nations.

"Business Benefits of Trade Facilitation"[5] highlights the importance of the rising incidence of transaction costs as documentation to enable exports and imports become more complicated. It points out the importance of error-free operations for international trade transactions as even minor errors may halt the entire transaction, or at least multiply the compliance costs due to possible repetitive error corrections, re-keying, and re-filing. Risks of error would be multiplied as the number of participants in trade transactions increase and their requirements become more complicated.

Another facet of Trade facilitation dealt with in this report involves lost business opportunity costs (i.e. business foregone). Due to the direct and indirect transaction costs involved in facilitating trade, enterprises often lose business opportunities. For example, for a company operating a just-in-time, low-inventory production network across countries, a delay in one country may cause stagnation in the entire global production chain, with potentially enormous lost business. Another example can be seen when a cash poor company foresees payment delays and high capital costs may

---

4. *Maritime Transport Costs and Port Efficiency*, Ximena Clark, David Dollar, and Alejandro Micco, World Bank, 2001.
5. "Business Benefits of Trade Facilitation", *OECD Working Paper for the Committee on Trade*, 2002.

drive it to give up a trade contract. In addition to importers and exporters of goods, suppliers of trade-related services (such as express airfreight operators) may also lose business opportunities if their clients foresee critical delays due to the procedural requirements for the delivery of their services.

The most important finding of this report involves the asymmetric effect that the lack of proper trade facilitation has on SMEs (small and medium enterprises), especially those operating in developing countries. The report concludes that while large players are often able to find ways and means to operate in any system given their large resource base, SMEs are adversely affected by the lack of proper channels of trade. When the necessary information on applicable regulations is not readily available, trade operators have to spend additional resources to obtain that information. Enterprises operating in an non-transparent business environment, as is often the case in developing countries, would need to spend more resources or time to obtain regulatory and market information. To this time and resources they will frequently have to add expenses for bribes, penalties and administrative or judicial appeals. As these additional expenses do not usually vary according to the value of the goods or the volume of the sales, they drive the operational costs per product unit quite high and put SMEs in a weaker position than larger enterprises.

Such asymmetric impacts of the lack of transparent and effective trade facilitation measures deter SMEs in developing countries from seeking to expand in international markets. According to Arichi in "*Trade Facilitation Efforts of ASEM and Japan*"[6] this may be one of the reasons why the bulk of exports today are made by a small number of large firms. This tendency is assumed to have been stronger in the past, which might have contributed to past under-estimations of trade transaction costs.

The findings of this OECD report are all the more important in the Indian context for three primary reasons:

---

6. "Trade Facilitation Efforts of ASEM and Japan" by Arichi Hiroshi in Schiavo-Campo, Salvatore (ed.), *Simplification of Customs Procedures - Reducing Transaction Costs for Efficiency, Integrity and Trade Facilitation* (Asian Development Bank).

1. Some of India's niche areas in the export sector i.e. gems and jewelry, carpets, processed marine and food products, leather goods etc. are mostly run by small and medium scale players, and the dynamism of India's exports are probably hampered due to lack of proper trade facilitation measures.
2. India is looking to leverage the abolition of MFA come 2005 to give textiles related exports a boost. If India can successfully access the global textiles market, it means billions of USD worth of export earnings and millions of new jobs in this sector. Given the fact that this sector is in the hands of small and medium players, trade facilitation will yet again play a role in the success or failure of India to emerge as textiles and clothing super power.
3. To compete in global supply chains that feed into global production process, Indian manufacturing will have to ensure 'just in time' delivery modules. If, given the high per unit cost of trade facilitation, such modules will become very expensive and Indian manufacturers will be priced out of the market. This will be especially true of many successful medium-scale engineering manufacturers who have recently shown incredible initiative to latch on the world market for parts and components.

The above review of literature on the subject of Trade Facilitation presents the most important aspects and dimensions on the topic. Based on this review, it is possible to identify the issues and methodology for the study of trade facilitation in an Indian context.

Trade Facilitation and Transaction Costs: The Case of India

The aim of this section is the following: The broad areas that come under Trade Facilitation (and germane to Indian conditions) are presented, followed by a description of India's shortcomings in this area expressed in physical units. This is then translated into financial costs.

1a) Areas Requiring Reform (The Domestic Agenda)

The ambit of Trade Facilitation is very broad and touches upon several areas. While some of these falls directly under initiatives that need to be taken by the Government, others involve a partnership between private stakeholders and Government initiatives. The main indicators of trade facilitation and the areas of reform required in them are briefly presented below.

Port Logistics

- Cargo Dwell time,
- Warehousing facilities (including refrigerated warehouses for perishables),
- Rail and road links from hinterland to ports.

Customs Procedures

- Electronic Data Interface (EDI),
- Signature-less, Internet-based process for filing customs related documents,
- Trust-based systems,
- Post-clearance audit,
- Pre-Shipment Inspection Agreements (PSI),
- Risk-analysis and assessment.

Standards Harmonisation

- Reform of domestic Standards-setting and monitoring authorities,
- Moving towards regional and global convergence on standards,
- Mutual Recognitions Agreements on standards.

Business Mobility

- Movement of Professionals and transparent visa systems,
- Adequate Financial systems including Banking, Insurance and Clearance mechanism.

Trade Information and E-business Facilities

- Proper channels and access to market information, legal systems and standards and regulations,
- Availability of information electronically through the internet,
- E-Business infrastructure to enable to business to business contacts.

Administrative Transparency and Professionalism

- Simple and transparent procedures for export and import,
- Non-discriminatory approach to enforcement based on risk assessment techniques,
- Public Private cooperation and information sharing to improve enforcement and compliance.

b) Trade Facilitation in the Multilateral Context

The principle behind the multilateral framework of WTO lies in the formation of a rules-based trading framework for all countries. The WTO has achieved remarkable success in this direction in reference to trade liberalisation and removal of barriers in terms of tariffs, and to some extent Non-Tariff barriers. The time has come for the WTO to explore areas beyond tariffs and NTB's that are impeding trade. Trade Facilitation is definitely one area that all countries will have to cooperate in for their mutual benefit, and multilateral framework of the WTO provides an excellent forum to explore this issue. But it should be recognised clearly at the outset, that removal of impediments to trade facilitation would take time in most developing countries, given their lack of essential capacity to undertake reforms. Multilateral and bilateral institutions must earmark provisions of substantial resources towards capacity building process in developing countries.

A Brief Background

Trade facilitation came rushing to the foreground of WTO issues as the international business community increasingly expressed concern for greater transparency, efficiency, and procedural uniformity of cross-border transportation of goods. Trade Facilitation came into the WTO agenda after some important studies done by APEC, World Bank and UNCTAD came up with the conclusions that:

- Clearing the red tape at country borders would generate approximately twice as much gain to GDP than tariff liberalisation would.
- Trade facilitation measures would particularly benefit developing countries, where the inefficiencies are sometimes more costly to industries than are tariff barriers.

In response, WTO members added trade facilitation to the agenda at the Singapore Ministerial Meeting in 1996. The Singapore Ministerial Declaration calls upon the Council for Trade in Goods (CTG) to conduct exploratory research into cross-border barriers, and analyse the effects of those barriers on traders and consumers.

Aspects of Trade Facilitation are not new as issues in WTO/GATT. Even though Trade facilitation was first included at the 1996 WTO Ministerial Conference, there are several GATT provisions that are related to trade facilitation. In addition to Article VII (Valuation for Customs Purposes), Article VIII (International Standards, Fees and Documentation) and Article X (Marks of Origin and Publication/Information issues) a number of specific agreements have been negotiated during the Uruguay Round that are directly relevant to trade facilitation *viz.*

- **Customs Valuation Agreement**: It sets out rules and guidelines for customs valuation.
- **Agreement on Rules of Origin**: It contains principles for origin determination in a neutral transparent, non-trade restricting manner. However actual origin rules are yet to be finalised for which intense negotiations are going on for the last seven years.
- **Agreement on Pre-shipment Inspection (PSI)**. It provides for pre-shipment inspection to avoid delays and to resolve disputes.
- **Agreement on Import Licensing Procedures**. It lays down rules for issuance of import licenses in respect of goods requiring license.
- **Agreement on Technical Barriers to Trade (TBT)**. It provides that product standards should be based on scientific

information and evidence and should not be so applied as to cause unnecessary obstacles to trade.

- **Agreement on the Application of Sanitary and Phyto-sanitary (SPS) measures**. It provides that sanitary and phyto-sanitary regulations are not so formulated and applied as to create unnecessary obstacles to trade.

2. The Current State of Trade-Facilitation in India

In this section we will briefly outline the state of trade facilitation in India and describe certain aspects in physical units. We will also outline some proposals and see how far India has acted in this respect. India has several problem areas in Trade Facilitation and there are substantive Transaction Costs involved in trading with India. While some impressive gains have been made over the last decade in terms of eradicating transaction costs, a lot of work still needs to be done to bring India up to the global standards in this area. The major work will involve simplification of export/import procedures and streamlining customs procedures and improving port logistics. Another major area of work will involve bilateral and multilateral initiatives that work towards agreements on Mutual Recognition (MRA) of Standards and Pre-Shipment Inspection (PSI).

Export and Import Procedures

In spite of major trade liberalisation introduced since June 1991, the administrative procedures associated with trade are probably the most complex and irrational procedure-bound in the world. Table 21.1 shows that in order to export, one needs to obtain 258 signatures, make 118 copies of the same information, keypunching of which takes 22 hours. It of course, involves dealing with a multitude of GoI agencies separately. This evokes hardly a protest from established exporters who have a knack of going around the system and having prompt clearance by paying bribes. But for the new global players, this is posing a major irritant. Moreover, the Government should promptly remove a major source of complex administrative procedures and corrupt practice. Table 21.1 illustrates the sheer wastage of time (and escalations of costs involved with wastage of time) to get export clearance in India:

Table 21.1

Documents Required for Export Clearance

Documents	*No. of Copies*	*No. of Signatures Required*	*Time Required for Typing*
1. Proforma Inv.	4	4	1 hour
2. Buyers Order	8	16	1 hour
3. Letter of Credit	1	4	**1 hour**
Total	**13**	**24**	**3 hours**
Shipper's Documents			
4. Shipping Instructions	2	2	1/2 hour
5. Commercial Invoice	11	27	2 hours
6. Packing List	10	26	2 hours
7. GRI (Exch. Cont.)	2	4	1/2 hour
8. Freight Certificate	2	2	5 minutes
9. Origin Cert. Form 'A'	2	2	1/2 hour
10. AR4/AR4A	2	4	1/2 hour
11. G. Receipt	3	6	15 minutes
12. AR4 or AR4A	4 or 5	16 or 20	1/2 hour
13. T. Tax (BAHETI)	2	2	10 minutes
14. Inspection Certificate	2	2	15 minutes
15. Insurance	3	3	**2 hours**
Total	**46**	**101**	**9 hrs. 15 min.**
Clearing Agent			
16. Shipping Bill	10	72	1 hour
17. Carting Order	1	5	15 minutes
18. Forwarding Note	2	7	10 minutes
19. SPL. Custom Inv. (Visa)	2	4	15 minutes
20. G.S.P.	4	4	1 hour
21. Meas. Certificate	4	4	1 hour
22. Fumigation Certificate	3	3	15 minutes
23. Container Load Plan (CLP)	3	3	1/2 hour
Total	31	105	3 hrs. 40 min.
GRAND TOTAL*	**118**	**258**	**22 hours**

Source: Roy[7] * Grand Total greater than the sum of displayed components as the latter are not exhaustively listed.

7. "Towards International Norms for Indirect Taxes and Trade Facilitation in India", Paper prepared by Dr. Jayanta Roy for the *Task Force on Indirect Taxes*, Government of India, 2002.

Cargo Dwell Time and Port/Airport Logistics

The current performance of India's Ports and Airports are far below global norms, and remain an impediment to India's greater integration with the world economy.

Table 21.2

Typical Cargo Dwell Time

Transaction	*Location*	*Norm*
Air Freight	*Delhi Airport*	
Export	2.5 days	Less than 12 hours
Import	15 days	Less than 12 hours
Containerised Sea Freight	Mumbai	
Ship Waiting Time	3-5 days	Less than 6 hours
Export Dwell Time	3-5 days	Less than 18 hours
Import Dwell Time	7-14 days	Less than 24 hours

Source: Roy[8]

Table 21.2 clearly shows that premier Indian entry points i.e. Delhi and Mumbai perform far below par of International norms, and thus reforms are urgently needed.

Proposals for Trade Facilitation in WTO in the Indian Context

a) Article X of the GATT

Article X requires Members to publish all laws, regulations, judicial decisions and administrative rulings relevant to importing and exporting in a manner as to enable governments and traders to become acquainted with them. The text of Article X further elaborates what the laws, regulations, judicial decisions and administrative rulings could pertain to. These include classification or valuation of products, rates of duty, taxes or other charges; requirements, restrictions or prohibitions on import or export; on

8. "Trade Facilitation and Transaction Costs as an Agenda for Global Trade Negotiations", Presentation by Dr. Jayanta Roy at the *Workshop on Major Issues in the WTO and their Implications for India,* April 30 and May 1, Administrative Staff College of India and The European Commission.

transfer of payments related to imports or exports and on sale, distribution, transportation, insurance, warehousing, inspection, exhibition, processing, mixing and others related to export or import. Article X also requires Members should publish all trade agreements affecting international trade policy.

Proposals Based on Article X

Countries that have given proposals on Article X include the European Communities (G/C/W/363), Japan (G/C/W/376), Korea (G/C/W/377) and Canada (G/C/W/379). The key issues in the proposals are related to:

- Advance rulings,
- Use of electronic media,
- Enquiry points,
- Consultative mechanism,
- Appeals.

Advance Rulings

India has set up the Authority for Advance Ruling by the Finance Act 1999. The scheme of advance ruling has become fully operational from 4th February 2004. The ruling by the Authority can be on classification, valuation and applicability of duty exemption in respect of export, import, production and manufacture. Despite this positive move, the scope of advance ruling has been limited. Only foreign firms which want to invest in India through joint ventures or wholly owned subsidiaries, or Indians who are getting into joint ventures with foreign firms can ask for advance ruling. Such a provision is not made available to a solely-Indian owned company. While this sends a very strong signal to foreign investors into the Indian market, it does not objectively address the concern of Trade Facilitation. Solely Indian-owned companies, many of which are small to medium scale players, undertake most of India's importation. It is also accepted that small to medium scale companies are far more susceptible to high transaction costs than larger players. Keeping such Indian stakeholders outside the purview of the Authority for Advance Ruling will be counter productive to the goals of trade facilitation.

Use of Electronic Media

The CBEC (Central Board of Excise and Customs), the DGFT (Directorate General of Foreign Trade) and the Reserve Bank of India are using the electronic media very widely for dissemination of information, though there is room for improvement. Some positive suggestions are the use of online training modules for private stakeholders, guidelines for best practices on the website and interfaces for information at the regional Port/Airport level.

Enquiry Point

As of now there is no officially designated inquiry point for traders. India should immediately start work on creating such a single window enquiry point that is online (this feeds into the use of electronic media). Such a single window system will go a long way in reducing information costs of trade in India.

Consultative Mechanism

The Kelkar Committee Report recognised the acute need for a consultative mechanism. The Kelkar Committee has thus recommended, 'An institutional mechanism, namely Standing Committee on Procedures chaired by Chairman CBEC and including trade and industry representatives, should be established to identify and resolve the problem areas in present procedures and evolve new procedures on a need basis'. While the Government has accepted the recommendations of the Kelkar Committee Report, it is yet to fully implement many recommendations made by it.

Appeals

India has an excellent institutional mechanism dealing with appeals protesting the decision of authorities dealing with customs and related assessment problems. The mechanism allows appeals at various levels up to the highest of Supreme Court. The right to make such appeals is enshrined legally under the aegis of the Customs Act of 1962. However, it must be kept in mind that the transaction costs (including the cost 'time' element) in legal disputes in India are substantial and are often beyond small to medium players. Initiative should be taken to evolve some sort of mechanism whereby most minor disputes in terms of valuation and assessment are dealt with expeditiously.

Article VIII of the GATT

Article VIII of the GATT requires contracting parties to impose fees and charges in relation to import and export in a manner that it is limited to the cost of service provided. It also requires parties to recognise the need for reducing the number and diversity of fees and charges and the incidence and complexity of import and export formalities. Article VIII also provides an illustrative list of the types of fees and charges, formalities and requirements relating to consular transactions, statistical services, analysis and inspection, and licensing which are imposed by governmental authorities beyond Customs.

Proposals Based on Article VIII

Proposals regarding fees and formalities were made by Canada (G/C/W/397), Colombia (G/C/W/425), European Communities (G/C/W/394), Hong Kong, China (G/C/W/398), Japan (G/C/W/401) and Korea (G/C/W/403).

The key proposals relate to:

- The levy of fees and charges,
- Provisions to reduce documentation requirements,
- Standard processing times, and
- The use of international standards.

Levy of Fees and Charges

The GATT requires that fees and charges related to Import/Export be based on the actual cost of service provided by the Government, not on *ad valorem* basis. While most fees and charges imposed by authorities in India are indeed nominal and based on the cost of actual services provided, there are some anomalies i.e. some fees and charges are based on the value of goods (i.e *ad valorem*). It is important that such anomalies are removed from the system.

Provisions to Reduce Documentation Requirements

India has taken a significant towards reducing documentation requirements through the harmonisation of the customs code. Since February 2003, classification codes at the eight-digit level used by the CBEC (for purposes of tariff), the DGFT (for purposes of determining importability/exportability) and DGCI&S Director

General for Commercial Intelligence and Statistics (for statistical purposes) have been unified to evolve a Combined Nomenclature based on the HS classification.

Standard Processing Times

The CBEC has set basic guidelines on standard processing times. However, it must be kept in mind that such guidelines serve only as an intent on the part of CBEC. India has several customs stations and the level of infrastructure varies considerably between them. In order for India to fully implement such guidelines, substantial investment will have to be made in various fronts, including the provision of physical infrastructure and training for personnel. It is obvious that India will require help on such capacity building activity.

The Use of International Standards

In order to fully meet International Standards as set by the Revised Kyoto Convention, India will need to implement several reforms in the area of customs administration. Such reforms will involve the following:

- Upgrading the existing EDI system to move towards a totally paperless mechanism for declaration. It should also create mechanisms to incorporate the latest technology for online payment of duty. Another major feature should be an interface that allows interconnectivity of the EDI to all ports and airports, not stand-alone system as are now in place.
- Incorporating the best practices of risk management and assessment systems in the customs administration, as envisaged by the Kelkar Committee recommendations.
- Move towards an universal Green Channel system.

Trade transaction costs can vary also according to characteristics of the trader, such as the size of the trading firms. Smaller firms, which engage less frequently than bigger competitors in cross-border transactions, have several disadvantages:

- They will tend to have fewer specialised personnel, so that they might have to devote relatively more resources towards acquiring knowledge on trade formalities and administering cross-border procedures

- They might have weaker capital reserves, so that unforeseen delays at the border, tying-up a part of their working capital, can affect their liquidity and force them to seek expensive interim financing
- Small firms might not have a sufficiently rich track record with customs authorities, so that they might be classified in a higher risk category and, hence, more frequently subjected to costly documentary and physical cargo checks.

A Point Overlooked: The Case of Article V

The peculiar shape of India caused by the partition of Bengal when she was granted independence meant that transport links with the North East India and rest of India became far more difficult than it used to be. Apart from this, tea from Assam (India's principal export at the time of independence) had to be transported by rail all the way to Calcutta for export. Similarly machinery for the tea factories had to transported along such a circuitous route from the Calcutta port. The North East is effectively landlocked although it belongs to a working party that itself is not land-locked. A simpler route would be through the Dhaka port which would save firms located in Assam quite a bit through reduced transport costs. As things stand today, this is not yet a reality. Thus it may be argued that Nepal (a land-locked entity) has better access to the sea (through the Raxaul-Kolkata corridor) than the North East.

Can Article V of the GATT be used/benefit to India's and especially the North East's benefit ? A simple reading of the article, especially clause 2, leaves little doubt as to the intention of the article, '*There shall be freedom of transit through the territory of each contracting party, via the routes most convenient for international transit, for traffic in transit to or from the territory of other contracting parties......*'. This gives the impression that given this tenor Bangladesh is obligated to give India passage its North East. However clause 3 states that '*Any contracting party may require that traffic in transit through its territory be entered at the proper custom's house..*' Thus Bangladesh can legally designate a customs house on any place on its border with West Bengal and leave the North East high and dry. Clearly, this article in its present form/interpretation is not satisfactory. What the North East requires is the establishment of a Bangladeshi custom house not on the West Bengal-Bangladesh border but on a road/rail/water way that connects the North East to Bangladesh. Thus the point where Brahmaputra enters Bangladesh (i.e. near the town of Dhubri) could be such a point. The Pratapgarh/Pyrdiwah village on the Meghalaya-Bangladesh border could be another point.

This development if not supported any interpretation of article V of GATT, may require the amendment of this clause by introducing a new term *'regionally landlocked entities'* where by contracting parties describe/list some of its regions as being *regionally landlocked*. Then clause 3 of article V has to be read in this light and the custom house stipulated must be situated on the border with this landlocked region. To be sure, the entire benefits of allowing freedom of transit may be borne by the contracting party that posses the landlocked region and all the costs borne by the contracting party providing transit privileges. This is unfair and the latter must be compensated by the former as per clause 4 of article V. But there is definitely scope for improving trade linkages by a fresh re-reading of this article and it is in India's interest to take up the lead in this respect.

Indeed, the opening up of Central Asia to India through the Tibet Autonomous Region and Xinjiang of the People's Republic of China may also critically depend on the progress made on Trade Facilitation. Currently none of the Central Asian ex-Soviet Republics are WTO members whereas India and China are. But as these countries become members, a comprehensive agreement on Trade Facilitation will ensure that India is able to compete with the People's Republic of China for the region's hydrocarbon resources as well as for the potentially enormous hydel resources of Tajikistan and Kyrghizstan. To secure India's interests from this region, India might think of the inclusion of a clause whereby the output that comes about as a result of Contracting Party A's investment (e.g. US investment) in country B (e.g. Tajikistan) and input that this investment requires should be allowed to avail of transit through the territory of a contracting party say C (e.g. China), via the routes most convenient for international transit, for traffic in transit to or from the territory of other contracting parties D (e.g. India) *even if country B is not a Member country*. The customs house on D and B should be designated by D and B respectively with C compensated for use of infrastructure and territory. Thus India would be able to compete for Central Asia's hydrocarbon resources as well as its potentially enormous Hydel resources.

3. The Financial Costs of India's Trading Infrastructure and Red Tape

This chapter has at some length pointed out to the shortcomings in India's Infrastructure (especially that proportion related to trade) as well those related to its procedures. All these so far have been expressed in physical terms but have a corresponding financial cost.

The Exim Bank study[9] translates the physical measures to costs to exporters. The results, we argue are disturbing for a host of reasons. Table 21.3 given below (reproduced from the same study) gives certain numbers regarding transaction costs measured as a proportion of exports as well as projected growth rates of a number of sectors based on an interview of 111 firms.

Table 21.3[10]

Commodity Group	*Transaction Costs (as percentage of export revenue)*	*Projected Export Growth (firms' projections)*
Agro-commodities	7	19
Chemicals	14	16
Engineering	10	28
Fish & Marine	8.5	34
Gems & Jewellery	0.8	15
Jute	7	21
Leather	6.5	33
Pharmaceuticals	10	10
Rubber & Allied Products	7	38
Software	10	10
Tea	3	10
Textiles	15	26
Other	6	18

Firstly, transactions costs are high for areas like textiles where India possesses a natural competitive advantage and where expected and actual growth rates are pretty high. Thus, it could be argued that this labour absorbing sector could do much more with lower transaction costs with profound implications for growth and employment.

9. Exim Bank Report *op cit.*
10. *ibid*

Secondly India's technologically dynamic industries like chemicals, pharmaceuticals and engineering are also with hobbled high transaction costs which means that their ability to compete with well-entrenched competitors from developed countries is impaired at source to begin with. This too has profound implications for India's ability to move up the technology ladder.

Thirdly, India's ability to take advantage of the existing attitude towards the environmentally friendly products that militate against the purchase of products like plastic bags is severely compromised by the fact that jute exports too face high transaction costs.

Fourthly, what is made clear in this study is the fact that transaction costs are not scale and technology neutral. In general the small and medium enterprises (the typical firm in the textiles and garments) bear higher transactions costs as compared to their larger or more technologically advanced counterparts in engineering and software respectively. Given the fact that the SMEs have so far been the sword-arm of India's export thrust this bodes ill for the future of the economy given the current economic regime that relies of export to drive aggregate demand.

It must be noted that these figures understate the problem created by poor infrastructure and cumbersome regulations. What it does not calculate (and indeed it is difficult to do so) is the amount of FDI that does not come to India on account of high transaction costs. Similarly it doe not (if it were possible) calculate what Indian exporters lose out for being prevented in setting up market networks in the destination of exports as a result of the uncertainty of supply that India's trade infrastructure entails.

A Brief Note on the Costs of Trade Facilitation

This chapter does not go deeply into the costs of trade facilitation. However, it is extremely easy to overstate the costs of implementing the required measures. To be sure measures that aim at enhancing port capacity, widening and increasing rail and road networks are capital intensive. But there are others that deal with the streamlining of procedure and changing the methods of checking. These are heavily dependent on the ICT revolution and telecommunications and thus not very expensive given India's expertise in these sectors.

The software required can be easily designed and replicated. A unified database that is upgraded all the time can come out with relevant information required to carry out checks or set customs duties quickens the time taken to dispose cases. Secondly, even remote places e.g. in the North East that share borders with other countries may become custom houses with modern telecommunications which gives them access to a unified databases that contains all the regulations, required definitions that enables the local customs house to set duties on imports or record exports etc. While modern infrastructure is desirable, it may be pointed out that its absence is not necessarily fatal. Standby power, satellite communications and automated electronic devices can make the 'remote' customs house operated by a skeletal staff a reality.[11] The rules in question even if not the duty structure must be simple so that it can be interpreted without recourse to litigation. Complex rules can hold up business if it creates scope for myriad interpretations which have to be harmonised anyway. If complex rules holds up decision making by making harmonisation a slow process, bottlenecks are once more created. Thus the costs of trade facilitation cannot be measured independently of the nature of the regulatory regime that it enforces. This said, it is likely, that the costs of implementing Trade Facilitation measures are likely to be considerably less than the benefits that accrue from it.

Conclusion and a Proposed Further Course of Action

To sum up, there are two aspects to the programme of Trade Facilitation. One refers to the costs associated with Trade Facilitation (which we have not dealt with in this chapter); the other refers to the benefits that accrue from it. This chapter argues in so far as trade facilitation also covers activities and investments that the Indian economy would have to undertake anyway to promote economic development not necessarily related to export (but affecting trade prospects favourably anyway) the actual cost must be equal to the difference between the investment that trade facilitation (under a global multilateral agreement) requires and the investment that the

11. For an example of how an sophisticated e-venture can run in an area with no power or telecommunications, see ITC's *e-chaupals* operate successfully and profitably in certain part of rural India, www.itcportal.com.

government of India needs to carry out to maximise economic growth. This is likely to be measurable as studies can be carried out that put numbers to both entities. Secondly, a part of the cost that trade facilitation brings about cannot be measured independently of the import and regulatory regime in place; i.e. the more convoluted the regime the higher is the cost of managing it. This is more difficult to measure but well within the capacity of the government.

The methodology that the government should adopt would be to look at studies that detail its own investment plans in the field of trade-oriented infrastructure, calculate what proportion of a plausible Trade Facilitation commitment this investment covers. The actual cost of Trade Facilitation then is the cost of the uncovered portion of the plausible Trade Facilitation commitment. This too will come from studies that have already been performed in the case of some countries that include India.

The likely benefits would accrue from a number of sources, one is the reduction in costs as setting up businesses as time required reduces for projects that crucially require imports, e.g. imported capital goods, the second is the costs saved by firms as the process of importing becomes easier and transparent and the third is the benefit from the increase in competition as a more level playing field ensures that not just the bigger firms but also the smaller firms have the access to imports in a regime with low transaction costs. Similarly the FDI that would flow in as a result of implementing trade facilitation measures would also have direct and indirect benefits on the economy. The ability of domestic firms to market their goods abroad would enable them to earn more per unit of good exported than they do currently. The first two sources are easily measurable while the latter three present more difficult cases for measurement. But this exercise is indispensable to carry out a cost-benefit analysis of the various models of a Trade Facilitation Agreement that may be proposed and the one that India finally pushes for should be one that yields the maximum net benefit.

Seen in its entirety, Trade Facilitation is an issue that India stands to gain from. While India's ability to exports will be enhanced, it will also lead to enhanced FDI and may contribute to the overall evolution of Indian firms from merely suppliers to global players with their own networks. For this and more should India be on the offensive on issue of Trade Facilititation. India should broaden the scope of some of the articles of GATT particularly Article V given certain important points overlooked which in turn are critical to India's interests.

References

Finger, J Michael and Philip Schuler, "Implementation of Uruguay Round Challenges: The Development Challenge," *Policy Research Working Paper Series 2258*, World Bank.

Bagai, Shweta, Richard Newfarmer and John S. Wilson, *Trade Facilitation: Ways WTO Disciplines Could Promote Development*, May 2004.

Taneja, Nisha, *Trade Facilitation in the WTO: Implications for India*, ICRIER, 2004.

Hummels, David, *Time as a Trade Barrier*, Department of Economics, Indiana: Purdue University Press 2001.

22

Government Procurement System in India[1]

SANDWIP KUMAR DAS

Background

The general perception that prevails in India is that corruption pervades every sphere of government activity and government procurement is no exception to this dictum. The government departments operate under rules and procedures that have been made extremely complicated and cumbersome purposefully so that irregular activities can be hidden in a non-transparent environment. Since government procurement rules are non-transparent, a greater transparency is likely to lead to a lessened amount of corruption. Given that both the officials and firms may be motivated by a desire to use the procurement process as a vehicle for creating rents, there seems to be *a priori* ground for greater transparency. A firm may decide to reduce the competition for contracts by 'rigging' the prices it submits to the government, with the understanding that other firms will take turns in winning government contracts so that they can divide the spoils. Firms could attempt to bribe or otherwise induce government officials to view their tenders favourably. Such corruption has been extensively researched (Bardhan, 1997 and Rose-ackerman, 1999). The general view is that procurement rules should be designed to take account of the danger of corruption, though it may be difficult to make the rules entirely corruption resistant. But the scenario could be improved by forcing public entities to make their decisions in a transparent manner - including banning firms that have indulged in bribery, protecting the whistle-blowers and conducting random public and ex-post audits of procurement decisions that explicitly take into account comparisons with similar transactions in the private sector. Quite a few developing countries

1. The author is grateful to Consumer Unity & Trust Society, Jaipur for funding this research. The research assistant for this project was Mr. Sayantan Banerjee.

have benefited from transparency in the procurement rules. Box 22.1 provides some instances of these benefits, indicating that transparency either reduces corruption or inefficiency or both.

Box 22.1

Transparent Procurement Rules Can Reduce Corruption and Save Cost

(i) 43 per cent saving in the purchase of medicine by Guatemala's Ministry of Health (USAID, 1999).

(ii) 47 per cent cost saving in the procurement of military goods by the Colombian Ministry of Defence (USAID, 1999).

(iii) Reduction in pharmaceutical budget of Nicaraguan government from $21 million to $13 million from 1992-93 (Cohen, 2000).

(iv) A saving of more than $3.1 million for the Karachi Water and Sewerage Board in Pakistan (Transparency International, 2002).

(v) Reduction of electricity prices at less than US$0.03 per kilowatt-hour in Bangladesh, roughly half the price of directly negotiated deals in Indonesia (Lovei and McKechnie, 2000).

Theoretical Issues in Government Procurement

A preliminary search of the theoretical literature (Cartier-Bresson, 2000, Kaufman, 1997, Klitgaard, 1990, Mauro, 1997, Rege, 2001, Rose-Ackerman, 1999, Tanzi, 1998, Tanzi and Davoodi, 1997, Wei, 1997, 1999) on government procurement gives one the impression that transparency will definitely promote competition, efficiency and reduce corruption. Transparency has its costs in terms of monitoring, establishment of new institutions and procurement regimes, training of personnel etc., but there seems to be a general agreement that the benefits would outweigh these costs. What are the possible costs of introducing transparency in government procurement?[2] First, there are the costs of switching over from the existing procurement regime.

2. For a cost benefit study in the Indian context see Srivastava (1999), which mentions two potential sources of benefit for the signatories to the GPA. One source of gain is through better market access and gains from trade and the second is through the cost saving and quality gains, likely to result from the disciplines imposed by the GPA. The benefit estimates are based on the assumption that gains from market access are likely to be small and that the only significant source of gain is from the potential saving of government resources. The benefits are estimated to be in the range of Rs. 67.5 billion - Rs. 90 billion. The economic costs of switching are predicted to be small. The paper concludes that India should have no hesitation in negotiating a transparency agreement.

This depends on the divergence of the existing procurement policies from those required by the Government Procurement Agreement (henceforth GPA) and the number of entities involved. For India, these costs could potentially be high in view of its federal structure, the number of sub-central entities and the large number of central and state public sector enterprises. Debroy and Pursell (1997) state that although there would be no problem for India to have joined the Tokyo Round GPA, this is not true for the current GPA (signed in Marrakesh on 15 April 1994) because of its extension to sub-central and other public entities and to the purchase of services. An attempt needs to be made to estimate the changes involved and to examine what exclusions, if any, might be justified on these grounds.

There are some theoretically justifiable arguments for preferential treatment in government procurement. Developments in international trade theory during the 1980s have showed[3] that in the presence of imperfect competition and increasing returns to scale, interventions in trade could be used to shift profits to domestic firms or to generate positive externalities. Some of these arguments can be extended to the case of government procurement. In addition, there are certain other possible justifications for preferential government procurement. These include the possibility of increasing competition through price preferences (McAfee and McMillan 1989), reducing price-cost margins by expanding domestic output (Chen 1995), problems of contract enforcement (Laffont and Tirole 1991), and economies in the presence of asymmetric information. Although such "strategic" interventions are difficult to accurately target, and the potential benefits are likely to be small, they are popular with governments and businessmen. Another argument against the GPA suggests that discrimination does not significantly restrict trade and the gains from non-discrimination are consequently small. Mattoo (1996) has pointed out that the benefits may not be insignificant if government demand is large, domestic and foreign goods and services are not perfect substitutes and if there is imperfect competition. The crucial question is whether markets have become more competitive and trade freer, because in that case it would become easier to conform to the discipline of the GPA. With the public sector being subject to harder budget constraints, procurement

3. See Helpman and Krugman (1986).

by these entities would automatically become more efficient. On the other hand, with trade restricted through tariffs and non-tariff barriers the GPA may not achieve much. Thus, it seems that the effectiveness of GPA depends a great deal on the international trading environment.

Objective of the Study

The purpose of this chapter is to make a critical review of the rules and procedures applicable to government procurement in India. The chapter also focuses on government procurement policy (or absence of it) in India and its implementation and explores the role of transparency in reducing corruption in government procurement. The existence of corruption can be proved indirectly if it is shown that transparency leads to an increase in efficiency and cost saving and this method is followed by many OECD studies. Since Indian economy is a federal one with multiple tiers of government procurement, we explore whether there is a need for harmonisation of procurement rules and procedures. We also review the functioning of the regulatory bodies and grievance redressal mechanism. Our objective is to find out the extent to which the government procurement rules and practices are transparent and to recommend measures for improving it further. Finally, it should be mentioned that the study is based entirely on secondary source materials drawn from several World Bank and OECD studies. We have also relied heavily on Srivastava (1999) for data on different aspects of government procurement system in India.

Size of Government Procurement

Public procurement in India at the time of independence was confined to purchase of office equipment and construction of office buildings and roads. Since independence government activity has grown manifold, including setting up of a vast number of public sector undertakings in every sector of the economy in pursuance of social democracy, planned development and a command economy. Public procurement grew exponentially and now covers all type of goods and services and is carried out by a large number of agencies all over the country. Since the nineties the government has embarked upon an economic liberalisation path including gradual disinvestment in the public undertakings. However the implementation is slow and government procurement continues to remain large in volume and all pervasive. Ministries, departments, municipal and other local bodies, statutory corporations and public undertakings both in the Centre and in the States, carry out procurement of goods and services. The public procurement policies, procedures and practices of the Centre, States and the Public Enterprises have a tremendous impact on the economy and the business community, particularly in the construction sector, which depends largely on public works contracts. The public perception of integrity and efficiency of the government is to a large extent swayed by the transparency and integrity of public procurement. Table 22.1 gives some idea of the size of government procurement in India. It shows estimates of the range of government procurement in two years and it highlights the relative importance of public sector enterprises. The industries that are dominated by PSEs can be listed in order of market shares (i.e., share of PSEs in total sales of all public sector and private sector firms in the industry in 2000-2001). These are Crude oil and natural gas (99.17 per cent), Coal and lignite (98.2 per cent), Financial services (80.3 per cent), Transport service (76.7 per cent), Electricity generation and distribution (73.31 per cent), Communication (62.6 per cent) and Chemicals (64.79 per cent).[4]

Table 22.1

Government Procurement Estimates (in Billion Rupees)

Sector	*1998-99 Min*	*1998-99 Max*	*1999-2000 Max*	*1999-2000 Max*
Central Government	*40.95*	*68.24*	*48.13*	*80.22*
Railways	*36.35*	*72.71*	*38.8*	*77.61*
Telecommunication	*27.06*	*54.12*	*33.62*	*67.25*
Total Central Government	**104.35**	**195.07**	**120.55**	**225.08**
Share in GDP (per cent)	*0.59*	*1.1*	*0.6*	*1.13*
State government	*32.99*	*65.98*	*37.94*	*75.88*
Total Government	**137.35**	**261.06**	**158.5**	**300.97**
PSEs	*431.09*	*664.38*	*482.82*	*744.11*
Grand Total	**609.65**	**1003.78**	**688.87**	**1135.40**
Share in GDP (per cent)	*3.43*	*5.65*	*3.44*	*5.68*

Source: Srivastava(1999). Figures in italics are estimated/extrapolated.

4. Shares are estimated by the author of this paper from CMIE's Prowess database.

Table 22.1 above shows significant increases in the share of government expenditure estimates in GDP. The question that should be asked is whether the government is acquiring more goods and services per rupee spent or not. This study has done some rough estimates by looking at total expenditure of the Central Government which includes consumption expenditure, gross capital formation, transfer payment to the rest of the economy (current plus capital expenditure) and financial investments and loans to the rest of the economy. Then it has taken the data on gross capital formation from budgetary resources of the Central Government which includes fixed assets, works stores, increases in the stocks of foodgrains and fertilisers and gross financial assistance for capital formation to state governments, public undertakings operated by autonomous corporations and companies and loans and grants to local authorities for capital formation. The ratio between the two will roughly tell us the value of every rupee spent by the Central Government and Table 22.2 shows a steady downward trend in this ratio. It should be noted that the decline could not be due to the inflation factor. We could deflate both expenditure and capital formation by separate price indexes if these were available. Deflating both by wholesale price index, which is available, would not alter the ratio. A large part of this decrease in the value of money spent by the Central Government is caused by the increase in the wages and salaries. But a decrease from 42 per cent in 1981-82 to 19 per cent in 2002-03 does not give much credit to the procurement policy.

(a) Public Procurement Policies

Article 298 of the Constitution of India authorises the Central and the State governments to contract for goods and services and also requires the executive to protect the fundamental rights of all citizens to be treated equally (while soliciting tenders), but beyond that it does not provide any guidance on public procurement principles, policies or procedures. There is no Central or State legislation on public procurement, except for two States, Tamil Nadu[5] and Karnataka[6], which have recently enacted legislation on

5. Tamil Nadu Transparency in Tenders Act, 1998, implemented from 2000.

6. The Karnataka Transparency in Public Procurement Act, 1999.

Table 22.2

Value of Government Expenditure

Year	Government Expenditure (Rs. Crore)	Capital Formation (Rs. Crore)	Value for Money (per cent) (Capital Formation Per Rupee Spent)
1981-82	25401.2	10799.1	42.51
1982-83	30493.7	12404.0	40.68
1983-84	35987.7	14701.0	40.85
1984-85	43878.9	17551.2	40.00
1985-86	53112.4	21477.2	40.44
1986-87	64023.1	24319.7	37.99
1987-88	70304.6	25770.1	36.65
1988-89	81402.3	28977.4	35.60
1989-90	95049.4	33012.7	34.73
1990-91	104972.9	35057.4	33.40
1991-92	112730.7	35164.6	31.19
1992-93	125926.9	37648.6	29.90
1993-94	145788.0	45050.5	30.90
1994-95	166998.4	54199.9	32.46
1995-96	185232.8	55275.6	29.84
1996-97	211259.6	60950.3	28.85
1997-98	224866.0	54185.0	24.10
1998-99	263755.0	57806.5	21.92
1999-00	307509.1	67601.5	21.98
2000-01	328264.7	66959.4	20.40
2001-02	361334.7	69238.8	19.16
2002-03	409581.7	77930.5	19.03

Data Source: Economic Survey, 2002-03.

'Transparency in Public Procurement'. The policies, procedures, guidelines and delegation of authority relating to procurement are issued by the executive branch of the government through primarily, the Finance Ministry, but also through the Industry and other Ministries. The same laws that govern private contracts govern government contracts. There is no department or agency in the Centre or State exclusively responsible for framing policies or regulating public procurement. Nor is any department entrusted with the responsibility of overseeing public procurement in respect to its compliance with the laid down policies and procedures, or its efficiency and transparency. The *ex-post* audit of government expenditures carried out by the Comptroller and Auditor General of India (CAG) including government and public sector procurements is essentially for checking the budget authority for expenditures and adherence to laid down procedures. Unauthorised and wasteful expenditures are highlighted in CAG's annual report. The reports are published and are discussed in the Parliament and State legislatures. All this shows that India does not have a procurement policy in the form of an act of the parliament. Public procurement is a matter for executive branch of the government. Only two states have recently started to implement transparency acts passed by the respective legislatures.

(b) Evolution of Procurement Rules

The broad principles of financial propriety in incurring government expenditures including expenditure in the procurement of goods and services are formulated by the Ministry of Finance in the Centre and the Department of Finance in the States. The procuring agencies expand these principles into detailed rules and procedures. Besides, Finance and other Ministries such as Industry, Public Works, Environment, Agriculture, State Enterprises also issue directives on government procurement relevant to their portfolio, e.g., encouragement of small scale industry, environmental standards in government procurement, procedures for purchase of commodities, preferences for state owned enterprises and so on.

Initially the Ministry of Supply in the Centre and Central Stores Purchase Organisation in the States and the Public Works Department (PWD) in the Center and the States served as the lead agencies to formulate detailed procedures for the purchase of goods and works respectively, which were followed by other departments, agencies and state undertakings, However as the government expanded its activities and set up multitude of state enterprises, each ministry, agency and particularly state enterprises introduced innovations and improvements. As a result of this, there is no single uniform law that governs procurements by all of these entities.

The scope of government procurement covers purchases of goods and services made by government entities using funds allocated to them from either budgetary resources or international donor agencies as aid.[7] The central government, the state governments and the three tiers of local government - village, intermediate and district make up the various levels of government in India. As mentioned earlier in this paper, Centre and state-owned enterprises are big buyers. Central government procurements are governed by the **General Financial Rules** (GFRs) of the Ministry of Finance. The procurement practices of different companies have evolved owing to these GFRs. The *Directorate General of Supplies and Disposal* (DGS&D) is the central purchasing organisation in India. The role of DGS&D has declined in recent years, but it is still used to finalise the rate contracts for "common use" products. According to a scheme of decentralisation[8], procurement against *ad hoc* indents was transferred from DGS&D to the indenting Ministries/Departments. The declining importance of DGS&D is however evident from the fact that the purchases made by the directorate have fallen from Rs.24 billion in 1995-96 to Rs. 16.6 billion in 1998-99.[9] State governments and state owned enterprises (SOEs) have the power to make their own purchases and follow different procedures. Different states and SOEs have different targets and instruments to achieve them. The procedures followed by the state governments are based on the states' financial rules. Multiple rules applied at different levels of the federal government can be regarded as a source of inconvenience for suppliers but it is not necessarily a source of corruption. The current GPA provides for uniform rules of procurement which would require a costly change of procurement regime in India - a point which has been made by Srivastava (1999). But it is clear from the available evidence that there is an urgent need for harmonisation of procurement methods and procedures in the federal economy of India.

Procurement Methods

Open tender (purchases based on advertisements), limited tender (direct invitation to a limited number of firms) and single tender (invitation to one firm only) are the methods of procurement and

7. Rege (2001).
8. See Government of India (2003).
9. Source: Ministry of Finance.

the rules provide for negotiation with one or more firms.[10] Tender notices are generally publicised through the **Indian Trade Journal** a monthly bulletin issued by the DGS&D and are now available on the Internet. For global tenders, notices are also published or disseminated through Indian embassies. *In the case of the railways, all tenders above a value of Rs.0.3 million are invited by open advertisements in the national newspapers.*

The specifications for procurement are drafted normally on the basis of national or international standard specifications.[11] There is a well-defined registration procedure to establish "reliable and regular sources" of supply for government purchases. The DGS&D registers firms interested in government purchases as approved contractors for supply of stores of various descriptions. Similarly, the **National Small Industries Corporation** registers such firms in the small-scale sector and Indian Railways also has a similar registration procedure.

Preferential Treatment

India does not discriminate between domestic and international bidders and no preference is given to domestic suppliers.[12] According to the Indian government, *"domestic bidders are treated at par with foreign bidders and the ultimate price available to the user department is the determining criterion"*[13]. However, preferential treatment is allowed with a view to encouraging the small-scale sector, village industries, certain kinds of women's organisations and public enterprises. However, such preferential treatment discriminates against domestic as well as foreign firms not belonging to these categories and in this sense, foreign firms get "national treatment". Debroy and Pursell *(1997)* have provided a comprehensive review of the policy. In what follows we briefly discuss these preferences.

10. The general rules apply to all departments regarding stores required for use in "the public service". Special rules apply to Defense, Railways, Post and Telegraphs, Public Works, Central Purchase.
11. The Bureau of Indian Standards formulates Indian Standard specifications.
12. This is not true for all state governments.
13. See the Government of India's response to Question 9 of the WTO Questionnaire on Government Procurement Services (Document S/WPGR/W/11/add.Jan 17, 1997).

(a) Preference for Public Sector

A large public sector developed in India as a result of the policies initiated in 1956.[14] Prior to the reforms initiated in 1991, public sector enterprises (PSEs) were not only protected from competition through reservation, but price and purchase preferences were operated in favour of the public sector. The preference for the public sector also applied to construction and service enterprises and was extended to state-level PSEs. Since that time some significant changes have occurred. The list of industries reserved for the public sector has now been reduced significantly. After 1991, the list of industries reserved for public sector has undergone radical changes. There were 17 industries reserved in the public sector prior to July 1991. The New Industrial Policy reduced it to eight industries. More industries, namely mining of iron ore, manganese ore, chrome ore, gypsum, sulphur, gold and diamond and mining of copper, lead, zinc, tin, molybdenum and wolfram were dereserved since March 26, 1993 and Coal and Lignite and Mineral oils were dereserved from June 1998. Now the reserved list contains only three sectors: Atomic Energy, Minerals specified in Schedule to Atomic energy and Railway Transport.[15] The system of price preferences has been discontinued. The system of purchase preference continued with some modifications until March 31, 2000.

(b) Preference for the Small-Scale Sector

The small-scale sector is protected through compulsory purchase and price preference on procurement imposed on Central Government Ministries, departments and PSEs. The purchase-preference system requires that specified products be procured exclusively from small-scale firms. In addition, a system of price preference exists: if the price offered by the small-scale unit is not more than 15 per cent above the price offered by a large unit, the product has to be purchased from small-scale sector. This condition applies not only to Central Ministries and Departments, but also to Central public undertakings. If the competition is with the duty-

14. In March 1998 there were 240 Central PSEs (see Department of Public Enterprises 1998) and almost 1000 State PSEs, including electricity boards.

15. Source: Websites of Ministry of Company Affairs and Ministry of Disinvestments (*http://www.divest.nic.in*).

inclusive price of imports, the implied preferential margin is higher with respect to the duty-free price of imports. As in the case of the public sector, the small-scale sector is exempted from the payment of earnest money and tender fees. So far, the protection of artisans and small-scale firms, and the subsidies and preferences directed to them, have not been touched by the reforms. Between 1994-95 and 1998-99, purchases by DGS&D from the small sector were about 8-10 per cent of the Directorate's total purchases.

(c) Preferences for Indigenous Production

Before 1991 foreign direct investment in India was subjected to procedural restrictions and maximum foreign equity permitted in joint ventures was 40 per cent. Government procurement was used directly to favour indigenous production over imports. Both a price and purchase preference in favour of domestic production used to exist. The system of Price Preference was abolished in 1992. Purchase Preference was also scrapped. In some cases, however, the preference for Indian providers of services, if not of goods, continues to apply.

Regulation and Dispute Settlement

There is a standing review committee functioning under the DGS&D. Unresolved issues pertaining to contracts are settled through arbitration. In order to curb corrupt practices in all Central Government departments and its public enterprises as well as local authorities, Government of India has constituted Central Vigilance Commission (CVC) in 1999 through an ordinance and it has been strengthened through an act of parliament entitled the Central Vigilance Commission Act 2003. The function of CVC is to investigate offences alleged to have been committed under the Prevention of Corruption Act, 1988 or to act on a reference made by the central government. As already mentioned, the role of CAG is limited to carrying out *ex-post* audit of government expenditures including government and public sector procurements essentially for checking the budget authority for expenditures and adherence to laid down procedures. The Santhanam Committee set up by the Central Government in 1966 had recommended setting up of an *ombudsman* in the centre and in every state to investigate charges of corruption against officials and politicians. Some states have set up the mechanism. Others, including the Centre, have not done so.

All this makes the challenge procedure rather weak in India. Assessing Indian financial accountability, analysts from the World Bank (Sahgal and Chakrapani, 2002) have stated that incidence of fraud, waste and abuse of public funds is reportedly widespread. In a World Bank/Confederation of Indian Industries (CII) survey of 210 private sector firms carried out in 1999 responded that a bribe of 2 to 25 per cent of the price is necessary to secure government contracts.[16]

(a) Discrimination

India is known for a two-envelope system under which bidders submit all administrative, qualification and technical response in one envelope and the price in the second envelope. The first envelope is publicly opened first and reviewed, and all bids, which are not in full compliance with tender requirement, are rejected. In the second sitting, the price envelopes of the rest are opened publicly, evaluated and decided. There is some logic behind this procedure, which automatically eliminates non-conforming bids. However, the procedure has some disadvantages. Firstly, the delay in opening price envelopes, which can be a week to months in many cases, gives the purchaser the opportunity to switch envelopes and this obviously is a great potential for corruption. Secondly, the tender conditions and technical specifications may be deliberatively or otherwise drafted in favor of some bidders. The approving authority and auditors are prevented from knowing the additional price paid for a trivial or avoidable requirement. The procedure obviously has great scope for discrimination.

(b) Public Works Contracting

Public works contracting has an established tradition but suffers from antiquated procedures. The PWD manual is the Bible for works contracting procedures for all government departments, agencies, corporations and enterprises. But the manual outlines procedures

16. Reported in *India: Country Procurement Assessment Report*, The World Bank, 2003.

that were relevant when contractors were mostly illiterate and essentially labour contractors. Some of the problems in works contracting analysed in the World Bank report are summarised below.[17]

Each PWD maintains a data book, some times district-wise, which provides the rate for each standard item of work. The rates are based on material, labour and overheads. Departmental estimates for works and the Schedule of Rates for tendering are based on these rates in the data book. However, the data books are generally out of date. The situation varies. The Central PWD is reasonably up to date. In most States, the data books have not been updated for years. Also, whenever taken up, often the rates are merely updated for inflation but not reworked using the new materials, methods of construction, plant depreciation, overheads and reasonable profit. The result is that the departmental estimates are generally unreliable and out of date. Works are taken up without adequate funding, often under political pressure, which languish for years. Contracts are awarded when land acquisition is far from initiation. Some PWDs even put the responsibility for land acquisition and clearance of the site on the contractor. Advertised tenders are opened only to approved registered contractors, whose qualifications and capacity have been verified. But the registration process has become a vehicle for political patronage and once a contractor is registered, he is automatically deemed qualified. Even for good qualified contractors, the works on hand and consequent available capacity to take on new works is not examined. Bad performers are not systematically eliminated from the list. Powers of approval of awards are linked to the departmental estimates, based on data books, which as mentioned earlier, are outdated. This provides one excuse for negotiation to 'bring prices closer to the departmental estimate'. Even when prices are below the departmental estimate, negotiation is often resorted 'to get further savings to public funds'. Major contractors sub-contract the entire works or a major portion to unqualified sub-contractors with the silent support of the department. The payments are based on entries in "measurement books" in the handwriting of the supervising departmental engineer, and test checked by his superiors at the site

17. Source: The World Bank (2003).

(mostly in theory). Monthly bills are actually prepared by the departmental engineers but signed by the contractors. Every month, each item in the bill of quantities is reentered in the measurement book with full description, and then, the measured quantity. Even if an outside consultant is employed for works supervision, the measurement book is still entered by the department, as stipulated in the 'public works manual'. The whole system is antiquated, repetitive and based on technology and office systems available fifty years ago, with practically no modernisation.

Contracts do not provide for adequate price adjustment mechanism and fair claim and dispute resolution mechanisms. Contract supervision is spotty and subject to pervasive corruption. In fact, there are frequent press reports of wide spread corruption in many PWDs. It appears from this World Bank study that a part of corruption in public works contracting is due to the fact that the existing rates are outdated and too low for work to be done in today's world.

(c) Multiple Tender Documents

According to one estimate, there are more than 150 different contract formats used by the government and its agencies.[18] Obviously, this causes confusion in the minds of bidders. Also, some are of poor quality. Even when instructions are issued standardising a document, each ministry/department has a tendency to tailor the document, add/subtract clauses, repeat the same provisions in different clauses, defeating the purpose of the standardisation. The situation in the States is much worse. For the same work, say, for construction of a road, the tender document is different if it is issued by the Public Works Department or the Municipal Corporation or the Metropolitan Urban Development Authority or the State Road Development Corporation. The qualification requirements, selection criteria, the payment terms, the dispute settlement mechanism are all different for no conceivable reason. It is essential to develop and publish a set of Standard Tender Documents and Contract Conditions for mandatory use by all ministries, agencies and enterprises for similar procurements.

18. Reported in World Bank (2003).

(d) Negotiation

India has a system of post-bid negotiation. The procuring agency negotiates with the lowest bidder for further concessions. Instructions regarding negotiation of price with the lowest, or with others as well are confusing. Many ministries and agencies issue them.[19] The officials and the auditors believe that negotiation results in savings to the public exchequer and in fact encourage negotiation, at least with the lowest bidder. Obviously, the bidders include a cushion in their bid price to give up when called for negotiation and the system of post-bid negotiation provides them an opportunity to earn supernormal profit even in a competitive bidding system because they never give up more than what they have included, often less. Negotiation provides the best opportunity for corruption at the cost of the public exchequer. If all the bidders are absolutely sure that no negotiation will be held under any circumstance, they are forced to quote the lowest price to be competitive. World Bank procurement prohibits negotiation to merely push down the competitively quoted price. In India some agencies conduct negotiations with *all* the bidders requiring them to 'match' the price of the lowest or quote a revised lower price, making a mockery of the tender process. The World Bank report recommends negotiation only in exceptional cases and only by a committee, and based on mutual concessions.

(e) Delay in Tender Processing and Award Decision

Delay occurs in almost all countries in tender processing, particularly at the time of evaluation and selection. In procurement, the longer the time taken for the decision, greater is the chance of political pressures and corruption and eventually, a decision becomes very difficult. This often results in re-tender, which is probably what the rejected bidders would like most. Good bidders are discouraged from participating in re-tender and the rejected bidders raise their bids. Government officials and auditors do not have an adequate appreciation of the cost of delays. Even though delay is a universal problem, the average time taken in implementation of projects in India is much longer compared to countries like China, Mexico, Indonesia and Brazil mainly due to delays in procurement.[20]

19. DFID Report (2002).

20. As reported in World Bank (2003).

India's Procurement Policy and the GPA

There are two models of government procurement. One is UNCITRAL model law published in 1980, which acted as a model for East European and ex-Soviet Union countries. The other is the government procurement agreement of the World Trade Organisation. In defining transparency Evenett and Hoekman point out[21], " A procurement process is said to be transparent if (i) the terms upon which the procurement process will be conducted and the criteria upon which any decisions are to be made are codified to the greatest extent possible and made widely available, (ii) the eventual procurement award decision (and, where possible, any intermediate decisions...) is made publicly available as are the reasons given for these decisions, and (iii) it is possible to verify expeditiously that the codified procedures and criteria in (i) were indeed applied and that the claims made in (ii) are in fact true." Effectively, transparency ensures that information be made available to suppliers and in essence, the right to access information in matters of procurement is guaranteed on policies, rules and methods, practices and opportunities.

Government procurement in India has major differences with respect to the national treatment, transparency, and challenge, and review provisions of the GPA.[22] Since India has price and purchase preferences, procurement policies are at odds with the requirements of Article III (National Treatment and Non-discrimination). Although Article V (Special and Differential Treatment for Developing Countries) provides some flexibility to developing countries and exclusions are possible, the long-term objective of the GPA is do away with any kind of preferential treatment in purchases. To promote greater transparency in transactions, Article XVIII (Information and Review as Regards Obligations of Entities) requires that information on winning contracts be made public. It also makes it mandatory for each entity, on request, to provide pertinent information concerning the reasons for rejection and the

---

21. Evenett, S.J. and B.M. Hoekman. "Transparency in Procurement Regimes: What Can We Expect from International Trade Agreements." in Sue Arrowsmith and Martin Trybus (eds.) *Public Procurement: The Continuing Revolution*, Kluwer Law International 2003.

22. Appendix A provides the texts of the relevant clauses.

characteristics and relative advantages of the selected tender. This could be a major problem area because the procurement policies in India do not have any such provision. In general India has the reputation of being one of the most opaque countries in which to do business. The GPA lays down a detailed challenge procedure (Article XX: Challenge Procedures), which has no parallel in the existing rules and procedure in India. There is no independent adjudicating authority and the concerned department generally deals with disputes. An aggrieved party obviously always has access to regular court of law. It is common knowledge that Indian courts are overloaded with litigation and justice is slow. *In our view, the absence of a proper challenge procedure is a potential source of corruption.* It should however be mentioned that the state of things in the OECD countries in this regards is only better in some degree. Court proceedings subsequent to procurement appeals have taken as long as one and a half to five years in OECD countries and interim suspension measures are not always granted. The only exception is Canada where appeals are dealt by a quasi-judicial independent review body, the Canadian International Trade Tribunal that is in charge of federal procurement matters.[23]

India's Negotiating Position in WTO Ministerial Meetings

India did not sign the Tokyo Round GPA and is not a signatory to the current GPA. India, however, has dropped its opposition to a multilateral agreement on transparency in government procurement. Government procurement is one of the new issues that has arisen from the initiatives of the **Singapore Ministerial Conference** of December 1996 and is likely to be part of the Millennium Round negotiations. The working Group on Transparency in Government Procurement had been set up by the Singapore Ministerial Conference to study the existing practices and develop elements for inclusion in a suitable agreement. In the Geneva round of Ministerial conference held in 2004, three Singapore issues (competition policy, trade and investment and government procurement) have been put on a backburner till 2005 and negotiations are going to take place only on trade facilitation.

23. OECD (2003).

"National treatment" requirement is India's biggest problem with any agreement on government procurement. As noted above, the procurement policies of the government give preference to various categories of companies based on size and location. Such practices are based on the view that government procurement is an important instrument for directing investment to "desirable" sectors, less privileged social groups and underdeveloped regions of the country. In view of these concerns, the Indian government is only willing to go along with a suitable transparency agreement that steers clear of market–access issues.

With regard to the definition and scope of government procurement, it is felt that a broad definition that includes government entities at the sub-central level and other public entities would be difficult for a quasi-federal state like India with multiple levels of government and with a large number of public sector enterprises. Any agreement should be restricted to the Central Government. It is also held that the service sector and lease arrangements should be beyond the purview of the agreement. Further, it is believed that the methods of procurement have no bearing on transparency, and that there should be no restriction on the choice of procurement method other than those placed by domestic legislation. In addition, it is felt that existing domestic review and appeal procedures are available and should not be a part of any transparency agreement. Last, India maintains that the proposed transparency agreement should recognise the special needs of developing countries and should incorporate a special clause in this regard.[24] Although the existing Plurilateral GPA provides for exemptions from national treatment for certain categories of industries, these exemptions have to be negotiated with the other members. Finally, the government feels applying the WTO dispute-settlement mechanism to any transparency arrangement is unwarranted, and that effective domestic review procedures should suffice in any such agreement.

Conclusions and Recommendations

Public procurement in India is chaotic. Preference being offered to certain sectors of the economy in government procurement is an

24. Similar to Article V of the current GPA.

issue that can be debated. But there does not seem to be a scope for debate on transparency in government procurement. There is an immediate need for legislation on government procurement providing for uniform rules and procedures for government procurement to be followed by every organ of the government. Such a public procurement law should, as a minimum, cover the objectives, substantive procedural requirements to achieve them, debriefing of unsuccessful bidders, publication of contract awards and an appeal/challenge mechanism. The law may also cover post-award issues in contract implementation such as securities, timely payment, penalties and damages, dispute resolution and termination of contract for default or convenience.

The absence of a nodal agency in the government to evolve public procurement policies and to oversee their functioning has contributed to the present multiplicity of procedures, rules, practices and documents. It has also resulted in the absence of leadership in the government to deal with public procurement issues with the international financial institutions, bilateral donors and other international bodies. A Government Procurement Commission along the lines of the recently established Competition Commission may serve as a nodal agency.

In WTO negotiations the government of India has not shown concern regarding the transparency aspect in any future agreement on government procurement. This shows that the government wants procurement to be corruption-free and the reason for its opposition to GPA lies somewhere else. The government is definitely opposed to market access in order to safeguard the interest of selected economic groups and it is also opposed to uniform rules of procurement for the federal economy.

The study has clearly established the need of rationalisation and harmonisation of procurement rules. But one cannot correlate transparency with lessened corruption. There are studies on government procurement in India claiming prevalence of corruption. But in this study's opinion poll of officials dealing with government procurement, one gets the picture of sporadic rather than pervasive corruption mainly due to the rigidity of the system and fear of vigilance. It should however be mentioned that a similar survey at the state, local or municipal level may bring out a completely different picture. The broad conclusions of this study are:

1. So far as the procurement rules and practices are concerned, there is no significant difference between Indian case and current GPA. But a drastic modernisation of procurement rules and procedures is required. Apparently, an agreement on transparency will not make much difference, which is the Indian official position. However, given India's record, greater transparency in government procurement may reduce corruption. A world economic forum survey ranks India 45th out of 49 countries on honesty of its officials and 44th in the effectiveness of laws protecting the shareholders.[25]
2. In the light of the experience of other developing countries which have followed transparent procurement rules, it can be said that an agreement will be cost-saving for India and a part of this cost-saving can be taken as saving due to transfer of rent from the corrupt officials to the parties in a transaction.
3. Divergent procurement rules in the federal economy of India are likely to be a source of inefficiency but not perhaps a source of corruption. Indian's federal economy comprising multiple layers of state-level decision-making is like a common market. A uniform set of procurement rules followed at all levels would result in efficient purchase as well as trade creation. This requires a drastic change of procurement regime, which is costly but justifiable in the long run.
4. The argument against GPA is a protectionist argument, which loses much of its force in an era of globalisation. India is going through a process of dereservation in public sector and small-scale sector. Disinvestment in public enterprises is the rule of the day and is likely to continue even under the new regime. Since India does not have objection against transparency *per se*, it can be guessed that India's opposition to GPA is *strategic* in the multilateral negotiations under WTO.

25. Source: Perspective. "India's Road Ahead", Investor's Business Daily, April 7, 1998.

5. Publication of contract awards in news media and the web is a very useful step to improve transparency. The public and the bidders have a right to know the outcome of a public tender. The publication will also reveal the time taken by the purchaser in finalising the award, which will encourage quick decisions. The Tamil Nadu and Karnataka Acts provide for this. The publication can be in the official gazette, bulletin and website, and for large contracts, in the press as well.
6. Transparency alone may not be able to curb corruption or political favouritism. The procuring unit may design the procurement process in favour of a particular firm, interpret the prerequisites with corrupt intensions during the process and manipulate the evaluation process for achieving the desired outcome. A properly designed challenge procedure that delivers justice without delay can go a long way in controlling corruption. The study has identified the inadequate challenge procedure in India as a possible source of corruption in government procurement. But it is doubtful whether a GPA can solve this problem, as the experience of OECD countries in this regard is not very encouraging.
7. Standardisation of tender document is urgently needed. In 1998, the Government of India, Ministry of Finance, in consultation with the World Bank, developed a set of standard documents for National Competitive Bidding (NCB) in Bank projects, and circulated them to the Central Ministries and the States, advocating their use in non-Bank funded procurement as well. These documents can be the starting point, and can be updated in the light of experience gained in their use.
8. The multi-layered review and approval process, particularly for large value contracts, should be simplified to expedite the process and minimise opportunities for malpractice and corruption. The tender committee alone shall evaluate and compare the bids, and its recommendation should go directly to the approving authority with no intermediate reviewers. The approving authority may seek clarifications from the tender committee or reject the recommendation, giving its reasons for the tender committee to re-examine, but shall

not itself re-evaluate the bids. If a decision is not reached within one extension of bid validity, the tender should be cancelled.

9. In line with a study by Transparency International (2002) we recommend frequent public opinion polls on corruption issues to control corrupt practices. The media and the non-governmental organisations can play a constructive role and perform this task.
10. Registration of contractors shall apply only to contracts up to Rs. 10 million. Larger contracts shall be open to all contractors, irrespective of their registration status, who meet specific qualification criteria in order to be considered. Also registration of contractors should be centralised in one agency.

References

Bardhan, P.K. (1997). "Corruption and Development", *Journal of Economic Literature*, September Issue.

Cartier-Bresson, J. (2000). "Economics of Corruption", *OECD Observer.*

Chen, Xianquin (1995). "Directing Government Procurement as an Incentive of Production", *Journal of Economic Integration*, 10, pp. 130-140.

Cohen, J.C. (2000). *The LAC Pharmaceutical Region*, The World Bank.

Debroy, Bibek and Gary Pursell (1997). "Government Procurement Policies in India", in Hoekman, Bernard and Petros Mavroidis (eds.) (1997), *Law and Policy in Public Purchasing: The WTO Agreement on Government Procurement*, University of Michigan Press.

Department for International Development(DFID) (2002). *Government of Andhra Pradesh-Public Procurement Review*, United Kingdom.

Evenett, S.J. and B.M. Hoekman (2003). "Transparency in Procurement Regimes: What Can We Expect from International Trade Agreements." in Sue Arrowsmith and Martin Trybus (eds) *Public Procurement: The Continuing Revolution*, Kluwer Law International.

Government of India (2003). *Report of the Task Force on Revision of Norms for Procurement of Goods and Services by Government*, Ministry of Finance, New Delhi.

Helpman, Elhanan and Paul Krugman (1986). *Market Structure and Foreign Trade*, Cambridge, Mass: MIT Press.

Kaufman, D. (1997). "Corruption: Some Myths and Facts", *Foreign Policy*, Summer, pp.114-131.

Klitgaard, R. (1990). *Tropical Gangsters*, Basic Books.

Laffont, J.J., and Jean Tirole (1991). "Auction Design and Favouritism", *International Journal of Industrial Organisation*, 9, pp. 9-42.

Lovei, L. and A. McKechnie (2000). *The Cost of Corruption for the Poor-The Energy Sector*, The World Bank.

Mattoo, Aaditya (1996). "The Government Procurement Agreement: Implications of Economic Theory", *The World Economy*, Vol, 19, No. 6, pp. 695-720.

Mauro, P. (1997). *Why Worry About Corruption*, IMF.

McAfee, R. Preston and John Mcmillan (1989). "Government Procurement and International Trade", *Journal of International Economics*, 26, pp. 291-308.

OECD (2002). *The Size of Government Procurement Markets*, Paris.

OECD (2003). *Transparency in Government Procurement: The Benefits of Efficient Governance and Orientation for Achieving It*, Working Party of the Trade Committee, Paris.

Rege, V. (2001). "Transparency in Government Procurement: Issues of Concern and Interest to Developing Countries", *Journal of World Trade*, 35(4): 489-515.

Rose-ackerman, Susan (1999). *Corruption and Government: Causes, Consequences and Reform*, Cambridge University Press.

Sahgal V. and D. Chakrapani (2002). "India: Evaluating Bank Assistance for Public Financial Accountability in the 1990s", *OED Working Paper*, The World Bank.

Srivastava, Vivek (1999). *India's Accession to the GPA: Identifying Costs and Benefits*, National Council of Applied Economic Research, New Delhi.

Tanzi, V. and H. Davoodi (1997). "Corruption Public Investment and Growth", *IMF Working Paper.*

Tanzi, V. (1998). "Corruption Around the World: Causes, Consequences, Scope and Cures", *IMF Staff Paper.*

Transparency International (2002). "Karachi Integrity Pact Saves 75 per cent in Consulting Fees", *Press Release*.

Transparency International (2002). *Corruption in South Asia*.

USAID (1999). "Ensuring Transparency and Accountability in Hurricane Reconstruction and Transformation", USAID Discussion Paper for the *Consultative Group for the Reconstruction and Transformation of Central America*.

Wei, S.J. (1997). "How Taxing is Corruption on International Investors?", *NBER Working Paper No. 6030*.

Wei, S.J. (1999). "Corruption in Economic Development: Beneficial Grease, Minor Annoyance, or Major Obstacle", *World Bank Policy Research Working Paper No. 2048*.

World Bank (2003). *India: Country Procurement Assessment Report*.

23

Multilateral Competition Framework: Is WTO the Only Alternative?

PRADEEP S. MEHTA
NITYA NANDA
ALICE PHAM

Introduction

The issue of competition problems, both domestic and cross-border, is not new and is increasing as the world heads towards greater economic integration. Whilst countries are adopting competition laws, their capacity to deal with competition issues, which have their roots outside their borders, continues to remain an enigma. To deal with such issues, the national competition authorities would need cooperation from foreign competition authorities, but how far such cooperation will be available is a debatable proposition.

The need for a multilateral approach to competition policy was recognised in the Havana Charter of 1948, of which efforts to set up an International Trade Organisation (ITO) just after the Second World War did not succeed due to intransigence of the US. The General Agreement on Tariffs and Trade (GATT), which emerged instead, was based on the Havana Charter. Competition issues, however, remained outside the GATT framework.

As the Charter was not adopted, efforts were made at the GATT, the UN and later UNCTAD, to remedy the absence of rules on anti-competitive practices. In December 1980, the UN General Assembly adopted the "Set of Multilaterally Equitable Agreed Principles and Rules for the Control of Restrictive Business Practices" (popularly known as the Set). But, the developed countries distanced themselves from the instrument, probably due to the liberalisation in the approach to competition matters in the EU and the US. Developing countries, however, continued to support the idea of international rules on restrictive practices.

The issues pertaining to competition, and measures to deal with restrictive business practices were raised in the Uruguay Round negotiations, and finally entered the WTO arena through the Singapore Ministerial Declaration, in 1996. At the Doha Ministerial Meeting it made further progress, though conditional, as the need for a multilateral framework on trade and competition was recognised in the Declaration. There was huge pressure from the EU, and some other countries, to launch negotiations on the issue at the Fifth Ministerial held at Cancun in September 2003. Following the collapse of the Cancun Ministerial, during the July 2004 negotiations at Geneva—to revive the Doha Round—it was agreed to launch negotiations on trade facilitation, and to drop the competition and other three Singapore issues from the negotiating agenda.

Be that as it may, one cannot overlook the fact that, with the opening up of domestic markets to foreign competition, countries have become increasingly vulnerable to anti-competitive practices that originate outside their own territory. A recent study on the infamous vitamin cartel has validated this (Clarke and Evenett 2002).

How do competition authorities in developing countries deal with these cross-border (international) challenges? When competition authorities from highly developed countries/blocs, like the European Union, face difficulties in handling cases with a cross-border dimension, it is clear that the authorities in developing countries face even greater and more serious problems. Against this backdrop, this chapter makes an effort to critically look into the desirability of a multilateral framework and particularly, whether the WTO is an appropriate forum to host such a framework.

Types of Cross-border Practices

Before we look further into the issue of tackling cross-border, anti-competitive practices, let us briefly look into the various types of such practices that affect countries. There is no simple formula by which one can estimate the damage that these cross-border anti-competitive practices are causing. However, one can get a fair idea of the nature and dimensions of the problems through the analysis of anecdotal evidence. These issues can broadly be classified into four groups:[1]

- Market power in global or export markets;
- Barriers to import competition;
- Foreign investment; and
- Intellectual property rights

Market Power in Global or Export Markets

The anti-competitive practices under this category are:

- International cartels,
- Export cartels and related arrangements,
- International mergers or mergers with international spillovers,
- Abuse of dominance in overseas markets,
- Cross-border predatory pricing, and
- Price discrimination.

International Cartels

The 1990s saw the uncovering of several international cartels, all of which were constituted by producers mostly from industrialised countries. In a background paper prepared for the World Bank's *World Development Report 2001*, Levenstein and Suslow (2001) identified the international trade flows, in 1997, that best matched the products sold by sixteen international cartels, which operated during the 1990s. Developing countries' imports of these goods in 1997 amounted to US$81.1bn, an amount that represents 6.7 per cent of these countries' imports and 1.2 per cent of their national incomes.

However, this is just one side of the story. Cartelisation is not only about loss in consumer welfare; it hampers the development of poor countries, and growth of their firms, in several ways. Levenstein and Suslow (2001) found that international cartels used various

1. This categorisation is borrowed from "Special Study on Trade and Competition Policy" as included in Chapter Four of *WTO Annual Report* for 1997.

techniques, ranging from the threat of retaliatory price wars, use of common sales or distribution agency (i.e. vertical foreclosure), to patent pooling, that effectively blocked developing country competitors' entry into the relevant international product markets.

Export Cartels[2]

Export cartels have been categorised as 'officially sanctioned restraints on trade'. Many governments follow a 'beggar thy neighbour' policy by legally permitting their own private firms to cartelise in export markets, as long as affected markets are outside the country. Generally, these cartels attempt to raise prices in their export markets to the detriment of overseas consumers.

The story of US soda ash producers portrays an interesting case in this area. Attempts by the competition authorities in India, South Africa and Venezuela, to deal with the American Natural Soda Ash Corporation (ANSAC) cartel, have led to serious problems. The US Government threatened to take "actions" in completely unrelated areas, even as a similar action by the European Community against ANSAC was complied with, without much ado.

Mergers & Acquisitions With International Dimensions

Large companies merge in the developed world and consequently their subsidiaries and associates in developing countries too end up in new combinations. This can create positions of dominance for merging firms having a potential of subsequent abuse. Moreover, developing countries may also be affected by merger and acquisition (M&A) activities that take place outside their territory, without any local presence.

Developing countries, to our knowledge, have dealt only with the first type of cases, i.e. subsidiaries merging, as a result of a merger between parent companies, internationally. Although, even stopping the subsidiaries from merging would not serve any purpose, as both will continue to be controlled by the same parent company. Thus, the

2. At the beginning of this part, it is important to note a particular case of (international) export cartel, which is not included for discussion hereby, despite their makeup – the Organisation of Petroleum Exporting Countries (OPEC). The oil cartel is supposedly outside the realm of antitrust action, as it is a sovereign activity of governments.

issue could possibly be dealt with appropriately only through the application of the "effects doctrine," and regulating the merger in the home country. The question remains whether a developing country could enforce any such action on the parent companies in the home country.

Anti-Competitive Practices by Foreign-Based or Globally Dominant Companies

Other than collusion or combinations, the size and scope of TNCs make it possible for them to engage in a variety of anti-competitive practices. Take the example of Microsoft. The company has been hauled up for indulging in anti-competitive practices time and again in the US and the EU. By and large, it has not faced such action in other jurisdictions, especially in the developing world, where the effects of Microsoft's conduct have been increasing at the same pace as its business; but where people are mostly unaware and ill-equipped to deal with cases of the same nature.

The market for agricultural products is another case in point. It is very often considered to be an example of a perfectly competitive market. However, the farmers do not reach the consumers directly as there is a chain of intermediaries. Unfortunately, this set of intermediaries, especially when they happen to be huge transnational agribusiness groups and retail chains, does not always work in a competitive manner. Hence, a huge gap exists between the prices the consumers pay, and the prices the primary producers receive.

A World Bank report estimated that the divergence between producer and consumer prices may have cost commodity-exporting countries more than US$100bn a year; and suggests that imperfect competition at the intermediary level is the key factor (Morriset 1997). The maritime transport industry is another area where, even collectively, shippers from developing countries are not able to counter the various cartel-like arrangements, often made up as *conferences*, between developed-country liners. Fink, Mattoo, and Neagu (2001) found that a break-up of cooperative working agreements, and price-fixing arrangements amongst the major private carriers could reduce transport prices by 20 per cent on US routes, with savings of $2bn or more.

Cross-Border Predatory Pricing

Cross-border predatory pricing can also lead to market distortions. Due to some striking similarities, cross-border predatory pricing is very often equated with dumping and, thus, action is usually taken under anti-dumping legislation. However, the principle underlying anti-dumping is different from that underlying competition law in that it *prima facie* seeks to protect competitors and not competition. However, in most developing countries, due to the small size of markets and low levels of market contestability, there is a greater convergence between anti-dumping and anti-predatory actions. Ironically, until recently, the main users of anti-dumping laws were developed countries, though increasingly developing countries too are taking recourse to these laws (WTO 2001).

The case of the American Natural Soda Ash Corporation (ANSAC) mentioned earlier, serves as a good example of a typical cross-border predatory pricing case. Though the Indian MRTP Commission did not conclusively assert the charge of predatory pricing, it observed that the pricing pattern of ANSAC's export shows "inference of predatory pricing".

Earlier, the soda ash producers in Europe also brought forward an anti-dumping complaint before the European Commission, alleging that US exporters were following an aggressive pricing policy. After an investigation in 1995, the European Commission imposed an anti-dumping duty on the imports of Soda Ash originating from the USA. Unfortunately, it has not been that easy for developing country authorities to do so in similar cases.[3]

Barriers to Import Competition

Import cartels, vertical market restraints creating import barriers, private standard setting activities, abuse of monopsonistic dominance (dominance of a buyer), etc., may fall under this category. Import cartels formed by domestic importers or buyers, and similar arrangements (such as boycotts of, or collective refusals to deal with, foreign competitors) may be a threat to maintaining competition in a market. In principle, a national competition law may normally be able to tackle such market-access barriers to foreign supplies and

3. As mentioned previously.

suppliers. Although, in practice those barriers have been very much deliberately tolerated. In some cases, import cartels were allowed to counter export cartels.

A well-known example, in this regard, is the dispute between Japan and the US, where it was alleged that Fuji effectively prevented Kodak's exports to the Japanese market by controlling the distribution channels.

Foreign Investment

Foreign Direct Investment (FDI) has always been recognised as having complex effects on host countries' market structure and competition. At first glance, Greenfield investment may add to the number of enterprises – potential competitors – in a host country, reducing market concentration; or even an acquisition may actually not reduce the number of firms. The net effect on market structure is, however, more complex than this. M&As, in particular, can be used to reduce competition via "monopolising mergers and acquisitions" (UNCTAD 1997), which can occur when (UNCTAD 2000):

- The acquiring firm was exporting substantially to a market before it buys a competing firm in it;
- A foreign firm with an affiliate, already in the market, acquires another, thereby acquiring a dominant or monopolistic market share;
- The investing TNC acquires a market leader with which it had previously competed;
- The acquisition is intended to suppress rather than develop the competitive potential of the acquired firm.

Intellectual Property Rights

Without a suitable and sufficiently strong legal framework in place, to check the anti-competitive behaviour of these IPRs holders, the possibility that TNCs will be tempted to abuse their market power cannot be ruled out. Agriculture, for example, represents an overwhelming portion of the economy in the South. However, with the internationally recognised protection of seed patents or *sui generis* plant variety protection, billions of farmers in the developing countries are having to pay high prices for patented seeds, and are being prevented from reusing the seed freely.

To make matters worse, though the TRIPS Agreement enables the broad framework, for all countries, to take necessary action if an IPR is abused, leading to anti-competitive outcomes, it does not 'empower' all of them to do so. The suggested remedy of compulsory licensing would not be available to a country that does not have domestic production capacity. The Doha Declaration on TRIPs and Public Health has taken care of this problem in the case of medicines that have public health dimensions. However, abuses of IPR would not be limited to medicines only. Of greater concern are seeds, which will affect the food security of the poor countries.

Existing and Proposed Cooperation Arrangements

Whether it is to deal with anti-competitive practices that occur at national level, or those that have international dimensions, having a strong and well-oiled competition regime is an essential prerequisite. This requires that competition authorities in developing countries have adequate resources, and competition law enforcement officials are technically competent.

Even so, a strong competition regime, at national levels, may not be enough to tackle cross-border anti-competitive practices that are affecting developing countries. Indeed, it would be a good idea to have provisions for extra-territorial jurisdiction in their legislation, on the "effects doctrine," to legally empower competition authorities to deal with such cases.

Nevertheless, most developing countries will not have enough muscle to actually enforce such provisions. Therefore, there are some *prima-facie* arguments to suggest that a multilateral framework can help weaker nations too.

Quite clearly, the need for seeking across-the-border cooperation has increased in line with the globalisation of economies. International cooperation is particularly important in four areas:

i) Strengthening the institutions and promoting competition culture;

ii) Reducing the costs of transactions for transnational mergers;

iii) Promoting market access by reducing/eliminating private barriers; and

iv) Fighting international cartels and other anticompetitive practices.

Realising this, attempts have been made to promote cooperation amongst the competition authorities (or countries) through bilateral, regional, as well as multilateral channels. Some of these are formal whilst others are more of informal initiatives.

Bilateral and Tripartite Tracks

The US, the EU and Canada, have signed a number of bilateral agreements with other countries to cooperate in the area of competition enforcement. Whilst the US has such agreements with Australia, Brazil, Canada, Germany, Israel, Japan and Mexico; the EU has such an agreement with Canada. Similarly, Canada has signed bilateral agreements with Chile and Mexico. It has also entered into a trilateral cooperation agreement with Australia and New Zealand, which between them have a strong bilateral agreement.

Similarly, there is a tripartite agreement between Denmark, Norway and Iceland. France has an agreement with Germany. China has bilateral agreements with Russia and Kazakhstan. Taiwan has such agreements with Australia and New Zealand. Papua New Guinea has an agreement with Australia, which makes a lot of sense, as its economy is heavily dependent on Australia.

Regional Approach

A comprehensive, regional approach to competition policy was first adopted by the EU and, subsequently, by CARICOM (Caribbean Community). The primary objective of adopting a regional competition policy within the EU was to use it as a vehicle to further integrate the common market. The main objective of the CARICOM regional competition policy is to apply competition rules in respect of cross-border anti-competitive business conduct; promote competition in the Community; and coordinate the implementation of the Community Competition Policy. Such an approach is at various stages of discussion/adoption in many other regional groupings. For example, in MERCOSUR (Common Market of the South, also known as Southern Cone); COMESA (Common Market for Eastern and Southern Africa); SADC (Southern African Development Community); EAC (East African Community); CEMAC (Economic and Monetary Community of Central Africa), etc.

Global Initiatives

Over the last few years, several global initiatives have been taken up to deal with competition problems, especially those having international dimensions.

UNCTAD – The United Nations Conference on Trade and Development

As noted before, in December 1980, the UN General Assembly adopted, by resolution, a Set of Multilaterally Equitable Agreed Principles and Rules for the Control of Restrictive Business Practices. The importance of the Set and UNCTAD, in this area of work, cannot be underestimated. The adoption of the Set was an extremely far-sighted move by the international community, and has stood UNCTAD in good stead in helping developing countries to adopt comprehensive competition laws. UNCTAD has been very active in providing technical assistance to developing countries.

OECD's Global Forum – Organisation on Economic Cooperation and Development

The OECD has been regularly cooperating with a variety of non-OECD countries to provide capacity building. With the advent of its Global Forum on Competition, the OECD claims that its cooperation with non-OECD countries will extend beyond capacity building, to include high-level policy dialogues to build mutual understanding; identify 'best practices'; and provide informal advice and feedback on the entire gamut of competition-policy issues. The forum can also be used to promote cooperation amongst countries.

ICN - International Competition Network

The ICN is a membership body of competition authorities of the world. ICN is intended to encourage the dissemination of competition experience and best practices, promote the advocacy role of competition agencies and to facilitate international cooperation.

ICN is not intended to replace or coordinate the work of other organisations, nor will it exercise any rule-making function. However, it is working as an informal platform for promoting cooperation and the exchange of information amongst competition authorities.

WTO – World Trade Organisation

Competition policy is not a new issue in the GATT/WTO framework. The issues pertaining to competition were raised in the Uruguay Round negotiations. Although no agreement on trade and competition policy was signed, the issue is very much present in many of the provisions of the existing WTO Agreements. Amongst all the global level forums, the WTO, until recently, has been most active in discussing a multilateral agreement on competition. Hence, the proposals at the WTO are discussed in greater detail in the next Section.

The Proposal at WTO and its Implications

The proposals, under the Doha Development Agenda, are a statement of core principles, on transparency; non-discrimination; procedural fairness; recognition of the ills of hard-core cartels; and development of flexible cooperation modalities and technical cooperation.

Transparency has been one of the core principles of the GATT system since its inception. In the context of competition, transparency is likely to mean that the administration of competition regulation must be based on published laws, regulations and guidelines.

The reasons why a competition agency may decide to pursue an individual enforcement action would have to rely on confidential action that cannot be disclosed. Procedures in competition law and its administration differ across countries. Thus, transparency in the competition context is not entirely clear; and what constitutes a transparent competition regime may be a cause of controversy.

Non-discrimination is, again, a fundamental tenet of the WTO. The WTO jurisprudence of non-discrimination has clarified that equality of competitive opportunity (not outcome) underpins this concept - a perspective that is also relevant in the competition policy context.

Many of the existing WTO agreements already contain the procedural fairness obligation. Due process does not require any given institutional structure. But, in the competition context, one may presume that the decisions made by the competition authorities or courts must be well reasoned and published; and the competition law must be applied in a non-discriminatory manner.

The proposal says hardcore cartels are to be banned. Technically this will include price-fixing domestic cartels, international cartels, export cartels and import cartels. Although export cartels and import cartels are exempt in much jurisdiction, such exemptions may not be allowed if the agreement was to be developed on the proposed lines.

Cooperation, to be extended amongst the members, will be voluntary in nature. The cooperation will be exchanged for building capacity, especially of developing countries, as well as providing specific information and assistance in dealing with cases.

Now, the question that assumes importance is how far an agreement, designed on the above lines, will help in tackling the different types of cross-border anti-competitive practices, especially from the perspective of developing countries.

International Cartels

The international cartel has been considered to be the most injurious anti-competitive practice affecting the developing countries. However, since the task of enforcement on hard-core cartels would be on a national rather than international basis, it will not be easy for developing countries, which do not have resources and the required technical expertise, to break international cartels. Even in some developing countries, with substantial experience of implementing a competition law, the record of busting domestic cartels is abysmally poor. The experience in winning cooperation, by a developing country, for dealing with international cartels so far is not at all satisfactory.

Developed countries have already warned that developing countries should not expect much on this front because much of the information collected by them, in this regard, is confidential and cannot be passed on. Moreover, in most of the cartel cases, it is argued that information collected through a leniency programme cannot be passed to other countries, as that will undermine the effectiveness of their leniency programme. Given the existing discourse, the proposed agreement will not be able to provide any credible mechanism to tackle international cartels.

Export Cartels

If hardcore cartels were banned, an affected country, subjected to non-discrimination, would be able to force the country of origin of an export cartel to take measures. However, this would require the affected country to have sufficient evidence to prove that an export cartel exists, and this would not be an easy task for a developing country.

It should, nevertheless, be noted that, in this era of globalisation, it would be quite difficult for an export cartel (where all the players are from one single country) to make any substantial impact on any particular market. There is little information in the public domain on the existence of export cartels except, ANSAC.

Tackling export cartels through the effects doctrine, however, runs another risk. If an export cartel is banned from exporting into a particular market, the cure could be worse than the disease, as post-ban there will be a lesser number of players and, hence, reduced competition in the market. ANSAC was, of course, a cartel of a different nature that was allegedly engaged in predatory pricing rather than charging higher prices.

Import Cartels

These should also be banned. However, just like export cartels, the affected country must have sufficient evidence to prove that an import cartel exists in the importing country's market. This will definitely prove to be difficult for developing countries. Moreover, the impact of import cartels operating in developing countries may not be all that bad. Import cartels that try to get better bargains from foreign exporters may be welfare enhancing, especially in developing countries where there is no production base in many sectors. Nevertheless, even such beneficial import cartels will be forced to disband.

M&As with International Spillovers

The effective remedy in this area would depend on the level of international cooperation that could be ensured. Thus, only mandatory cooperation with positive and negative comities can ensure that. Voluntary cooperation, even with positive and negative comities, will not be sufficient.

Typically, when two companies with presence in multiple markets merge, the costs due to the lessening of competition fall on all such markets. However, the benefits of efficiency gains tend to get concentrated in the home country/countries of the merging companies. Thus, cooperation can be promoted only, if a suitable solution is found to distribute the gains as well as losses equitably, in all affected markets. But this is easier said than done. The US and the EU found such a solution in the Boeing/McDonnel Douglas case. However, they could not agree in the GE/Honeywell case as they had different perceptions about the costs and the benefits, and this led to the breakdown of cooperation. Effectively, the EU used its muscle power to block the merger. Obviously, it would not be easy to take such actions by smaller countries, which would simply be ignored by such big merging companies or their authorities.

Another concern that may be noted, in this context, is the issue of national champions and public interest, especially in developing countries. Many developing countries think that their domestic companies are very small compared to global players and, hence, mergers between domestic companies need to be dealt with leniently to promote national champions. However, if their national competition laws become subject to non-discrimination, using differential standards may be difficult.

Anti-Competitive Practices by Foreign-Based or Globally Dominant Companies

These kinds of problems can be best handled through an international enforcement mechanism which is not envisaged in the proposal. Similarly, the abusive practices of agribusiness, in the markets of both primary products as well as processed final products, will continue to remain unchecked even if the existing proposals at the WTO get adopted. Such a problem can hardly be tackled with national level enforcement.

Cross-Border Predatory Pricing

As mentioned before, due to some striking similarities, cross-border predatory pricing is very often equated with dumping and, thus, action is taken under anti-dumping legislation. Indeed the scope of taking anti-dumping actions under the GATT is quite broad and, hence, it is capable of taking care of predatory pricing as well. However, this is again a case of the cure being worse than the disease. Indeed, developing country exporters are more affected by arbitrary anti-dumping actions by developed country governments. Of late, some developing countries have also shown high tendency to take misguided anti-dumping actions, which subverts the process of competition rather than protecting it. The proposals do not mention the predatory dumping issue, and it appears difficult to hope for the issue to be discussed under the existing framework.

Foreign Investment

Anti-competitive practices arising out of FDI operations can, by and large, be tackled by domestic competition authorities if they have adequate legal provisions and institutional capability related to merger control. This may, however, be problematic in smaller countries where governments are rather weak whilst the TNCs concerned can be powerful. The proposals at the WTO would not provide any remedy in this regard.

IPR - Intellectual Property Rights

The proposed agreement on competition would have no impact on this type of anticompetitive, abusive practice. Such IPR abuses will continue to be governed by the TRIPs framework, which as explained before, is not fully equipped to deal with the fairness of such practices.

Based on the above analysis, it can reasonably be said that the proposals at the WTO do not offer solutions on the whole range of cross-border anti-competitive practices. In fact, except for export and import cartels, all other problems will remain, by and large, unattended. Even in these two types of practices, developing countries would be in a comparatively disadvantageous position to utilise them effectively, due to incapability of enforcement and lack of cooperation from foreign countries. If one considers that, in this era of globalisation, export cartels operating from a single country are unlikely to pose any major challenge, the expected gains for developing countries will remain elusive.

The Way Forward

As anti-competitive practices on a global scale are quite prevalent, consumers world-wide are losing out everyday due to absence of a global regulatory framework. Whilst the governments continue to debate whether to have a MCF within the WTO or not, consumers continue to lose. There is, by and large, an overall consensus that there is a case for a multilateral competition framework, but there is no agreement as to:

- What should be its scope and contours, and
- Where it should be situated.

A comprehensive, multilateral competition framework that can effectively meet international competition challenges should ideally contain:

- the core competition principles, including prohibition of hard-core cartels, control of vertical restraints, and abuse of dominance as well as regulation of M&As,
- enforceable special and differential treatment for developing countries,
- cooperation rules, including positive comity, exchange of information, including confidentiality safeguards, peer review, and
- some sort of dispute settlement or mediation mechanism.

There is also a good case for including predatory dumping rules in this framework.

Regarding the forum, some suggest that UNCTAD already has a long history of dealing with competition issues and is a non-controversial forum. It has also been suggested, to have it in an independent forum, away from the UNCTAD and the WTO. UNCTAD is considered to be pro-developing countries, hence, the rich do not like it much or they just about tolerate it. On the other hand, the WTO is considered to be pro-rich countries. Looking at the state of affairs in the geopolitical arena, it is therefore, quite unlikely that such an agreement can be adopted at the WTO in the near future. Moreover, even if such an agreement is adopted at the WTO it is quite unlikely that the desired level of cooperation, which is the most substantial remedy for most of the cross-border anticompetitive practices, could be ensured. With this in mind, only the ICN would qualify to host the MCF, though it would require substantial transformation in its structure and functioning.

In view of these points, the advocates of a multilateral approach for competition policy must seek an alternative way out, rather than sticking to existing 'sticky' proposals. The hosting forum could be a completely new body. For a suitable structure, some of the existing arrangements dealing with similar multilateral issues could be looked at. In this paper we explore two models of international cooperation, which may help to move the agenda. These are the World Intellectual Property Organisation (WIPO) and the International Criminal Police Organisation (Interpol). Indeed, combining the features of both of these organisations, as well as borrowing specific ideas from other multilateral fora could evolve the proposed structure.

WIPO is one of the specialised agencies of the United Nations system of organisations. WIPO's principal objective is to promote the protection of intellectual property throughout the world through cooperation amongst States, and, where appropriate, in collaboration with other international organisations. It administers 23 international treaties, dealing with different aspects of intellectual property protection. The Organisation counts 180 nations as its members. Looking at various aspects of WIPO, such a model may be an optimal structure for an international organisation administering a possible MCF. Considering that the UN General Assembly has been amongst the pioneers to recommend the Set, there should be no problem with such an initiative under the auspices of the UN.

The WTO has often been criticised for not being democratic enough, and development-friendly in its functioning. Having a WIPO-type model, for multilateral cooperation on competition, would possibly help to eliminate this drawback for the protection of developing country interests against more powerful trading partners. One should note that the decision-making mechanism designed for

WIPO, has enabled developing countries to block expansions to intellectual property treaties. These treaties (such as universal pharmaceutical patents) might have occurred through WIPO during the 1960s and 70s, in the context of the significant North-South divide in the politics of intellectual property[4].

WIPO has an Arbitration and Mediation Centre, which was established in 1994, to offer Alternative Dispute Resolution (ADR) options including arbitration and mediation service, for the resolution of cross-border commercial disputes between private parties.

Whilst WIPO does not have an investigation arm, to supply the dispute settlement body with evidence and facts, a multilateral competition organisation should be equipped with this power, complementary to its adjudicative power, to overcome this drawback. An Interpol-type investigation body, incorporated into such a forum, will help to solidify the possibility that violations are brought to light and justice carried out.

In short, the sentiments in developing countries are, by and large, against a WTO agreement on competition; developed countries are either seeking a pro-market access approach or putting on an indifferent attitude (as they have no big concerns of interests being damaged). With such approaches, at this stage, it is difficult to come out with anything concrete. Recommendations as given above, with respect to building an appropriate forum for administering a possible multilateral competition framework, still remain at a very preliminary level. Further details need to be worked out, to build up a feasible proposal, which can resolve the current geo-political dilemma, so that legitimate interests of consumers and producers, all over the world, are not sacrificed.

---

4. In the 1980s, this lead to the United States "forum shifting" intellectual property standard-setting out of WIPO and into the General Agreement on Tariffs and Trade (GATT) (later the WTO), where the North had greater control of the agenda. This strategy paid dividends with the enactment of the Agreement on Trade-Related Aspects Intellectual Property Rights (TRIPS).

References

Clarke, Julian and Simon J. Evenett (2002). *The Deterrent Effects of National Anti-Cartel Laws: Evidence from the International Vitamins Cartel*, World Trade Institute, Berne.

Fink, C., A. Mattoo, and I.C. Neagu. (2001). "Trade in International Maritime Services: How Much Does Policy Matter?" *World Bank Economic Review* 16: 81–108.

Levenstein, Margaret, and V. Suslow (2001). "Private International Cartels and Their Effects on Developing Countries." Background Paper for the World Bank's *World Development Report 2001*. World Bank, Washington.

Morriset J. (1997). *Unfair Trade? Empirical Evidence in World Commodity Markets Over the Past 25 Years*. Foreign Investment Advisory Services

(www.worldbank.org/html/dec/Publications/Workpapers/WPS1800series/wps1815/wps1815.pdf)

UNCTAD (1997). *World Investment Report 1997: Transnational Corporations, Market Structure and Competition Policy*. New York and Geneva: United Nations.

———. (2000). *World Investment Report 2000: Cross-border Mergers and Acquisitions and Development*. New York and Geneva: United Nations.

WTO (2001). *Market Access: Unfinished Business, Post-Uruguay Round Inventory and Issue*, World Trade Organisation, Geneva.